T0305321

Additional Praise for *Energy and Power Risk Management*

"Eydeland and Wolyniec give a very detailed, yet quite readable, presentation of the risk management tools in energy markets. The book will be a valuable resource for anyone studying or participating in energy markets."
—Severin Borenstein
  E.T. Grether Professor of Business Administration and Public Policy, Haas School of Business, University of California, Berkeley
  Director, University of California Energy Institute

"Activity in the power sector exposes all participants to complex and unique risk. Deregulation and the collapse of Enron have only increased the need to understand and control these risks. Covering the spectrum of risk and valuation, from the fundamentals of price movement and modeling with poor data, to physical asset valuation and the complex energy derivatives, this book offers a firm foundation from which to solve real world problems."
—Dr. Chris Harris
  General Manager, Commercial Operations, InnogyOne

Founded in 1807, John Wiley & Sons is the oldest independent publishing company in the United States. With offices in North America, Europe, Australia, and Asia, Wiley is globally committed to developing and marketing print and electronic products and services for our customers' professional and personal knowledge and understanding.

The Wiley Finance series contains books written specifically for finance and investment professionals as well as sophisticated individual investors and their financial advisors. Book topics range from portfolio management to e-commerce, risk management, financial engineering, valuation and financial instrument analysis, as well as much more.

For a list of available titles, please visit our web site at www.WileyFinance.com.

Energy and Power Risk Management

New Developments in Modeling, Pricing, and Hedging

ALEXANDER EYDELAND

KRZYSZTOF WOLYNIEC

John Wiley & Sons, Inc.

Library of Congress Cataloging-in-Publication Data:
Eydeland, Alexander.
    Energy and power risk management: new developments in modeling, pricing, and hedging / Alexander Eydeland, Krzysztof Wolyniec.
        p. cm.
    ISBN 0-471-10400-0 (cloth)
    1. Energy industries—United States—Finance. 2. Portfolio management—United States. 3. Risk—United States. I. Wolyniec, Krzysztof. II. Title.
    HD9502.U52 E97 2003
    333.79'068'1—dc21

                                                            2002013581

10 9 8 7 6

To Alla, Becky, and Celia
—A.E.

To Alec and Ewan
—K.W.

contents

acknowledgments

We would like to express our gratitude to Boris Chibisov, Yan Gao, and Uriel Scott who have made conceptual contribution to this volume. Without their insights our understanding of the subject would have been significantly poorer. We would also like to thank our colleagues, Travis West, Dan Mahoney, Roman Kosecki, Harald Ullrich, and Tsvetan Stoyanov, who have influenced our views on the risk management in energy markets or contributed in other ways. Special thanks to Doug Tinkler, Sailesh Ramamurtie, Jay Catasein, Chris Hemschot, Mark Breese, and Vance Mullis for many stimulating discussions and to Eddie Anderson, Tim Kennedy, Jiri Hoogland, and Olaf Honerkamp for the assistance they have given to this project. We are particularly grateful to Holly Harkness for her expert help in preparing this book. Last but not least, we are thankful to Mirant Corp. for giving us an opportunity to witness firsthand the spectacular evolution of energy markets and for letting us use the historical data. Needless to say, the responsibility for all errors is solely ours.

introduction

Few will argue that these are interesting times for the energy industry. Deregulation of natural gas, initiated in the United States in the early 1990s, is slowly but inexorably moving into Europe and Asia. Simultaneously, deregulation of the power industry, launched in Scandinavian countries and continued in the United Kingdom and Australia, is taking root in North America. Introduction of the competitive natural gas markets in the United States and Canada has been an indisputable success from the point of view of liquidity, efficiency, and transparency. Power markets, on the other hand, are still too young to be judged with any degree of confidence. Due to geographical constraints and market idiosyncrasies their development has been, to say the least, uneven. The data thus far strongly argues that the effect of competition on power prices in general has been positive, manifesting itself in a substantial drop of wholesale prices in many regions. The failures, however, are also well known and publicized. Needless to say, the debate about competitive markets versus regulation still rages. We leave this fascinating topic outside the pages of our book—it is too big and too peripheral to our subject. (It is worth noting, though, that in our opinion, the advantages of competition are beyond doubt.)

The subject of this book is assessing and managing the risks of complex derivative structures arising in energy markets. It is natural to ask: Why do energy derivatives merit special attention and what is so unusual about them that we cannot use the familiar and well-developed risk management tools of the financial markets?

Energy Derivatives Are Unique. A number of energy derivative products cannot be found in any other markets. For example, various volumetric options, such as swing, recall, and nominational, which have been developed to manage risks associated with meeting the demand in natural gas or power, have no parallel in financial markets. Similarly exceptional are all kinds of load serving structures. To be sure, there are standard products—futures, forwards, swaps, options, but even they have unique features due to their predominantly physical nature. They settle differently and are defined differently. Even the commodities underlying these products are different. For example, electricity seems like a perfect commodity, since all electrons are naturally identical, but the impression is deceptive. Power delivered at any particular hour, block of hours, day, week, month, and so on, represents a different commodity because electricity cannot be stored and thus must be studied independently. Nonstorability of power is also a reason why most of the well-known financial theories may not be applicable to electricity derivatives. Finally, energy derivatives include structures whose complexity may surpass anything that one encounters elsewhere, namely, energy assets, such as power plants and gas storage. These assets are equivalent to a complex portfolio of options whose definition requires understanding of a great variety of economic, operational, environmental, regulatory, and other issues. Note that the complex features of energy derivatives are neither artificial nor avoidable; rather, the complexity is a natural consequence of the needs and challenges of the energy markets.

The Price Evolution Processes Are Unique.   Even a superficial analysis of the empirical data reveals the truly unusual characteristics of energy prices. What captures the eye first is their extraordinarily high volatility. Indeed, the volatility of energy prices, such as crude, natural gas, and especially electricity, is an order of magnitude higher than the volatility of foreign exchange rates, interest rates, or equity prices. Just compare the typical volatility of dollar/yen or dollar/euro exchange rates (10%–20%), LIBOR rates (10%–20%), SP500 index (20%–30%), NASDAQ (30%–50%) with the volatility of natural gas prices (50%–100%) and electricity (100%–500% and higher). In addition to high volatility, energy prices exhibit pervasive spikes of extraordinary magnitude, mean reversion, regime switching, stochastic volatility, volatility smiles, and the host of other interesting properties that make processes describing the evolution of energy prices very different from their more standard financial counterparts. Correlation is another distinguishing feature. As will be clear from the book, energy derivatives usually involve spreads and, therefore, the importance of joint distributions is impossible to underestimate. Consequently we pay great attention to correlations and the ability of price processes to capture accurately their structural characteristics.

The Derivative Payoffs Are Unique.   Typical derivative valuation methodologies involve computing expectations of the derivative payoff functions with respect to some probability distribution. As a rule, the payoffs of financial derivatives, even the most complex ones, are well-defined functions of the underlying price paths. In contrast, the cash flows associated with energy assets, such as power plants, are determined as solutions of complicated dynamic programming problems subject to a number of operational and environmental constraints. It makes the task of valuation and particularly hedging, exceptionally difficult and nonstandard.

Energy Derivatives Require Special Risk Management Tools.   The undisputed success of quantitative models in financial markets has naturally led to efforts to adapt these models for the needs of the energy markets. Indeed, initial and influential publications on the subject of modeling for pricing and managing energy derivatives are based on such expansion of the scope of financial models. Although there is no doubt that there are many similarities between the energy and financial markets, their differences are so fundamental and difficult to ignore that they demand development of new powerful analytical tools tailor-made to address distinct characteristics and challenges of the energy markets. Conceptually, these modeling methodologies should be able to combine the best characteristics of the financial models with the fundamental models used in the energy industry to manage energy assets.

The purpose of this book is to answer this challenge and to share with the reader the practical experience of building the pricing and hedging models specifically for energy applications. Throughout the book, a number of models will be proposed and analyzed. One important point should be emphasized: No matter what modeling methodology is chosen, it is always market-based, in the sense that the forward-looking market data is used as a reference against which all products are priced. This is a crucial distinction of the models discussed in the book. Indeed, some risk management exists even in the regulated world where the hedging is done through fuel clauses and various rate formulas. In contrast, the risk management methods developed in this book are decidedly market-based.

The modeling approaches we pursue in depth are nested in the commercial and empirical framework of the energy industry. One of the most salient challenges in modeling energy (and especially power) markets is the limited amount of historical and forward-looking price information. This forces us to augment the standard techniques to extract as much as possible from other sources of information. This issue is central to many analytical strategies we pursue. The overriding goal of our analysis is to develop modeling and trading approaches that are commercially viable and have operational meaning. In this, our approach differs significantly from the academic analysis of financial derivatives. The issues of valuation, hedging, model estimation, and the like are closely intertwined and cannot be always separated into independent steps.

The structure of the book is as follows.

Chapter 1. Markets—description of the basic energy market structures

Chapter 2. Basic Products and Structures—introduction to the products most frequently encountered in the energy markets and some of their applications

Chapter 3. Data—analysis of historical data and the empirical properties of the market prices

Chapter 4. Reduced-form Processes—overview of the reduced-form price models including mean-reverting and jump-diffusion processes, processes with stochastic volatility, and with regime switching

Chapter 5. Forward Price Processes—an introduction to models describing the forward curve evolution, such as HJM, BGM, and string models

Chapter 6. Correlation—an overview of a host of issues involved in modeling, using and misusing correlations, and other concepts of dependence

Chapter 7. Hybrid Process for Power Prices—a modeling technique based on combining fundamental and market-based quantitative methodologies with the purpose of capturing a number of important empirical characteristics of power prices

Chapter 8. Structured Products: Fuels and Other Commodities—an overview of several key structures, from simple to the most complex. The issues addressed include pricing, hedging, and application. The topics covered range from simple swaps to storage facilities to load-serving contracts

Chapter 9. Power Plants and Other Cross-commodity Derivatives—an overview of valuation and hedging of cross-commodity energy derivatives with particular emphasis given to power plants

Chapter 10. Risk Management—systematic analysis of general issues of risk-adjustment, risk-measurement, and hedging

Markets

Energy markets are a collection of commodities that are quite different in nature. It's helpful to break them into three groups:

1. Fuels: oil, gas, coal, and their derivatives and byproducts
2. Electricity
3. Weather, emissions, pulp and paper, and forced outage insurance

This classification roughly corresponds to the historical pace at which these markets were opened. Fuel markets, and especially oil and gas markets, opened for competition in the 1980s at the wholesale level. Electricity markets followed in several states in the early and mid-1990s. Finally, the late 1990s saw the quickening pace of trading in new types of commodities related to electricity such as weather and emissions.

The term "fuels" might suggest an electricity-centric perspective. Obviously, oil and gas are also used for direct consumption, and, in fact, their demand as heating fuels drives their price formation.

Before we look more closely at the differences between fuel and electricity markets, let's examine what they have in common.

FUELS AND ELECTRICITY AS PHYSICAL COMMODITIES

As with any physical commodity that has independent value apart from its investment value, the markets involve three sets of activities: production, distribution, and consumption. Those activities give rise to several types of services. For example, distribution in gas markets involves moving physical gas from the wellhead, through the gathering system, to a processing facility, and then on through the main line to receipt points—with possible stops along the way at storage facilities for balancing purposes. Before deregulation, this complex activity was often managed by one entity that had control over a significant portion of the local distribution system. Naturally, this arrangement led to concerns about monopoly power and resulted in heavy regulation that both controlled and sustained the problem.

Concerns about the enormous inefficiency of this situation led to the onset of deregulation. The process has entailed two things: an (often forced) unbundling of the services and the creation of markets to mediate the provision of the services. Those unbundled services are the commodities that form the proper subject of this book.

The extent of deregulation varies with commodities and locations. The degree to which the interaction among the components of the value chain is handled through markets or by public utilities also varies considerably.

Below we review the most pertinent features of the different markets. Our quick tour is not meant to be exhaustive; the topic itself warrants—and indeed has warranted—separate volumes. We supply the references as we go along.

One point worth making here is that the organizational details of the physical markets have a substantial impact on the workings of the corresponding forward and derivative markets. Given the complexity of some of those markets—a perfect example is the electricity market that trades several cash products—understanding the interaction of optionality, risk, and expectations within and between the different markets presents a challenge that should not be underestimated.

FUEL MARKETS: OIL AND GAS

Oil

Crude

Although we put oil and natural gas together under the heading of fuels, their respective markets operate quite differently. The market prices had been effectively fixed until 1985, when the OPEC pricing regime collapsed. This led to the creation of active forward and spot markets.

The crude oil market is the largest commodity market in the world. The most significant trading hubs are New York, London, and Singapore. These markets trade crude oil as well as refined products such as gasoline and heating oil.

Crude oil comes in a wide variety of grades, determined by its gravity and sulfur content. The world benchmark crude oil is the Brent crude pumped from the North Sea oil wells. Estimates indicate that up to two-thirds of the world supply is priced with reference to this benchmark. In the United States the benchmark is West Texas Intermediate (WTI) crude oil.

The forward markets in the United States are conducted on the New York Mercantile Exchange (NYMEX). The NYMEX crude price most often quoted is the price of light, sweet crude oil. "Sweet" refers not to its flavor, but to its sulfur content. Oil with sulfur content below 0.5% is referred to as "sweet," while oil with higher sulfur content is called "sour."

The spot markets tend to be rather thin, with the bulk of the transactions concentrated in the financial and physical forward contracts.

Refined Products

Crude oil needs to be processed (refined) in order to yield products that can be directly consumed. The most popular refined product is obviously gasoline. Heating oil and fuel oil are often used by utilities. Kerosene (jet fuel) powers the airline industry.

Heating oil and fuel oil of various grades have extensive forward markets, both exchange-based (NYMEX) and OTC. The liquidity in those markets varies substantially.

Natural Gas

The gas markets were steadily opened to competition during the 1980s and early 1990s. The final act of this process was the Federal Energy Regulatory Commission (FERC) Order 636 issued on April 9, 1992. In that order the FERC mandated open access to the pipeline system used for transporting natural gas.

Before we dive into the details of the existing markets, let's look at the demand characteristic for this commodity. It will help us later understand the main price trends and the shape of the forward curve.

Factors Affecting Demand

Industrial customers consume around 38% of natural gas; 37% goes to residential and commercial customers, while a fast-growing share of 14% is used for generation of electricity.

The heaviest residential consumption is during winter months for home heating, reflected in the relatively high winter prices and low summer prices. It's worth noting that the relative consumption of natural gas in summer and winter might be affected in the future by the growing stock of gas-powered electrical generation. Since the bulk of seasonal variation in electricity consumption is driven by the demand for air-conditioning, electricity consumption is highest during summer. This could lead to a relative shift in natural gas demand towards the summer months.

Markets

There are five categories of market participants:

- Gas producers
- Pipeline companies
- Local delivery companies
- Consumers
- Marketers

The first four market players have well-defined roles along the value chain of the industry. Marketers serve as intermediaries, managing the interactions of the other parties.

Transactions in the natural gas physical markets are conducted daily or monthly. Transactions in the monthly market are often conducted during *bid-week,* the last week of the month preceding the contract month. These transactions procure supply for the predictable part of the consumer demand, while the daily market nets out the balance. The bid-week monthly market establishes the benchmark, or *index price,* for the transactions. This is not the price of a specific contract. Rather, it represents an average price at which monthly contracts have transacted. The price is determined by a telephone survey conducted by industry publications, most often *Inside FERC's Gas Market Report.* The index for a given delivery location or hub is published on the first day of the month. In the following chapters we will discuss the different financial products that are based on index prices, as well as the relationship between forward and futures prices and index prices.

The natural gas market is a collection of locations at which the delivery and receipt of the commodity takes place. The participating parties contract for two services:

- Delivery and receipt of natural gas at a given location
- Transportation of natural gas between two different locations

Depending on their position in the pipeline system, these locations experience different volumes of transactions. Some locations have developed into significant trading hubs. In the eastern United States the major location is Henry Hub in southern Louisiana. The western United States has its main trading hub at Waha Hub in west Texas.

Delivery

Three types of transactions commonly govern delivery of natural gas. (For details, see Sturm, 1997).

Baseload Firm.   In this transaction the delivering party is expected to perform according to the contract under any conditions (with the exception of *force majeure*). Liquidated damages and financial penalties are imposed for nonperformance. Also referred to as "firm."

Baseload Interruptible.   Delivery can be interrupted; interruptibility conditions may or may not be specified in the contract. Also referred to as "baseload."

Swing.   The volume of delivered gas is adjusted daily at the buyer's discretion. Swing contracts are typically used for daily pipeline volume balancing requirements.

Transportation

Natural gas transportation transactions have similar contractual provisions. There are two categories of the transportation services:

Firm Transportation Service (FTS).   The highest priority service.

Interruptible Transportation Contract.   Under this contract a pipeline has an option to interrupt the service on short notice without a penalty. The interruption generally occurs in peak-load seasons as a result of demands from firm service customers. Also referred to as "best efforts."

Although most of the firm capacity is subscribed, there is an active "secondary market" trading this capacity. When a holder of the firm space on a pipeline sells some of the capacity, the transaction is referred to as *capacity release*.

POWER MARKETS

The design of efficiently functioning electricity markets has proven to be a challenging undertaking. The physical characteristics of the commodity are quite unlike those in the fuel markets. One of the crucial features of electricity markets—and one that differentiates it from other commodity markets—is the need for real-time balancing of locational supply and demand. This requirement flows from the technological characteristics of supply and distribution. Since electricity cannot be stored, instantaneous supply and demand must always be in balance; otherwise the integrity of the whole system might be compromised.

This peculiar feature of the electricity markets introduces the need for an additional set of services beyond production and distribution: balancing and reserve resources. Therefore, the supply of electricity involves three types of activities:

- Generation
- Transmission
- Ancillary services (balancing)

Across the United States and around the world, there are considerable differences in the extent to which these activities are mediated through markets and/or public utilities.

The common feature of virtually all solutions is the presence of an independent system operator (ISO), which maintains the system. In the United States these are public utilities regulated by the individual states and FERC.

The services can then be managed by either a highly centralized market under the control of the ISO, or through a sequence of bilateral markets, with the ISO only playing a limited role as a sole buyer of some of the services.

The solutions include a system where the ISO manages provision, contracting, and infrastructure for all the activities of the electricity markets—generation, transmission, and balancing. ISO New England is a prime example. In other markets, the ISO is mainly involved in the procurement of generation (the energy market) while transmission is left to bilateral markets with only a rudimentary presence of the ISO as the buyer of the final product. The initial design of the California market, since abandoned, was one example of this approach. Finally, some markets are purely bilateral, with only a symbolic presence of the system operator.

Primary Market Structures

The cash market takes on two contracting structures: pools and bilateral markets.

Pools. The main characteristic of the pool market is the formal establishment of the market (system) clearing price at which all cash (energy) transactions clear. Examples include the Nordic Power Exchange (Nord Pool), New England Power Pool (NEPOOL), New York Intrastate Access Settlement Pool (NYPOOL), and the California Independent System Operator (CAISO).

Bilateral Markets. All transactions are entered into by two parties and are independent of any other transactions in the market. Examples include the Electric Reliability Council of Texas (ERCOT), the East Central Area Reliability Council (ECAR), and the Southeastern Electric Reliability Council (SERC).

The products offered by pool markets vary widely from market to market. Several markets trade the main energy cash products as well as the ancillary services.

Contracting for the physical product can be handled through a single or multiple settlement system. The next section defines the terms used in those systems and provides a detailed example of the multisettlement system.

Energy Cash Markets

The different energy cash markets are:

Day-ahead. This market transacts for generation of energy the next day. Every hour is transacted separately. In some markets, the structure of the bid is very simple; in other markets startup and no-load bids can also be transacted.

Day-of. This market transacts for generation of energy for the rest of the day. Every hour is transacted separately.

Hour-ahead. This market transacts for generation of energy for the next hour.

TABLE 1.1   PJM Energy Bidding Timeline

Timeline	Event	Description
12 noon: Day-Ahead Market closes	Submit energy offers and demand bids for next operating day.	• Offer curves can be up to 10 points. • Generation offer must not exceed $1000/MWh (megawatt-hour) • Can submit offer data up to seven days in the future.
	Bilateral transactions (physical) Increment offers/decrement bids (financial instrument)	• Hourly MW (megawatt) demand quantities by location (node).
4:00 PM	PJM posts Day-Ahead results	• PJM publishes hourly LMPs (Locational Marginal Prices), hourly generation/demand schedules, transmission limitations, Inc/Dec schedules, energy transaction schedules, external energy schedules, and net tie schedules.
6:00 PM: Balancing Market closes	Balancing Market	• Rebidding period to submit updated generation offers only. Can only modify bids for units not selected by PJM in first settlement.

Ex-post (or Real-time).   This is a reconciliation market that clears any deviations from the predicted schedules entered in the earlier markets.

A market that has more than one cash market is referred to as *multisettlement market*. Table 1.1 provides an example of a multimarket scheme timeline for the Pennsylvania-New Jersey-Maryland (PJM) market.

Energy Forward Markets

Forward markets are markets in which the parties contract for the delivery of energy in the future. The future in question can be near (e.g., balance-of-the-week and balance-of the-month products) or quite far (e.g., monthly forward contracts that cover periods months or even years into the future). The next chapter provides detailed descriptions of those products. Here we take a quick look at the mechanics of the market.

The forward markets take on three basic forms:

Bilateral or Broker-based (Over-the-Counter).   The trading involves either direct contact between two parties or contact mediated by a broker (possibly an electronic broker like InterContinental Exchange Trade or Spark).

Market Maker-based.   The trading is centered around a market maker who posts two-sided (for buying and selling) quotes, stands behind every transaction, and can carry inventory (examples include the once omnipresent EnronOnLine, DynegyDirect, and UBSWEnergy.com).

Exchange-based.   The trading centers around a central exchange that matches up buyers and sellers and guarantees the performance of the transaction without taking an outright position and carrying inventory (NYMEX).

Types of Traded Power

On the surface, electricity seems to fit the definition of an almost ideal commodity, but the reality is far from that. Indeed, since it cannot be stored, power sold in the morning is completely different from power sold in the same location in the evening. For this reason there are many varieties of products traded in the power markets, making the study of these markets even more difficult. Frequently encountered power products include:

On-peak Power.   In the East and Central regions on-peak is defined as 5×16 power, that is, power for 16 hours a day (for example, 8:00–23:00 EST in PJM, 7:00–22:00 CST in ECAR) for five days a week (Monday–Friday) for the delivery period excluding North American Electric Reliability Council (NERC) holidays. In the West, the standard forward product is 6×16 power, that is, power for 16 hours a day for six days a week (Monday–Saturday) for the delivery period, excluding NERC holidays.

Off-peak Power.   Power during the low-demand periods (complementary to on-peak).
    Other products include, 2-, 4-, 8-, or 16-hour blocks of power, next-day power, balance-of-the-week power, next-week power, balance-of-the-month power, and next-month power.

Ancillary Services and Ancillary Services Markets

As mentioned previously, in electricity markets, instantaneous supply and demand must always be in balance; otherwise the integrity of the whole system might be compromised. This creates the need to hold reserves to balance instantaneous variations in load. The way this need is handled depends on the market design. In some NERC regions, such as ERCOT, the need is satisfied by requiring generators to withhold part of their generation capacity of committed units for the so-called spinning reserve. In practice this means that a generation unit does not ramp up to full capacity unless called upon by the market administrators (ISOs) to help balance the system in a contingency.

Another solution is to create a market that supplies those services. A number of pool markets, including PJM, NEPOOL, and CAISO use this method. In the market-based scheme, the generators have the choice of committing their available capacity either to the energy market or to one of the ancillary services markets. In some regions, ancillary services markets are composed of as many as seven products. A typical list includes:

Spinning Reserves.   Resources synchronized to the system that are available immediately and that can be brought to full capacity within ten minutes.

Non-spinning Reserves.   Resources not synchronized to the system that are available immediately and can be brought to full capacity within ten minutes.

Operating Reserve.   The resources that can be brought to full capacity within 30 minutes.

Energy Imbalance.   Resources needed for correcting supply/demand imbalances.

Regulation.   Reactive energy to maintain the phase angle of the system.

Reactive Power Supply.   Services to maintain voltage of transmission lines. As such, it is locationally specific.

Installed Capacity Markets (ICAP)

In some markets, the long-term reliability of the system is managed through capacity markets. These arose from the need for all load-serving entities to show the availability of physical supply from which the load will be served. This type of market assures a long-term reliability, and short-term reliability is handled through the ancillary services markets. The ICAP requirement is usually specified as excess to the peak load. It differs from market to market, but it can be as high as 110% of the peak load.

In a market with capacity requirements, the additional revenues for the generators will induce more entry and lead to higher *reserve margins,* defined as the difference between the maximum system capacity and the peak system load. This has consequences not only for reliability but also for the behavior of energy prices themselves. When we analyze the economics of power markets more extensively, we will show how reserve margins have a substantial impact on the probability and amplitude of price spikes.

Price spikes are useful in two ways:

- On the demand side, they help to signal shortages and encourage customers to reduce their usage in times of stress.
- On the supply side, they signal shortages and help bring in more supply/additional entry.

On the other hand, extreme price spikes can be very disruptive, as we explain in later chapters. Many market designs strive to retain the features mentioned above without having actual spikes. The capacity market should have the effect of encouraging entry (supply side), thus preventing spikes while maintaining sufficient reserve margins. However, demand-side signaling cannot be achieved by this mechanism—a moot point since there is currently almost no disaggregated demand-side metering. Consequently, no price signals can be sent to the customer, no matter what the market design is. For more extensive analysis of those issues see papers by Borenstein, Bushnell, and Stoft (2000).

The structure of the capacity markets, detailed bidding rules, and coverage periods differ from market to market. For details see the Web pages of the appropriate ISOs.

Spatial Markets: Zonal, LBMP, and FTRs

All the previous analyses of the market relied on the assumption that there is effectively one central location at which the market clears. However, one of the biggest challenges of organizing electricity markets is assuring the delivery of a sufficient amount of energy to the right location. This is compounded by the fact that power supply and demand must be in balance all the time. Therefore, the availability of generation in one location is of no value if the transmission system is not sufficient to move the power to where it's needed. The presence of congestion can lead to significant opportunity cost differentials between locations. Not recognizing those differentials in pricing the underlying commodity can lead to significant inefficiencies. This motivates the development of schemes to differentiate prices; the two most popular are zonal and nodal schemes.

Before we take a closer look, one consideration is worth mentioning: the downside of fragmenting a given region into submarkets is the possibility of local market power. A large generator in a congested subsystem might be able to influence prices, hence the introduction of various mitigating mechanisms (reliability-must-run contracts in CAISO, for example). This problem afflicts the two popular designs, although nodal prices are naturally under more strategic influence than their zonal counterparts.

Here are short descriptions of zonal and nodal markets:

Zonal Prices. In this scheme, the region is divided into several large zones with separate energy and ancillary services markets. There are different mechanisms to manage exchange between zones (zonal interfaces). The interzone flow is typically managed with physical transmission rights. An example is CAISO.

This design represents the complexity of the transmission system in a very simplified manner. Its advantage is precisely its simplicity, which offers market participants a relatively low number of submarkets with the attendant high liquidity. Its drawback is the very same thing: simplicity. The workings of the transmission system are misrepresented, leading to inefficient dispatch and perverse incentives.

Nodal Prices: LBMP/LMP (Locational Marginal Price). In this scheme, every location (every bus) has its own price, representative of the congestion in the system. In an unconstrained system the prices are identical throughout the system. The risks of the price differentials are managed through financial transmission rights: FTRs (fixed/firm transmission rights).

The clear advantage of a nodal market is the faithful representation of the opportunity cost differentials. The significant downside is the resulting illiquidity in the fragmented market, and with that the threat of the exercise of local market power.

A detailed description of the way locational-based market pricing (LBMP) prices are calculated can be found in tutorials available on the Web pages of NYPOOL and PJM Pool.

In decentralized market schemes, generators bid in "incremental" and "decremental" markets. The system operator uses the bids to adjust locational generation to manage congestion in the system. In centralized schemes, the optimization of the energy, transmission, and balancing systems happens at one time. Decentralized markets optimize each system in sequence.

The usual timeline of markets in decentralized systems involves, first, long-term contracting in bilateral markets for forward energy. As the next step, the day-ahead energy markets open to adjust the delivery schedules contracted for in the forward market. Given the universe of all those contracts, a balanced schedule is constructed by the system operator. If the resulting schedule results in congestion, another market opens for transmission capacity. Additionally, the system operator will conduct an auction to purchase the required reliability/balancing resources.

In some markets balancing needs are managed through the imposition of a specific reserve requirement on all the participants in the energy market (i.e., the old ERCOT setup, PJM). The system operator can order the generators to increment or decrement their generation without an explicit pricing mechanism for those services. Obviously, the option held by the system operator is not free; its cost tends to be reflected in the energy market prices.

In many centralized schemes, the bidding is performed at the same time in the energy and balancing markets (e.g., NEPOOL).

OTHER MARKETS: EMISSIONS, WEATHER, COAL, AND FORCED OUTAGES

Emissions

Emissions markets arose as a consequence of the imposition of controls on nitrogen oxides (NO_x) and sulfur oxides (SO_x) through the Clean Air Act.

The Act established nationwide limits on SO_2 emissions and allocated emission credits to generators. To manage the optimal use of resources while meeting the environmental restrictions allowance, the Act permits the free exchange of allowance credits. This has led to the creation of a market for emission allowances or credits. Allowances correspond to annual caps on emissions, and they trade in over-the-counter markets. The SO_2 restrictions affect all generating plants with capacity over 25 MW.

This credit market is just one tool available in maintaining compliance. There are several new technologies (such as scrubbers) as well as operating decisions (lower unit utilization, switching to a different fuel grade) that allow a reduction in emissions. The market allows generators to make more optimal decisions in committing to often expensive solutions. The market prices for allowances can be very volatile due to several factors. Significant regulatory and legal uncertainty due to ongoing litigation (the New Source Review pursued by the EPA against several utilities) and changing laws (SIP Call) affect the market behavior markedly. We will examine the evidence in later chapters.

A regional market also exists for NO_x allowances; it covers 11 states, mainly in the Northeast and the East, participating in the Ozone Transport Region. The Environmental Protection Agency (EPA) intends to extend the program to Midwestern states in coming years (SIP Call). The allowance market that appeared in the wake of regulation covers the summer ozone period (May 1 through September 30). The market trades over-the-counter.

Weather

The market in weather products is a relatively recent development. The first trades appeared in 1997 in the over-the-counter market. The premise of the market is the significant weather-driven volumetric exposure of various participants in the energy markets. The electric load and gas demand exhibit significant correlation with ambient temperatures and other factors such as humidity. This led a number of power marketers and other financial institutions to develop weather-related products. Among the most popular are:

HDD/CDD Swaps. Heating (cooling) degree swap is a swap of a fixed cash flow for the floating leg that is calculated by the sum of heating degree days under (over) 65 degrees Fahrenheit, with the sum covering the whole swap period.

HDD/CDD Calls and Puts. Calls (puts) on heating/cooling degree-days.

The promise of the market has not yet been fulfilled, with the main trading activity occurring mainly in the over-the-counter market between the power marketers. The Chicago Board of Trade (CBOT) attempted to create an organized forward market; however, the concept did not find acceptance and the hoped-for liquidity has never arrived.

Coal

Coal is widely used in older generation plants. A significant portion of the generation stock in the United States is still coal-based. There are several grades of coal available with the sulfur content determining the quality. However, the market is mainly regional with different types of coal available in different parts of the country.

The market is dominated by long-term delivery contracts between producers and generators. There is an over-the-counter spot market, and in the summer of 2001, NYMEX started a coal futures market.

Forced Outage

One of the significant challenges of risk management in electricity markets is forced outage. An unplanned failure of a generation unit in spiking markets can have catastrophic financial consequences. This has created a market for forced-outage products, though there is no one market that trades them. We can distinguish the shape of the emerging markets through the appearance of a number of structured products marketed by power marketers, and insurance marketed by insurance companies.

THE ECONOMICS OF ELECTRICITY MARKETS

In this section we provide a short overview of the economics and technologies of electricity markets. Understanding the basics helps us understand the behavior of energy prices in general.

Technologies

On the supply side of the business, the following technologies currently dominate electricity generation:

- Nuclear
- Coal–Steam

TABLE 1.2 Fuel Mix in Some NERC Regions

	PJM	NEPOOL	NYPOOL–J,K	ERCOT	California
Gas	31%	32%	90%	75%	46%
Oil	21%	28%	74%	38%	1%
Coal	37%	9%	0%	21%	0%
Nuclear	21%	16%	0%	7%	9%
Hydro	5%	12%	1%	1%	23%
Other	1%	2%	0%	0%	21%

- Gas/Oil–Steam
- Combined Cycle (CC)
- Combustion Turbine (CT)
- Hydro
- Renewables

Different regions of the country have different mixes of technologies. The most prevalent ones are coal, nuclear, and natural gas–based technologies. The last category is quickly gaining in importance, since almost all substantial new generation being built in the United States is based on natural gas. The importance of natural gas lies in its relative environmental advantages and low cost. In certain seasons, hydrological resources can be of significant importance in regions such as the Western Systems Coordinating Council (WSCC), NEPOOL, and NYPOOL. Table 1.2 shows the fuel mix in some NERC regions. (The numbers do not total 100% because many gas units have dual oil generation capability.)

The characteristics that determine cost of generation are listed below. Detailed explanations can be found in Chapter 9:

Capacity.   Maximum power output of the unit expressed in MW (megawatts).

Heat Rate.   A measure of efficiency of the unit, that is, its ability to convert fuel energy content, expressed in British thermal units (Btus), into electrical energy, expressed in KWh (kilowatt-hour).

Variable O&M Costs.   Variable operational and maintenance costs (per unit of generation).

Min/max Generation Level.   Maximum generation level is the unit's capacity. Minimum generation level is the technically feasible minimum level.

Scheduled Outages.   Planned downtime for maintenance.

Forced Outages.   Unplanned downtime caused by a technical failure of the unit.

Ramp Rates.   The rate at which the generation level can be changed, expressed in MW per minute.

Startup/shutdown Costs.   The costs of starting up or shutting down a unit.

Min/max Runtime, Min/max Offline Time.   For technical reasons, various restrictions on the length of runtime and/or offline time can be present.

Costs

Operational costs of units are affected by the following items:

- Fuel costs
- Variable O&M
- Emissions costs/emissions restrictions (they can have cumulative instead of marginal character)
- Transmission costs (depending on the market design)

Knowing the unit characteristics and the cost items above, we can calculate the marginal cost of generation for all the units in a given region. By stacking the units in "merit order," that is, from the lowest to the highest cost, we can form what we call a *supply stack*.

The marginal cost of a unit depends not only on current fuel costs, but also on the previous states of the unit. The operating characteristics mentioned above (startup costs, min runtime) can create dependencies between different unit states at different points of time. This obviously suggests that the marginal cost will be path-dependent (more about those issues in later chapters).

If we ignore the above subtleties, we can form the supply stack by considering only the marginal fuel costs (and variable O&M). The supply stack is then a potentially multidimensional surface that shows us the marginal fuel cost for the different system generation levels and fuel prices.

Figures 1.1 and 1.2 show three-dimensional stack surfaces for different regions. We plot the dependence of the marginal system cost on the system generation level and main (marginal) fuel. In almost all regions, the marginal fuel (the fuel that sets the price most often) tends to be natural gas.

The marginal fuel cost stack surface (generation stack) may not be necessarily equivalent to the actual bid stack submitted for optimization in different pools. For certain regions we have at our disposal the actual bid stack used. Consequently we can compare the marginal fuel stack with the actual bid stack used in determining system price.

The importance of this exercise lies in the fact that the structure of the stack helps us understand the behavior of power and fuel prices. For that to be a viable option, we must reasonably expect that the structure of the marginal fuel stack is close to the actual bid stack.

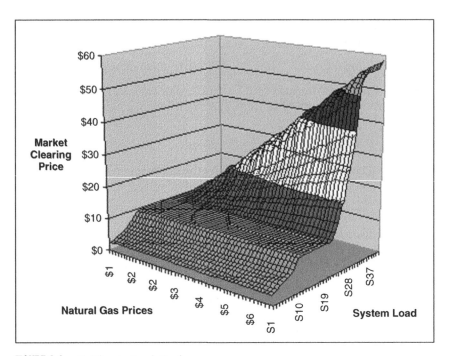

FIGURE 1.1 California Stack Surface

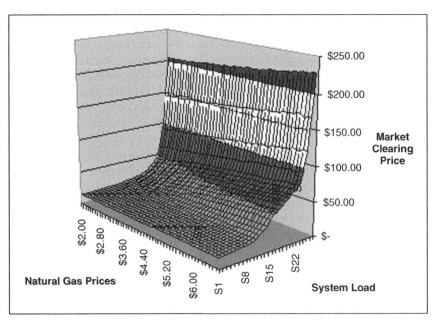

FIGURE 1.2 PJM Stack Surface

The differences in the fuel and bid stack are due to several factors. The actual marginal costs of the different generators can be influenced by a number of physical constraints, and in some situations, this might make fuel cost an insufficient proxy for the actual marginal cost of generation. Furthermore, the differences can be induced by strategic behavior by the bidders. This topic has received a substantial amount of scrutiny in the wake of the California power crisis of 2000 to 2001. So far, the results of academic research into the topic remain inconclusive (see research article collection at the Web page of the University of California, Berkeley Energy Institute, available online).

CHAPTER 2

Basic Products and Structures

In this chapter we briefly describe standard derivative products, often called "plain vanilla," as well as their more exotic relatives used for risk management of energy transactions. Many of these products were first developed for financial market applications, and then naturally migrated to the energy markets as the risk management objectives common to both markets became evident. Simultaneously, a whole class of derivative products with a unique "energy flavor" were developed to address the special needs of risk management in energy markets. Table 2.1 contains examples of frequently encountered energy derivatives. We describe several of these products and their applications in this chapter (see also Chapters 8 and 9).

STANDARD RISK MANAGEMENT INSTRUMENTS

Futures contracts, forward contracts, swaps, and options are the most frequently used risk management tools. The popularity of these contracts stems from the fact that they are standardized, well understood, and are, without exception, the most liquid instruments available to a risk manager.

Futures

Futures are highly standardized exchange-traded contracts for purchase or sale of an underlying commodity or financial product at a specified price over a certain future period of time. Commodity futures, which typically call for a physical settlement, require the following characteristics to be defined:

- Volume
- Price
- Delivery location
- Delivery period
- Last trading day or settlement date

TABLE 2.1 Energy Derivatives

Physical				Financial	
Standard	Exotic		Assets	Standard	Exotic
	Price-based	Volumetric		Futures	American Options
Futures	American	Swing options	Storage	Forwards	Asian options
Forwards	options	(recall,	Power plants	swaps	Swaptions
Swaps	Asian options	nominational,	Transmission	European	
European	Swaptions	etc.)		options	Spread
options	Spread options	Load following			options,
	Tolling, etc.				etc.

One of the main attractions of futures contracts is the virtual elimination of counterparty credit risk, because the financial performance and commodity delivery are guaranteed by the exchange. Another frequently mentioned benefit of futures is the reduction of transaction costs due to contract standardization. Finally, because they are settled daily, computing the mark-to-market value of futures contracts does not require discounting, making them much simpler to evaluate than their close cousins: forwards and swaps.

Electricity Futures

The first North American electricity futures contracts were introduced in 1996 by the New York Mercantile Exchange (NYMEX) for delivery in two locations: the California-Oregon border and Palo Verde, Arizona. In subsequent years futures contracts with delivery locations around the United States were introduced for trading on NYMEX, CBOT, and the Minnesota Grain Exchange (MGE). Nord Pool, the Nordic Power Exchange, was the earliest power market in Europe; it started trading financially settled futures contracts in the Scandinavian countries in 1993. Later, other exchanges such as International Petroleum Exchange (IPE) in London and Energy Exchange (EEX) in Frankfurt introduced their own electricity futures contracts.

Unfortunately, for a variety of reasons, after the initial burst of activity market participants lost interest in exchange-traded futures contracts in favor of over-the-counter forward contracts. In March 2002, NYMEX delisted electricity futures, and soon after that CBOT and IPE stopped trading their contracts. MGE is still trading electricity futures but the volumes are small. Today only EEX, and particularly, Nord Pool maintain a high level of trading activity in futures. As an example, consider one of the MGE electricity futures contracts, which by design is very close to the original NYMEX contract.

EXAMPLE 2.1   *Twin Cities electricity on-peak futures contract specifications*

Volume: 736 MWh

Price quotation: $/MWh

Delivery location: Twin Cities Hub

Delivery period: From the first day of the delivery month to the last day of the delivery month

Delivery Rate: 2 MWh during the consecutive on-peak hours of the delivery month

Last trading day: The sixth business day preceding the first delivery day

NYMEX Gas Futures

Gas futures are primarily traded on NYMEX.

Specifications:

Volume: 10,000 MMBtu (Million British thermal units)

Price quotation: $/MMBtu

Delivery location: Sabine Pipeline Company's Henry Hub in Louisiana

Delivery period: From the first day of the delivery month to the last day of the delivery month

Delivery rate: As uniform as possible

Last trading day: Six business days prior to the first calendar day of the delivery month

Following the lead of NYMEX, other exchanges launched gas futures similar to NYMEX contracts, but with new delivery locations. For example, Kansas City Board of Trade has introduced a new gas contract for delivery at the Volero pipeline in West Texas.

Hedging with Futures

The application of futures as a hedging tool is well documented in finance literature (see Kolb, 1997; Hull, 1999). Here we illustrate the hedging procedure on a simple but useful example.

Value of a Fixed-Price Forward Contract

Our goal is to evaluate, at any given time t, a contract for delivery of a commodity at some future month in exchange for a fixed payment of X $/unit of commodity. This is typically called a *fixed-price forward contract*.

To avoid unnecessary complications, we assume that the delivery conditions of this contract agree with those of the futures contract for the same month. The price of this futures contract at time t is denoted by $F_{t,T}$, where T is the expiration time of the contract.

Our goal is to show that the value at time t of the fixed-price forward contract for a party that at delivery pays a fixed price X and receives one unit of the commodity is

$$V(t, F_{t,T}) = e^{-r(T-t)}(F_{t,T} - X) \tag{2.1}$$

where r is the risk-free rate.

Alternatively, the value of this contract for a party that delivers one unit of the commodity in exchange for a fixed payment is

$$V(t, F_{t,T}) = e^{-r(T-t)}(X - F_{t,T}) \tag{2.2}$$

The proof of the relations (2.1) and (2.2) is based on one crucial and widely used assumption of the convergence of futures and spot prices at the futures expiration date.

Convergence Assumption

For a given time t, let $F_{t,T}$ denote the price of the futures contract expiring at T. It is assumed that at expiration the futures price converges to the spot price S_T of the asset underlying the futures contract,

$$F_{T,T} = S_T \tag{2.3}$$

The condition (2.3) is called the *convergence assumption*.

We are now ready to prove equalities (2.1) and (2.2). For this we use the delta hedging procedure with hedges applied at certain times $t_0, t_1, \ldots, t_n = T$. Successful delta hedging is equivalent to the following equality, which in case of (2.1) and (2.2) can be proved directly:

$$V(T, F_{T,T}) + e^{r(T-t_1)}\delta_0\Delta F_0 + e^{r(T-t_2)}\delta_1\Delta F_1$$
$$+ \ldots + e^{r(T-t_{i+1})}\delta_i\Delta F_i + \ldots + \delta_{n-1}\Delta F_{n-1} = e^{r(T-t_0)}V(t_0, F_{t_0,T}) \tag{2.4}$$

where

$$\delta_i = \frac{\partial V}{\partial F}(t_i, F_{t,T}) \quad \text{and} \quad \Delta F_i = F_{t_{i+1},T} - F_{t_i,T}$$

Delta Hedging.   The equality (2.4) is the essence of dynamic or delta hedging with futures: the asset value at the beginning of hedging period is equal to the asset value plus the value of the hedges at the end of the period (all adjusted for the accrued interest). In other words, delta hedging preserves the value of the asset by ensuring that the value of the portfolio consisting of the asset and the hedges does not change with time.

Note that (2.4) is a strict equality only because the value function $V(t, F_{t,T})$ in (2.1) and (2.2) is linear. Generally (e.g., in the case of options) discrete delta hedging will result only in an approximate equality (2.4). More specifically, the equality will be valid up to higher-order terms in Δt_i—the length of interval between consecutive instances of re-hedging. The smaller Δt_i, that is, the more frequent the instances of re-hedging, the closer we are to the exact equality (2.4) and, thus, to preserving the initial asset value. (This is a somewhat idealized picture since we have ignored the transaction costs associated with hedging, which in general should not be.)

Recalling the convergence assumption (2.3), $F_{T,T} = S_T$, the monthly spot commodity price, we finally have

$$(S_T - X) + e^{r(T - t_1)} \delta_0 \Delta F_0 + \ldots + \delta_{n-1} \Delta F_{n-1} = (F_{t_0,T} - X) \quad (2.5)$$

in the case of the fixed-price payer and

$$(X - S_T) + e^{r(T - t_1)} \delta_0 \Delta F_0 + \ldots + \delta_{n-1} \Delta F_{n-1} = (X - F_{t_0,T}) \quad (2.6)$$

in the case of the fixed-price receiver.

Assume now that marketer XYZ wants to trade a forward contract on a certain commodity but does not agree with the payer's forward contract evaluation (2.1) or with the receiver's contract value (2.2).

■ **CASE 1.**   XYZ is confident that the value at t_0 of the receiver's forward contract (XYZ receives a fixed payment) is greater than the one given by (2.2),

$$V_{XYZ}(t_0) > e^{-r(T - t_0)} (X - F_{t_0,T}) \quad (2.7)$$

Here, $V_{XYZ}(t_0)$ denotes the value of the contract from XYZ's point of view. This means that at time t_0 XYZ is willing to pay us $V_{XYZ}(t_0)$ for the right to deliver a commodity in the future month and to receive a fixed payment X. After entering into the contract with XYZ, we immediately implement the delta hedging strategy, assuming that (2.2) is the correct value of the contract. (From our point of view, it is a payer's contract; that is, at every time t_i the hedge position is $\delta_i = -e^{r(T - t_i)}$ per unit of commodity.) At expiration time T we pay XYZ the fixed payment X, and receive the commodity that we promptly sell at the spot market for S_T. Thus, at expiration our total cash flow per unit of commodity consists of the following components:

$+S_T$ is the sale of the commodity at the spot market

$-X$ is the fixed payment

$e^{r(T-t_0)} \delta_0 \Delta F_0 + \ldots + \delta_{n-1} \Delta F_{n-1}$ is the futures margin account

$+e^{r(T-t_0)} V_{XYZ}(t_0)$ is the initial payment from XYZ at the inception of the contract

Our total P&L from the contract is

$$\Pi = (S_T - X) + e^{r(T-t_1)} \delta_0 \Delta F_0 + \ldots + \delta_{n-1} \Delta F_{n-1} + e^{r(T-t_0)} V_{XYZ}(t_0)$$

Using (2.5) we obtain that

$$\Pi = e^{r(T-t_0)} [V_{XYZ}(t_0) + e^{-r(T-t_0)} (F_{t_0,T} - X)]$$

By (2.7)

$$V_{XYZ}(t_0) + e^{-r(T-t_0)} (F_{t_0,T} - X) > 0$$

Therefore, at expiration we guarantee ourselves a profit regardless of market behavior. It makes no difference if we have to pay cash into a futures margin account, or if we have to pay XYZ at t_0 in case of negative $V_{XYZ}(t_0)$—we just borrow the necessary cash and repay the debt at expiration. But as long as $V_{XYZ}(t_0)$ is greater than the value given by (2.2), we will make a riskless profit without ever using our own cash.

Creating a riskless profit is called *arbitrage*. A common and frequently justifiable assumption is that arbitrage cannot exist for a long period of time. Indeed, once XYZ shows that he values the contract at a level allowing others to make riskless profit, many offers to enter the contract appear, and XYZ will realize that he has overvalued the contract and adjust the value.

■ ■ ■

■ **CASE 2.** Assume now that XYZ believes that

$$V_{XYZ}(t_0) < e^{-r(T-t_0)} (X - F_{t_0,T}) \tag{2.8}$$

Thus, if we are interested in entering into a receiver's contract with XYZ (we receive a fixed payment), we will be happy to learn that XYZ values this contract lower than we do. Therefore, XYZ will accept the payment of $V_{XYZ}(t_0)$ for agreeing to receive the commodity in the specified future month in exchange for paying the fixed payment X. After this we implement delta hedging, assuming that (2.2) holds.

At futures expiration time T our cash flow consists of the following components:

$- S_T$ stands for buying commodity at the spot market to delivering it to XYZ

$+ X$ is the fixed payment from XYZ

$e^{r(T-t_1)} \delta_0 \Delta F_0 + \ldots + \delta_{n-1} \Delta F_{n-1}$ represents the futures margin account

$-e^{r(T-t_0)} V_{XYZ}(t_0)$ is the payment to XYZ for entering the contract (borrowed money, hence accrued interest)

Total P&L at T is

$$\Pi = (X - S_T) + e^{r(T-t_1)} \delta_0 \Delta F_0 + \ldots + \delta_{n-1} \Delta F_{n-1} = e^{r(T-t_0)} V_{XYZ}(t_0)$$

By (2.6)

$$\Pi = e^{r(T-t_0)} [e^{-r(T-t_0)} (X - F_{t_0,T}) - V_{XYZ}(t_0)]$$

Recalling the assumption (2.8) we obtain that $\Pi > 0$. We have again achieved a riskless profit, which means that (2.8) cannot last for long.

■ ■ ■

Thus, both inequalities (2.7) and (2.8) cannot hold for long, and we must conclude that the value of the receiver's fixed forward contract should be (2.2). By the same token, (2.1) should give us the value of the payer's fixed forward contract. This completes the derivation of valuation formulas for the forward contract.

The equalities (2.1) and (2.2) imply that a fair fixed price for a forward contract at any time t is

$$X = F_{t,T} \tag{2.9}$$

Indeed, at this price the present value of the contract is zero; therefore, parties negotiating the contract at time t should accept this price and enter the contract without any up-front cash payment. Price transparency is one of the most important consequences of a liquid futures market.

It is important to emphasize that the ability to hedge is the main reason why both parties can and will agree on the pricing of a forward contract. Furthermore, there are other valuable consequences that follow from the availability of a hedging strategy.

1. First and foremost, a hedging strategy offers the ability to manage market risk. With a good hedge it is possible to lock in the initial value of a deal despite adverse market movements.

2. A hedging strategy offers the ability to value deals. Hedging allows one to use the arbitrage argument in valuation procedures, just as it was used above to value forward contracts.

3. A hedging strategy means the ability to agree on fair pricing of the deal. What would be the fair price of the forward contract if we did not or could not hedge? Clearly, it would be an expectation at time t of the forward spot prices S_T,

$$X = E_t\,(S_T) \tag{2.10}$$

This expected value would most likely be a result of statistical analysis of historical data, or a product of one of the numerous forecasting models. In any case, it is subjective, with a high possibility that different parties had different estimates of the expected value. By contrast, a hedging strategy results in everyone agreeing on the forward price, since any deviation will be arbitraged away. By (2.9) the uniformly accepted forward price is the futures price $F_{t,T}$. Thus, the ability to hedge eliminates the necessity to seek the expectation of spot prices in the future. Instead of these expectations, based on subjective distributions of spot prices in the real world, we can now use the transparent prices of exchange-traded futures. Hedging removes the burden of having an argument about "correct" distributions in the real, or physical world, as it is frequently called, and allows us, instead, to use futures in place of expected spot prices.

This is *not* equivalent to saying that futures prices *are equal* to the physical-world expectations of spot prices. For pricing purposes, and only in the presence of a hedging strategy, we can and should use futures prices instead of physical-world expectations.

In the financial literature the difference between forward expectations of spot prices and corresponding futures prices is called *risk premium*. The ability to hedge allows us to move away from the physical world and consider solutions of pricing problems in the conventional world, where expectations of spot prices in the future are equal to futures prices, that is, the world without the risk premium. This world is commonly called the *risk-neutral world,* and evaluation in this world is called *risk-neutral evaluation.*

To illustrate hedging with futures we provide the following example.

EXAMPLE 2.2   *Hedging with futures*

A load-serving entity (LSE) in the Twin Cities area is searching for ways to provide power to its clients during summer months. The LSE has concerns that the summer power prices may be high, and it wants to shield itself from the price volatility. The best solution is to lock in the summer prices as early as possible, say on January 1. The LSE enters into the negotiations with an energy trading and marketing company (ETM) to ensure the supply of power at a fixed price for the month of July. On January 1 (we will denote this date by t_0) the July futures price $F_{t_0}^{TC} = \$50/\text{MWh}$. Therefore, both parties agree that in July the ETM will deliver a contracted amount of on-peak power, say, 73,600 MWh, and the LSE will pay the fixed price $X = \$50/\text{MWh}$ for this power. Clearly, with this deal the LSE has reached its goal of minimizing its risk due to volatile summer prices by shifting it to the ETM. In order to manage this risk and to meet its obligations, the ETM has immediately implemented the dynamic hedging strategy. Table 2.2 illustrates the behavior of the hedges through the life of the deal under two scenarios of rising and falling prices. (Contract and hedge values are given from ETM's point of view.)

The scenarios presented in this table precisely demonstrate our point that with the help of dynamic hedging the ETM is able to meet its obligations to the LSE at the end of the contract. In particular, the prices in Scenario 1 moved against the ETM, and at the end of June it was facing a loss of $3,680,000, having had to buy power at the spot market at a much higher price than the \$50/MWh it received from the LSE. However, the cash accumulated on the futures margin account nullified this loss. Similarly, in Scenario 2 the debt of $1,695,434.31 accumulated to cover margin requirements was paid off from the profits earned by delivering power purchased at the spot market for \$27/MWh, and sold for the contractual \$50/MWh.

Another important observation is related to the significance of the margin account. Suppose that instead of dynamic hedging the ETM chose a different strategy to protect itself, and at the outset of the contract it bought futures for the full amount of power it was obligated to deliver to the LSE. In this case, that would be 73,600 MWh or 100 futures contracts priced at \$50/MWh. (This strategy is sometimes suggested in the literature.) On the surface it looks like a good protection, since at the futures expiration the ETM will take delivery on its long futures position of 73,600 MWh paying \$50/MWh. Then the ETM will deliver this power to the LSE, receiving \$50/MWh, thus covering its expenditures at the futures delivery. In reality, this static hedging strategy has some risks as is demonstrated in Table 2.3, where the strategy is applied to Scenario 2 from Table 2.2.

TABLE 2.2 Behavior of Hedges in Rising and Falling Prices

Scenario 1: Increasing futures prices

Hedge number	Date	Futures price	Contract value	Change in contract value	Delta Hedge (MWh)	Futures hedge (contracts)	Futures margin account[1]	Change in margin
1	1-Jan	$50.00	$0.00		71,501.15	97	0	
2	1-Feb	$55.00	– $359,332.20	($359,332.20)	71,866.44	98	$358,783.67	$358,783.67
3	1-Mar	$60.00	– $721,979.86	($362,647.65)	72,197.99	98	$722,742.62	$363,958.95
4	1-Apr	$70.00	– $1,451,336.76	($729,356.90)	72,566.84	99	$1,451,399.99	$728,657.36
5	1-May	$80.00	– $2,187,767.57	($736,430.81)	72,925.59	99	$2,190,817.42	$739,417.43
6	1-Jun	$90.00	– $2,931,926.20	($744,158.63)	73,298.15	100	$2,934,372.63	$743,555.21
Expiration	26-Jun	$100.00	– $3,680,000.00	($748,073.80)			$3,685,487.39	$751,114.76

Scenario 2: Decreasing futures prices

Hedge number	Date	Futures price	Contract value	Change in contract value	Delta Hedge (MWh)	Futures hedge (contracts)	Futures margin account[1]	Change in margin
1	1-Jan	$50.00	$0.00		71,501.15	97	0	
2	1-Feb	$47.00	$215,599.32	$215,599.32	71,866.44	98	($215,270.20)	($215,270.20)
3	1-Mar	$43.00	$505,385.90	$289,786.58	72,197.99	98	($506,106.33)	($290,836.12)
4	1-Apr	$40.00	$725,668.38	$220,282.48	72,566.84	99	($726,181.45)	($220,075.13)
5	1-May	$35.00	$1,093,883.78	$368,215.41	72,925.59	99	($1,095,892.55)	($369,711.10)
6	1-Jun	$33.00	$1,246,068.63	$152,184.85	73,298.15	100	($1,247,963.86)	($152,071.31)
Expiration	26-Jun	$27.00	$1,692,800.00	$446,731.37			($1,696,521.56)	($448,557.70)

[1]To avoid unnecessary complications, we assume that the futures price changes occur at the beginning of each hedging period so that the interest is accrued through the entire period.

TABLE 2.3 Static Hedging Applied to Scenario 2 in Table 2.2

Hedge number	Date	Futures price	Contract value	Change in Contract value	Delta hedge (MWh)	Futures hedge (Contracts)	Futures margin account[1]	Change in margin
1	1-Jan	$50.00	$0.00		71,501.15	100	0	
2	1-Feb	$47.00	$215,599.32	$215,599.32	71,866.44	100	($221,928.04)	($221,928.04)
3	1-Mar	$43.00	$505,385.90	$289,786.58	72,197.99	100	($518,710.05)	($296,782.00)
4	1-Apr	$40.00	$725,668.38	$220,282.48	72,566.84	100	($743,288.13)	($224,578.08)
5	1-May	$35.00	$1,093,883.78	$368,215.41	72,925.59	100	($1,116,781.99)	($373,493.86)
6	1-Jun	$33.00	$1,246,068.63	$152,184.85	73,298.15	100	($1,270,439.54)	($153,657.55)
Expiration	26-Jun	$27.00	$1,692,800.00	$446,731.37			($1,719,089.80)	($448,650.26)

[1]To avoid unnecessary complications, we assume that the futures price changes occur at the beginning of each hedging period so that the interest is accrued through the entire period.

28

As is clear from this table, the ETM will have a deficit of $23,698.57 at futures expiration, and will not be able to cover margin requirements with proceeds from its contract with the LSE.

Is $23,698.57 a substantial quantity for us to be concerned with?

As a percentage of the total contract value or margin account value it is indeed small—less than 1.5%—but this comparison is misleading. A correct approach is to compare this quantity with the profit the ETM expects to net from this deal. At its inception, the value of the deal is zero. A perfect hedging strategy, as we have demonstrated above, will only preserve this zero value under market movements. Therefore, if the ETM decides to hedge, the only way for it to profit is through its presumably superior trading executions. That is, if $50/MWh was the mid-price of the July futures on Jan. 1 (mid-price is the middle point between bid and offer prices), and if $49/MWh and $51/MWh were, respectively, the bid and offer prices of the same contract, then the ETM expected to make at least half of the $2/MWh spread by buying futures closer to the bid size. Thus, the ETM expected to make at most $73,600 on its contract with the LSE. Suddenly, the reduction of the profits by $23,698.57 does not look so small. We can lose almost a third of our expected profits by carrying out, instead of a dynamic hedging strategy, a simpler but defective static hedge. What hurt us was the interest accumulated on the margin account.

Failure to implement a correct hedging strategy is just one of many risks in managing deals even as simple as a standard fixed-price forward contract. Other common and often interrelated risks include:

Execution Risk

- Inability to execute futures trades at the quoted price
- Inability to execute trades of necessary size

Basis Risk

- At expiration the futures prices may not exactly converge to the spot prices
- The delivery conditions of the hedged forward contract may be somewhat different from those of the futures contract.

Liquidity Risk

- Inability to hedge at the right time, at the right price, at the right size (similar to execution risk)

Credit Risk

- Inability to borrow cash to meet margin requirements

The last risk is crucial, because inability to borrow can literally ruin a company. (The case of Metallgesellschaft is one of the most famous examples.) Analysis of the availability of cash to meet margin requirements under a variety of scenarios is essential to the development of successful futures hedging strategies (Culp and Miller, 1999).

Termination of a Futures Contract

The termination of a futures contract is important, among other reasons, due to its relation to the convergence assumption (2.3), which played the key role in the application of the no-arbitrage argument. The termination of futures typically occurs in three ways (see Kolb, 1997).

1. Closing a futures contract by entering the offsetting futures position
2. Exchanging futures for physical (EFP). An EFP is an agreement between a party with a long futures position and a party with the equal size short position to enter a bilateral contract specifying the terms of physical delivery (location and price). The futures positions for both parties are terminated under the terms of the contract.
3. Keeping the contract until expiration for physical delivery

The third method of termination needs to be examined in greater detail. When the futures contract expires, the owner of the long position becomes the buyer of the commodity at the futures settlement price. To monetize this commodity position, the owner should sell it at the spot market. Alternatively, the holder of the short futures position must buy the commodity at the spot market to deliver and receive the futures settlement price. Since in most cases the delivery of an energy commodity is uniformly spread over the delivery month (e.g., daily delivery), the holder of the futures contract is exposed to the differential between the settled futures price and the average of the spot prices inside the deliverer period. To analyze this differential, it is convenient to split it into two parts.

The first part involves a differential between the futures price and the price of a physical deal that closely matches the futures contract. For example, in the case of natural gas, when futures contracts require monthly delivery, the monthly physical contracts are actively traded during the bid-week when the price of gas for the next month delivery is determined. Due to the need to match futures and monthly physical contracts, it's no accident that bid-week overlaps the futures settlement period and that the greatest activity in trading monthly contracts coincides with the futures expiration dates. As the result, the monthly indexes such as *Inside FERC's Gas Market Report* (IFGMR) are quite close to the futures settlement price.

The second part of the differential involves the spread between the monthly physical index (e.g., IFGMR) and the average daily spot prices. This difference can be rather large. More precisely, the distribution of this difference has a substantial standard deviation while the mean of this distribution on average is close to zero.

Thus, the spread between the settled futures prices and the average spot prices can be also substantial, although its expectation may be close to zero. The existence of this spread implies that the convergence assumption (2.3) is valid only on average and that the holder of the futures contract is exposed to potentially a significant basis risk.

Forward Contracts

Forward contracts, like futures, are agreements to buy or sell a commodity at a future time. The price to be paid at delivery is specified in advance, when the contract is made. Specifications may vary, but the most common are as follows:

- Delivery price is fixed at the inception of the contract *or*
- At the outset, the formula is agreed upon by which the price will be determined at the delivery time. This formula may be based on the futures price at expiration; or on the futures prices during the period before expiration. For example, it can be an average of closing futures prices during the week preceding the expiration date. Or it can be based on an index other than the futures price, for example, an index distributed by a respectable publication, such as *Inside FERC's Gas Market Report, Gas Daily,* or *Megawatt Daily.*

As follows from Figure 2.1, a forward contract, similar to a futures contract, must specify the following characteristics:

- Delivery details (total quantity, per day/hour quantity, firm/non-firm, and so on)
- Delivery price or formula for computing delivery price
- Delivery period and time of delivery during this period
- Delivery location

Date: March 1, 2001

Buyer:	ABC	**Seller:**	XYZ
Quantity (MW):	50	**Quantity (MWh):**	16,800
Price ($/MWh):	40.50	**Type of energy:**	Firm (LD)
Start Date:	April 1, 2001	**End Date:**	April 30, 2001
Day of Week:	Mon–Fri, Peak hours Excluding NERC Holidays	**Hours:**	HE 0700–2200 CPT
Delivery Point:	Seller's choice into Cinergy interface		

FIGURE 2.1 Example of a Fixed-price Forward Contract for a Power Delivery

There are, however, important differences between forward and futures contracts.

1. Unlike exchange-traded futures, forward contracts are over-the-counter (OTC) products. They need not be standardized, and they can be structured in the way most convenient to the counterparties. This flexibility is one of the reasons why electricity forward contracts are currently more popular than futures. Consider, for example, the electricity futures delivery volume, which is fixed at 736 MWh all on-peak hours during the contract month with the rate of delivery fixed at 2 MWh. Since the amount of on-peak hours differs from month to month, sometimes Saturdays are added to fit the contractual obligations. Therefore, if the goal is to supply power only during on-peak hours (or during a certain block of on-peak hours, or during off-peak hours, and so on), forward contracts provide a much more flexible tool than futures to meet this goal. It is of no surprise then that in the power market, with its multitude of contractual needs, forward contracts have completely taken over and are at present the most liquid and widely used risk management tool.

2. Forward contracts can be
- Physically or financially settled
- Yearly, seasonal, quarterly, monthly, daily, hourly, etc.
- Defined in any geographical location

3. Forward contracts, unlike futures, are not settled daily. On the positive side, this means that a contract holder does not have to worry about having daily access to cash to satisfy margin requirements. On the negative side, if the market moves in the right direction (i.e., the contract ends up being in-the-money), the contract holder becomes exposed to counterparty credit risk.

Value of a Forward Contract

We have established that the value of a fixed-price forward contract for future delivery of a unit of commodity, with delivery terms identical to those of a futures contract, is expressed by

$$V_f(t, F_{t,T}) = e^{-r(T-t)} (F_{t,T} - X)$$

In reality, the valuation formula even for such a simple contract is more complicated and should be

$$V_f(t, F_{t,T}) = N \cdot e^{-r(t, T_{pay})(T_{pay}-t)} \cdot (F_{t,T} - X) \qquad (2.11)$$

In this formula:

t is the time at which the contract is evaluated

X is a contractual fixed price to be paid for one unit of the delivered commodity

T_{pay} is the payment time (it can be different from the contract settlement time)

$r(t, T_{pay})$ is an annualized, continuously compounded discount rate from t to T_{pay}

$e^{-r(t, T_{pay})(T_{pay}-t)}$ is the correspondent discount factor

N is the number of commodity units to be delivered under the contract

$F_{t,T}$ is the price at time t of the futures contract settled at the same time as the forward contract

$V_f(t, F_{t,T})$ is the value of a fixed-price forward contract at time t

The sign convention is as follows: a positive N corresponds to the payer's fixed-price forward contract (we pay a fixed price and receive a commodity), and a negative N corresponds to the receiver's forward contract (we deliver commodity and receive a fixed price).

We have assumed that the delivery conditions of a forward contract are similar to those of a futures contract. What if there is a discrepancy in the delivery conditions? What if a forward contract has a different delivery location, starting time, daily amounts, and so on? All these differences, particularly the geographical ones, are typically accounted for through the introduction of a spread with respect to the futures prices. The forward values of the spreads are either extrapolated from the historical data or provided by the markets. In many instances spreads are actively traded, and spread-based products, such as basis swaps, are almost as liquid as the futures or forward contracts. Denoting this spread by d_t and representing the forward price of a commodity under general delivery conditions as $F_{t,T} + d_t$, we can now modify the equality (2.11) to reflect a more general case of a forward contract:

$$V_f(t, F_{t,T}, d_t) = N \cdot e^{-r(t,T_{pay})(T_{pay}-t)} \cdot (F_{t,T} + d_t - X) \qquad (2.12)$$

The proof of this equality is similar to the one we have used to justify equalities (2.8) and (2.9). The only difference is that now the value depends on two variables, F_t and d_t, and therefore hedging should now be performed using futures, as well as spread-based instruments. Finally, we note that X in the equation (2.11) can represent any index, and not just a fixed price. For example, X can be a fixed price plus a geographical spread

$$X = Y + d_t$$

It is easy to see that, in this case, the equality (2.12) goes back to the form (2.11),

$$V_f(t, F_{t,T}) = N \cdot e^{-r(t,T_{pay})(T_{pay}-t)} \cdot (F_{t,T} - Y)$$

On the other hand, if X is defined in the contract as a fixed spread of the futures price,

$$X = F_{t,T} + D$$

then

$$V_f(t,F_t) = N \cdot e^{-r(t,T_{pay})(T_{pay}-t)} \cdot (d_t - D)$$

Application: Hedging with Forward Contracts

The use of forward contracts for dynamic hedging is as common as that of futures, particularly in electricity markets, where forward contracts currently represent the majority of instruments used for risk management. As in hedging with futures, in order to hedge a complex structure whose value depends on a number of random factors, we must first find a set of forward contracts dependent on the same factors. Then we will determine the contract sizes by matching the sensitivities of the structure, or deltas, of these factors with those of the hedge portfolio. To illustrate this approach, we consider an example of a structure whose value

$$V(t,F_{t,T})$$

depends only on time and futures prices.

Then a correct hedge at time t_i is the one that negates the term

$$\frac{\partial V}{\partial F}(t_i, F_{t_i,T})(F_{t_{i+1},T} - F_{t_i,T})$$

Suppose we want to hedge with a fixed-price forward contract whose value at any time t is expressed by (2.11). The change of value for this forward contract between times t_i and t_{i+1} is

$$N \cdot e^{-r(t_i,T_{pay})(T_{pay} - t_i)}(F_{t_{i+1},T} - F_{t_i,T})$$

Therefore, to achieve a correct hedge at time t_i, we need to enter in a forward contract on

$$N_i = -\frac{\partial V}{\partial F}(t_i, F_{t_i,T}) \cdot e^{r(t_i,T_{pay})(T_{pay} - t_i)} \tag{2.13}$$

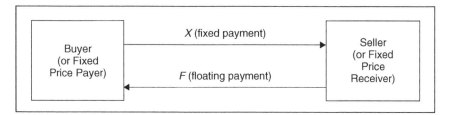

FIGURE 2.2   Fixed-price Swap

units of commodity. As in (2.11), a positive N_i corresponds to the payer's forward contract, and a negative N_i corresponds to the receiver's forward contract. Note the difference between the futures hedge size

$$\delta_i = -\frac{\partial V}{\partial F}(t_i, F_{t,T})$$

and the size of the hedge involving forwards given by (2.13). This is clearly a result of the different settlement characteristics of both contracts, and is yet another indication that futures and forwards, while similar, have distinct attributes, behaviors, and risk factors.

Swaps

There are a number of reasons that explain the phenomenal popularity of swaps in virtually all markets. Here are just a few:

1. Swaps are flexible, OTC, easily customizable transactions.
2. Swaps are typically financially settled (do not involve physical delivery), off-balance sheet and nonregulated.
3. Swaps are uniquely suited for hedging applications.

Swaps in energy markets are similar to swaps in financial markets and are natural generalizations of forward contracts (which themselves can be viewed as a one-period swap). The most frequently encountered is a fixed-price swap in which for a period of several months or years one counterparty pays another a fixed payment and in exchange receives a payment linked to a certain floating index. Graphically, this periodic transaction can be represented as shown in Figure 2.2.

The fixed payment may be the same every period or vary according to a specified schedule. The floating payment is typically connected to a commodity spot price or price index. It is not difficult to see how swaps can be used for hedging.

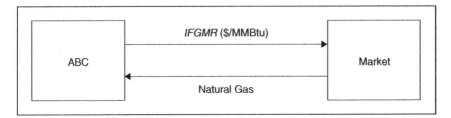

FIGURE 2.3   ABC's Procurement Contract

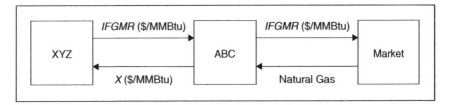

FIGURE 2.4   ABC's Hedged Procurement Business

EXAMPLE 2.3   *Hedging with swaps*

An industrial corporation, ABC, procures its monthly natural gas supply at the spot market paying the *Inside FERC's Gas Market Report* (*IFGMR*) index for each MMBtu delivered. Schematically, ABC's procurement contract looks like Figure 2.3.

At some point ABC concludes that the index volatility is too high and decides to eliminate price risk from its procurement contract. As a result of this decision, ABC and marketer XYZ enter into a financial swap in which ABC agrees to be a payer of the fixed payment and a receiver of the *IFGMR*. The exchange of payments will occur every month. Now, ABC's procurement business looks like Figure 2.4.

As is clear from this diagram, ABC is no longer exposed to the spot price fluctuations, since the floating payments it is required to make are now supplied by marketer XYZ on a monthly basis—ABC is only passing them through to the market. ABC's obligations are now limited to paying fixed payments to XYZ. Thus, by entering the swap ABC has completely removed its price exposure and shifted it to XYZ who is probably much better equipped to manage the price risk.

This type of swap can be typically represented as a strip of monthly fixed-price forward contracts. This representation, together with the expression (2.11) for valuation of forward contracts, allows us to derive a formula for the value of the swap.

$$PV_{swap}(t) = \Sigma_i N_i \cdot [f_i \cdot DF(t, T_{i,pay}^{float}) - X \cdot DF(t, T_{i,pay}^{fixed})] \qquad (2.14)$$

The notation is standard:

N_i is the volume

$f_i = F_{t,T_i}$ is the forward price at the valuation time t of the commodity for delivery in the i-th month, which by (2.9) is the price of the corresponding futures contract

$DF(t,T_{i,pay}^{float}) = e^{-r_i(t,T_i)(T_i-t)}$ is the discount factor from t to time $T_{i,pay}^{float}$, the time of payment for the commodity delivered during the i-th month

$DF(t,T_{i,pay}^{fixed})$ is the discount factor from t to the fixed-price payment time $T_{i,pay}^{fixed}$

$PV(t)$ is the present value of the swap at time t

Using the equality (2.14) we can now derive an expression for a fair value of the fixed payment X, the value that delivers a zero swap present value. This value of X is called a *swap price* and is key in the origination and analysis of swaps. Setting the left side of (2.14) to zero and solving for X, we obtain the following expression for the swap price:

$$SP(t) = \frac{\Sigma_i N_i \cdot f_i \cdot DF(t,T_{i,pay}^{float})}{\Sigma_i N_i \cdot DF(t,T_{i,pay}^{fixed})} \qquad (2.15)$$

The formula (2.14) assumes that the frequency of fixed and floating payments is the same, which is a rather natural assumption in the case of energy swaps. (Financial swaps, on the other hand, often have different payment frequencies.) In the general case, instead of (2.14) one should use the following formula for the present value of a swap:

$$PV_{swap}(t) = \sum_{i_{fl}} N_{i_{fl}} \cdot f_{i_{fl}} \cdot DF(t, T_{i_{fl},pay}^{float}) - \sum_{i_{fx}} N_{i_{fx}} \cdot X \cdot DF(t, T_{i_{fx},pay}^{fixed}) \quad (2.16)$$

where i_{fl} and i_{fx} are the indexes for floating and fixed payment periods respectively. The swap price is then expressed by:

$$SP(t) = \frac{\sum_{i_{fl}} N_{i_{fl}} \cdot f_{i_{fl}} \cdot DF(t,T_{i_{fl},pay}^{float})}{\sum_{i_{fx}} N_{i_{fx}} \cdot DF(t,T_{i_{fx},pay}^{fixed})}$$

TABLE 2.4   Market and Contractual Conditions

Month	Volume of MMBtu	Cash payment dates	Discount factors	Forward prices per MMBtu
Nov	600,000	20-Dec	0.96734	$4.20
Dec	620,000	20-Jan	0.96242	$4.30
Jan	620,000	20-Feb	0.95753	$4.50
Feb	560,000	20-Mar	0.95313	$5.10
Mar	620,000	20-Apr	0.94829	$5.00

Applications of Swaps

As a risk management tool, swaps are indispensable. The flexibility of swaps allows a risk manager to structure them so that they closely approximate a target risk profile. This is much easier to achieve than with futures whose delivery and settlement requirements add unnecessary rigidity to the task of risk management. Swaps are amenable to any accounting treatment, accrual, or mark-to-market, and need not be rolled or actively managed.

EXAMPLE 2.4   *Swap price*

At the beginning of the summer, say June 1, a local distribution company (LDC) decides to secure the baseload supply of gas for the coming winter. It is known that the winter demand is 20,000 MMBtu/day. The LDC wants to pay one fixed price for the gas supply. Find this price, assuming the following market and contractual conditions shown in Table 2.4.

From the equality (2.15) it follows that the swap price is

$$SP = (600{,}000 \cdot 4.20 \cdot .96734 + 620{,}000 \cdot 4.30 \cdot .96242 + 620{,}000 \cdot$$
$$4.50 \cdot .95753 + 560{,}000 \cdot 5.10 \cdot .95313 + 620{,}000 \cdot 5.00 \cdot$$
$$.94829)/(600{,}000 \cdot .96734 + 620{,}000 \cdot .96242 + 620{,}000 \cdot .95753 +$$
$$560{,}000 \cdot .95313 + 620{,}000 \cdot .94829) = 4.61$$

Thus, a fair fixed price that the LDC should agree to pay on June 1 for the winter gas supply is $4.61 /MMBtu.

Flexible, versatile, manageable, and widely used, swaps have been extensively covered in the literature (e.g., see Kolb, 1999; Beidleman, 1990; Clewlow and Strickland, 2000). In Chapter 8 we will return to this subject again and discuss a number of useful energy applications of swaps and their derivatives.

Plain-vanilla Options

Standard Power and Natural Gas Options

After futures, forwards, and swaps, standard options, such as calls and puts, are the most frequently used risk management instruments. The literature on options is quite extensive (e.g., see McMillan, 1992; Hull, 1999; Cox and Rubinstein, 1985), and to date options are well studied and understood. Therefore, we are not going to spend much time on their analysis. We remind the reader that in energy markets a *call option* is the right, but not the obligation, to buy energy at a predetermined strike price, and a *put option* is the right, but not the obligation, to sell energy at a predetermined strike price. European-style options are exercised only once, at the specified exercise day, while American options can be exercised any time before the exercise date.

Thus, by definition, there is not much difference between calls and puts in energy markets and calls and puts in all other markets. What sets them apart is an unusual diversity of traded energy options, a natural consequence of the diversity in the underlying commodity, especially power (see Chapter 1). Typically, energy option specifications include:

- Location
- Exercise time
- Delivery conditions, for example, in the case of power, the type of delivered power (on-peak, off-peak, round-the-clock)
- Strike
- Volume

In order to illustrate the variety of energy options consider the following option classes.

Calendar-year, Quarterly, and Monthly Physical Options

These options are exercised only once, on or before the exercise date (depending if the option style is European or American), and the exercise decision is applied to the whole delivery period.

EXAMPLE 2.5 *Power options*

Monthly option: 50 MW ERCOT on-peak June 2002 $60 CALL

Quarterly option: 100 MW PJM off-peak Q3 2002 $25 CALL

Calendar-year option: 50 MW Cinergy round-the-clock CAL2002 $35 PUT

The owner of the first option has the right, but not the obligation, to call on the seller of the option to deliver 50 MW of power for each on-peak hour (from 7 AM until 11 PM) during the month of June in the ERCOT region at 60 $/MWh. If this is a European-style option, it is exercised specifically on the exercise day, May 29, 2002. If it is an American-style option, it can be exercised any time before that date.

The second option in the above example gives its owner the right to call on 100 MW of power for each off-peak hour (from 11 PM until 7 AM) of the third quarter of 2002 for delivery in the PJM region at $25/MWh. The option is exercised on or before June 28, 2002.

Finally, the third option gives its owner the right to sell (to put) 50 MW of power in a Midwestern location (Cinergy) round-the-clock for the whole year 2002 and to receive 35 $/MWh for this power. The exercise date is typically several business days before the beginning of the year.

European Option Exercise Payoffs

To understand the payoff at the option exercise, we must separate financially settled options from physically settled ones.

Financially Settled Option. For options to be settled financially, there must be a widely accepted financial index against which the options are exercised. In the gas market, there are indexes such as *Inside FERC's Gas Market Report,* and therefore, the financial settlement of gas options is common.

The payoff of a financially settled European call on energy is not different from any other financially settled call. That is, if K is the strike price, and S is the price of the index against which the option is settled, the call's payoff is given by

$$\Pi_{call} = \begin{cases} S - K & \text{if } S \geq K \\ 0 & \text{if } S < K \end{cases}$$

or

$$\Pi_{call} = \max\{S - K, 0\}$$

Similarly,

$$\Pi_{put} = \begin{cases} K - S & \text{if } S \leq K \\ 0 & \text{if } S > K \end{cases}$$

or

$$\Pi_{put} = \max\{K - S, 0\}$$

Physically Settled Options. Physical settlement is particularly relevant for power options, since the power markets have not yet developed a solid financial index for financial settlement.

Consider, for example, a monthly call option. Physical settlement means that the option holder has the right, but not the obligation, to buy, paying the strike price K, the commodity for the period of one month. Buying the commodity is only the first step in extracting the value from the option. To realize the option payoff, the option owner must now sell the commodity at the spot market. This situation is similar to the one for futures settlement discussed in the section on termination of a futures contract. The option is then effectively an option on the average spot price inside the contractual month.

As we explained, we can try to proxy for this average in two ways. In one approach we use a convergence argument and represent the average spot price as a value to which monthly forward prices converge at expiration. The advantage of this approach is that forward prices in most energy markets are quoted and reliable. The disadvantage of this approach is that the time-basis between the settlement of the forward price (at the beginning of the contract month) and the time the average settles (end of the contract month) can be very significant in power markets (as high as 100$/MWh). This disqualifies the use of forward prices as a proxy in power option pricing. Incidentally, for forward contract pricing, whether settled physically or financially, the use of the forward price is not a problem as the forward price at expiration and the average spot price are statistically (on average) equal. However, for option pricing statistical equality is not enough. The above consideration is very important for power markets. In natural gas markets, the use of forward prices as a proxy for value seems to work well.

In the second approach, we use an average of daily spot prices over the delivery month. Again, the daily spot prices are rather transparent in most markets. This approach corresponds to taking the commodity into the month and trading it on a daily basis at daily spot prices. The justification for this approach is based on the assumption that the monthly average of daily prices should be close to the monthly spot index (in natural gas markets). In reality, the average of daily prices is a random variable. Its relation to another random variable, the monthly spot index, and their joint behavior must be thoroughly studied and properly modeled.

Once we have chosen the method of representing the price S at which we can sell the commodity at the spot market, the option payoff is the same as for the financially settled options, namely,

$$\Pi_{call} = \max\{S - K, 0\} \text{ and } \Pi_{put} = \max\{K - S, 0\}$$

Fixed-Strike(Daily) and Floating-Strike(Index or Cash) Options on the Spot Commodity

In this section we consider another popular group of options—options on the spot commodity. As a rule, these options can be exercised daily. This group is typically divided into two subgroups.

Fixed-Strike Option (a.k.a. Daily Option). An option exercised every day during the exercise month. It allows its owner to make daily decisions during the exercise month about buying (call option) or selling (put option) spot gas or power at a fixed strike price.

Floating-Strike Option (a.k.a. Index or Cash Option). An option exercised every day during the exercise month with a specified monthly index as a strike price. It allows its owner to make daily decisions during the exercise month about buying (call option) or selling (put option) spot gas or power at a strike price determined at the beginning of the month as a settled value of the monthly index.

Options on the spot commodity are very common among energy derivatives, because they answer the real need to manage price risks on a daily basis. They are typically structured as a strip of options exercised daily during a certain time period (month, quarter, season, and so on). Therefore, their payoffs can be represented as

$$\Pi_{daily\_call} = \sum_{i = day\_in\_period} \max \{S_i - K, 0\}$$

$$\Pi_{daily\_put} = \sum_{i = days\_in\_period} \max \{K - S_i, 0\}$$

The strike is either fixed or linked to a floating index, which, as a rule, is set at the beginning of each month. A typical floating strike in the gas daily options is *Inside FERC's Gas Market Report*. It is worth noting also that there are some differences between gas and power daily options. Gas options are typically financially settled against a specified financial spot price index, such as the *Gas Daily Index*. Power daily options are typically physically settled and therefore the variable *S* in the above payoffs represents the spot price in the physical power markets.

Hourly Options

Currently hourly options are a purely power market phenomenon, responding to the needs of managing power price risks. These options are financially settled against the real-time hourly prices (in the U.S. markets while some European markets trade in 15-minute intervals).

In power markets, forward options are not widely traded. The only exceptions are ATM options, which are actively traded in the over-the-counter (OTC) market in several regions. Their liquidity depends on how volatile and how high the power prices are—those two facts are connected (see Chapter 4 for a discussion of the inverse leverage effect in the energy markets). For very low volatilities, the market seems to lose interest in the protection offered by options and the liquidity dries up. Conversely, when the prices are very high and volatility becomes very large, few players are willing to write calls. The risks associated with a short volatility position become unmanageable, and the liquidity virtually disappears.

It is worth noting here that as the markets are transacted OTC, the size of the bid-ask spread might not be a good measure of liquidity. In extreme situations, market participants are willing to buy calls (for insurance purposes), while hardly anyone is interested in selling them. The market becomes one-sided with nobody capable of making a two-sided market. Consequently the reported bid-ask spread becomes quite narrow, indicating only the prices at which the exchange between few sellers and many willing buyers will occur.

It might seem puzzling that no one is willing to make a two-way market (at least since the demise of Enron). At some substantial premium, there should be a willing participant. It has to be understood however, that selling an option in a high price environment is very risky since the standard strategy of writing a covered call might not be feasible due to the inability to buy the underlying in a very constrained system. These are precisely the circumstances under which the prices and volatility will be very high. One will not be able to buy the physical power at any price. Under those conditions, the only possibility is to price those structures at a high actuarial premium, which makes option pricing techniques largely irrelevant.

The same factors have an even greater impact on the ability to effectively trade daily power options. The result is that the liquidity of OTM (out-of-the-money) and even ATM (at-the-money) forward and daily options is quite spotty. The market is awaiting the entry of well-capitalized speculators, willing to take on the enormous risks and earn the attendant returns (and glory).

Option Valuation

Option pricing is one of the most extensively covered subjects in the financial literature. There are numerous publications devoted to analysis of different valuation methodologies. (We refer the reader to Wilmott (2000) for the details and bibliography.) For illustration purposes, we consider Black's formula for options on futures in this section. This is the case of monthly call and put options described in the previous section whose payoffs at the expiration time T are

$$\Pi_{call} = \max \{F_{T,T} - K, 0\} \text{ and } \Pi_{put} = \max \{K - F_{T,T}, 0\}$$

where, as before, $F_{t,T}$ denotes the futures price at a given time t.

Black's valuation formula for options on futures is developed under certain assumptions about the instantaneous changes of futures prices, specifically, that the price change at time t

$$\Delta F_{t,T} \equiv F_{t+\Delta t,T} - F_{t,T} = \sigma F_{t,T}\sqrt{\Delta t}\,\varepsilon \tag{2.17}$$

where the parameter σ is called volatility, and ε is a normally distributed random variable with expectation zero and standard deviation one. Under this condition, the values of the futures call and put are given by the formulas (Black, 1976)

$$V_{call}(t,F_{t,T}) = e^{-r(T-t)}\,[F_{t,T}N(d_1) - KN(d_2)] \tag{2.18}$$

$$V_{put}(t,F_{t,T}) = e^{-r(T-t)}\,[KN(d_1) - F_{t,T}N(d_2)] \tag{2.19}$$

where

$$d_1 = \frac{\ln(F_{t,T}/K) + \sigma^2(T-t)/2}{\sigma\sqrt{T-t}}$$

$$d_2 = \frac{\ln(F_{t,T}/K) - \sigma^2(T-t)/2}{\sigma\sqrt{T-t}}$$

It is easy to verify that under the assumption (2.17) $V_{call}(t,F_{t,T})$ and $V_{put}(t,F_{t,T})$ satisfy the equality (2.4) up to higher terms in Δt. This means that the delta hedging procedure can be successfully applied to standard options (see Hull, 1999, and the discussion following the equality (2.4)).

As we know, the most important consequence of the ability to hedge is that market participants must agree with the options values given by (2.18) and (2.19), as long as they agree with the futures price movement assumption (2.17). Moreover, anyone selling options at time t and collecting premia (2.18) and (2.19), and then executing delta hedging, is guaranteed to be able to meet their obligations to the option buyer at the option expiration time T. Conversely, if one borrows money to buy an option, the option payoff at the exercise date, combined with the value of the hedge portfolio, will be sufficient to repay the loan. Again, this is true under the assumption that market movements follow the equation (2.17).

In natural gas and oil markets the forward options are very actively traded for a variety of monthly forward contracts and strike prices. As we shall see, the implied volatilities exhibit significant dependence on the strike price. This strongly suggests that the underlying process for forward prices cannot be described by (2.17). Consequently, pricing and hedging of those structures require the more sophisticated models described in Chapter 4. Thanks to a significant number of available tradables, hedging a given vanilla structure can be performed quite effectively.

Hedging Daily Options with Forwards

A forward contract in energy markets is simply a fixed-for-float swap with the floating leg set by the average cash (spot) price. In natural gas markets, the cash price is given by the *Gas Daily* index for a given liquid point, while in power (especially pool) markets it is usually given by the average on-peak price (either day-ahead or day-of) for a given day.

Since the forward/futures contracts expire before the beginning of the month, there is no convergence between the forward price at expiration and the average inside-the-month spot prices. Consequently, there is no put-call parity with the forward contract. The portfolio of a long daily call and a short daily put is not equal to the forward price, although it can be the case on average. While it should be possible, but not simple, to delta hedge the monthly option, hedging daily options is seriously impeded by the (time) basis between the value of the underlying swap at expiration (end of the contract month) and its value at the beginning of the month (when the forward option expires).

The daily contracts are extensively used to manage the exposures associated with physical assets and demands. By trading in the option markets, volatility-sensitive assets such as gas storage or generation plants can exploit the existing option markets to monetize the value of the associated optionality. As we will see later, a physical asset faces significantly more complex volatility exposure than simple vanilla products. Nevertheless, should the need arise, one can build complex structures from the vanilla products.

Applications: Risk Management

Daily and especially cash options in energy markets have a very different character from similar option structures in financial markets. They are not derivative products as such, since the underlying of those options is not traded directly. These options can be viewed as the basic tradables of the energy markets along with forward/futures contracts. This is especially pertinent in power markets where the spot commodity itself does not exist. Indeed, unlike corn or copper, power purchased on one day cannot be resold on another. The situation is analogous (although not as extreme) to the weather market in which the spot commodity can be observed but cannot be traded.

In pricing and risk management of cash and daily options we cannot rely on the replication argument, because the replicating portfolio does not exist. We can still achieve an approximate replication by using other spot "derivative" contracts (e.g., forwards, forward options). The residual, though, is very substantial. Consequently, the market makers supply a primary economic service. To a degree, the option market makers can be seen as intermediaries mediating the process of risk allocation that cannot be achieved in any other way (e.g., by trading in the underlying).

In truth the above distinction between financial and energy markets is one of degree and not of the essence of the process. Options in financial markets may not be fully replicable either. But in energy markets the issue is much more pronounced.

Applications: Hedging with Options

Hedging with options is very common in energy applications simply because options are frequently the only instrument to address risk management needs. For example, as we will see in Chapter 3, price spikes of high magnitude are a frequent reality in power markets and consequently, a source of great concern for power marketers who need to buy spot power to fulfill their obligations to the customer. To protect themselves against exceptionally high prices, they often buy call options. If the power prices greatly increase, the marketer will exercise the option and pay only the option strike for the power.

EXAMPLE 2.6   *Hedging as insurance against an extraordinary event*

The marketer XYZ wants protection from the power price spikes during the month of August. For that purpose, XYZ buys a daily call option with the strike $200/MWh. The option premium is $10/MWh per day. Hence the total premium is $310/MWh per month. If in the month of August there is at least one day with $1,000/MWh and every other day the price is below $200/MWh, just by exercising the option during the high-price day, XYZ saves $1,000/MWh $-$ $200/MWh = $800/MWh in power prices. Taking into account the option premium, the total saving is $800/MWh $-$ $310/MWh = $490/MWh.

In this example an option is used as an insurance against extraordinary events. These are typically low-probability events with possibly devastating effects on the company. Because of their almost discrete nature they are not very amenable to the standard hedging techniques (such as dynamic hedging), and therefore buying options/insurance is a more appropriate course of action in this circumstance.

The use of standard options for managing risk will be discussed throughout this book, and particularly in Chapter 8. Here we will list some of the most typical energy applications:

■ Meeting load obligations, ensuring supply under adverse weather conditions
■ Protecting against unexpected events, such as forced outages, price spikes, and so on.
■ Capping exposure on the upside as well as downside

For an extensive presentation of options as the hedging tool in the energy markets we refer the reader to Krapels (2000), *Managing Energy Price Risk* (2000), Clewlow and Strickland (2000), Pilipovic (1997).

Applications: Speculative and Arbitrage Strategies

Options are frequently recommended as an efficient speculative tool, allowing one to achieve high leverage in directional bets with limited loss potential—an option buyer cannot lose more than an option premium. If options are correctly priced (the option markets are efficient), buying an option (or any combination of options) is a game with zero risk-adjusted profit expectation, like playing heads or tails. Consequently, the value of those strategies comes from the differences in risk appetites of the market participants. The option market can also be an attractive investment in the case when options are not correctly priced (i.e., replicated). In other words, when the option markets are inefficient, careful investment can be very beneficial. For example, option strategies may rely on exploiting relative mispricing, or discovering an arbitrage between different option markets, or developing a better estimation of volatility. Needless to say, these strategies are quite different from simple directional bets.

EXOTIC OPTIONS

Vincent Kaminski and Stinson Gibner in their 1997 paper, "Exotic Options," gave an excellent introduction to exotic options and presented the reasons behind their increased popularity in energy. In summary, the use of complex energy derivative products can be explained by their ability to capture complex structural characteristics of energy deals and assets, and to provide a powerful tool for managing relevant price risks. These derivatives are not a product of analysts' whims, but are naturally embedded in the most common energy contracts and organically enter into practically every aspect of energy trading, marketing, asset management, and risk management.

There is no shortage of publications on exotic options, their applications, and pricing methodologies, particularly as financial markets are concerned. (For examples, see Wilmott, 2000; *Over the Rainbow,* 1995; Nelken, 1999; Rebonato, 1998.) In this book we will concentrate on a particular subgroup of exotic options that, in our opinion, has the greatest relevance in energy markets. As a starting point, in this chapter we consider *spreads* and *spread options*.

Other important classes of exotic options will be considered in Chapter 8.

Spreads

The spread, both as a product and a concept, is probably the most useful, prevalent, and important structure in the world of energy. Indeed, spreads are used to describe power plants, refineries, storage facilities, and transmission lines. Practically every aspect of energy production and delivery can be explained using spreads. As a trading tool, they are used to stabilize operational cash flows, to mitigate geographical and calendar risks, and to arbitrage market inefficiencies. In this section we will introduce several important and frequently encountered spreads and give examples of their applications.

A spread is a price differential between two commodities. Below we present several common classes of spreads.

> **Intracommodity spread or quality spread.** For example, *sweet versus sour crude oil spread* represents the difference between the spot prices of different grades of crude.
>
> **Geographic spread.** For example, *Sonat versus Henry Hub spread* represents the difference between prices in two particular locations.
>
> **Time or calendar spread.** For example, *July '02 versus November '02 natural gas futures spread* represents the difference between futures prices of different expiration.
>
> **Intercommodity spread.** This is by far the most important class of spreads and we are going to consider it in detail in the next section.

Intercommodity Spreads

Definition: Price differential between two different, but related commodities.

In the energy markets one encounters a great variety of intercommodity spreads. Most frequently they are connected to a certain operational process.

> **Spread between operational inputs.** For example, *#6 residual fuel oil versus natural gas spread* represents the spread between power plant input fuels.
>
> **Spread between operational outputs.** *Gasoline versus #2 heating oil spread* represents the spread between the refinery outputs.
>
> **Spread between outputs and inputs (processing spread).** This class of spreads contains two most frequently encountered spreads, the crack spread and the spark spread.

Crack Spread

Definition: Differential between the prices of refining products (outputs) and the price of crude oil (input).

TABLE 2.5   Heat Rate Data

	Heat rate Btu/kWh	Efficiency (%)
"Ideal" Power Plant	3,412	100
Combined Cycle Combustion Turbine	6,250–7,200	55
Base Load Unit	10,000–12,000	30–35
Single Cycle Gas Turbine	12,000–19,000	20–30

Unleaded gasoline (UG) and #2 heating oil (HO) are the most profitable refining products. Eighty percent of the crude feedstock goes into the production of UG and HO.

Application of Crack Spread: "Paper Refinery."   The crack spread is used to financially replicate the physical reality of a refinery, that is, to replicate a short position in crude oil and a long position in the refined products. Refineries use the crack spread to lock into their production margins. Crack spreads are being traded over-the-counter and on NYMEX.

Spark Spread

Definition: Differential between the price of electricity (output) and the prices of its primary fuels (inputs).

Primary fuels are natural gas, coal, #6 residual fuel oil, and uranium. The spark spread between electricity and natural gas is the most common. Spark spreads are traded over-the-counter.

Application of a Spark Spread: "Paper Power Plant."   The spark spread can be used to financially replicate the physical reality of a power plant, that is, to replicate a short position in fuels and a long position in electricity. Merchant plants can use the spark spread to lock into their production margin. To better understand the mechanics of spark spread utilization it is necessary to introduce an important characteristic of a power plant, the heat rate.

Heat Rate

Definition: Number of Btus needed to make 1 kWh of electricity.

Heat rate is a measure of how efficiently the generating unit converts the energy content of the primary fuel into power. Ideally, in the absence of any inefficiency, it would take 3412 Btu to produce 1 kWh of electricity. Table 2.5 contains heat rate data for some frequently encountered power plants.

It is important to note that when heat rate is presented as a constant, it is done to simplify matters and is merely an approximation. In reality the heat rate varies with a number of parameters, particularly the ambient

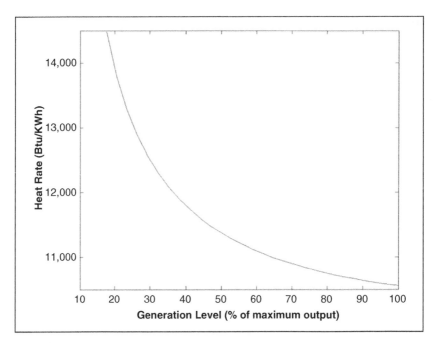

FIGURE 2.5   An Example of Heat Rate of a Single Cycle Gas Turbine As a Function of Generation Output

temperature and the plant generation level. Figure 2.5 presents an example of heat rate dependence on the generation output.

Thus, when we say that a heat rate of a particular plant is 7,000 Btu/kWh, we mean that on average it will take 7,000 Btu to produce 1 kWh (or 7 MMBtu to produce 1 MWh). If we want to be more precise, we must determine the generation level, ambient temperature, and so on, find the corresponding heat rate, and use that rate to determine the number of Btus necessary to produce 1 kWh under these conditions.

Another use of the heat rate (HR), particularly important in financial applications, is to determine the cost of fuel needed to generate one unit of power. Indeed, if it takes HR Btu to produce 1 kWh of power and the price of 1 Btu of fuel is

$$P_{fuel}\left(\frac{\$}{Btu}\right)$$

then the fuel cost of generation of 1 kWh of power is

$$Fuel\_Cost_{power}\left(\frac{\$}{kWh}\right) = HR\left(\frac{Btu}{kWh}\right) \cdot P_{fuel}\left(\frac{\$}{Btu}\right) \qquad (2.20)$$

or, after simple arithmetic manipulations,

$$Fuel\_Cost_{power}\left(\frac{\$}{MWh}\right) = \frac{1,000\left(\frac{kWh}{MWh}\right)}{1,000,000\left(\frac{Btu}{MMBtu}\right)} \cdot HR\left(\frac{Btu}{kWh}\right) \cdot P_{fuel}\left(\frac{\$}{MMBtu}\right)$$

$$= \frac{1}{1,000} \cdot HR\left(\frac{Btu}{kWh}\right) \cdot P_{fuel}\left(\frac{\$}{MMBtu}\right)$$

EXAMPLE 2.7 *Fuel cost of generating 1 MWh of power*

Assume that the heat rate of a gas-fired power plant is 7,000 Btu/kWh, and that currently the cost of 1 MMBtu of natural gas is $3/MMBtu. Then, the cost of fuel needed to generate 1 MWh of power is

$$\frac{7,000}{1,000} \cdot \$3/MMBtu = \$21/MWh$$

Table 2.6 contains examples of cost of generating 1 MWh of electricity for different types of fuel and corresponding generic plants.

Thus, the significance of the heat rate is that it provides a conversion factor between fuels used to generate power and the power itself. This allows us to compare the corresponding energy contents. Furthermore, it allows us to compare fuel and power prices expressing them in the same units, typically in $/MWh. Once the heat rate is specified, the spark spread can be defined as

$$Spark\_Spread = Power\_Price - Heat\_Rate \cdot Fuel\_Price$$

TABLE 2.6 Cost of Power Generation for Different Fuel Types

Fuel	Fuel units	Fuel cost ($/unit)	Heat content (MMBtu/unit)	Fuel cost ($/MMBtu)	Heat rate (Btu/kWh)	Fuel cost ($/MWh)
Coal	Tons	25	20	1.25	9,500	12
Gas	1,000 CF	3	1	3	10,000	30
#6 Oil	Barrel	16	6	2.67	12,000	32
Nuclear	KG	32,000	64,000	.5	10,000	5

Quoting the Spark Spread

As a rule, electricity is quoted in \$/MWh, gas is quoted in \$/MMBtu, and heat rate is quoted in Btu/kWh. Hence,

$$Spread\left(\frac{\$}{MWh}\right) = P_{power}\left(\frac{\$}{MWh}\right) - \frac{1,000 \frac{kWh}{MWh}}{1,000,000 \frac{Btu}{MMBtu}} \cdot HR\left(\frac{Btu}{kWh}\right) \cdot P_{fuel}\left(\frac{\$}{MMBtu}\right)$$

or, in a more simple form,

$$Spread\left(\frac{\$}{MWh}\right) = P_{power}\left(\frac{\$}{MWh}\right) - \frac{1}{1,000} \cdot HR\left(\frac{Btu}{kWh}\right) \cdot P_{fuel}\left(\frac{\$}{MMBtu}\right)$$

$$(2.21)$$

Sometimes, it is required to express the spread in \$/MMBtu:

$$Spread\left(\frac{\$}{MMBtu}\right) = \frac{P_{power}\left(\frac{\$}{MWh}\right)}{Heat\_Rate\left(\frac{Btu}{kWh}\right) \times \frac{1}{1,000}} - P_{gas}\left(\frac{\$}{MMBtu}\right)$$

EXAMPLE 2.8   *Computing spark spread*

Assume that the price of electricity is 40.50 \$/MWh, the price of natural gas is 3.00 \$/MMBtu and the heat rate is 8,152 Btu/kWh. Then, by (2.21), the spread quoted in \$/MWh is:

$$Spread\left(\frac{\$}{MWh}\right) = 40.50\left(\frac{\$}{MWh}\right) - \frac{1}{1,000} \cdot 8,152\left(\frac{Btu}{KWh}\right) \cdot 3.00\left(\frac{\$}{MMBtu}\right)$$

$$= 16.04\left(\frac{\$}{MWh}\right)$$

Simple Arbitrage

Consider an example of a gas-fired plant serving a regional load. The heat rate of the plant is $HR = 10,000$ Btu/kWh. The plant receives X \$/MWh according to the service contract. The plant dispatcher has two alternatives in serving the load:

1. Burn gas, generate power, and serve the load.
2. Buy power from the grid (at spot prices) and serve the load.

In the first strategy the plant's profit/loss (P&L) is

$$\Pi_1 = X - HR \cdot G \ \$/MWh$$

with G being the price of gas. The second strategy P&L is

$$\Pi_2 = X - P \ \$/MWh$$

with P being the spot power price. The difference between strategies,

$$\Pi_1 - \Pi_2 = P - HR \cdot G$$

is exactly the value of the spark spread. Thus, the dispatcher's strategy is to determine the current spark spread by computing it directly or consulting a publication such as *Megawatt Daily*. If the spark spread is positive, the first alternative is better, and the dispatcher must run the plant to serve the load. Otherwise, the power should be bought from the grid. For example, if the natural gas price is currently \$3/MMBtu and power price is \$40/MWh, then the spark spread is \$40 − 10 × \$3 = \$10/MWh. The positive spark spread means that it is economical to run the plant.

This example is given for illustration purposes only. In practice, the dispatch decision is much more complex and will be discussed in detail in Chapter 9.

Forward Spark Spread

Since the spark spread is an approximate financial representation of a physical power plant, it is not surprising that it is frequently used to hedge merchant power plant operator's exposure to the market prices. As with any other hedging application, to manage power plant's forward price risks we need a forward spark spread. To define a forward spark spread we must specify:

- Delivery date
- Size (typically in MWh)
- Heat rate

Fundamentally, a forward spark spread contract is a combination of forward contracts in electricity and fuel. Specifying a forward spark contract is equivalent to specifying each of its standard components.

Buying the forward spark spread is equivalent to buying electricity forward and selling gas forward. The payoff from a long position in the forward spark spread is the difference between the spot spark spread at maturity and the contractual delivery price.

Selling the forward spark spread is equivalent to selling electricity forward and buying gas forward. The payoff from a short position in the forward spark spread is the difference between the contractual delivery price and the spot spark spread at maturity.

EXAMPLE 2.9   *Using a forward spark spread to manage the price risk*

An operator of a merchant power plant wants to protect himself from the fluctuation of gas and power prices during the future months of August. Assume that the August forward power price is $40/MWh and forward gas price is $3/MMBtu. The plant's heat rate is 10,000 Btu/kWh and total August power output is 100,000 MWh. In order to achieve his objective of locking into the margins implied by today's gas and power forward prices, the operator employs the following strategy:

- Sell the financially settled forward spark spreads totaling 100,000 MWh. By definition, to sell 1 MWh spark spread = sell 1 MWh of power + buy 10 MMBtu of gas. Total: sell 100,000 MWh of power and buy 1,000,000 MMBtu of gas.
- At maturity (end of July) of the forward spark spread contract, buy gas and sell electricity into the spot market for monthly delivery.

By selling the forward spark spread the operator has ensured operational margins equal to the value of the forward spread, that is $10/MWh (for simplicity we ignored here a number of costs one should take into account in calculating margins, see Chapter 9). The spread value is obtained using the following calculation:

$$Spread\left(\frac{\$}{MWh}\right) = 40\left(\frac{\$}{MWh}\right) - 10 \times 3.00\left(\frac{\$}{MMBtu}\right) = 10\left(\frac{\$}{MWh}\right)$$

According to the strategy, at the end of July the operator settles the spread and simultaneously buys natural gas and sells power at the spot market for monthly delivery. We shall now demonstrate that with this strategy, $10/MWh is indeed a guaranteed operational margin regardless of August spot prices. Consider two scenarios.

Scenario 1.   August spot power price is $45/MWh and the spot gas price is $4/MMBtu. Hence, the August spot spark spread is $45/MWh − 10 × $4/MMBtu = $5/MWh. The total P&L per 1 MWh will consist of two components:

Settle spread position:	$10.00/MWh − $5/MWh = $ 5/MWh
Buy 10 MMBtu of gas	
and sell 1 MWh of power	
at the spot market:	$5/MWh
Total:	$10/MWh

Scenario 2.   August spot power price is $35/MWh and the spot gas price is $2/MMBtu. Hence, the August spot spark spread is $35/MWh − 10 × $2/MMBtu = $15/MWh. The P&L per 1 MWh:

Settle spread position:	$10.00/MWh − $15/MWh = − $ 5/MWh
Buy 10 MMBtu of gas	
and sell 1 MWh of power	
at the spot market:	$15/MWh
Total:	$10/MWh

We can conclude that no matter what the spot prices are at maturity, the operational margins are locked at $10/MWh, and the total operational margins for the month of August are locked at 100,000 MWh × $10/MWh = $1,000,000.

Next we show some more profitable spread option–based strategies for operating merchant plants.

Spread Options

It is impossible to underestimate the significance of spread options in the energy markets. Practically every energy asset and every structured deal has a spread option embedded in it. By definition, a spread option is an option on a spread, that is, an option holder has the right but not the obligation to enter into a forward or spot spread contract. Typically, it is a call or a put option, similar to the one considered earlier in this chapter, with the exception that the underlying is now a two-commodity portfolio, instead of a single contract.

EXAMPLE 2.10   *Payoffs of standard spread options*

Consider the example of an options on the spread between forward prices of power and natural gas. Let

F_{power} = forward price of electricity (*$/MWh*)

F_{gas} = forward price of natural gas times heat rate (*$/MWh*)

Then by the definition, the payoff at maturity of the call option on the spread is

$$\prod_{call} = \max \{(F_{power} - F_{gas}) - X, 0\}$$

and the payoff of the put on the spread is

$$\prod_{put} = \max \{X - (F_{power} - F_{gas}), 0\}$$

with X being the strike price.

Valuation of spread options is more complex than the valuation of plain-vanilla puts and calls and it will be analyzed at length in Chapter 8 and 9. Here we will demonstrate the ubiquitous nature of spread options by considering a number of key examples.

Power Plants

It is not difficult to see that in principle a merchant power plant is a spark spread option, that is an option on the spread between power and fuel prices. Indeed, if P is the spot price of power, G is the price of fuel, HR is the heat rate, and V is variable cost of running the plant (ex-fuel), then the decision to run or not to run the plant is rather straightforward. Consider two cases:

1. If $P - HR \cdot G - V \geq 0$, then run the plant. In this case buying fuel and paying variable costs $(HR \cdot G + V)$ to run the plant and then selling the generated power for P results in the positive gain.
2. If $P - HR \cdot G - V < 0$, do not run the plant. In this case buying fuel and paying variable costs to run the plant will not be compensated by sold power. It is better not to generate and receive zero than to generate at a loss.

Combining these two cases together, we can represent the operational margins from running the plant following this strategy as

$$\prod = \max \{P - HR \cdot G - V, 0\} \tag{2.22}$$

Note that this is exactly the payoff of the call option on the spread between power and fuel with the variable cost being the strike.

Once we have established that a power plant can be viewed as a spread option, we can suggest how to improve the operational strategy described in Example 2.9.

EXAMPLE 2.11   *Using spark spread options to manage price risk*

Assume that the market and plant characteristics are the same as in Example 2.9. The objective is also the same: to ensure constant operational margins in August regardless of the levels of spot prices. The strategy, however, will be different now. Instead of selling the forward spread, the operator will sell the option on the forward spread. Selling spread option is better than selling the spread itself, because the option value always exceeds the value of the spread. In the subsequent chapters we will explain why this is the case. Here we will only mention that the spread (if it is positive) is equal to the intrinsic value of the options. At the same time, the total value of the option consists of the intrinsic value and, on top of that, the time value which depends on time to expiration, volatility, and so on (see Hull, 1999 for details.) Therefore, the operator can expect to get more than $10/MWh—the value of the forward spark spread—if he or she sells the spread option. Assume that the spread option is sold for $12/MWh. Let us consider again two scenarios from Example 2.9, and verify if the objectives of protecting against price fluctuations are achieved.

Scenario 1.   The August spot power price is $45/MWh, the spot gas price is $4/MMBtu, and the August spot spark spread is $5/MWh. The P&L per 1 MWh is

Premium from selling the spark spread option:	$ 12/MWh
Payment to the spread option holder:	− $ 5/MWh
Buy 10 MMBtu of gas and sell 1 MWh of power at the spot market:	$5/MWh
Total:	$12/MWh

Scenario 2.   The August spot power price is $35/MWh, the spot gas price is $2/MMBtu, and the August spot spark spread is $15/MWh. The P&L:

Premium from selling the spark spread option:	$ 12/MWh
Payment to the spread option holder:	− $ 15/MWh
Buy 10 MMBtu of gas and sell 1 MWh of power at the spot market:	$15/MWh
Total:	$12/MWh

This example demonstrates that selling the options guarantees protection against price fluctuation and provides higher margins than selling the forward spread. All obligations with respect to the option buyer are fulfilled through running the plant.

Needless to say that the use of spread options to represent a power plant is only an approximation presented above for illustration purposes only. A real-life representation requires taking into account a large number of operational, environmental, market, transmission, and many other considerations to be effective. However, there exist rather popular products for which spread option representation may be more appropriate.

Tolling Agreements

One of the most popular power products, *the tolling agreement,* comes in different shapes and forms. The simplest way to represent this agreement is to view it as a call option on power with a floating strike linked to fuel prices. In real life applications the tolling contracts can be interpreted as leasing contracts on a plant wherein the "toller," the buyer of the call option, has the right to the plant output at his or her discretion. A typical tolling agreement has the following characteristics:

- The length of the contract is typically short-to-medium (up to several years).
- The toller has the right (but not obligation) to use the plant and to call, if he or she so chooses, for the firm delivery of energy on a specified time basis (for example, on a day ahead basis).
- Whenever the toller decides to exercise this right and to call for energy, he or she should pay for the energy according to the contractual arrangements. Typically, the payment is computed according to the formula

$$Heat\_Rate \times Fuel\_Price + VOM$$

The first term in the formula represents the fuel costs (see the definition (2.20)), while the second term, represents additional costs, frequently (but not always) variable costs of running the plant.

- The Toller has to pay regular (monthly, quarterly, and so on) premium to the plant owner for having the right to the plant output. This option premium is frequently called a *capacity payment.*

The tolling contracts do not belong exclusively to the world of power. In fact, the word "tolling" comes from the oil industry where similar arrangements allow the toller after paying a certain fee to have the right to use refinery (supply crude and receive refined products).

Viewing the tolling agreement as a call option with a fuel-linked strike price allows us to write the payoff of this option as

$$\Pi_{tolling} = \max \{P - HR \cdot W - VOM, 0\} \qquad (2.23)$$

where P is the spot (day ahead) price of power, W is a spot price of fuel (e.g., *Gas Daily Index*), and *VOM* denotes variable and other contractual costs. This payoff is identical to (2.22), that is, it is a payoff of an option on a spread between power and fuel prices with *VOM* being the strike. The value of this option is what determines the premium, or capacity payment, paid by the toller to the plant operator.

Reverse Tolling Agreement

If the tolling agreement can be represented as a call on power struck at the fuel cost of power, the reverse tolling agreement is a call on fuel struck at the cost of power that could be generated with this fuel. Thus, under this agreement the reverse toller can call on the fuel, but should pay for this with the equivalent quantity of power delivered to the plant operator to compensate for not running the plant. The payoff of the reverse tolling can be written as:

$$\Pi_{reverse\_tolling} = \max \{HR \cdot W + VOM - P, 0\} \qquad (2.24)$$

From this expression it is clear that reverse tolling is an option on the spread between fuel and power prices.

Gas Storage

The connection between gas storage and calendar spreads of futures prices is clear even in the case of the most straightforward approach to storage utilization. To illustrate this approach we consider the following example.

EXAMPLE 2.12   *Gas storage as a spread option*

On January 1 a gas marketer XYZ is evaluating a gas storage lease contract for two future months, October and November. Observing that October futures are traded at $4.50/MMBtu and November futures are $4.70/MMBtu, XYZ devises the following strategy to extract the value from the storage.

Strategy 1.   January 1: Sell the October–November futures spread, that is establish the following futures position:

- Long October contract
- Short November contract

October 1: Use October contract to buy gas, pay $4.50/MMBtu and put the delivered gas into the storage;

- Keep the gas in the storage during the month of October

- November 1: Use November contract to sell gas from storage at $4.70/MMBtu
- Lock the profit, $.20/MMBtu. (For simplicity, we have ignored injection/withdrawal costs and financing costs.)

We have just demonstrated that the value of the October–November storage is at least equal to the October–November futures spread. In reality, it is higher. To extract this higher value we need to employ a different strategy.

Strategy 2. January 1: Sell October–November spread option. This is an option on the October–November spread, and at the expiration date, say, October 1, it will pay

$$\max \{F_{Nov} - F_{Oct}, 0\}.$$

The key fact is that on January 1 the value of the spread option is higher than the value of the futures spread itself. The reason for this is a well-known result from the option theory stating that before expiration the option value is always higher than or equal to its intrinsic value, the difference being a non-zero option time value. This should not be confused with the value of the current forward spread, which can be higher than the option value, due to discounting effects. Of course, the option value, as well its time value, will depend on many factors, such as volatility, time to expiration, and so on. For example, in the case of $F_{Oct} = \$4.50/MMBtu$, $F_{Nov} = \$4.70/MMBtu$, volatility of each contract being 50%, correlation coefficient being equal to .95 and discount rate being 6%, on January 1 the value of the October–November spread option will be $0.35/MMBtu. Clearly, the earlier the start of the strategy, the greater the difference between the spread option and the futures spread proper.

Consider now possible scenarios at option expiration date October 1:

■ CASE 1.

$$F_{Oct} = \$4.80, \ F_{Nov} = \$5.50$$

Spread option loss: ($.70/MMBtu)

Availability of the storage allows us to buy October gas for $4.80/MMBtu, short the November contract, store gas, and sell it in November for $5.50/MMBtu. Profit: $0.70/MMBtu. We have met our obligation to the option owner. (Again, we ignore storage and other costs.)

Our total P&L = $0.35/MMBtu (spread option premium).

■ ■ ■

▥ CASE 2.

$$F_{Oct} = \$2.70, F_{Nov} = \$2.50$$

Spread option expires worthless; we do nothing and keep $0.35/MMBtu premium. Total P&L = $0.35/MMBtu.

▥ ▥ ▥

The implication of this strategy is that the storage is a hedge for a spread option. Therefore, its value should be at least as high as that of the spread option.

Example 2.12 has demonstrated that to evaluate gas storage one may use the value of the gas futures spread options. In the example, we have only considered a simple case of having storage only for two months, leading to evaluation of one spread option. In reality, gas storage is evaluated for a period of many years requiring evaluation of a complex portfolio of spread options, and not just spread options on futures, but options on a wide variety of spreads. Although it significantly increases the complexity of the problem, it does not change the fact that gas storage is in principle a combination of calendar spread options and should be valued as such. (See Chapter 8 for a detailed discussion of gas storage issues.)

Transmission Lines, Pipelines

Consider a frequently encountered transmission contract: a right to move power or gas from a liquid point A to a liquid point B. It is easy to show that the value of this contract is simply a value of the option on the spread between endpoint prices. Indeed, let P^A and P^B be the prices of a unit of power or gas at the endpoints of a transmission line or a pipeline. Let T^{AB} be the tariff on moving a unit of power or gas from A to B. Then, if at a time t_i the price at the endpoint B is greater than the price at the endpoint A plus the tariff, that is

$$P_i^B - P_i^A - T_i^{AB} > 0$$

it is worth buying the commodity at A, moving it through the transmission line, selling it at B, and collecting the profit. If the above does not hold we do nothing.

Combining these two cases together, we conclude that the cash flow generated by the transmission contract can be expressed as

$$\Pi_i = \max \{P_i^B - P_i^A - T_i^{AB}, 0\}$$

Therefore, if the decision on using a transmission line or a pipeline is made on a monthly, daily, or hourly basis, then the total value of the transmission contract is

$$\Pi = \sum_i \max\{P_i^B - P_i^A - T_i^{AB}, 0\}$$

This equality means that the evaluation of the transmission contract of moving power or gas from A to B can be reduced to evaluation of a series of options on the spread between endpoint prices, with the strike being a transmission line tariff.

EXAMPLE 2.13   *Valuing a transmission contract*

On January 1, XYZ, an owner of the transmission line, wants to sell a unidirectional transmission right contract for the month of September. The contract will allow the transmission right holder to move power from point A to point B, paying a tariff of $5/MWh. On January 1 the September forward prices at the endpoints of the line are $40/MWh and $45/MWh. Knowing that the volatility of these prices is 50%, correlation coefficient between them is 0.9 and risk-free rate is 6%, XYZ can compute the value of the spread option between these prices with tariff being a strike. It is equal to $3.23/MWh (see Chapter 8 for details on valuations of spread options.)

This concludes the overview of the most popular structures in the energy markets. Detailed analysis of pricing and hedging can be found in Chapters 8 and 9.

CHAPTER 3

Data

Analysis of the available data is the first, and potentially one of the most important, steps in understanding and quantifying the essential features of a particular market. Without thorough data analysis it is impossible to design models that capture crucial market drivers, describe unique market characteristics, and reflect particular market realities. Only through exhaustive data analysis can we select the most appropriate pricing model and understand its strengths and weaknesses, as well as the limits of its application. Model calibration and parameterization—a critical step in the model development process, yet frequently ignored in the literature—is impossible without data analysis based on the relevant statistical tools and methodologies. In this chapter we will focus on understanding the special properties of data used in energy models, as well as on the tools used to achieve this understanding.

STATISTICAL METHODS FOR DATA ANALYSIS

Estimation of Sample Mean, Variance, and Higher Moments

Estimation of mean, variance, and to a lesser degree correlation coefficients is clearly among the most frequently used statistical procedures. Although the formulas for these estimates are well known, they can easily be misused if one does not pay attention to the limits of their applicability. These limits are especially important in the case of financial and econometric data, which is often nonnormal, nonstationary, and autocorrelated. We will review these commonly used estimation formulas and provide confidence intervals for some of the estimates.

Everywhere in this section $(X_1, X_2, \ldots, X_n)$ denotes a random sample from the population with population mean μ, variance σ^2 and higher moments $\mu^{(k)}$, $k > 2$. In a multidimensional case X_i are vectors; the population mean vector is denoted by $\bar{\mu}$; and the covariance matrix is denoted by Σ. A useful interpretation of X_i: they are realizations or samples of a random variable X, characterized by a certain distribution with moments μ, σ, and $\mu^{(k)}$. This distribution may be unknown, or it may belong to a known family of distributions (for example, a family of normal distributions), but its parameters may still be unknown. The goal is to use the random sample to estimate the distribution or its parameters.

The Mean and the Variance.   The estimates of the population mean μ and variance σ^2 are given by the familiar expressions:

$$\overline{X} = \frac{1}{n}\sum_{i=1}^{n} X_i \tag{3.1}$$

$$s_x^2 = \frac{1}{n-1}\sum_{i=1}^{n} (X_i - \overline{X})^2 \tag{3.2}$$

Once the estimates are computed, a natural question follows: How good are these estimates? The answer is typically expressed in the form of a confidence interval. This is an interval that contains, with a required degree of certainty, the parameter of population distribution we set out to estimate (i.e., population mean, variance, etc.).

The confidence interval bounds are readily available if the sample is taken from a normally distributed population (e.g., see Hahn and Meeker, 1991). With the assumption of normality, the confidence interval bounds for the population mean μ are given by the following expression:

$$\Pr\left\{\overline{X} - t_{1-\alpha/2,n-1}\frac{s_x}{\sqrt{n-1}} < \mu < \overline{X} + t_{1-\alpha/2,n-1}\frac{s_x}{\sqrt{n-1}}\right\} > 1 - \alpha \tag{3.3}$$

Here $t_{1-\alpha/2,n-1}$ is a $1 - \alpha/2$ percentile of the $t-$ distribution with $n-1$ degrees of freedom, and α is a given confidence level.

The confidence interval for estimate (3.2) of a normally distributed population variance can be written in the form

$$\Pr\left\{s_x^2\frac{n-1}{\chi_{1-\alpha/2,n-1}^2} < \sigma^2 < s_x^2\frac{n-1}{\chi_{\alpha/2,n-1}^2}\right\} > 1 - \alpha \tag{3.4}$$

Here

$$\chi_{1-\alpha/2,n-1}^2$$

and

$$\chi_{\alpha/2,n-1}^2$$

are respectively $1 - \alpha/2$ and $\alpha/2$ percentiles of the chi-square distribution with $n - 1$ degrees of freedom. Thus, the $100(1 - \alpha)\%$ confidence interval for the population variance σ^2 is

$$\left[s_x^2 \frac{n - 1}{\chi_{1 - \alpha/2, \, n - 1}^2}, \, s_x^2 \frac{n - 1}{\chi_{\alpha/2, \, n - 1}^2} \right] \tag{3.5}$$

Remember that the expressions (3.3) to (3.5) for confidence intervals were derived under the assumption of normality of the population distribution. What if this assumption does not hold? Several approaches are frequently employed in this case.

1. As long as the individual observations are independent, it is acceptable for a sufficiently large n to use the interval (3.3) as the confidence interval for the estimate of the mean. It is an approximation, of course, but it can be validated by the central limit theorem, which allows us to treat the estimate $\overline{X}$ as normally distributed.

2. For small samples with a general population distribution, one can attempt to find a nonlinear transformation of the data such that the transformed population has a distribution much closer to normal. The transformations are typically chosen from, but certainly not restricted to, the Box-Cox family of mappings (see Box and Cox 1964) of the form

$$f(X) = \begin{cases} X^\gamma, & \gamma > 0 \\ \ln X, & \gamma = 0 \end{cases}$$

Once an appropriate transformation is found, confidence intervals (3.3) and (3.5) can be used for the estimates in the transformed space. If necessary, these confidence intervals can then be mapped back to obtain confidence intervals for the estimates related to the original population distribution.

3. Confidence intervals can be also determined using a distribution-free methodology, that is, a methodology that does not depend on any particular population distribution. Intervals obtained with this approach are usually wider than those derived using a specific distribution, but the approach itself is more general and flexible. We refer the reader to Hahn and Meeker (1991) for a detailed description of this and other methodologies, and their extensive bibliography on the subject of statistical estimation.

Bootstrapping techniques are an example. Their disadvantage lies in their ability to give us an idea of the confidence interval for finite samples. These can differ substantially from the asymptotic normal confidence interval.

The importance of the confidence intervals in data analysis can be illustrated by the following example.

EXAMPLE 3.1   *Empirical analysis of the expectation hypothesis for electricity prices*

The expectation hypothesis states that the forward price is an unbiased estimate of the expected future spot prices. Our goal is to determine if the current data support or refute this conjecture for electricity prices.

In this example we will test a slightly modified version of the expectation hypothesis: We will determine whether there is a drift in either daily changes or daily returns of futures prices of electricity. Although it is not precisely equivalent to the expectation hypothesis, the presence of a discernable nonzero drift in either of these cases can lead to the conclusion that the expectation hypothesis does not hold. In our test we will analyze the forward electricity prices for the PJM West region. The first test will be applied to price changes and is set as follows.

Let $F_{t,T}$ denote the forward price of electricity at time t for delivery at T. For each forward contract we use a historical series of daily prices $F_{t_i,T}$, $i = 1, \ldots, n$ and introduce the sequence of daily changes,

$$X_{i,T} = F_{t_i+1,T} - F_{t_i,T}$$

The average $\overline{X}_T$ will be our estimate of a drift μ_T of the forward price changes for a particular contract. Once $\overline{X}_T$ is computed, the only remaining question is whether this estimate implies that $\mu_T \neq 0$, and that we should reject the expectation hypothesis.

From (3.3) we have the following condition for rejecting the hypothesis of zero drift (corresponding to 95% confidence level):

$$\left| \sqrt{n-1} \, \frac{\overline{X}}{s_x} \right| > 2.0$$

The expression

$$u = \sqrt{n-1} \, \frac{\overline{X}}{s_x}$$

is called a *t*-statistic and is often used for testing hypotheses about expectations.

Table 3.1 shows the results of the drift test described above for PJM West forward contracts from June to August 1998. As is seen from the last column of the table, none of the forward contracts has a *t*-statistic greater

TABLE 3.1 Test of the Drift of Forward Price Changes

Contract	Number of observations	Average of daily price changes	Standard deviation of daily price changes	t-statistic
Jun-98	19	0.16140	0.67360	1.04
Jul-98	44	0.69460	2.45393	1.88
Aug-98	66	0.13605	4.32712	0.26

TABLE 3.2 Drift Test Applied to Returns

Contract	Number of observations	Average of daily price changes	Standard deviation of daily returns	t-statistic
Jun-98	19	0.00571	0.02325	1.07
Jul-98	44	0.01217	0.04373	1.85
Aug-98	66	0.00335	0.06903	0.39

than 2.0; therefore we cannot conclude that returns of PJM forward contracts exhibit a discernable nonzero drift. Thus, the expectation hypothesis cannot be rejected with 95% confidence.

The second test is applied to forward price returns. For this test we define daily returns as

$$X_{i,T} = \frac{F_{t_{i+1},T}}{F_{t_i,T}} - 1$$

Table 3.2 contains the results of this test. The forward price data used in this table is the same as in Table 3.1. As in the first test, we cannot conclude with confidence that any of the contracts has returns with a discernable nonzero drift.

Note that without a careful statistical analysis, but just looking at the averages of price changes or returns, we probably would have concluded that forward contracts are drifting upward with time. This in turn would imply that buying a forward contract and waiting until expiration would be a successful trading strategy. Table 3.3 contains the result of implementing exactly this strategy: buying forward contracts one year before expiration and closing position when the contract settles.

Table 3.3 shows that the trading profits are not as stellar as the averages led us to believe. Undoubtedly we could have anticipated a problem if in addition to return averages, we had considered their variances, and ultimately, their t-statistic, which would have given us an indication that average estimates should have been treated with caution.

TABLE 3.3   Profitability Test

Contract	Forward price one year before contract expiration	Average spot during the contract month	P&L average spot—forward
Jun-99	26.50	48.88	22.3
Jul-99	43.00	135.21	92.2
Aug-99	59.00	58.77	−0.2
Sep-99	27.50	27.92	0.4
Oct-99	25.65	26.01	0.3
Nov-99	26.40	23.05	−3.3
Dec-99	27.10	24.06	−3.0
Jan-00	27.10	31.53	4.4
Feb-00	31.00	26.98	−4.0
Mar-00	23.80	26.87	3.0
Apr-00	23.50	31.75	8.2
May-00	28.00	49.92	21.9
Jun-00	40.75	44.95	4.2
Jul-00	81.00	37.80	−43.2
Aug-00	74.25	48.42	−25.8
Sep-00	34.40	31.62	−2.7
Oct-00	25.90	39.26	13.3
Nov-00	26.75	44.93	18.1
Dec-00	26.35	65.70	39.3
Jan-01	30.29	51.25	20.9
Feb-01	29.15	36.93	7.7
Mar-01	26.13	44.42	18.2
Apr-01	26.39	48.02	21.6
May-01	32.60	40.30	7.7
Jun-01	57.00	42.51	−14.4
Jul-01	107.00	41.31	−65.6

The Higher Moments.   Equations (3.1) and (3.2) provide estimates for the first two moments of distribution. The estimates of higher moments are given by the expression

$$\mu^{(k)} = E(X - \overline{X})^k = \frac{1}{n} \sum_{i=1}^{n} (X_i - \overline{X})^k \tag{3.6}$$

Distribution Tests

To say that understanding the distribution properties of underlying variables is essential for the success of any stochastic model is to state the obvious. Modeling methodologies, model testing and acceptance routines, and, finally, model parameters all depend to a great extent on the choice of relevant distributions. If we focus on financial pricing models, we discover that a great majority of them are based on an assumption of the normality or log-normality of underlying price distributions.

Theoretical and computational convenience is certainly a beneficial characteristic of a model. However, it must be carefully weighed against the model's ability to realistically represent different aspects of empirical data, particularly price distributions. Needless to say, if there is a clear difference between empirical and model distributions, an effort should be made to modify the models with the purpose of achieving better agreement. There is a vast body of work devoted to empirical analysis of the properties of price distributions in different markets, and to development of models that incorporate these properties, most of which clearly abandon normality assumptions. A description of these models in any detail is obviously beyond the scope of this book. The reader can find examples of new modeling developments in equity, fixed income, and FX markets in Briys et al. (1998), Jarrow (1995), and Lipton (2001).

The analysis of empirical price distributions is especially important in the energy markets. Even a cursory look at sample histograms of electricity price returns (see Figure 3.5) is sufficient to make one apprehensive of the normality assumption for these returns. We obviously need a tool that allows us to quantify our intuition and to provide a formal foundation for acceptance or rejection of a particular choice of distributions built into our pricing models. More precisely, we need a test of the hypothesis that a sample $(X_1, X_2, \ldots, X_n)$ belongs to a population with a particular population distribution. In this section we introduce two useful tests frequently used to answer distribution-related questions. They are the Jarque-Bera test and Kolmogorov-Smirnov test.

The Jarque-Bera (JB) Test of Normality.   This test is used to test the normality hypothesis; it uses the following statistic:

$$JB = n\left[\frac{S^2}{6} + \frac{(K - 3)^2}{24}\right]$$

where S and K are skewness and kurtosis respectively:

$$S = \frac{\mu^{(3)}}{s_x^3}$$

and

$$K = \frac{\mu^{(4)}}{s_x^4}$$

The third and fourth moments $\mu^{(3)}$ and $\mu^{(4)}$ are defined in (3.6), and the variance s_x is defined in (3.2). For large sample sizes the JB statistic follows the chi-square distribution with 2 degrees of freedom, χ_2^2.

For normal distributions $S = 0$ and $K = 3$, and hence JB $= 0$. If the JB statistic is sufficiently large (greater than 6.0 at 5% significance level), the null hypothesis of population distribution normality is rejected.

The Kolmogorov-Smirnov test is more general and allows one to test an arbitrary distribution hypothesis, not necessarily normal distribution.

Kolmogorov-Smirnov Test.   This test is designed to determine whether a function $F(x)$ is a population distribution function. First, the sample $(X_1, X_2, \ldots, X_n)$ is used to define a sample distribution function

$$F_n(x) = \frac{1}{n} \sum_{j=1}^{n} 1_{\{X_i < x\}}, \text{ for } \infty < x < \infty$$

In other words, $F_n(x)$ is a piecewise constant function whose value for every x is defined as a number of sample elements less than x (ultimately divided by n to make it equal to 1 at ∞). Then a Kolmogorov-Smirnov statistic is computed as follows:

$$D_n = \sup_x |F_n(x) - F(x)|$$

The distribution of D_n is well understood; it can be computed for every n, using readily available formulas or can be obtained from the tables. Most importantly, this distribution does not depend on $F(x)$—a very useful feature, since it allows us to define universal acceptance limits that can be applied to any population distribution function. For the majority of values of n and for a number of significance levels, these limits are computed and tabulated (see Hahn and Meeker, 1991); here we give only their asymptotic values for large values of n (see Table 3.4).

The application of the Kolmogorov-Smirnov test is straightforward. First, the statistic D_n is computed, the acceptance level α is chosen, and the acceptance limit corresponding to n and α is determined. If D_n exceeds the acceptance level, then the hypothesis H_0—that the sample $X_1, X_2, \ldots, X_n$ belongs to a population with population distribution $F(x)$—is rejected at the level α. The smaller the value of α, the greater the acceptance level, and the more confident we are when the test forces us to reject the hypothesis H_0.

We use the Jarque-Bera and Kolmogorov-Smirnov tests in this section to build our intuition about distributions of energy prices. Our goal is to demonstrate how strikingly different they are from price distributions in more traditional markets. As references for comparison, we use the distri-

TABLE 3.4 Asymptotic Acceptance Limits for the Kolmogorov-Smirnov Test

Significance level:	.20	.15	.10	.05	.01
Acceptance limit:	$\frac{1.07}{\sqrt{n}}$	$\frac{1.14}{\sqrt{n}}$	$\frac{1.22}{\sqrt{n}}$	$\frac{1.36}{\sqrt{n}}$	$\frac{1.63}{\sqrt{n}}$

TABLE 3.5 JB and KS Statistics for the Log-returns in Example 3.2

	JB statistic	KS statistic
SP500	599.6	.053
JPY/USD	5488.1	.063
WTI	1924.9	.068

butions of Standard & Poor's 500 equity index values (SP500), Japanese yen/U.S. dollar exchange rates (JPY/USD), and crude oil spot prices (WTI).

EXAMPLE 3.2 *Analysis of distributions of equity, FX, and commodity products*

Our sample consists of the daily closing values of the SP500, JPY/USD, and WTI considered over a six-year period, from 01/01/1996 to 12/31/2001; a period whose beginning corresponds approximately to the opening of power markets. We want to test the hypothesis that log-returns of these values are normally distributed. Log-returns for a sequence of prices S_i are defined as

$$X_i = \ln \frac{S_{i+1}}{S_i} \qquad (3.7)$$

Table 3.5 contains the values of JB and KS statistics for the log-returns. The statistic D_n for SP500 is equal to .053. As follows from Table 3.4, the 10% acceptance limit for the distribution hypothesis for sample size $n = 1363$ is equal to

$$1.07/\sqrt{1363} = .029$$

Since $D_n > .029$, the hypothesis that the log-returns of the SP500 index are normally distributed should be rejected at the 10% acceptance level, and in fact, even at the 1% rejection level (= .044). However, it is clear that the

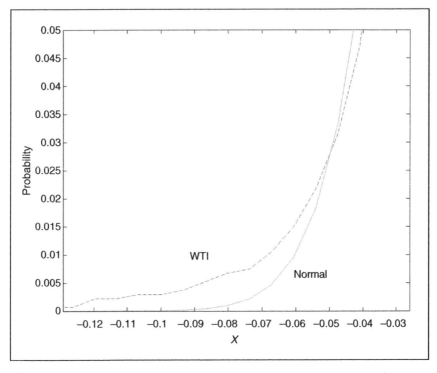

FIGURE 3.1   The Left Tail of the Cumulative Distribution Function (c.d.f.) for WTI Log-returns versus Normal Distribution

distribution of log-returns of the SP500 is closer to normal than the distributions of JPY and WTI.

How does the nonnormality manifest itself? If we analyze the graph in Figure 3.1 we can conclude that the most characteristic feature of the distribution of crude oil log-returns separating it from the normal distribution is the fatness of its tails. The fat tails can also be deduced from the magnitude of the distribution kurtosis. In the case of WTI it is equal to 8.1, which is significantly higher than 3, the value of the kurtosis for the normal distribution. The third distribution moment, skewness, can also be quite different from the skewness of the normal distribution, but as we will see, in the case of energy prices it is the distribution kurtosis (or tail fatness, or spikiness) that is the main cause of nonnormality (see Figure 3.1).

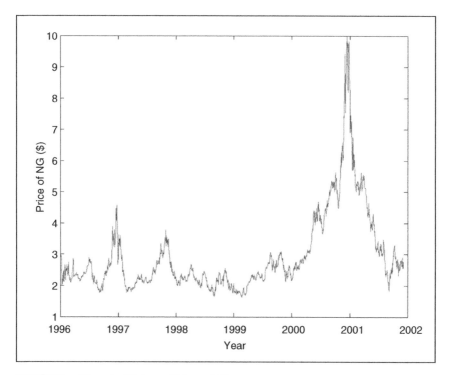

FIGURE 3.2   Historical Prices of Natural Gas

ANALYSIS OF NATURAL GAS AND ELECTRICITY DATA

Now we apply the statistical tools introduced in the previous section to the data from the energy markets.

Distribution of Natural Gas Prices

Spot Prices. We start with an analysis of the six-year history (01/01/96–12/31/2001) of the natural gas daily spot prices at Henry Hub. Figure 3.2 displays the time series of these prices and Figure 3.3 presents the histogram of their log-returns. The definition of the log-returns of spot prices S_i is given by equation (3.7).

Table 3.6 contains the values of the first four moments of the sample distribution, and two statistics we use for testing the normality hypothesis.

The spikiness of the prices in Figure 3.2 provides an obvious explanation of the fat tails of the histogram on Figure 3.3. Therefore, it is not surprising that the JB and KS statistics are as high as they are in Table 3.6.

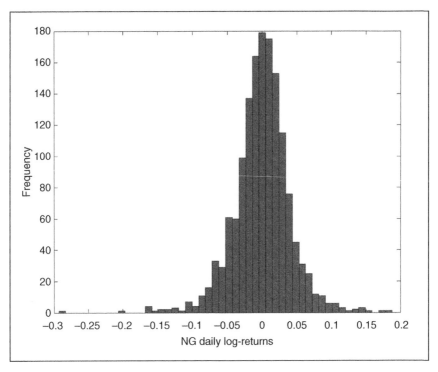

FIGURE 3.3 Histogram of Daily Log-returns of Natural Gas

TABLE 3.6 Quantitative Measures of the Sample Distribution of the Natural Gas Prices

n	Mean	Standard deviation	Variance	Skewness	Kurtosis	JB	KS
1582	$-.00007$	.04	.0016	$-.38$	7.03	1040.6	.06

According to the criteria introduced in "Distribution Tests" earlier, both statistics imply that the normality hypothesis for the log-returns should be rejected at a 1% rejection level. (In the world of econometric data analysis, this means absolute confidence.) The qualitative notion of fat tails is clearly supported by the high value of the kurtosis. On the other hand, the skewness of the distribution is reasonable, and not far from the skewness of the normal distribution (which is equal to zero).

Forward Prices. The same analysis as above can be applied to the prices of NYMEX natural gas futures contracts. Table 3.7 contains the results of an analysis of the two-year history of some of the contracts.

TABLE 3.7   Analysis of Log-returns of the NYMEX Futures Prices

Contract	n	JB	KS
Mar 2000	500	565.8	.12
June 2000	500	563.8	.11
Sep 2000	499	1136.2	.12
Dec 2000	499	501.5	.14
Mar 2001	499	2466.3	.18
Jun 2001	499	204.5	.13
Sep 2001	499	172.9	.12
Dec 2001	515	148.5	.12

The first impression of the results in the table is that the distribution of log-returns of futures prices is not normal. This inference may not be correct, however, and may stem from the misuse of a statistical methodology, especially when the main assumptions underlying a particular method are not valid. In testing distribution hypotheses, the principal assumption is that each sample element X_i is taken from the same population, or is a realization of the same random variable X (see the preceding section "Estimation of Sample Mean, Variance, and Higher Moments"). In particular, if a time series is used as a sample realization of a random variable, each element of the time series must have the same distribution. This is precisely the assumption we have implicitly made analyzing the data for Table 3.7. That is, we have assumed that for a given contract the distribution of its log-returns are the same for all moments of time. (These distributions, of course, may differ from contract to contract.) In other words, we have assumed some form of stationarity of the futures price evolution.

As we will see from the results presented in the upcoming section "Historical Volatility of Natural Gas and Power Forward Prices," this assumption is almost always wrong, and distributions of futures or forward prices are changing as we approach the contract expiration. Therefore, it is important to recognize this nonstationarity and to minimize the cumulative error that arises from sampling prices of a certain futures contract at different moments in time, and then using these samples to reach conclusions about the statistical properties of the prices at one particular time. How do we reduce the effect of nonstationarity? One solution is to find a data transformation such that the transformed time series is stationary (or is at least less nonstationary than the original time series). Once it is found, then applying the hypothesis testing procedures to the transformed data is more justifiable. Needless to say, finding this transformation is not easy, and success usually depends on understanding the nature of the data and its intrinsic properties.

TABLE 3.8   Scaled Log-return Time Series

Contract	n	JB	KS
Mar 2000	500	345	.06
June 2000	500	413	.07
Sep 2000	499	519	.06
Dec 2000	499	215	.06
Mar 2001	499	267	.05
Jun 2001	499	22	.08
Sep 2001	499	24	.07
Dec 2001	515	108	.04

For example, as will be shown in the upcoming sections "Implied Volatility Structure of Natural Gas and Power Forward Prices" and "Historical Volatility of Natural Gas and Power Forward Prices", futures price volatility increases as we approach expiration. Therefore, we can reasonably expect that scaling log-returns with a time-dependent function may improve the statistical properties of the time series. Consider, for example, the scaling function of the form $1/(T - t + \text{Const})$, and perform the same analysis as presented in Table 3.7. (The choice of this function is suggested by historical data, for example see Figure 3.17). The new results are displayed in Table 3.8, where it is clear that the transformed data is closer to normal distribution than the original data.

There are also more sophisticated ways of accounting for the varying volatilities. We discuss some of those techniques in Chapter 4 when we analyze GARCH models.

Distribution of Power Prices

At the present time a definitive analysis of the price data available in the U.S. electricity markets faces several considerable obstacles. First, as is clear from Chapter 1, the structural differences between the geographically distinct U.S. power markets mean that we must study each one separately and draw individual conclusions about each one. Most of these markets are relatively new, and price data is scarce and often unreliable. Second, a frequent regulatory intervention in some markets cannot but affect the statistical properties of electricity prices—sometimes severely. The introduction and reintroduction of price caps, changes in the rules of bidding in energy and auxiliary markets, and frequent redefinition of the market structure all quickly render the historical data obsolete, and prevent accumulation of a data set of necessary size. Finally, the emerging power markets often lack

TABLE 3.9 Analysis of the Distribution of the Log-returns of PJM Spot Prices

n	Mean	Standard deviation	Variance	Skewness	Kurtosis	JB	KS
975	.0002	.025	.0006	.36	14.1	5054.4	.14

transparency, due to their illiquidity and frequent inconsistency among the sources of price data.

Therefore, it is of no surprise that for the most part, in this chapter and throughout the book we will use price data from the PJM market. It is one of the few markets that has operated in a stable fashion for several years, and it seems to have the least number of the previously-mentioned problems. In many aspects PJM has been an exemplary market, whose principal features have been imitated in a number of other power markets. Because of that, we hope that the results of our analysis of PJM data may prove to be equally useful for the markets outside PJM. We will not restrict ourselves solely to PJM data, and whenever possible, will use data from other power markets.

As in the case of natural gas, we will analyze both spot and forward prices.

Spot Prices

For our analysis, we will take the history of PJM daily prices from April 1998 to December 2001, the period spanning the entire life of the PJM power market. Table 3.9 contains the results of an analysis of the log-returns of these prices.

From the JB and KS statistics we can conclude that this distribution is remarkably nonnormal. Its departure from the normal distribution is even higher than that of natural gas or oil. The plot of the price history (Figure 3.4) and the histogram of the log-returns (Figure 3.5) provide the explanation for this nonnormality: the enormous price spikes yield the exceptional fat tails of the histogram and the nonnormality follows.

Forward Prices

Statistical properties of the PJM forward contracts are presented in Table 3.10. For each contract we have used two years of prices, or in the absence of that data, the maximum available price history.

The values of JB and KS statistics for each contract suggest that distributions of log-returns deviate significantly from the normal distribution. (Remember that for the normality hypothesis to be rejected at the 1% level, it is enough for the KS statistic to be greater than .07.) However, the comments we made in the preceding section "Distribution of Natural Gas Prices" concerning the results in Table 3.7 are valid here as well, and our conclusions may be biased by the nonstationarity of the empirical data.

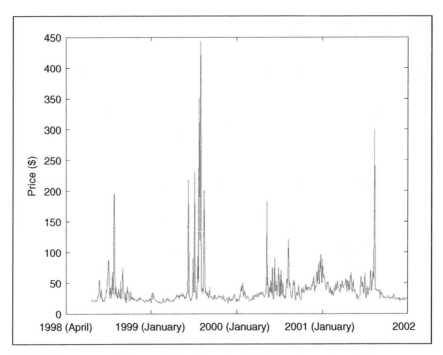

FIGURE 3.4 PJM Daily Power Prices from April 1998 to December 2001

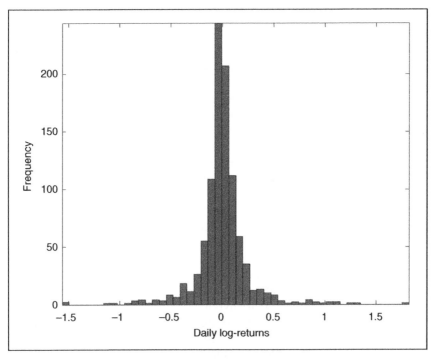

FIGURE 3.5 Histogram of Daily Log-returns for PJM Prices

TABLE 3.10 Analysis of Log-returns of PJM Forward Prices

Month	n	Mean	Standard deviation	Skewness	Kurtosis	JB	KS
Mar 2001	549	.00009	.023	1.7	36.1	25307	.23
Jun 2001	551	.0001	.026	.38	15.1	3345.5	.19
Sep 2001	551	0	.024	−.004	11.4	1621.7	.20
Dec 2001	523	0	.022	.19	14.8	3041.4	.14

FORWARD CURVES

In this section we investigate the empirical characteristics of natural gas and power forward curves. Recall that for a given time t, a forward curve $F(t,T)$ as a function of T is defined by the prices of forward contracts maturing at T, $T \geq t$. In other words, a forward curve is a term structure of forward prices observed in the market at time t. This definition is rather vague; of course, a complete definition specifies the particular properties of the forward contracts, such as the delivery period, the nature of the delivered commodity (e.g., on-peak power, off-peak power), and the delivery point. Typically, observed forward prices in the energy markets have monthly resolution in the near years, and possibly finer resolution in the near months. In the far end of the curve they are quoted on a quarterly or yearly basis. These nonhomogeneous quotes are then used as inputs of an interpolation procedure that generates a forward curve with more uniform resolution. For example, each point of the resulting interpolated curve may correspond to a price of monthly contracts with specified delivery conditions.

Figures 3.6 and 3.7 show examples of forward on-peak power price curves in different regions observed at two dates, 05/03/1999 and 11/01/1999, and Figure 3.8 shows the Henry Hub NYMEX futures price curves for the same dates.

These graphs illustrate several common features of forward curves, which we list below and examine in greater detail later in this chapter.

1. Seasonality. Unlike forward curves in the financial markets, power and natural gas curves have a pronounced seasonal character. The particular seasonal shape differs from region to region and depends on factors such as regional weather conditions, current and future supply characteristics, demand growth, and demand structure.

2. Due to the geographically distinct nature of power markets, at present, the correlation between forward curve movements in different NERC regions is not strong, so the evolution of the curves in these regions may be studied separately.

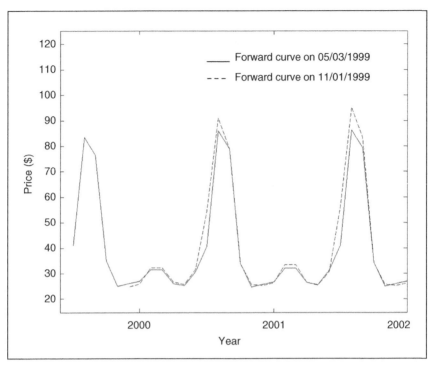

FIGURE 3.6   PJM West Forward On-peak Curves on 05/03/1999 and 11/01/1999

3. Intertemporal correlation, that is, correlation among movements of different parts of a forward curve, is very strong, particularly in the far segments of the curve, for fuel curves. For power curves the correlation in the early parts of the curve is quite weak.

VOLATILITY STRUCTURE

In the world of financial derivatives the notion of volatility is generally understood, and the methodology for its measurement is well established (see Rebonato, 1999). In the broadest sense, price volatility is a measure of the randomness of price changes: the higher the degree of randomness, the greater the volatility. To be useful, the definition of volatility must be quantifiable, so in most applications volatility is associated with certain parameters of stochastic processes used for modeling the evolution of the underlying prices. This in turn yields a natural connection between the volatility and the price distribution moments, particularly the second moment.

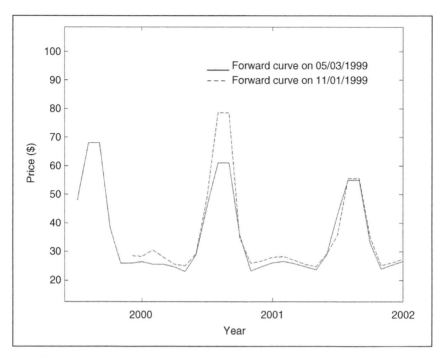

FIGURE 3.7   ERCOT (Texas) Forward On-peak Curves on 05/03/1999 and 11/01/1999

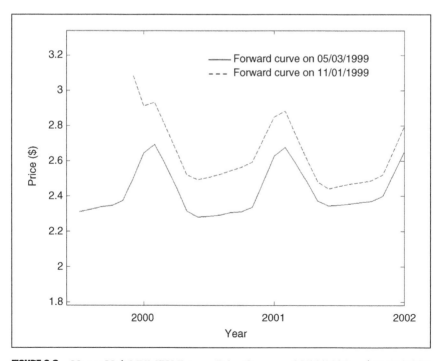

FIGURE 3.8   Henry Hub NYMEX Futures Price Curve on 05/03/1999 and 11/01/1999

In financial applications volatility is most commonly associated with the standard deviation of the distribution of the logarithms of prices. This association is based on a widespread assumption—broadly supported by the empirical data—that prices are lognormally distributed, or, equivalently, that price logarithms are normally distributed. Naturally, this assumption yields a well-known procedure for estimating volatility from the time series of historical prices.

Estimation of Price Volatility from the Historical Data: Lognormal Case

Let $\{P_i\}$ be a time series of historical prices observed at times $t_i, i = 0, \ldots, n$. We assume that the increments $\log P_i - \log P_{i+1} \equiv \log P_i/P_{i+1}$ are independent (not correlated) and normally distributed, and that the standard deviation of this distribution is proportional to the square root of time between observations; that is it can be represented as

$$\sigma \sqrt{t_i - t_{i-1}}$$

The parameter σ is called return volatility, and it can be estimated using formula (3.2) after we introduce the normalized variables

$$X_i = (\log P_i - \log P_{i-1})/\sqrt{t_i - t_{i-1}} \tag{3.8}$$

Then

$$\sigma = \sqrt{\frac{1}{n-1} \sum_{i=1}^{n} \left(\frac{\log P_i - \log P_{i-1}}{\sqrt{t_i - t_{i-1}}} - \frac{1}{n} \sum_{i=1}^{n} \frac{\log P_i - \log P_{i-1}}{\sqrt{t_i - t_{i-1}}} \right)^2} \tag{3.9}$$

The expression (3.9) needs a little clarification, since we have not specified how we measure time. It is customary to represent time increments $t_i - t_{i-1}$ as year fractions. In this case σ is called the annualized price volatility. It is most frequently encountered in applications, although other volatility types (e.g., monthly, daily, etc.) are also used.

EXAMPLE 3.3   *Estimating volatility*

Consider a time series of prices presented in Table 3.11.

TABLE 3.11 Time Series of Prices

Date (t_i)	$t_i - t_{i-1}$ (days)	$t_i - t_{i-1}$ (fraction of the year)	Price ($)
5/1/2001		0.0000	67.25
5/2/2001	1	0.0027	66.50
5/3/2001	1	0.0027	65.00
5/4/2001	1	0.0027	66.00
5/7/2001	3	0.0082	62.00
5/8/2001	1	0.0027	64.50
5/9/2001	1	0.0027	61.50
5/10/2001	1	0.0027	62.25
5/11/2001	1	0.0027	62.00
5/14/2001	3	0.0082	62.00
5/15/2001	1	0.0027	64.75
5/16/2001	1	0.0027	62.00
5/17/2001	1	0.0027	60.50
5/18/2001	1	0.0027	59.00
5/21/2001	3	0.0082	56.00
5/22/2001	1	0.0027	55.50
5/23/2001	1	0.0027	58.75
5/24/2001	1	0.0027	61.00
5/25/2001	1	0.0027	56.00
5/29/2001	4	0.0110	54.00
5/30/2001	1	0.0027	47.00
5/31/2001	1	0.0027	43.00

Applying formula (3.9) we obtain that the annualized volatility of the observed prices is equal to 90.37%.

In the example above, the length of the interval between observations is computed in calendar days, and to represent it as a year fraction, we must divide it by 365. It is often proposed that one should use only the data observed during business days, and therefore, divide by 250 to compute the year fraction. Both approaches have their advantages and drawbacks. (See Hull, 1999, for the extensive discussion of this issue.) Whatever the choice, however, it has to be applied consistently to avoid mismatching errors. In forward energy markets (gas, power, and crude), the data indicates that the proper scaling for volatility should use the number of trading days and not the number of calendar days. As an example, consider the scaling properties of the returns of the January 2000 forward Henry Hub contract. To derive the implied number of days we use the square root of time rule for scaling

TABLE 3.12 Implied Volatility Scaling

Returns	Daily	Weekly	Biweekly	Monthly
Sample Volatility	1.4%	3.2%	4.1%	5.9%
Implied Number of days		5.41	8.73	17.95

volatility. As we can see in Table 3.12, the implied number of days is much closer to the number of trading days.

It is important at this moment to recall that the estimate (3.9) is based on implicit assumptions that the normalized increments of price logarithms given in (3.8) have the same standard deviation. (The estimate also requires their independence, an important condition that is typically assumed to hold unless specifically stated otherwise.) What do you do if this assumption does not hold? For example, what if the standard deviation changes with time, that is, if $\sigma = \sigma(t)$? A common approach in this case is to assume that volatility is constant at least for a relatively short period of time (typically, 20 to 30 days). Then for any time t, the volatility estimate (3.9) uses only a specified number of observations at times that precede t and fall into the window of constant volatility. This approach is often called the *moving window method*, since the data set used for estimation moves together with the time at which volatility is estimated. In the moving window approach, the volatility estimate at a given time t_k is given by the expression

$$\sigma(t_k) = \sqrt{\frac{1}{m-1} \sum_{i=k-m+1}^{k} \left(\frac{\log P_i - \log P_{i-1}}{\sqrt{t_i - t_{i-1}}} - \frac{1}{m} \sum_{i=k-m+1}^{k} \frac{\log P_i - \log P_{i-1}}{\sqrt{t_i - t_{i-1}}} \right)^2}$$

(3.10)

Here m is the width of the moving window, that is, a specified number of observations preceding t_k used to estimate volatility.

Implied Volatility

Expressions (3.9) and (3.10) are volatility measures based on historical prices, and the volatility computed with their help is commonly called *historical price volatility*. It has the obvious shortcoming of being based solely on past price data, making it impossible to incorporate information about future price behavior. Therefore, a forward-looking volatility measure based on option prices has been developed. It is called *implied volatility* and can be described as an anticipated volatility of prices in the future, such that option prices derived using this volatility match the market quotes. More specifically, under the log-normality condition an option value is

$$V_{option} = f(F_T, X, t, T, r, \sigma)$$

See equations (2.18) and (2.19).

This means that the option value is a function of the forward price F_T, strike X, time t at which the option is evaluated, exercise time T, interest rate r, and finally, of the volatility σ. The parameter σ reflects market consensus on the anticipated random behavior of prices on the interval $[t,T]$. Now, for any given market option quote V_{option}^{market}, the corresponding implied volatility $\sigma^{implied}$ is defined as the value of the parameter σ, such that

$$V_{option}^{market} = f(F_T, X, t, T, r, \sigma^{implied}) \tag{3.11}$$

Applying standard techniques, such as Newton's method, to solve equation (3.11), we obtain the implied volatility

$$\sigma^{implied} = \sigma(t, T, X, F_T, r, V_{option}^{market})$$

Recall that in the simplified world of the Black-Scholes option pricing model, it is required that the implied volatility is constant,

$$\sigma_{Black\text{-}Scholes}^{implied}(t, T, X) \equiv Constant$$

As we show in the next section, this assumption is resolutely invalid in the case of energy derivatives. Consequently, to create realistic pricing models in energy markets, it is essential to understand the behavior of implied volatility as well as the historical volatility of energy prices. We will use empirical data to illustrate some of the important characteristics of energy price volatility. These characteristics will be used later in the model selection.

Volatility of Natural Gas and Power Prices

Historical Volatility of Natural Gas and Power Spot Prices

A brief examination of Figure 3.9 is sufficient to conclude that the volatility of spot prices of natural gas, and particularly of electricity, is nothing like that of the prices of other commodities or equities, or of FX or interest rates. Indeed, the volatility of energy prices is consistently and significantly higher than that of other products; their spikes are more violent, and the nonstationary behavior is much more pronounced. Note that to create these graphs we used the volatility estimate (3.10) with the 60-day moving window.

From this figure it is clear that the volatility of electricity prices is exceptional even by energy market standards. In Figure 3.9 we have used the PJM electricity prices, but the same behavior is exhibited by power prices in virtually any other market (see Figure 3.10).

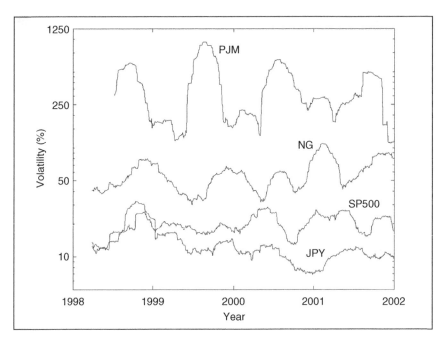

FIGURE 3.9 Annualized Spot Price Volatility for JPY, SP500, NG, and PJM (Logarithmic Scale, 60-Day Moving Window)

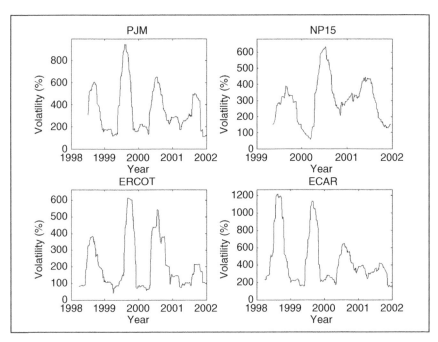

FIGURE 3.10 Volatility of Power Prices: PJM, California (NP15), ERCOT, and ECAR (Cinergy)

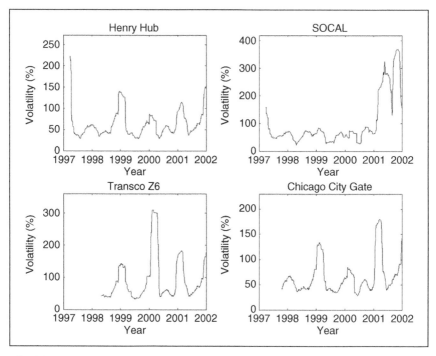

FIGURE 3.11 Volatility of Natural Gas Prices at Henry Hub, California (SOCAL), Transco Z6, and Chicago City Gate

Similarly, the volatility behavior of natural gas prices in different locations is no better than at Henry Hub, as seen in Figure 3.11.

Implied Volatility Structure of Natural Gas and Power Forward Prices

As we have demonstrated, the volatility of energy spot prices has a complex and frequently unpredictable character. The volatility of forward prices, on the other hand, exhibits a more consistent behavior, which we show now by analyzing the structure of their implied volatility. We will study the dependence of the implied volatility on the following parameters:

t, the current valuation date

T, the settlement date of a forward contract. (In (3.11) T denoted the expiration date of the option on the forward contract, which is directly connected to the contract's settlement date. Both can be used interchangeably.)

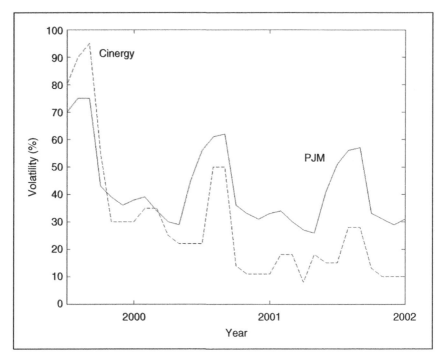

FIGURE 3.12   Implied Volatility Curve As a Function of Forward Contract Maturity. Date: 05/03/1999. Locations: PJM and Cinergy

X, the strike of the option used to define implied volatility (typically, the at-the-money option is used, so this strike is equal to the current forward price)

Note that in an analysis of implied volatility it is also common to use a relative time measure $\tau = T - t$, called time to expiration. For example, one can fix the valuation time t_0, and examine the behavior of $\sigma^{implied}(t_0, \tau)$ as a function of the forward contract settlement date relative to t_0. Similarly, one can select a contract with settlement time T_0, and study $\sigma^{implied}(t, \tau) \equiv \sigma^{implied}(t, T_0 - t)$ as a function of the time remaining to the contract expiration.

Figures 3.12 through 3.19 show the implied volatility curves for different natural gas and power forward contracts.

Analysis of these graphs allows us to make the following conclusions regarding the structure of the implied volatility of forward prices:

1. Seasonality of the implied volatility as a function of the forward contract settlement date. Figures 3.12, 3.13, and 3.16 demonstrate that regardless of valuation date t, the implied volatility essentially preserves its shape as a

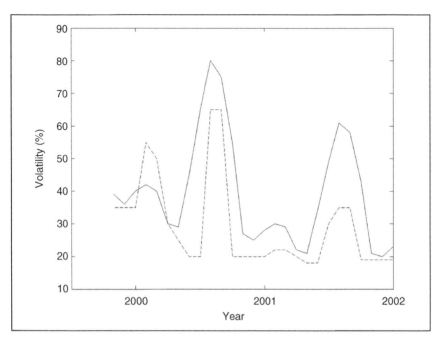

FIGURE 3.13 The Same Graphs as Figure 3.12 at a Different Valuation Time. Date: 09/01/1999

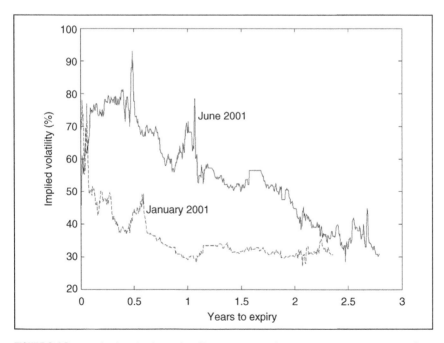

FIGURE 3.14 Implied Volatility of Different Forward Contracts As a Function of Time to Expiration (PJM)

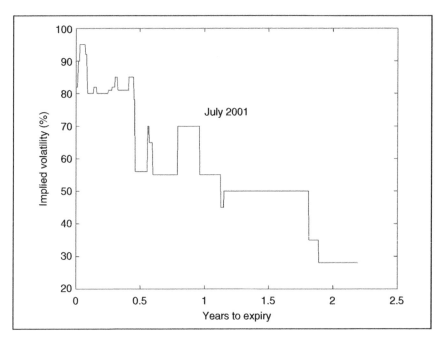

FIGURE 3.15 Implied Volatility of Cinergy July 2001 Contract As a Function of Time to Expiration (Note the lower liquidity compared to PJM.)

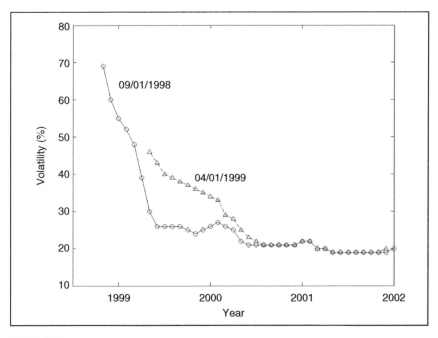

FIGURE 3.16 Implied Volatility Curves of NYNEX Futures Options on 09/01/1998 and 04/01/1999

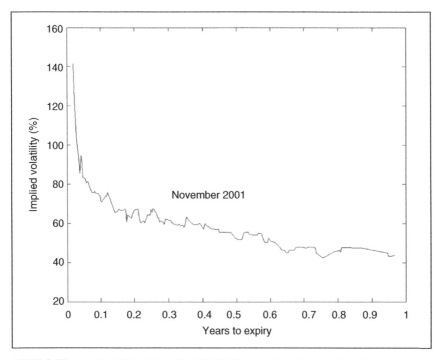

FIGURE 3.17 Implied Volatility of NYMEX Natural Gas Futures As a Function of Time to Expiration

function of settlement time T, although the magnitude of peaks and troughs of the volatility profile may change. The stability of the shape is mainly due to the stability of the relation between regional supply and demand, the principal drivers defining forward volatility.

   2. Samuelson effect. The volatility of any given forward contract is generally a decreasing function of the time to expiration (see Figures 3.14, 3.15, and 3.17). This property of the volatility structure is called the *Samuelson effect* (see Samuelson, 1965) and is also exhibited by the volatility of forward contracts in other markets. However, in the case of energy contracts this effect is especially pronounced, with a particularly steep increase in volatility occurring in the last six to twelve months of the life of the contract.

   3. Volatility surface. The two properties described above indicate that in order to achieve a more complete description of implied volatility, we must consider it as a function of both valuation time t and contract expiration time T. A simplified representation

$$\sigma^{implied}(t, T) = \sigma^{implied}(T - t)$$

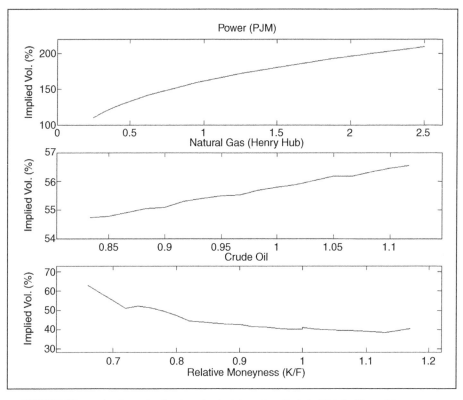

FIGURE 3.18 Volatility "Smiles" and "Smirks": Implied Call Volatility of Power, Natural Gas, and Crude Oil Prices As a Function of Relative Moneyness (Strike/Forward Price)

frequently used in financial markets, is likely to fail when applied to energy contracts.

4. **Volatility "smile."** Analysis of Figures 3.18 and 3.19 makes it clear that one more variable is needed for a reasonable representation of the implied volatility, namely, the strike. Recall that in the trader's vernacular, option strikes are typically divided into three groups. Strikes of at-the-money (ATM) options are concentrated close to the corresponding forward price. Strikes of out-of-the-money (OTM) options are significantly below the forward price for call options and above the forward price for put options. Alternatively, in-the-money (ITM) calls have their strikes below the forward price, and the strikes of ITM puts are above the forward price. Values of OTM options are lower than values of ATM options, which, in turn, are lower than values of ITM options. The dependence of implied volatility on strike is generally referred to as a *volatility smile,* although terms like

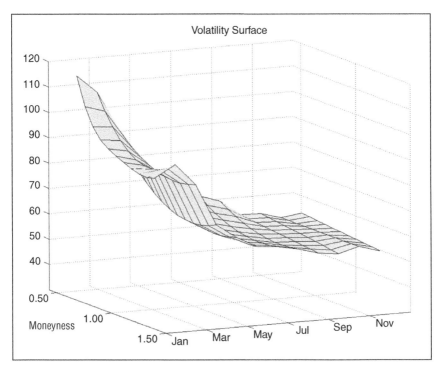

FIGURE 3.19 Volatility Surface: Implied Volatility of Natural Gas NYMEX Futures Contracts As a Function of Time to Expiration and Relative Moneyness

"smirk" and "frown" are also frequently encountered. These more precise grades of facial expressions are used to better describe the dependence of volatility on strike. "Smile" means that the implied volatility of OTM and ITM options is higher than that of ATM options. "Smirk" means that the volatility of OTM options is higher than that of ATM options, which, in turn, is higher than that of ITM options, or vice versa. "Frown" is the opposite of smile, meaning that the volatilities of OTM and ITM options are lower than the volatility of the ATM options.

What does it mean that implied volatility has a smile, or more precisely, what does it mean that implied volatility depends on the option strike? Earlier we introduced implied volatility as a parameter in a certain option pricing formula. For any traded option, its corresponding implied volatility is defined so that the option price generated by the pricing model matches the option market quote. Thus, the value of the implied volatility is directly connected with the choice of option pricing methodology.

The most common pricing formula for options on futures and forwards is given by the expressions (2.18) or (2.19)—Black's formula. This formula assumes a lognormal distribution of the underlying futures or forward prices with constant volatility parameter σ. If market prices were indeed lognormally distributed, then the option pricing formula would match the market option quotes at any strike, and the implied volatility at any strike must therefore be constant. The fact that option quotes in energy markets do not yield constant implied volatility is a clear indication of the non-lognormality of energy prices (see previous section "Implied Volatility"). Moreover, the implied volatility of call options grows with the strike (see Figures 3.17 and 3.18) indicating that a real-life price distribution has a fatter tail at high prices than the lognormal distribution. What is the real-life distribution and how do we model it? We will discuss some answers to these questions in Chapters 4, 5, and 7.

Historical Volatility of Natural Gas and Power Forward Prices

As we mentioned previously, implied volatility is a forward-looking measure of price uncertainty deduced from option prices. Therefore, it directly depends on the choice of the option pricing formula and on the parameters and assumptions underlying that formula, such as strike, interest rate, and lognormality assumption. The situation seems to be simpler in the case of historical volatility, which is typically computed with the help of equations (3.9) or (3.10), applied to the time series of realized prices. However, difficulties arise even in this case.

The problem is that equations (3.9) and (3.10) may not be well suited for energy prices. These formulas were developed under the conditions of the normality and independence of price log-returns, and only under these conditions are they really meaningful. Of course, these expressions can be computed for any process underlying price evolution, but the interpretation of the results would be difficult, if not impossible, in the general case. Despite these words of caution we nevertheless use the moving window expression (3.10) to produce graphs illustrating the behavior of historical volatility. We do so for three reasons.

1. The formula (3.10), despite the above-mentioned reservations, is used most frequently in energy trading, probably because it is also a standard formula in financial market applications.
2. This formula for computing historical volatility, from the point of view of underlying assumptions, is in agreement with the formula for computing implied volatility discussed in the previous section, which provides justification for the comparison of two volatilities.
3. Finally, the qualitative properties of historical volatility that we want to emphasize with the following graphs (Figures 3.20 through 3.22) most likely will be preserved by any reasonable volatility measure.

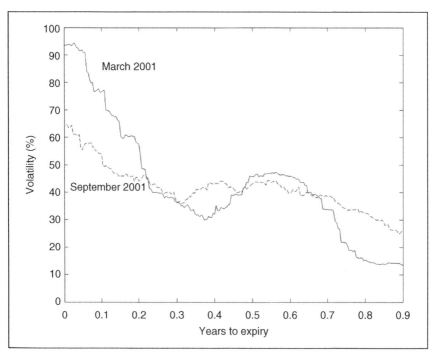

FIGURE 3.20 Historical Volatility of Natural Gas Forward Contracts As a Function of Time to Expiration: March 2001 and September 2001

Let us now examine the historical volatility graphs for different energy prices series. To compute historical volatility we use the moving window formula (3.10) with the window width $m = 60$ days. For any given forward contract with the expiration time T, we consider the times series $P_k = F(t_k, T)$, where $F(t_k, T)$ is the price of the forward contract at time t_k. Formula (3.10) is then applied to this time series to compute $\sigma^{historical}(t_k, T)$ for any t_k. For convenience, Figures 3.20 through 3.22 plot historical volatility not as a function of absolute time t, but as a function of time to expiration, $\tau = T - t$.

The graphs indicate that the historical volatility of energy prices has a structure quite similar to that of implied volatility. First, for any given time to expiration, both exhibit the same seasonal dependence on the contract expiration time. Second, for any given contract, both demonstrate comparable behavior with respect to time to expiration (the Samuelson effect). This similarity becomes even more pronounced if we recall that the implied volatility is a cumulative characteristic of price movements. This means that in order to correctly compare implied and realized volatilities, we should

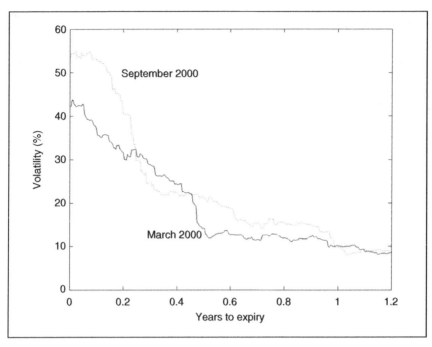

FIGURE 3.21 Historical Volatility of Natural Gas Forward Contracts As a Function of Time to Expiration: March 2000 and September 2000

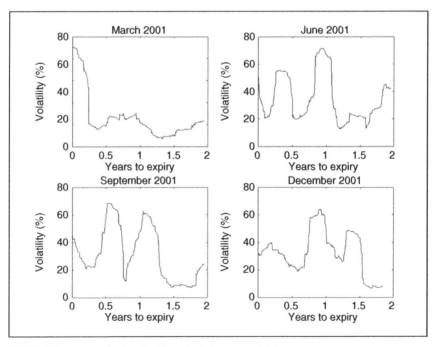

FIGURE 3.22 Historical Volatility of PJM Forward Prices

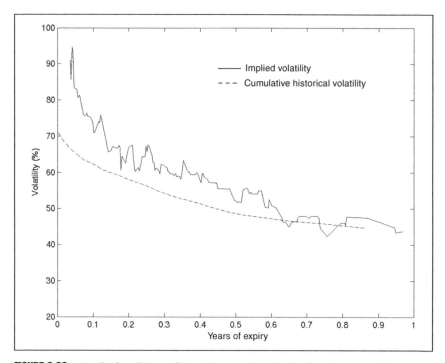

FIGURE 3.23 Implied and Cumulative Historical Volatility for the November 2001 Natural Gas Contract

compare $\sigma^{implied}\,(t,T)$ (implied volatility of ATM options) with the cumulative historical (realized) volatility

$$\frac{1}{T-t}\int_t^T \sigma^{historical}(s,T)\,ds.$$

See Figures 3.23 and 3.24.

Correlation Data

In energy markets, unlike in financial markets, the importance of the joint behavior of various prices is crucial for the proper valuation and hedging of energy derivatives. The canonical examples are generation assets and storage facilities. One very popular measure of dependence between prices (among others) is linear correlation. Here we briefly outline the available evidence on the behavior of correlations in energy markets; in later chapters, we spend more time analyzing correlation and its limitations for pricing and hedging.

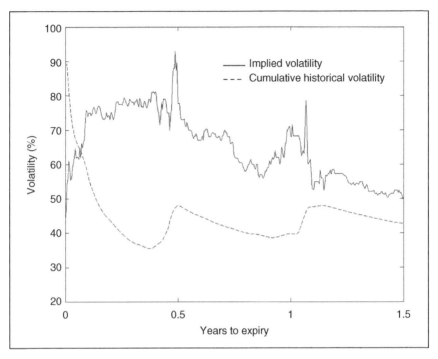

FIGURE 3.24   Implied and Cumulative Historical Volatility for a June 2001 PJM Contract

It is well known that correlations in financial markets tend to be quite unstable (Wilmott, 2000; Rebonato, 1998). However, the situation in energy markets is much more extreme. Correlations between spot power prices and the corresponding spot fuel prices exhibit instabilities not seen in any other markets.

Cash Power/Fuels Correlations (Natural Gas, Oil)

We can see in Figure 3.25 that correlations can spike to higher levels, and then quickly drop to lower values. Even if we eliminate spikes from our data to analyze correlations under the "normal" conditions, we can see that a great deal of variability remains in the correlations. Actually, we see much more of it than we see in other markets. We attempt to analyze the structure by looking at seasonal variation of correlation. The rolling window we use is over 100 days long. We cannot use shorter periods because of significant standard error of correlation estimates for shorter periods. This points to the inherent problem of analyzing correlation: too much averaging (over longer windows, for example) will hide the object of our study from view (i.e., changes in cor-

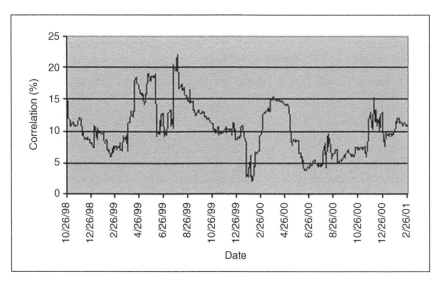

FIGURE 3.25   Rolling Correlation of the PJM Spot Prices and Transco Z6 Spot Gas Prices

relations). Shorter windows unduly skew our picture by overwhelming our estimates with rare events and noise. The example suggests that correlation as a concept has limited direct usefulness, and the world of electricity prices (as opposed to the wider world of energy prices) is not a hospitable environment for it. We can still use correlations, but we have to be careful how we do it. We address those issues in detail in Chapter 6.

The seasonal structure is not nearly enough to explain the variation in correlation. We briefly analyzed the structure of the supply curve earlier; the correlation between the marginal fuel and the power prices is affected by which part of the supply curve is on the margin. If the system load were such that the marginal unit comes from the flat part of the stack, then one would expect the variability of power prices to be driven by changes in the marginal fuel price, and not by load or outage variability. This obviously suggests that the return volatilities of power and fuel prices will be close, and that the correlation of returns will be high. Conversely, if the load finds itself on the steep part of the supply stack, power price variability will be mainly due to load and outage variability and consequently the power returns volatility will be unrelated to the marginal fuel return volatility. Similarly, one would expect the correlations to be low. Note that this example is reasonable only if we have just one main fuel in the system; we can expect this behavior to be most common in markets like ERCOT or California, where natural gas dominates across a wide range of system generation levels.

TABLE 3.13   Example for ERCOT Market

Implied heat rate range	Return correlation	95% confidence interval for correlation
[5, 10]	98%	[97.8%, 98.7%]
[10, 20]	90%	[88%, 92%]
[10, 100]	39%	[16%, 57%]

This discussion suggests that we might elicit more robust patterns from a time series of correlations if we could condition them on a proxy for the location in the supply curve. The simplest choice is to use seasonal proxies (summer, winters, etc). We can, however, be more direct. A natural choice would be the implied heat rate, that is, P/G, daily on-peak power price divided by daily gas price. Table 3.13 shows a simple example for the ERCOT market.

The data used in estimation were the on-peak day-ahead ERCOT prices and the daily Houston Ship Channel daily gas index. The period covered was January 1998 through April 2001. We include 95% confidence-level bounds on the estimate. Note that they can be very wide: For lower correlations the average distance between the estimate and the lower or upper bound is over 40%. Unfortunately, this cannot be easily rectified. Even if we double the size of the window, the average size of the difference drops only to 30%. On the other hand, as per the previous discussion, we have every reason to expect changing conditions to affect the correlation. Therefore, it is crucial to understand the temporal drivers of correlation before we even look at the available data. We are unlikely to understand its structure from the time series of correlation alone. Further chapters will address these issues in detail.

Forward Power/Fuels Correlations (Natural Gas, Oil)

Figure 3.26 shows the time series of correlation between a gas forward contract for Transco Z6 and a power forward contract for PJM West. As we can see, the correlations are much more stable than those of spot products, and they also tend to be higher with a tendency to increase closer to expiration (a correlation Samuelson effect).

Cash and Forward Fuel/Fuel Correlations (Natural Gas, Oil)

Figure 3.27 shows rolling window correlations between various cash gas indexes, which tend to be relatively high and stable except for occasional significant dips. This behavior is reminiscent of the correlation plots for equities and other financial markets.

The next series shows correlations between oil and gas prices, which are relatively low and unstable.

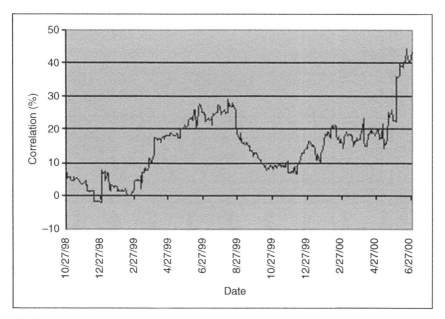

FIGURE 3.26 Forward Power and Gas Correlations for July 2000 PJM versus Transco Z6 Forward Prices

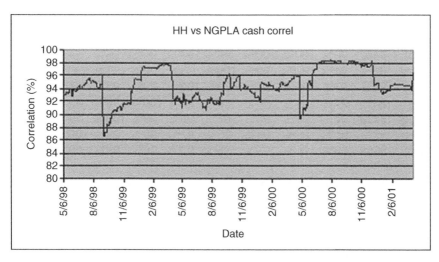

FIGURE 3.27 Cash Gas-to-Gas Correlations

We concentrate on forward correlations, since the cash crude oil prices are not very liquid (see Figure 3.28).

Finally, the correlations between different NYMEX forward contracts are shown in Figure 3.29. The correlations tend to be very high, and fall off

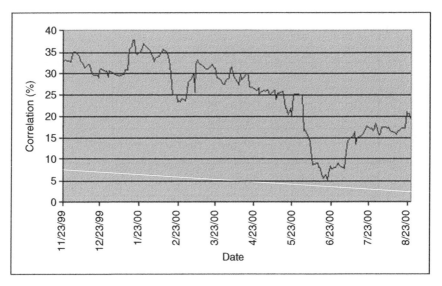

FIGURE 3.28   Forward Gas-to-Oil Correlations

	Jan	Feb	Mar	Apr	May	Jun	Jul	Aug	Sep	Oct
Jan	**100%**	99%	97%	94%	92%	90%	88%	87%	87%	85%
Feb	99%	**100%**	99%	96%	94%	93%	91%	90%	90%	88%
Mar	97%	99%	**100%**	99%	97%	95%	94%	92%	92%	91%
Apr	94%	96%	99%	**100%**	99%	97%	96%	95%	94%	93%
May	92%	94%	97%	99%	**100%**	99%	98%	97%	96%	95%
Jun	90%	93%	95%	97%	99%	**100%**	99%	98%	97%	97%
Jul	88%	91%	94%	96%	98%	99%	**100%**	99%	99%	98%
Aug	87%	90%	92%	95%	97%	98%	99%	**100%**	99%	99%
Sep	87%	90%	92%	94%	96%	97%	99%	99%	**100%**	99%
Oct	85%	88%	91%	93%	95%	97%	98%	99%	99%	**100%**

FIGURE 3.29   Intertemporal Forward Gas-to-Gas Correlations

for more distant contracts. In addition, they tend to increase with time to expiration, because individual contracts trade as a strip. The time structure of
forward correlations can be characterized in the following way:

- For time periods of more than two years to expiration, intertemporal
  fuel-to-fuel (local, see Chapter 6) correlations tend to be very high, because those contracts trade as strips; that is, traders do not differentiate
  between July and August of 2010, and if they quote them, they will

quote one price for them. That implies perfect correlation. This is generally true for all fuel-to-fuel correlation within the same calendar year, and even for correlations between marginal fuel and power price in the medium term. The latter arises because power contracts, in the medium term, trade at a heat rate to the marginal fuel.

■ For shorter time periods the correlations drop, but are still very high. They do exhibit a pronounced term structure. We will analyze those issues in Chapter 6.

WEATHER DATA

It is obvious that weather, and particularly temperature, has a great deal of influence on gas and power demand, as well as on their prices. Therefore it is not surprising that one of the most successful pricing models described in this book uses temperature as a principal factor in the price evolution. This, in turn, requires a thorough analysis of temperature behavior, including analysis of daily and hourly temperature distributions, seasonal patterns, short-term and long-term autocorrelations, and locational correlations. Fortunately, a vast amount of temperature data is available for analysis. In the United States this data is provided by the National Climatic Data Center on a daily basis for more than 200 weather stations, going back 50 years or more. Private companies take the raw government data and clean it, fill the gaps, and sometimes "de-trend" it on request, thus reducing concern about the quality and increasing confidence in the results.

In this section we concentrate on one important problem for our modeling efforts, the statistical properties of the fluctuations of daily average temperatures. The question is, can we use normal distribution to describe deviations of the daily temperatures from some historical norms? The normality assumption is common in papers on weather models, see Davis (2001), for example. Our own approach to modeling temperature is similar to that of Davis.

We view temperature evolution as a combination of two processes. One is a low-frequency process, evolving on a seasonal or even yearly time scale. The other is a high-frequency process of daily, or sometimes hourly, temperature fluctuations around the first process. In other words, for any given year, the temperature at time t (measured as a fraction of a year) is denoted by $\Im(t)$, and is calculated by the formula

$$\Im(t) = \sum_{k=0}^{m} a_k \sin(2\pi kt + \varphi_k) + \varepsilon_t \qquad (3.12)$$

The first term in this expression characterizes the low-frequency (monthly or seasonal) temperature behavior, with m being a small integer. The random variables ε_t represent daily temperature fluctuations.

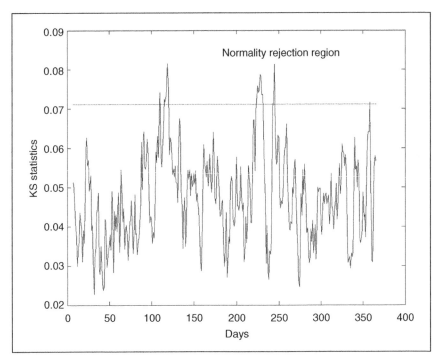

FIGURE 3.30   KS Statistics for Temperature Residuals

Are ε_t normally distributed? In order to answer this question, we take 42 years of temperature history (from 1960 to 2002), and for each year J, we compute the best low-frequency approximation to the temperature within the year (the first term in (3.12), with $m = 1$). The difference between the daily temperature and this approximation represents the sample

$$\varepsilon_{t_i}^J$$

$J = 1,\ldots,42$, of the random variable ε_t for each day t_i

Figure 3.30 represents the KS statistics for the distributions of ε_t computed using the Philadelphia temperature data. To increase the sample size in the test, we pool the data from seven consecutive days. Thus, each KS statistics on this graph corresponds to $42 * 7 = 294$ data points. The KS rejection criterion is set at a rather generous 10% level, which the normality hypothesis is rejected if KS > .071.

Figure 3.31 represents the JB statistics for the same locations.

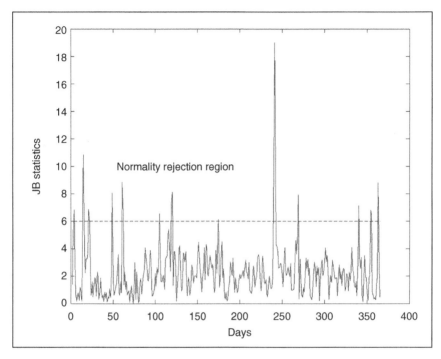

FIGURE 3.31 JB Statistics

As can be seen from these graphs, most of the time we cannot reject the normality hypothesis—and as is customary in the applied statistics, this reason is good enough to accept normality.

Undoubtedly, an assumption of normality of temperature fluctuations will greatly aid our modeling efforts, and our statistical tests indicate that historically it holds in most cases. But one must exercise caution using these tests, particularly for energy models.

The problem arises from the fact that tests like KS or JB use integrated statistics, and although as a whole these statistics may indicate that sample distribution is not far from normal, they may miss a much greater difference at the tails. In turn, the difference in the tails can lead to significant errors in pricing deals related to an important class of power plants called *peakers*. To alleviate these concerns about the tails, we conduct one more test in which we examine the probability of temperature exceeding 98°F under normality assumptions, and compare that probability with the historical frequency of this event. The results of this comparison are compiled in Table 3.14.

As we can see from the table, the results are quite close; they further justify the validity of using normal distributions for temperature fluctuations in energy models.

TABLE 3.14   Comparison of Probabilities of Temperature Being Above 98°F Under Normality Assumption and Determined from the Historical Data

Station	Empirical probability (temp>98)	Theoretical probability (temp>98)
Phoenix Sky Harbor Airport	.2564	.2616
Sacramento Executive Airport	.0335	.0369
Las Vegas McCarran Airport	.2290	.2318
Wichita Falls Airport	.1067	.1108

To complete our analysis, we now examine the autocorrelation properties of daily temperature data: we compute correlation coefficients $\rho(\varepsilon_t, \varepsilon_{t+\tau})$, where the displacement

$$\tau = \tfrac{1}{365}, \tfrac{2}{365}, \ldots$$

Since time is measured in years, this corresponds to a displacement of one day, two days, etc. Figure 3.32 represents these correlation coefficients as a function of τ.

The coefficients were computed for each year separately, using the yearly temperature data. The graph shows the average of correlation coefficients over 42 years, as well as their one-sigma bounds.

The correlation between daily temperature movements drops considerably during the first three days, and is negligible after five days. More precisely,

$$\rho(\varepsilon_t, \varepsilon_t + \tau) = .67, .34, .20, .12, .09 \ldots$$

Although these results represent only one geographical location, other locations exhibit similar behavior, with minor local differences in the speed of decay of correlation coefficients. Regarding different locations, we should not forget interlocational correlations. Figure 3.33 shows that these correlations may be quite high and stable. The graphs we plot here are those of

$$\rho(\varepsilon_t^{loc_1}, \varepsilon_t^{loc_2})$$

While temperature plays a critical role in energy models, it is not the only climate variable we should study. Precipitation, too, can be extremely important in building models for hydropower plants. Another interesting parameter is wind-chill factor. Studying the climate variables in their entirety is an important undertaking, but its complexity puts it beyond the scope of this book.

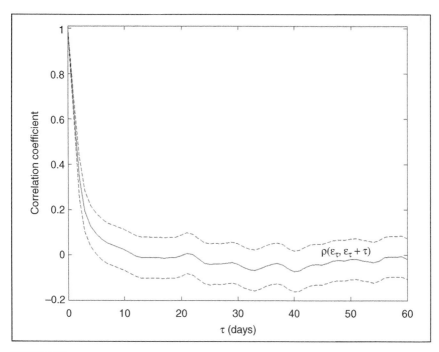

FIGURE 3.32   Estimates of Correlation Coefficients $\rho(\varepsilon_t, \varepsilon_{t+\tau})$ for Philadelphia Temperatures and Their One-sigma Bounds

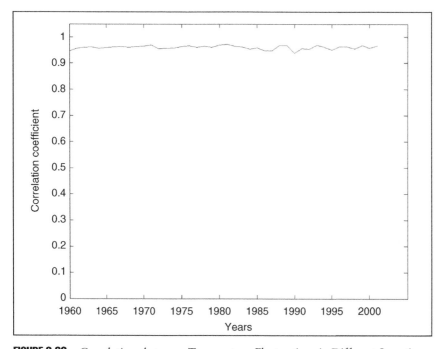

FIGURE 3.33   Correlations between Temperature Fluctuations in Different Locations

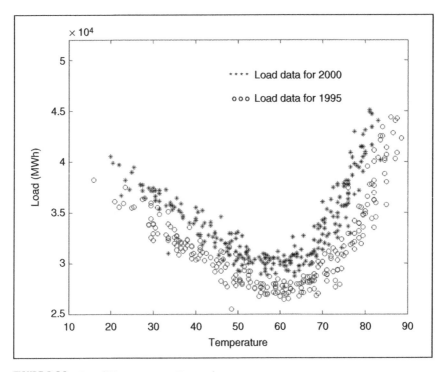

FIGURE 3.34   Load/Temperature Dependence

DEMAND

Sources of power demand data include government agencies and utilities. Hourly demand data is generally available, but frequently of low quality and limited volume. Nevertheless, because of its stable statistical properties, demand behavior is fairly well understood and reasonably modeled (see Stoll, 1989).

The demand for electricity, or load, is typically divided into three categories—residential, commercial, and industrial. Each load class has its own characteristics and statistical properties. For example, industrial load is the most stable and has the lowest sensitivity to temperature. On the other hand, residential load is most affected by the weather conditions, and hence shows the greatest variations. Analysis of each of these categories is particularly important for load-serving entities, since the load shape and variability significantly affect the economics of load obligations.

Figure 3.34 depicts the load/temperature dependence graphs in the NEPOOL region for two different years. Both graphs have frequently encountered parabolic shapes indicating increased power consumption at high and low temperatures. These graphs also indicate that projecting the future loads requires an understanding of the following two components:

1. Load growth relative to a certain base (reference) year, for example the current year. Modeling load growth requires an extensive analysis of economic, demographic, technological and other trends in a region. Although the growth rates are stable on the large scale, they may be nonconstant, even as a function of temperature.

2. The basic load/temperature shape function. Figure 3.34 suggests that a polynomial approximation of this function may be quite reasonable. However, other representations may be used as well. For example, regions with hot summers have a characteristic saturation behavior at high temperatures, when the load slows its growth with temperature and eventually becomes almost flat. For such profiles polynomial approximations may not be optimal and other choices should be considered.

OUTAGES

Outages can have a substantial impact on power prices, especially in a period of high demand. Understanding outages, therefore, is critical for developing realistic power price models. In North America the main source of power plant outage data is the NERC's Generating Availability Data System (GADS), the most comprehensive database on generating unit availability for more than 90% of the total installed capacity of North America.

GADS tracks a large number of parameters describing unit operation and outage conditions in an exceptionally detailed fashion. For example, in dealing with forced outages such as unplanned unit failures, it distinguishes among immediate, delayed, and postponed outages. It differentiates among various kinds of forced derating, or unplanned reduction of the load, and tracks planned and maintenance outages. It would be a major undertaking to present a complete description of the GADS data, but the price models introduced in following chapters use only a few of its critical parameters.

The most important of these parameters is the Equivalent Forced Outage Rate (EFOR), the hours of unit failure as the percentage of the total hours of unit availability. When the hours of complete failure are modified by the hours of partial failure, EFOR is the result. Derated hours are recalculated to arrive at the equivalent representation as if they were complete outages, and hence are called *equivalent forced derated hours,* or EFDH. According to the formal definition

$$EFOR = \frac{\text{Unplanned (Forced) Outage Hours} + \text{Equivalent Unplanned (Forced) Derated Hours}}{\text{Unplanned (Forced) Outage Hours} + \text{Service Hours} + \text{Equivalent Unplanned (Forced) Derated Hours}} \times 100\%$$

TABLE 3.15   Ranges of EFOR

Name	FOR	EFOR
Coal	4.8%	7%
Oil	8.5%	11.5%
Gas	7.5%	9.7%
Nuclear	9.0%	10%
Geothermal	3.3%	23%

In this formula

Unplanned (Forced) Outage Hours = total number of forced outages over a period of time (year)

Service Hours = total number of hours a unit is connected to the grid

Equivalent Unplanned (Forced) Derated Hours = the product of Forced Derated Hours and the size of derating, divided by the maximum capacity

Table 3.15 contains typical values of EFOR for several common classes of units. We have also included the corresponding values of Forced Outage Rates (FOR), in order to demonstrate the effect of derates on unit performance. The difference between FOR and EFOR is that FOR requires that only pure (100%) forced outage are included in its calculation:

$$FOR = \frac{\text{Unplanned (Forced) Outage Hours}}{\text{Unplanned (Forced) Outage Hours + Service Hours}} \times 100\%$$

MEAN REVERSION

For power and natural gas, as with any consumable commodity, one expects the long-term marginal cost to prevail in equilibrium. In industries where technology changes rapidly, it's not easy to identify what the long-term marginal cost of production will be, but in the medium-term we expect energy prices to exhibit mean reversion. In this section we look at the available evidence for electricity, gas, and oil prices. The effects of mean reversion in weather, demand, and the like will be reviewed separately. In later chapters we will examine the impact of mean reversion on the pricing of energy derivatives.

Estimation

Estimation of the effects of mean reversion can be done in several ways depending on the choice of mean-reverting model and the presence of such other effects as jumps and stochastic volatility. Here, we perform estimation of mean reversion assuming a simple model of constant volatility and no autocorrelation. We look at specifications of mean reversion in prices, log-returns, and returns. We find the methods give roughly the same results, although one may be more suitable for a particular region than another one. We can estimate a model of this form by running a simple lagged regression:

$$x_t = a + bx_{t-1} + \sigma_t \varepsilon_t$$

where x is the variable in question (i.e., price, return or log of price), a and b are the coefficients to be estimated, epsilon is a standard normal variate, and

$$\sigma_t = \sigma$$

is a constant. (Some of our tests do not depend on this fact.) The estimate of the mean-reversion coefficient is then given by

$$\mu = b - 1$$

For the model to be sensible, that is, truly mean-reverting and not mean-exploding, we must have $b-1 < 0$ or $b < 1$.

(Care must also be taken not to mix prices changes with changing time intervals. For example, if we want to look at daily changes, we should not include changes over the weekends unless we scale them appropriately, or make sure that the returns are affected only by trading time flow, and not by calendar time. In practice, scaling price changes by time intervals or by the square root of time intervals seems to work well.)

The actual regression we run in our examples has the following form

$$\Delta x_t = a + \mu x_{t-1} + \sigma \varepsilon_t$$

To test the model, we perform a statistical test to confirm whether the coefficient μ is negative, as required by the assumption of mean reversion. The test is the standard t-test, the ratio of the estimate divided by standard error of the estimate. Many statistical and spreadsheet packages (including Excel) have built-in functions to perform this test. The standard for significance (under normality) is usually around 2 (or -2). That is, if the absolute value of the t-statistics exceeds 2, the result is deemed significant. However, the regression is peculiar in that a higher value is required for significance. This is the so-called Dickey-Fuller test.

The critical values for acceptance in this test are higher; how much higher depends on the size of the sample. For samples of energy data, the critical value is usually closer to 3 for a 5% confidence interval. For a far more lenient

TABLE 3.16   Critical Values

Significance	"t-statistic" critical value
1%	3.4
5%	2.88
10%	2.56

criterion of acceptance of 10%, the critical value is still over 2.5. Consequently, the p-values reported in the packages for the t-tests should not be used for this regression. Using the so-called Phillips-Perron unit-root test (see Davidson and MacKinnon, 1993), we apply the following critical values for the different levels of significance in the standard regression (as produced by Excel or other popular spreadsheet packages) (see Table 3.16).

We will shortly see that the difference between choosing 2 or 3 as a critical value has quite an impact on our conclusions about the presence of mean reversion.

In the following sections we estimate this model and show the statistical significance of the estimates to identify the presence of mean-reversion in the energy time series. Before we proceed, a word of caution: the significance tests can be greatly affected by the presence of varying volatility, so one must be careful interpreting the following results.

It might seem surprising that, after arguing about the likely misspecification of the evolution process for the energy prices, and especially for electricity prices, we insist on using a very simple and potentially misleading specification. Wouldn't it be better to offer some general mean-reverting, stochastic-volatility, jump-diffusion model, and estimate it directly? The answer is no, for two reasons:

1. Simplicity and practicality: estimation of such processes tends to be cumbersome and complex. The simple test we advocate here (with some revisions), can give us a general picture and, in most situations, a robust estimate of the parameters in question.

2. Applicability: complex reduced-formed models do not necessarily offer a much better fit. The specification of a model in terms of jumps, stochastic volatility, and the like is not a natural description of the underlying process. While we can get better fit with some complex functional specifications, the performance of those models out-of-sample is poor, and the parameters are unstable.

Crude Oil

As shown in Pindyck (1999), the standard unit-root tests tend to reject the presence of mean reversion in short- and medium-term samples. Mean re-

TABLE 3.17 Mean-Reversion Rate and Corresponding *t*-statistics for the Spot Henry Hub Prices

Time period	Mean-reversion coefficient (per day)	*t*-statistic
Whole sample	−.00442	−1.06
Winter 98–99	−.015	−.56
Summer 99	−.03577	−2.09

version shows up, however, if we consider very long time series, as long as a hundred years. The inability to distinguish between nonstationary and mean-reverting processes in relatively large samples (as long as thirty years) indicates that the mean-reversion coefficient is very small, and is unlikely to have much impact on pricing in the short and medium terms. Clearly, as long as we are not concerned about writing options with a 100-year maturity, we can safely assume that the underlying prices are not mean-reverting.

On the other hand, modified models that assume a stochastic long-term price to which the prices revert perform quite well in recovering crude price behavior (see Pindyck, 1999). This suggests that the tests we use for detecting mean-reversion can be misleading. However, in the same paper it is shown that for other commodity prices (natural gas, coal), the performance of those models out-of-sample is poor.

Natural Gas

The evidence for the presence of mean reversion in natural gas spot prices is quite mixed. The results depend on the index and the season. We will first look at the major U.S. gas hub, Henry Hub. Table 3.17 shows the estimate of the mean-reversion rate and its corresponding *t*-statistics for the spot Henry Hub prices for the period of January 1998 through April 2001:

The pattern is similar for other subperiods. Overall the estimates of coefficients are not statistically insignificant at a 5% confidence level, or even at an aggressive 10% confidence level. The exceptions are summer prices, where the estimates tend to be consistently significant at the 10% confidence level. However, even when the estimates are significant, they are unstable. Additionally, when we perform more sophisticated tests that account for serial correlation in errors (ADF and Phillips-Perron), the results cease to be significant even at 10%.

Similar patterns prevail for many other major hubs: NGPL LA, Transco Zone 6 (Non–New York), Tennessee 800, PG&E City Gate. Some of the estimates tend to be of the wrong sign, i.e., they show negative mean reversion. This suggests either a resounding confirmation of the null hypothesis,

TABLE 3.18   Mean-Reversion Estimates for Transco Zone 6

Time period	Mean-reversion coefficient (per day)	t-statistic
Whole sample	.0067	−2.07
Jan 98–Sept 99	.053	−3.73
Sept 99–April 01	.0096	−1.96

TABLE 3.19   Mean-Reversion Estimates for Houston Ship Channel

Time period	Mean-reversion coefficient (per day)	t-statistic
Winter 98–99	.20	−3.03
Winter 99–00	.075	−2.73
Winter 00–01	.041	−1.79

that the true mean reversion is zero, or, more likely, that the model is mis-specified, and even the removal of serial correlation is not sufficient.

Some significant exceptions include the winter of '98 in Transco Zone 6 and the Houston Ship Channel (see Table 3.18).

Unlike in the other regions, the evidence here for mean reversion is much stronger for the winter seasons and weaker in the summers. Again, however, whenever the estimates are significant they are also unstable. The same holds for HSC as shown in Table 3.19.

For different winters, the conclusions about significance vary along with the numerical estimate for mean reversion.

Power

Cash Products

The evidence for the presence of mean reversion in electricity spot prices is mixed, and the results depend on the region and the season. We will look at some of the major U.S. electricity regions: PJM West, ERCOT, NEPOOL, and COB, and analyze the day-ahead on-peak power prices for the period January 1998 through April 2001.

Analysis of mean reversion in power prices is more questionable than for other commodities, because of the presence of spikes in the price evolution. Unlike jumps in financial time series, spikes are characterized by significant upward moves followed closely by sharp drops. It is quite clear that if we apply our constant volatility mean-reverting estimate procedure to electricity data, we are likely to find significant mean reversion. However, this kind of mean reversion is just a reflection of the spiky nature of power prices—not exactly what we are after.

TABLE 3.20   PJM and ERCOT

Market/Period	Estimate	*t*-statistic
PJM West/ whole sample	−.126	−7.5
ERCOT/ whole sample	−.046	−4.8
COB/ whole sample	−.019	−2.7 (not significant even at 10%)
PJM West/ winter 99–00	−.12	−2.87
ERCOT/ winter 99–00	−.01	−.4
COB/ winter 99–00	−.034	−1.1
PJM West/ summer 99	−.16	−2.8
ERCOT/ summer 99	−.08	−1.93
COB/ summer 99	−.30	−3.84

There are two ways around this problem, short of specifying a full-blown "spiky" price model (which we attempt in later chapters). One is to concentrate on periods with few if any spikes; in some markets those correspond to winter periods, but this is not true for all regions. The other solution is to censor the data by removing the spikes. Here we pursue the former first.

We first look at two U.S. markets: PJM and ERCOT (see Table 3.20).

As expected, we find very strong evidence of mean reversion for the whole sample. Strikingly, PJM winter prices show significant evidence of mean reversion, while ERCOT prices do not. This might seem to complicate our story of the subversive spikes skewing our estimation techniques, but we will see later, that this result is not surprising. The winter PJM prices are spikier, especially for higher gas prices (this deepening mystery is cleared up in Chapter 7 on hybrid models). On the other hand, ERCOT prices do not tend to exhibit any spikes in winter; the difference is due to the different structure of the supply stack. We will also investigate this phenomenon more closely in subsequent chapters.

Similar behavior can be observed in other markets, with the exception of the COB market, which seems to exhibit no mean reversion, spike-driven or otherwise. This result is puzzling, since others (Knittel and Roberts, 2001) who have estimated similar models for the NP15 market find statistically significant evidence of mean reversion. The difference between their study and our material is that they look at hourly prices, while we investigate on-peak block prices.

Escribano et al. (2001) find evidence of mean reversion in several overseas markets after accounting for spikes and GARCH (heteroskedasticity) effects. They analyze Nord Pool, Argentine, Australian, New Zealand, and Spanish markets.

As it turns out, once spikes are removed from the sample, the significant results for mean reversion disappear. Also, we can see in the data that removing just a couple of the biggest spikes makes the estimate of mean reversion insignificant.

A more sophisticated analysis of mean reversion in the presence of spikes can be found in Arranz et al. (2000) (see Escribano et al. (2001). The idea of those tests is similar to our simple filter. Another set, the presence of near-integrated process for volatility, is considered in Boswijk (2000).

These facts suggest that to estimate mean reversion in power prices we require, at minimum, models that account for varying volatility and spikes; otherwise, the estimate can be significantly biased. We will consider a model of this type in Chapter 4. The general conclusion that emerges is that even if we can find a significant estimate of mean reversion, it will be strongly dependent on the model chosen to represent the behavior of power prices. Additionally, we find that resulting estimates are quite unstable over different periods of times for more complex models of price evolution. This last fact makes the application of mean-reverting models quite challenging. In later chapters we will see that under certain circumstances we can avoid the problem altogether.

Finally, the seeming absence of mean reversion in our samples obviously does not prove that there is no mean reversion in power prices. What it does seem to suggest, however, is that it is insignificant for the medium term, which is exactly where the greatest interest in pricing and managing energy derivatives lies.

Forward Prices

Before we analyze the presence of mean reversion in forward prices, we must clear up some confusion about mean reversion in forward prices and its relationship to mean reversion in the corresponding cash product.

Despite appearances, mean reversion in commodity spot prices does not imply mean reversion in forward prices (in the absence of straightforward cash-and-carry arbitrage; see the next chapter for details). Spot mean reversion is induced by the equilibrating forces present in any commodity (as opposed to purely financial products). On the other hand, futures/forwards can be thought of as information about spot price behavior. There is no reason to think that the information about future conditions will be itself mean-reverting, as long as the market incorporates information about spot prices reasonably quickly; that is, if it is efficient. Incidentally, tests for mean reversion can be thought of as tests of the efficiency of the market.

The above should not be confused with option pricing theory, which imposes the condition that under the pricing measure, forward prices do not exhibit any drift (which obviously precludes any mean reversion). This fact holds as long as we can form replicating portfolios. It is not dependent on the statistical properties of any given market, but only on the available asset structure (see Rebonato, 1999). In other words, even if we could detect the presence of mean reversion in forward prices, this would by itself have no

TABLE 3.21   Results of Test for Four Markets

Market/contract	Coefficient estimate	t-statistic
PJM West/Jan 00	−.0092	−.64
NEPOOL/Jan 00	−.016	−1.88
HenryHub/Jan 00	−.0097	−1.04
TranscoZ6/Jan 00	−.0079	−1.01
PJMWest/Jul 00	−.00752	−1.08
NEPOOL/Jul 00	−.004	−.56
HenryHub/Jul 00	−.004	−.52
TranscoZ6/Jul 00	−.017	−1.87

impact on derivative pricing (well, almost none—it has an important impact on the term-structure of volatility (see Chapter 4)).

We will look now at the results of tests for mean reversion for different power and fuel forward prices. Because of liquidity issues, we include only one year of data before expiry.

Table 3.21 shows the results of our test for four markets: Henry Hub, Transco Zone 6 Non-New York, NEPOOL and PJM West. We cannot find evidence of the presence of mean reversion in any of those markets, even for a 10% confidence interval. Introducing more sophisticated tests to account for autocorrelations in returns (augmented Dickey-Fuller and Phillips-Perron) produces identical conclusions. We cannot reject the null hypothesis of unit-root (i.e., absence of mean reversion) even with the generous 10% confidence assumption. It's worth mentioning that the more sophisticated tests tend to give significantly different estimates of the coefficient than the naïve OLS does. This suggests that the autocorrelation in errors can significantly skew the result.

Conclusion

As expected, our analysis shows that forward contracts do not exhibit mean reversion—in other words they are relatively efficient. Somewhat unexpectedly, we show that there is very little evidence for the presence of mean reversion in gas and even power spot prices. This finding is quite striking, since simple arguments about the structure of the commodity markets suggest that some mean reversion should be present. The possible explanation is that, similarly to the results of Pindyck for oil, the mean reversion in those markets is very slow, and we do not have enough data to form tests with enough power to detect it.

In practical terms then, it seems that we do not have to worry about the presence of mean reversion in gas markets with the possible exception of some locations. For power spot prices, the evidence is mixed and strongly indicative of a misspecification of the process. In the following chapter we show how to specify a spot process for power more appropriately.

CHAPTER 4

Reduced-form Processes

MODELING PRICE PROCESS

Modeling energy prices, especially in deregulated markets, can be quite different from the approaches utilities have adopted for planning purposes in a regulated environment. Moreover, the methods currently used are substantially different from those initially transplanted from Wall Street.

This chapter deals with what are usually called reduced-form models. The modeling approach consists of specifying a stochastic process of price evolution by selecting it from a parameterized family of processes (e.g., geometric Brownian motion, jump-diffusion process, and so on). The next step is to determine the requisite parameters, either through estimation, based on historical prices, or through inference from the available forward-looking information, such as option or forward quotes. This chapter concentrates on the most frequently encountered classes of reduced-form models. Fundamental and hybrid models will be discussed in subsequent chapters.

Before proceeding with the details, we should examine the criteria we use in choosing a model. By defining what a "good model" is we have a basis for judging the plethora of approaches presented in the following pages.

Let's start by stating what modeling in energy markets is not: *It is not price forecasting.* This fact is fundamental to the business of risk management, which proceeds on the assumption that prices cannot be reliably and consistently forecasted. If they could, there would be no need for risk management. We adopt this assumption as a central tenet of our approach.

Modeling Process

We start with an idealized modeling process that typically consists of the following steps:

1. Consider the market's qualitative properties, such as spikes, mean reversion, jumps.
2. Select a model—parametric, fundamental, or hybrid—that matches the qualitative properties identified in Step 1.

3. Estimate the parameters based on historical data.
4. Check the performance of the selected model out-of-sample.
5. Make the model's pricing of liquid contracts match the market quotes (options, forwards, and so on) and use other forward-looking information consistently.
6. Price away everything that comes your way.
7. Hedge away.

This standard approach is often impossible to follow, especially in power markets. The dearth of available historical information turns the crucial step of estimation and validation of models, especially reduced-form models, into a daunting task.

Reduced-form models have the special problem of dealing effectively with non–price-based forward-looking information. Even though available traded contracts will be affected by these pieces of information, we cannot differentiate them sufficiently to price structured products. The information is too aggregated.

Consider the following example. It comes to our attention that 10,000 MW of extra capacity is due to be added to the generation stack of a certain region. Obviously, this information is reflected in the summer forward and ATM option prices—the contracts that usually trade with some liquidity. However, knowing those new prices doesn't tell us what the price of a deep OTM daily call should be. Unless our model can directly condition on this kind of information—we will address indirect conditioning later—we cannot consistently use it.

In financial markets we would have had a number of strike prices quoted so the impact could be easily discerned, but this is not the case for some energy markets, especially power markets. Energy markets suffer from a scarcity of historical as well as forward-looking information, with significant consequences for the modeling process.

Our revised (more realistic) approach is generally the following:

1. Look at the qualitative properties of the structure you want to price and hedge.
2. Identify, if possible, the static hedges (model independent).
3. Investigate the dependence of the residual between the structure and the static hedge portfolio, based on the qualitative features of the market (model dependent).
4. Model the properties in Step 3.
5. If data is insufficient to reliably model the properties in question, consider approximations that do not have a high impact on the price *and* on the hedges. If this fails, give up—that is, have the trader guess the missing parameters—at least you have achieved risk-factor separation.

6. If the model works, return to Step 3 and go through the rest of the process again, and repeat this until the static hedges and the model are consistent.
7. Price and hedge away.

EXAMPLE 4.1   *Valuation of options on temporal forward spreads for natural gas contracts in the presence of mean reversion*

The valuation of options on spreads between forward contracts often arises in the valuation of storage facilities. The value of the option is given by the following generic formula:

$$V = E[\max(F_2 - F_1, 0)] \tag{4.1}$$

We will see in later chapters that if we can assume prices are described by joint-lognormal distribution, then price is expressed by the Margrabe formula (see Chapter 8 and Margrabe, 1978) that depends on current forward prices, cumulative volatilities, and correlation. If the underlying exhibits mean reversion, both the volatilities and the correlation are affected.

The standard approach calls for estimating the relevant mean-reversion parameter, and then use it to arrive at the correct volatilities and correlation. Estimation of the mean-reversion parameter can become quite tricky, as we saw in Chapter 3. The usual response to this problem is to ignore it—estimate the mean reversion directly, bias or no bias, put it into the relevant formulas, and live with the consequences.

We can fare much better, however, by following our revised approach to valuation. First, note that we can get rid of exposure to assumptions about the impact of mean reversion on volatilities by using implied volatilities from the options traded on the individual legs of our transaction. This is equivalent to assuming that we will form a hedge with the standard calls on the individual legs. This strategy corresponds to Step 3 in our revised approach, and it also results in the separation of the problem—at least as long as the implied volatilities exhibit no significant smiles.

Now we can concern ourselves with only the cumulative correlation (Step 4 of the revised approach). It seems we have not escaped the curse of mean-reversion estimation after all—the cumulative correlation depends on the correct value of the parameter (see Chapter 6). Since spread option prices are sensitive to the choice of the correlation parameter, the problem is not a trivial one. However, this dependence on the mean-reversion parameter arises only through the cumulative correlation, not directly. If we can find a way of estimating the cumulative correlation itself, we might avoid the problem completely.

It turns out that there is a way of doing it. As we discuss extensively in Chapter 6, the standard estimate of correlation estimates the cumulative correlation itself. Consequently, if we choose our sample for estimation carefully, so that it corresponds to the maturity period of the option (admittedly, this is not always possible), we can obtain an unbiased and consistent estimate of the correlation in question.

Thus we have managed to find a robust estimate of the option's value, even though we have no idea what the true mean-reversion parameter is; that information is not required to properly value the spread option.

Although we have not escaped modeling choices completely, the problem is greatly simplified if the prices are jointly lognormal. In the presence of significant implied volatility smiles, this example is not valid; a detailed discussion of how to treat the problem under those conditions can again be found in Chapter 6.

Example 4.1 gives a flavor for what is involved in the modeling process. We can now concentrate on defining the desired features of a model. A good model must meet the following criteria:

- It must be a good fit to the historical data, and be able to recover the historical distribution (out-of-sample).
- It must be an exact match to the current prices of liquidly traded contracts.
- It must make efficient and consistent use of nonprice conditional information—especially important in power markets.
- It must have stable parameters (no appreciable variation with changing market conditions). This requires an efficient estimation of parameters.
- The resulting prices *and* hedges must have low sensitivity to the choice of the remaining free parameters.
- The representation must be efficient. We should strive to have as few free parameters as possible, unless we can clearly and independently obtain their values from somewhere else (e.g., implied volatility, implied correlation, and so on).
- It must include time-efficient evaluation of prices and hedges.

To illustrate the problems that can appear, consider the following example.

EXAMPLE 4.2 *Estimation and application of jump-diffusion models*

In the first wave of electricity deregulation in 1997, jump-diffusion models gained popularity, stemming from their ability to replicate, at least qualitatively, the spiky nature of electricity spot prices. The trouble was the inefficient and unstable estimates of jump properties. Depending on which summers were used for calibration, the resulting parameters varied significantly. This instability was due partially to the misspecification problem, which we will discuss later, but more directly to the scarcity of available data on which to estimate the model. Only a few significant spikes occur each year, and estimation based on such a limited data set produces unreliable estimates.

This is not the end of the problem, however. Even if we could reliably estimate the unconditional distribution of jumps, given a sufficient data set, jump-diffusion models still present a problem in giving us the conditional distribution of jumps. Therefore, the model does not perform very well on out-of-sample tests, and there is no natural way of incorporating non–price-based forward-looking information. Going back to the example above, the addition of capacity in the market can have a dramatic impact on the probability of a price spike. Any information about price spikes we can infer from ATM options (the only options liquidly trading) or forward contracts will be too aggregated to provide us much insight; consequently, the model will have difficulty using this information to account for capacity additions.

In principle we might specify a model in which the jump distribution is a function of exogenous variables such as capacity additions. Although this approach can potentially address our second concern, it can do so only by exacerbating our first one (estimation of unconditional distribution). To reliably estimate or calibrate the conditional structure of a jump distribution requires significantly more data—which we usually don't have.

It might seem that the problem described above is the fundamental problem of any modeling approach in power markets. But that's not the case; the trick is to use nonprice information to effectively extend our data set. How this is done is the subject of Chapter 7, where we discuss hybrid models.

Model Selection: Model Rejection

How to determine if the model is "bad"? Below we identify several common problems that can significantly damage model applicability. Although we suggest the ways to repair the problems, nevertheless, serious concerns should be raised if models exhibiting such behavior should be used at all, particularly in stand-alone (i.e., with no ad hoc expert guidance) pricing and hedging applications.

> *Problem:* There are several parameters for which we cannot find a stable estimate, and which have a dramatic impact on value and hedges.
>
> *Advice:* Once the model exhibits this type of behavior, it clearly cannot be used on a stand-alone basis for pricing and hedging. The only way for it to be used is as an auxiliary model, for example, in combination with or in support of an expert opinion. Furthermore, it is advisable to create a version of the model that, while reasonable, has only one such unstable parameter. Have the trader guess its value.

Problem: The model has stable parameters that cannot fit the market quotes. (You must price the underlying correctly before you start pricing the derivative.)

Advice: Try an approximate fitting through some distance function (e.g., least squares). Most likely, this approach will not work well, because approximation procedures tend to be unstable, and hence unreliable.

Problem: The model has stable estimates of parameters, capable of matching market quotes through the choice of free parameters, or calibration, but this calibration changes abruptly with market changes.

Advice: That kind of model may be sufficient for static hedging, if we have enough liquid instruments, but it will perform quite poorly in dynamic hedging. Use it only as a last resort.

By now we should have sufficiently convinced the reader that energy prices in general, and power prices in particular, exhibit behavior significantly different from other commodities or financial products. Strong seasonality and dependence on time to expiration for both forward prices and option volatility, extreme and frequent price spikes, uniquely pronounced "fat tails" of price distributions, nonstationarity of correlations, and volatility smiles are some of the properties that make modeling the evolution of energy prices so difficult and challenging. Having said that, we should immediately add that there is hardly a shortage of pricing models for energy products. Most of them are more or less direct adaptations of the models used in financial markets, although, as energy markets mature, new pricing methodologies with a distinct energy flavor are also emerging.

Here we provide a review, albeit incomplete, of the principal approaches to modeling energy price evolution. We focus on typical choices of stochastic processes that define random movements in time of either spot or forward prices, we describe the corresponding calibration procedures, and finally, we will analyze the pros and cons of particular models.

Model Selection: Estimation and Calibration

The challenge of complex models is the large set of parameters we must estimate. We can easily fall victim to the problem of an overfit: the more parameters, the easier it is to fit the data without gaining any explanatory benefit whatsoever. There are two ways of testing for an overfit:

1. Always test your models out-of-sample, and measure the closeness of fit.
2. Perform stability tests: estimate the model on two subsamples and compare your estimates. If they differ widely, be suspicious of the model in question. We can perform this test more systematically by resampling—randomly drawing from the original sample and reestimating the model.

This procedure results in a robust calculation of the standard errors in a finite sample; the alternative of using asymptotic normal standard errors can be highly misleading.

In practice we find that the complex models examined in the rest of the chapter suffer from significant instability of the estimates: mean reversion, correlation between volatility and returns, and jump rates tend to be particularly unstable. The problem is especially acute in power prices, since the limited size of samples limits our ability to differentiate estimation noise from changes in the underlying process.

In-sample estimates can be obtained through a variety of methods. We review the most popular ones.

Maximum Likelihood

The most popular technique for estimating models is the maximum likelihood approach (see Greene, 2000). Its principle is simple: find a model that the probability of the data originating from the model is the highest.

We have a set of observations $\{x_i\}_1^N$ assumed to be drawn independently from the same distribution. We want to find the best model to describe the available data. We might choose a family of probability distributions $f(x|\theta)$ indexed by the vector of parameters θ, for example, the normal distribution indexed by the mean and variance. We now try to find a set of parameters θ^* that gives us the highest probability for our sample to come from. If we assume that the observations are independent, the probability that they came from the distribution $f(x|\theta)$ is given by the product of individual probabilities:

$$P(\{x_i\}_1^N; \vec{\theta}) = f(x_1|\vec{\theta})\, f(x_2|\vec{\theta}) \ldots f(x_N|\vec{\theta}) \qquad (4.2)$$

This function is called likelihood function. If the sample observed is not independent, and the individual observations are not drawn from the same distribution, we must redefine our likelihood function to account for that fact

$$P(\{x_i\}_1^N; \vec{\theta}) = f_1(x_1|\vec{\theta})\, f_2(x_2|x_1; \vec{\theta}) \ldots f_N(x_N|x_{N-1}; \vec{\theta}) \qquad (4.3)$$

Estimates are now calculated by finding the set, if it exists, of θ^* for which the above function achieves its maximum. In practice, instead of using the likelihood function, we use the logarithm of the likelihood function: the loglikelihood function. The maximum estimates are identical, but the mathematical manipulation is much easier. The maximum likelihood (ML) estimates are given by θ^* such that

$$\vec{\theta}_{MLE} = \vec{\theta}^* = \arg\max_{\vec{\theta}}(\log\{P(\{x_i\}_1^N; \vec{\theta})\}) =$$

$$= \arg \max_{\vec{\theta}} \left(\sum_{i=1}^{N} f(x_i | \vec{\theta}) \right) \qquad (4.4)$$

If the distribution function satisfies certain regularity conditions, the solution in (4.4) is given by the first order condition:

$$\frac{\partial \log \{P(\{x_i\}_1^N; \vec{\theta})\}}{\partial \vec{\theta}} = \vec{0} \qquad (4.5)$$

The function on the left side of the equation (4.5) is also called the score function (vector). In the majority of practical problems (4.5) and (4.4) are equivalent. There are situations, however, where the solution to (4.5) does not exist, even though we can find a solution to (4.4); for example problems exist with regard to uniform distributions (see Davidson and MacKinnon, 1993).

EXAMPLE 4.3 *Maximum likelihood estimation with normal distribution*

In this example we consider estimation with normal distribution. The distribution function for a normal variable is given by

$$\phi(x|\mu, \sigma^2) = \frac{1}{\sigma \sqrt{2\pi}} e^{-\frac{(x-\mu)^2}{2\sigma^2}} \qquad (4.6)$$

The loglikelihood function is given by

$$\ln\{P(\{x_i\}_1^N; \vec{\theta})\} = -\frac{N}{2} \ln(2\pi) - N \ln(\sigma) - \frac{1}{2} \sum_{i=1}^{N} \left(\frac{x_i - \mu}{\sigma} \right)^2 \qquad (4.7)$$

Differentiating with respect to the mean and standard deviation gives us the ML estimates:

$$\hat{\mu}_{MLE} = \frac{1}{N} \sum_{i=1}^{N} x_i$$

$$\hat{\sigma}_{MLE} = \sqrt{\frac{\sum_{i=1}^{N} (x_i - \hat{\mu}_{MLE})^2}{N}} \qquad (4.8)$$

Note that the standard unbiased estimator of standard deviation has $N-1$ in the denominator. This difference underscores the fact that ML estimates can be biased.

Maximum likelihood estimators enjoy many useful properties. They are:

- Consistent, that is, they converge to the true parameter for large samples.
- Asymptotically efficient; for large samples, the standard error of the estimates converges to the minimum possible size.
- Asymptotically normal.

All these results have asymptotic character, that is, they give us a desirable structure for our estimates in large samples. The finite-sample properties of ML estimators are usually unknown and can differ substantially from asymptotic behavior.

One of the key requirements of the methodology is knowledge of the likelihood function. For many of the processes we consider here, we have no explicit formula for the likelihood function. The usual solutions involve approximations; for example, in jump-diffusion models the distribution function for returns is given by

$$\ln\{P(\{x_i\}_1^N; \vec{\theta})\} = \sum_{i=1}^{N} \ln\left\{\sum_{n=0}^{\infty} \frac{e^{-\lambda \Delta t}(\lambda \Delta t)^n}{n!} \phi\left[x_i; \left(\mu - \frac{1}{2}\sigma^2\right)\Delta t, \sqrt{\sigma^2 \Delta t + n\delta^2}\right]\right\}$$

(4.9)

We can get rid of the unpleasant infinite sum in the function, however, by noting that return analysis usually involves time intervals of a day or even an hour. An infinite number of jumps within such short periods of time is virtually impossible and can be safely ignored. Consequently, we can truncate the sum at a finite number; in practice five to ten terms will suffice.

Another solution is to approximate the distribution by simulation and perform the optimization by resimulating the process. Not surprisingly, this method is computationally expensive.

Goodness-of-fit can be measured by the likelihood function itself. We can perform a number of statistical tests on the observed estimate of the likelihood to test for restrictions of model parameters (Lagrange multiplier, Wald, and likelihood ratio tests, see Davidson and MacKinnon 1993). We can nest various models within a complex one (e.g., stochastic volatility within stochastic volatility jump-diffusion), and compare the models by comparing submodels. The problem with this approach is that more complex models tend to perform better in such tests, an obvious reflection of an issue mentioned earlier: all the tests we perform are in-sample ones. We are therefore likely to achieve a better fit from a model with many parameters. To control for this problem, we can use so-called information criteria that explicitly penalize the introduction of additional parameters (Akaike and Schwartz, see Davidson and MacKinnon, 1993).

Quasi Maximum Likelihood

The maximum likelihood estimation procedure relies on knowing the right family of distributions to use. Since we always deal with models that are at best only approximately true, we need to know how robust the procedure is to misspecifications. Obviously, if we consider Example 4.3, we can easily see that if the true distribution is, for example *t*-distribution, the ML estimates will not have the desirable properties. However, it turns out that in certain cases the improperly specified model retains the consistency and asymptotic normality properties. For example, nonlinear least squares estimates (which are ML estimates under normality) will be consistent and asymptotically normal even if the error disturbances are not normal. Similarly, we later analyze GARCH processes with normal and *t* innovations. We will see that models with *t* innovations offer a better fit. The natural question in this context is, what happens to the estimate of the GARCH coefficients when we use normal innovations. The estimates are generally consistent, although they may be biased. For large enough samples, the misspecified coefficients might still be useful as will the standard tests for significance (since they rely on normality).

The procedure therefore involves estimating models always assuming that the error terms (innovations) are normally distributed (see Gourieroux and Jasiak, 2001). The procedure works well as long as we are dealing with large samples. In energy price markets, it is unlikely that we will have enough data points to trust this procedure. Some data sets however can be easily handled in this way, such as temperature and other weather data, and possibly some load data.

However, it turns out that for many models used in derivative pricing, QMLE tends to perform much better in coefficient estimates and specification tests than even the exact maximum likelihood method (see Zhou, 2001). Even though, theoretically, MLE should be better, this is only assured for asymptotic behavior. In finite samples, there is no guarantee that MLE performs better. The Monte Carlo studies for selected processes show that QMLE performs much better for typical sample sizes (500 to 1,500 observations) than MLE or other more sophisticated methods we mention later. The method has the added advantage of relative simplicity and ease of implementation. As long as we can find explicit formulas for the first two moments of the conditional (transition) distribution, QMLE is the preferred method. Again, even if we have explicit expression for the transition distribution, we should only use the information about the first two moments and ignore the rest.

Incidentally, Zhou's paper shows that as soon as we introduce more complex volatility structures (compared to GBM), the estimation of mean reversion in finite samples cannot be reliably performed, even if we know precisely the data-generating process.

Method of Moments and Its Extensions

The broad alternative to ML estimation methods is method of moments. This idea is also simple: instead of looking at and comparing the whole distributions, we compare only some moments of the sample distribution and the theoretical distribution. Consider our theoretical distribution $f(x|\theta)$. We can derive a set of L moments as a function of the model parameters

$$\mu_f^1(\vec{\theta}), \mu_f^2(\vec{\theta}) \ldots \mu_f^L(\vec{\theta})$$

We can also calculate the analogous moments from the sample:

$$\mu_{sample}^1(\{x_i\}_1^N), \mu_{sample}^2(\{x_i\}_1^N) \ldots \mu_{sample}^L(\{x_i\}_1^N)$$

Now we can choose the parameters in such a way that the theoretical moments are equal or close to the sample moments.

If we analyze time series data with dependent observations, we may need to consider conditional moments instead of marginal ones. This can pose a problem, since marginal moments are much easier to estimate from the data than conditional ones, but the problem can often be solved by the use of instrumental variables that can turn the conditional moment restrictions into unconditional ones. (See Gourieroux and Jasiak, 2001.)

Our models can generate more valid moment restrictions than the available number of parameters. In such a situation we perform an optimization to find estimates "closest" to the available data. The standard technique is generalized method of moments (GMM), which uses a quadratic objective function with an appropriate weighting matrix (see Davidson and MacKinnon, 1993). It yields consistent and asymptotically normal estimates.

The significant advantage of the method of moments is that it uses only a subset of all the possible restrictions that full knowledge of the underlying distribution implies. One benefit of this is a computational one. We can often find an explicit expression for the moments of the distribution, even though we don't explicitly know the likelihood function. For example, the class of affine jump-diffusion models (the Heston model belongs to this class) does not offer explicit formulas for the distribution function. On the other hand, for many members of the class we can find an explicit expression for the characteristic function of the distribution function (see Duffie, Pan, and Singleton, 2000) and knowing the characteristic function is equivalent to knowing explicit expressions for the moments of the distribution. Even if we don't know the moments explicitly, using approximate or simulation methods is much more computationally efficient than ML estimation. In recent years there has been an explosion of new methods of moments used for estimation in derivative pricing; examples include simulated method of moments, efficient method of moments, and indirect inference (see Gourieroux and Jasiak, 2001).

We can often choose moment conditions for estimation that are important from the standpoint of pricing and hedging certain energy derivatives. For example, under some but not all circumstances, kurtosis (scaled fourth moment) can be a good measure of the steepness of a symmetric smile in implied volatility. If we are interested only in pricing butterflies with little level and ATM volatility exposure, we can choose a model that recovers the observed kurtosis robustly, without much concern about how it performs in recovering other parts of the distribution.

Calibration: Matching Market Data

The approach in the previous sections consisted of estimating the parameters of the objective/historical distribution to be used for pricing and hedging of derivative products. However, proper pricing requires an adjustment of the objective process by the price of risk to arrive at the so-called risk-neutral process (see Chapter 10 for details). Instead of following the indirect route of obtaining risk-neutral parameters, we may be able to obtain them directly by recovering them from the prices of liquidly traded products (forwards, options, and so on).

This method of calibrating the parameters of a price evolution process is typically used as the method of last resort. It is simple and universal, but it possesses unpleasant numerical properties. The method can be described as follows.

Let the process governing the price evolution depend on the vector of parameters $\Theta = (\theta_1, \theta_2, \ldots, \theta_n)$. For example, in (4.79) this is vector $(\kappa, \theta, \lambda, k, \sigma)$. Assume that at a given moment of time we observe a number of traded products, and denote their prices by $P = (p_1, p_2, \ldots, p_N)$. These products can be forward contracts, swaps, options, strips of options, swaptions, and so on; the principal condition is that they can be valued with the help of the governing process under consideration. For a given parameter vector Θ, the values generated by the process are denoted by $\Pi(\Theta) = (\pi_1(\Theta), \pi_2(\Theta), \ldots, \pi_N(\Theta))$. Note that these values can be determined by analytical formulas or through simulations. The goal is to find a certain set of parameters Θ^* to ensure that the process-generated values match the observed prices. Since this problem can rarely be solved exactly, we formulate it as a nonlinear least squares optimization problem:

$$\Theta^* \to \min_{(\theta_1, \theta_2,\, k \ldots, \theta_n)} \sum_{i=1}^{N} [\pi_i(\theta_1, \theta_2, \ldots, \theta_n) - p_i]^2 \qquad (4.10)$$

That is, we are looking for parameters that provide the best approximation of the market prices by the model-generated values. This calibration procedure, although easy to understand and implement, has the problem that it can be numerically ill-conditioned, and most frequently is. Specifically, the minimization problem (4.10) may not have a unique solution. Moreover, the solution set may have a rather complex structure. Further and most importantly, the objective function, that is, the right side of (4.10), may be so flat in the neighborhood of its minimum that its value may be very close to the minimum value even for parameters significantly removed from the optimal ones. This, in turn, means that the computational procedures chosen to solve the problem (4.10) may end too early and too far from the solution. Because of that, even small perturbations of market data may lead to a large perturbation of the parameter estimates, causing parameter instability. A numerical problem with such characteristics is called ill-conditioned.

Obviously, if the objective function is very flat in the neighborhood of the solution, the value of the structures to which we calibrate our process is not very sensitive to the choice of parameters. Consequently, one could argue against undue concern for the true value of the parameters under consideration. But even though one structure is not very sensitive to a parameter, it does not mean that another structure will retain this property. For example, we can calibrate a jump-diffusion model to ATM option prices. In practice, estimates of jump amplitude and jump frequency tend to be very unstable, implying that ATM options are not overly sensitive to the choice of amplitude and frequency parameters, and that what counts is the product of the two. (However, deep OTM options *are* sensitive to assumptions about these parameters, and not just their product). In practice, calibrating parameters to price liquid instruments is of little interest, since we know the prices already; we calibrate them precisely to understand the behavior of illiquid products (e.g., OTM options).

BUILDING REDUCED-FORM MODELS FOR ENERGY APPLICATIONS: THE BASICS

We start with a simple but essential question. Let t_0 be a given initial time, say January 1. What is the distribution of spot (daily) prices of energy P_T at some future time T, say August 15, conditional on the information available at t_0?

Consider two possible approaches to determining the distribution.

1. Using the information available at t_0, construct an appropriate process for the evolution of spot prices on the interval $[t_0, T]$, and apply this process to obtain the required distribution at the right-end point of the interval.

2. Develop this process for August monthly forward prices, with the information at t_0, and use it to determine the distribution of the August monthly forward prices at expiration (July 31). Combine this process with the evolution of spot prices in August, conditional on the settled price of the monthly August contract. In other words

$$\Pr(S_T) = \Pr(S_T | F_{exp}^{Aug}) \, \Pr(F_{exp}^{Aug}) \qquad (4.11)$$

where F_{exp}^{Aug} denotes the price of the August monthly forward contract at the expiration date.

The spot price inside a particular month is frequently called the *spot (or cash) price*. Thus, according to the second approach, the simulation of daily prices on August 15 is achieved by first simulating the evolution of August forward prices up to July 31, and then continuing each forward price scenario by evolving the cash prices inside August up to August 15, conditional on the settled price of the forward contract on July 31.

The first approach results in a pure spot price evolution process, while the second is a combination of forward and spot evolution processes. Which one is better? Most likely, the first approach will be a favorite in financial applications, but the situation is not so clear in energy applications. The applicability of the pure spot process is rather limited at present and we strongly favor the second approach for the following reasons:

- Hedgeability
- Shortage of data
- Calibration

We elaborate on these reasons as follows.

Hedgeability. Risk management of energy structures is very demanding and presents a number of challenges. This is primarily because these structures—whether these are energy assets such as power plants and fuel storage, or structured products such as tolling agreements and swing options—are remarkably complex. To make things worse, the set of tools available for active risk management is still quite limited, primarily because of liquidity issues. On top of that, the existing tools frequently do not match hedging needs, sometimes leaving us with no way to neutralize significant sources of risk. Developing models in such an imperfect environment requires utmost attention to maximizing the efficiency, transparency, and implementation flexibility of the resulting hedging procedures.

It is precisely for this reason that we prefer the forward/spot model to the pure spot model. Indeed, the principal disadvantage of the pure spot model, particularly in power applications, is that spot products cannot be used for hedging, due to the nonstorability of power. Therefore, any model that uses spot prices as an underlying, and generates hedges in terms of spot products, must also provide mapping from spot to some other tradable products—for example, forward or balance-of-the-month (BOM) contracts. Obtaining this mapping is a challenge, especially because in power markets the well-known relation between the spot and forward prices cannot be established with the no-arbitrage argument commonly used in other markets. Obviously, the situation is no different in the forward/spot approach; we still have to determine this relationship for effective hedging. However, the significant difference is that we get rid of the part of the price evolution that is unimportant for pricing or hedging. The model description is more parsimonious.

The forward/spot process models the greater part of price evolution, namely, from t_0 to the expiration date of the forward contract T_{exp}, using the price of a tradable product, the forward contract. In the case of the example above, this means that if a cash flow of a certain structure depends on the spot price on August 15, we can hedge the variability of its mark-to-market value for January 1 to July 31 using the forward contract. Even assuming that we have no tradable products inside the month to manage the fluctuations in value (in reality, BOM, balance-of-the-week, and possibly other contracts are frequently available), we are fortunate to face only a 15-day exposure, a fraction of the total period. Granted, the exposure in the last 15 days can be substantial, particularly for power. Yet even in the most extreme cases, we are assured a significant reduction of the total variance of the cash flow over the January 1 to August 15 period.

This variance reduction will be even greater if we use BOM contracts to hedge the cash period exposure. That requires a small modification of the methodology: Instead of a forward/spot process, we must develop forward/BOM process that, conceptually, is a comparable undertaking. This separation of the problem corresponds to modeling the residual part of our exposure.

The Shortage of Data.   The strong seasonal behavior of energy prices necessitates separation of spot price modeling by seasons, and even by months. This means that it is probably incorrect to use the February data to calibrate the evolution process of August spot prices; a better approach is to use August data from the previous years. However, here lies the problem: We have only few available seasons of market data, even for natural gas, which makes the calibration of a pure spot process unstable and unreliable. The effect of this data shortage is particularly serious in the case of the convenience yield, which is a key parameter in modeling spot prices. Complex models are frequently proposed to describe its evolution, but at present there is not sufficient data to estimate them reliably.

The forward/spot approach allows us to enhance a data set by adding forward-looking information about the behavior of forward prices implied by traded liquid monthly forward contracts and options on forwards. Using this data, we can confidently calibrate the process for forward prices; after that, what remains is modeling prices inside the cash period—a task made simpler and more manageable by the shortness of the modeling period.

Calibration.   The forward/spot approach makes the task of model calibration significantly easier. To illustrate this point, consider the process of matching option prices. In Chapter 2 we introduced commonly traded options—monthly, daily, and index. Recall that a monthly option is a fixed strike option, whose exercise decision and cash flow are determined by the settlement value of a specified monthly index. A daily option is a fixed strike option exercised daily inside a specified month, with a daily spot price as underlying. Finally, an index option is an option with daily spot prices as underlying and a settled monthly index as a price. These three types of options imply three types of volatilities:

1. Monthly options imply the volatility of monthly forwards (monthly volatility)
2. Index options imply the volatility inside the month (cash volatility)
3. Daily options imply daily volatility

Since all these volatilities are linked to the same month, they cannot be arbitrary. There is a certain structural relation between them that must be captured by a reasonable model. As we will explain later, the pure spot processes have a difficult time representing this relation. On the other hand, the forward/spot approach is naturally fit for this purpose, and here's why.

The relationship of the three options is based on the following identity

$$\text{var}_t(P_T) = \text{var}_t(E[P_T|F_{\text{exp}}]) + E_t[\text{var}(P_T|F_{\text{exp}})] \qquad (4.12)$$

where F_{exp} is the settled price of the monthly forward prices (in our example it is the price of August contract at expiration) and P_T is the spot price at time T (the August 15 price). The variance $\text{var}_t (P_T)$ means the total variance of the (August 15) spot price as estimated at time t (January 1). The quantities $E\left[P_T\middle|F_{\text{exp}}\right]$ and $\text{var}\left[P_T\middle|F_{\text{exp}}\right]$ are expectation and variance, respectively, of the inside-the-month spot price P_T, conditional on the settled price F_{exp}. That is, they are two moments of the conditional distribution $\Pr\left(P_T\middle|F_{\text{exp}}\right)$ introduced in (4.11). Conditional expectation and variance are functions of the random variable F_{exp}, and the expected value and variance of these functions with respect to the distribution of F_{exp} (with the distribution determined at time t) are denoted by $E_t[\text{var}(P_T|F_{\text{exp}})]$ and $\text{var}_t(E[P_T|F_{\text{exp}}])$ respectively.

The proof of equality (4.12) follows directly from the definition of conditional variance and the law of iterated expectations. One can show that (4.12) is an identity, that is, it is completely independent of any distributional assumptions.

Despite its complex appearance, the meaning of this identity can be intuitively understood. Indeed, let us assume that

$$E\left[P_T\middle|F_{\text{exp}}\right] = F_{\text{exp}}$$

and

$$\mathrm{var}\left[P_T\middle|F_{\mathrm{exp}}\right] = \upsilon_C\left(T - T_{\mathrm{exp}}\right)$$

where T_{exp} is the expiration time of the forward contract.

The first equality means that at expiration monthly forward prices are unbiased predictors of spot prices inside the month. The second equality means that the variance of spot prices inside the cash period, the cash variance, is a function only of time inside the cash period, and is not dependent on the prices of monthly forwards. Under these assumptions the equality (4.12) can be written as

$$\mathrm{var}_t\,(P_T) = \mathrm{var}_t\,(F_{\mathrm{exp}}) + \upsilon_C\,(T - T_{\mathrm{exp}}) \qquad (4.13)$$

The left side of this equality is the estimate at time t of the total variance of spot prices at time T (i.e., it is the measure of the uncertainty of spot prices on August 15, as determined on January 1). This variance is the one that has a direct effect on the value of daily options. The first term on the right side of the equality is the variance of the monthly forward prices—the quantity that is linked to the value of monthly options. The second term is the variance inside the cash period, which affects the value of index options.

This equality thus illustrates the connection among the three types of traded options. Under certain conditions, such as lognormality, the relation between options can be made more precisely, as will be demonstrated next. We can see that simulation of the movement of spot prices over the whole period $[t,T]$ can be done by first simulating the movement of monthly forward prices over the period $[t, T_{exp}]$, and then simulating the movement of cash prices over a short "cash" period $[T_{exp},T]$ inside the month.

The expression (4.12) is too general to be useful, but its usefulness increases once we impose conditions on the statistical behavior of prices. Of particular interest is the lognormal case, in which the equality (4.12) leads to the standard relation between implied volatilities of monthly, daily, and index options.

In the lognormal case (more precisely, the geometric Brownian motion case), each option is associated with the constant volatility; σ_F is the volatility of the monthly option, σ_D is the volatility of the daily option, and σ_C is the "cash" volatility, that is, the volatility of the index option (see Chapter 2).

To derive the relation between these volatilities we can rewrite expression (4.12) in terms of the logarithms of daily prices:

$$\mathrm{var}_t(\log P_T) = \mathrm{var}_{t,F_{\mathrm{exp}}}(E[\log P_T|F_{\mathrm{exp}}]) + E_{t,F_{\mathrm{exp}}}[\mathrm{var}(\log P_T|F_{\mathrm{exp}})] \quad (4.14)$$

As before, assume that

$$E\left[P_T \middle| F_{\exp}\right] = F_{\exp}$$

Note that in principle this is not a bad assumption, and is supported by available empirical evidence for both gas and power. Moreover, our conclusions will not change even if there are risk premia in the forward contracts as long as the premia are not random:

$$E\left[P_T \middle| F_{\exp}\right] - F_{\exp} = \text{const}$$

By the lognormality assumption

$$E[\log P_T | F_{\exp}] = \log F_{\exp} + \frac{\text{var}(\log P_T | F_{\exp})}{2}$$

By the definition of the "cash" volatility, the variance is

$$\text{var}(\log P_T | F_{\exp}) = \sigma_C^2 \cdot (T - T_{\exp})$$

If we can assume that the "cash" variance is not dependent on forward price at expiry (an assumption often violated for power prices, and more mildly for natural gas prices), then we get

$$\text{var}_t(\log P_T) = \text{var}_t(\log F_{\exp} + \tfrac{1}{2}\sigma_C^2 \cdot (T - T_{\exp})) + E_t[\sigma_C^2 \cdot (T - T_{\exp})]$$

$$= \text{var}_t(\log F_{\exp}) + \sigma_C^2 \cdot (T - T_{\exp})$$

Since, by assumption, the forward price follows a geometric Brownian motion, we have

$$\text{var}_t(\log P_T) = \text{var}_{F_t}(\log F_{\exp}) + \sigma_C^2 \cdot (T - T_{\exp})$$

$$= \sigma_F^2 \cdot (T_{\exp} - t) + \sigma_C^2 \cdot (T - T_{\exp})$$

By the definition of the daily volatility the variance is

$$\text{var}_t(\log P_T) = \sigma_D^2 \cdot (T - t) = \sigma_F^2 \cdot (T_{\exp} - t) + \sigma_C^2 \cdot (T - T_{\exp}) \qquad (4.15)$$

If the options are fairly valued *and* all the assumptions are met, the equality (4.15) describes the relationship among the implied volatilities of various option contracts, and consequently among the values of those option contracts.

Needless to say, lognormality is a bad assumption for natural gas prices and an even worse one for power prices. But the relation (4.15) is frequently used, with necessary adjustments, to imply, for example, cash volatility in a case where only daily and monthly option quotes are available. After cash volatility is estimated, the forward/spot modeling procedure can be used to simulate spot prices. It is clear that with the forward/spot approach, matching option prices are easily achieved—monthly option prices are matched because the forwards are evolved with monthly volatility, index options are matched because the prices inside the cash month are evolving with cash volatility, and daily options are matched because of the relation (4.15).

EXAMPLE 4.4   *Replacing spot with forward-cash for robust modeling of mean reversion*

In Chapter 3 we analyzed the presence of mean reversion in spot and forward prices of energy commodities. We noted there that it was difficult to find the evidence for the presence of mean reversion, and even if we did find it, the estimates turned out to be very unstable. The overall picture was unclear for spot prices where we expected mean reversion. For forward prices, where we do not expect mean reversion, little evidence of mean reversion showed up.

An alternative way of investigating the presence of mean reversion in spot prices is to try to extract it from the term structure of forward prices (for an example, see Bessembinder, et al., 1999) and implied volatilities. The speed of mean reversion can be read off the slope of the long-term forward curve (after accounting for seasonality effects). As we indicated above, the presence of mean reversion induces a declining pattern in the term structure of volatility, which agrees with the observed regularities in power and natural gas markets (see Chapter 3). Consequently, using the calibration techniques we mentioned earlier we can expect to recover estimates for the mean-reversion coefficients. In practice, the estimates also tend to be quite unstable. This may be a reflection of a misspecification of the precise form of the process we assume for the mean-reverting process or possibly the fact that the patterns of the term structure are induced by other causes (for example, scaling of volatility is different from the square-root). Note, if we use the spot modeling approach, it is crucial to find the appropriate specification of the process, otherwise we cannot price anything. On the other hand, if we use the forward-cash approach, and as long as the mean-reversion effects are not likely to assert themselves within the tenor of the forward contract (a month in the United States, a week in Scandinavia), the need to know the mean-reversion coefficients or even the precise form or the process disappears. We replace the requirement to specify the spot process with the specification of the evolution of the forward and cash prices conditioned on forward prices. The big advantage of this approach is that forward prices are directly observable, and we usually have a number of quoted tradables to give us insight into the evolution (ATM and OTM forward options). Similarly, we tend to have information on the evolution of the cash process (index options). This enables us to develop a robust understanding of the behavior of prices without ever needing to understand the mean reversion of underlying prices. All the important facts are implicit in our tradables, so we can consistently account for them without ever knowing what they are. The same options can be used to reconstruct the dynamics of spot prices; however, this requires explicit modeling. Furthermore, the availability of tradables gives us a direct way of forming hedging strategies.

It might seem that the proposed approach that we've just described completely solves the problem of understanding mean reversion in energy markets. In truth, it is merely an intelligent way of avoiding the problem. Naturally, if we are dealing with a structure that is sensitive to the mean-reversion effects within the forward contract tenor, the proposed methodology will be useless.

To summarize, the three items discussed above provide justification for modeling spot price distribution as a two-step procedure: first modeling the evolution of forward monthly prices, and then modeling the evolution of spot prices. This procedure can be modified to include other liquidly traded products, such as BOM contracts.

Finally, we present one more argument in support of our cautious attitude toward using pure spot models, particularly for power. It is well known that for financial products (equity indexes, currencies, and so on), the relation between the spot price at time t, S_t, and the price of the forward contract maturing at time T, $F_{t,T}$, is given by the relation

$$F_{t,T} = S_t e^{r(T-t)} \qquad (4.16)$$

where r is a risk-free rate adjusted for dividends, foreign exchange rates, etc.

The proof of this relation is typically based on the no-arbitrage argument (e.g., see Hull, 1999), along the following lines: If the relation (4.16) does not hold, one can construct a portfolio combining the spot product and the forward contract, wait until expiration of the forward contract, unwind the portfolio, and extract a riskless profit.

This argument typically works in financial markets. But can we use it in the case of power? Since it cannot be stored, any strategy requiring the purchase and maintenance of spot power in a portfolio until some opportune time is impossible to implement. The standard proof for the relation (4.16) does not hold for power—so one must be cautious about using this relation. For power, all spot-based pricing models derived with the help of the no-arbitrage argument are suspect and should be carefully examined. Moreover, if a spot price process is used in models for hedging power derivatives, these models cannot be implemented, strictly speaking, since hedging requires combining derivative and spot products in one portfolio, holding it for some time, and unwinding it in the future. Spot power is consumed immediately and cannot be kept in the portfolio for any period of time (with rare exceptions, which are not currently important).

Nevertheless, there is a way, although not a particularly elegant or precise one, to circumvent the issue of power's nonstorability. It proceeds as follows. First, we look for a financial product whose prices historically correlate closely with spot prices—a balance-of-the-month contract, or the nearest futures contract, or something else. Once we find this product, we can develop our pricing and hedging models based on spot price evolution processes. Whenever these models require that a spot product is bought and kept for some time in a hedge portfolio, we use the surrogate financial product to satisfy this requirement. Clearly, this approach leaves us with potentially significant residual errors, but at least it provides us with some justification for the development of spot price models.

Regardless of the choice of modeling methodology, the question remains: What process should we use to model the evolution of the underlying of a reduced-form model? The rest of this chapter and the next are devoted to answering this question. In the next chapter, we examine reduced-form processes that can be applied to modeling both forward and cash prices. We start with the simplest and the most popular process of them all.

GEOMETRIC BROWNIAN MOTION FOR SPOT PRICES

The use of geometric Brownian motion (GBM) for modeling price evolution goes back to the works of Samuelson (1965). At present, GBM is as common and as well understood as standard Brownian motion, with the additional benefit of generating only positive random numbers—an important property for financial applications when these numbers represent prices.

In its most standard form the GBM process is presented as

$$dS_t = \mu S_t dt + \sigma S_t dW_t \tag{4.17}$$

Here, dS_t denotes a random movement of the spot price S_t over a small time interval $[t, t + dt]$, the constants μ and σ are respectively drift and volatility parameters, and dW_t denotes the increments of standard Brownian motion over the same period of time. It is useful to recall the three properties that characterize Brownian motion:

1. Increments dW_t are normally distributed random variables with mean zero and standard deviation $\sqrt{dt}$, i.e., $dW_t \sim \phi\left(0, \sqrt{dt}\right)$

2. For any two time moments t_1, t_2 the increments dW_{t_1}, dW_{t_2} are independent random variables, which, in particular, implies that $E(dW_{t_1} \cdot dW_{t_2}) = 0$.
3. The Brownian path W_t is almost always continuous.

A frequently used equivalent form of the equation (4.17) is obtained via the change of variables

$$Z_t = \log S_t \tag{4.18}$$

Then

$$dZ_t = \left(\mu - \frac{1}{2}\sigma^2\right)dt + \sigma dW_t \tag{4.19}$$

Note that the equation (4.19) is obtained from (4.17) with the help of Ito's lemma, which states that if S_t is the stochastic process governed by the equation

$$dS = a(t,S)dt + b(t,S)dW_t$$

and if the new variable $Z = Z(t,S)$ (and by inversion $S = S(t,Z)$), then Z is governed by the equation

$$dZ = \left(\frac{\partial Z}{\partial t} + \frac{\partial Z}{\partial S}a + \frac{1}{2}\frac{\partial^2 Z}{\partial S^2}b^2\right)dt + b\frac{\partial Z}{\partial S}dW$$

with all coefficients evaluated at $S = S(t,Z)$ and t.

If the value of Z_t is known at some initial time t, then equation (4.19) implies that for any future time T, $T \geq t$, the variable Z_T is normally distributed,

$$Z_T \sim \phi\left[Z_t + \left(\mu - \frac{1}{2}\sigma^2\right)(T - t), \sigma\sqrt{T - t}\right] \tag{4.20}$$

where $\varphi(m,s)$ is a shorthand notation for the probability density function $\varphi(x;m,s)$ for the normal distribution with expectation m and standard deviation s,

$$\phi(x;m,s) = \frac{1}{\sqrt{2\pi s}}e^{-\frac{(x-m)^2}{2s^2}} \tag{4.21}$$

Indeed, dividing the interval $[t_0,T]$ into small subintervals

$$t = t_0, t_0 + \Delta t, t_0 + 2\Delta t, \ldots, t_0 + n\Delta t = T$$

we have from equation (4.18) that on each subinterval the increment

$$\Delta Z_k = Z_{t+(k+1)\Delta t} - Z_{t+k\Delta t}$$

is a normally distributed variable,

$$\Delta Z_k \sim \phi\left[\left(\mu - \frac{1}{2}\sigma^2\right)\Delta t, \sigma\sqrt{\Delta t}\right] \tag{4.22}$$

By the definition of Brownian motion all random variables ΔZ_k are independent. Therefore the variable

$$Z_T - Z_t = \sum_{k=0}^{n-1} \Delta Z_k$$

is the sum of independent normally distributed random variables, and hence is normally distributed with the mean equal to the sum of means of variables ΔZ_k, and variance equal to the sum of their variances. This proves the relation (4.20).

By definition (4.18) spot price $S_T = \exp(Z_T)$, and therefore it is lognormally distributed. Below we give the expression for the distribution of S_T conditional on initial spot price S_t at t,

$$\Pr(S_T = x|S_t) = \frac{1}{\sqrt{2\pi(T-t)}\sigma x} e^{-\frac{1}{2}\left(\frac{\log x - \log S_t - \mu(T-t)}{\sigma\sqrt{T-t}}\right)^2} \tag{4.23}$$

The expectation and variance are given by the following expressions:

$$E(S_T|S_t) = S_t e^{\mu(T-t)} \tag{4.24}$$

$$\text{var}(S_T|S_t) = S_t^2 e^{2\mu(T-t)}\left[e^{\sigma^2(T-t)} - 1\right] \tag{4.25}$$

Spot Price Processes and Forward Prices

It is appropriate now, using GBM as an example, to briefly review how spot processes are used to price standard derivative products. We begin with the problem of determining the price of the forward contract maturing at time T, given the known spot price at a certain time t. The spot price at t is denoted by S_t and the forward price is denoted by $F_{t,T}$.

In the financial world, the relation between spot and forward prices is given by a familiar formula

$$F_{t,T} = S_t e^{(r-q)(T-t)} \tag{4.26}$$

where r is the risk-free rate and q is a dividend yield, in the case of equity products, or foreign interest rates in the case of currencies. The proof of (4.26) is usually based on the no-arbitrage argument (see Hull, 1999).

There is an interesting interpretation of the relation (4.26), which we present here under the assumption that the evolution of spot prices S_t is governed by GBM. In this case we can use the equality (4.24) and rewrite (4.26) as

$$F_{t,T} = E(S_T | S_t) \qquad (4.27)$$

where the expectation is taken over all paths of the GBM of the form

$$dS_t = (r - q)S_t dt + \sigma S_t dW_t \qquad (4.28)$$

Recall that computing the expected value of a random cash flow with the help of the process (4.28) is called a *risk-neutral* evaluation, or an evaluation in the *risk-neutral* world. The term *risk-neutral* is introduced to emphasize the difference between processes describing the evolution of spot prices in the actual physical world, and processes such as (4.28) that are used for pricing derivatives. Suppose that the physical world process, determined after statistical analysis of the empirical data, is also a GBM of the form

$$dS_t = \mu_P S_t dt + \sigma_P S_t dW_t \qquad (4.29)$$

The equality (4.26) maintains that this process cannot be used to find forward prices as expectations with respect to its paths. The process should first be modified by changing its physical drift μ_P to the drift $(r-q)$ of the process (4.28) while retaining volatility, $\sigma = \sigma_P$. This explains why the risk-neutral evaluation is so attractive: It requires no knowledge of the actual drift rate to compute the value of the derivative—an important benefit, since computing this drift and projecting it forward can be a complex undertaking. The risk-neutral evaluation requires only the knowledge of a risk-free rate and a dividend yield, parameters that can both be determined relatively easily.

Thus, in the financial world, the correct drift term needed for computing the prices of forward and other derivative contracts is a risk-free rate with necessary adjustments. In the world of commodities the situation is less simple, even if we assume that the evolution of commodity prices is governed by GBM. Below are several cases that lead to different drift rates, depending on the assumptions we are willing to accept with respect to the physical commodity.

In Chapter 2, we developed the general no-arbitrage argument for pricing forward contracts. The crucial assumption was the ability to borrow (short) commodity without cost. It is clear that for commodities such as gas and oil, the assumptions are not very realistic. First, the cost of storing these commodities, which we denote by U, can be substantial. Second, the owners of a commodity may require a premium for selling it, even if they are guaranteed that they will regain ownership in the future. This premium is a measure of the benefits of physical ownership of a commodity, when the purpose of such ownership is not just investment but consumption as well. For example, the owners may be reluctant to sell the commodity because they anticipate shortages between the time of sale and the time when they recover ownership, and they will consequently require an additional premium to entice them to sell. Under these conditions, the relation between spot and forward prices is not as simple. Moreover, in actuality, the most we can prove is that this relation is an inequality.

$$F_{t,T} \leq (S_t + U)e^{r(T-t)} \tag{4.30}$$

Again, to prove (4.30) we will use the no-arbitrage argument. Assume that (4.30) does not hold and that $F_{t,T} > (S_t + U)e^{r(T-t)}$. Then we can employ the following arbitrage strategy.

At time t:

- Borrow $S_t + U$ at the risk-free rate to buy the commodity at the spot market and to pay storage costs.
- Short the forward contract at $F_{t,T}$.
- Keep the commodity in storage until expiration of the forward contract.

At time T:

- Exercise the forward contract: sell the commodity and receive $+ F_{t,T}$.
- Return borrowed cash with interest: $- (S_t + U)e^{r(T-t)}$.
- Realize a riskless profit $F_{t,T} - (S_t + U)e^{r(T-t)} > 0$.

Since we presume that riskless arbitrage strategies will not last for long, $F_{t,T}$ cannot be greater than $(S_t + U)e^{r(T-t)}$, and (4.30) is the only valid alternative. The question remains: Why cannot we show, as in Chapter 2, that it is also impossible for $F_{t,T}$ to be strictly less than $(S_t + U)e^{r(T-t)}$, thus ensuring the equality in (4.30)? The answer is that now the commodity owners require an additional premium for parting with the commodity and waiting for its return at some future time. This premium, denoted by Y, is a measure of the importance of owning a commodity when the purpose of ownership is not just investment but consumption as well. Therefore, the arbitrage strategy of the previous section will be attractive to commodity owners only if

$$F_{t,T} < (S_t + U)e^{r(T-t)} - Y \tag{4.31}$$

If this holds, they will employ the following strategy.

At time t:

- Sell the commodity and invest the proceeds S_t, together with the released storage cost U, at the risk-free rate.
- Enter a long forward contract at $F_{t,T}$.

At time T:

- Close the cash account: $+ (S_t + U)e^{r(T-t)}$.

- Exercise the forward contract and buy back the commodity: $- F_{t,T}$.
- Realize a riskless profit $(S_t + U)e^{r(T-t)} - F_{t,T} > Y$ (see (4.31)).

Thus, the guaranteed profit from the strategy is sufficient to overcome the commodity owners' need to hold on to the commodity, and therefore they will quickly eliminate this arbitrage opportunity and bring spot and forward prices to the level that

$$Y \geq (S_t + U)e^{r(T-t)} - F_{t,T} > 0 \tag{4.32}$$

Inside these bounds, although the arbitrage strategy exists, the profits are not large enough to motivate its employment.

Relation (4.32) is most commonly represented with the help of an auxiliary parameter y in the following way

$$(S_t + U)e^{r(T-t)} = F(t,T)e^{y(T-t)}$$

Parameter y is called *convenience yield;* similar to premium Y, it measures the benefits of the physical ownership of a commodity. With the help of convenience yield we can express the spot/forward price relation in the following way:

$$F(t,T) = (S_t + U)e^{(r-y)(T-t)} \tag{4.33}$$

Noting that storage costs are typically proportional to time, and introducing a parameter u by the equality

$$1 + \frac{U}{S_t} = e^{u(T-t)}$$

we arrive at the convenient and frequently used representation of (4.33)

$$F_{t,T} = S_t e^{(r+u-y)(T-t)} \tag{4.34}$$

This relation is particularly useful and attractive if storage and convenience yields u and y are constants. In this case equality (4.34) is similar to (4.26) and forward prices are therefore given as an expectation of the spot prices in the risk-neutral world, where the evolution of spot prices is governed by the process

$$dS_t = (r + u - y)S_t dt + \sigma S_t dW_t \tag{4.35}$$

Of course, an assumption that u and y are constants is often just a crude approximation. In recent years a number of papers have presented models for the term structure and stochastic nature of the convenience yield (see survey in Seppi, 1999).

As an example of such models, consider the one proposed in Schwartz (1997), in which GBM is used to describe the price evolution, and the standard Brownian motion with mean reversion is used to describe the evolution of the convenience yield. Thus,

$$dS = (r - \delta)Sdt + \sigma_1 S\, dW_1$$

$$d\delta = [\kappa(\alpha - \delta) - \lambda]dt + \sigma_2 dW_2$$

$$dW_1\, dW_2 = \rho\, dt$$

where

δ denotes random convenience yield.

Parameters κ, α, σ_2 are, respectively, the strength of the mean reversion for convenience yield, the long-term value of convenience yield, and the instantaneous volatility of convenience yield.

Constant λ is the market price of risk associated with convenience yield, introduced to account for the fact the convenience yield cannot be hedged.

Under this process the forward price is given by the equality

$$F_{t,T} = S_t \exp\left[-\delta\,\frac{1 - e^{-\kappa(T-t)}}{\kappa} + A(t,T)\right]$$

$$A(t,T) = \left(r - \alpha + \frac{\lambda}{\kappa} + \frac{1}{2}\frac{\sigma_2^2}{\kappa^2} - \frac{\sigma_1\sigma_2\rho}{\kappa}\right)(T - t) + \frac{1}{4}\sigma_2^2\,\frac{1 - e^{2\kappa(T-t)}}{\kappa^3}$$

$$+ \left[\left(\alpha - \frac{\lambda}{\kappa}\right)\kappa + \sigma_1\sigma_2\rho - \frac{\sigma_2^2}{\kappa}\right]\frac{1 - e^{-\kappa(T-t)}}{\kappa^2}$$

Using this expression and historical data for forward prices, we can derive the parameters defining the stochastic process for convenience yield. It is still an open question whether this or any other convenience yield model has features superior to those of alternative price models. For example, it would be beneficial if convenience yield models had more stable parameterization, particularly in energy applications. Only time and more data will tell. In the meantime we continue to focus on GBM with constant coefficients to further investigate the properties of spot price processes.

Lastly, the relations between spot and forward prices discussed in this section are applicable only to storable commodities, and thus can almost never be used in the case of power.

Valuation of European Call and Put Options

There is no need to spend much time on derivation of formulas for European call and put options in the case of GBM, they are well-known and have been extensively analyzed (e.g., see Wilmott, 2000). For storable commodities like natural gas and crude oil, under the assumptions of no storage costs and zero convenience yield, we can use a dynamic hedging technique similar to the one described in Chapter 2, except that this hedging is undertaken using spot products and not forward contracts. Our ability to use dynamic hedging yields familiar conclusions:

- Regardless of the drift of spot prices in the physical world, the options should be priced in the risk-neutral world.
- For a given time t and underlying spot price S, let $C(t,S) \equiv C(t,S;T,X,r,\sigma)$ be the value of the call option with strike X and time of exercise T. Then $C(t,S)$ satisfies the Black-Scholes equation

$$\frac{\partial C}{\partial t} + r\frac{\partial C}{\partial S} + \frac{1}{2}\sigma^2 S^2 \frac{\partial^2 C}{\partial S^2} = rC$$

with the initial conditions

$$C(T,S_T;T,X,r,\sigma) = \max(S_T - X, 0)$$

where r is the risk-free rate and σ is volatility.
- Correspondingly, the put option $P(t,S) = P(t,S;T,X,r,\sigma)$ satisfies the same equation with different initial conditions:

$$P(T,S_T;T,X,r,\sigma) = \max(X - S_T, 0)$$

- The value of the call and put options is given by the following equalities:

$$C_{BS} \equiv C_{BS}(t,S;T,X,r,\sigma) = SN(d_1) - Xe^{-r(T-t)}N(d_2) \qquad (4.36)$$

$$P_{BS} \equiv P_{BS}(t,S;T,X,r,\sigma) = Xe^{-r(T-t)}N(-d_2) - SN(-d_1) \qquad (4.37)$$

$$d_1 = \frac{\log(S/X) + (r + \sigma^2/2)T}{\sigma\sqrt{T}}$$

$$d_2 = \frac{\log(S/X) + (r - \sigma^2/2)T}{\sigma\sqrt{T}} = d_1 - \sigma\sqrt{T}$$

As in the previous section, we now introduce storage costs and nonzero convenience yield, and option formulas (4.36) and (4.37) must be slightly modified to account for these.

$$C = C_{BS}\,(t,Se^{(u-y)(T-t)};T,X,r,\sigma) \tag{4.38}$$

$$P = P_{BS}\,(t,Se^{(u-y)(T-t)};T,X,r,\sigma) \tag{4.39}$$

It is worth pointing out that using relation (4.34) we can rewrite the equalities (4.38) and (4.39) in terms of futures prices:

$$C = C_{BS}\,(t,F_T e^{-r(T-t)};T,X,r,\sigma)$$

$$P = P_{BS}\,(t,F_T e^{-r(T-t)};T,X,r,\sigma)$$

The benefit of this representation is that it does not require the knowledge of the convenience yield for option valuation (it is incorporated into the futures prices). This is yet another argument in favor of models based on forward prices.

Finally, we note a useful generalization of these valuation formulas in the case of nonconstant volatility. If volatility is a function of time, $\sigma = \sigma\,(t)$, then the pricing formulas (4.36) to (4.39) are still valid with only one modification: Parameter σ should be replaced with

$$\bar{\sigma} = \sqrt{\frac{1}{T-t}\int_t^T \sigma^2(u)\,du} \tag{4.40}$$

This result can be proved by reasoning similar to (4.20). Assuming that on each interval $[t,t+\Delta t]$, the evolution process is GBM with constant volatility $\sigma\,(t)$, we again have that the variables $\Delta Z = Z_{t+\Delta t} - Z_t$ are normally distributed and independent for each t, and therefore their sum Z_T is normally distributed with annualized standard deviation (4.40). Moreover, on each interval $[t,t+\Delta t]$ we can use the strategy designed to hedge options with constant volatility, but now the volatility will change from interval to interval.

Parameter Calibration

As we have seen, in order to price forward contracts or standard European options we use GBM processes of the form (4.17). The task of finding parameters for these processes is particularly easy if the drift of that process is known and the only parameter that needs to be determined is volatility σ.

If we adopt the forward-spot approach, then the option values can be expressed in terms of forward contracts. This obviates the need to know the convenience yield or even the need to know the exact model.

We will now describe two commonly used approaches to computing parameter σ, which is called *instantaneous volatility* since it measures instantaneous spot price movements over period of time $[t, t + \Delta t]$. In practice, these are price movements over small and discrete periods of time, say, over one day.

Deriving Volatility Estimates from Historical Data

The procedures of Chapter 3 can be applied now to historical spot price data to calibrate the volatility parameter in process (4.17). Let S_i denote spot prices at discrete times t_i, $i = 1, \ldots, m$ (e.g., S_i can be prices at the closing of each day). Prices S_i represent historical data measured at m time points prior to the current valuation date (e.g., prices at the closing of m trading days before today). We know from (4.22) that under GBM the differences of logarithms of spot prices are normally distributed,

$$\Delta Z_i \equiv \log S_{i+1} - \log S_i \sim \phi\left(\left(M - \frac{1}{2}\sigma^2\right)\Delta t_i, \sigma\sqrt{\Delta t_i}\right) \quad (4.41)$$

where $\Delta t_i = t_{i+1} - t_i$, and $\mu = r + u - y$ in the case of (4.35). Moreover, by the definition of GBM all random variables ΔZ_i are independent. Therefore, we can directly apply formula (3.10) and get the volatility estimate

$$\sigma = \sqrt{\frac{1}{m-1}\sum_{i=1}^{m}\left(\frac{\log S_i - \log S_{i-1}}{\sqrt{t_i - t_{i-1}}} - \frac{1}{m}\sum_{i=1}^{m}\frac{\log S_i - \log S_{i-1}}{\sqrt{t_i - t_{i-1}}}\right)^2} \quad (4.42)$$

The confidence interval for this estimate is given by (3.6).

Deriving Volatility Estimates from Option Prices

We described in Chapter 3 how option prices can be used to derive implied volatility, whose benefit, as compared to volatility based on historical data, resides in the fact that it is a forward-looking measure of price uncertainty—the best (or close to the best) market estimate of price volatility between to-day and the time of option expiration. When spot price evolution is governed by GBM, implied volatility σ_I satisfies the equation

$$C_{t,T,X}^{Market} = C(t, S_t; T, X, r, \sigma_I) \quad (4.43)$$

The left side of this equation is the market quote of the call with strike X and exercise time T. The right side is the same option evaluated using option-pricing formulas from "Valuation of European Call and Put Options." Implied volatility is then the value of parameter σ in (4.36) or (4.38), which makes both values agree.

Note that market quotes for ATM options are most frequently used for estimates of implied volatility. Also, although in (4.43) we utilized calls to derive the implied volatility, the straddles (i.e., combinations of call and put options with the same strike) are used just as often for this purpose.

EXAMPLE 4.5 *Computing implied volatility*

Assume that the current price of natural gas is $2.50. The ATM straddle, strike $2.50, expiring 6 months from now is quoted at $0.42. The risk-free rate is 5%. Our goal is to find the implied volatility under the assumption that the spot price evolution is governed by GBM; thus we must find a value σ_I such that

$$C(0,\$2.50;.5,\$2.50,5\%,\sigma_I) + P(0,\$2.50;.5,\$2.50,5\%,\sigma_I) = \$0.42$$

where call and put values are given by (4.36) and (4.37). Using a standard numerical algorithm, we can solve this equation and find that $\sigma_I = 30\%$.

This approach for computing a volatility parameter in GBM, while simple and straightforward, also faces some inherent problems. To understand the source of these problems, recall that implied volatility has a distinct term structure, that is, dependence on time to expiration (see Chapter 3 section titled, "Volatility of Natural Gas and Power Prices"). Therefore, using prices of options with different expiration dates to derive implied volatility can lead to contradictory results. Consider Example 4.5 with two options.

EXAMPLE 4.6 *Computing implied volatility for different maturities*

Option 1
$t = 0, S_0 = \$2.50, T_1 = .5, X_1 = \$2.50, r = 5\%$ Call Value: $C_1 = \$0.24$

Option 2
$t = 0, S_0 = \$2.50, T_2 = 1, X_2 = \$2.70, r = 5\%$ Call Value: $C_2 = \$0.37$

If (4.36) is used as an option pricing formula, then it can be easily shown that the volatilities implied by the two options are respectively

$$\sigma_I(T_1) = 30\%, \qquad \sigma_I(T_2) = 40\%$$

Clearly, in this example, the market data precludes us from using a constant volatility parameter, so an obvious solution is to assume that instantaneous volatility is time-dependent, $\sigma = \sigma(t)$. As follows from (4.40), the implied volatility of European options is a measure of the cumulative effect of instantaneous spot price movements, and only when instantaneous volatility is constant will it be equal to implied volatility. Introduction of time dependence naturally affords us greater flexibility in matching market data. Indeed, returning to the example above, we should look for a function $\sigma(t)$ that yields correct cumulative variances at times T_1 and T_2. By (4.40), this means that

$$\int_0^{T_1} \sigma^2(s)ds = T_1\sigma_I^2(T_1) \quad \text{and} \quad \int_0^{T_2} \sigma^2(s)ds = T_2\sigma_I^2(T_2) \qquad (4.44)$$

or, after substitution,

$$\int_0^{T_1} \sigma^2(s)ds = .5 \cdot .3^2 \quad \text{and} \quad \int_0^{T_2} \sigma^2(s)ds = .4^2$$

Infinitely many functions $\sigma(t)$ satisfy these equalities, of course; for example, a piecewise constant function

$$\sigma(t) \equiv .3 \text{ for } 0 \le t < T_1 \quad \text{and} \quad \sigma(t) \equiv .48 \text{ for } T_1 \le t < T_2$$

If implied volatility $\sigma_I(T)$ is given for every time T, then instantaneous volatility $\sigma(t)$ should satisfy the equation

$$\int_0^T \sigma^2(t)dt = T\sigma_I^2(T) \qquad (4.45)$$

or

$$\sigma^2(T) = \frac{\partial}{\partial T}[T\sigma_I^2(T)] \qquad (4.46)$$

Note that for this equality to make sense, the derivative on the right side must be positive, which means that the function $T\sigma_I^2(T)$ should be a monotone increasing function of T.

Here lies the principal limitation of using spot price GBM. Even if we allow for a time-dependent volatility parameter in process (4.35), we cannot generally match an arbitrary term structure of implied volatility. Indeed, if in the above example market option prices corresponded to implied volatilities

$$\sigma_I(T_1) = 60\%, \qquad \sigma_I(T_2) = 28\%$$

then no function $\sigma(t)$ could satisfy (4.44), since in this case

$$\int_{T_1}^{T_2} \sigma^2(t)dt = -0.1$$

And this is not an exceptional situation, particularly in the case of energy commodities. In Chapter 3 we saw examples of how implied volatility of gas and power options depends on time to expiration. This dependence has a distinct periodic structure. It is not difficult to show that for such structures the equalities in (4.44) may be inconsistent for some T_1 and T_2, making the correct parameterization of GBM impossible.

The parameter calibration problem described above stems from potentially inconsistent option quotes corresponding to different months, seasons, or years. In practice this problem is typically overcome (or ignored) by using different processes for different options. Thus, the process to price and hedge options expiring in August a year from today, is different from that for options expiring two years from now. The parameters for both processes will be chosen to match implied volatilities corresponding to options in the summer of the next year and the year after that respectively. Of course, this may result in inconsistencies because we have two processes, potentially different, describing the evolution of the same spot prices over the time interval common for both options. These inconsistencies may be overlooked in the case of European options, since for their pricing we need only terminal, or cumulative, spot price distribution—although correct hedging requires a more refined modeling of price movement. But for more exotic, path-dependent options or swaptions this approach will not work, as a rule; and other modeling methods are required, which we describe further in the chapter.

Monthly, Daily, and Cash Volatilities

We have described the difficulties in matching option prices corresponding to different months or seasons. As we know from the previous section "Building Reduced-form Models for Energy Applications: The Basics," additional problems arise on the monthly scale, because for any given month there are several pieces of overlapping market information related to power and natural gas prices. These are usually quotes on options whose payoffs are determined by inside-the-month daily prices, and the challenge of model calibration consists in reconciling these market quotes. Consider, for example, two options that were introduced in Chapter 2 in the section "Fixed-Strike(Daily) and Floating-Strike(Index or Cash) Options on the Spot Commodity":

Fixed-strike daily option—an option exercised every day during the exercise month.

Floating-strike daily option (index option in natural gas markets)—an option exercised every day during the exercise month with a specified monthly index as a strike price.

The payoffs of both options depend on the settlement of daily prices inside a given month. The options are very different, however. The cumulative movement of spot prices from the current date to the expiration date determines the value of the first option. On the other hand, the value of the second option is determined only by the movement of these prices inside the exercise month. Indeed, the strike of a floating-strike option is determined at the beginning of the exercise month, and therefore the option price depends only on spot price movements occurring after that date.

These two options imply two types of volatility associated with a given exercise month (see "Building Reduced-form Models for Energy Applications: The Basics"):

σ_D—volatility of daily prices, called *daily volatility;* it characterizes distribution of daily prices throughout the exercise month.

σ_C—volatility of daily prices, called *cash volatility* or inside-the-month volatility; it characterizes distribution of daily prices conditional on the value of the monthly index at the beginning of the month.

EXAMPLE 4.7 *Implied volatility of fixed-strike and floating-strike daily options*

We need to find implied volatilities for the following "into Cinergy" power options.

Valuation date: $t_0 = 12/08/1998$

Underlying $S_0 = \$23.50$

Risk-free rate $r = 5\%$

1. March 1999 daily call, strike \$25.00: $C_{Daily} = \$4.25$
2. March 1999 daily call, strike FOM (first-of-the-month index): $C_{FOM} = \$4.25$

The first option is a fixed-price daily option and its payoff for 1 MWh of power is

$$\Pi_1 = \sum_{i=1}^{31} \max\left(P_i - X, 0\right)$$

where P_i is the average daily power price per 1 MWh for the month of March. According to convention the option is quoted as the average of daily call values,

$$C_{Daily} = \frac{1}{31}\sum_{i=1}^{31} C_{BS}\left(t_0, S_0; T_i, X, r, \sigma\right)$$

where T_i represents the expiration date of each daily option running over every day in March, and the call value is given by (4.36). For the given values of t_0, T_i, X, and r the value of daily implied volatility σ_D is determined as a solution of this equation with respect to parameter σ. It is easy to show that in this case $\sigma_D = 98\%$.

Deriving cash volatility from floating-strike option prices is more complicated, because it generally it requires modeling the evolution of the spot and the floating strike simultaneously. Here we sidestep this issue by assuming the convergence of the spot price and monthly index at the beginning of the month. Under this condition, the floating strike is simply the value S_1 of the spot price at t_1, the first day of March. We set the strike at this day, and can compute the option value conditional on the value of S_1 as

$$C_{FOM}(S_1) = \tfrac{1}{31} \sum_{i=1}^{31} C_{BS}(t_1,S_1;T_i,S_1,r,\sigma)$$

We complete computing the option value at the current time t_0 by taking an expectation of the values $C_{FOM}(S_1)$ with respect to the distribution of S_1 and discounting it to t_0

$$C_{FOM} = e^{-r(t_1-t_0)} E_{S_1}[C_{FOM}(S_1)] = e^{-r(t_1-t_0)} \int_{S_1} C_{FOM}(S_1)\Pr(S_1)dS_1$$

From (4.36) we have that

$$C_{BS}(t_1,S_1;T_i,S_1,r,\sigma) = S_1[N(d_1) - e^{-r(T_i-t_1)} N(d_2)]$$

and therefore

$$C_{FOM}(S_1) = S_1 \cdot \left\{ \tfrac{1}{31} \sum_{i=1}^{31} [N(d_1) - e^{-r(T_i-t_1)}N(d_2)] \right\}$$

Under simple GBM rules, the risk-neutral expected value

$$E(S_1) = e^{r(t_1-t_0)} S_0$$

This value is independent of the volatility of spot prices on the interval $[t_0,t_1]$. Thus,

$$C_{FOM} = S_0 \cdot \left\{ \tfrac{1}{31} \sum_{i=1}^{31} [N(d_1) - e^{-r(T_i-t_1)}N(d_2)] \right\}$$

As noted earlier, this value depends only on inside-the-month volatility. The value of the parameter σ that provides the solution to this equation is the cash volatility, $\sigma_C = 245\%$.

This example indicates a serious problem we might face in calibrating spot processes for energy prices. Namely, for each month we may, and usually do, have to match two or more option quotes, which are defined on overlapping intervals. As in the example above, the first option may depend upon price behavior on interval $[t_0, T]$, with T being a day inside the month, and the second option upon price behavior on interval $[t_1, T]$. As before, t_0 is the current time and t_1 is the first day of the exercise month.

As we saw in "Building Reduced-form Models for Energy Applications: The Basics," the complexity of finding the right parameters for a spot price process increases even more when we attempt to take into account one more option, namely the monthly option.

Monthly Option. An option that allows its owner to buy (call) or sell (put) gas or power for whole months at a specified strike price.

One variable underlying this option is usually an accepted monthly index, such as the *Inside FERC's Gas Market Report,* and a monthly option is exercised when the index is greater (in the case of the call) or less (in the case of the put) than the strike price. A monthly option naturally introduces an implied volatility

σ_M—volatility of a monthly index, or simply *monthly volatility.*

In the case of gas this volatility is strongly correlated, and often identified, with the volatility of the monthly average of daily prices, which is induced by any process we use to model spot prices (see Chapter 8). Obviously, if we decide to reconcile these two volatilities by choosing the right parameters in the process, our overall parameterization task becomes very complex. Indeed, for any given month we must match implied volatilities of daily options, inside-the-month options, and options on monthly averages. These option data overlap, making it exceedingly difficult to find the right parameters for a spot process. This is the reason why the forward/spot approach of "Building Reduced-form Models for Energy Applications: The Basics" is appealing—under that process, the mechanism of matching implied volatilities is much more natural.

Drift

As is apparent from the previous section, estimating a volatility parameter in (4.17) can be a complex undertaking. On the other hand, it seems that the choice of the drift parameter for the purpose of pricing derivatives should be rather simple: it is a risk-free rate, or possibly a risk-free rate adjusted for storage and convenience yield. However, after closer examination a more complicated picture emerges.

For example, hedging may not exactly match the indexes defining the payoff function of a particular derivative product. This means that no hedging strategy can completely eliminate variability in the value of the derivative. This problem is particularly common in the case of energy derivatives, with their multitude of underlying indexes: consider the case of electricity options, which can be monthly, daily, hourly, on-peak, off-peak, round-the-clock, firm, interruptible, and so on. The situation is similar for natural gas options.

EXAMPLE 4.8   *Divergence between prices that underly options and hedges*

A trader wants to hedge a July daily off-peak power option, that is, an option on off-peak power exercised every business day of the month of July. The trader uses the formula (4.36) to determine the value of the option and then the value of hedge parameters. The option value, and hence the hedges, are given in terms of spot price. As was pointed out in the beginning of this chapter, the nonstorability of power prevents direct implementation of spot hedges. Financial surrogates must therefore be used, creating a mismatch between the index underlying the option payoff (in this case, a daily off-peak price) and the price of the hedging instrument (e.g., a balance-of-the-month contract).

Although this mismatch is important, let's focus on another source of residual risk. Off-peak products are not very liquid in most power markets, so it is common, after investigating the correlation between off-peak power prices and the prices for on-peak power, natural gas, or oil, to use these commodities for hedging. The divergence between the prices underlying the option and the hedge can be substantial, weakening the effectiveness of the hedging procedure.

This inability to fully hedge a derivative undermines the argument for using the risk-free rate in pricing models. Despite this drawback, the rate is commonly used in practical applications on the grounds that the residual risks are relatively small. A more correct approach would be to introduce the price of risk for sources of unhedged uncertainty, and use it to adjust the drift rate by a quantity representing the excess return required by investors for the risk they take. Thus for a risk-neutral evaluation, the real-world return in (4.29) should be replaced with

$$\mu_P - \Sigma \lambda_i s_i \tag{4.47}$$

where λ_i is the price of risk for a particular source of unhedgeable uncertainty, the uncertainty defined by a random factor with volatility s_i. (In the example above this factor is the spread between on-peak and off-peak power, or the spread between spot prices of power and the prices of instruments used as their surrogates for hedging purposes.) How to choose the parameters is discussed in Chapter 10. The main challenge of the adjustment is to separate the hedgeable and unhedgeable risk factors.

If all factors are hedgeable the following relation holds:

$$\mu_P - \Sigma \lambda_j s_j = r - u + y$$

Assuming that risk-free rate r and storage rate u are known, the only parameter we must estimate is convenience yield y. Of course, estimation of this yield can be a very difficult problem in itself and, as we have seen before, a special stochastic process may be needed to describe its evolution.

On the other hand, if one wants to avoid complex processes for the convenience yield, a simple approach is frequently used to compute drift in the risk-neutral world, and it doesn't require computing the prices of risk or convenience yield. It is based on the assumption of a liquid forward curve, and on the fact that in the risk-neutral world any forward price $F_{t,T}$ which for convenience we prefer to denote here by $F(t,T)$ is the expectation of future spot prices S_T, conditional on the current price S_t (see (4.27)). To simplify notation, we assume that current time $t = 0$, and hence the forward curve is simply $F(T) \equiv F(0,T)$ where T, as always, is the expiration time. Denoting the risk-neutral drift by $m \equiv r + u - y$, we now make a key assumption—that it is a deterministic function of time, $m = m(t)$—and thus the price evolution process takes the form

$$dS_t = m(t) S_t \, dt + \sigma S_t \, dW_t \qquad (4.48)$$

It is not difficult to show that in the case of a time-dependent drift, the relation (4.34) connecting spot and forward prices can be generalized as follows,

$$F(T) = S_0 e^{\int_0^T m(s)ds} \qquad (4.49)$$

and therefore,

$$m(t) = \frac{\partial}{\partial T}[\log F(T)]\Big|_{T=t} \qquad (4.50)$$

This equality assumes that the forward curve, which is typically given as a sequence of discrete points, is smoothly interpolated so that it can be differentiated at any point. The drift $m(t)$ computed in (4.50) is then used in (4.48) to generate paths for pricing derivatives in the risk-neutral world. One obvious drawback of this approach: it presumes that the derivative of the logarithm of the forward curve does not change with time, so the time-dependent drift coefficient computed today will not differ from the one computed tomorrow.

This assumption, although clearly an idealization, is not too different from the usual assumptions of the Black-Scholes pricing formula, which requires a constant risk-free rate and volatility. And as in the case of the Black-Scholes formula, a good understanding of benefits and limitations of the methodology is a prerequisite to the successful use of the equations (4.48) to (4.50).

Modifications of GBM: Mean Reversion and Seasonality

At the present time there is little argument that GBM in its standard form (4.17) is not well suited to describe evolution of energy prices. Various modifications of this process have been proposed with the goal of a more realistic representation of these prices; the majority emphasize two essential attributes of spot prices in energy markets, namely, mean reversion and seasonality.

Mean Reversion

A quantity is said to be mean reverting toward a certain level, called a long-term mean, if it exhibits the following property: the further it moves away from this level, the higher the probability that in the future it will move back toward it. Empirical evidence of mean reversion can be found in a number of markets. For example, historical data supports the claim that interest rates in the United States mean revert to a long-term mean level somewhere between 7% and 7.5%.

Note that the process (4.17) cannot be mean-reverting because, first, it contains no information on the long-term mean and, second, as follows from (4.22), the distribution of the future changes in the price logarithms is the same, independent of their current level. Several modifications of the GBM have been proposed to accommodate mean reversion, of which the following two are probably the most common.

Mean Reversion to the Long-term Price.   In this version of the mean-reverting process, it is assumed that spot prices on average travel toward their long-term mean, and that the sign of the price drift is therefore changing, depending on whether prices are above or below the long-term mean level. More formally, the evolution of spot prices is represented by the following modification of (4.17)

$$\frac{dS_t}{S_t} = \kappa(S_\infty - S_t)dt + \sigma dW_t \tag{4.51}$$

where S_∞ is the long-term mean of spot prices, and κ is the strength of mean reversion. The left side of this equation is the instantaneous rate of change in spot prices. The first term on the right side represents deterministic drift of spot prices, which is positive when spot prices are below the long-term mean S_∞, and negative when they are above it—thus always skewing the probability of price changes at the next time period in the direction of the long-term mean. The parameter κ determines the strength with which the long-term mean attracts spot prices: the larger its value, the greater the skewness of the probability of price changes in the direction of S_∞.

Mean Reversion to the Long-term Price Logarithm. A mean-reverting process now has the following form

$$\frac{dS_t}{S_t} = \kappa(\theta - \log S_t)dt + \sigma dW_t \tag{4.52}$$

Here $\theta - \dfrac{1}{2\kappa}\sigma^2$ is the long-term mean of logarithms of spot prices, and κ is again the strength of mean reversion. Processes (4.51) and (4.52) are intuitively quite similar, and if one is used, a strong qualitative argument can be given in favor of the other. The only advantage of (4.52) is that it allows a closed-form solution for the distributions of logarithms of prices similar to (4.20) and (4.22). Indeed, after the familiar change of variables

$$Z_t = \log S_t$$

and the use of Ito's lemma (see remark after (4.19)) process (4.52) can be written as

$$dZ_t = \kappa\left(\theta - \frac{1}{2\kappa}\sigma^2 - Z_t\right)dt + \sigma dW_t \tag{4.53}$$

Now we introduce a new variable

$$Y_t = e^{\kappa t} Z_t \tag{4.54}$$

and, again with Ito's lemma, process (4.53) takes the form

$$dY_t = \kappa e^{\kappa t} Z_t + e^{\kappa t} dZ_t = \kappa\left(\theta - \frac{1}{2\kappa}\sigma^2\right)e^{\kappa t}dt + \sigma e^{\kappa t} dW_t$$

Since for every t the increment dY_t is a normal variable, the approach we used to derive the distributions (4.20) can be applied here as well. Thus, summing these increments from current time t to future time T, we obtain that the random variable

$$Y_T \sim \phi \left[Y_t + \left(\theta - \frac{1}{2\kappa}\sigma^2 \right)(e^{\kappa T} - e^{\kappa t}), \sigma \sqrt{\frac{e^{2\kappa T} - e^{2\kappa t}}{2\kappa}} \right]$$

Hence, by (4.54),

$$Z_T \sim \phi \left[e^{-\kappa(T-t)}Z_t + \left(\theta - \frac{1}{2\kappa}\sigma^2 \right)(1 - e^{-\kappa(T-t)}), \sigma \sqrt{\frac{1 - e^{-2\kappa(T-t)}}{2\kappa}} \right] \quad (4.55)$$

As expected variable Z_t is a normally distributed random variable, whose standard deviation converges to the standard deviation of the distribution (4.20) if the values of the mean-reversion strength parameter κ are small. For the larger values of κ, the standard deviation in (4.55) is smaller in comparison with that of the GBM—the clamping effect of the mean reversion. This characteristic of terminal distributions is consistent with the behavior of a typical implied volatility curve, which as a rule slopes downward.

Valuation of European Options under Mean-Reversion Process

In order to price European options we must first modify the drift in (4.53) to make risk-neutral valuation possible. From the discussion in the earlier section "Drift," we know that this can be achieved either by finding an appropriate convenience yield and estimating the price of risk, or by calibrating drift using the forward curve. We will follow the latter approach.

Let t_0 be the current time and assume that the long-term log-of-price parameter θ depends deterministically on time, $\theta = \theta(t)$. The strength of mean reversion κ is constant and assumed to be determined from the historical data. Introducing again the variable Y_t as in (4.54), we can show that Y_t is normally distributed with the expectation

$$E(Y_t) = \int_{t_0}^{t} \kappa e^{\kappa s} \left[\theta(s) - \frac{1}{2\kappa}\sigma^2 \right] ds \quad (4.56)$$

and the variance

$$\text{var}(Y_t) = \sigma^2 \frac{e^{2\kappa t} - e^{2\kappa t_0}}{2\kappa} \quad (4.57)$$

From (4.56)

$$\theta(t) = \frac{1}{\kappa}e^{-\kappa t}\frac{\partial}{\partial t}E(Y_t) + \frac{1}{2\kappa}\sigma^2$$

and hence, recalling (4.54)

$$\theta(t) = \frac{1}{\kappa}e^{-\kappa t}\frac{\partial}{\partial t}E(e^{\kappa t}Z_t) + \frac{1}{2\kappa}\sigma^2 = E(Z_t) + \frac{1}{\kappa}\frac{\partial}{\partial t}E(Z_t) + \frac{1}{2\kappa}\sigma^2$$

In the risk-neutral world $F(t_0,t) = E(S_t)$, where $F(t_0,t)$ is the forward curve at the current time t_0, and t being a parameter along the curve. The terminal price S_t is lognormally distributed because, according to (4.55), the distribution of its logarithm is normal. Using the standard result for the expectation of lognormally distributed variables, we obtain

$$E(Z_t) \equiv E(\log S_t) = \log[F(t_0,t)] - \tfrac{1}{2}\text{var}(Z_t)$$

By (4.57)

$$\text{var}(Z_t) = \sigma^2\frac{1 - e^{-2\kappa(t-t_0)}}{2\kappa} \tag{4.58}$$

and hence

$$\theta(t) = \frac{1}{\kappa}e^{-\kappa t}\frac{\partial}{\partial t}E\left(e^{\kappa t}Z_t\right) + \frac{1}{2\kappa}\sigma^2$$

$$= \log F_{t_0,t} + \frac{1}{\kappa}\frac{1}{F_{t_0,t}}\frac{\partial}{\partial t}F(t_0,t) + \frac{\sigma^2}{4\kappa}(1 - e^{-2\kappa(t-t_0)}) \tag{4.59}$$

The European call option with expiration time T and strike X

$$C(t_0,S_0;T,X,\theta,\kappa,r,\sigma) = e^{-r(T-t_0)}E(\max\{S_T - X,0\}) \tag{4.60}$$

where the expectation is computed under process (4.52), with the time-dependent parameter $\theta(t)$ defined in (4.59) and S_0 being the initial spot price at t_0. The terminal price S_T, as was demonstrated above, is lognormally distributed, and by the construction of $\theta(t)$ its expectation is $F(t_0,T)$. The standard deviation of the logarithm of S_T is

$$\tilde{\sigma}_T = \sigma\sqrt{\frac{1 - e^{-2\kappa(T-t_0)}}{2\kappa}} \tag{4.61}$$

Therefore, computing the expectation in (4.60) will result in a Black-Scholes–type formula for European calls. Indeed, it is a simple exercise to show that

$$C(t_0,S_0;T,X,\theta,\kappa,\sigma) = C_{BS}(t_0,e^{-r(T-t_0)}F(t_0,T);T,X,r,\tilde{\sigma}_T)$$

where the right side uses the Black-Scholes formula.

Seasonality

As is clear from the examples of the previous chapter, seasonality is one of the most typical characteristics of energy prices, and any realistic model must incorporate this characteristic. In the method described above, seasonality is modeled implicitly, as the model parameters are calibrated on the forward curve, and the forward curve naturally includes the property of seasonality. There are also more direct approaches, such as the one used in Pilipovic (1997), which is based on modeling prices as perturbations of explicitly defined seasonal averages. In both approaches, price seasonality affects the drift of the underlying price process.

It's worth remembering that the approach we have taken to derive option pricing formulas is based on the assumption that, in the risk-neutral world, spot and forward prices are connected by a relation of the type (4.34). This assumption allows us to calibrate the parameters of the underlying mean-reverting process so that it can be used for risk-neutral valuations. As we mentioned, there exists another method to achieve the same goal. It consists of first developing a realistic process for spot-price evolution in the physical world, and then modifying the drift to incorporate the price of risk for risk-neutral valuation. Essentially, this is an approach used by Pilipovic to develop a model for pricing energy derivatives .

Pilipovic's model employs a process of the form (4.52) as a basis for physical-world price evolution. In the model, the long-term price logarithm θ is not deterministic but is governed by its own stochastic process. Also, specific assumptions about the relation between the price of risk and spot and long-term prices, are made to facilitate the calibration of model parameters on forward prices and historical data. It's a complex model, incorporating such important features of energy prices as mean reversion and seasonality. Moreover, it is analytically tractable and, like the models described in this section, results in the lognormal distribution of terminal prices, thus providing a closed-form solution to the problem of pricing European options. Note also that Pilipovic's model is equivalent to Schwartz's model, which we examined earlier in this chapter.

The fact that processes of the type (4.52) lead to lognormal terminal distributions is a matter of great convenience and a principal *raison-d'être* for such models. But it is also their main drawback, since there is a wealth of empirical data (as seen in Chapter 3), indicating that energy prices and particularly power prices should not be modeled with a lognormal distribution. Real-life distributions have much fatter tails, or, more formally, they significantly differ from lognormal distribution when higher moments are concerned.

Pros and Cons

What are the benefits and drawbacks of using geometric Brownian motion as a process to model spot-price evolution for energy commodities? Many characteristics we present in answer to this question are applicable not only to GBM but to a larger class of spot price processes.

Pros

One of the clearest benefits of GBM is that it is an industry standard. It leads to the Black-Scholes option pricing model, which has become more than just a valuation procedure; it has become a language. Option traders interpret prices and markets in terms of Black-Scholes volatility, and this interpretation is widely accepted and understood.

As a stochastic process, GBM is popular in a great number of applications. It has been extensively studied and its properties are well known. It is easy to work with, and it is very amenable to efficient computer implementations.

GBM allows us to quickly build simple but efficient models. It is particularly useful for modeling cross-commodity correlations, essential for pricing spread options—one of the most frequently encountered and important options in the energy applications. For example, if the processes of the type (4.35) are used to model evolution of gas and power prices, a simple linear transformation will be sufficient to introduce an arbitrary correlation between these two commodities.

Cons

We start with the review of shortcomings common for all spot processes and then discuss the limitations of GBM.

One of the biggest weaknesses of the spot processes is that it is very difficult to justify their use for pricing power products. The problem resides in the nonstorability of power, which makes it impossible to use the standard no-arbitrage argument to validate even the most common pricing formulas, such as the formulas for pricing forward contracts and standard European options. The same problem is an obstacle to implementing hedges, thus, rendering the dynamic hedging approach to option valuation suspicious, if not completely useless.

Even in the case of storable commodities, such as natural gas or crude oil, we have to deal with such nebulous concepts as convenience yield, designed to account for certain, frequently nonquantifiable market intangibles and to capture the behavior driven more by psychological than economic considerations. It is still an open question if the convenience yield of energy products exhibits stable statistical properties, not to mention the lack of data for calibrating the convenience yield models.

If a spot process is chosen as a modeling tool, its calibration is difficult to implement due to the significant amount of overlapping market data for energy derivatives, and there are few degrees of freedom in the spot processes to match this data.

The equality (4.34) clearly shows that spot processes may experience significant difficulties matching arbitrary correlation structures between forward contracts, since all forward contracts are linked to the same driver: the initial spot price. This can be a serious weakness when we deal with calendar spread options such as gas or oil storage. Note that for one-factor models the correlation coefficients induced by spot processes are equal to one (see equation 4.34). For many-factor models (Pilipovic, 1997; Schwartz, 1997) the allowed correlation structure can be restrictive.

It is difficult for spot processes to capture the complex volatility structures inherent to energy products (see Chapter 3) or to match overlapping market volatility data. Again, too few degrees of freedom is an impediment.

In addition to the above drawbacks applicable to all spot processes, GBM has problems of its own. The principal weakness of applying GBM to energy products is that it does not allow us to model the fat tails of the price distributions. As we have learned from Chapter 3, the high kurtosis is one of the most distinct features of energy prices and the same must be required from the prices generated by any reasonable model. A related issue is price spikes. Even the most superficial comparison of GBM price paths with the historical data reveals that it is impossible for GBM to generate as many spikes with the magnitude observed in energy markets. This is particularly true for natural gas and power prices. Finally, it is impossible for GBM to capture the complex structure of power/gas correlation described in Chapter 3, a structure essential to pricing spark-spread options such as power plants.

MODELS WITH MORE REALISTIC PRICE DISTRIBUTIONS

Now we will investigate classes of models capable of generating more realistic price distributions. As mentioned before the major drawback of GBM is the inability to recover the statistical properties of energy prices we described in Chapter 3, that is, pronounced skewness and kurtosis. But we have to be careful about drawing conclusions. Estimated excess kurtosis and nonzero skewness of time series of returns can be induced by varying deterministic volatilities. If this is the case, the terminal distribution of prices may still be lognormal.

Important information is provided by the implied volatility surface of energy option prices. In power prices, we can usually observe pronounced skews or smiles. In natural gas prices, we observe smiles and skews. These characteristics can only be due to non-lognormal terminal distributions, and therefore invalidate the use of GBM.

The two possible deviations from the lognormality assumptions of GBM are stochastic volatility or the presence of jumps in the price process. These processes represent two types of deviation from GBM (including excess kurtosis and nonzero skewness): stochastic parameters of conditional normal transition distribution (stoch vol) and condition nonnormality (jumps). Those processes belong to a richer class of levy processes (see Raible, 2000). It might seem easy to identify what particular deviations drive the process. One look at spot power prices will convince anyone that jumps (or spikes) are an important feature of the price process.

On the other hand, it is also easy to see that implied volatilities are changing over time, often unpredictably, but this can be explained by either jumps or stochastic volatility. Moreover, even the clear-cut case of power price evolution might hide both effects: the obvious jumps and the latent stochastic volatility.

Several estimation methods described earlier will help us find the parameters and judge the fit of the jump and stochastic volatility models. However, these methods are limited because they tend to be most efficient when we know precisely the way the processes are specified. As we will see, many models can be classified as either stochastic volatility or jump models.

Can we somehow infer from the available data the likely explanation for deviations from lognormality without committing ourselves to a specific parameterization? The answer is a partial yes, and we will present the general rules to help make the initial choice.

As shown in Das and Sundaram (1999), we can differentiate jumps from stochastic volatility by looking at the following characteristics of returns:

- For jump models, the excess kurtosis of returns decreases with the length of the return. For example, if we can see that daily returns have higher excess kurtosis than weekly returns, and those in turn are still higher than monthly returns, then the most likely mechanism is a jump-process.
- For stochastic volatility, the excess kurtosis shows the opposite pattern. It increases with the length of the return, at least initially. It will start decreasing again only for very long returns. A similar pattern prevails if the volatility only varies in the sample only deterministically (e.g. seasonal volatility or mean-reversion effects).

These facts are also evident in the implied volatility surface (see Rebonato, 1999). If the smile (or the skew) is the steepest for prompt contracts, and then gradually flattens out, jumps are the most likely explanation. On the other hand, if the smile is flat for the near contracts and increases for the later contracts, then stochastic volatility is the likely explanation. Note that this behavior cannot be explained by deterministically varying volatility (seasonality, mean reversion).

In practice we can encounter both effects at the same time (e.g., equities). In the natural gas markets, the forward volatility smile follows the first pattern, suggesting jumps. However, the volatility seasonality effects are likely to affect our conclusions. On the other hand, the direct analysis of returns of

TABLE 4.1 Excess Kurtosis of Henry Hub Futures Contracts as a Function of Length of the Return

	Daily returns	Weekly returns	Biweekly returns	Monthly returns
Excess Kurtosis	7.79	3.91	1.54	8.90

different horizons for natural gas futures contracts shown in Table 4.1 indicates the presence of both effects. The excess kurtosis drops for the returns up to two weeks, but starts increasing again for monthly returns.

We can also look at the problem from a different perspective. A trader managing the risks associated with power plants or other real assets often employs the dynamic delta-hedging strategies to limit the price risk. We've shown that the correct delta hedge is dependent on the volatility of the price product (forward or balance-of-the-month contract). Two problems often appear. The first one is what volatility to use. The often-accepted answer is that the implied ATM volatility is the appropriate one to use. This choice works well, despite some theoretical drawbacks. But we might have further concerns, since the implied volatility itself is not constant over time, and its changes are unpredictable. This will lead our delta hedges to change unpredictably themselves, leaving us in doubt about how robust our hedging strategy is.

One way to answer this concern is to introduce models that, unlike the Black-Scholes model, will be able to incorporate the changes. There are many mechanisms that can induce changes in implied volatility: jumps in price returns and volatility of volatility (not to be confused with implied volatility), for example. In the next two sections we discuss first, stochastic volatility models and then, jump diffusions.

We will impose some structure on the process driving volatility to see whether we can get models broadly in agreement with the available empirical evidence. Once we have this in place, we will look more closely at our models to see what we can find about valuation and our hedging strategies.

PROCESSES WITH STOCHASTIC VOLATILITY

Volatility in Energy Markets

Modeling volatility is of fundamental importance in modeling option prices and all contingent claims. We will present overview of available techniques, then review their ability to capture empirical regularities we analyzed in Chapter 3, and finally, gauge their applicability for properly valuing and hedging both cash/daily and forward options. Given the vastness of the topic, we can only give a glimpse of what the approaches can yield. We refer the reader to the existing literature on this topic in financial markets, and we encourage the user to experiment with the different approaches in energy markets, guided by the experience of the investment world.

There are a number of reduced-form volatility models that deviate from the standard Black-Scholes assumption of constant return volatility. There is voluminous literature on those models (see Hobson, 1996; Frey, 1996). We will describe a selection of these and analyze their applicability to the energy markets.

Constant Elasticity of Volatility Models (CEV)

The standard Black-Scholes model is described by the following stochastic differential equation (SDE):

$$\frac{dS}{S} = rdt + \sigma dW$$

where r and σ are constants. We know from available data that the return volatility does not remain constant, directly contradicting the assumption of the Black-Scholes model. The simplest assumption, then, is to assume that instantaneous volatility depends on the prices themselves, that is,

$$\frac{dS}{S} = rdt + \sigma(S)dW$$

For example, if we want to represent the fact that volatility is positively correlated with price levels we could assume the following model:

$$\frac{dS}{S} = rdt + \sigma(S)dW = rdt + \sigma S^\alpha dW$$

If $\alpha > 0$, the correlation between volatility and price will be positive. If the opposite holds, the correlation will be negative.

A model of this type will easily capture the inverse "leverage effect" present in energy prices. The volatility of power prices tends to increase with the level of the prices.

As we have seen in Chapter 3, the implied volatility surfaces tend to exhibit both pronounced (symmetric) volatility smile and asymmetric skews, especially for the prompt contracts. Over time volatility smiles can turn into skews and vice versa. Constant elasticity of volatility models (CEV) generally induce skews, not smiles, in the implied volatility surface, indicating that they are not well suited for representing the behavior of natural gas prices—similar conclusions hold for crude oil option prices. Because of this, we

choose not to fully analyze the CEV model, and proceed to the richer specifications of stochastic volatility models that produce option price behavior
(implied volatility surfaces) that is more consistent with the observed facts.
For readers who wish to pursue the CEV models in more detail, we recommend the paper by Schroder (1989).

Local Volatility Models

Our discussion of the CEV model made an explicit assumption about the
functional form of the deterministic dependence of volatility on time and the
price level. Since this kind of model is not suitable in fuel option markets due
to the unrealistic shapes of the implied volatility surface it produces, is it possible to specify the local volatility function $\sigma(p,t)$ so that we can recover the
implied volatility surfaces given by the quoted option prices?

The answer to the question is positive; it's almost always possible to calibrate the local volatility function in the following equation so that we recover the implied volatility surface:

$$\frac{dS}{S} = \mu(t)dt + \sigma(S, t)dW$$

The method of implied trees achieves precisely this without any explicit assumptions about the functional form of the local volatility function (see
Derman and Kani, 1994, and Hull, 1999, for a simple introduction to the
method; and see Rubinstein, 1994, and Rebonato, 1999, for more numerically robust approaches). There is also an explicit formula due to Dupire
(see Gatheral, 2001), that relates the implied volatility surface to the local
volatility:

$$\sigma^2(K,t,S_0) = \frac{\dfrac{\partial C}{\partial t} - \mu(t)\left[C(K,t,S_0) - K\dfrac{\partial C}{\partial K}\right]}{.5*K^2\dfrac{\partial^2 C}{\partial K^2}}$$

where

   $C(K, t, S_0)$ is the option price with maturity t, strike price K, and
   initial price S_0

   $\mu(t)$ is the risk-neutral drift

If we express all the values as a function of the forward price F_0 then the
formula simplifies with the explicit reference to the drift dropping out. Thus

$$\sigma^2(K,t,F_0) = \frac{2\dfrac{\partial C}{\partial t}}{K^2 \dfrac{\partial^2 C}{\partial K^2}}$$

The problem of fitting the local volatility surface is technically a delicate one. The above formula gives the exact relationship, but it also requires the continuity of option quotes across all maturities and strike prices. In practice this requirement is never met even approximately and one has to be careful in trying to achieve a robust fit, especially for deep out-of-the-money options (see Gatheral, 2001; Rebonato, 1999; and Rubinstein, 1994 for details).

It appears that this tool allows us to recover the characteristics of the natural gas prices/crude oil prices—at the very least forward prices—as implied from the option prices. Unfortunately, we are still far away from a satisfactory solution, because the local volatility functions calibrated with the methods above perform badly in recovering the dynamics of the implied volatility surface (e.g., see, Dumas, Fleming, and Whaley, 1998; Buraschi and Jackwerth, 1998). In other words, the calibration of the local volatility function performed one day can be misleading a couple days later. We will not be able to recover the new implied volatility surface in the near future.

This failure of the model flows from the misspecification problem: The true underlying process does not have a deterministic local volatility structure, but instead it is likely to have a stochastic volatility structure (and possibly jumps and switching regimes; more about that later). We can show that the local volatility function gives us the conditional expectation of the stochastic variance (see Gatheral, 2001). That is, assuming that the true process is described by the following equation:

$$dF_{t,T} = \sqrt{v_t}\, F_{t,T}\, dW_t$$

where v_t is the variance process (having any given dynamics), then we have:

$$\sigma^2(K,T,F_0) = E[v_T | F_T = K]$$

We can see that using local volatilities amounts to using expectations of the volatility process in place of the full distribution of the true volatility process.

This limitation does not have to be a crippling blow to the methodology. As long as we are using the local volatility function calibration to form static hedges with the quoted option (vanilla) contracts, we do not have to worry about the wrong dynamics. This is easy to see if we consider a European option whose value depends only on the terminal (risk-neutral) distribution of the underlying(s) ϕ. The distribution can be recovered from the current option quotes through the following relationship (up to discounting):

$$\frac{\partial^2 C(K,T,F_0)}{\partial K^2} = \varphi(K,T,F_0)$$

In other words, the second derivative of the option prices with respect to the strike price gives us the pricing distribution. This shows that we can effectively replicate any option with a combination of vanilla options. In practice, we do not have option prices at all strikes; we also must deal with many path-dependent options. Nevertheless, the replication procedure seems to perform well as long as the payoffs are not too discontinuous and the volatility of volatility is not too high. (See Toft, 1998.)

If we attempt (or are forced) to delta hedge our structure with the underlying, the hedges will perform poorly. In reality they might be worse than just using the simple Black-Scholes model with ATM volatility. (See Rebonato, 1999; Gatheral, 2001; Dumas, Fleming, and Whaley, 1998.)

In many situations, the liquidity at various strikes is quite limited, and we generate the implied volatility surface by interpolation. In those cases, one might be tempted to use delta hedging with the Black OTM implied volatility Δ_{Black}, but it can be easily shown that the true delta should be given by the following expression:

$$\Delta_{True} = \Delta_{Black} + \kappa \cdot \frac{\partial \sigma_{IV}}{\partial F}$$

where κ is the volatility sensitivity (vega) and $\sigma_{IV} = \sigma_{IV}(K,T,F_0)$ is the implied volatility surface. The second term can be significant, which can make the naïve delta-hedging methodology quite dangerous.

We can see from the above expression that the only thing standing between us and the correct delta hedge—we can derive all the other terms from the current implied volatility surface—is knowledge of

$$D = \frac{\partial \sigma_{IV}}{\partial F}$$

This term may remind us of the slope of the implied volatility skew:

$$Slope = \frac{\partial \sigma_{IV}}{\partial K}$$

But these terms are quite different. The latter describes the shape of the current static volatility skew while the former describes the dynamics of the volatility skew. The latter can be read off from the current shape of the volatility surface, while the former cannot.

Can we imply something about the dynamics of the smile from the static implied volatility surface and if so how can we do it? The answer to the question is a qualified no. The technique that attempts to solve the problem is precisely the local volatility surface, and we know from the empirical evidence for equity markets that the method does not describe the dynamics of the volatility surface very well (see Derman, 1999).

The usual solution to the problem is to adopt certain rules of thumb concerning the evolution of the volatility smile with the changes of the underlying. The standard rules are:

Sticky Strike. This assumes that the implied volatility remains the same for any given strike. In other words, we start with an ATM option with some volatility, say 50%. The market then moves so that our original option is no longer at-the-money, but the implied volatility does not change. This rule is also called sticky smile. It implies that $D = 0$ and hence the Black deltas are the correct ones and no adjustment for smile is required beyond the volatility level.

Sticky Delta. This assumes that the implied volatility remains the same for any given moneyness of the option. For example, if we start with an OTM option, the market moves so that the option becomes at-the-money, then its implied volatility changes to the level of the ATM option. In other words, the ATM implied volatility stays the same. This rule implies that $D \cong$ slope.

Sticky Tree. This assumes that the local volatility surface remains the same with the movements of the underlying. This rule is clearly implied by the local volatility approach. It also implies $D \cong -$slope. One of the very unpleasant consequences of these models is that the smile moves in the opposite direction of the price movements. That is, if the price goes up, the center of the smile will actually move down. This behavior contradicts the empirical behavior of smiles and broadly disqualifies the model for delta hedging.

There is ample evidence that both regimes hold in equity markets (see Derman, 1999; research by Dumas, Fleming, and Whaley, 1998). On the other hand, Dumas, Fleming, and Whaley (1998) show that the local volatility approaches do not perform as well as simple Black-Scholes in equity markets. With a different approach, Buraschi and Jackwerth (1998) show that one-factor models cannot explain the variability of the volatility smiles in equity markets, effectively rejecting the local volatility models.

According to our research and the experience of traders in natural gas forward markets, the sticky delta rule seems to be a good description of the evolution of the implied volatility smile. Electricity markets present a tougher challenge, since the limited liquidity of OTM options prevents us from drawing clear conclusions.

The behavior implied by the first two rules cannot be described by the local volatility function. In point of fact, there is no diffusive one-dimensional process that could recover this behavior (see Reiner, 1998). The alternative is to introduce more (diffusive) dimensions (e.g., stochastic volatility models), or resort to the inclusion of jumps.

HIGHER-DIMENSIONAL MODELS

Before we consider the higher-dimensional models, let's review the motivation for proceeding. We have discovered that static fits of even complicated one-dimensional models do not perform well in dynamic hedging of nonvanilla products. While this is partially because not all vanilla products trade liquidly (or offer reliable price discovery), we still cannot effectively dynamically hedge (dynamically synthesize) vanilla options that do not trade.

Hence the idea arises of developing the model that will recover/match the dynamics of the implied volatility surface. For example, for natural gas futures we would like to have a model that can reproduce the sticky delta properties of the quoted implied volatility surface. Before we proceed we need to ask ourselves whether the prices of the quoted options are fair. Can we replicate the vanilla options at the cost suggested by the market quotes? It may be that the sticky trading rules are simply helpful approximations traders use to manage the complexity of the problem. If that's the case, matching the perceived dynamics can be a misdirected effort. If the dynamics of the surface are suspect, then the static values themselves cannot be trusted, since they need to be a result of dynamic replication. Effectively, the question we are asking here is about the efficiency of the (vanilla) option market itself. Ultimately then, it's a question of trading opportunities present in the vanilla market.

We cannot provide the reader with references to studies proving the issue one way or the other. First, it's unlikely that studies demonstrating profitable trading rules would become widely available before the opportunity is fully exhausted. Secondly, in very liquid markets offering a rich selection of vanilla and exotic products, there is little likelihood that substantial opportunities still remain in play. That suggests looking at markets of relatively lower liquidity (like energy markets). Of course, the absence of liquidity might reflect the presence of unmanageable or hard to quantify risks—again, energy markets, and especially power markets are a perfect example. This leads us to the third consideration, that is, disentangling risk premia from inefficiencies, which can be very tricky. As the argument over the capital asset pricing model (CAPM) shows, everything can become evidence of risk premia.

GARCH-type Models

Now we will discuss the relationship between GARCH and simpler volatility estimation techniques.

GARCH and Exponential Smoothing

In Chapter 3 we discussed in passing the uses and misuses of moving average estimates of volatilities and correlation. Here we look more closely at exactly how exponential smoothing is done, and how certain natural extensions of the procedure lead us into modern financial econometrics.

Exponential smoothing is a procedure in which the estimate of volatility or variance uses the available observations with different weights. For comparison we show the expression for a moving average, and compare it with the one for the smoothed estimate:

$$\text{var}_{t-d}^t(\varepsilon) = \sum_{i=t-d}^{t} \frac{\varepsilon_i^2}{d-1}$$

$$\text{var}_\lambda^t(\varepsilon) = \sum_{i=0}^{t} \frac{\lambda^{t+1-i}\varepsilon_i^2}{t-1}$$

$$0 < \lambda < 1$$

where d is the length of the averaging window, while λ is the smoothing coefficient. We can see that exponential smoothing gives more weight to the recent observation than the older observations. Unlike moving average, however, there is no set cutoff point; all the available data are included. The particular choice of the persistence probability, or the smoothing coefficient, can be done by minimizing the one-step forecasting error, using standard optimization tools in Microsoft® Excel, such as Solver. The procedure is used in the estimation of volatilities in RiskMetrics™, the VaR estimation technology used and popularized by J.P. Morgan. The optimized value of lambda, used in their system is 0.94.

One useful way we can rewrite the formula for the exponentially smoothed estimate of variance is

$$\text{var}_\lambda^t(\varepsilon) = \sum_{i=0}^{t} \frac{\lambda^{t+1-i}\varepsilon_i^2}{t-1} = \lambda\text{var}_\lambda^{t-1}(\varepsilon) + (1-\lambda)\varepsilon_t^2$$

We can see today's estimate as the weighted average of yesterday's estimate and today's observation. If we assumed that there is some long-term variance to which the observed variance is returning (mean-reverting variance model), we could express it by adding an additional term to the above expression for the estimate of variance:

$$\text{var}^t(\varepsilon) = a\,\text{var}^{t-1}(\varepsilon) + b\varepsilon_t^2 + (1-a-b)V$$

The estimate is a weighted average of the previous estimate, current observation, and the long-term variance V. This model for variance is the *generalized autoregressive conditional heteroskedasticity model* (GARCH), to be more specific, it's the GARCH(1,1) model.

The model above gives us the following recursive description of the evolution of returns over time:

$$r_t = \sqrt{var^t}\, \varepsilon_t$$

$$var^t = a\, var^{t-1} + b\varepsilon_t^2 + (1 - a - b)V$$

Other Members of the GARCH Family

The equation for the return itself can be more complex. We can introduce autoregressive terms, exogenous variables (e.g., seasonal mean adjustments), and so on. For example, we find that the AR(1)-GARCH(1,1) model for temperature-time series performs quite well.

We can also use a more complex representation of the evolution equation for variance; for example we can introduce additional autoregressive lags (GARCH (n, m) models). Other sets of extensions include changes to the structure of the variance equation. We can specify the autoregressive form not for the variance itself but for the log of variance (EGARCH model). This ensures that the variance process is always positive, and it also induces a skewed distribution of returns.

A simple alternative to EGARCH, which also generates a skewed distribution of returns, is the NGARCH model. The variance equation is given by the following:

$$var^t(\varepsilon) = a\, var^{t-1}(\varepsilon) + b(\varepsilon_t - c)^2 + (1 - a - b)V \qquad (4.62)$$

As we can see the only difference from the standard GARCH process is the presence of the constant c. Positive (negative) c induces negative (positive) correlation between variance and returns.

Estimation, Pricing, and Energy Markets

We will now concentrate on the estimation of the GARCH model and analyze its applicability to energy markets. There is also an explicit pricing formula for calls under GARCH-type processes due to Heston and Nandi (1997). Since this formula is related to the Heston model, which we consider later, we do not reproduce it here. Since GARCH models can be seen as discrete time approximations of the continuous-time stochastic volatility models, we analyze GARCH models as tools for estimation of continuous-time models, which we then use for pricing after appropriate risk-adjustment. Incidentally, we mentioned that (static) implied trees perform worse than the recalibrated Black-Scholes model in hedging and pricing. Heston and Nandi

(1997) report that static GARCH models outperform recalibrated Black-Scholes for S&P500 index options.

GARCH model estimates often yield IGARCH(1,1) model (integrated GARCH model), that is, a model where a + b = 1. This feature implies that the variance process is persistent, and there is no long-term volatility to which the process reverts—in other words, the exponential smoothing seems to be an appropriate estimation technique for the variance process. However, we need to mention that in the presence of jumps, GARCH estimates tend to be skewed toward the integrated process. Consequently, the results can be due to a misspecification of the process. Additionally, the residuals of the model exhibit substantial kurtosis and skewness, suggesting that, even conditionally, the distribution of returns is not normal. Indeed, using the GARCH specification with t-distributed (fat-tailed) innovations can improve the in-sample fit (as measured by loglikelihood or the information criteria) to some degree for natural gas and power prices. The GARCH-type models help remove unconditional skewness and excess kurtosis from the data only. We require explicit modeling of conditional returns to deal with conditional excess kurtosis and skewness.

Next, we present the conclusion of a number of studies we performed on gas and power prices. The results can be found in Chibisov, Scott, Stoyanov, and Wolyniec (2001).

We examined natural gas prices from 1998 through 2001 in several locations (Henry Hub, Transco Z6 [Non-New York], and NGPLA). In natural gas prices, GARCH models successfully eliminate the majority of deviations from normality for the conditional distributions of spot prices in summer (April through September). In winter months, the models are not nearly as successful, suggesting a nonnormal process for innovations. GARCH models with t-distributed innovations usually offer a better in-sample fit. We also find evidence that in some periods at certain locations the conditional volatility structure (GARCH) disappears, and any deviation from normality is driven by the excess kurtosis of the innovations (jumps). Also, it is worth mentioning that testing for the presence of mean reversion in the presence of conditional volatility models tends to offer a more ambiguous picture than the one we analyzed in Chapter 3. In some periods we can find statistically significant estimates of nonzero mean reversion. However, as usual the estimates are quite unstable from one period to another.

For power cash prices, however, the GARCH models are not nearly as successful. The improvement in fit tends to be small. This effect is to be expected since the conditional distribution of power prices is unlikely to be normal. We must introduce spikes/jumps to successfully account for the power price behavior.

Somewhat surprisingly, GARCH models do not manage to eliminate the conditional skewness and kurtosis from forward power prices (PJM,

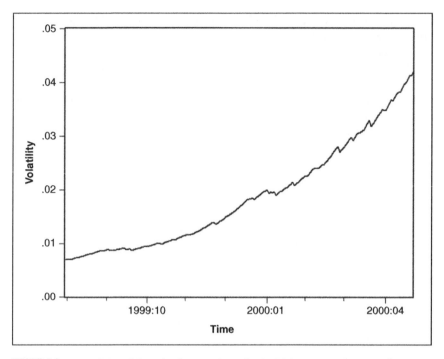

FIGURE 4.1   Conditional Standard Deviation of July 2001 NYMEX Natural Gas Forward Contract

NEPOOL, ERCOT). On the other hand, natural gas forward contracts seem to be essentially normal after accounting for GARCH effects.

Figure 4.1 shows that GARCH-type models consistently recover the Samuelson effect we talked about in Chapter 3.

Figure 4.1 shows an unambiguous upward trend. In fact, the GARCH estimate gives us an autoregressive term greater than one and a very small moving average term. This suggests that the underlying process has deterministic increasing volatility (with shorter term to expiry). The result allows us to sort out the issue of the presence of unconditional skewness and kurtosis in forward returns, which we noted in Chapter 3. We repeat, the presence of unconditional kurtosis may not be due to the underlying nonnormality; deterministic changes in (local) volatility can induce this effect. GARCH models offer us a way to untangle the drivers. In the case of the forward contract in the analysis, we can see that all the kurtosis disappears once we accounted for the deterministic trend in volatility (i.e., using cumulative volatility, see earlier in this chapter). Deterministic trends in volatility enable us to use the Black-Scholes model with a simple modification of the ATM volatility, since the prices are still lognormal. This is in direct conflict with the presence of volatility smiles, since they indicate deviations from the lognormality assumption. The explanation for the discrepancy is twofold:

- Conditional excess kurtosis, although close to zero for many contracts, can be statistically significantly different from zero for others. In other words, while for some contracts the price distribution is approximately normal, for others it is not necessarily true.
- The nice behavior of forward prices usually prevails within one year before expiration. If we include earlier data points in our sample, the structure of the return series becomes fundamentally nonnormal.

The first item points out why we can have significant volatility skew even though the realized distribution is approximately normal. Since the implied volatilities are risk-adjusted expectations of future realized (local) volatility (see discussion on implied trees in the "Local Volatility Models" section), they also incorporate the possibility of nonnormal behavior of returns.

We also test the out-of-sample fit of the models, and we find poor performance for several cash price samples. On the other hand, the AR(1)-GARCH(1,1) specification for the temperature process offers a good in-sample fit, judging by the autocorrelograms of returns and squared-returns, and a satisfactory out-of-sample fit.

The relatively poor fit of the GARCH models for electricity prices is not surprising. The presence of large spikes in the process severely impacts any estimate of variance. In other words, the GARCH (and any stochastic volatility specification) may not be appropriate.

Our results are in general agreement with those reported in similar studies by Duffie, Gray, and Hoang (1999).

Continuous-Time Stochastic Volatility Models

The distinction between GARCH-type models and stochastic volatility models is not a clean one. To a degree, GARCH models can be seen as a discrete approximation of a subclass of stochastic volatility models (see Nelson, 1990), suggesting that GARCH models can be useful in estimation of continuous-time stochastic volatility models. However, there are delicate issues involved (see Ghysels, Harvey, and Renault, 1997 on this topic). As mentioned above, for certain assumptions about the stochastic behavior of innovations, there are semi–closed-formed solutions for option pricing for GARCH models—up to the inversion of the generalized Fourier transform (see Duan, 1995). Similarly, we can develop analogous formulas for the continuous-time limits of GARCH processes. One would expect that the pricing and hedging results would be quite close (see Duffie and Protter, 1992), so the choice of a particular approach hinges on the ease of mathematical manipulation and the ease of estimation.

Naturally, GARCH models are easier to estimate, since we deal with discrete data only, while the limits are easier to use in mathematical transformations. The suggested strategy then would be to develop pricing models for products with the continuous-time versions of stochastic volatility models and estimate their parameters with the discrete-time approximations and test the specification on the discrete model. For example, the Heston model (see p. 178) is the limit of the NGARCH model. Consequently, we can use the estimation strategies described in the section on GARCH for some of the models described here. However, the estimation only helps us with the qualitative choice of the model; we generally cannot use the GARCH parameters in the pricing formulas if the true process is a continuous one. *It does matter* whether the true process has discrete or continuous structure. Estimating a true continuous process on discrete data can lead to significant biases in estimation (see Gourieroux and Jasiak, 2001) if we use naïve discretisation schemes.

Since the GARCH process has a nonlinear structure, the time aggregation properties of the GARCH models are not very attractive (estimation for different return horizons will result in different estimates of the parameters).

An alternative solution is to use some of the estimation techniques we described previously. Again, the problem with maximum likelihood methods as applied to stochastic volatility models is the fact that we usually do not have an explicit expression for the likelihood function. We can resort to methods of moments (SMM, EMM, Spectral GMM). For a review of direct estimation and calibration techniques see Chernov and Ghysels (2000).

One of the challenges of estimation of stochastic volatility models (and in general all reduced-form models) is the ability to use historical underlying price data along with the historical option (and other derivative) prices. Historical estimates on the underlying prices yield the objective/historical process, while calibration to derivative prices (see Chapter 3) yields the risk-neutral process. Reconciling the two estimates and/or using the two data sets at the same time is a challenging problem. For a review of possible solutions in the case of stochastic volatility models see Chernov and Ghysels (2000), and Pan (2002).

Stochastic volatility models usually take on the following form:

$$\frac{dS}{S} = \mu(S, t)dt + \sigma dW_1$$

$$dm(\sigma) = \gamma(\sigma, t)dt + \phi(\sigma, t)dW_2$$

$$dW_1 dW_2 = \rho dt$$

This form represents a number of popular models, but it is not the most general. Here we do not offer an exhaustive review (Hobson, 1996). We look at two canonical models that illustrate the issues involved in modeling stochastic volatility. We also review the applicability of those specific models to energy markets.

There are a wide variety of possible specifications of stochastic volatility models. We will consider two of them: the oldest, known as the Hull-White model and the one currently most popular in the financial world, the Heston model. From the modeling standpoint, the most important difference between them is the treatment of the correlation between return and volatility. The Hull-White model makes the assumption that the correlation is zero. This makes the analysis a great deal simpler.

Hull-White Model

The Hull-White model is described by the following equations:

$$\frac{dS}{S} = \mu dt + \sigma dW_1$$

$$\frac{d\sigma}{\sigma} = \gamma dt + \eta dW_2$$

$$dW_1 dW_2 = 0$$

The volatility process is described by geometric Brownian motion, while the price process itself will no longer be geometric Brownian motion. However, conditioned on the realized path of volatility, the process will be still *described* by geometric Brownian motion. In other words, the terminal distribution of returns will be given by a mixture of normals. This observation may seem unimportant until we remember that for European options, the value of the derivative depends only on the cumulative volatility between the evaluation time and expiration:

$$\int_t^T \sigma_s^2 ds$$

The value of any derivative given the realized path of volatility, then, will be given by the standard formulas for geometric Brownian motion (the whole family of Black-Scholes formulas) with the

$$\sqrt{\frac{\int_t^T \sigma_s^2 ds}{(T-t)}}$$

used as the input volatility. From the conditional formula there is only one simple step to get the value under stochastic volatility:

$$V_{StochVol} = E_{\sigma,s}[f(s)] = E_\sigma\left\{E_{S_i}\left(f(S)\mid\sqrt{\int_t^T \sigma_s^2 ds}\right)\right\}$$

where $f(p)$ is the payoff function. For the standard call option, the value will be given by the weighted average of the Black-Scholes formula over the possible realizations of volatilities:

$$C_{StochVol} = E_{\sigma,s}[\max(S - K, 0)] = E_\sigma\left[BS\left(\frac{\sqrt{\int_t^T \sigma_s^2 ds}}{\sqrt{T - t}}\right)\right]$$

The elegant result does not yield any elegant pricing formulas. The solution requires numerical methods such as simulation, finite difference, or expansion based methods. Hull and White (1987) offer a Taylor expansion approximation for small η (volatility of volatility).

Apart from the fairly quick development of pricing formulas, what is the motivation for using the Hull-White models? The model does have some attractive features:

- As we can see from the process specification, the volatility process will be unbounded (nonstationary). This is in agreement with our GARCH estimates for fuel prices where we found the volatility process to be integrated (nonstationary). However, we have to be careful with the conclusion, because the integrated process estimate can be caused by the biases introduced by jumps in the underlying process.
- The shape of the smile for natural gas forward prices is at times broadly symmetric. As shown by Renault and Touzi (1996), in the absence of correlation between prices and volatility, the smile will be perfectly symmetric. Consequently, the model can recover the shape of volatility smiles in natural gas and oil markets under certain circumstances. Note that the model can only produce symmetric smiles. The lack of correlation between price and volatility is a serious drawback, since we know from both the analysis of returns and the shape of volatility smiles that there should be a positive correlation between the two.

Heston Model

The crucial difference between the Heston model and the Hull-White model is the assumption of nonzero correlation between the price and volatility process.

$$\frac{dp}{p} = \mu dt + \sigma dW_1$$

$$d\sigma^2 = \kappa(\theta - \sigma^2)dt + \eta\sigma dW_2$$

$$dW_1 dW_2 = \rho dt$$

The variance process is described by the mean-reverting square-root process. The model's popularity arises less from its empirical performance and more from its relative tractability. The introduction of nonzero correlation greatly complicates the analysis of stochastic volatility models. Consequently, the tractability issue should not be underestimated. The choice of the square-root process has the advantage of ensuring that the variance process can never be negative or reach zero in finite time. If the true process has the diffusive component of power 1 or 2, the variance process can become negative. Furthermore, the square-root process belongs to the class of the so-called affine models that makes it relatively tractable in mathematical transformations and in estimation (see Duffie, Pan, and Singleton, 2000).

On the other hand, the Heston model is consistently rejected in tests on historical returns (equity markets). Those tests suggest that the diffusive coefficient for the volatility process is more likely to be of power 1 or 2, rather than the square-root assumed in the Heston model (Chacko and Viceira, 2001). There is one problem with those kinds of models because for some exponents of the diffusive volatility term (e.g., 3/2) the process becomes explosive and the volatility can go to infinity in a finite time—a rather undesirable feature. Other studies show that if we estimate a joint stochastic volatility jump-diffusion process, the estimates of the power of the stochastic volatility coefficient indeed turn out to be close to one half.

In energy markets (forward gas and power contracts), the evidence is mixed. The stability of estimates is quite limited. Actually, this effect is not that surprising since some term structure of both conditional (local) skewness, kurtosis and volatility seems to exist in energy forward markets. Time-homogenous models have problems recovering the dynamics of the underlying.

Despite all these drawbacks, the model has more luck recovering the dynamics of the smile than implied trees approaches do. The fit of the Heston model is very good, and over time the stability of the fit to the relative smile (i.e., implied smile scaled by ATM volatility), is also reasonable under most circumstances. We say *"most* circumstances" because natural gas implied volatilities curves exhibit a tendency to switch between symmetric smiles and asymmetric skews, implying changes in the return-volatility correlation. Since the implied volatilities also reflect risk adjustment, it is possible that the correlation flips are driven by the trader's outlook and not by any fundamental distributional changes.

When we talk about combined models at the end of this chapter, we will present some comparative results of the goodness-of-fit of the models to the dynamics of implied volatility smiles in natural gas markets.

The Heston model can yield semi-analytical expressions for the value of call options. The formula is given in terms of the inverse Fourier transform of the characteristic function of the Heston process. It turns out that this characteristic function has an analytical representation. Consequently, the pricing of calls (and puts) under the model comes down to the numerical inversion of the Fourier transform, which can be done very efficiently (see Heston, 1993). It is worth noting here that the Heston formula can be also applied to the Hull-White model, as it is a special case of the Heston model (for certain parameter choices).

The price of an European call under the stochastic volatility assumptions can be written in the following form:

$$C_{StochVol} = E_t^* [\max(S_T - K,0)] = S_t P_1 - e^{-r(T-t)} P_2 \qquad (4.63)$$

The Ps are the risk-neutralized probabilities of ending in-the-money at expiration. There are no explicit formulas for the probabilities. We can, however, express the characteristic functions of the probability $f_j, j = 1, 2$, in closed form:

$$P_j(x,v,T; \ln K) = \Pr(\ln S_T \geq \ln K | \ln S_t = x, v_t = v)$$

$$f_j = e^{i\phi x}$$

$$f_j = \exp\{C_j(T - t;\phi) + D_j(T - t;\phi) + i\phi x\}$$

$$C_j(\tau;\phi) = r\phi i\tau + \frac{\kappa\theta}{\eta^2}\left[(\kappa_j - \eta\rho\phi i + d) - 2\ln\left(\frac{1 - ge^{dr}}{1 - g}\right)\right]$$

$$D_j(\tau;\phi) = \frac{\kappa_j - \eta\rho\phi i + d}{\eta^2}\left(\frac{1 - e^{dr}}{1 - ge^{dr}}\right)$$

$$g = \frac{\kappa_j - \eta\rho\phi i + d}{\kappa_j - \eta\rho\phi i - d}$$

$$d = \sqrt{(\eta\rho\phi i - \kappa_j)^2 - \eta^2(2u_j\phi i - \phi^2)}$$

$$\kappa_1 = \kappa + \lambda - \eta\rho$$

$$\kappa_2 = \kappa + \lambda$$
$$u_1 = .5$$
$$u_2 = -.5 \tag{4.64}$$

With all these definitions in hand, one can now invert the formulas:

$$P_j(x,v,T; \ln K) = \frac{1}{2} + \frac{1}{\pi} \int_0^\infty \mathrm{Re} \left(\frac{e^{-i\phi \ln K} f_j}{i\phi} \right) d\phi \tag{4.65}$$

Now we can put (4.65) into (4.63). Similar expressions can be developed for other structures.

JUMP-DIFFUSION PROCESSES

Since the pioneering work of Merton (1976) jump-diffusion processes (JDPs) have been used for modeling price evolution in financial markets [see the survey in Bates (1996) for references]. Interest in these processes increased dramatically after the 1987 stock market crash—the event that has underscored the inability of pure diffusion models, such as GBM, to capture big market movement correctly.

In recent years these processes started appearing more and more frequently in energy applications, because of the ubiquitous nature of price spikes in the energy markets. Record natural gas prices in Chicago in the winter of 1995 and in California in the winter of 2000; the hundredfold increase in the electricity prices in the Midwest in the summer of 1998; the exceptional price levels in Texas in 1999, California in 2000, New England in 2001, Europe in 2000—all indicate that price spikes are inherent to energy markets and must be incorporated into price evolution models. This leads naturally to jump-diffusion processes.

An additional advantage of a JDP is that it captures the fat tails of energy price distributions quite well—not only better than GBM, but also better than stochastic volatility processes. Therefore it's no surprise that JDP has gained considerable popularity as a modeling tool for energy applications.

A typical JDP is a combination of a diffusion process of the type (4.17) and a jump process. Although many processes can be used to represent discontinuous jumps, the Poisson process is chosen most frequently. We recall that the Poisson process, q_t, is characterized by the following property: On any small interval of length dt, either no jumps arrive or a jump of magnitude one arrives with a probability proportional to the length of the interval. The arrival of two or more jumps on a small interval is unlikely. More precisely, for any time t, an increment of the Poisson process dq_t, on the interval $(t, t + dt)$ is defined by the following relations

$$\Pr(dq_t = 0) = 1 - \lambda\, dt$$

$$\Pr(dq_t = 1) = \lambda\, dt$$

$$\Pr(dq_t > 1) = o(dt) \tag{4.66}$$

In addition, it is assumed that increments of the Poisson process on any two nonoverlapping intervals are independent. The parameter λ in the above definition is called the intensity of the Poisson process. Below are some useful facts about the Poisson process.

$$E(q_t) = \lambda t \tag{4.67}$$

$$\mathrm{var}(q_t) = \lambda t \tag{4.68}$$

If $T_1, T_2, \dots, T_n, \dots$ are the arrival times of jumps, then the random variables $X_i = T_{i+1} - T_i$, the lengths of intervals between jumps, are independent and have exponential distribution with parameter λ, that is

$$\Pr(X_i < x) = \begin{cases} 1 - e^{-\lambda x} & \text{for } x \geq 0 \\ 0 & \text{for } x < 0 \end{cases} \tag{4.69}$$

By definition, all jumps in the Poisson process have a magnitude of one. Since jumps of *constant* magnitude are not realistic, jumps of *random* magnitude are typically introduced in pricing models. In the financial applications the most frequently used representation of the jump-diffusion processes is

$$\frac{dS_t}{S_t} = (\mu - \lambda k)dt + \sigma dW_t + (Y_t - 1)dq_t \tag{4.70}$$

or after the usual substitution $Z_t = \log S_t$,

$$dZ_t = \left(\mu - \lambda k - \frac{1}{2}\sigma^2\right)dt + \sigma dW_t + \log(Y_t)dq_t \tag{4.71}$$

In these equations we used the following notation:

S_t spot price

W_t standard Brownian motion

μ expected instantaneous rate of relative changes in the spot prices

σ volatility of relative changes of the spot prices on any interval not containing jumps

q_t the Poisson process

λ the intensity of the Poisson process

$Y_t - 1$ a random variable representing the magnitude of jumps in price returns, $Y_t \geq 0$

k the expected jump magnitude, $E(Y_t - 1)$

The drift adjustment in the diffusive part of (4.71) is made to ensure that the total expected rate of relative price changes (a sum of the expected diffusive drift and expected rate of relative changes from the jumps) is equal to μ.

Jump-diffusion Processes with Lognormally Distributed Jump Size

A question remains how to choose the distribution for the jump magnitude. A typical choice in the financial applications is

$$\log(Y_t) \sim \phi\,(\gamma, \delta) \tag{4.72}$$

That is, the random sizes of jumps in (4.71) are normally distributed with expectation γ and standard deviation δ. The probability density function φ is defined in (4.21) and

$$\gamma = \log(1 + k) - \frac{\delta^2}{2}$$

With this choice of the jump size distribution it is now possible to answer the question about the distribution of the spot prices S_t or their logarithms Z_t and to establish the analogs of the relations (4.20), (4.22) in the case of JDPs. Consider an interval $(t, t + \Delta t)$ and the increment $\Delta Z_t = Z_{t + \Delta t} - Z_t$. Conditional on exactly n jumps of the interval $(t, t + \Delta t)$ we have from (4.71) that

$$\Pr(\Delta Z_t = x | \#\text{jumps} = n) = \phi\left[x; \left(\mu - \lambda k - \frac{1}{2}\sigma^2 \right)\Delta t + n\gamma, \ \sqrt{\sigma^2 \Delta t + n\delta^2} \right]$$

From the definition of the Poisson process we can show that the probability of n jumps on the interval $(t, t + \Delta t)$ is

$$\frac{e^{-\lambda \Delta t}(\lambda \Delta t)^n}{n!}$$

and therefore, the following relation gives unconditional distribution of the increment ΔZ_t of the logarithm of the spot prices in the JDP:

$$\Delta Z_t \sim \sum_{n=0}^{\infty} \frac{e^{-\lambda \Delta t}(\lambda \Delta t)^n}{n!} \phi\left[\left(\mu - \lambda k - \frac{1}{2}\sigma^2 \right)\Delta t + n\gamma, \ \sqrt{\sigma^2 \Delta t + n\delta^2} \right] \tag{4.73}$$

By analogy, we can show that on any interval (t,T) the distribution of the terminal value Z_T of the JDP conditional on the known initial point Z_t at the current time t, is given by the relation

$$Z_T \sim \sum_{n=0}^{\infty} \frac{e^{-\lambda\tau}(\lambda\tau)^n}{n!} \phi\left[Z_t + \left(\mu - \lambda k - \frac{1}{2}\sigma^2\right)\tau + n\gamma, \sqrt{\sigma^2\tau + n\delta^2}\right] \quad (4.74)$$

where $\tau = T - t$.

This expression is very much like (4.20), so a logical next step is to try to replicate the results we obtained in the earlier sections "Spot Price Processes and Forward Prices" and "Valuation of European Call and Put Options," and to price forward contracts and European calls and puts.

To do this we present an argument that, for the pricing purposes, the drift μ in equations (4.70) and (4.71) can be replaced with the risk-free rate r. Recall that the argument in the section "Modeling Price Process" justifying such replacement in the case of the geometric Brownian motion was based on the ability to replicate the terminal payoffs of the forward contracts or options, thus eliminating any payoff uncertainty. Only two product was used for the replication: the underlying commodity bought or sold at the spot market. It was not a coincidence that there was also exactly one source of uncertainty in the price evolution equation (4.17), namely, the small diffusive shocks $\sigma S_t dW_t$ continuously and randomly affecting the prices. At least one additional traded product is generally required to eliminate one additional source of uncertainty, and that is why a replicating (or hedging) strategy is working for geometric Brownian motion.

The situation is entirely different in the case of JDPs. There are infinite sources of random shocks affecting the instantaneous price changes in equations (4.70) or (4.71), as becomes immediately clear after comparison of (4.22) with (4.73). The success of the risk-neutral methodology in this case depends on the ability to hedge away the totality of these random shocks. Two alternatives are frequently considered to address this problem.

One stems from the Merton (1976) paper where jump-diffusion processes were used to model the evolution of stock prices. The critical assumption of the paper is that jumps are specific to the location and not correlated with the movements of the market as a whole. In other words, they represent nonsystematic risk. Under the assumption of Merton's paper the option values can be computed as the expectations of the option payoffs in the risk-neutral world, in which price evolution is governed by the process

$$\frac{dS_t}{S_t} = (r - \lambda k)dt + \sigma dW_t + (Y_t - 1)dq_t \quad (4.75)$$

The other approach (e.g., see Jones, 1984 and Bates, 1988) assumes the existence of an infinite number of independently traded products (e.g., the commodity, commodity options with different strikes, and so on). Using these products, one can create a portfolio to neutralize both diffusive and discontinuous random shocks (jumps). In the end, this approach also results in the process (4.75) as the one required for risk-neutral valuation of the derivative products.

Completeness

If a certain market satisfies the condition that for each source of random shocks affecting the prices, there is at least one traded product that hedges this source of uncertainty, then this market is called complete. The question of market completeness is a question of the richness of the traded product set. One source of randomness in the GBM requires only two hedging products—yet another reason for GBM's popularity, markets are typically complete under this process. It is much more difficult to ensure completeness when a market is governed by a jump-diffusion process with an infinite number of sources of random shocks. In this case either incompleteness is accepted, and then, under certain conditions, circumvented (as in Merton's paper), or additional assumptions are made about existence of a large number of tradables to ensure completeness (as in Jones, 1984).

What if neither of these approaches is applicable and the market is incomplete? In this case not all sources of risk can be hedged away, so there is no justification for using a risk-free rate to price derivative products, such as options. However, this problem can be addressed. An established approach (see Hull, 1999) follows familiar lines: option prices are computed as the expectation of option payoffs along the paths of a certain process. This process differs from the physical world process (4.70) only by the drift rate, obtained by subtracting from the physical world drift rate μ, a cumulative price of risk associated with all sources of uncertainty. The resulting "risk-adjusted" process for the JDP (4.70) will have the form

$$\frac{dS_t}{S_t} = (\mu - \Lambda - \lambda k)dt + \sigma dW_t + (Y_t - 1)dq_t \qquad (4.76)$$

where Λ is the price of risk.

In an economy where all risks can be hedged, the term $\mu - \Lambda = r$ (the risk-free rate) and the process (4.76) define the risk-neutral valuation. Not surprisingly, when the market is incomplete, the derivative pricing methodology based on the process (4.76) is also called, albeit somewhat inaccurately, risk-neutral valuation. Finally, it is important to note that a cumulative price of risk is not a well-defined, stable, or universal parameter, but is rather elusive and even subjective. It is usually computed from historical data by comparing real-life returns (typically for a given industry or sector) with the risk-free rate. We discuss those issues in more detail in Chapter 10.

Forward Prices and Values of European Options Under Jump-diffusion Processes

Once the process underlying the risk-neutral valuation (e.g., the process [4.75]) is determined, computing forward prices and the values of European calls and puts is a fairly straightforward exercise. The payoffs of these contracts depend only on the terminal values of the paths generated by the process, therefore the valuation involves computing the expectation with respect to the terminal value distribution. In the case of the process (4.75) the terminal distribution of the logarithms of the prices is given by the expression (4.74) in which the physical rate of return μ is replaced with the risk-free rate r. Computing the expectations (as always, conditional on the current spot price S_t) we obtain that the forward price

$$F(t,T) = E(S_T) = e^{r(T-t)}S_t$$

the European call with the strike X is

$$C_{JDP} = \sum_{n=0}^{\infty} \frac{e^{-\lambda\Delta t}(\lambda\Delta t)^n}{n!} \, C_{BS}\left(t,S;T,X,r - \lambda k + \frac{n\lambda}{T}, \sqrt{\sigma^2 + \frac{n\delta^2}{T}}\right) \qquad (4.77)$$

and the European put is

$$P_{JDP} = \sum_{n=0}^{\infty} \frac{e^{-\lambda\Delta t}(\lambda\Delta t)^n}{n!} \, P_{BS}\left(t,S;T,X,r - \lambda k + \frac{n\gamma}{T}, \sqrt{\sigma^2 + \frac{n\delta^2}{T}}\right) \qquad (4.78)$$

where C_{BS} and P_{BS} are Black-Scholes call and put prices, respectively.

Modeling Spikes: Jump-diffusion Process with Mean Reversion

The processes described so far, although able to capture certain features of energy prices, still cannot model one of the most characteristic features of power prices, namely, spikes. Indeed, JDPs are useful in modeling sudden discontinuities in the price behavior, that is, jumps. However, once the jumps have occurred and the prices have moved to a new level, the JDP tends to keep them on that level until a new jump arrives. It is sufficient to look at the graphs in "Distribution of Power Prices" section in Chapter 3 to realize that this is definitely not a behavior of power prices. Instead of jumps, these prices exhibit spikes—after a discontinuous move the prices quickly return to their normal level. This strongly indicates that we should add mean reversion to the set of phenomena the model must capture. Thus, the resulting process will be a JDP with mean reversion. Processes of this type, in the context of energy models, have been studied by Deng (1998). In the simplest form the process can be represented as

$$\frac{dS_t}{S_t} = \kappa(\theta - \lambda k - \log S_t)dt + \sigma dW_t + (Y_t - 1)dq_t \qquad (4.79)$$

Here the parameters κ and θ are the same as in the mean-reverting process (4.52):

$\theta - \lambda k - \dfrac{1}{2\kappa}\sigma^2$ is the long-term mean of logarithms of spot prices

κ is the strength of mean reversion

The parameters λ, k, and the random variable Y_t represent the jump component, as in (4.70):

q_t is the Poisson process

λ is the intensity of the Poisson process

$Y_t - 1$ is a random variable representing the magnitude of jumps in price returns; $Y_t \geq 0$, in the simplest case log (Y_t) is normally distributed with standard deviation δ)

k is the expected jump magnitude; $k = E(Y_t - 1)$

σ is the instantaneous volatility of the diffusion part of the price process

In principle, the process (4.79) captures all the essential features of power prices, but it has one serious drawback: the necessity to determine at least six parameters, κ, θ, λ, σ, k, δ. Additionally, if we want to reconcile the estimation of the model on historical underlying price data and the calibration to the available derivative prices, we also must explicitly estimate the (market) price of risk, which adds another parameter(s). And ultimately, this is where the problem resides: The number of parameters is just too large for reliable and stable calibration with the available data. The problem will get even worse if the time dependence is introduced, as in (4.59). The example in the upcoming section "Estimation of Jump-Diffusion Processes" will illustrate some of the difficulties of parameter estimation for the process (4.79).

Other Families of Jump-diffusion Processes

The attraction of jump-diffusion processes with lognormally distributed jump sizes is that under certain conditions, they can lead to relatively simple closed-form valuation formulas for various derivatives. But these processes are not the only ones that have such properties. A different class of processes, with the distribution of jumps belonging to a certain exponential family of distributions, has been introduced by Kou and Wang (2001) who have been also able to construct analytically tractable option valuation formulas. Essentially, their process has the form (4.70) with the only difference that now log (Y_t) has a distribution $f(y)$ where

$$f(y) = \begin{cases} p\eta_1 e^{-\eta_1 y} & y \geq 0 \\ (1 - p)\eta_2 e^{-\eta_2 y} & y < 0 \end{cases}$$

where p, η_1, η_2 are positive constants.

The advantage of this distribution compared to the lognormal distribution is that it has fatter tails, making it more useful for energy applications, particularly for modeling power prices. The obvious disadvantage is that its specification adds one more parameter to the long list of parameters we need to estimate, using the sparse and unreliable historical and/or market data.

Estimation of Jump-diffusion Processes

In this section we present the results of maximum likelihood estimation of JDP parameters for California on-peak prices in the summers of 1999, 2000, and 2001.

EXAMPLE 4.9   *Calibration of the JDP with mean reversion for California data*

We can see from Table 4.2 that the year of crisis in California (2000) differs markedly from the other two years. The summers of 1999 and 2001 yield

TABLE 4.2   Parameter Estimates for JDP in Returns

Parameters	Whole sample	Summer '99	Summer '00	Summer '01
Theta	3.637	3.509	4.592	3.521
κ	0.052	0.299	0.104	0.110
Sigma	0.111	0.160	0.132	0.134
Jump mean	0.054	0.410	0.039	0.438
Jump volatility	0.296	0.019	0.297	0.024
Lambda	0.695	0.071	1.132	0.143
Likelihood	(5.266)	15.244	(24.220)	20.649

similar estimates of diffusive volatility, jump mean, and jump volatility. There are significant differences in the estimate of the rate of mean reversion and jump intensity.

Pros and Cons of Estimation of Jump-diffusion Processes

Pros

The benefits of jump-diffusion processes for modeling energy prices are obvious. They are much better suited than pure diffusion processes to capture the important characteristics of those prices, such as spikes and distribution of fat tails. Hence, it is no surprise that JDPs are gaining popularity as important modeling tools in the world of energy derivatives.

Cons

In addition to the issues discussed earlier, jump-diffusion processes have problems of their own. As was mentioned above, the major complication of a JDP is parameter calibration. There is typically not enough data to estimate six or more parameters defining the process, and the results change significantly when new data sets are added. Moreover, procedures used to compute these parameters, for example, the maximum likelihood method or the nonlinear least-squares approach, have poor numerical properties. The minimization procedures tend to converge slowly; the objective function may be very flat in the neighborhood of the solution set resulting in unstable parameter estimates.

There is another drawback, common to all processes discussed in this chapter, but particularly severe in the case of JDP and JDP with mean reversion. These processes are unable to incorporate certain critical information about the future, in particular, information about the load growth or addition of new generation.

REGIME-SWITCHING MODELS

As we have seen, while jump-diffusion models with strong mean reversion can produce a realistic "spiky" price process, we must introduce a very strong mean-reversion component to make the price jumps transitory. This leads to the misspecification of the diffusive part of the price evolution. It would be useful if we could introduce various mean reversions depending on the state of the system. The idea can be extended to other price process characteristics. The natural way to handle such a process is by introducing regime-switching models.

Regime-switching models are models in which we specify a number of regimes, or states, among which the process moves. This flexible method allows the price process to behave in any way desirable in any given regime. The next step is the introduction of some probability distribution of switches between regimes.

We will illustrate the above with a simple example of a two-state continuous-time Markov process. Assume that the return process follows geometric Brownian motions in both states. The two states will have different return volatilities, drifts, and starting points.

Because the model is in continuous time instead of using the probabilities of transition, we characterize the model with the probability rates per unit of time (transition rates). If we assume that the rates are constant, we will essentially deal with a Poisson-distributed Markov chain. Despite the parallels with two-jump jump-diffusion models, the symmetry is not complete. Jump-diffusion models are more restrictive in specifying the dynamics of the diffusion in the two states. Here we assume the process transitions to a different level with different drift and volatility. The process is given by:

$$\frac{dS}{S} = \begin{cases} \mu_L dt + \sigma_L dW_L \rightarrow P_L = 1 - \lambda_{LU} dt \\ \mu_0 + \mu_U dt + \sigma_U dW_U \rightarrow P_U = 1 - \lambda_{UL} dt \end{cases} \tag{4.80}$$

The probability transition matrix is given by:

$$P = \begin{pmatrix} 1 - \lambda_{LU} dt & \lambda_{LU} dt \\ \lambda_{UL} dt & 1 - \lambda_{UL} dt \end{pmatrix} \tag{4.81}$$

In the matrix, the diagonal terms give the probability of remaining in any given state. The off-diagonal terms represent the probability of transitioning to the other state. For example, λ_{UL} represents the transition rate from the state v to state L (high and low price regimes respectively).

If we integrate the process for some terminal time T, the return distribution will be a mixture of normals given by:

$$\text{Ln}(P_T/P_0) \sim \frac{\lambda_{21}}{\lambda_{21} + \lambda_{12}} \phi(\mu_1 T, \sigma_1^2 T) + \frac{\lambda_{12}}{\lambda_{21} + \lambda_{12}} \phi(\mu_1 + \mu_2 T, \sigma_2^2 T) \tag{4.82}$$

If instead of specifying the regime switching for returns, we specify the switching regime for price levels, the resulting distribution will be a mixture of lognormal terms. Note that this specification has the advantage of providing pricing formulas for European options in the form of mixtures of the standard Black-Scholes results. We will illustrate this situation shortly.

The model has a natural appeal, since the histograms of the mixed distributions handily produce bimodal graphs in broad agreement with the his-

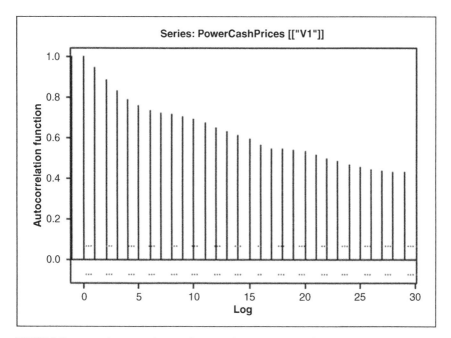

FIGURE 4.2   Correlogram of Log of On-peak Power Prices for ERCOT

tograms of empirical distributions of power prices (see Chapter 3). Histograms, however, have the disadvantage of giving valuable insights only for terminal distributions—sufficient for pricing European options. To investigate the dynamics of the process—crucial for pricing path dependent and American options as well for hedging—we produce the graph (Figure 4.2) of the correlogram of log of on-peak power prices for the ERCOT market.

Figure 4.2 exhibits strong initial hyperbolic decline, which then levels off and declines more or less linearly. This behavior is a characteristic of regime-switching models (see Gourieroux and Jasiak, 2001). This casual empiricism indicates that regime-switching models might be a suitable choice for representing power price dynamics.

If we choose the rate of transition from the lower to the upper state λ_{LU} to be low, while the transition rate from the upper state to λ_{UL} to be high, we will qualitatively recover the behavior of power prices of infrequent price spikes followed shortly by reversion to the normal level.

The significant advantage of this process formulation is separation of the spike regime from the normal diffusive regime. As we recall, to simulate spikes with jump-diffusion models we need to introduce a significant mean reversion. However, a strong mean-reversion effect is present whether prices spike or not, an undesirable feature of jump-diffusion models. It is doubtful that the mean reversion from the spike will have anything to do with the mean reversion in normal conditions. The regime-switching models allow precisely that separation (see Chapter 3 on mean-reversion estimation for the discussion of the problem).

In formulation (4.80) we did not specify mean reversion in any of the regimes, but this would be a straight forward process.

Estimation of Regime-switching Models

There is no limit to how many states we can introduce in our modeling approach. While the methodology is flexible enough to handle widely varying behavior, this is not necessarily an unequivocal blessing. With the ability to represent rich behavior comes many more parameters of the process. On the other hand, the more parameters we are dealing with, the more severe the requirements for the data sets used for estimation. As we have argued, the available data sets are quite short and the way the price-formation process works changes frequently, limiting the way historical data can be used for forward projections.

The standard method for estimation of regime-switching models (in discrete time) is the maximum likelihood method, possibly with Kalman filtering methods for filtering latent (unobservable) variables such as states. We do not have the space here to offer a detailed analysis. The interested reader should consult Chapter 22 in Hamilton (1994).

An example of ML estimation of regime-switching models for energy markets can be found in the paper by Huisman and Mahieu (2001) (also see Geman and Roncoroni, 2002). They compare regime-switching and jump-diffusion models for CALPX, several European spot power markets, and some fuel markets. Their results are mixed, however. Even though the regime-switching model produces statistically significant and reasonable—from the standpoint of the underlying economics—estimates of parameters, and the jump-diffusion models result in very counterintuitive results (positive mean-explosion), the overall in-sample fit (as measured by log-likelihood or information criteria) is significantly worse for the regime-switching models compared to the jump-diffusion models in all power markets studied. Strikingly, regime-switching models perform better in oil markets (Brent and NYMEX Light Sweet Crude) while performing worse in natural gas (Henry Hub), strongly suggesting that even the regime-switching models are misspecified.

One possibility is the presence of stochastic volatility, which will bias the estimates of the coefficients (if the true process is nonlinear in squared innovations) and make them inefficient. This might account for the counterintuitive results of the jump-diffusion estimation. We will consider this topic in more detail below when we talk about estimating compound/complex models that include all these effects at the same time (jumps, regime-switching, mean reversion, stochastic volatility).

Pricing

Here we consider the simple example of pricing European daily calls on on-peak power prices. We assume a version of the regime-switching model (4.80) in prices. The terminal distribution of prices will be given by the following density:

$$S_T \sim \frac{\lambda_{UL}}{\lambda_{UL} + \lambda_{LU}} LN(\mu_0^L + \mu_L T, \sigma_L^2 T) + \frac{\lambda_{LU}}{\lambda_{UL} + \lambda_{LU}} LN(\mu_0^U + \mu_U T, \sigma_U^2 T)$$

(4.83)

where $LN(\mu\ \sigma)$ are the lognormal cumulative distribution function. Assuming we can fully hedge the option with some appropriate forward contract—which we cannot always do—we will have:

$$F_0 = \frac{\lambda_{UL}}{\lambda_{UL} + \lambda_{LU}} \exp\left(\mu_0^L + \frac{\sigma_L^2 T}{2}\right) + \frac{\lambda_{LU}}{\lambda_{UL} + \lambda_{LU}} \exp\left(\mu_0^U + \frac{\sigma_U^2 T}{2}\right)$$

(4.84)

where F_0 is today's price of our hedging instrument (the underlying). In practice, all the parameters of the model are estimated except for $\mu_0{}^L$, which is then used to match the forward price.

Given the distribution, we can now try to value the call in question:

$$V = E_{P_T}[\max(P_T - K, 0)] \int_0^\infty \max(P_T - K, 0) f(P_T) dP_T =$$

$$= \frac{\lambda_{UL}}{\lambda_{UL} + \lambda_{LU}} \int_0^\infty \max(P_T - K, 0) dLN(\mu_0^L + \mu_L T, \sigma_L^2 T) +$$

$$+ \frac{\lambda_{LU}}{\lambda_{UL} + \lambda_{LU}} \int_0^\infty \max(P_T - K, 0) dLN(\mu_0^U + \mu_U T, \sigma_U^2 T) =$$

$$= \frac{\lambda_{UL}}{\lambda_{UL} + \lambda_{LU}} C_{BS}\left(e^{\mu_0^L + \frac{\sigma_L^2 T}{2}}, K, \mu_L, \sigma_L, T\right) + \frac{\lambda_{LU}}{\lambda_{UL} + \lambda_{LU}} C_{BS}\left(e^{\mu_0^U + \frac{\sigma_U^2 T}{2}}, K, \mu_U, \sigma_U, T\right)$$

(4.85)

As we can see, the value of the option is given by a weighted average of two Black-Scholes formulas.

Introduction of mean reversion in both or any of the regimes would be a trivial extension. The effect will be to change the expectation and volatility term, but structurally the expression would not change.

For more complex specification of component processes, we can apply Monte Carlo simulations or some transform-based techniques. (For affine jump-diffusion specifications, see Deng, 2000.)

Hedging

In the discussion on jump-diffusion models we pointed out that if the amplitude of the jump is stochastic, there is no dynamic hedging strategy to eliminate all the risk (see Rebonato, 1999, for the proof). A similar conclusion applies to regime-switching processes. However, under certain conditions, we can simplify the hedging of regime-switching processes. The same result holds for jump processes given some restrictions on the amplitude. However, regime-switching models offer us a more natural way to represent the behavior, as Example 4.9 illustrates.

EXAMPLE 4.10   *Hedging in two-state regime-switching markets*

Consider an example of a market similar to ERCOT but with only two regimes:

- A mean-reverting diffusive state with the long-term mean price of $30 per MWh, mean-reversion speed of .05, and return volatility of 20% per year
- A spike state with the price centered around $100, with standard deviation of the state location of $10

Assuming the process does not undergo any spikes, hedging any derivatives written on the process would involve the standard delta-hedging approach, using either underlying, or if not available, we could use proxies like BOM contracts. To hedge out the spike risk we must have one other instrument. The best solution would be OTM call options, but ATM options would suffice. The smaller the standard deviation of the spike-state, the more effective the hedge is. In the limit, when the standard deviation is zero, we could form the perfect hedge (see Rebonato, 1999).

EXTENSIONS

In this section we consider the estimation, valuation, and hedging issues for combined models that include many effects together. We will review two types of modeling techniques: stochastic volatility (mean-reverting) jump-diffusion models and models with exogenous variables.

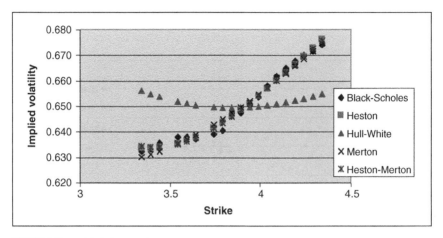

FIGURE 4.3 Initial Curve Fit

Stochastic Volatility Jump-diffusion Models

The primary motivation for considering stochastic volatility jump-diffusions models is the evidence from historical data that the simpler models lead to biases in estimation of parameters. In other words, when we estimate a jump-diffusion model, the parameters of jump distribution can be biased by the presence of stochastic volatility. It is well known fact that estimation of jumps with maximum-likelihood methods causes the model to calibrate to the frequent, small amplitude jumps easily explained by stochastic volatility effects. We have some casual evidence that both effects will be present in natural gas prices. It is worthwhile, then, to at least investigate whether the systematic separation of these effects can add to the explanatory power of the model and stability of its parameters.

We consider the following stochastic volatility jump-diffusion model:

$$\frac{dS}{S} = \theta(\mu - \ln P)dt + \sqrt{V}dW_1 + (Y - 1)dN$$

$$\frac{dV}{V} = \theta(\omega - \ln V)dt + \eta\sqrt{V}\,dW_2 \qquad (4.86)$$

$$dW_1 dW_2 = \rho dt$$

Here we perform a comparison of the fit to the natural gas forward volatility smile. Figure 4.3 shows the original fit and Figure 4.4 shows how the different models fit the same volatility curve a month later without recalibration. Figure 4.4 shows how well each version of the models perform in recovering the dynamics of prices.

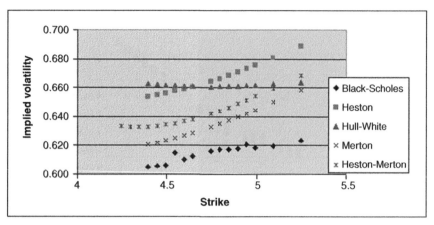

FIGURE 4.4 The Original Fit in Figure 4.3 a Month Later

We can see that the volatility smile flattens out considerably. The models do not recover this flattening. As we argued before, the excess kurtosis of the underlying distribution decreases with the time to maturity for jump-diffusion processes and it increases, at least for reasonable time horizons, for stochastic volatility models. That is why the Merton (jump-diffusion) model does not flatten out closer to maturity, while the stochastic volatility model does. The calibration results suggest that there is some term structure of kurtosis in addition to the term structure of ATM volatility (Samuelson effect, see Chapter 3).

Instead of implying the model parameters from option prices, which will result in risk-neutral estimates, we can perform estimation on the historical returns. Historical estimation yields the so-called objective/historical distribution that cannot be used directly for pricing derivatives. The risk adjustment required is discussed at length in Chapter 10.

In Tables 4.3 and 4.4 we present the results of estimation of the various models presented in this chapter by using the specification in (4.86). We estimate the models on natural gas and power prices.

In general we can observe that the more complex models offer better fit even if we penalize explicitly for the use of the additional parameters by using the Akaike and Schwartz information criteria. However, the estimates (especially for the mean-reversion and jump intensity parameters) change significantly between different time periods and under different models. This has significant implications for the application of those models in pricing and hedging. As a practical matter, unstable parameters render the models hard to use. Similar results have been obtained for the overseas markets (Europe and Australia) by Escribano, Peñta, and Villaplana (2001).

TABLE 4.3 Complex Model Estimation Results: Natural Gas

	Whole sample	1st half	2nd half
Theta	0.423	0.339	(0.126)
Mu	1.244	1.241	0.974
Sigma	1.266	1.171	0.617
Psi	0.838	0.792	0.771
Omega	1.221	1.125	0.862
Eta	0.940	0.873	0.870
Rho	(0.284)	(0.349)	(0.844)
Jump frequency	0.846	0.748	(0.192)
Jump amplitude	0.446	0.439	0.129
Jump volatility	0.026	0.020	0.082

TABLE 4.4 Complex Model Estimation Results: Power Prices

	Whole sample	1st half	2nd half
Theta	0.042	0.52	0.20
Mu	3.543	3.81	2.99
Sigma	0.43	1.31	1.08
Psi	0.127	1.00	0.71
Omega	0.23	0.35	(0.09)
Eta	0.54	1.20	0.47
Rho	−0.73	(0.06)	(0.62)
Jump frequency	0.02	0.70	0.02
Jump amplitude	0.23	0.26	(0.20)
Jump volatility	0.02	0.09	0.09

CHAPTER 5

Forward Price Processes

In Chapter 4 we showed that energy models based on spot processes—no matter how powerful, elegant, or efficient—have several fundamental drawbacks. One of them is the necessity to use the convenience yield. In energy markets, the convenience yield is not observable, and the amount of historical data is not large enough to deduce a model for its evolution in a stable and reliable manner. Using liquidly traded products (such as forward contracts and standard options) for calibrating convenience yield models can be misleading and may result in mispricing of common structures such as recall options, as will be demonstrated in Chapter 8.

Another drawback is the difficulty of using spot models for computing and implementing hedges, particularly for power models. The section in Chapter 4 "Building Reduced-form Models for Energy Applications: The Basics" provides a compelling argument in favor of using forward price models to avoid these difficulties. Indeed, forward models do not require knowledge of the convenience yield for risk-neutral valuation, and hedges based on forward contracts can be readily implemented. On the negative side, these models are usually more technically complex than their spot counterparts. Moreover, standardized futures and forward contracts may lack the flexibility to replicate, and hence, to accurately hedge some of the most important energy structures such as power plants, tolling agreements, and load-following deals.

SIMPLE MODELS

In Chapter 2 we discussed a model describing the evolution of forward prices, namely the Black model. As a variation of the Black-Scholes methodology, it is by far the most widely used model for pricing standard options of futures. In this model, the prices of a particular futures contract in the risk-neutral world are governed by GBM with zero drift:

$$\frac{dF_{t,T}}{F_{t,T}} = \sigma dW_t, \quad t_0 \leq t \leq T \tag{5.1}$$

where parameter T denotes the expiration time of the contract. It's important to remember that process (5.1) is the one to use for pricing derivatives (risk-neutral valuations) and that it is different from a process describing the evolution of futures prices in the physical (actual) world. A justification of the zero drift of the futures prices in the risk-neutral world follows directly from equation (4.36) in the case of constant or time-dependent deterministic convenience yield. Zero drift can be also demonstrated under more complex conditions (see e.g., Ross, 1999). The zero drift property is what explains the appeal of models based on futures, rather than on spot prices. These models do not require knowledge of the convenience yield, since this yield is incorporated in the futures prices.

The applicability of process (5.1) is limited, however, because it describes the dynamics of prices of a given futures contract without taking into account how this contract interrelates with other futures. In financial applications, particularly complex derivatives, knowing this interrelation is frequently critical for developing accurate valuation models. This is because in many applications the derivative cash flow depends not just on one futures price, but on the whole term structure of forward prices at a given time, that is on the forward curve. Therefore, a number of interest rate models have been developed—culminating with the Heath-Jarrow-Morton (HJM) modeling methodology (see Heath, Jarrow, and Morton, 1992)—which focus on the dynamics of the forward curve as a whole, rather than on the evolution of a single contract.

Similarly, many energy applications require the evolution process of the whole forward curve; an important example is the valuation of gas or oil storage. As will be shown in Chapter 8, at any given time, the storage value depends on the spreads between contracts along the curve, hence, the need to know the whole curve at any time, that is, the need to model the forward curve evolution.

CONTINUOUS FORWARD CURVE MODELS

Forward curve processes, such as the ones used in HJM-type models, generally have the following form:

$$dF_{t,T} = \mu(t, T, F_{t,T})dt + \sum_j \sigma_j(t, T, F_{t,T})dW_t^j, \quad 0 \le t \le T \quad (5.2)$$

For a given time t this equation defines the change of forward curve $F_{t,T} \equiv F_t(T)$ on the interval $[t, t + \Delta t]$. The change is represented as a linear combination of random perturbations applied to the curve. Each perturbation is specified as a deterministic shape function $\sigma_j(t,T,F_{t,T})$ multiplied by a Gaussian factor dW_t^j. In the interest-rate world, the risk-neutral drift function μ exhibits complex dependence on the whole forward curve and is uniquely determined by the volatility surface. This is due to the no-arbitrage relationships between various zero-coupon bonds and the definition of the forward rate (see Rebonato, 1996). Due to the stochastic convenience yield, no relationships of this type obtain in energy markets. Since the forward contracts are directly traded (unlike forward rates in the interest-rate world), their risk-neutral drift must be equal to zero (see Duffie, 1992, and Dixit and Pindyck, 1994).

An aside here: The zero risk-neutral drift result relies on replication arguments, that is, on our ability to replicate the payoff of the forward contract by trading in the underlying. Among others, the argument relies on the convergence of the forward price and the spot price at expiration. As we know from previous chapters, in energy markets we have no convergence in the strict sense: The value of the underlying (given by the average spot price in the contract month) and the forward price at expiration can be very different (especially for power). Although the difference is close to zero on average, this time basis can be as high as several multiples of the forward price. Consequently, we cannot rely on replication arguments and we must introduce risk premia explicitly in the parameterization of the forward process (see Chapter 10).

For energy commodities, the forward curve models have the following form:

$$dF_{t,T} = \sum_j \sigma_j(t, T, F_{t,T})dW_t^j, \quad 0 \le t \le T \tag{5.3}$$

Example 5.1 illustrates a forward curve model of this type.

EXAMPLE 5.1   *A two-factor forward curve dynamics model (Schwartz-Smith, 2000)*

This model describes the evolution of the forward curve in the risk-neutral world. It is similar to (5.3), with the additional benefit that it can be explicitly integrated to obtain the following expression for the forward curve at any time t

$$\log(F_{t,T}) = e^{-\kappa(T-t)}\chi_t + \xi_t + A(T - t) \tag{5.4}$$

where random variables χ_t and ξ_t are linked to the spot price by the equation

$$\log(S_t) = \chi_t + \xi_t \tag{5.5}$$

and are governed by the processes

$$d\chi_t = (-\kappa\chi_t - \lambda_\chi)dt + \sigma_\chi dW_t^\chi$$

$$d\xi_t = (\mu_\xi - \lambda_\xi)dt + \sigma_\xi dW_t^\xi$$

$$E(dW_t^\chi \, dW_t^\xi) = \rho_{\chi,\xi}dt$$

The function

$$A(\tau) = \mu_\xi\tau - (1 - e^{-\kappa\tau})\frac{\lambda_\chi}{\kappa} + \frac{1}{2}\left[(1 - e^{-2\kappa\tau})\frac{\sigma_\chi^2}{2\kappa} + \sigma_\chi^2\tau + 2(1 - e^{-\kappa\tau})\frac{\rho_{\chi\xi}\sigma_\chi\sigma_\xi}{\kappa}\right]$$

Parameters (κ, σ_χ, μ_ξ, σ_ξ, $\rho_{\chi,\xi}$) have their usual meaning, and λ_χ, λ_ξ are risk premia introduced for proper risk adjustment. This model is attractive because the factors χ_t, ξ_t, in addition to being simply random coefficients in the decomposition of the logarithm of the forward curve, have their own separate interpretation. The variable ξ_t characterizes a long-term behavior of spot prices, while χ_t, by virtue of (5.5), represents the short-term deviation of spot prices from the long-term levels. This interpretation helps us to make and to justify the choice of an appropriate evolution process. Another benefit is the lognormality of the forward prices (as is evident from [5.4]), since it leads to closed-form formulas for the options on futures. On the other hand, as we know from Chapter 3, lognormality is not the most standard feature of energy prices and, therefore, one has to carefully weigh all pros and cons before using lognormal models in energy applications.

Another possible drawback of this approach is that it may not precisely match the initial forward curve. Moreover, despite natural interpretation, the factors determining the forward curve evolution are not observable. Therefore, we must estimate the model parameters using historical data, which leads, in the case of power applications, to our usual concerns about nonstationarity and the insufficiency of data. It is worth noting however, that Schwartz and Smith applied their methodology to oil prices quite successfully.

Returning to process (5.3), note that a simpler version is likely to be used in practice, namely

$$\frac{dF_{t,T}}{F_{t,T}} = \sum_j \sigma_j(t,T)dW_t^j \qquad (5.6)$$

The left side of this equation represents the change in the logarithm of the forward curve, while the right side is the combination of random shocks specifying this change. Since the complexity of the algorithm depends on the number of shocks, the question is how to determine them in the most efficient way.

In interest rate models one typically distinguishes three types of shocks: (1) parallel shift, which explains the biggest percentage by far of the forward curve daily movement; (2) twist; and (3) change of curvature. Numerically, these shocks are determined as the principal components of the historical forward curve movements. It is important to note that success in finding principal components for the movements of interest rate curves is due to a great extent to the large amount of historical data available for analysis. A word of caution: One should not expect that these principal components are universal. For example, what works well in the case of U.S. rates may not work in Japan.

Needless to say, finding principal perturbations in the case of energy commodities is much more problematic, again because of lack of data and nonstationarity. Moreover, the number of principal components may be quite high. For example, in their analysis of the forward curve dynamics in the Nordic electricity market, Koekebakker and Ollmar (2001) showed that as many as ten factors are needed to explain 95% of the variation of price data. In the case of natural gas or oil, the situation is not quite that hopeless, but clearly the principal component analysis for power cannot be performed reliably at the present time. For natural gas and oil, the most likely candidate for the first principal component is a seasonally shaped parallel shift, while "twist" is frequently used as a second principal component.

It is important to note that the interpretation of principal components in the interest-rate world as shifts, twists, and so on, applies only to forward rates. In energy markets those correspond to logs of forward priers. A parallel shift in logs of forward prices is not related to the parallel shift in the forward prices. One must be careful not to confuse the two.

We now present an example of the model of the type (5.6).

EXAMPLE 5.2   *A multifactor model for energy derivatives*

For the simplest example of the HJM model, consider process (5.6)

$$\frac{dF_{t,T}}{F_{t,T}} = \sum_j \sigma_j(t,T) dW_t^j, \quad 0 \le t \le T \tag{5.7}$$

This equation can be explicitly integrated, which is the main attraction of these processes, and of the majority of processes considered in Chapter 4. The result is the expression for the forward curve at any time t:

$$F_{t,T} = F_{0,T} \exp\left\{ \sum_j \left[-\frac{1}{2} \int_0^t \sigma_j^2(u,T) du + \int_0^t \sigma_j(u,T) dW_t^j \right] \right\} \tag{5.8}$$

Note that this equality ensures matching the initial forward curve at $t = 0$, since this curve is the initial condition for process (5.7).

Process (5.7), like any other forward price process, implies the process for the spot prices through the relation $S_t = F_{t,t}$. Using this relation together with (5.8), Clewlow and Strickland (1999) showed that the Schwartz (1997) model (also discussed in the section "Spot Price Processes and Forward Prices" in Chapter 4) is equivalent to a two-factor model such as (5.7) with

$$\sigma_1(t,T) = \sigma_1 - \rho\sigma_2\frac{1 - e^{-\kappa(T-t)}}{\kappa}$$

$$\sigma_2(t,T) = -\sigma_2\sqrt{1 - \rho^2}\frac{1 - e^{-\kappa(T-t)}}{\kappa} \tag{5.9}$$

The first perturbation function $\sigma_1(t,T)$ represents a parallel shift—it is a decaying function, with the rate of decay dependent on a parameter κ. The smaller this parameter the closer the perturbation is to a true parallel shift. The second perturbation $\sigma_2(t,T)$ represents twist—zero at the beginning of the curve and nonzero at the end.

We pause here to make an important observation. Although Schwartz's spot model is explicitly mean-reverting, there is no explicit modeling of mean reversion in the forward curve model. The explanation is simple: The mean reversion of spot prices is a natural consequence of the decaying shape of the principal perturbations of the forward curve, with the strength of the mean reversion dependent on the rate of decay. So we can conclude that the phenomenon we usually call mean reversion of spot prices can also be captured through the time dependence of the forward volatility term structure (specifically, the decay of the implied volatility curve).

One of our main concerns with respect to processes such as (5.3), (5.6), or (5.7) is that once the perturbation functions are chosen, they automatically induce the correlation structure between different contracts along the forward curve.

Consider an example of (5.7) with one random shock function:

$$dF_{t,T} = \sigma(t,T)F_{t,T}dW_t$$

For any two points T_1 and T_2, the correlation coefficient between $\log F_{t,T_1}$ and $\log F_{t,T_2}$ is

$$\rho(t,T_1,T_2) = 1$$

In the case of two shock functions

$$dF_{t,T} = \sigma_1(t,T)F_{t,T}dW_t^1 + \sigma_2(t,T) F_{t,T}dW_t^2 \tag{5.10}$$

the correlation coefficient between $\log F_{t,T_1}$ and $\log F_{t,T_2}$ is

$$\rho(t,T_1,T_2) = \frac{\sigma_1(t,T_1)\sigma_1(t,T_2) + \sigma_2(t,T_1)\sigma_2(t,T_2)}{\sqrt{\sigma_1^2(t,T_1) + \sigma_2^2(t,T_1)}\sqrt{\sigma_1^2(t,T_2) + \sigma_2^2(t,T_2)}}$$

EXAMPLE 5.3   *Induced correlation structure*

Assume that the forward curve evolution is governed by (5.10) with perturbation functions of the form (5.9), the parallel shift is

$$\sigma_1(t,T) = a - b(1 - e^{-\alpha(T-t)})$$

The twist is

$$\sigma_2(t,T) = c(1 - e^{-\alpha(T-t)})$$

Then

$$\rho(t,T_1,T_2) =$$

$$\frac{a^2 - ab(2 - e^{-\alpha(T_1-t)} - e^{-\alpha(T_2-t)}) + (b^2 + c^2)(1 - e^{-\alpha(T_1-t)})(1 - e^{-\alpha(T_2-t)})}{\sqrt{a^2 - 2ab(1 - e^{-\alpha(T_1-t)}) + (b^2 + c^2)(1 - e^{-\alpha(T_1-t)})^2}\sqrt{a^2 - 2ab(1 - e^{-\alpha(T_2-t)}) + (b^2 + c^2)(1 - e^{-\alpha(T_2-t)})^2}}$$

It is clear that the shock functions chosen in this example capture certain qualitative characteristics of the futures prices: decrease of the correlation with the increase of the distance between contracts, and the increase of the correlation coefficients as the time t approaches the first expiration date. On the other hand, this example demonstrates that with the choice of perturbation functions comes the fixing of the correlation structure between different parts of the forward curve. This lack of flexibility in imposing a correlation structure may be dangerous in pricing certain derivatives, such as storage, since they are known to be very sensitive to a small perturbation of correlation coefficients.

One way to achieve this flexibility is to increase the number of shock functions in (5.7), but this requires even more historical data, making it unrealistic for energy models. Another approach is to enhance the available data set by adding to it the forward-looking market data. In this approach the market data, rather than being simply used for testing historical analysis and as a target of calibration, becomes an integral part of the model itself.

MARKET MODELS

The HJM model we considered earlier specifies the evolution of the continuum of forward contracts for all the possible expirations. Since most of these contracts are not traded in the markets, instead of building models for nonexistent products, it is natural to try to develop a version of the HJM model that specifies the dynamics only for tradable contracts. The dynamics would be then described by the following equation:

$$dF_{t,k} = \sum_j \sigma_j(t, j, F_{t,k}) dW_t^j, \quad 0 \le t \le T \tag{5.11}$$

where $F_{t,k} \equiv F_{t,T_k}$ is the $k-$th tradable forward contract.

This structure defines the market models. A detailed description of market models in the interest-rate world can be found in Brace, Gatarek, and Musiela (1997). The volatility functions in (5.11) are specific to the contracts in question. The random factors dW_t^j follow standard Brownian motion and are uncorrelated. If the volatility and drift functions are linear functions of the forward prices, (5.11) can be rewritten as

$$\frac{dF_{t,k}}{F_{t,k}} = \sum_{j=1}^J \eta_{j,k}(t) dW_t^j, \quad k = 1, \ldots, K \tag{5.12}$$

This is obviously a multivariate GBM representation of the forward curve dynamics.

If the number of common (uncorrelated) factors J, is equal to the number of contracts K, then we can represent the dynamics of the forward curve by using K-correlated contract-specific factors:

$$\frac{dF_{t,k}}{F_{t,k}} = v_k(t) d\tilde{W}_{t,k}, \quad k = 1, \ldots, K \tag{5.13}$$

where the factors

$$d\tilde{W}_{t,kM}$$

are governed by the standard Brownian motion. For any t and an index pair k_1, k_2 they satisfy a given correlation condition

$$E(d\widetilde{W}_{t,k_1}, d\widetilde{W}_{t,k_2}) = \rho(t,k_1,k_2)$$

These are the discrete string models. A general study of string models can be found in Kennedy (1997).

The market models and discrete string models are equivalent only under joint lognormality and if the number of factors is chosen to be the same in both cases. Even though we arrived at the string models as a variation on the original HJM formalism, those models in our opinion are frequently superior to their predecessors, especially in some energy markets.

Unlike the other models, the factors in string models are *directly observable* in historical data, and the parameters of the distribution can be directly implied from other available contracts (e.g., forward ATM and OTM options). In principle, we can extract forward-looking information about the parameters of the models for the other representations as well. However, empirical estimation using both historical and forward-looking information becomes much more complex.

If we have enough data, and we *know* that the forward contracts are jointly lognormally distributed, then it doesn't matter which representation we choose. However, if any of those conditions fail, string models are the only natural choice, because they offer us direct access to the driving factors without data-intensive transformations of the representation. This is especially pertinent when we do not have a significant amount of historical data, as with power forward markets.

Even if we have enough data, the equivalence between representations fails in the presence of volatility skews and smiles (see Chapter 4). Principal component techniques generally apply only to jointly normal (lognormal variables). In the presence of stochastic volatility or jumps, those methods are only an approximation that can be very misleading (see Wolyniec, 2001). Again, power forward contracts exhibit substantial nonnormalities (see Chapter 3 and 4); therefore techniques such as the method of principal components should be used with caution. Pronounced smiles are present in natural gas and crude oil forward markets, suggesting that principal factor techniques (and any models with common factors, for example, HJM) must be carefully investigated before implementing.

Given the limitation of market models (and HJM), it is usually advisable to use string models, especially for structures for which the smile effects are nontrivial (OTM swaptions, multiperiod swing options, and so on; see Chapter 8). The estimation and representation advantages of string models should be weighed against the models with only a small number of common factors, since these have clear computational advantages. For example, using a small number of common factors (as we did in Examples 5.1 and 5.2) to represent the movements of natural gas or oil forward curves seems to work well for standard structures.

IMPLEMENTATION OF MARKET MODELS FOR MULTI-COMMODITY CASES

We now apply the string model methodology to a multi-commodity case, since our goal is the development of processes that govern multi-fuel evolution to be used in the power models of the upcoming chapters. We know that the key characteristic of market models is the use of observed tradables as the model variables. Clearly, different markets have different tradables, but for energy applications we narrow the choice of variables to prices of monthly forward contracts.

Assume that we have N commodities (fuels). Consider now the i-th commodity. The evolution of monthly forward prices $F^i_{t,k}$ as a function of t, with k being the index of the forward contract, is given by the equation

$$dF^i_{t,k} = \sigma^i_k (t,T,F_{t,k})d\tilde{W}^i_{t,k}, \quad t \geq 0, \quad i = 1,...,N, \ k = 1,..., K \ (5.14)$$

where again the factors $d\tilde{W}^i_{t,k}$ are governed by the standard Brownian motion and are correlated. The equation (5.14) also implies the evolution of the spot prices S^i_t of the i-th commodity via the relation

$$S^i_t = F^i_{t,t}, \tag{5.15}$$

To complete the model, we need to specify the initial conditions and the set of market data (market constraints) that will be used to calibrate the process parameters.

Initial Conditions

$$F^i_{0,k} \tag{5.16}$$

is the current forward curve for the commodity i, and $i = 1, \ldots, N$.

Market Constraints

For the risk-neutral evaluations it is required to match the following market data.

■ **The current forward curve:**

$$E(F_{t,k}^i) = F_{0,k}^i \text{ for every } t \geq 0 \qquad (5.17)$$

■ **Option prices:** A set of market data used for model calibration includes prices of options on monthly forward contracts:

$$C_M^i = C_B(F_{0,k}^i; T_k, X_k^i, r_k, \sigma_M^i) \qquad (5.18)$$

where C_M^i is a quoted option price of the i-th commodity, F_{0k}^i is the current price of the monthly forward contract on this commodity with T_k being its settlement time, X_k^i is the option strike, r_k is the risk-free rate, and σ_M^i is the volatility of the monthly forward prices. The current time is assumed to be $t = 0$. The option value is computed using Black's option pricing formula.

Note that in any given month there can be a number of monthly market option quotes corresponding to different strikes, although ATM option prices are quoted most frequently.

■ **Matching total correlation structure:** It is desirable to match correlations between log-returns for different forward contracts for the same commodity, as well as the correlations between different commodities. Therefore, for any two forward settlement times T_1 and T_2, and for any two commodities i and j we want to match the following correlation structure

$$\frac{E[d \log(F_{t,T_1}^i) \cdot d \log(F_{t,T_2}^j)]}{\sqrt{\text{var}[d \log(F_{t,T_1}^i)]} \sqrt{\text{var}[d \log(F_{t,T_2}^j)]}} = \rho^{i,j}(t,T_1,T_2) \qquad (5.19)$$

Lognormal Model of Multi-commodity Price Evolution: The Case of Monthly Prices

This example offers a particular implementation of the above model for monthly forward prices under the assumption that the governing process (5.14) is geometric Brownian motion. Assume that $T = (T_1, T_2, \ldots, T_K)$ is the set of expiration dates of the monthly forward contracts. The corresponding vector of monthly forward prices at time t for $i = 1, \ldots, N$ is denoted by

$$F_t = [F_{t,T_1}^1 \ldots F_{t,T_K}^1 \ F_{t,T_1}^2 \ldots F_{t,T_K}^2 \ldots F_{t,T_1}^N \ldots F_{t,T_K}^N]'$$

(As usual the apostrophe denotes transposition.) Since the governing process is GBM, the system of stochastic equations representing the evolution of the vector F_t is of the type (5.13) and can be written as

$$\frac{dF^i_{t,T_k}}{F^i_{t,T_k}} = \sigma^i(t,T_k)d\tilde{W}_{t,k}, \quad t \geq 0, \quad i = 1,\ldots,N, \quad k = 1,\ldots,K \quad (5.20)$$

The market conditions (5.16)–(5.19) impose the following constraints on the stochastic properties of the forward prices and their changes across all expiration times and all fuels.

1. Matching current forward prices.

$$E(F^i_{t,T_k}) = F^i_{0,T_k} \quad \text{for every } t \geq 0, \quad i = 1,\ldots,N, \quad k = 1,\ldots,K$$

where F^i_{0,T_k} is the term structure of the monthly forward prices at the current time $t = 0$.

2. Matching current option prices. In the lognormal case the option prices can be represented by the implied volatility (see Section 4.3.3). Our goal then is to find for each i and k a coefficient $\sigma^i(t,T_k)$ in (5.20) such that

$$\frac{1}{T_k - t}\int_t^{T_k} [\sigma^i(s, T_k)]^2 ds = \sigma^i_M(t,T_k)$$

where for every commodity i, $\sigma^i_M(t,T_k)$ is the implied volatility of the monthly options with expiration date T_k. (Typically, they are ATM calls or straddles, with the price of the monthly forward contract as the underlying variable.) Therefore,

$$[\sigma^i(t, T_k)]^2 = -\frac{\partial}{\partial t}\left\{T_k - t[\sigma^i_M(t,T_k)]^2\right\} \quad (5.21)$$

This approach provides the flexibility to handle a general implied volatility structure, even in a typically restrictive lognormal case. Indeed, it clearly allows us to introduce an arbitrary dependence of the implied volatility on T_k (seasonal term structure). Moreover, under a fairly general assumption about the growth rate of the implied volatility as a function of the time to expiration, it captures the dependence of the implied volatility of a given forward contract on t (Samuelson effect).

3. Matching the correlation structure. The condition (5.19) requires that for each $t \geq 0$ we match the given matrix of correlation coefficients

$$\frac{E(d \log F^i_{t,T_k} \cdot d \log F^j_{t,T_l})}{\sqrt{\text{var}(d \log F^i_{t,T_k})}\sqrt{\text{var}(d \log F^j_{t,T_l})}} = \rho^{i,j}(t,T_k,T_l) \equiv R^{i,j}_{k,l} \quad (5.22)$$

$$i, j = 1, \ldots, N, \quad k,l = 1, \ldots, K$$

This equality specifies a covariance matrix for the changes in logarithms of forward prices for all expiration dates and all commodities.

Thus, the equations (5.21) and (5.22) specify a variance-covariance structure that must be matched at every step of process (5.20) governing the evolution of the forward prices. Appendix A shows how to implement the Monte Carlo procedure to simulate the paths of the stochastic process, while enforcing a given covariance structure.

CHAPTER 6

Correlation

It is well known that correlation is a crucial quantity in the valuation of many energy derivatives and assets. The canonical example is the spark-spread option: the option on the spread between power and fuel prices, most commonly gas prices. In the Black-Scholes world (see Chapter 8), there exists a closed-form formula for the valuation of this option (developed by Margrabe, 1978). It requires the usual inputs: current prices, term of the option, discount rates, volatilities, and most crucially the correlation between the two. We have discussed at length the other inputs to the model, and by now we should have a good grasp on what those should be—with one exception, the correlation. What correlation should we use? Unlike with volatility, we do not usually have liquid markets in correlation, so we cannot rely on implied correlation for input.

In Chapter 3 we showed a number of graphs illustrating the unstable character of correlations over time. In this chapter we discuss whether instability is important, what numbers we should use for correlations, and how to find those numbers when pricing and hedging energy derivatives and contracts.

As is the case with volatilities and other parameters of marginal distribution, we face a serious problem of limited data, coupled with the nonstationarity of the little data we do have. Furthermore, the applicability of historically derived correlations to future conditions is often quite limited.

When analyzing correlation we must bear in mind that it cannot be done independently from analyzing volatility.

BASIC FACTS

Definition

The standard definition of linear correlation is given by the following formula:

$$\rho = \frac{\text{cov}(X, Y)}{\sqrt{\text{var}(X)}\sqrt{\text{var}(Y)}} = \frac{E[XY] - E[X]E[Y]}{\sqrt{E[X^2] - E[X]^2}\sqrt{E[Y^2] - E[Y]^2}} \quad (6.1)$$

The range of possible values covers the interval $[-1, 1]$.

Range of Applicability

Correlation is the proper measure of dependence between two random variables for a limited set of joint distributions. These include joint normal, lognormal, *t*, *F*, chi-2, and a number of others—the so-called elliptical family of joint distributions.

It is often loosely stated that correlation is not an appropriate measure of dependence for distributions with fat tails. Strictly speaking this is not correct, as shown by the example of the *t* distribution. However, there is a kernel of truth in this statement. We don't have space in our book to treat this subject systematically in any depth, but we will address it to some degree in the rest of the chapter. The excellent book by Nelsen (1999) and papers by Embrechts (1997) offer a good introduction.

The possible values of correlation depend on the distributions of the variables we try to correlate. For example, if we calculate the correlation between a normal and lognormal variable, the maximum and minimum possible correlations are less than 1 and more than −1, respectively. Additionally, the bounds—so-called Frechet bounds (see Nelsen, 1999)—depend on the parameters of the marginal distributions (i.e., normal and lognormal). With increasing volatilities of the individual legs of the correlation relationship, the admissible set of correlation narrows more closely around zero. In the limit, the only possible correlation is zero. It is important to understand, however, that low correlations do not necessarily imply weak dependence. The maximum possible correlation corresponds to the perfect (positive) dependence. By "perfect dependence," we mean the ability to express one variable as a deterministic function of the other.

The above example can be dismissed with the comment that this behavior of correlation was only the result of an improper choice of variables to analyze. If we start by looking at the correlation between the normal variable and the logarithm of the lognormal variable, the whole problem disappears. This is true for the specific example, but we face a practical problem of not knowing what the transformation should be. This points to the necessity of understanding the marginal distribution before we attempt any correlation analysis. As we know from previous chapters, this problem is far from trivial. Consider the following example.

EXAMPLE 6.1 *Correlations under stochastic volatility*

We are analyzing oil and natural gas forward prices to determine the value of a spread option between the two (see Chapter 8). One of the parameters needed for valuation is the correlation between the prices (returns). Assume that natural gas prices follow a geometric Brownian motion (GBM), while oil prices follow the Hull-White stochastic volatility process (see Chapter 4).

If the model correlation parameter between the returns is 90%, what correlation will we observe (use the standard formula [6.1])? Assuming the volatilities are both 50%, the observed correlation will be 80%; the higher the volatility of volatility, the lower observed correlation will be.

To properly estimate the correlation, we need to scale our observation by the stochastic volatility. The procedure is exactly the transformation we talked about above. As we know, fitting the proper process for the evolution of individual prices, and consequently finding the transformation, is a challenge (see Chapters 3 and 4).

As serious as this may sound, we must ask whether the problem significantly impacts valuation and hedging considerations. What happens if we just ignore all those issues, estimate correlation directly, insert it into the Black-Scholes formula for spread options, and use appropriate implied volatilities to price our structure? The answer is that, surprisingly, this simple procedure is likely to work reasonably well. We will expand on this point in the second part of the chapter.

As we saw, we face the practical problem of finding the appropriate change of variables by which to measure correlations. However, we are potentially exposed to a more fundamental problem: *this transformation might not exist at all* (see Nelsen, 1999). This reflects the fact that in many cases, joint distribution cannot be described by correlation. The fact that correlation is not an appropriate measure can also manifest itself in other ways. For example, for certain distinctions, large differences in correlation do not imply large differences in the dependence structure. Consider the following example.

Two main conclusions emerge from the analysis in this section:

1. For nonlinear relationships, low correlation does not imply weak dependence. (This is simply a generalization of the well-known fact that correlation between a symmetrically distributed variable and its square is zero).
2. Observed correlation can be a function of the parameters of the marginal distributions (e.g. volatilities, etc.), and we may not be able to rectify the problem by changing variables, either for practical or more fundamental reasons.

The second issue may be very pertinent in energy markets, where we are faced with extreme volatilities.

The above analysis may seem a bit beside the point. After all, as we explained in the introduction to the chapter, the gravest challenge in dealing with correlation lies in its temporal instability. But there is a connection: As we noted, observed correlation depends on the parameters of the marginal distributions, and those, in turn, are known to evolve over time.

Consequently, under certain circumstances, the explanation for the instability can be found in the set of facts analyzed in the previous paragraphs.

Conditional Correlation: Time Evolution

Figure 3.26 showed us that correlation changes over time. The evolution can be due to the following four factors:

- Change in conditional correlation (i.e., the correlation coefficient is time-dependent or stochastic)
- Covariance nonstationarity of the underlying processes (i.e., unconditional correlation does not exist)
- Nonlinear dependence structure
- Estimation noise

Any or all of these factors can generate the patterns of correlation we saw in the graphs in Chapter 3.

From the fundamental analysis of the underlying process of price formation in energy markets (see Chapter 7), we expect that the correlation between prices will not be constant. We therefore expect time dependence of the conditional correlation.

Covariance nonstationarity is unlikely to be the culprit (see Alexander, 2001, for the overview of testing techniques) since the correlated time series are themselves stationary.

Nonlinear dependence is likely to be present. However determining its exact structure can be a challenge. We address this issue later in this chapter.

Estimation noise is a pervasive problem when estimating correlation. In energy markets, the limited availability of data seriously impedes the application of the standard econometric techniques. The next section addresses this issue in detail.

Estimation

The standard estimator of the unconditional correlation is given by the following formula:

$$\hat{\rho}_{x,y} = \frac{\dot{\text{cov}}(x,y)}{\hat{\sigma}_x \hat{\sigma}_y} = \frac{\frac{1}{N}\sum_{i=1}^{N}(x_i - \hat{x})(y_i - \hat{y})}{\hat{\sigma}_x \hat{\sigma}_y}$$

$$\hat{\sigma}_x^2 = \frac{1}{N-1}\sum_{i=1}^{N}(x_i - \hat{x})^2 \tag{6.2}$$

$$\hat{\sigma}_y^2 = \frac{1}{N-1}\sum_{i=1}^{N}(y_i - \hat{y})^2$$

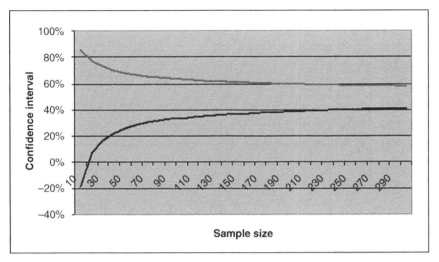

FIGURE 6.1 Confidence Intervals for Correlation Estimate of 50%

The 95% confidence interval for correlation is given by the following Fisher z transformation:

$$\underline{\rho} = \frac{e^{2\underline{z}} - 1}{e^{2\underline{z}} + 1}; \qquad \underline{z} = \hat{z} - \frac{1.96}{\sqrt{N - 3}}$$

$$\overline{\rho} = \frac{e^{2\overline{z}} - 1}{e^{2\overline{z}} + 1}; \qquad \overline{z} = \hat{z} + \frac{1.96}{\sqrt{N - 3}} \qquad (6.3)$$

$$\hat{z} = \frac{1}{2}\ln\left(\frac{1 + \hat{\rho}}{1 - \hat{\rho}}\right)$$

Figures 6.1 and 6.2 show the size of the 95% confidence interval for the estimate of a correlation of .5 and .9 for different sample sizes.

Figure 6.1 and Figure 6.2 clearly indicate that for relatively low estimates of correlations (around 50%, typical for an oil-gas relationship), a reliable sample requires hundreds of data points. The situation for higher estimated correlation may seem better, but in practice this is not the case. The major use of correlation analysis is in the valuation of multi-commodity derivatives. The sensitivity of those structures to correlation is highest at high correlation levels (see Chapter 8). Consequently, even though the confidence bounds for higher correlation seem tighter in absolute terms, they are not much better in relative terms.

The wide confidence intervals make analysis of the evolution of conditional correlation a very challenging undertaking. If we use rolling window estimates of the conditional correlation, we need to use an averaging period

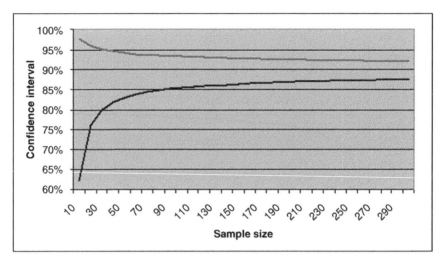

FIGURE 6.2   Confidence Intervals for Correlation Estimate of 90%

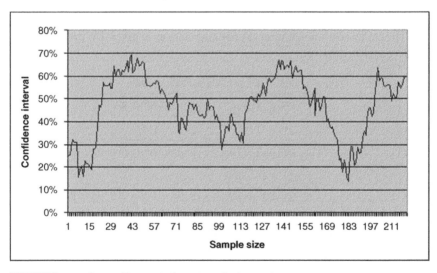

FIGURE 6.3   30-day Rolling Window Correlation Estimate

(the window) hundreds of observations long. (The situation is not much better if we use exponential smoothing). This means that we can only attempt to analyze seasonal changes in correlations. An attempt to drill down to finer time resolutions will be overwhelmed by noise. To make the concept more tangible, consider Figure 6.3.

It may seem that we are able to distinguish some seasonal correlation structure in the sample with correlations switching between the high and low level. However, all we are seeing is noise. The underlying sample is in fact a simulated one with a fixed correlation of 50%. The true correlation is constant throughout the sample.

Therefore we must analyze the data with some model in mind—hopefully motivated by some fundamental considerations. It is usually not possible to try to estimate complex multidimensional models with a fine time structure. There are exceptions to this rule. At times we can perform aggregation of the available data to increase the size of the sample and then test whether the aggregation leads to biases (see Scott and Wolyniec, 2002).

We will also shortly see that estimation of correlation cannot be separated from estimation of volatility. We can easily show that if volatility is not constant in the sample, the correlation estimate will be biased. However, this bias may not be a problem, and under certain circumstances, it can be very useful.

To analyze the interaction of correlation and volatility in a fruitful way, we must analyze a specific model, which obviously requires explicit assumptions about the behavior of the quantities we are interested in. As we will see in later chapters, making explicit assumptions might not be as limiting as it sounds, if the goal of the exercise is to use liquid contracts to hedge exposures or, equivalently, to sell risk along with assumptions about risk.

In the next sections we analyze the issue of estimation of correlation in the context of specific models. Armed with an understanding of the behavior of this correlation, we address the issue of relating correlation behavior to that of volatility in a more general setting.

Concepts of Correlation: Return versus Level Correlations

Thus far we have not been explicit about what variables are being measured by the correlations we are discussing. As we indicated in the previous section the choice of the variables can make all the difference. The standard practice in financial markets is to look at correlations between returns or logarithmic returns (return correlations):

$$\left(\frac{P_{t+1} - P_t}{P_t}, \frac{G_{t+1} - G_t}{G_t} \right)$$

$$\left[\ln\left(\frac{P_{t+1}}{P_t}\right), \ln\left(\frac{G_{t+1}}{G_t}\right) \right] \tag{6.4}$$

This is so primarily because of the standard models used in financial markets, which are expressed in terms of correlations of returns and related variables (e.g., geometric Brownian motion; see Chapter 4). The deeper reason for using return correlations and not, for example, price correlations or log price correlations is the fact that price-time series in financial markets are not stationary (neither variance nor covariance are nonstationary). Nonstationarity means roughly that volatilities and/or covariances grow without limit in time.

The fact that unconditional volatility or covariance is infinite in limit renders the concept of correlation meaningless.

In energy markets, we suspect that spot prices are stationary (mean-reverting). In principle, then, we could perform correlation analysis directly on prices. It turns out that it is still convenient to use return analysis. The motivation for that choice is twofold:

- **Convenience:** We can still formulate processes in terms of returns even for mean-reverting processes (we will see examples shortly).
- **Distributional choices:** Correlations are naturally defined for pairs of distributions of the same type. Since we often assume that the return process is normal (or a transformation of a normal variable), the natural choice of variables requires returns.
- **Autocorrelation structure:** For the simple models, the returns are sometimes not autocorrelated. Even for more complex models, it is easier to deal with the autocorrelation of returns than with prices.

The concept of correlation is specific to the model we assume for the representation of individual processes.

Consider a pair of processes that are correlated geometric Brownian motions:

$$\frac{ds}{s} = \mu_s dt + \sigma_s(t)dW_t^s$$

$$\frac{dg}{g} = \mu_g dt + \sigma_g(t)dW_t^g \tag{6.5}$$

$$dW_t^g dW_t^s = \rho(t)dt$$

Note that the volatilities and correlation in (6.5) can be stochastic processes themselves.

The quantity $\rho(t)$ is the *local* (*instantaneous*) correlation between the two processes. We can also define the *average* correlation by the following expression:

$$\rho_t^T = \frac{\displaystyle\int_t^T \rho(s)ds}{T - t} \tag{6.6}$$

And we can define the *terminal* (or *cumulative*) log correlation by the following expression:

$$\rho_{T;t}^* = \rho_{\ln s_T, \ln g_T} = \frac{E_t[\ln s_T \ln g_T] - E_t[\ln s_T]E_t[\ln g_T]}{\sqrt{\mathrm{var}_t[\ln s_T]}\sqrt{\mathrm{var}_t[\ln g_T]}} \tag{6.7}$$

Finally, we can define *implied correlation*. The concept is analogous to implied volatility we met in previous chapters. Obviously, implied correlation can have different meaning depending on what structure we use to extract the value from. As the canonical structure is a spread option, we will define implied correlation as the value of the correlation parameter used in the Black-Scholes valuation of spread options (i.e., the Margrabe model; see Chapter 8) that makes the value of the spread option equal to the value given independently after accounting for implied volatility. The "given independently" qualifier may refer to market quotes or valuations determined by some more complex models.

Next we will consider which of the above concepts is useful, and in what context.

Concepts of Correlation: Structured Products and Correlation

We use correlations for three main purposes:

- Pricing and hedging of non–path-dependent European options
- Pricing and hedging of path-dependent European options and American options
- VaR calculations

Non–Path-dependent European Options

The value of a two-asset non–path-dependent option can be expressed as follows:

$$V_t = DF \cdot E_t \left[f \left(X_T, Y_T \right) \right] \tag{6.8}$$

Where

DF is the discount factor

$f(,)$ is payoff function

X_T is the terminal value of the X process

Y_T is the terminal value of the Y process

Clearly the correlation of interest to us is the one between the terminal distributions, since we can easily see from the definition of the valuation problems that the only quantity affecting the value of the structure in question is the joint distribution of terminal prices.

Given those two facts, the correlation we need to find is the cumulative correlation. For the lognormal and related cases the joint distribution is fully described by the correlation of logs. Notice also that hedges also depend only on the cumulative correlation.

European Path-dependent and American Options

For path-dependent and American options, the situation is much more complex than for all the other cases. Depending on the payoff, the multivariate path-dependent option will depend nontrivially on the whole path of volatility and local correlation. We usually cannot describe the dependence structure by one parameter. In some cases, we can derive a satisfactory approximation where cumulative correlations and volatilities will play a role.

VaR Calculations

It is easy to show that the correlation needed for VaR correlation is again the cumulative correlation, as long as we are dealing with lognormal variables. However, the integration period will tend to be very short compared to the cumulative correlation used for valuation and hedging. VaR calculations usually involve price movements over 5- or 10-day periods. The cumulative correlation for such short periods tends to be close to the local correlation. In turn, the correlation for contracts with expiration longer than a couple of weeks will usually differ substantially from the cumulative correlation. This consideration leads us to develop two types of correlations: one for valuation and hedging and another one for VaR.

DETERMINISTIC COVARIANCE MATRIX

We start by first considering volatility and correlation depending—at worst, only deterministically—on time. We deal explicitly with models related to basic geometric Brownian motion. Obviously, these assumptions are quite restrictive and probably unrealistic in the energy markets. However, the issues arising from estimation of correlation and of volatility for the deterministic case are sufficiently complex as it is. To bring out the relevant structure, it's sufficient at this stage to consider the simpler case. We discuss its extension to stochastic volatility and correlation in the second part of the chapter. The additional complexity engendered by the stochastic character of the covariance matrix would obscure the issues that are quite clear at this point. Also, it's worth noting here that, in the stochastic case, the very concepts of correlation and volatility are unclear, as is the value of estimating them.

Correlation and the covariance matrix might not be sufficient to describe the joint behavior of the variables of interest to us. However, before we jump into an analysis of correlation in its full stochastic bloom, we will limit ourselves first to the nontrivial consequences of the time dependence of correlation and volatility. As it happens, for derivatives on fuel futures contracts such as natural gas and crude oil, the choice of models of this kind seems to be a reasonable description of reality at least as first approximation.

The starting point of the analysis should be the realization that estimating correlation is intimately connected with estimating volatility. This forces us to understand the behavior of volatility before we can approach the problem of analyzing correlation. Usually data shows the whole covariance matrix; the separation into volatility and correlation might not be straightforward, despite the importance of the task.

This is especially vexing, because we tend to have different sources of information for the different elements of the covariance matrix. The markets generally offer us forward-looking information about cumulative volatility, but to understand the conditional volatility structure and correlation, we must rely on historical time series. The challenge is to use the information from the disparate sources in an efficient and *meaningful* way.

Cumulative Correlation: Explicit Formula

As we explained, when valuing and hedging European options, the crucial quantity is the terminal, or cumulative, correlation. Under the assumptions of this section, we can derive an explicit expression for cumulative correlation (6.7).

The covariance term is given by the following (assuming that X and Y follow process (6.5):

$$E[\ln X_T \ln Y_T] - E[\ln X_T]E[\ln Y_T] =$$

$$E\left[\left(-\frac{\int \sigma_X^2(t)dt}{2} + \int \sigma_X(t)dW_t^X\right)\left(-\frac{\int \sigma_Y^2(t)dt}{2} + \int \sigma_Y(t)dW_t^Y\right)\right] -$$

$$E\left[-\frac{\int \sigma_Y^2(t)dt}{2} + \int \sigma_X(t)dW_t^X\right]E\left[-\frac{\int \sigma_Y^2(t)dt}{2} + \int \sigma_Y(t)dW_t^Y\right] =$$

$$E\left[\int \sigma_X(t)dW_t^X \int \sigma_Y(t)dW_t^Y\right] = E\left[\int \sigma_X(t)\sigma_Y(t)\rho(t)dt\right] = \int \sigma_X(t)\sigma_Y(t)\rho(t)dt$$

$$(6.9)$$

The first equality follows from Ito's lemma. The second follows from the standard properties of stochastic integration. The third follows from Ito's isometry (see Oksendal, 1998). In a similar manner, we can derive the expression for the volatilities in the denominator. Putting it all together, we get the following expression for the correlation of the terminal logarithms:

$$\rho_{T,t}^* = \frac{\displaystyle\int_t^T \sigma_X(s)\sigma_Y(s)\rho(s)ds}{\displaystyle\sqrt{\int_t^T \sigma_X^2(s)ds}\,\sqrt{\int_t^T \sigma_Y^2(s)ds}} \qquad (6.10)$$

The *T,t* indices indicate that the correlation depends on the expiration and evaluation time.

We have derived the formula for the case of "time-dependent" geometric Brownian motion. The result can be easily extended to the case of a mean-reverting process (in the logarithms), with a similar form of expression for the cumulative correlation:

$$\rho^*_{T,t} = \frac{\int e^{(\alpha_X + \alpha_Y)s}\sigma_X(s)\sigma_Y(s)\rho(s)ds}{\sqrt{\int e^{2\alpha_X s}\sigma_X^2(s)ds}\sqrt{\int e^{2\alpha_Y s}\sigma_Y^2(s)ds}} \tag{6.11}$$

where αs are the mean-reversion rates.

Obviously, the structural similarities for the two cases flow from the fact that both terminal price distributions will be lognormal. For other processes that do not contain irreducible stochasticity of volatility and correlation, such as mean reversion in price, CEV or GARCH processes, the situation is more complicated. We discuss these in later sections.

Given these facts, it seems reasonable to concentrate the estimation effort on the cumulative correlations and volatilities, since they should be sufficient to describe the relevant joint distributions.

Cumulative Correlation: Estimation

Before we proceed to the issues of estimation, it is worthwhile to focus for a moment on the properties of cumulative correlation. The insights gained here will illuminate estimation issues.

Properties of Cumulative Correlation

The following properties will be of interest later on:

$$\lim_{t \to T} \rho^*_{T,t} = \rho(T)$$

if

$$\sigma_X = \sigma_Y = const$$

$$\rho^*_{T,t} = \frac{\int_t^T \rho(s)ds}{T - t}$$

if

$$\rho(s) = \rho = const \tag{6.12}$$

$$|\rho^*_{T,t}| \leq |\rho|$$

and if

$$\frac{\sigma_X(t)}{\sigma_Y(t)} \neq const$$

$$|\rho^*_{T,t}| < |\rho|$$

TABLE 6.1 Cumulative Correlation

Regime	Length (days)	Local volatility 1 (annualized)	Local volatility 2 (annualized)	Local correlation	Cumulative correlation
1	325	20%	20%	100%	100%
2	10	20%	30%	100%	100%
3	10	20%	40%	100%	98%
4	10	20%	50%	100%	96%
5	10	20%	60%	100%	93%

The first property indicates that for small intervals, cumulative correlation is close to local correlation. This has a direct applicability to our analysis of VaR; it suggests that VaR analysis requires local correlation, while pricing and hedging requires cumulative correlation.

The second property shows that if volatilities are constant, the cumulative correlation is just the average correlation. Finally, the third property shows that if local correlation is constant, then the absolute value of cumulative correlation is no greater than the absolute value of the local correlation. The strict inequality follows if the ratio of volatilities is not constant.

As shown above, cumulative correlation is significantly affected by the presence of rapidly varying ratio of local volatilities. In those situations, even if local correlation is constant, it is crucial to understand the behavior of volatilities. Energy markets tend to exhibit a strong Samuelson effect: volatility decreases with time to expiration (see Chapter 3). This suggests that the differences between local constant correlations and cumulative correlations will be nontrivial—and this is indeed the case.

Consider the example in Table 6.1 of two variables that are (locally) perfectly correlated. One of the volatilities runs up at the end of the term. The effect is that the cumulative correlation for the whole period (1 year) drops from 100% to 93%. As a result, the value of an ATM spread option would double.

Estimating Cumulative Correlation

The usual procedure for estimation of correlation involves choosing a certain subset of historical data, forming a suitably scaled time series of returns, and calculating correlation on the sample thus formed. It is often assumed that this procedure results in a proper estimate of local correlations. However, this is true only under very special circumstances.

We can show that the estimated correlation is an unbiased and consistent estimate of the cumulative correlation realized in the historical subsample. To be more precise, let's introduce the following notation: t_1 and t_2 are the beginning and ending times, respectively, of the sample and $\hat{\rho}_N$ is the empirical estimate of correlation with N pairs of data points. Then we have:

$$E[\hat{\rho}_N] = \rho^*_{t_2, t_1}$$

$$\lim_{N \to \infty} \hat{\rho}_N = \rho^*_{t_2, t_1}$$

(6.13)

This shows that the standard procedure can arrive at the correct correlation if the behavior of local volatilities and correlations in the time period chosen corresponds to the future behavior of correlations and volatilities. However, this procedure can be highly misleading. If we estimate the cumulative correlation in the time period with slowly varying correlation and volatilities, then we are likely to get a good estimate of the local correlation. But this is wholly inadequate if we use the estimate to value derivatives with maturities extending over time periods with variable relative volatilities.

For example, consider natural gas futures contracts. It is well documented that volatilities tend to increase significantly in the last month or two of trading (see Chapter 3). This suggests that we should never try to estimate correlation for pricing derivatives without including the final months of the life of the contract in the sample; the last two months tend to have a significant effect on the estimate (see Table 6.1).

However, this does not tell us what time period to use. To properly weigh contributions from different volatility and correlation regimes, we should attempt to estimate from a sample covering the same time period as the one needed for valuation. There are several problems with this. First, it requires reestimating correlation continually as time to expiration shortens. Second, we might not have sufficient historical data to cover a wide choice of maturities. Finally, as is generally the case with historical data, we might be worried about the value of historical projections into the future. This last concern is all the more disconcerting, since we must make assumptions about future behavior not only of local correlations, but of local volatilities as well.

We can partially alleviate the last problem since, unlike with correlations, we tend to have some information about future volatility in the form of options quotes. However, for European options, the volatility implied from option prices is the cumulative volatility. On the other hand, it can be easily shown that the cumulative correlation does not depend on the total cumulative volatility, but only on the ratio of local volatilities. Consequently, the option quotes might be useless for the estimation process.

There are exceptions, however; for example, the use of forward-looking implied quotes can be useful, if the changes in implied volatilities reflect changes in the rate of change of local volatility with time. If higher cumulative volatility correlates with faster run-ups in the volatility with time to expiration, the forward quotes may be informative.

STOCHASTIC COVARIANCE MATRIX

We have seen the impact of changing volatilities on the use and estimation of correlation. Now we consider the impact of stochastic volatilities and correlations—driven by stochastic volatilities, jumps, nonlinearities, or other factors—on the estimation and application of correlation in pricing structured products. In principle we could approach the problem by assuming a sufficiently rich specification of the joint evolution of the variables in question, estimating it from available data and with the parameterization in hand, pricing and hedging whatever structure we are interested in.

This program turns out to be overly ambitious in many situations. We know that estimation of one-variable models with many factors presents a serious econometric and practical challenge. The problem is magnified when we attempt to extend the models to a multivariate setting.

We will quickly review the various extensions. The main thrust of our analysis is to see what qualitative impact the various considerations (jumps, etc.) have on the standard estimates of correlation, and whether those estimates—potentially biased or even misleading—can still be used in valuation of the popular multivariate structures. Our focus in the analysis of applicability is on spread options.

Stochastic Volatility

Consider a simple example of the valuation of a bivariate option:

$$V_t^B = e^{-r(T-t)} E_t^*[f(P_T, G_T)] \tag{6.14}$$

Assume that the evolution of the prices is given by the following:

$$\frac{dP}{P} = \mu_P dt + \sigma_P dW_t^P$$

$$\frac{d\sigma_P}{\sigma_P} = \alpha(t, \sigma_P)dt + \eta(t, \sigma_P)dW_t^{\sigma_P}$$

$$dW_t^{\sigma_P} dW_t^P = \rho_{\sigma p} dt \tag{6.15}$$

$$\frac{dG}{G} = \mu_G dt + \sigma_G dW_t^G$$

$$dW_t^G dW_t^P = \rho dt$$

$$dW_t^{\sigma_P} dW_t^G = \rho_{\sigma g} dt$$

We first analyze the version of the model where:

$$\rho_{\sigma p} = \rho_{\sigma g} = 0 \tag{6.16}$$

The p process is a stochastic volatility process, with volatility uncorrelated with p-returns, while the g process is a standard geometric Brownian motion.

We now analyze the impact of the stochastic volatility on the observed return correlation, and we also assume that the risk neutral drift of returns is zero. Given that the volatility and returns are not correlated, we can condition on realized volatility to get an expression for estimated correlation under stochastic volatility:

$$\sigma_T^{*;P} = \sqrt{\int_t^T (\sigma_s^P)^2 ds}$$

$$\sigma_T^{*;G} = \sqrt{\int_t^T (\sigma_s^G)^2 ds} \tag{6.17}$$

$$\text{cov}_t(\ln P_T, \ln G_T) = E_t[\text{cov}(\ln P_T, \ln G_T | \sigma_T^{*;P})] +$$

$$\text{cov}_t[E(\ln P_T | \sigma_T^{*;P}), E(\ln G_T | \sigma_T^{*;P})] =$$

$$E_t[\rho \sigma_T^{*;G} \sigma_T^{*;P}] + \text{cov}_t\left[\ln(P_0) - \frac{(\sigma_T^{*;P})^2}{2}, \ln G_0 - \frac{(\sigma_T^{*;G})^2}{2}\right] = \tag{6.18}$$

$$E_t[\rho \sigma_T^{*;G} \sigma_T^{*;P}] = \rho \sigma_T^{*;G} E_t(\sigma_T^{*;P})$$

We can express the covariance in terms of the local correlation, cumulative g volatility, and the expectation of the cumulative p volatility. The last quantity can be easily recovered from ATM option prices on P, since implied ATM volatility is an unbiased estimator of the expectation of volatility. (There is actually some slight downward bias, but in practice it is very small and can be safely ignored.)

To find the correlation we now need to find the individual variances:

$$\text{var}_t(\ln P_T) = E_t[\text{var}(\ln P_T | \sigma_T^{*;P})] + \text{var}_t[E(\ln P_T | \sigma_T^{*;P})] =$$

$$E_t[(\sigma_T^{*;P})^2] + \text{var}_t\left[\frac{(\sigma_T^{*;P})^2}{2}\right] \tag{6.19}$$

Since we have:

$$E_t[(\sigma_T^{*;P})^2] \geq E_t[\sigma_T^{*;P}]^2$$

$$\text{var}_t\left[\frac{(\sigma_T^{*;P})^2}{2}\right] \geq 0 \qquad (6.20)$$

then the cumulative correlation in the stochastic volatility case is always smaller than the cumulative correlation in the deterministic case, and also smaller than the local correlation:

$$\rho_{T,t}^* \leq \rho \qquad (6.21)$$

Note that the variance of variance term in (6.19) is related to the kurtosis of the return distribution. This gives us an idea of the magnitude of the adjustment by looking at the steepness of the volatility smile of the P options (if available).

The above analysis shows that the estimated (cumulative) correlation is smaller than the local correlation of the process (incidentally, the result explains Example 6.1). The crucial question at this stage is, can we use the estimated (biased) correlation in the valuation of our structures? We can reformulate this question in the following way: Given a spread option with a certain moneyness, can we follow the procedure below in estimating the value (and hedges) of the spread option?

1. Find appropriate implied volatilities for the moneyness of the spread option.
2. Estimate cumulative correlation directly with the standard procedure.
3. Put the values into an appropriate Black-Scholes–type formula (see Margrabe formula for spread options, Chapter 8).

The answer turns out to be positive. For the typical choices of parameters in power, gas, and oil markets, this procedure seems to work well. To illustrate, we present some numerical results in Table 6.2 from a simulation

TABLE 6.2 Hull-White ATM Implied Correlation

True correlation	Estimated correlation	Implied ATM correlation
90%	77%	79%
50%	43%	42%

TABLE 6.3 Heston ATM Implied Correlation

True correlation	Estimated correlation	Implied ATM correlation
90%	80%	79%
50%	44%	42%

of the bivariate Hull-White model (see Chapter 4). We compare estimated cumulative correlation to the implied correlation of spread options. We fit the individual legs of the bivariate Hull-White model to the observed forward volatility smiles (mainly of natural gas and oil, but also power, where available), and then run the model under various assumptions about the correlation(s) between the legs.

We can extend the previous analysis to the more general case of nonzero volatility correlations in (6.15) (see the Heston model in Chapter 4):

$$\rho_{\sigma p} \neq 0$$
$$\rho_{\sigma g} \neq 0 \tag{6.22}$$

Table 6.3 shows the results of simulation of bivariate Heston model.

The above results are for ATM spread options. We can also see that the procedure is broadly applicable for spread options with other strikes. The graphs in Figures 6.4 and 6.5 show the implied correlation skew for both the Hull-White and Heston model.

As we can see in Figure 6.4, there is some significant skew for a deep OTM spread option, especially for higher correlations. The implied correlation for a spread option 50% OTM is around 72% compared to the estimate of 77%. For the second case, the implied correlation for a 50% OTM option drops to 39% compared to the estimate of 43%.

We can see that the implied correlation skew is actually a frown for stochastic volatility models. The concavity of the shape is closely related to the convexity (the smile) of implied volatility generated by this kind of model. As stochastic volatility effectively increases the volatility of the spread, OTM (and ITM) implied correlations have to be lower than the ATM level to match up to the higher OTM (ITM) implied volatility. Note that this effect is in addition to the direct volatility smile effect.

In our calculations of implied correlations we account for the implied volatility level for the appropriate moneyness level (the next section will address those issues in detail). It might be surprising that it is not sufficient to adjust only for implied volatilities, and that further adjustments in implied correlations are necessary. The reason for this is that implied correlation captures the effect of the whole volatility smile, not just one point on the volatility curve.

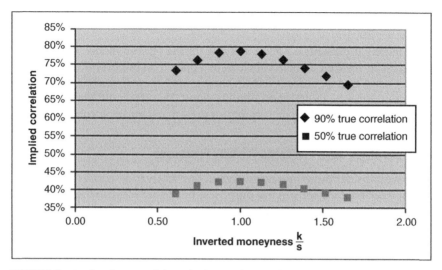

FIGURE 6.4   Hull-White Model Implied Correlation Skew As a Function of Inverted Moneyness

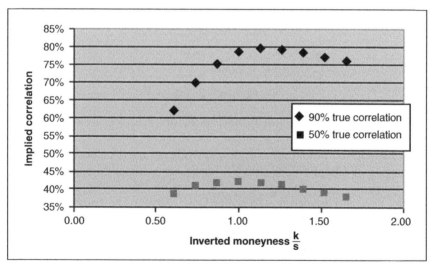

FIGURE 6.5   Heston Model Implied Correlation Skew

The lesson from this analysis is as follows. *To calculate the appropriate correlation in the presence of symmetric volatility smiles, we must first estimate the standard cumulative correlation on data. We can then use it directly for valuations of ATM spread options. For OTM or ITM options we must lower the correlation; the size of the adjustment should be proportional to the steepness of the volatility smile(s).* (For more formal analysis see Wolyniec, 2001.)

Figure 6.5 presents a similar analysis for the Heston model. As in Figure 6.4, we can see that similar conclusions apply. The important difference is the presence of a significant left (in-the-money) skew in correlation, which corresponds to the underlying volatility skew. This effect did not show up in the Hull-White model, since it cannot represent asymmetric volatility skew.

Jump and Mixed Jump-stochastic Volatility Processes

Next we consider jump processes. Again, our motivation is not to use a particular specification for pricing purposes, but to investigate the qualitative impact on estimation and pricing.

We use the affine jump-diffusion specification of the following form:

$$\frac{dP}{P} = \mu_P dt + \sigma_P dW_t^P + (Y^P - 1)dq_t^P$$

$$\frac{d\sigma_P}{\sigma_P} = \alpha(t,\sigma_P)dt + \eta(t,\sigma_P)dW_t^{\sigma P}$$

$$dW_t^{\sigma_P}dW_t^P = \rho_{\sigma_P}dt \qquad (6.23)$$

$$\frac{dG}{G} = \mu_G dt + \sigma_G dW_t^G + (Y^G - 1)dq_t^G$$

$$dW_t^G dW_t^P = \rho dt$$

$$dW_t^{\sigma_P}dW_t^G = \rho_{\sigma g}dt$$

Ys are stochastic amplitudes of jumps, while qs are the Poisson counting processes (see Chapter 4 for details). Jumps are assumed to be independent of the diffusive part of the process. (For more on affine jump-diffusion, see Duffie, Pan, and Singleton, 1999, and Deng, 1998.) The "affine" designation comes from the assumption that the drift and volatility functions are affine functions of prices and variances.

We continue the approach taken in the previous sections and consider an implied valuation example. In our model we have the long leg of the spread option modeled as an affine jump-diffusion model with stochastic volatility. The short side is modeled as a stochastic volatility process (Heston, 1993).

This setup roughly corresponds to the expected qualitative characteristics of power prices on the long side and a fuel, such as gas or oil, on the short side. The parameters of the model are again calibrated on the quoted volatility smiles. The results are compiled in Table 6.4.

TABLE 6.4 One-leg Mixed Jump-stochastic Volatility Models for ATM Implied Correlations

True correlation	Estimated correlation	Implied ATM correlation
90%	78%	74%
50%	43%	37%

TABLE 6.5 Two-leg Mixed Jump-stochastic Volatility Models for ATM Implied Correlations

True correlation	Estimated correlation	Implied ATM correlation
90%	67%	88%
50%	37%	64%

As we can see, the results are broadly similar to what we saw for the pure stochastic volatility models. However, this result is quite specific to the choice of representation; if we assumed that both legs of the option follow jump-diffusions, the results would be qualitatively different (see Table 6.5).

This result is not surprising. A jump component in the short leg is likely to lower the observed correlation further, however, it is also likely to decrease the value of the spread option. This has the consequence of increasing implied correlation. (Again, for formal results see Wolyniec, 2001.)

We can also compare the shape of implied correlation skews as shown in Figures 6.6 and 6.7. We can see that the shape of the implied correlation skew changes dramatically. In the money (ITM) options become much less valuable now, due to the possibility of a significant short jump that will bring the option OTM.

Therefore we can conclude: *The approximate procedure works also in the case of jump-diffusion models as long as the jumps are only on the long side of the spread.*

Multivariate GARCH Processes

An alternative specification of stochastic covariance models can be found through a large family of discrete time multivariate GARCH models. As we argued in Chapter 4, there is a connection between GARCH specifications and continuous time models. The Heston model is in fact the limit of the NGARCH model. The connections between multivariate volatility models and multivariate GARCH models are not straightforward, which is why we analyze those models as a separate topic from stochastic volatility.

The basic idea is to extend the concept of an ARMA (autoregressive moving average) process in squared innovations (GARCH)—or, in other words,

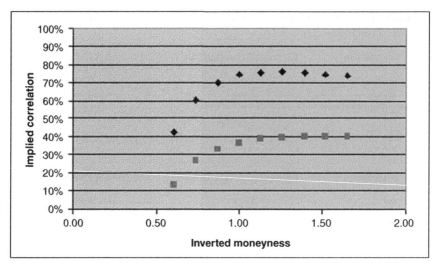

FIGURE 6.6   One-leg AJD Model Implied Correlation Skew

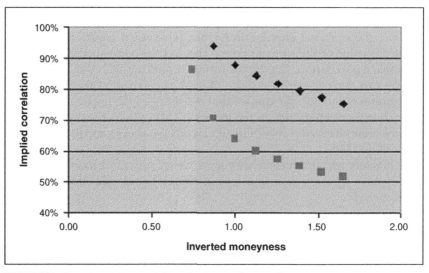

FIGURE 6.7   Two-leg AJD Model Implied Correlation Skew

to extend an ARMA process for the variance process to an ARMA process for the covariance matrix (see Chapter 4). We get the following expression:

$$\text{cov}_t(i,j) = a_{i,j} + \sum_{k \geq l} b_{k,l}\, \text{cov}_{t-1}(k,l) \tag{6.24}$$

As we can see, models of this type require a significant number of parameters; for the bivariate case we generally need 12 parameters. For more dimensions the number of parameters grows exponentially. There are a number of simplified versions of the general multivariate GARCH model that attempt to reduce the dimensionality by zeroing out certain parameters: diagonal models, constant conditional correlation models, BEKK models (based on spectral decomposition), and a host of others (see Gourieroux and Jasiak, 2001). Duffie (1998) presents some estimation results for energy markets. In our limited experience with those models, we found them quite unstable, with significant problems with estimation. In fact, in many cases we found them to be a poorer fit, both in-sample and out-of-sample, than simple univariate GARCH models.

Conditional Volatility and Correlation Models

The previous sections have used models that worked under the assumption that the true dependence structure is described by correlation (possibly varying deterministically with time). The fact that we saw the skew or term structure of the correlation was due to the use of inappropriate variables for analysis. We tried to avoid the hard problem of finding the correct variables by qualitatively analyzing the impact of various deviations from lognormality on pricing correlation dependent structures.

This approach may not always be justified, since we can have genuine changes in the dependence structure.

An alternative way of modeling correlation or covariance evolution over time is to assume that those quantities are stochastic quantities themselves. In the data chapter, we examined qualitatively the behavior of correlation over time. We saw that power-to-fuel correlations especially tend to be very unstable. The usual response is to consider models of uncertain or stochastic correlations; however, one must be very careful when using models of this type.

As we have seen, once we assume that volatility is stochastic, it might turn out that the concept does not describe anything meaningful. In these situations, it may be that only a detailed understanding of the process and the distribution is sufficient. Often we are able to eliminate this problem by introducing conditional volatility models (like GARCH or CEV), but in many cases that is not enough, and we end up introducing a wild zoo of stochastic volatility, jumps, jumps in volatility, stochastic volatility of volatility, and so on.

A similar situation arises when we deal with correlation. We can introduce conditional correlation models (multivariate GARCH, conditional stochastic correlation models), or try to model correlation in its full stochastic bloom. Not surprisingly, distinguishing among reasonable candidates can be difficult, but it is not hopeless. As we mentioned above, correlation is the proper measure of dependence only for a certain set of joint distributions. If the dependence structure is not described by one of the distributions, the calculated or estimated correlation depends not only on the nature of dependence, but also on the behavior of the marginal distributions. It follows then, that the stochastic nature of correlation might not be driven by the stochastic (or just time-dependent) nature of dependence, but by the changes in the behavior of the marginals.

To decide whether to introduce stochastic correlations and other members of the zoo, it would help to know whether we are dealing with constant noncorrelation dependence with varying marginals, or with a genuinely varying dependence structure (correlation- or non–correlation-driven).

Note that being able to distinguish between the two situations is greatly beneficial in terms of modeling. In the former case, we could reasonably expect that conditional models would work well. In the second case, we would have to expend ourselves much more.

It turns out that we are in luck. There are measures that, at least in population, are a function only of the nature of the dependence and not of the behavior of the marginals. This gives an immediate prescription for analyzing the question we posed above. If the measures tend to stay constant over time, this strongly suggests that whatever variability of correlation we are seeing is due not to the changes in the joint behavior, but only to changes in the marginals.

There are two measures that have the desired property and that share the virtue of being relatively easy to estimate. These are Kendal's tau and Spearman's rho (or rank correlation). It can be proven that these measures (for the population) depend only on the joint behavior and not on the marginals (Nelsen, 1999). These measures have been known for a long time. Their drawbacks as modeling tools are well known too. However, here we do not use them in this capacity, but as diagnostics to better select an appropriate and tractable model.

EXAMPLE 6.2 *Correlation and dependence*

Consider two variables representing power prices in two locations. To recover the qualitative characteristics of the power prices, we represent the behavior of the prices by a two-state regime-switching model (see Chapter 4). The dependence is characterized by the Gumbell copula (see Nelsen, 1999) with Kendal tau of 0.9. We set up the example so that the measured correlation is 80%. If we lower the volatility of the lower state from 80% to 60%, then the observed correlation will drop from 80% to 60%. However, the dependence structure remains unchanged.

As we argued earlier, the fact that the true dependence between the variables is nonlinear manifests itself in the dependence of correlation on the levels of prices, volatilities, and possibly other characteristics of the marginal price distributions. However, it is crucial to understand that this dependence will only show up for variables that are not normally distributed. If any of the variables we are considering is normally distributed, then its correlation with any other variable, no matter what the marginal distribution is, cannot depend on the mean and variance of the normal variable. This follows from the simple fact that for the normal variable the following holds:

$$F_{a,b}(bX + a) = F_{0,1}(X) \qquad (6.25)$$

where $F_{a,b}$ is the c.d.f. (cumulative distribution function) of the normal distribution with mean, a, and standard deviation, b.

As we have shown in previous sections, the estimate of correlation generally depends on the volatilities, even for normal variables. The dependence, however, is induced by sampling from different normal distributions, and will show up even if the true correlation is constant.

In practical terms, distinguishing the estimation bias from the true nonlinearity might not be so easy. We can be fairly confident that cash power prices, and possibly cash natural gas prices, are not lognormally distributed. This conclusion is not as straightforward for the corresponding forward prices. However, even if we are fairly confident that normality does not hold, we still need to distinguish the estimation bias from the nonlinearity effect. One practical way to check it is to look at how closely equation (6.25) is satisfied for the distributions we have in mind for our marginals. This test is of a negative nature only; it tells us that if equation (6.25) holds approximately, nonlinearity cannot be responsible for inducing the dependence of correlation on the marginals. The culprit must be then the estimation bias.

One other insight emerges from this analysis. Even if the dependence structure is described by correlation (Gaussian copula, see Nelsen, 1999), as long as the marginals do not satisfy equation (6.25), the calculated correlation will depend on the means and volatilities of the marginal distribution.

Fortunately, as we have shown above, the estimation bias will have the biggest impact for highly correlated variables (close to one). On the other hand, the variables for which equation (6.25) does not hold, cannot have high correlations (due to Frechet bounds, see Nelsen, 1999). This neatly sorts out the problem for us, because in the energy markets correlations with the highest variability tend to span the range. Hence, it's unlikely the estimation bias is the problem.

Incidentally, the above analysis sheds some light on modeling energy markets with stochastic correlation models. For this approach to be feasible, we would have to be reasonably sure the marginals themselves are normal. Even if the joint structure is described by Gaussian copula, the dependence parameter—we do not call it correlation—will differ from the observed correlation. Observed correlation will have a stochastic nature induced by the evolution of the nonnormal components. Imposing a process on the correlation that we know is only approximately true, might make the correlation process and the marginal process inconsistent. It will be hard to disentangle the stochastic and nonlinear effects.

An example of a conditional nonlinear correlation model is considered in Chapter 7 where we analyze hybrid models of power price evolution.

Implied Correlations

In the previous section we analyzed various models that are consistent with observed behavior of prices to determine what implications the various models have for pricing multi-commodity structures as well as for the correlation estimation issues. Our conclusion is that in the presence of non-lognormalities, the standard estimation techniques, and even the standard concept of correlation, may not apply. The primary evidence that makes us consider non-lognormal models for valuation and hedging, apart from historical data, is the presence of forward volatility skew (see Chapters 3 and 4). The models of the previous section are developed in such a way so they match the observed volatility skew. In the present section, we invert the procedure. Instead of modeling volatility skew first and seeing the consequences for correlation(s), we take the volatility skew as given, put it into relevant pricing formulas, and we look at what additional inputs (or adjustments) we need to properly price for example spread options. The missing link is the implied correlation. Different structures entail different implied correlations. Here we concentrate on implied correlations recovered from spread options (see Chapter 8 for details). Our goal is to find what kind of correlations we need to use to price spread options consistently in the presence of quoted or modeled volatility structure.

In this section we analyze the different dimensions of pricing and hedging for correlation-dependent derivatives. We will use the concept of correlation surface to tackle this problem.

One objection to this line of analysis is that we have argued that the concept of correlation can be a misleading and inappropriate tool for analyzing dependence. We could try justifying the approach, if the implied correlation skew actually traded to any degree of liquidity. Unfortunately there is no deep market for standardized spread options across various strike prices, and hence, no liquid implied correlation skew.

Given the above, why don't we introduce models that model the dependence structure directly without bothering with its significance for correlations? The answer is twofold:

- First, the market uses the Margrabe model as a convenient tool for pricing (see Chapter 8). Like implied volatilities, the practice is to a degree simply a quotation convention. However, for many market participants, the best way to express insights from more complex models is to relate them to the Margrabe benchmark. Traders are likely to think about pricing and hedging in terms of deviations from the Margrabe analysis. This alone would make the present exercise worthwhile.

■ Second and more importantly, even though the implied correlation skew does not trade, the implied volatility skew does. So we are faced with the task of decomposing the various risks (and hedging issues) into price levels (delta and gamma hedges), volatilities (vegas/kappas and gamma hedges), and the rest. The rest, however, is exactly the correlation skew.

Consequently, the approach allows us to decompose price, volatility, and dependence risks in a manner consistent with the available hedging instruments and in a language of the market convention. That's why we pursue it here.

Correlation Levels (Forward versus Historical Correlations)

In previous sections we have extensively reviewed the estimation of correlation on historical data. The question we try to answer here is: How relevant is past data for forward estimates of correlation (and other dependence parameters)?

Usually, we do not have enough data to build extensive models of conditional correlation from data alone. Even if we had enough data, it would not be easy to get a model that could properly condition on all the available forward-looking information (price-based and non–price-based).

On the other hand, in some situations, we have a good reason to expect that the correlation in the future will be different from historically estimated ones. In power markets, significant new additions of efficient generation in the absence of significant system load growth are likely to lead to an increase in the correlation between power and the primary fuel. We expand on this point in Chapter 7.

Knowing the direction of the likely change is usually not enough. We need reasonable estimates of the new value (or values). There are two ways of looking in the future and both are model-dependent:

■ Extract correlation projections from currently quoted forward and option prices.
■ Build fundamental models of price formation, project the future behavior of fundamental drivers, and extract information about correlations from the model.

The first approach relies on the existence of a functional relationship between volatilities (or volatility skews) and correlation. We pursued this approach in the two previous sections.

We can build hybrid models that try to integrate the two approaches. In Chapter 7 we present a model of this kind. The significant challenge we face is how to systematically use historical information for forward projections. As we argued, ultimately the issue comes down to choosing an appropriate model that gives us an idea about the relationship of forward and historical information.

Next we present an extended example of using historical data for the forward analysis, and try to flesh out the practical issues that come with interpreting the data. The particular example is well-suited for power markets. We introduce the concept of cash and forward covariance as a direct analogy to the concepts of cash and forward volatilities that we analyzed in Chapter 4.

Forward and Historical Covariance

Assume we are interested in the expected cost-to-serve of a load contract (see Chapter 8 for more details):

$$E_t[P_T L_T] = E_t[P_T]E[L_T] + \text{cov}_t(P_T, L_T) \tag{6.26}$$

We are focusing here on the covariance part of the above expression. The term is the conditional covariance at time t, of the terminal variables at time T. As in Chapter 4, we can decompose the ("daily") covariance term into the cash and forward component:

$$\text{cov}_t(P_T, L_T) = E_t[\text{cov}(P_T, L_T | F_{\text{exp}}, \sigma_{\text{exp}})] + \text{cov}_t(E[P_T | F_{\text{exp}}, \sigma_{\text{exp}}], E[L_T | F_{\text{exp}}, \sigma_{\text{exp}}]) \tag{6.27}$$

We condition on the forward prices and volatilities at expiration, where:

$E_t[\text{cov}(P_T, L_T | F_{\text{exp}})]$ is the conditional expectation at time t of the covariance of price, P, and load, L, conditioned on the forward information at expiration. It will be called *cash covariance*.

$\text{cov}_t(E[P_T | F_{\text{exp}}], E[L_T | F_{\text{exp}}])$ is the conditional covariance at time t of the expected price, P_T, conditioned on the forward information at expiration and the expected mean of the load conditioned on the same information set. It will be called forward *covariance*.

The choice of the conditioning information needs some explanation. In principle we can choose to condition the behavior of prices on any variable we find informative. If the monthly snow runoff in the Rockies is useful, we can proceed accordingly. We usually find forward prices more informative about the future behavior of prices (and demand), however ultimately this is not the deciding issue. Unlike our Rockies example, forward prices also tell us what to do to lock in our expectations. Forward information allows us to form hedges. In other words, forward information allows us to perform *rel-*

ative pricing in terms of tradables, instead of *absolute* pricing in terms of expectations. However, the limitation of the argument is that the efficiency of the forward hedge is constrained by the fact that there are only approximate arbitrage relationships between the forward prices and the spot prices we are attempting to hedge. This is why we are also interested in the information content of the forward data.

The usual practice involves calculating correlation (and covariance in general) using the realized spot prices inside of the month. Because of the limited data availability, the practice involves forming a sample aggregating data from several "similar" months (say, all the summer months, or from all the months of August we have available) and calculating one correlation (covariance). The unspoken assumption here is that the covariance term will not depend on the forward information at expiration in a "bad way," otherwise, our estimates of covariance will be biased. This, in turn, flows from the fact that the different months we aggregate correspond to different forward prices at expiry. Our procedure is only consistent if the covariance term depends, at most, linearly on the forward price (or does not depend on the forward price at all). This condition is actually not as restrictive as it seems. It admits, among others, the situation in which the price volatility and correlation depend on the forward volatility but the product (the covariance) does not.

The procedure described in the previous paragraph estimates the first term in the covariance decomposition $E_t[\mathrm{cov}(P_T, L_T | F_{\exp})]$. If we can assume that the conditional covariance depends only linearly on the forward price then the first term is given by:

$$E_t[\mathrm{cov}(P_T, L_T | F_{\exp})] = E_t[F_{\exp}]\frac{\mathrm{cov}_{\mathrm{Hist}}}{F_{\mathrm{Hist}}} = \frac{F_t}{F_{\mathrm{Hist}}}\mathrm{cov}_{\mathrm{Hist}} \qquad (6.28)$$

F_{Hist} is the forward price at expiry for the sample on which we estimate our historical covariance. In the case when we form a sample composed of many months, the consistent way to estimate historical covariance is by calculating the sample covariance where the individual prices are divided by the price of the corresponding forward contract at expiry $\mathrm{cov}^*_{\mathrm{Hist}} = \mathrm{cov}(P/F_{\mathrm{Hist}}, L)$. Then our expression will take on the following form:

$$E_t[\mathrm{cov}(P_T, L_T | F_{\exp})] = F_t \mathrm{cov}^*_{\mathrm{Hist}} \qquad (6.29)$$

The conditional covariance term is given by the historical estimate times the expected forward price at expiry. This expectation will be given by today's forward price under the risk-neutral expectation. (We use the risk-neutral expectation as we can easily hedge out the forward risk.)

The second term in the decomposition, $\mathrm{cov}_t(E[P_T | F_{\exp}], E[L_T | F_{\exp}])$, gives the contribution of the forward covariance. If we can assume that the forward price differs by a constant quantity from the expectation of the spot price:

$$F_{\exp} = E[P_T|F_{\exp}] + RP$$

where RP is a constant risk premium, we have to estimate the following term:

$$\text{cov}_t(E[P_T|F_{\exp}], E[L_T|F_{\exp}]) = \text{cov}_t(F_{\exp}, E[L_T|F_{\exp}])$$

Now we need to estimate the covariance of the forward price at expiry and the load conditional on the very same forward price. If the conditional load itself does not depend on the forward price (at expiry), then the covariance is zero, and we will not have any contribution to the total covariance from the forward covariance.

If we accept all the above assumptions we will have the following expression for the conditional covariance:

$$\text{cov}_t(P_T, L) = E_t[\text{cov}(P_T, L_T|F_{\exp})] + \text{cov}_t(E[P_T|F_{\exp}], E[L_T|F_{\exp}])$$
$$= F_t \, \text{cov}^*_{\text{Hist}} + \text{cov}_t(F_{\exp}, E[L_T|F_{\exp}]) = F_t \, \text{cov}^*_{\text{Hist}} \qquad (6.30)$$

This gives us an explicit expression for the conditional covariance in terms of historical estimates and current observable forward prices. We could incorporate option prices and other information in our formulas depending on need and on the availability of hedging instruments.

We can apply the above procedure to any type of derivative product that requires historical estimation for forward projections. The issue can become much more complex for other structures. The general comment is that the choice of the historical values to estimate is quite important. We did not use the concept of correlation in the above formulation for a reason. It turns out that the direct estimation of the covariance matrix is much more natural in the context. The choice of variables is driven by the choice of the conditioning information (i.e., hedges). If we decided to use daily and forward options for hedging, we would have to analyze forward and cash correlation instead of the corresponding variances.

The issue is especially pertinent when we discuss the valuation of spot spread options (for example in valuation of generation, see Chapter 9).

Forward, Cash, and Historical Correlation

We have shown in the previous (section "Deterministic Covariance Matrix") that correlation estimated directly on data could serve as a good approximation for the implied correlation to be used in the valuation of spread options. That analysis, however, did not take into account the structure of the hedging instruments we have at our disposal. Proceeding on the assumption that the directly estimated correlation(s) can be a proper proxy for the correct implied correlation, we can again start with the decomposition of covariance into the cash and forward part:

$$
\begin{aligned}
\mathrm{cov}_t(\ln P_T, \ln G_T) &= E_t[\mathrm{cov}(\ln P_T, \ln G_T | F_{\exp}, \sigma_{\exp}^{Forward}, \sigma_{\exp}^{Daily})] \\
&+ \mathrm{cov}_t[E(\ln P_T | F_{\exp}, \sigma_{\exp}^{Forward}, \sigma_{\exp}^{Daily}), E(\ln G_T | F_{\exp}, \sigma_{\exp}^{Forward}, \sigma_{\exp}^{Daily})]
\end{aligned} \quad (6.31)
$$

Again, the first term is the cash covariance. As we are using explicit quotes for the daily volatility at expiration (cash volatility), we decompose the cash covariance term in the following way:

$$
E_t[\mathrm{cov}(\ln P_T, \ln G_T | F_{\exp}, \sigma_{\exp}^{Forward}, \sigma_{\exp}^{Daily})] = E\left(\int_{\exp}^{T} \rho^{Cash} \sigma_{\exp}^{Daily;P} \sigma_{\exp}^{Daily;G} ds \right) \quad (6.32)
$$

If the cash correlation is constant, that is, does not depend on the daily volatilities or forward prices at expiration, then we can bring the correlation out from under the expectation operator.

The usual procedure for the estimation of cash correlation involves forming a sample from a collection of months deemed similar. For example, we can aggregate the data from all the summers or all the Augusts to estimate the correlation. Even if we can assume that the correlation is a constant, independent of all the conditional information, we might still face a significant problem in estimation. If the sample contains a collection of subperiods in which the ratio of gas and power cash volatilities is significantly different, our estimate of correlation will be biased downward (see equation [6.12]). This is an issue, which we ignored in the section, "Deterministic Covariance Matrix" when we discussed approximating implied correlations with estimated correlations. We make a tacit assumption that our estimate is done on a sample in which the ratio of volatilities behaves in the same way the future volatilities will behave (as suggested by the implied volatility surfaces, if any). Note that in the "Deterministic Covariance Matrix" section we did not have to worry about this consideration, because, by assumption, volatilities had the same deterministic structure and our cumulative correlation estimate implicitly contained it.

The impact of the decorrelation mechanism, due to varying relative volatilities, weakens with declining correlations. For correlations below 50% the effect is small. For high correlations this issue can become significant. Therefore, we need to be concerned about the problem in markets of high correlation between the legs. In some power markets (ERCOT, California), the problem can become an issue in winter and shoulder months.

A simple remedy for the problem is to scale the subsample correlations by the products of realized historical volatilities. The forward covariance, under mild assumptions about the underlying process can be written in the following form:

$$\text{cov}_t\big[E(\ln P_T|F_{\exp}, \sigma_{\exp}^{Forward}, \sigma_{\exp}^{Daily}), E(\ln G_T|F_{\exp}, \sigma_{\exp}^{Forward}, \sigma_{\exp}^{Daily})\big] =$$

$$= \text{cov}_t\bigg(\ln F_{\exp}^P - \frac{1}{2}\int_{\exp}^{T} \sigma_{\exp}^{Daily;P} ds, \ln F_{\exp}^G - \frac{1}{2}\int_{\exp}^{T} \sigma_{\exp}^{Daily;G} ds\bigg) =$$

$$= \text{cov}_t(\ln F_{\exp}^P, \ln F_{\exp}^G) + \frac{1}{4}\text{cov}_t\bigg(\int_{\exp}^{T} \sigma_{\exp}^{Daily;P} ds, \int_{\exp}^{T} \sigma_{\exp}^{Daily;G} ds\bigg) + \tag{6.33}$$

$$-\frac{1}{2}\text{cov}_t\bigg(\ln F_{\exp}^P, \int_{\exp}^{T} \sigma_{\exp}^{Daily;G} ds\bigg) - \frac{1}{2}\text{cov}_t\bigg(\ln F_{\exp}^G, \int_{\exp}^{T} \sigma_{\exp}^{Daily;P} ds\bigg)$$

The first term corresponds to the covariance of the forward contracts:

$$\text{cov}_t(\ln F_{\exp}^P, \ln F_{\exp}^G) = E_t\bigg(\int_{t}^{\exp} \rho^{Forward} \sigma_s^{Forward;P} \sigma_s^{Forward;G} ds\bigg) \tag{6.34}$$

In estimating the forward correlation, the issues of volatility-induced biases should be considered as well. If (cash) volatility is deterministic, then the additional terms have no contribution. Overall, even though daily volatility variability might not be high, the two can move together; we see that, for example, in some gas and power markets.

We can now define the overall correlation, which by analogy with the volatility case, we call daily correlation (see Chapter 4):

$$\rho^{Daily} = \frac{\text{cov}(\ln P_T, \ln G_T)}{\sqrt{\text{var}(\ln P_T)}\sqrt{\text{var}(\ln G_T)}} =$$

$$\frac{E_t\bigg(\int_{\exp}^{T} \rho^{Cash} \sigma_{\exp}^{Daily;P} \sigma_{\exp}^{Daily;G} ds\bigg) + E_t\bigg(\int_{t}^{\exp} \rho^{Forward} \sigma_s^{Forward;P} \sigma_s^{Forward;G} ds\bigg)}{\sqrt{\text{var}(\ln P_T)}\sqrt{\text{var}(\ln G_T)}} \tag{6.35}$$

We assumed zero covariance between volatilities. If volatilities are deterministic, the above is just the cumulative correlation we defined in equation (6.10) with two regimes (forward and cash). We can now use the above correlation in valuation of daily spark spread options directly (especially for options close to ATM). The procedure is then:

- Calculate the above correlation.
- Calculate the effective daily volatility smiles/skews by combining forward and cash (index) quotes (see "Asian Options" section in Chapter 8).
- Put the quantities into the Black-Scholes formula for spread options (Margrabe formula).

This procedure assures that the pricing of the spread option is consistent with the quoted forward and daily (and possibly cash) option prices.

Correlation Term Structure (Induced by Varying Volatilities)

The term structure of correlation can be naturally induced by a term structure of local correlation. Varying relative volatilities can also induce a term structure. Continuing an example we gave in the section "Implied Correlations," we can show that even with constant correlation, terminal correlation is going to evolve over time (see Figure 6.8).

In Figure 6.8, we assumed that the local correlation was perfect and that the volatilities ran up towards the end of the term. We can contrast that with the behavior of correlation for a neighboring natural gas Henry Hub futures contract as shown in Figure 6.9. Structurally Figures 6.8 and 6.9 look similar, suggesting the presence of volatility effects. Incidentally, this effect may account for the correlation Samuelson effect we mentioned in Chapter 3.

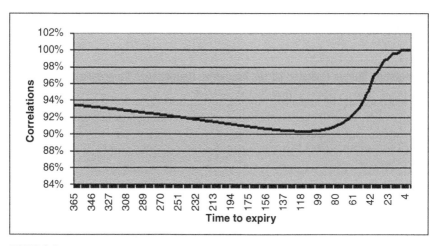

FIGURE 6.8 Term Structure Induced by Relative Volatilities

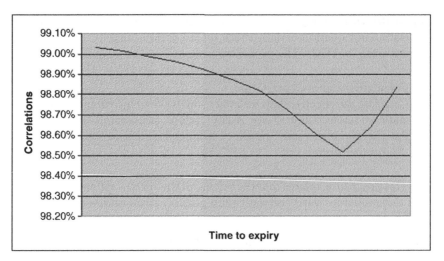

FIGURE 6.9   Term Structure of Henry Hub Correlations

We can attempt to account for changes in future correlation relationships by using fundamental or hybrid models in which we directly model price formation in terms of the underlying drivers (see Chapter 7). This kind of model enables us to assess the impact of nonprice information on, among others, correlation. We can again mention the immortal example of significant stack additions that can easily increase future correlation to levels unseen in historical data. This issue is a frequent consideration when we analyze power–fuel correlations.

By the very same fundamental consideration we can also expect that the stack additions will bring volatility down. The fact suggests that we could infer higher correlation from lower volatilities.

Correlation Skews (Induced by the Nonlinear Dependence Structure)

We will look at the so-called implied correlation skew for spread options. In other words, we will express the value of the spread option in terms of implied correlation as a function of its moneyness. By moneyness of a spread option with a payoff, $\max(P - H^*G, 0)$, we understand the constant H. If H is given by

$$H_{ATM} = \frac{F_P}{F_G} \tag{6.36}$$

then the option is at-the-money. In power markets, this ratio is called implied heat rate.

We've shown that the dependence of correlation on means and volatilities (henceforth, *realized correlation skew*) can only appear if the individual prices are not lognormal. In other words, realized correlation skew can only exist in the presence of implied volatility skews, or smiles. Flat volatility skew implies a flat realized correlation skew and vice versa.

However, the same does not hold for the *implied correlation skew*. Implied correlation skew is the curve of implied correlations from the prices of spread options with different moneyness. Even in the absence of implied volatility skew, implied correlation skew can appear. As we demonstrated in Chapter 3, implied volatility surfaces show significant smiles for cash and forward products. Consequently we should expect implied correlation skew regardless, and, strikingly, we must account for the implied correlation skew, even if there is no evidence of realized correlation skew in the data.

Since liquidity in spread options is quite limited, no such skew exists in a tradable form. The examples below come from models for the joint evolution of the prices. In a sense, these are estimates of the "fair" correlation skew, without any adjustments for the market price of the correlation risk. As we argue elsewhere in the book (Chapter 10), this adjustment is not necessary for trading—although risk adjustment as such is necessary.

In the section "Stochastic Covariance Matrix" we presented examples of implied correlation skew induced by various reduced-form models. Below we show some examples of implied correlation skew generated from hybrid models (see Chapter 7) for power–natural gas implied correlation.

We believe the model used to generate Figures 6.10 and 6.11 offers a fairly robust representation of the correlation skew. NERC regions exhibit two major types of power–natural gas correlation skew.

The two markets exhibit distinct patterns of implied correlation skew. ERCOT shows significant skew for OTM spread options, while PJM has a significant skew for ITM options. The facts are driven by the respective stack structures in the two markets. They have obvious consequences for generation plant investment decisions. We analyze these issues extensively in Chapter 7.

The valuation issues, as important as they are, are only one of the motivations for this exercise. Given that we cannot easily trade the spread options, understanding the behavior of correlation is especially useful from the hedging perspective. If implied correlation exhibits strong dependence on the implied heat rate and component volatilities, the hedging strategies we employ have to account for the regularity. Given the high sensitivity of spread options to correlation, the ability to hedge its variation can be of paramount importance.

The question we face is: What kind of hedges in the underlying and volatility we should put on, in light of the presence of the correlation skew?

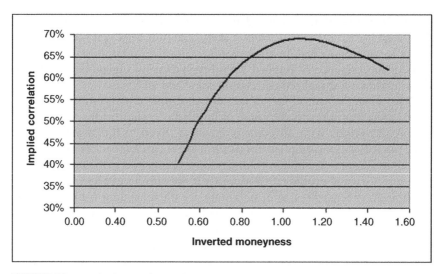

FIGURE 6.10   Implied Correlation for PJM Generated through Hybrid Models

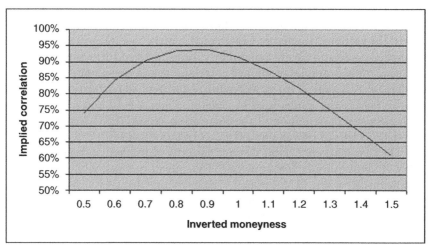

FIGURE 6.11   Implied Correlation for ERCOT Generated through Hybrid Models

Paralleling the analysis for stochastic volatility, we can write the correct delta hedges (for both legs) as follows:

$$\Delta_H^P = \Delta_{Mar}^P(\rho_{I;H}) - \kappa_H\left(\frac{\sigma_P - \rho_{I;H}\sigma_G}{\sigma}\frac{\partial\sigma_P}{\partial E[P]} + \frac{\sigma_P\sigma_G}{\sigma}\frac{\partial\rho_{I;H}}{\partial IHR}\frac{\partial IHR}{\partial E[P]}\right)$$

$$\sigma = \sqrt{\sigma_P^2 + \sigma_G^2 - 2\sigma_P\sigma_G\rho_I} \qquad (6.37)$$

Where

Δ_{Mar} is the delta for the standard Black-Scholes–based model for spread options: the Margrabe model

κ is the sensitivity of the spread option with respect to the "volatility" of the spread given by σ

IHR stands for the implied heat rate.

The implied correlation is indexed by moneyness H, as is the kappa (vega) of the option.

There are three terms in the equation. The first corresponds to the standard Margrabe delta, with correlations and volatilities properly adjusted for moneyness. The second term represents the adjustment for the volatility skew (see Chapter 4 on stochastic volatility models). Here it is a slightly different form from the one we saw previously, due to the fact that we are dealing with spread options. The final term accounts for the implied correlation skew.

We express the implied correlation as a function of implied heat rate, and not directly of any of the component prices. For many reasonable models of power–natural gas markets, the implied correlation shows the direct dependence on the implied heat rate. This is not surprising, considering the basic economics of power generation. We will investigate this point in more detail in Chapter 7, when we cover hybrid models of power markets.

With equation (6.37) in hand, we need just three things to arrive at the correct delta hedge:

- The correct volatilities
- The dynamics of the volatility skews
- The dynamics of the correlation skew

The first and most important question is what implied volatilities to use. The straightforward suggestion is to use the implied volatilities corresponding to the strike prices for the standard calls and puts on the component assets:

$$K_P = HF_P$$

$$K_G = \frac{F_G}{H} \tag{6.38}$$

Those choices will be consistent in the limit. This is to say that for the power call, if we assume that the volatility of the other leg goes to zero, our spread option will become a standard call with the strike price given by (6.38). Similarly, if the volatility of the P-leg goes to zero, the spread option will become a put on G struck at K_G.

Although this choice is a reasonable one, it is not the only one. The value of the spread option will depend on the whole implied volatility skew, and not only on one point on the skew. We hide this complex dependence in the implied correlation skew. This is one of the sources of the difference between implied correlation skew and realized correlation skew. Even if the true dependence is described by a constant Gaussian dependence structure, the implied correlation skew will appear as long as the marginals exhibit a volatility skew. We discussed the dynamics of the volatility skew and the various trading rules associated with them in Chapter 4 on stochastic volatility.

We can analyze the dynamics of the implied correlation skew by considering three possibilities:

$$\frac{\partial \rho_{I;H}}{\partial IHR} = 0 \tag{6.39}$$

$$\frac{\partial \rho_{I;H}}{\partial IHR} = -\frac{\partial \rho_{I;H}}{\partial H} \tag{6.40}$$

$$\frac{\partial \rho_{I;H}}{\partial IHR} = \frac{\partial \rho_{I;H}}{\partial H} \tag{6.41}$$

These three cases correspond roughly to the "sticky strike," "sticky tree," and "sticky delta" rules we encountered when talking about implied volatility skews and smiles. As with volatility we have to somehow relate the implied correlation skew to the dynamics of the various correlations.

We can see that the presence of the correlation skew asserts itself in two ways. First, the initial term in (6.37) is the standard delta calculated with the correlation appropriate for the moneyness. Second, we have an additional term driven by the dynamics of the implied correlation skew. (For more formal analysis, see Wolyniec, 2001).

MULTIVARIATE CORRELATIONS

In all the previous sections we were not explicit about the dimension of the problem we were considering, although a majority of our examples considered bivariate cases. The analysis of correlation extends to the multivariate case in largely unchanged form. One significant difference is that there are certain consistency conditions that have to be satisfied by sets of correlations.

Consider a portfolio composed of N assets. Let A be the N by N correlation matrix, describing the correlations among the various assets of the portfolio. As the overall portfolio variance has to be always positive, we need to make sure that whatever volatilities we use with our correlation matrix the portfolio variance (or volatility) is always positive. This leads to the condition that:

$$\underline{\sigma}' \underline{\underline{A}} \underline{\sigma} \geq 0 \tag{6.42}$$

where σ is a vector of volatilities (positive or negative depending on whether we are long or short an asset). The above condition is simply a requirement that the matrix A is positive semi-definite.

There are a variety of techniques used for checking the condition. One of the more popular ones is Cholesky decomposition. The literature on the topic is vast and we suggest the reader consult the references for further details (e.g., see Press, et al., 2002).

If we estimate the correlation matrix A on the same sample with paired-up observation, the matrix is always positive semi-definite. The problem may appear when we try to combine various correlation estimates from different sources.

CORRELATION VERSUS COINTEGRATION

In this section, we briefly describe the concept of cointegration and analyze its usefulness for derivative pricing in energy markets. (For more extensive yet accessible coverage of cointegration see Alexander, 2001.)

Definition. We have two nonstationary stochastic processes $\{x_t\}_0^\infty$, $\{y_t\}_0^\infty$. The two processes are said to be cointegrated if there exists at least one pair of coefficients (α, β) such that process $\{z_t\}_0^\infty$, defined by the equation below is stationary:

$$z_t = \alpha x_t + \beta y_t$$

In plainer language, we can say that cointegration is a rigorous way of defining stable long-term relationships between variables. It says that even though in the short term the variables can wander far from each other, they tend to wander back, given enough time. If we put it this way, informally, an immediate question arises about the definition of the short and long terms. In practice, econometric studies show that the cointegration effects show up on the time scale of years or even decades. So those effects will tend to have an impact only on really long-term assets, such as generation assets.

The concepts of correlation and cointegration are not directly related. There can be situations of high cointegration and low correlation and vice versa. It would seem then, that cointegration would be ideally suited for the analysis of generation assets and other long-term contracts. However, there are two problems with this approach; one is of a practical nature, the other is more fundamental.

We will start with the former. The practical problem is the one we have run into throughout the whole book: the availability of data. To test out long-term relationships, we require sufficiently long time series. These simply do not exist for power, and will not be available for a long time. It's a significant shortcoming of the methodology.

More fundamentally, the usefulness of cointegration for risk management, despite the enthusiasm of many (Wilmott, 1998; Alexander, 2001), is quite limited. Risk management requires local control of risk. The knowledge that the variables in question are likely to eventually come back closer to each other is of little comfort if you are not around to enjoy the fruits of your prescience. So even though, thanks to cointegrating relationships, you know that the variables you are betting on will never stray far from each other, they might still stray far enough to bankrupt you. The cautionary adventures of MetallGesselshaft (see Schwartz and Smith, 1998), LTCM (see Lowenstern, 2001) and many others offer a handy warning. Relying on long-term equilibrium relationships can be quite dangerous and should be only contemplated by entities with deep pockets, and even deeper patience resources.

LTCM is especially instructive. We have no doubt (although we do not really know) that if one runs cointegration analysis on the swap and treasury rate, one will find a significant cointegrating relationship; however, this information turned out to be of little value to LTCM. One bad September, with the swap rate wandering far away from the treasuries, did the hedge fund in. When you run a mark-to-market operation, especially with significant leverage, you have to be right about your bet every day, and not only at the end. This issue is as relevant to asset ownership as it is to swap rates.

Those considerations lead us to believe that you will always need some local measures of dependence, be they correlation or something more general (e.g., copulas), for a successful risk management of energy assets or any financial assets. Cointegration analysis may still be useful as an additional issue. A model developed by Duan and Pliska (2000) shows that in the presence of stochastic volatility, cointegration has an impact on spread option valuation. However, the presence of the cointegrating effects does not change the fact that we have to understand correlation structure to effectively hedge the option.

The biggest challenge in management of energy derivatives is understanding this local dependence structure. Furthermore, by now we are quite convinced that the seeming limitations of correlation, which we amply demonstrated with empirical data and theoretical analysis, are due to the fundamentally nonlinear relationship between energy tradables.

CHAPTER 7

Hybrid Process
for Power Prices

The processes described in the previous chapters, while quite effective in financial applications, entail substantial difficulties when used to model the evolution of power prices. The main issues that complicate modeling efforts are as follows:

1. A reasonable evolution process should be able to capture important properties of energy prices such as:
   - Spikes
   - Mean reversion
   - Fat tails of the price distributions
   - Seasonality
2. A process must be able to represent:
   - Volatility surface
   - Correlation structure between different forward contracts for a given commodity
   - Cross-commodity correlation structure between different commodities, particularly between natural gas and power
3. The variables underlying the process should have stable statistical properties. There should be some degree of confidence that the basic parameters defining the process will not significantly change with every new month of price data. Also, in a reasonable model a small move in market prices should not cause a large change in the process parameters.

The pure-price processes of Chapters 4 and 5 fail to deliver these properties. Item 3 in the list is the most serious obstacle due to the current lack of a substantial (for the purposes of parameter calibration) price history in the energy markets, particularly in the power markets. In many power markets there are presently no more than a few seasons of reliable price data. Thus, any method that requires estimation of a significant number of parameters risks producing meaningless results.

On the other hand, the requirements of items 1 and 2 suggest the need for greater flexibility in defining a process, and therefore, a large number of parameters for its specification.

This seemingly unsolvable dilemma provides an incentive to look for new approaches to modeling energy prices. We obviously do not want to reject market-based financial models, which have many important characteristics we want to preserve. Ultimately, only with these models can we expect to produce correct hedging, in addition to correct valuation methodologies. But we need to augment their power and effectiveness and compensate for the data shortage by incorporating certain important features derived from the fundamental supply/demand models successfully used in the energy industry for many years.

PRODUCTION COST AND FUNDAMENTAL EQUILIBRIUM MODELS

In the most general terms the production cost models can be described as optimization procedures whose objective is to minimize the cost of generating power required to meet the demand in a certain region, while satisfying operational and environmental constraints. From this definition it is clear that these models require

- Accurate specification of the generation capabilities in the region (supply), including capacities, both existing and projected, heat rates, fuel, and other costs
- An understanding of the load (demand) characteristics based on the economic, demographic, and statistical analysis
- Specification of the constraints, including
  - Transmission constraints, such as capacity, topology, costs, and losses
  - Environmental constraints, such as pollution allowances, pollution rates, and costs
  - Operational constraints, such as maximum and minimum operational levels, start-up times, ramp-up/down rates, outage rates, and reserves

The production cost models are widely used by regulated utilities for short-term dispatch as well as for long-term planning purposes (see Stoll, 1989; Wood and Wollenberg, 1984). Long-term planning is of particular interest to us because it addresses many issues important to our modeling efforts, specifically, modeling load growth, load uncertainty, generation capacity additions, outages, and a number of other important parameters required to model future power prices.

Production cost models are often used to project short- and long-term expected spot prices, but, unfortunately, this is often difficult to achieve.

These models usually attempt to faithfully represent the details of the operations of the market, involving large-scale optimization problems that extend the runtimes by hours or even days. To generate reliable price forecasts one must account for the uncertainty around the future values of the driving factors (i.e., load, fuel prices, outages). It is not enough to project the expected values of the factors and put them into the optimization engine. Since the transformation between the factors and the power price is highly nonlinear, the expected power price can be only derived through explicit simulation of the factors and reoptimization of the system for different outcomes. This approach, however, employs extremely intensive computations, rendering production cost models unsuitable for power price projections of more than a couple of days—this is to say for time periods where the volatility effects become significant.

The attraction of production cost models is their focus on finding certain primary factors as drivers of power prices. With knowledge of these drivers it is only natural to develop a methodology in which the evolution process for power prices is not a starting point of the modeling routine, but rather is induced by the evolution of the primary drivers. The challenge, of course, is in reconciling this methodology with market-price information, since production cost models are not typically concerned with market data. (It is worth noting that from the risk management point of view, the biggest weakness of production cost models is that, as a rule, they do not capture such important characteristics of price evolution as volatility or higher moments of price distributions.)

Similarly, the goal of the fundamental equilibrium methodology is to model supply/demand relations and to obtain the power prices as a solution of certain optimization—or to be more precise, equilibrium—problems. The difference between this and the production cost methodology is that now the optimization problems include market information and trading activity, they are not limited by the assumption of cost minimization. For example, Bessembinder and Lemmon (2001) propose a method in which forward prices are found using the condition that they provide equilibrium in demand for forward contracts. In the paper by Supatgiat, Zhang, and Birge (2001) market clearing prices are determined by solving a Nash equilibrium problem for the bidding strategies of market participants. These techniques have drawbacks, however, because they often fail to recover the dynamics of power-price formation in a robust quantitative manner. They can be still useful for a wide range of applications, especially qualitative analysis of price behavior. However, as in the case of production cost models, the challenge is that these models are not designed to capture the price dynamics, which is ultimately what we need to develop effective hedging and risk-management tools.

HYBRID MODELS

Introduction and Motivation

In this chapter we attempt to address this challenge and to develop a process that fuses the benefits of different modeling methodologies. It can be characterized as a hybrid process, with distinctive features of both fundamental as well as pure stochastic models: the efficient use of information of the former and the rigor and market-data awareness of the latter. The fundamental methodology is used to represent supply/demand relations, while stochastic techniques are used to represent the evolution of the underlying drivers. Unlike the models in financial markets that focus primarily on answering the question of how prices move, our hybrid method, and in particular its fundamental component, attempt to look beyond prices. Its goal is to answer the question of what causes the prices to move, to find primary variables that describe the movements in a robust and stable way, and to model the evolution of these variables. It is important to emphasize, however, that the most important feature of financial models—namely, matching the market data—is also preserved in the hybrid approach.

Ultimately, the motivation for employing the hybrid models is threefold:

- Natural representation of the dynamics of the power prices
- Consistent and explicit use of nonprice forward-looking information (e.g., generation stack additions)
- Ability to extend the available data set from historical (and forward looking) power prices to information on fuel prices, historical load, temperature, outage, and so on

The first consideration is a matter of convenience and is not the overriding one (although it is important), since it can be also recovered through sufficiently high-dimensional reduced-form models. The second and the third considerations are of paramount importance. We noted several times in Chapters 4 and 5 that the scarcity of historical power price information severely limits the applicability of the reduced-form models. The distinct advantage of the hybrid models is their ability to exploit major new sources of information. The price we pay for the additional information is the significant expansion in the number of parameters of the model—usually something to avoid if only possible. However, in this case, with the growing set of parameters our ability to fix them is also increasing.

Two approaches are commonly used in practice for statistical modeling of a complicated phenomenon, such as the behavior of power prices.

The first consists of testing a variety of distributions, sometimes quite exotic and defined by many parameters, and identifying the one distribution that provides the best approximation to the available empirical data. This is precisely the methodology described in Chapters 4 and 5. There, we went through a family of increasingly complex stochastic processes to match as many observed properties of the energy prices as possible.

Another approach, which can be traced back to the Box-Cox paper (1964), is based on the assumption that a complex behavior can be modeled as a nonlinear transformation of a certain number of random variables, with each variable described by a standard distribution, such as normal or uniform. This approach is particularly appealing when the choice of these random variables is clear from the physical nature of the phenomenon. Then the only remaining problem is to find an appropriate transformation—for instance, using a polynomial approximation—such that the transformed variables have the right properties.

We will show that the transformation approach works very well in the case of power prices.

Formal Representation

Formally, hybrid models are represented in the following way:

$$p_T = s(D_T, g_T, l_T, \overrightarrow{\Omega_T}, \overrightarrow{E_T}, \overrightarrow{\Im_T}; \overrightarrow{OPC_T}, T) + \varepsilon_T \qquad (7.1)$$

where the following are dynamic variables (random variables):

D_T is the system demand at time T

g_T is the natural gas price at time T

l_T is the oil price at time T

Ω_T is the vector of outages at time T

E_T is the vector of emission prices at time T

$\Im_T$ is the vector of weather at time T

ε_T is the stochastic error term

The deterministic parameters are the following:

OPC_t is the vector of operational characteristics of the stack at time t that parameterizes the stack transformation; and

s is the deterministic stack transformation, which is potentially a deterministic function of time. This assumption corresponds to the situation where we know both the transformation between the dynamic factors and the market clearing price (MCP) with certainty. The transformation may have a stochastic nature, especially for longer-term valuations; new stack additions can change the nature of the transformation, and we cannot be certain what those are beyond a two-year horizon. However, the deterministic assumption is crucial to the viability of the whole methodology. Indeed, testing (on historical data) a stochastic transformation function would be extremely difficult.

The formula above yields the dynamics of the power price as a function of the dynamics of the underlying factors. Since we are interested in the forward evaluation of power contracts, the dynamics of the factors will be a function of the corresponding tradables:

$$D_T = d(T) + \varepsilon_T^D$$

$$g_T = g(BOM^{gas}, \overrightarrow{C^{GasMonthly}}, \overrightarrow{C^{GasDaily}}; T) + \varepsilon_T^g$$

$$l_T = g(F^{oil}, \overrightarrow{C^{OilMonthly}}; T) + \varepsilon_T^l \qquad (7.2)$$

$$E_T = E(F^{Emissions}; T) + \varepsilon_T^E$$

$$\Im_T = \Im(Swap^{HDD}, Swap^{HDD}; T) + \varepsilon_T^\Im$$

The notation is standard:

BOM is the balance-of-the-month contract

F is the forward contract

$\overrightarrow{C}$ is the vector of monthly and daily options

This formulation allows us to develop a hedging and risk-adjustment strategy directly. We explore this in Chapter 10.

Since some of the factors cannot be hedged out (e.g., load, forced outages, even natural gas prices), and the relationship between the underlying factors and the power price is not deterministic (we denote it by including the stochastic basis ε_T), the available power tradables (forwards and option prices) cannot be risklessly replicated solely by using the factor tradables (i.e., natural gas options, oil forward contracts, and so on). Consequently, we must be sure that we adjust the power price p_T given by (7.1) so that the power tradables are exactly matched:

$$p_T^* = \aleph(p_T, BOM^{Power}, \overrightarrow{C^{PowerMonthly}}, \overrightarrow{C^{PowerDaily}})$$

s.t.

$$E_t[p_T^*] = E_t[\aleph(p_T, BOM^{Power}, \overrightarrow{C^{PowerMonthly}}, \overrightarrow{C^{PowerDaily}})] = F_t^{Power}$$

$$E_t[\max(p_T^* - K_i, 0)] = C_t^{K_i} \text{ for every } i \qquad (7.3)$$

where $C_t^{K_i}$ is the price of a call option with strike K_i.

The choice of the matching transformation is such that if we price the forward contracts and the available options under the power price distribution generated by p^*, we recover their current prices exactly.

This setup enables us to price and hedge any power contract, derivative, or asset, consistently with the current prices of the liquid power and factor tradables.

The aim of this strategy is to reduce the inherent nonstationarity of power prices by explicitly accounting for the dynamic factors that induce it. In lay terms, we attempt to find the factors that cause the vastly different behavior of distributional characteristics in different periods of time.

There are a number of mechanisms that can achieve the above-stated restrictions. The choice of one is more art than science and can be dependent on the market in question. However, it is obvious that the chosen solution needs to be very stable over time for the model to have any meaning.

The parsimony of the quotes-matching described above has some downsides that must be clearly understood.

The above model implicitly fixes the following dimensions of the valuation problem:

- Conditional evolution of the power-market tradables
- Risk-adjustment mechanisms for the different risk factors
- The conditional evolution of the power tradables, such as the forward price, forward "volatility," or daily volatility are determined by the conditional evolution of the underlying drivers: fuels, loads, temperatures, and outages. In as much as some of those factors have a trivial conditional structure, they do not contribute anything. Ready examples are temperature that does not exhibit much of a conditional evolution until three months from the expiration date. Similarly, outages do not show much in the way of conditional structure until one is close to the time in question.

This analysis has the following practical implications. The model, in some sense is assumed to be a very comprehensive one. We attempt to explain the behavior of all the tradables and spot products in terms of the evolution of the underlying factors and *static* adjustments to the resulting terminal distribution. We can easily see that it implies that we are not going to use any historical information on the evolution of the tradables and spot products in the calibration of the model. This does not mean that we do not use the historical information in the model development. Quite the contrary, the information is fundamental in the model validation. However, validation is a binary process. We either find that the model satisfactorily explains the behavior of *all* the tradables and spot products or not. If it doesn't, we must change the model; we cannot adjust some parameters to make use of the historical information. In other words, we cannot calibrate.

Obviously, the technique described earlier is not as rigid as suggested. There are always some free parameters that allow adjustments. However, as opposed to the case of the reduced form-models, the parameters describe some characteristics of the mapping of the underlying factors into the power price in a wholesale manner. We cannot easily adjust means, volatilities, correlations, and the kurtosis of the joint distribution independently of each other. Since the free parameters are not available in the parameter space of the resulting distribution, our freedom to choose them is severely limited. *In other words, the hybrid models can be thought of as not a model of specific volatilities, correlation and the like, but as a model of the relationship among all the parameters of the joint distribution.* We fix specific values by choosing the free parameters and adjusting to the static market quotes.

The preceding representation is a formal one. In the rest of this chapter we provide examples of how to choose the transformations, and what issues should be considered when doing so.

Depending on how we determine the function s, we can distinguish two types of hybrid models. The classification depends on how we determine the transformation:

- **Reduced-form hybrid models:** the transformation is implied (calibrated on) from the historical prices
- **Fundamental hybrid models:** the transformation is implied from the structure of the market and is only tested on the historical prices

The second approach uses the available price information more efficiently— a distinct advantage at the current stage of the market development. We will devote a good part of the rest of the chapter to analyzing the fundamental hybrid models in detail. First, however, we quickly look at a simple example of a reduced-form hybrid model and its motivation.

REDUCED-FORM HYBRID MODELS

Different versions of the method have appeared in a number of works including Pirrong and Jermakyan (1999), Eydeland and Geman (1999), Johnson and Barz (1999), Skantze and Ilic (2001), and Davison et al. (2001). They differ in the choice of the underlying drivers, which correspond more or less faithfully to the fundamental drivers of the power price formation.

Although the proposed implementations may differ significantly in their technical details, the principal idea of modeling power prices not directly, but through transformation of a set of variables with better statistical properties, underlies all the implementations. In all the above implementations, the transformation function is calibrated from the available historical (and/or forward-looking prices).

To understand the logic of those models consider the example discussed in the next few paragraphs.

When we talked about jump-diffusion models in the introduction to Chapter 4 we showed examples when they are not capable of incorporating nonprice information. The solution to this problem might be the introduction of exogenous variables into the evolution equation. We can introduce the jump parameters as functions of the reserve margin, load, or other similar measure that might help better use of information. While the introduction of more structure results in more demands on the available data, since we simply have more parameters to estimate, somewhat surprisingly this can help us with the estimation problem by expanding the data set. To examine how it happens, we analyze a specific example of a hybrid model.

We specify the following stochastic volatility jump-diffusion model:

$$\frac{dP}{P} = \theta(\mu - \ln P)dt + \sqrt{V}\,dW_1 + (Y - 1)dq$$

$$dV = \partial(\theta - V)dt + \eta\sqrt{V}\,dW_2 \qquad (7.4)$$

$$dW_1 dW_2 = \rho dt$$

$$\lambda_t = \lambda(V_t)$$

This is the standard Merton jump-diffusion model combined with the Heston stochastic volatility model. The only nonstandard feature is the dependence of the jump rate λ_t on the variance. We are not interested in the solution of the above equations and the pricing results (see Deng, 1998). We are only interested in the motivation for the choice of the specification and the efficient (stable) estimation.

The reason for conditioning the rate of jumps on volatility is the simple economics of power generation. The probability of a price spike is not constant and depends on the market conditions.

More specifically, a spike only occurs if the system is significantly constrained, and this happens only in systems where the reserve margin is below 10% to begin with. These types of systems, under hot weather conditions where majority of generation is dispatched and disruptions in generation (i.e., transmission congestion, outages), will result in significant spike prices, because very expensive quick-start generation will be forced on-line to protect the stability of the system.

This scenario strongly suggests that the probability of the jump depends on the weather conditions, such as temperature $\Im$. On the other hand, the volatility of the diffusive part of the process also depends on the weather. Consequently we might decide to condition the jump probability on the variance of the process.

If we get the correct distribution of the diffusive variance and the correct functional dependence between λ and V, then we will recover a model equivalent to the one with the following specification:

$$\frac{dP}{P} = \theta(\mu - \ln P)dt + \sqrt{V}\,dW_1 + (Y - 1)dq$$

$$\frac{dV}{V} = \partial(\omega - \ln V)dt + \eta\sqrt{V}\,dW_2$$

$$d\Im = \pi(\psi(t) - \Im)dt + \zeta dW_3$$

$$dW_1 dW_2 = \rho_{12}dt \tag{7.5}$$

$$dW_1 dW_3 = \rho_{13}dt$$

$$dW_2 dW_3 = \rho_{23}dt$$

$$\lambda_t = f(\Im_t)$$

The great advantage of equation (7.4) is that it is much more parsimonious; equation (7.5) requires several additional parameters. We have argued that, the more parsimonious models are, the more preferable, but this is not the case here.

Notice that the volatility process is a latent process for which we do not have any independent observations. We must estimate it on the available price data, which are limited. Consequently, our estimates of complex processes like equation (7.4) are not going to be very efficient (stable). Our understanding of the volatility distribution will be very limited. On the other hand, the distribution of temperature is much better known. We have, in some cases, almost 50 years worth of data. Consequently, choosing parameterization (7.5) effectively significantly expands our data sample. We still have to estimate the $f(\ )$ function from the price data. However, for equation (7.4) we would have to do the same thing plus calculate the distribution of volatility from the same data set.

The approach illustrated above achieves an effective separation of the estimation problem into two independent steps:

- Estimation of the conditional response function conditioned on the dynamic factors (e.g., fuel prices, loads, etc.)—usually on price data
- Estimation of the unconditional distribution—usually on nonprice or other price data (e.g., fuel)

The toy model we considered in this section illustrates the fundamental advantage of hybrid models: efficient use of disparate sources of information. Consider the procedure for the estimation of the parameters of the jump distribution in the two models. Under the reduced-form model (7.4), to get proper estimates of the distribution of jumps we would have to use price data to estimate the price process, the volatility process, and the response function to volatility. In the hybrid model (7.5), we use price and temperature data only to estimate the price process parameters and the response function $f(\ )$. To arrive at the distribution of jumps we need also to estimate the temperature process. For this purpose, however, we can use the temperature data only. We can see then, that introducing another factor (temperature) increases the total number of parameters we must estimate. However, the number of parameters we need to estimate on price data actually drops. This fact is a significant advantage of all hybrid models. The scarce price data are used much more efficiently.

FUNDAMENTAL HYBRID MODELS

The major limitation of reduced-form hybrid models is the need to rely on limited historical price data to imply the transformation. The situation is different for fundamental hybrid models. Typically, random drivers for these models, that is, underlying variables with standard distributions, are readily identifiable. Furthermore and most importantly, the transformation of these variables that generate power prices follows naturally from the physical realities of a given market. For these and other reasons that will be described next, the approach has been gaining popularity in recent years.

Price Formation Mechanism

The first and most important step in developing the approach we call the hybrid method is to understand how power prices are formed in competitive markets. Most of the price formation principles have been already outlined in Chapter 1. To avoid getting bogged down in unnecessary details, we focus on the pool market and consider its price setting procedures. In a typical pool market, the price is determined through the auction mechanism, in

TABLE 7.1   Sample Bid for a Given Hour

Price ($/MWh)	20	25	30	35	50
Volume (MWh)	50	100	200	400	600

which the role of the auctioneer is frequently, but not always, played by the ISO. Thus, the ISO typically performs a dual function: determination of the MCP and system dispatch. In general terms the procedure to determine the MCP can be described as follows.

1. The generators and power marketers submit power supply bids to the ISO. The bid is a set of pairs, {Price, Volume}, from which a bid curve for a particular power supplier is constructed. The bid curve is the function of the form *Price* = F(*Volume*) which determines at which price a generator is willing to supply a given volume.

EXAMPLE 7.1   *Bid curve*

A generator is bidding its three units A (100 MW), B (100 MW), and C (400 MW) into the market. A sample bid for a given hour may have the form shown in Table 7.1.

According to this bid, the generator is willing to produce the first 50 MWh of power at $20/MWh. If a greater volume is needed then the generator will produce any amount of energy from zero up to 100 MWh at $25/MWh, up to 200 MWh at $30/MWh, up to 400 MWh at $35/MWh, and finally up to 600 MWh at $50/MWh.

Note that it is not necessary that the number of bids be equal to the number of units. In fact, it can be significantly higher than the number of units, depending on the allowed granularity of the bids. Also, in this example the bid is assumed to be piecewise constant. For example, any amount of power between 200 MWh and 400 MWh will be generated at the constant rate of $35/MWh. Sometimes market rules require that the price of generation between bid points be determined by a linear interpolation. In any case, the result is a curve showing the prices at which the generator is willing to run at certain levels up to its maximum capacity.

---

2. The ISO collects the bids from all the generators and sorts them by price to obtain the system bid stack. Simultaneously, the demand is determined either from the demand bids or by other means.

TABLE 7.2 Bids

Generator 1

Price ($/MWh)	20	25	30	35	50
Volume (MWh)	50	100	200	400	600

Generator 2

Price ($/MWh)	18	40	100		
Volume (MWh)	100	200	500		

TABLE 7.3 System Bid Stack

Price ($/MWh)	18	20	25	30	35	40	50	100
Volume (MWh)	100	150	200	300	500	600	800	1,100

3. Next the MCP is determined as the highest price on the system bid stack at which the total generation will match the demand.

EXAMPLE 7.2 *System bid curve*

Assume that the system consists of two generators, and that they bid for a particular hour according to Table 7.2.

Combining these bids together and sorting by price, we obtain the system bid stack shown in Table 7.3.

Figure 7.1 depicts this bid stack.

Now, if the projected demand at the given hour is 130 MWh, the MCP for this hour will be $20/MWh, for which price Generator 2 will supply 100 MWh, and Generator 1 will supply 30 MWh. Note that Generator 1 supplies the last megawatt of power to meet the demand. In this case, the power from Generator 1 is said to be on the margin, or marginal, and it is the bid from this marginal generator that determines the MCP. Thus, if the demand is equal to 350 MWh, then the MCP is $35/MWh, and if demand is 870 MWh, the MCP is $100/MWh.

This procedure of computing the MCP describes how energy prices are usually formed. Note that after the MCP is set, additional markets will open to handle any system constraints such as those upon transmission or system integrity. These are separate commodity markets (e.g., ancillary services markets) that employ similar procedures, such as auctions and bids.

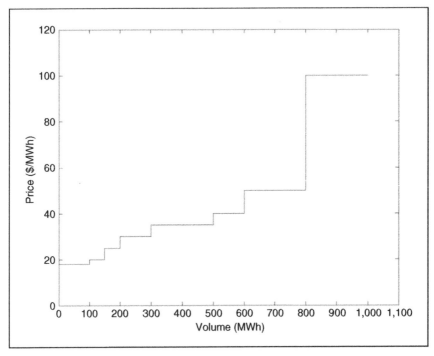

FIGURE 7.1   The Bid Stack

Chapter 1 describes other price formation mechanisms, zonal and nodal. In the case of zonal pricing it is possible to generalize a pool market methodology involving a single bid stack to a multi-stack case, and to develop, after taking into account interzonal transmission constraints, a reasonable representation of zonal prices. A similar approach can be used in the case of nodal pricing, with the understanding that it results in an approximation of the pricing mechanism, the accuracy of which depends directly on the degree of congestion in the market.

In the rest of the chapter, we analyze a hybrid model with only one stack (example of such a market would be NEPOOL). Extensions to multistack markets would not be hard but they would require a much more cumbersome notation and increased level of complexity without providing additional insights into the modeling approach.

Underlying Random Drivers

Once we have an idea of how the procedure that determines the market prices works, the next step is to establish what constitutes the inputs into this procedure (i.e., What are the underlying random drivers that ultimately affect power prices?) It is natural to assume that in determining their bids, the generators take into consideration the cost of power generation for each unit. This cost is primarily dependent on the price of fuel (or fuels, if fuel switching is possible) and the variable costs of running the generation unit. In fact, recalling the definition of the heat rate from Chapter 2, the cost of generating 1 MWh can be written as

$$C = HR \cdot P_{fuel} + VC \qquad (7.6)$$

where

HR is the heat rate

P_{fuel} is the spot price of the fuel in \$/MMBtu

VC denotes the variable costs in \$/MWh

Remember that HR is usually not a constant, but may vary with ambient temperature, generation level, and so on, although here we ignore these details. The variable costs can be split into many components, but to avoid overmodeling, we will only separate out emission costs and combine all others in one block of operational costs. Thus we have identified the first drivers affecting the bids: the fuel price and the variable costs of generation.

Next, the availability of the units is clearly a factor that influences bidding decisions. As we know from Chapter 3, there are two kinds of unit outages: planned and forced (unplanned random outage). We assume here that planned outages, mostly due to maintenance, follow a schedule and can be described in a deterministic way. (In reality, in many cases their schedule is not known with certainty and should be modeled stochastically. But in this case there is little difference between planned and forced outages from the modeling point of view.) As for forced outages, they may have a tremendous impact on prices and so special attention must be paid to their modeling. Forced outages are clearly among the critical drivers of power prices. Finally, demand, or load, directly affects power prices and should be included in the list of drivers.

Figures 7.2 and 7.3 demonstrate a typical strong relation between demand and prices and provide a justification for using demand as a primary driver and, in fact, for the modeling approach as a whole. Note the deterioration of this relation in the region of high demand. The most plausible explanation is that in this region forced outages start playing a greater role in affecting prices, not to mention that forced outage rates may increase due to high operating levels. Naturally, there are exceptions, and in some markets the demand/price relation is quite weak. This is the case in some European markets (see Pirrong and Jermakyan, 1999) and a few markets in the United States (e.g., SERC). These exceptions notwithstanding, in the majority of markets demand is by far the most important factor affecting price.

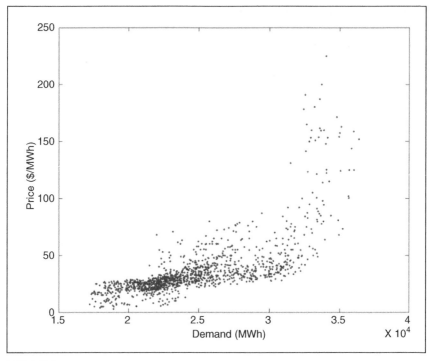

FIGURE 7.2   Power Prices versus Power Demand in California (04/01/98–01/31/00, Hours 16 and 18)

As will be demonstrated later in this chapter, it is frequently advantageous to represent demand as a function of temperature (and possibly other weather related parameters such as humidity). In this case temperature will be used as a primary driver instead of demand.

In summary, the random variables that are identified as the primary drivers determining power prices are

- Fuel prices
- Outages
- Demand or temperature
- Variable operational and emission costs

Transformation of Underlying Drivers into Power Prices

It is clear that power prices can be represented as

$$P_t = s^{bid}(D_t) \tag{7.7}$$

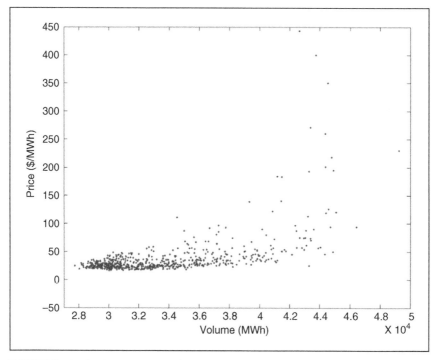

FIGURE 7.3 Daily Average On-peak Prices versus On-peak Average Demand in PJM

where

   P_t is the price of power for a given moment of time

   D_t is demand at that time

   $s^{bid}(D)$ is the bid stack function for a given region

The main question is how to determine or approximate this function. It turns out that using the *generation stack* as an approximation of the bid stack function works very well. Due to the important role the generation stack plays in the development of our model, it makes sense to discuss this concept in greater detail. There are several ways to introduce the generation, or supply stack, but for the purpose of this presentation a generation stack is a particular realization of a bid stack, when generators bid into the market precisely the generation costs of their units. Thus, to obtain a generation stack at a given time we need to sort units by their generation costs.

TABLE 7.4 System Unit Specifications

Unit Number	1	2	3	4	5
Capacity (MW)	200	100	200	300	500
Fuel	#6 Oil	Nat. Gas	Nat. Gas	#6 Oil	Nat. Gas
Heat Rate (Btu/kWh)	10,000	12,000	8,000	10,000	7,000
Fuel Price ($/MMBtu)	3	2.5	2.5	3	2.5
Variable Costs ($/MWh)	10	3	4	12	2
Generation Cost ($/MWh)	40	33	24	32	19.5

TABLE 7.5 Generation Stack

Unit Number	1	2	3	4	5
Cost ($/MWh)	19.5	24	32	33	40
Volume (MWh)	500	700	1,000	1,100	1,300

EXAMPLE 7.3 *Generation stack*

Assume that the system units have the specifications shown in Table 7.4. Viewing these costs as bids, after sorting them we obtain the generation stack shown in Table 7.5.

To understand the relation between the generation stack and the bid stack consider the graphs on Figure 7.4 depicting both stacks in the NEPOOL region. Note that the generation stack presented in this figure reflects the effect of outages. Namely, it is the expectation of generation stacks with respect to random outages. The interruptible rate (i.e., the price of power in the case when the load exceeds the generation capacity due to the outages) is assumed to be $500.

Figure 7.4 clearly suggests that there are similarities between the bid and generation stacks, and in fact these similarities are not accidental. We find time and again bid stacks to be a result of rather simple transformations of the generation stack. These transformations typically can be approximated by a combination of multiplication and scaling operators, with the best results achieved for the segments of the stacks corresponding to medium-to-high demand. In the low demand segment, the structure of transformation may be less obvious, but fortunately it is not important since the units in that section (low-cost baseload units) rarely set the MCP, so their impact on the price distribution is minimal. Here lies the key to understanding the relation

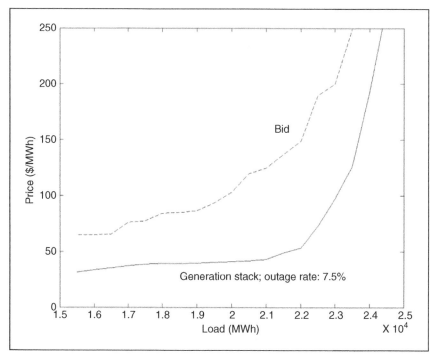

FIGURE 7.4 The Generation Stack versus the Bid Stack in the NEPOOL Region

between the generation stack and the bid stack. If the higher-demand segment of the stack is responsible for setting the MCP, and therefore for the price distribution, then multiplication and scaling transformations should not significantly affect the higher normalized moments of distributions, particularly the third (skewness) and fourth (kurtosis) normalized moments, where

$$skewness = \frac{E[X - E(X)]^3}{\sigma_X^3}$$

$$kurtosis = \frac{E[X - E(X)]^4}{\sigma_X^4} - 3 \qquad (7.8)$$

$$\sigma_X^2 = \text{var}(X)$$

That the multiplication and scaling of the stack preserves the higher normalized moments can be easily proved analytically in the case when the MCP-setting segment of the stack is linear. In real life the assumption of stack linearity is, of course, an approximation, and we expect the skewness and kurtosis to be preserved only approximately. Thus, if our empirical understanding of the relation between the generation and bid stacks is correct, we should also see the agreement between the higher normalized moments of price distributions generated by both stacks. More formally, consider the prices, called marginal generation costs, created using the generation stack by the expression

$$\tilde{P}_t = s^{gen}(D_t) \tag{7.9}$$

Now compare the distribution of the marginal costs $\tilde{P}_t$ with the distribution of power prices P_t generated in (7.7) via the bid stack, that is, with the distribution of market clearing prices. If we are correct, then the higher normalized moments (such as skewness and kurtosis) of both distributions are approximately the same.

This is precisely what we persistently observe in the historical data—the distributions of market clearing prices and marginal costs have approximately the same skewness and kurtosis coefficients (see details in the later section "Justification of the Hybrid Model"). This means that both distributions, while having different expectations and variances, are structurally similar with the same asymmetry characteristics (skewness) and the same measure of fat tails (kurtosis).

This empirical similarity is the foundation of our modeling approach to power prices, which can be described in general terms as follows.

1. With the help of the generation stack and the distribution of demand, determine the distribution of the marginal generation costs $\tilde{P}_t$ using (7.9).
2. Find a transformation $\Phi: \tilde{P}_t \rightarrow P_t$, with P_t being the MCP of power, such that the following conditions are satisfied.
   a. The distribution of power prices P_t is such that the prices of market instruments used for calibration (i.e., forward contracts, options) are matched.
   b. The normalized higher moments, particularly skewness and kurtosis, are preserved (at least approximately).

The class of transformations Φ with the required properties is quite extensive. As was mentioned above, a possible (but not the only) choice can be a family of transformations induced by the multiplication and stack scaling operators.

How do we justify this approach? So far we know that by virtue of item 2a in the preceding list we match market data. Then, by virtue of item 2b, the normalized higher moments of the power prices (i.e., market clearing prices) agree with those of the marginal generation costs. To complete the justification argument, we need to show that the normalized higher moments of the marginal costs agree with the normalized higher moments derived from historical data. (This agreement will be demonstrated in the section "Justification of the Hybrid Model.") Once that is done, our goal is attained. We have generated power prices whose distributions on one hand agree with the market data, and on the other hand accurately capture unique properties of the empirical power price distributions, for example, their extraordinary (even for energy commodities) fat tails as measured by the kurtosis.

Note that historical prices have never been used to calibrate the model, only to test its soundness. This is a subtle but crucial distinction of our approach, separating it from the models introduced in Chapter 4 and other bid stack models (e.g., reduced-form hybrid models). To understand why this is important, consider, for example, a jump-diffusion model from Chapter 4.

This model is typically defined by at least five parameters. Two of these parameters can be estimated to match forward and option prices. But remaining three parameters, particularly those related to jumps can only be calibrated by the historical data. We have already mentioned why this is not a good idea in the case of energy prices—too little data exists, the historical distributions are nonstationary, the parameter estimates are nonstable. Pulling data from different years together may help to increase the sample size, but then the calibration becomes unconditional, that is, it does not differentiate among specific structural conditions present in a given year. This undermines our confidence in the correctness of the properties of the future price distributions generated by this model, because we do not know how model parameters change in response to future structural changes (e.g., anticipated stack changes or changes in demand).

It is not sufficient to claim that the information on the future changes is reflected in the market prices used to calibrate the model. Indeed, having only a forward price and ATM option means having only two integral constraints on a price distribution. But we need to know more about distribution, particularly about its tails, especially when peaking units are concerned. Ideally, if our model is able to match *all* higher normalized moments plus two market constraints (a forward price and the ATM option), then we can be sure that we have captured the whole distribution. In practice, getting skewness and kurtosis right, even approximately, can be considered a success and allows us to be confident in the model distributions.

The hybrid model introduced in this chapter is calibrated using market data, while historical data is used only for back-testing (out-of-sample testing) to validate the approach and to confirm that it continues to correctly capture the empirical properties of power price distributions. Since our model uses structural variables such as supply and demand, it can naturally incorporate projected structural changes.

To summarize, the principal advantage of the hybrid model is that it generates a distribution of power prices using only the available market data and technical characteristics of the generation units, and does not require the use of historical data for calibration. The accuracy of higher normalized moments of this distribution (skewness and kurtosis) is supported by the empirical data. The question of the accuracy of lower moments (i.e., expectation and variance) of the distribution is not relevant, since their values are functions of the prices of traded instruments, and therefore their impact on the values of power derivatives can be hedged.

This completes a general outline of our modeling approach. Following the Box-Cox (1964) methodology, it represents power prices as a transformation of primary variables. The transformation is derived as a simple perturbation of the generation stack. Thus, we now have all the necessary ingredients to give a detailed presentation of the hybrid model. But before we do so, it is worth making a brief digression to explain why there is a difference between the bid stack and the pure generation stack, or, in other words, what precludes generators from always bidding their generation costs. See Harvey and Hogan (2001) for a more comprehensive discussion of the topic; here we focus only on certain issues that, although important, are rarely discussed in the literature.

The Effect of Outages

Outages complicate the definition of the generation stack, because in the presence of random outages, the generation stack itself becomes a random function. In this case the proposition that an operator bidding its next-day generation should bid its production costs requires clarification. Indeed, due to the uncertainty of unit availability, we may have a number of possible generation stacks, each with a probability attached to it. Then, if we want to bid a generation stack, which of the many probable ones should we use? One solution is bidding the probability-weighted sum of all generation stacks, that is, bidding the expected generation stack over all possible outage outcomes. A bid stack constructed in this way may be considerably different from a simple generation stack.

In summary, a generator bidding its generation forward, say, day-ahead, should take into account the uncertainty in available generating capacity. As a rule, this would result in the bid curve being different from the generation stack, most likely higher. Needless to say, outages are not the only source of divergence between the bid and generation curves. The effect of the optionality due to a number of operational and environmental constraints is another important source.

Operational Optionality

To illustrate how operational constraints affect the bidding process, consider the following example.

Assume that a particular generating unit cannot be run more than a certain amount of hours per year. The upper bound on the total run-time can originate from technical specifications or total emission constraints or something else. Then, an operator bidding this unit should always take into account that running the unit on any particular day reduces the possibility of running it later, at a more opportune time. Therefore, a rational decision is to bid higher than in the nonconstrained case, to compensate for the loss of opportunity. This procedure is similar to the early exercise of American options carried out only when the price of the underlying asset is sufficiently far from the strike, thus providing a profit big enough to justify the exercise decision. The only difference is that in the case of power plants we face a much more complex problem, since the number of exercise decisions is significantly greater than just one.

This issue of opportunity loss is particularly acute in the case of peaking plants whose total run-time limits can be rather tight. Consider a realistic case, in which a peaking unit is not allowed to run more than 300 hours per year. This translates into approximately 20 days of running the plant during on-peak hours or 40 to 60 days of running it during super-peak hours. If there is a nonzero probability that the unit is needed during 120 days in a given year, it means that the unit operator has 120 options that can be exercised not more than 20 (or 40 or 60) times. This optionality has value, sometimes substantial, and a rational bid should be able to extract this value. Thus, even if bidding generating costs some time in June guarantees us a profit of $10/MWh, that does not mean this is a rational bid. First, we must determine whether this profit is sufficient to compensate for the loss of opportunity to run the plant sometime, in August or September, since there is a probability of generating greater profits at that time. This probability of expected future profits may not be high enough, and we may still decide that $10/MWh is a worthwhile profit. This decision is not arbitrary, however, but is reached by solving a complex dynamic programming problem, similar to the American option problem. The solution to this problem provides a required level for the rational bid.

The operational constraint optionality described above causes bids to be higher than generating costs. There are also situations when operational constraints move the bid lower. For example, when a unit has a long ramp-up time and start-up costs, it is sometimes necessary to bid below generating costs, just to start the unit—losing money today to win more tomorrow and beyond.

There are many, probably even more important, reasons, in addition to the ones introduced above, why the bid curve may be different from the short-term marginal cost curve, that is, the generating stack curve. We refer a reader to the work of Harvey and Hogan (2001) for a comprehensive analysis of this and related issues. Here we can only give a cursory outline of some of the key structural characteristics affecting the bid curve.

Ancillary Services Markets. Ancillary services markets were introduced to ensure and to manage system reliability. Generators have the choice between bidding in the energy markets or ancillary services markets. Hence, their energy bid curve may differ from the generation stack, since a certain part of generation capacity may be used in the ancillary services markets. (For example, see Zhu, Jordan, and Ihara (2000) for a discussion of the impact of spinning reserve on the energy prices.)

Real-time Market. The existence of the real-time market is another reason why the bid curve in the day-ahead market may differ from the generation stack. A generator may decide that it is more advantageous not to bid all the units in the day-ahead market, but to keep some capacity for bidding in the real-time market.

Environmental Constraints. Environmental constraints may prevent generators from bidding their total capacity and may affect the bidding decisions. These constraints have to do with the impact of generating plants on the environment, including the air quality, temperature (or its rate change) of the adjacent water resources, and so on.

Self-insurance Premium. This is a premium that may be added to the generation costs in order to provide protection against the losses associated with forced outages. (This premium is commonly present as a component of early settlement prices in multi-settlement markets.)

THE MODEL

Following the guidelines outlined in the previous section we now can build a model describing the evolution of power prices in a certain region. We start with the processes for the primary drivers, such as fuels, outages and temperature/demand, then construct the "bid stack" transformation, and finally obtain the process for power prices. Schematically, the model is presented in Figure 7.5.

Note that in this model, temperature is regarded as a primary driver and not the power demand, as is the case, for example, in Skantze and Ilic (2001). Although in principle these choices are equivalent, we prefer to use temperature for the following reasons. First, there is substantially more historical data available for temperature than for demand. Second, there is a reasonably active market of temperature products, which allows us to use forward-looking market data in addition to the historical information, to calibrate our model. On the other hand, the market for demand products is still in a nascent state.

Throughout the chapter we will use the following notation:

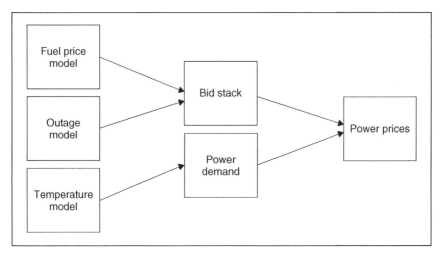

FIGURE 7.5   A Hybrid Model for Power Prices

t and T denote time; $0 \leq t \leq T$; $t = 0$ is the current time

$F_{0,T}^{P}$ is the current (at $t = 0$) forward power curve as a function of time to expiration T

$F_{t,T}^{P}$ is the simulated forward power curve at a certain time t as a function of time to expiration T

$P_T \equiv F_{T,T}^{P}$ is the spot power price at the time T

$U = (u_1, u_2, \ldots, u_{N_f})$ is the set of Group 1 fuels (see the section "Fuel Model")

$F_{0,T}^{u_i}$ is the current (at $t = 0$) forward curve as a function of the time to expiration T and specified for each fuel u_i

$F_{t,T}^{u_i}$ is the simulated forward curve at a certain time t as a function of the time to expiration T for the fuel u_i

$U_T^i \equiv F_{T,T}^{u_i}$ is the spot price of the fuel u_i at time T

$F_{t,T}^{\Im}$ is the forward (forecasted) temperature curve at time t as a function of the expiration time T

$\Im_T \equiv F_{T,T}^{\Im}$ the temperature at time T

$D_T = d(T, \Im_T)$ power demand at time T as a function of the temperature $\Im_T$

$\Omega_T(\lambda) = (\omega_{T,1}, \omega_{T,2}, \ldots, \omega_{\ell,T}, \ldots, \omega_{T,L_{gen}})$ is the outage indicator vector at time T

TABLE 7.6   Two Categories of Fuels

Group 1	Group 2
Natural gas	Nuclear
#2 Heating oil	Hydro
#6 Fuel oil (with different sulfur concentration)	Solar
Coal	Wind
Jet fuel	Biomass
Diesel	Etc.
Methane	
Liquefied natural gas (LNG)	
Etc.	

where

$\omega_{\ell,T} = 0, 1$

$\omega_{\ell,T} = 0$ is the ℓ-th unit is out

$\omega_{\ell, T} = 1$ is the ℓ-th unit is on $\lambda = (\lambda_1, \lambda_2, \ldots \lambda_\ell, \ldots \lambda_{L_{gen}})'$ a vector of outage arrival rates with λ_ℓ being the average outage arrival rate for the unit ℓ in the stack, and L_{gen}, the total number of units in the generation stack

Fuel Model

The first step in our modeling effort is to represent the fuel-related costs of generating power. In order to do this it is useful to split fuels into two categories as seen in Table 7.6.

The distinct feature of the fuels in Group 1 is that they are tradable commodities. They are traded both in the spot and forward markets in the form of futures, forward contracts, swaps, and options. Forward contracts and swaps allow one to construct forward curves that frequently reach up to ten years and beyond, while options imply forward-looking volatility term structures for these fuels. Both forward and volatility curves are then used to estimate parameters of the process governing the fuel price evolution. It is worth noting that in practical applications it is common to model only the evolution of natural gas, heating oil, and coal prices, and then to express the prices of other fuels in Group 1 as a spread of the prices of these principal fuels. As was discussed in Chapter 2, the relation between Group 1 fuel prices and the corresponding fuel related costs of power generation is given by the equality

$$Fuel\_Cost\ (\$/MWh) = \frac{Heat\_Rate\ (Btu/KWh)}{1000} \cdot Fuel\_Price\ (\$/MMBtu)$$

$$(7.10)$$

As for Group 2, at present there is no liquid market for the fuels in this group, so they will be treated differently. Namely, we are not going to model their prices but simply identify generating costs (usually constant) related to these fuels and treat them as a part of variable costs.

EXAMPLE 7.4 *Fuel costs*

For a natural gas-fired power plant with a heat rate of 7,000 Btu/kWh, the fuel-related generation cost is \$21/MWh if the price of natural gas is \$3/MMBtu. It will be \$35/MWh if the natural gas price moves up to \$5. On the other hand, in our calculation the fuel cost of the nuclear plant will be a plant-dependent constant whose value is usually very low (frequently it is set to \$0.00/MWh).

Evolution Process for the Fuels in Group 1

Let the following equation denote the set of Group 1 fuels used in generation plants of a particular region.

$$U = (u_1, u_2, \ldots, u_{N_f})$$

It does not matter whether this set includes all fuels or only the principal fuels mentioned above (natural gas, heating oil, and coal)—the general model methodology remains the same. It consists of specifying the evolution process for the spot or forward prices, and the set of market data used for the process calibration.

Price Evolution Process

There is no shortage of stochastic processes that can be used to describe the evolution of fuel prices; some of these were presented in Chapters 4 and 5. As a rule, we recommend to use processes for the forward price term structure (see Chapter 5). These processes, although more computationally complex than the spot price processes, provide a greater flexibility for matching market data, in particular volatility and correlation data. For any given fuel u_i, a forward term structure model offers a process for evolving forward prices $F_{t,T}^{u_i}$ as a function of t, with the parameter T denoting forward contract expiration times.

Thus, we propose to use the HJM (Heath-Jarrow-Morton) modeling methodology, or its discrete version such as BGM (Brace-Gatarek-Musiela) or string model should we choose T to be a discrete index (see Chapter 5), to model the evolution of the forward curves for different fuels. Depending on the forward curve granularity we need to achieve, T may correspond to the settlement of monthly contracts, weekly contracts, or even daily contracts. A typical example is the process of the form (5.14) with the appropriately chosen drift and volatility coefficients.

The process for forward prices also implies the evolution of fuel spot prices via the relation

$$U_t^i = F_{t,T}^{u_i} \qquad\qquad (7.11)$$

where U_t^i denotes the spot price of the fuel u_i. Alternatively, one can, and frequently does, directly use spot price processes described in Chapter 4 to model the evolution of U_t^i, provided that the spot price is all that is required to compute cash flows. Spot processes are easier to implement but, as was discussed in Chapter 4, are significantly less flexible than forward price processes when matching market data.

Market Data and Model Calibration

Below we describe a typical set of market data used to calibrate fuel price models. Although by no means exhaustive, this set of market constraints gives a good idea about the challenges one faces in practical applications.

Initial Condition.   The condition (5.16) specifies the forward prices at $t = 0$.

Market Constraints

■ **Matching the current forward curve.** The condition of the type (5.17) imposes a constraint on the drift term of a forward price process. Particularly, in the risk-neutral world the drift is zero. Together with (5.15) this condition also specifies the constraint on the drift of the spot price process.

■ **Matching options prices.** This condition has been extensively discussed in Chapter 5. Typically, fuel markets supply prices of monthly and sometimes daily options. As a rule, these are at-the-money options, although in some markets out-of-the-money options are also actively traded. In Appendix A we demonstrate how to match these prices in the lognormal case. Matching option prices generally requires solving a system of nonlinear equations—a conceptually straightforward, but computationally complex problem.

■ **Matching total fuel correlation structure.** The condition (5.19) imposes constraints on the correlation between different contracts for the same fuel, as well as on the correlation between different fuels. The importance of correct representation of the joint fuel evolution can be explained by, among other reasons, the fact that the ordering of the generation stack to a significant degree depends on fuel prices. Hence, misrepresentation of the joint fuel behavior may, in extreme cases, lead to a qualitatively wrong distribution of the power prices. The importance of capturing joint behavior becomes even more apparent if we recall that many power plants have duel fuel capabilities, and therefore a wrong model for the joint evolution may lead to an incorrect dispatch of those plants and ultimately to wrong cash flow projections. In Appendix A we show how to match the correlation structure in the lognormal case. Clearly, this problem becomes much more technically difficult in the case of more general processes.

Temperature Model

Stable statistical properties and the abundance of historical data significantly facilitate the task of modeling temperature. As follows from the section "Weather Data" Chapter 3, temperature behavior in many locations can be described with the help of normal distribution, which considerably simplifies the modeling efforts. In typical implementations the focus is on modeling the variable $\Im_t$ (see equation [3.15]). This variable is a representation of the temperature at time t, and can be, for example, a daily average temperature, daily maximum, daily minimum, and so on. By analogy with other markets, we call $\Im_t$ the spot temperature, which is used as an index against which weather products are settled. Together with the spot temperature we can introduce the forward-looking temperature term structure $F_{t,T}^{\Im}$ It can be interpreted as a forecast at time t of the temperatures at the future times T at a given location. Another interpretation, valid for liquid market locations, is that it is a term structure of prices of the traded forward temperature contracts.

When modeling temperature behavior, one should pay a special attention to capturing the seasonality of its statistical characteristics, such as temperature mean and variation. A common approach is to represent the daily temperature as a deviation from the historical mean and model the evolution of this deviation using, for example, the standard Brownian motion:

$$\Im_t = \psi(t) + \tau_t$$

$$d\tau_t = \sigma(t)dW_t$$

The choice of the function $\psi(t)$ should not be confined solely to historical means. More sophisticated models may incorporate long-term temperature trends, cycles, and other particularities, or even introduce a separate stochastic process for the evolution of the function $\psi(t)$. It is important, however, not to lose sight of the final goal of the modeling efforts, since ultimately this goal determines the need or relevance of more complex models. For example, temperature models with long-term trends may not be necessary for hedging purposes, because long-term trends may have been already reflected in the price structure.

Alternatively, we may develop a process for the forward temperature term structure $F_{t,T}^{\Im}$ using the HJM-type approach:

$$dF_{t,T}^{\Im} = \mu^{\Im}\left(t,T\right) dt + \sigma^{\Im}\left(t,T\right) dW_t \tag{7.12}$$

With the appropriate choice of the coefficients $\mu^{\Im}(t,T)$ and $\sigma^{\Im}(t,T)$ we can capture a complex trending and volatility behavior, as well as a general temperature correlation structure between different times and locations. In that respect modeling temperature is not significantly different from modeling fuels. As expected, in this case the evolution of the spot temperature is given by the relation

$$\Im_t \equiv F_{t,t}^{\Im}$$

Demand Model

Models for power demand, or load (both terms are used interchangeably), are well developed and understood. Utilities have been perfecting these models for many years to improve short-term forecasts of their loads. A typical short-term load model is a complex multi-parameter nonlinear function dependent on weather variables—temperature, humidity, wind-chill factor—as well as on economic and demographic data, and the data on load composition. This degree of detail may not be necessary for building a longer-term stochastic process for demand evolution. Indeed, there is little advantage in trying to capture each and every factor affecting the power demand while lacking sufficient information to accurately model the evolution of these factors. Moreover, short- and long-term models have significantly different objectives. The purpose of short-term models is to provide an accurate load forecast, while long-term models are mostly used for hedging and risk management purposes. Therefore, if our intention is to build a demand process for a pricing and hedging model, we should focus on correctly capturing the load distribution at a given time, rather than predicting load at that time.

Various techniques are used to model load distributions. Pirrong and Jermakyan (1999) and Skantze and Ilic (2001) chose to model it directly. Other methodologies favor first representing the load as the response function to a number (usually small) of primary factors, such as temperature and humidity. After that the load distribution is implied by the distribution of the primary factors.

We prefer the factor approach to the direct representation of load distribution for the following reasons. First, the primary factors frequently have more stable and manageable statistical properties than the load and are therefore easier to model. Second, there is typically substantially more data available for these factors. Third, unlike load, some of these factors, especially temperature, are traded in the forward markets, and hence can be used for hedging purposes, thus making modeling in terms of these factors very attractive. Finally, using the factor approach we can easily model different load configurations in the same region since, most likely, they are dependent on the same primary factors.

For example, suppose we have built a distribution of the New England regional load through modeling the distribution of an appropriate temperature index, and determining the response of the total regional load to temperature. After that very little is required to generate, for instance, the distribution of the residential load in the region. Indeed, the only modification we have to make is to find a response this time of the regional residential load to the same temperature index. Once that is done, the already known temperature distribution can be used to compute the distribution of the residential load. In contrast, the direct approach to load modeling requires that we develop the residential load distribution from scratch using historical data. This distinction between two modeling approaches is especially evident when a power plant's cash flow is determined by a combination of loads. For example, the total regional load may affect cash flow through pool power prices, whereas the residential load may have an impact via power purchase agreements or other contracts. Therefore, cash flow evaluation requires simultaneous simulation of both total load and residential load. If the direct approach to modeling loads is used, then the simultaneous simulations need the development of the joint distribution of these loads, which often is a challenging statistical problem due to the lack of data and the complexity of the joint distribution. On the other hand, the factor approach automatically implies the joint distribution of loads from the joint distribution of the primary factors, which as a rule is not difficult to find due to the availability of data. This property is particularly useful when the number of factors is small (one or two).

Caveat: It is imperative to test the resulting joint distribution of loads against the historical data. Note that without this test, we can only claim an empirical support of the marginal distributions of loads. Although it may seem that the joint distribution of loads is constructed naturally and must be correct, the test still must be carried out, since matching only marginal distribution ultimately is not enough to validate the joint distribution.

In this section we use only temperature as a primary factor describing the load distribution. This is done to simplify the exposition, and by no means implies that other factors, for example humidity, cannot be used in the model. (It is worth mentioning, however, that in many cases the temperature is actually all one needs to accurately describe distributions of power demand.) More formally, the power demand at time t, denoted by D_t, is represented as a function of time and temperature

$$D_t = d(t, \Im_t) \tag{7.13}$$

Typically, the demand function $d(t, \Im_t)$ is selected with the help of some statistical estimation technique (least squares, maximum likelihood, and so on) from a parametric family of functions. The choice of this family is usually suggested by the empirical data (see the section "Demand" in Chapter 3). For example, it can be a family of polynomials with respect to the temperature variable $\Im_t$ with polynomial coefficients dependent on time t as in Kosecki (1999). This form of the demand function is simple and flexible, and allows one to represent the long-term load growth as well as the fairly general temperature dependence. Polynomial representation is certainly not the only one that is used in practice. Other choices of the analytical form of the demand functions (e.g., piecewise polynomial family, logistic family, and so on) are available that may capture more efficiently the particular empirical properties of the temperature/load relationship. We leave this choice to the modeler's intuition and understanding of the specific properties of a given application.

Outages

Outages will be modeled independently for each unit in a given regional generation stack. Our goal is to develop a procedure that generates random outages in agreement with technical and empirical data, and to use this procedure to determine the availability of generating units at any given time T.

Consider a unit ℓ in the regional generation stack, $\ell = 1, 2, \ldots, L_{gen}$. The procedure for modeling outages generally consists of the following two steps.

1. Model random time intervals between the forced outages, that is, the availability periods,

$$\Delta t_{1,\ell}^{avail}, \Delta t_{2,\ell}^{avail}, \ldots, \Delta t_{m,\ell}^{avail}, \ldots$$

2. Model the length of each outage

$$\Delta t_{1,\ell}^{out}, \Delta t_{2,\ell}^{out}, \ldots, \Delta t_{m,\ell}^{out}, \ldots$$

In order to implement this procedure for each generation unit we use the following forced outage characteristics:

- Equivalent Forced Outage Rate (EFOR), an average forced outage time of a given unit measured as a fraction of the total time the unit has been connected to the system during a certain measurement period (typically, a year).

■ Parameters specifying the distribution of time under repairs for a given unit, for example, repair time mean and variance.

These technical characteristics will allow us to derive the parameters necessary to model the availability intervals $\Delta t_{m,\ell}^{avail}$ for each unit ℓ. Indeed, consider an example wherein a particular unit is expected to experience forced outages on average 30 days out of the 330 days it is connected to the system, and assume that the expected repair time is

$$E\left(\Delta t_{m,\ell}^{out}\right) = 3 \text{ days}$$

In this case, an average length of the availability interval is

$$E\left(\Delta t_{m,\ell}^{avail}\right) = 30 \text{ days}$$

The average number of outages per measurement period is 10 and the average outage arrival rate is

$$\lambda_\ell = \frac{10}{330} = 0.03 \text{ per day}$$

Knowing average outage arrival rates λ_ℓ may be sufficient to specify certain commonly used processes and use them to model outages. For example, we may choose a Poisson process to govern the outages. (Other distributions, [e.g., uniform] have also been used in some applications.) Under the Poisson process, the time periods between the outages have exponential distribution:

$$\Pr(\Delta t_{m,\ell}^{avail} \leq x) = 1 - e^{-\lambda_\ell x}, \quad x \geq 0, \quad \ell = 1, 2, \ldots, L_{gen}, \quad m = 1, 2, \ldots$$
$$(7.14)$$

where

$$\lambda = (\lambda_1, \lambda_2, \ldots \lambda_\ell, \ldots \lambda_{L_{gen}})'$$

is a vector of outage arrival rates, with λ_ℓ being the average rate for unit ℓ in the stack.

Combining this process (or any other process used to model outage arrivals) with the process specifying the outage length allows us to determine the availability of any unit at any time. More formally, an outage model generates for any time T, an outage indicator vector

$$\Omega_T (\lambda) = (\omega_{T,1}, \ldots \omega_{T,L_{gen}})$$

defined as follows

$$\omega_{T,\ell} = \begin{cases} 0 & \text{if at time } T \text{ the unit } \ell \text{ is experiencing forced outage} \\ 1 & \text{otherwise} \end{cases}$$

Frequently in practical implementation this vector is allowed to assume values between 0 and 1 in order to take care of partial forced outages, otherwise called *derates*. Modeling derates is not substantially different from modeling forced outages. However, it requires specific data, which is sometimes difficult to find.

Finally, we modify the indicator vector $\Omega_T (\lambda)$ to incorporate the planned outages by setting to zero the components of this vector that correspond to units scheduled for outage at time T. After this, the vector $\Omega_T (\lambda)$ gives us a complete picture of the generating unit availability, no matter the nature of the outage, random forced or deterministic scheduled. When the planned outage schedule of a particular unit is not known, we have no choice but to build a stochastic model for the planned outages, which can be done using the same techniques as were developed to model the forced outages.

In summary, the outage model generates an indicator vector $\Omega_T (\lambda)$ with the following properties. If for a particular unit ℓ the component $\Omega_{T,\ell}(\lambda) = 1$, then this unit is available for generation at time T, and if $\Omega_{T,\ell}(\lambda) = 0$, it is not. The value between 0 and 1 indicates that the unit is partially available due to derates.

Stack Function

The equation (7.7) suggests an approach to modeling power prices as a function of the demand. We called it a *bid stack function*, $s^{bid} (D)$, and it plays a crucial role in our model. In this book we propose one method for deriving this function. The principal idea underlying the method is to look for the bid stack as a certain transformation of the generation stack function. The generation stack has been introduced earlier, together with an argument supporting its use as an approximation of the bid stack. In this section we give a more detailed description of the generation stack and suggest a class of generation stack transformations that may be useful in representing the bid stack.

At any given time T, building a regional generation stack typically means sorting power plants in the region according to their short-term generation costs. Conceptually, these costs are as follows.

Short-Term Generating Costs

Fuel Costs Associated with Group 1 Fuels. If the ℓ-th unit in the generation stack uses a Group 1 fuel u_{i_ℓ}, then the corresponding fuel cost is given by the product

$$Q_{T,\ell} = HR_{i_\ell,\ell} \cdot U_T^{i_\ell}$$

where

$U_T^{i_\ell}$ is the price of the fuel

u_{i_ℓ} at time T, and $HR_{i,\ell}$ is the unit's heat rate associated with this fuel. (As was mentioned before, this heat rate may not be a constant, but may depend on generation level.)

For a dual fuel unit, which can switch between fuel u_{i_ℓ} and fuel u_{j_ℓ} (e.g., between natural gas and oil, between oil and LNG, and so on), the fuel-related costs are given by the expression

$$Q_{T,\ell} = \min\left\{ HR_{i_\ell,\ell} \cdot U_T^{i_\ell}, HR_{j_\ell,\ell} \cdot U_T^{j_\ell} \right\}$$

Fuel Costs Associated with Group 2 Fuels. Since at present there is no liquid market for Group 2 fuels, so their prices are not readily available, we simply assign some constant value that approximates the cost of generating 1 MWh in the plants utilizing these fuels. Thus, if u_ℓ is a Group 2 fuel used in unit ℓ of the stack, the fuel cost associated with this fuel is denoted by Q_ℓ ($/MWh).

Emission Costs. These costs become an increasingly larger component of the total generating costs. They are typically quoted in dollars per ton of emitted pollutants (i.e., SOx, NOx, and so on). Therefore, we must first translate these quotes into $/MWh. To do this we need the following conversion coefficients:

- NOx Rate, SOx Rate [lbs/MMBtu]: plant-specific emission rates per MMBtu of the fuel
- Heat Rate [Btu/kWh]

With these coefficients

$$\text{NOx Price}\left[\frac{\$}{\text{MWh}}\right] = \frac{\text{Heat Rate}}{1000}\left[\frac{\text{MMBtu}}{\text{MWh}}\right] \cdot \text{NOx Rate}\left[\frac{\text{lbs}}{\text{MMBtu}}\right] \cdot \frac{1}{2000}\left[\frac{\text{ton}}{\text{lbs}}\right] \cdot \text{NOx Price}\left[\frac{\$}{\text{ton}}\right]$$

$$\text{SOx Price}\left[\frac{\$}{\text{MWh}}\right] = \frac{\text{Heat Rate}}{1000}\left[\frac{\text{MMBtu}}{\text{MWh}}\right] \cdot \text{SOx Rate}\left[\frac{\text{lbs}}{\text{MMBtu}}\right] \cdot \frac{1}{2000}\left[\frac{\text{ton}}{\text{lbs}}\right] \cdot \text{SOx Price}\left[\frac{\$}{\text{ton}}\right]$$

EXAMPLE 7.5   *Emission costs*

Consider a coal plant with the following characteristics:

$$\text{NOx Rate} = 0.62 \text{ [lbs/MMBtu]}, \text{SOx Rate} = 2.14 \text{ [lbs/MMBtu]}$$
$$\text{Heat Rate} = 7000 \text{ [Btu/kWh]}$$

If the June NOx contract be \$800/ton, then according to the above formula

$$\text{NOx Price [\$/MWh]} = 7 \times 0.62 \times (1/2000) \times 800 = 1.74 \text{ [\$/MWh]}$$

Similarly, if June SOx contract is quoted at \$160/ton, then

$$\text{SOx Price [\$/MWh]} = 7 \times 2.14 \times (1/2000) \times 160 = 1.20 \text{ [\$/MWh]}$$

Modeling emission costs can be as involved as modeling fuel prices. Indeed, there have been attempts to develop a stochastic model for the evolution of emission costs. However, at present, the success of these attempts has been limited by the lack of data and by the structural complexities of the market. In this presentation, for simplicity, emission costs are represented simply as a deterministic function of time (e.g., we can use the expectation of future emission costs derived with the help of the forward curve or some other technique). At a given time T, emission costs for the ℓth unit of a generation stack are denoted by $E_{T,\ell}$. They are quoted in \$/MWh, and are a combined measure of the emission costs associated with all pollutants produced during the run of the unit.

Other Variable Costs (VOM).   This category includes all variable costs (other than fuel and emission costs) that are incurred during the run of a generating unit and that can be directly connected the generating output. They are frequently called variable operation and management costs (VOM), although their definition and composition may be rather loose. They may include some labor costs, heating/cooling costs, or a certain fraction of the fixed costs. As a rule, in power price models these costs are not considered separately, but are combined in one quantity, which we denote by $VOM_{T,\ell}$ (\$/MWh). In a typical combined cycle plant, VOM costs may vary between .50 \$/MWh and 2 \$/MWh, while in a peaking unit they may exceed 3 \$/MWh.

To summarize, short-term generating costs of a unit ℓ at a given time T

$$W_{T,\ell} = \begin{cases} HR_{T,\ell}^{u_{i_\ell}} \cdot U_{T,\ell}^{i_\ell} + E_{T,\ell} + VOM_{T,\ell} & \text{if } u_{i_\ell} \text{ is a Group 1 fuel} \\ U_{T,\ell}^{i_\ell} + E_{T,\ell} + VOM_{T,\ell} & \text{if } u_{i_\ell} \text{ is a Group 2 fuel} \end{cases} \quad (7.15)$$

where

u_{i_ℓ} is the fuel used in the unit (or the cheapest fuel to use, in the case of dual-fuel units)

$HR^{i_\ell}_{T,\ell}$ is the unit's heat rate associated with the fuel

$U^{i_\ell}_{T,\ell}$ is the price of the fuel at time T

The Generation Stack

Once the generating costs are determined for each unit in the stack, we can approximate the generating stack function by sorting all available units according to their costs. More formally, the procedure of building the generating stack looks like this.

1. For given time T, obtain the prices of all fuels used by the stack units.
2. Compute the generating costs of each unit using (7.15).
3. Obtain the outage indicator vector Ω_T using the procedure from the section "Outages."
4. Use this vector to determine available units.

The generating stack is an ordering $\{\ell_1, \ell_2, \ldots, \ell_i, \ldots\}$ of the available generating units in such a way that the corresponding generating costs satisfy

$$W_{T,\ell_1} \leq W_{T,\ell_2} \leq \ldots \leq W_{T,\ell_i} \leq \ldots$$

This means that the units in the generating stack are ordered in the ascending order of their costs.

Following Example 7.3, we define the value of the generation stack function for a given demand as the generation cost of the last unit in the stack needed to meet this demand (the marginal cost). Assume that

$$C_{\ell_1}, C_{\ell_2}, \ldots C_{\ell_i}, \ldots$$

are the generating capacities of the ordered stack units. If the demand

$$D = C_{\ell_1}$$

then, by our definition, the value of the generation stack function is

$$s^{gen}(D) = W_{\ell_1}$$

The demand is met by the first plant in the stack, therefore, its cost is the value of the generation stack function for this demand. If

$$D = C_{\ell_1} + C_{\ell_2}$$

then

$$s^{gen}(D) = W_{\ell_2}$$

In this case we must run two units to meet the demand and W_{ℓ_2} is the higher of the two units' costs. Similarly, if

$$D = C_{\ell_1} + C_{\ell_2} + \dots + C_{\ell_i}$$

then

$$s^{gen}(D) = W_{\ell_i}$$

Thus, this procedure determines the generation stack function at the discrete points

Demand at T: $D_T = C_{\ell_1}, C_{\ell_1} + C_{\ell_2}, C_{\ell_1} + C_{\ell_2} + C_{\ell_3}, \dots, C_{\ell_1} + C_{\ell_2} + \dots + C_{\ell_i}, \dots$

Gen. Stack $s^{gen}(D_T) = W_{\ell_1} \quad W_{\ell_2} \qquad W_{\ell_3} \qquad\qquad W_{\ell_i} \qquad\qquad\qquad \dots$

If the demand falls between those points, then we use some interpolation procedure, such as piecewise constant interpolation, piecewise linear interpolation, and so on, to find the value of the generation stack function.

At the end we get the generation stack function defined for every demand up to the maximum stack capacity. From the construction procedure it is clear that the shape of this function at time T depends on the fuel price vector U_T, outage indicator vector $\Omega_T(\lambda)$, emission prices E_T, variable costs VOM_T, and, finally, on the vector of generating capacities C_T (which in turn, depends on various reserve requirements). Therefore the full notation for the generation stack function is

$$s^{gen}(D_T; T, U_T, \Omega_T(\lambda), E_T, VOM_T, C_T)$$

It is important to emphasize that the procedure above describes only an approximation of the generation stack function, because a more rigorous construction procedure requires taking into account a much greater set of technical parameters and constraints. They include start-up costs, ramp-up and ramp-down rates, maximum up and down times, minimum dispatch requirements, requirements on spinning reserves, transmission constraints, and so on. The resulting procedure is substantially more complex than the one described above and is beyond the scope of this book. On the other hand, since this function will be used as an approximation to the bid stack function, we may not need to describe it with the utmost precision. Indeed, accounting for every possible nuance may be unnecessary because the uncertainties and imprecision of our assumptions, statistical parameterization, and empirical data may (and most likely will) overcome whatever accuracy we achieve by building the exact generation stack function.

The Bid Stack

We are now ready to make the final step in constructing a demand-to-price function, a function that we call a bid stack. Following the earlier section "Transformation of Underlying Drivers into Power Prices," we will be looking for a bid stack as a transformation of the generation stack function. That section also suggests a particular form for this transformation, namely a combination of multiplication and scaling operators applied to the generation stack. More specifically, at any time T the bid stack is sought for in the following form

$$s_T^{bid}(D_T) = \alpha_1 s^{gen}(D_T; T, U_T, \Omega_T(\alpha_2\lambda), E_T, VOM_T, \alpha_3 C_T) \quad (7.16)$$

where α_1, α_2, α_3 are constants (for a given T, but may vary with time).

The justification for the transformation form has been given previously in the section "Transformation of Underlying Drivers into Power Prices." Remember that the main selling point there is that only market (tradable) data is used to parameterize this transformation. Unlike in other models, historical data is not used for model calibration. Nonetheless, the back tests demonstrate that the model price distributions agree with the empirical distributions, thus validating our modeling approach. Clearly serious attention should be paid to assure that a stack transformation preserves (at least approximately) higher normalized moments of price distributions. For example, in the section "Transformation of Underlying Drivers into Power Prices" we justified the choice transformation (7.16) when the stack is close to linear in a high load region. In the case of a very nonlinear stack, (7.16) may not be a good choice and other possible transformations should be considered. Ultimately, the "goodness" of transformation is verified by performing out-of-sample testing of simulated versus actual price distributions, as will be done in the section "Justification of the Hybrid Model."

It is also interesting at this point to provide some intuitive arguments to illuminate the choice of the transformation (7.16). As was discussed earlier, there are a number of reasons why the bid stack may differ from the generation stack. It is our goal to choose the transformation between both stacks so that it captures these differences. Thus a coefficient α_1 in (7.16) can be interpreted as a factor needed to capture premia added to (or subtracted from) the generating costs to account for numerous optionalities and market constraints. The adjustment of the stack capacities by α_3 is done to better represent frequently uncertain reserve levels and operational constraints.

Finally, the factor α_2 is introduced to capture the uncertainty about the operational characteristics of the plants in the stack. Thus, the representation of the type (7.16) sums up, albeit in aggregate form, the sources of deviation between power prices and generating costs.

Finally, we address the question of how accurate the representation of the generation stack in (7.16) should be. In general, the principal characteristics of the generation stack are known, including costs, average heat rates, outage rates, and so on. What are often not known are the details: minimum/maximum runtime, ramp-up/down rates, precise heat-rate curve, the strategies employed by the market participants relative to ancillary services, and so on. Knowing these details may or may not be important; as always, one should carefully examine the modeling goal. For example, ramp-up rates may be important for modeling off-peak prices and not for the on-peak prices. On the other hand, too many details in the representation of the generation stack, while failing to deliver any additional modeling precision, may result in substantial deterioration of computational efficiency of the model. Thus, in representing the generation stack one should look for a compromise between accuracy and efficiency of the model.

Power Prices

The complexity of modeling prices in power markets is caused by, among other reasons, the wide range of power prices. It is necessary first to clearly define which one of them is being modeled. As was mentioned in Chapter 2, there are on-peak prices (typically, from 7 AM to 11 PM weekdays), off-peak prices (11 PM to 7 AM weekdays), weekend prices, round-the-clock-prices, eight-hour on-peak block prices (7 AM to 3 PM and 3 PM to 11 PM), four-hour on-peak block prices, super-peak prices (block-prices for the highest demand hours), hourly prices, quarter-hour prices, and so on. These prices may have different statistical properties that must be carefully taken into consideration in a successful model. In addition, as in the case of fuel prices, the market price data and the modeled prices may not match (i.e., different resolution, delivery characteristics, and definition), which can cause further problems. Therefore, when modeling power prices special attention should be paid to the particular properties of these prices and of the input data used in the model calibration. To avoid overwhelming our readers with the implementation details, we only present a generic version of the power price model. However, it is worth noting that real-life applications may require model modifications designed to address issues concerning price specifications, input data, model constraints, and so on.

We start with describing a typical set of input data used to calibrate the power price model.

Input Data

Power

The market price quotes used to calibrate the model include

- Monthly Forward Prices
- Monthly option prices, that is, options exercised into the monthly forward contracts
- Daily option prices, that is, options that can be exercised daily during a certain future month

Fuel

The market price quotes used to calibrate fuel models are described in detail in the previous section "Fuel Models." As a rule, they include

- Monthly Forward Prices
- Monthly option prices, that is, options exercised into the monthly forward contracts
- Daily option prices, that is, options that can be exercised daily during a certain future month

In addition a variance-covariance matrix involving all forward contracts (different expiration dates and different fuels) must be matched. (See also the section "Fuel Models.")

Regional Generation Stack Data

For each generating unit in the stack the following information is supplied.

- Heat-rate curve for the fuels in Group 1 (as a function of the generation levels)
- Variable costs of generation per 1 MWh for fuels from Group 2
- Emission costs ($/MMBtu)
- Additional information (i.e., start-up costs, ramp-up and ramp-down rates, minimum uptime, minimum downtime, total emission constraints, and so on)

Outage Data

Equivalent Force Outage Rates (EFOR) are supplied for each generating unit in the regional stack.

Temperature

- Historical average daily temperatures. It is possible to instead use a forecasted daily forward temperature curve if better information is available

about future temperatures (such as an information about a probable El
Niño year).

▪ Historical standard deviation of daily temperatures.

Modeling Goal

Our goal is to describe the evolution of power and fuel prices, as well as daily
temperatures, so that

▪ Constraints imposed by the market data are satisfied.
▪ Distribution of the power prices has required properties.
▪ Joint distributions of power and fuel prices have required properties.

THE PROCESS FOR POWER PRICES

We now summarize the steps of the procedure introduced in this chapter to
model power prices.

Step 1.   **Simulating fuel prices.** The procedure presented in Chapter 5 yields
the evolution process for daily forward prices for each fuel in Group 1.
As a result, for each future time T and for each fuel u_i in Group 1 we
now have the process describing how the forward prices $F_{t,T}^{u_i}$ change
with time t, $0 \leq t \leq T$, while satisfying market constraints specified in
Chapter 5. This process also generates the evolution of spot prices for
these fuels by virtue of the relation

$$U_t^i \equiv F_{t,T}^{u_i}$$

Step 2.   **Simulating temperatures.** We use the process from Chapter 5 to describe the evolution of the temperature forecasts $F_{t,T}^{\Im}$ for every future
time T, $0 \leq t \leq T$. The evolution of daily temperatures is then obtained
with the help of the relation

$$\Im_T = F_{T,T}^{\Im}$$

Step 3.   **Simulating power demand.** Power demand or load is simulated using the relation (7.13)

$$D_T = d(T, \Im_T)$$

Step 4.   **Simulating outages.** The outage indicator vector $\Omega_T(\lambda)$ is generated
according to the procedure described in the section "Outages". Each
component of this vector indicates whether the corresponding stack unit

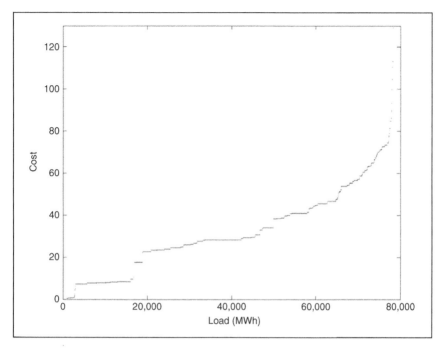

FIGURE 7.6   PJM Generation Stack

is available $[\Omega_{T,\ell}(\lambda) = 1]$ or not available $[\Omega_{T,\ell}(\lambda) = 0]$ for generation at time T. A component of the vector is set to zero, regardless of whether the corresponding unit is down as a result of forced or scheduled outages.

Step 5.   **Building the generation stack.** Until now we have focused on how to model the evolution of primary variables such as fuel prices, outages, and temperature/demand, and hence how to generate their distributions at each future time T. For a given random vector of fuel prices and outages, $[U_T, \Omega_T(\lambda)]'$, we use the procedure described earlier in this chapter to construct the generation stack

$$s_{T^{gen}, U_T, \Omega_T}(D_T) \equiv s^{gen}[D_T; T, U_T, \Omega_T(\lambda), E_T, VOM_T, C_T]$$

The additional parameters E_T, VOM_T, C_T denote emission prices, variable costs, and maximum capacities. An example of the generation stack is shown in Figure 7.6.

Step 6.   **Process for power prices.** We now have all the necessary ingredients to define the evolution of power prices. We compute spot power prices as the bid stack transformation of the demand, with the bid stack defined as a certain perturbation of the generation stack,

$$P_T = s_T^{bid}(D_T) \equiv \alpha_1 s^{gen}[D_T; T, U_T, \Omega_T(\alpha_2\lambda), E_T, VOM_T, \alpha_3 C_T] \quad (7.17)$$

For any fixed set of parameters $(\alpha_1, \alpha_2, \alpha_3)$, this expression defines a power price evolution process through the evolution processes for the primary variables $(U_T, \Omega_T, \Im_T)$. Having the process for P_T allows us to compute the values of the forward contracts and options, and check to see if they match the market quotes. This procedure is continued until we find the triplet $(\alpha_1, \alpha_2, \alpha_3)$, that delivers the best match of market data.

Process Calibration

Finding optimal α-parameters in (7.17) is a key step in calibrating the power price process. The calibration procedure involves matching as best as we can the input market data. (Historical data is not used in calibration for the reasons described in the earlier section "Formal Representation.") In practice it means solving nonlinear problems whose complexity directly depends on the structure and complexity of instruments used in calibration. Fortunately, the generation stack is by definition a monotone increasing function and that often helps to improve the efficiency of numerical solvers.

The parameters $(\alpha_1, \alpha_2, \alpha_3)$ are dependent on time T, which means that we must solve a large number of optimization problems to define the process. In practice the situation is somewhat more manageable due to the fact that most of the time the market data has the monthly resolution. For example, assume (in agreement with the practical experience) that the set of market instruments used in calibration includes monthly forward contracts, monthly options, and even daily options. The prices of these instruments are defined on a monthly scale, that is, for each month we have one quote for each of these instruments. (Note that the prices of daily options are quoted as monthly averages.) In this case the optimal α-parameters may be different for different months but should remain the same within a month, which reduces the number of optimization problems we need to solve in practice.

An important question is how stable these parameters are as we keep recalibrating the model with the passage of time. Needless to say, we prefer these parameters not to change dramatically from day to day, especially in the absence of big market moves. To date our experience with respect to the parameter stability has been positive: During any particular year the variation of parameters α_1, α_2, and α_3 is typically not exceeding ±10%. An empirical confirmation of the parameter stability is helpful in justifying our modeling approach, although, in general, one should expect α-parameters to fluctuate exactly as one expects the implied volatility of a particular option

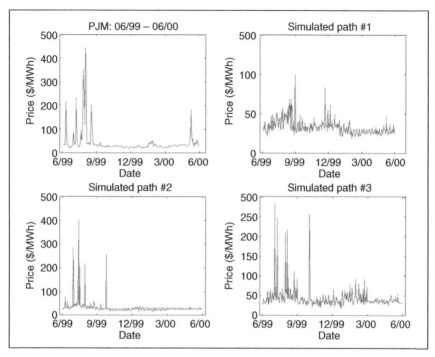

FIGURE 7.7 Actual and Simulated PJM Prices for the Period June 1999 to June 2000

to fluctuate. It is worth mentioning, however, that the fact that these parameters fluctuate is not of particular importance for pricing derivative products for the reasons discussed earlier. Namely, since they are determined using the prices of tradable instruments, the impact of the parameter fluctuation can be effectively hedged. On the other hand, hedging aside, a relative stability of parameters indicates the soundness of a modeling methodology and its ability to capture essential structural properties of a modeled phenomenon. That is why one should pay constant attention to the stability of model parameters. If at some point the tests start consistently showing a nonstable behavior of the parameters, it may signal the change in the market paradigm and may even force us to reconsider the whole modeling approach.

JUSTIFICATION OF THE HYBRID MODEL

The stability of the process parameters is a useful and necessary feature of the modeling approach presented in this chapter. However, in order to justify the model convincingly we need to demonstrate that it accurately represents the empirical properties of the power prices.

We start with the example of the price paths in the PJM region simulated by the hybrid model for the period June 1999 to June 2000. Figure 7.7 depicts these paths together with the path of the actual prices. Using these graphs as an illustration, we now outline the reasons why the power prices simulated by the hybrid model possess the empirically observed properties described in Chapter 3 and summarized at the beginning of this chapter.

Spikes

It is not an accident that the simulated prices on Figure 7.7 have spikes. The mechanism of spike formation is easy to understand since it is naturally embedded in the design of the hybrid model. In fact this is a fortuitous circumstance, since the behavior of spikes is quite complex. We saw in earlier graphs that for high levels of system demand, power prices tend to be high, but this relationship is very noisy. The hybrid model produces a natural explanation for this behavior. Indeed, by construction the power prices are modeled as a bid-stack function of the demand according to the expression (7.17). The bid stack, as well as the generation stack, are typically very steep in the area of high demand (e.g., see Figures 7.4 and 7.6), and hence, very sensitive to supply changes. This means that if demand is high, relatively small fluctuations in available supply can produce major changes in prices as the system operator is forced to bring expensive quick-start units online to meet the existing demand. A string of significant plant or transmission outages can lead to very significant increases in the power price. We can see that demand and outages drive spikes at the same time. This also explains why the probability of spike increases with high demand levels. Given the scarcity of historical data, it would be difficult to disentangle this relationship with econometric tools.

The hybrid fundamental model recovers the behavior in very natural and robust manner. For example, consider the bid stack in Figure 7.4. For this stack, an outage of 1,000 MW results in almost 100% price change. Similarly, looking at the rightmost segment of the generation stack on Figure 7.6 it is easy to see how spikes are formed in PJM when loads are sufficiently high.

Mean Reversion

The outage mechanism also explains the rapid reversion of power prices to normal levels. After a major outage, it can take several hours to bring on cheaper units to replace the outed facility. By that time the prices respond by dropping to close to the initial levels.

Additionally, a measure of mean reversion is induced by the mean-reversion property of the demand, which in turn, can be explained by the mean reversion of the temperature. Thus, if the model generates a power price increase due to a large upward demand fluctuation from the mean, eventually this increase will be corrected by the mean reverting demand/temperature. This explanation of the mean reversion works for high demand scenarios when demand is the main factor driving the high power prices.

In case of low demand (low power prices) the need for modeling mean reversion is less obvious. As was demonstrated in Chapter 3, mean reversion of power prices, as well as fuel prices, is far from certain, and until now empirical data has not provided strong support for this property—at least at short-to-medium time scale (up to several years). Nevertheless, in the absence of the convincing empirical data, mean reversion remains a modeling choice and if one chooses to introduce it in the fuel price model, it will induce mean reversion in the power price process as well. Note also that in the low price interval the effect of the demand mean reversion cannot be very strong, first, because in this interval power prices are not very sensitive to demand, and second, because the demand itself is rather noisy compared to the high demand region.

Fat Tails of the Price Distributions

Since power prices are modeled as an increasing (in some cases rather steeply) function of the demand or temperature, and since the temperature is a normally or almost normally distributed variable, it is no surprise that the power-price distribution has tails wider than those of normal distribution. This means that the distribution of model power prices should have kurtosis higher than zero (it is equal to zero for the normal distribution). The analysis of the distribution higher normalized moments and comparison with the empirical data will be presented later in this chapter.

Seasonality

Seasonality of power prices follows naturally from the seasonality of market data used for model calibration.

Volatility Structure

In Chapter 3 we described a number of empirical characteristics of the volatility of spot and forward prices. Most of these characteristics are preserved by the hybrid model simply because they are present at the market data used for calibration. For example, the dependence of the volatility on the expiration time of the forward contract is preserved by the use of option prices for calibrating the fuel as well as power price models. The dependence of the volatility of a given forward contract on the time to expiration (Samuelson effect) is captured in the fuel models if they are based on the evolution of the forward price term structure, see Chapter 5.

Correlation Structure between Different Forward Contracts for the Same Commodity

For the fuels this property again is the consequence of using the process for evolution of forward prices (see Chapter 5 for details).

So far we have demonstrated that many desired qualitative properties are present in the model prices because of the model structure or the attributes of the input data. We now examine if certain important characteristics of the model price distributions are in agreement with those of the empirical price distributions, while not being used in model calibration. Capturing these characteristics would be useful in supporting the soundness of our modeling approach.

Test of the Higher Normalized Moments of the Distribution

We start with one critical out-of-sample test of agreement between historical and model power price distributions. More precisely, this will be a test of the stack transformation used in the hybrid model. We know from equation (7.17) that the distribution of power prices is determined by the evolution of primary random drivers, as well as the shape of the bid stack transformation. Suppose that we are confident in our ability to capture the behavior of underlying factors, such as fuel prices, temperature, and outages, since statistically this behavior is rather stable and manageable. Then the only remaining concern is the impact of the stack transformation on the power-price distribution. To analyze this impact it must be isolated from the impact of primary drivers. To achieve that in this test we will not simulate primary drivers, but instead we take actual historical realization of the fuels, temperatures, and outages. These will be then substituted in equation (7.17) to generate the distribution of power prices. After that, the higher normalized moments of the distribution of simulated power prices are compared with those of the actual power price distribution.

Specifically, we will focus on the third (skewness) and the fourth (kurtosis) moments, see equation (7.8). Our goal is to demonstrate that they are in agreement with the corresponding normalized moments of the empirical distributions. The reason why we focus on the higher normalized moments was explained in the section "Transformation of Underlying Drivers into Power Prices." Of the higher normalized moments, kurtosis is of particular interest, since it is a measure of "fat tails"—one of the most prominent features of the power-price distributions, as we have seen in Chapter 3. If we are able to demonstrate the agreement between the normalized moments of the model and empirical distributions, achieved without special calibration effort, it will undoubtedly support the structural soundness of the model and

TABLE 7.7   Skewness and Kurtosis of PJM Price Distribution: Model versus Empirical Data

	Skewness		Kurtosis	
	Model Data	Empirical Data	Model Data	Empirical Data
Summer 2000	3.58	3.17	4.77	4.89
Summer 2001	18.13	14.65	25.83	26.46
Winter 2000	.68	1.32	2.02	1.19
Winter 2001	.18	1.54	5.48	1.98

TABLE 7.8   Skewness and Kurtosis of ERCOT Price Distribution: Model versus Empirical Data

	Skewness		Kurtosis	
	Model Data	Empirical Data	Model Data	Empirical Data
Calender year 1999	4.06	4.09	17.07	18.03
Calender year 2000	3.65	3.83	20.83	19.71
Summer 1999	2.05	2.09	3.33	3.91
Summer 2000	3.25	3.14	14.58	10.73

provide some validation to our approach. Tables 7.7 and 7.8 contain the model and empirical values of third and fourth normalized moments for different time periods for the PJM and ERCOT regions.

The numbers in these tables indicate precisely what we expect from our model, namely, the agreement of the higher normalized moments. As follows from the discussion in the earlier section "Transformation of Underlying Drivers into Power Prices," this agreement is particularly important due to the fact that the stack transformation has not been derived by matching historical price distributions, as in the reduced-form hybrid models, but has been constructed using fundamental market characteristics. Matching higher normalized moments increases our confidence in the accuracy of the simulated price distributions. Therefore, it is of no surprise that the graphs on Figures 7.8 and 7.9 exhibit the similarity of the simulated prices and the actual prices. And although the spikes of simulated prices may not exactly coincide in time with those of actual prices, the total number of spikes and their magnitudes are clearly close for both time series. This agreement in the spike price region, as well as in the normal price region, indicates the closeness of the price distributions.

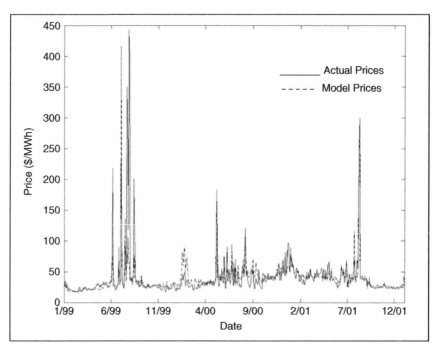

FIGURE 7.8 PJM Prices: Actual versus Model

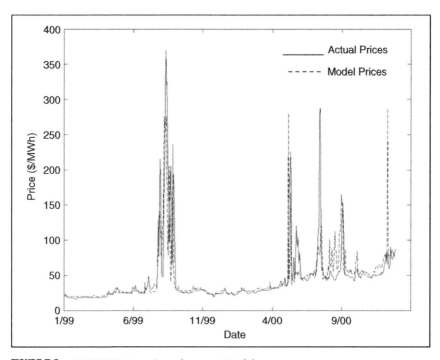

FIGURE 7.9 ERCOT Prices: Actual versus Model

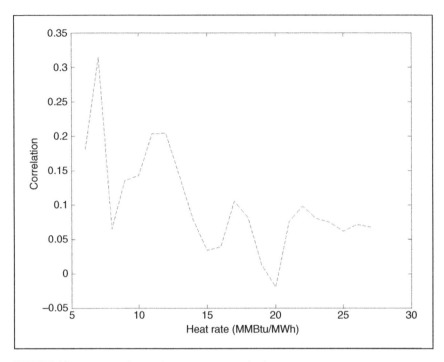

FIGURE 7.10   Historical Correlation versus Implied Heat Rate in NYPOOL Region

Test of Correlation between Power and Natural Gas Prices

Another important characteristic that sets apart prices of energy products is the correlation structure between power and fuel prices. It is critical to examine if the correlation structure generated by the model is consistent with the empirical data, since the power plant is essentially a spread option between power and fuel prices, and hence the correlation plays a key role in its valuation and hedging. In this section we will focus on the correlation between the power prices and the natural gas prices but similar analysis can be conducted for other fuels. Our goal is to show that the correlation structure induced by the model agrees with the empirical data. (Note that the power/fuel correlation structure has never been used for model calibration. Hence, an agreement with the empirical data means a success of a powerful out-of-sample testing experiment and consequently, a support to the modeling approach.) Figures 7.10 through 7.13 contain graphs of correlation coefficients as a function of the implied heat rate (i.e., ratio between the power and natural gas prices).

Figures 7.11 and 7.13 show that the correlation between power and gas prices computed using the data simulated by the hybrid model follows the same pattern: correlation coefficients are low for small values of the implied

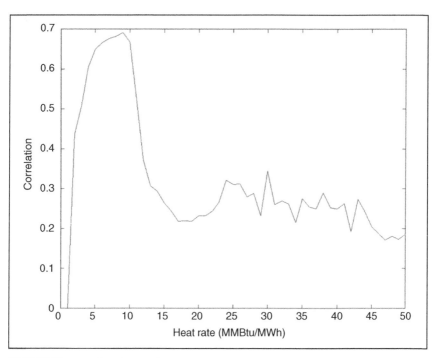

FIGURE 7.11   Simulated Correlation versus Implied Heat Rate in NYPOOL Region

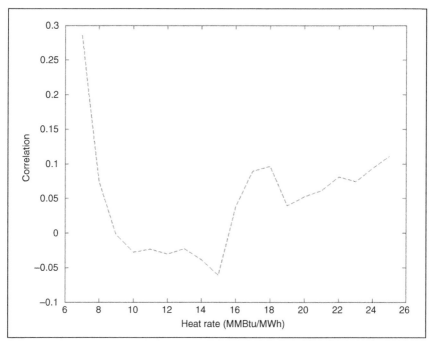

FIGURE 7.12   Historical Correlation versus Implied Heat Rate in PJM Region

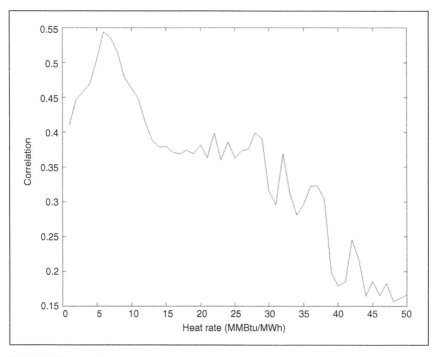

FIGURE 7.13   Simulated Correlation versus Implied Heat Rate in PJM Region

heat rate, then they increase, and then they drop again. Figures 7.10 and 7.12 indicate that historical correlations follow the same patterns. Moreover, we even can give a fundamental justification of this correlation structure. Indeed, low implied gas/power heat rate means that gas is not a marginal fuel and lower-cost units, such as coal plants, are setting the power price. Hence, we should not expect high correlation between power and gas in this case. Similarly, when implied heat rate is high, it means that demand is high and the power prices are set by high-cost units located on the steep segment at the end of the generation stack. In this case the power prices are mostly sensitive to changes in demand. It is the demand that drives the power prices, thus weakening the relation between gas and power and lowering the value of the correlation coefficient. When demand is not very high, price-setting units are located on the flat (i.e., insensitive to demand fluctuations) part of the generation stack. Only when demand is low and gas units are marginal can we expect high correlation between power and gas. This explains the shape of the graphs in Figures 7.10 to 7.13.

We are also interested to see if the hybrid model reproduces another important phenomenon observed empirically.

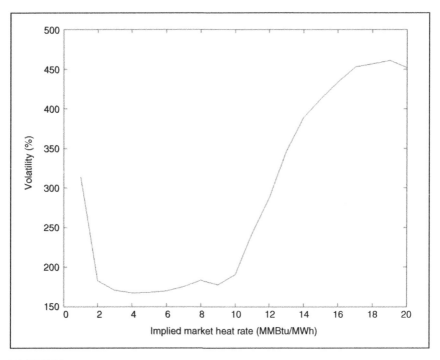

FIGURE 7.14 Dependence of Volatility of the Weekly Returns of the Simulated Prices on the Implied Heat Rate

Test of the Inverse-leverage Effect

The term *inverse-leverage effect* is used to specify the increase of power price volatility at higher levels of the implied heat rate. Again, qualitatively this phenomenon is easy to explain. Indeed, as we know, high levels of the implied heat rate correspond to the steep part of the stack where small demand variations may produce highly volatile behavior of power prices. Figure 7.14 demonstrates the dependence of the volatility of weekly returns of the simulated prices on the implied market heat rate. The weekly returns are used here to smooth out to some extent the effect of price jumps.

As is clear from Figure 7.14, the hybrid model is successful in capturing the inverse-leverage effect for high levels of the implied heat rate. Also interesting is the volatility increase for the low values of the implied heat rate. The explanation of that phenomenon is based on the fact that in PJM stack (see Figure 7.6) there is a gap between the production costs of low-cost generators (i.e., nuclear and coal). When the demand levels are such that these units are the marginal ones, the gap may cause a significant variability in the production costs. As the implied heat rate increases and the marginal units move further into the flatter segment of the stack corresponding to the coal units, the variations in production costs are getting smaller and the price return volatility drops, as the graph in Figure 7.14 above demonstrates.

The fact that the hybrid model captures a rather complicated structure of the power price volatility, as well as of the power/gas correlation coefficients, and does it without any special enforcing effort, is an indication that the model is fundamentally sound. In contrast, it is no surprise that the reduced-form processes of Chapter 4 will have problems when used in energy models. The correlation structure (and to a certain degree the volatility structure) is by and large not observable and strongly depends on the fundamental characteristics of the regional power supply. Hence, projecting this structure into the future using only price data, either historical or market, is a difficult, if not impossible task. As will be clear from the next two chapters, a correct representation of volatility and correlation structure is critical for a successful energy model.

CHAPTER **8**

Structured Products: Fuels and Other Commodities

In this chapter we present an analysis of the valuations of various energy derivative products. Our assumption throughout this presentation is the ability to use liquid hedging instruments. We do this to separate basic risks from complex risks, so that the values of energy derivatives are determined by relative pricing—relative to the prices of the underlying liquid instruments. Otherwise it would mean using derivative products to speculate on the prices of the underlying instruments, which can be done much more efficiently with the underlying instruments themselves, provided that they are liquid.

Thus, throughout the chapter the values of derivative structures will be expressed in terms of underlying liquid products, though sometimes we may not know, or may not be concerned with, what the underlying products are. A valuation approach based on relative pricing is much simpler than one based on absolute pricing. Additionally, it is always possible to perform absolute pricing of derivatives by combining relative pricing of derivatives with absolute pricing of the underlying instruments. Even if we do not intend to hedge anything, the results of this chapter can still be useful.

To make the distinction a tangible one consider the following example:

EXAMPLE 8.1 *Relative pricing of collars*

In the next section we discuss the pricing of collars. We show there that this structure can be decomposed into a strip of OTM calls and puts. Absolute pricing of the structure would involve assuming a properly calibrated process for the underlying price and pricing the payoff function of the collar with this process (given in Figure 8.1). Relative pricing would involve splitting the structure first into component puts and calls and either pricing the individual pieces or using market quotes for the individual options if available.

306

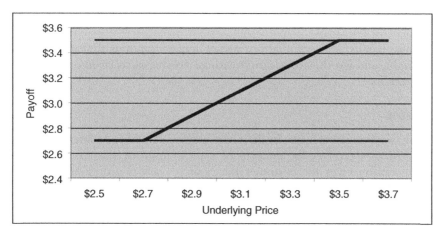

FIGURE 8.1   Collar Payoff

Example 8.1 is a very simple one as the decomposition of the structure is clear. This is usually not the case and we have to carefully analyze the behavior of the structure in question to understand how to decompose it through static (as above) or dynamic strategies (e.g., standard call on forwards).

CALLS, PUTS, AND COMBINATIONS (CAPS, FLOORS, AND COLLARS)

The fuel markets extensively trade standard calls and puts on both forward and cash products. We do not analyze the pricing and hedging to any large extent here, since we addressed this issue in Chapters 2 and 4. Instead, we give an example of a combination product.

Costless Collars

A customer demanding protection from high commodity prices might be unwilling to incur the significant cost of options needed for that protection. On the other hand, if the customer is willing to give up a possible gain from low prices to pay for the protection, the simple solution is to offer a collar. The payoff is given in Figure 8.1.

From the customer's point of view the collar consists of a long OTM call position, giving the protection, and a short OTM put position, reducing the cost of the call. The protection levels can be chosen so that the up-front cost will be zero, hence, "costless" collar.

SWINGS, RECALLS, AND NOMINATIONS

Swings, recalls, and nominations are volumetric options that give holder the right, and not the obligation, to adjust volume of received or delivered commodity.

Definition

The basic swing option can be defined as follows: We have N dates, at which the customer receives the delivery of a set amount of a commodity. The swing option gives the customer the right to vary the amount delivered within a certain range. This right can be exercised K ($< N$) times. The timing is at the discretion of the holder.

These options often arise in natural gas markets, where typical contractual arrangements call for flexibility in the amount delivered depending on the customer's need. The customer nominates a certain fixed amount to be delivered over time (baseload) and is also given the right to deviate from the requirement to receive the nominated volume (swing) within a certain range. On the other hand, the supplier has the right not to deliver, or *recall*, the nominated volume a couple of times during the period.

The structure of these contracts evolved from the supply and demand characteristics in the natural gas business. The average demand for gas over the next month is usually known with some certainty at the beginning of the month; that is why nomination rights are exercised within bid-week (see Chapter 1). However, demand can deviate from the average day-to-day, which is the motivation for holding the swing rights. They are used to adjust the volume taken as dictated by demand.

On the other hand, the supplier may face extreme conditions jeopardizing delivery, due to supply disruptions such as earthquakes or pipeline failures. The recall provision gives the supplier an escape clause. Since disruptions occur under exceptional circumstances, the recall rights tend to be few. The contract is also likely to contain provisions on minimum and maximum volumes taken over the life of the contract, called take-or-pay provisions. Violation of the constraint can be enforced by penalty payments or the requirement to make up for the violations physically—deliver or receive the shortfall amount of the commodity.

The structure above has been used to manage the interaction of supply and demand in energy markets. With the development of liquid markets, however, any operational decisions are based on the locational spot price. It is helpful to mention here that the optimal exercise of a swing option is independent of the holder's physical demand as long as the spot market is liquid and the bid-ask spread is not significant (see the section on asset management deals later in the chapter). Therefore, volumetric options can be effective tools for managing the risks associated with spot gas prices. However, many market participants still use volumetric contracts to manage and supply gas demand directly. This situation arises due to the limited liquidity of certain spot markets and to end-users' lack of knowledge about the available products.

This creates situations in which volumetric options can be exercised suboptimally. For example, an end user might call on the swing provision to increase the volume taken at a time when the spot market offers a lower price. This suboptimal policy is often called an uneconomic exercise. If the customer exercises the option only when the native demand of the customer requires it, we can value the contract as a load-serving contract with caps and floors. The nature of the derivative is quite different from a swing option. We refer the reader to the section on load contracts for details. More often than not, the exercise of the option is a mixture of economic and uneconomic exercise. In summary, when marketing, hedging, and valuing volumetric options, it's important to be aware of the nature of the customer. Putting aside the issues of economic versus uneconomic exercise, we proceed by assuming that all options are exercised optimally.

In our description above we considered a structure that had several volumetric embedded options. We will analyze them separately in the remainder of the section. However, it is worth pointing out that the above structure is not just a sum of three different options: nomination, swing, and recalls (see the following sections). Since optimally exercising the nomination option (nomination options will be discussed in detail later) should take into account the value of the swing and recall provisions, the above contractual arrangement is in fact a complex compound option. We will not analyze those structures, but simply point out the generic valuation techniques useful in handling those challenges.

Swings

Swing options give the right to the holder to adjust volume received within some range at some fixed price (nomination or swing strike). The number of swing rights can be less than or equal to the number of days within the period covered (typically, a month or a quarter) of the contract.

EXAMPLE 8.2 *Daily swing contract*

Power marketer GBH sells a contract with the following specifications: The supplier contracts to deliver 10,000 MMBtu/day of natural gas at Chicago City Gate. The tenor of the contract is the month of January. During this period, the recipient has the right to swing the volume of the gas taken between

5,000 MMBtu and 15,000 MMBtu a total of 10 times (days). The timing of the swings is at the discretion of the recipient. The recipient will pay first-of-the-month Chicago City Gate index plus $.10 for every MMBtu of gas actually delivered.

If the number of swing rights is equal to the number of days in the period, the value of the swing option is given by the value of strip of daily European call options struck at the nomination price. The number of options one holds is equal to the volume between the minimum and maximum swing level. We can see that the valuation boils down to the valuation of a strip of European daily calls and possibly puts.

In the subsequent analysis of the structure we assume that the nominated volume is 5,000 MMBtu/day, and we own K swing calls. The analysis for puts or combined calls and puts position would be very similar.

If the number of swing rights is less than the number of days, the valuation is considerably more challenging, because of the trade-off between the value of holding an exercise right in the future and the gain from exercising the right now. The main difficulty in pricing swing/recall options is precisely the same one we face when pricing American options in general. Consequently, the techniques developed for pricing American options can be modified to handle the more complex challenges of swing valuation.

Valuation of Basic Swing Structures

It is well known that the main analytical problem in pricing American options is the calculation of the optimal exercise boundary (see Hull, 1999; Duffie, 1992; Wilmott, 2000). The exercise boundary is the critical price that separates the continuation region and the exercise region. More specifically:

$$
\begin{aligned}
S > S^* (t) &\rightarrow exercise \\
S \leq S^* (t) &\rightarrow wait
\end{aligned}
\tag{8.1}
$$

The critical price is a function of time, since the opportunity cost of exercising changes the closer we come to expiration.

Similar logic applies to swing options. Assume we have a 30-day period and five swing rights. If we come to the 25th day of the month with all the swing rights intact, the exercise strategy becomes obvious. We must start exercising the options right away as long as they are in the money.

However, at the beginning of the month the situation is very different. We might require the option to move substantially in-the-money before we are willing to exercise one of the rights. This suggests that the critical price for swing options depends on time, similarly to American options. Moreover, our example suggests that the critical price also depends on the number of outstanding (unused) swing rights. If we arrive at the 25th day with one right instead of five, our willingness to exercise will be not as strong. Consequently, the major task in managing swing options is finding the following critical surface:

$$S^* = S^* (t, K) \tag{8.2}$$

where K is the number of remaining swing rights. Seen in this light, we can treat swing options as multiple American options with mutually exclusive exercises.

This also suggests the possible numerical algorithm for valuation of simple swing options. The algorithm is simply an extension of the standard binomial trees used for valuation of American options (see Hull, 1999 for a description of the binomial tree algorithm).

Note that, given that the cash flow from the exercise is linear in volume, the optimal exercise policy always leads to full volumetric exercise (unless there are special constraints such as cumulative constraints on the volume taken). In other words, it is never optimal to exercise less than the full volume of the swing right, that is, not to go to the maximum allowable level. Even if there are cumulative volumetric restrictions and penalties, we can still obtain some general pricing relationships. For example, Jaillet, Ronn, and Tompaidis (2001) show that:

$$V(cMinVol,cMaxVol,cS,cL,cP) = cV(MinVol,MaxVol,S,L,P) \tag{8.3}$$

where

L is the strike price and P is the (constant) unit penalty

S is the spot price

MinVol and MaxVol are minimum and maximum volumes respectively

This formula says that the value of the swing option does not depend on the scale (or units) of the problem. Technically, the value of the swing option is homogenous of degree one.

The algorithm for valuation of swing options involves building a two-dimensional tree. One dimension is the standard tree, while the other is the discrete tree of the number of available swing rights (see Figure 8.2).

Swing Tree Description

The valuation proceeds with the following steps.

1. We start at the last time node N in all the trees (indexed by the available swing rights). We evaluate the payoffs of the swing options in all the trees.

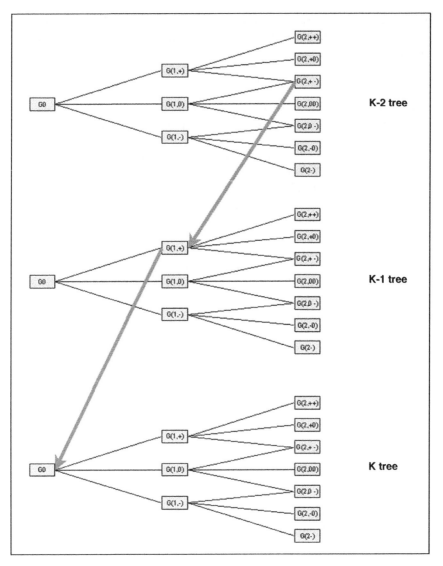

FIGURE 8.2   Trinomial Forest

2. We move one step back to time node $N - 1$. In every tree at every node we evaluate two expectations of the value of the option at expiration for the feasible pairs of swing rights. Assume we are looking at a node on the tree with k remaining swing rights, then we calculate the following expectations (S_N is the spot price at time-step N):

$$E[\,V(S_N,k)|S_{N-1},k\,]$$
$$E[\,V(S_N,k-1)|S_{N-1},k\,]$$

3. We compare the sum of the second expectation and the current exercise (intrinsic) value against the first expectation. This means comparing the strategy of exercising at time $N-1$ and arriving at time N with the $k-1$ available exercises with the strategy of not exercising at $N-1$. The value of the option at this node is given by the higher of the two quantities.
4. We roll back through the trees until time 0.

This procedure is a direct implementation of the backward induction method of solving the relevant stochastic dynamic program. We discuss the issues involved in Appendix B.

More detailed analysis of tree-based valuation of standard swing options with trinomial trees (for mean-reverting processes) can be found in Jaillet, Ronn, and Tompaidis (2001). The proof of the convergence of the procedure can be found in Lari-Lavassani, Simchi, and Ware (2001).

The limitation of the tree-based approaches is their inability to efficiently handle processes with many factors. The trees are well-suited for handling GBM with mean reversion or with a deterministically varying volatility structure. Also, we can easily apply implied trees (see Chapter 4) in the valuation. This allows us to capture the impact of volatility skews and smiles on the swing value. As usual with implied tree approach, the dynamics of the process will be misspecified, but this is of secondary importance. In energy markets, spot skew is not extensively traded and we do not have full volatility surface even for individual monthly contracts. We can try and extract information about the evolution of the spot from the shape of volatility skews and smiles for forward volatility contracts for neighboring months, but this procedure is unlikely to work for two reasons.

First, the monthly volatility skew is not fully informative about the (nontraded) cash volatility skew (although see the section "Forward Volatility Skew versus Daily/Index Volatility Skew"). Second, even if it were, the performance of the implied valuation methods (see Chapter 4) is conditioned on actively using the volatility contracts for hedging. If we just use the implied tree to value the swing option, and then use only delta hedging, we are not likely to be able to recover the theoretical value.

The alternative to using implied trees is to specify a multifactor spot model (e.g., stochastic volatility jump-diffusion model, etc.) and price the structure. However, tree-based methodologies do not efficiently represent processes of this type. The only feasible solution is to use Monte Carlo simulation.

Historically, valuation of American options with Monte Carlo techniques has been a difficult problem (see Broadie and Glasserman, 1997). Recently,

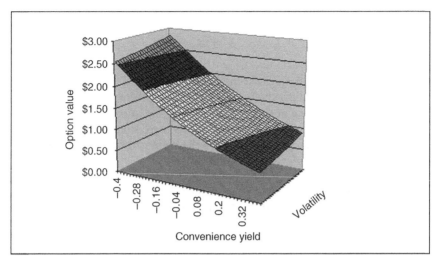

FIGURE 8.3   Swing Value As a Function of Parameters

Longstaff and Schwartz (2001) developed a numerical approach that can handle American options in Monte Carlo simulations in a simple and flexible manner. The basic idea is to approximate the critical boundary (the continuation value) by a set of polynomials (or other functions) in the underlying prices (factors) at every step of the simulation. The estimation of the coefficients of the polynomials is performed through a standard regression on the (Monte Carlo) simulated prices. This allows a great degree of flexibility in the choice of the process.

The methodology has been applied by Ghuieva, Lehoczky, and Seppi (2001) to the valuation of swing options. Their results are very encouraging. We refer the reader to this paper for details.

Valuation and Process Parameters: Volatility and Convenience Yield

Figure 8.3 shows the results of pricing simple one-month swing option with five swing rights. We present the pricing results as a function of the net convenience yield ("the dividend") and volatility.

In Figure 8.4 we compare the value of the swing options to the value of five European options at the end of the swing term (when the value of European option is the highest.) The purpose of this exercise is to see the size of the early exercise premium. We express it as a percentage of the European option value.

For negative convenience yield, the early exercise premium is zero (as it should be, see next paragraph). We can also see that the lower the volatility, the higher the early exercise premium is.

Convenience yield is often seen as secondary to the volatility. Unfortunately, it is of crucial importance. We say unfortunately, since it is often very

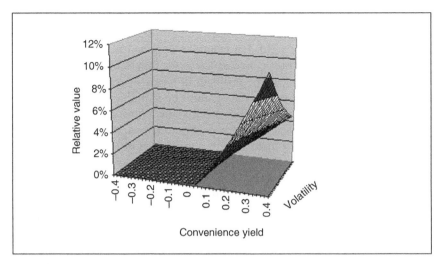

FIGURE 8.4 Early Exercise Value of the Swing Option As a Function of Parameters

hard to estimate. The importance of this parameter can be seen in the above graphs. To better understand why, we illuminate the issue by the following example.

Consider a contract with only one swing right. We can view the contract as an American option with expiration at the end of the term. Under what circumstances is it optimal to exercise the swing right early? As we know, early exercise of a standard American call option is only optimal if the convenience yield is not equal to zero. The logic of the rule is simple. If the benefits of owning a physical inventory of the commodity are now high enough, they might outweigh the savings on the cost of carry (financing and storage costs) and the benefits of the future volatility that a later exercise brings. An identical conclusion applies to swing options. We can now see that knowing the (net) convenience yield is crucial to valuation of swing options. Direct estimation of this quantity is difficult. An alternative way is to extract its mean value from forward prices (see equation 4.36):

$$\int_{t_n}^{t_{n+1}} (y_s - c_s)ds = -r(t_{n+1} - t_n) - \ln\left(\frac{F_{t_{n+1}}}{F_{t_n}}\right) \tag{8.4}$$

where

y_s is the instantaneous (marginal) convenience yield, c_s is the (marginal) storage cost, and $F(t_n)$ is the forward price of the nth month.

Formula (8.4) only gives us the (expected) average convenience yield inside the month of interest. Swing options can be very sensitive to the distribution of the convenience yield. For example, in power markets, large price spikes imply large (absolute) convenience yield. Obviously, in power markets, the very formulation of the problem in terms of convenience yield is only a formal trick. If the commodity cannot be stored, expressing the evolution of prices in terms of a spot process may be a bit misleading.

Despite the drawbacks, for storable commodities, the yield extracted from forward prices can at times give us a good idea of the likely contribution to the early exercise premium. On the other hand, for nonstorable commodities like power, yield extracted from forward prices can be very misleading. For example, July and August forward power prices usually trade closely to each other in the U.S. markets (implying zero average yield), but we would never advise anybody to sell swing options—for example, interruptible contracts—flat to corresponding European options. The early exercise premium can be very substantial.

We can avoid the issue of convenience yield entirely by calibrating some appropriate stochastic process directly on forward prices, and then valuing the option with the procedures described above. However, we must choose some appropriate risk-adjustment to the process. This is often the only viable way of getting valuations. (For example, see Jaillet, Ronn, and Tompaidis, 2001.)

Swing Options in Practice: Approximations and Shortcuts

As we argued in the introduction to Chapter 4, the crucial first step in a valuation procedure is to consider specific features of the structure we are dealing with.

Consider a generic swing option with N periods and K $(< N)$ swing rights. We can easily show that the value of the swing option per swing right will be bound by the following:

$$EC < Swing\_Option < AC \qquad (8.5)$$

In other words, the value per swing right of a swing call option must always be higher than the value of the European daily call for any given day and less than the American daily call. The first inequality follows because the swing option gives us the flexibility in timing the exercise. On the other hand, the K American daily calls can be exercised on any given day inside of the period. Given the linearity of the problem in the size of option position, they will be all exercised on the same day. However, swing options can be only exercised one at a time, so their value is lower.

We can see that if the number of the swing rights equals the number of the time periods, the value of the swing option will be equal to the strip of daily European calls. At the other extreme, if we have just one swing right the value is equal to that of the American option (actually Bermudan option). We can therefore quickly form an estimate of the value of the swing option by interpolating between the value of the American and European option with the interpolation expressed as a function of the number of swing rights.

Interestingly, in natural gas markets, for the usual ranges of volatilities and other conditional parameters, the spread between European and American calls (as calculated using GBM-based models) is relatively small, at most 10%. This allows us to evaluate the value of the swing option with the standard option pricing tools. Obviously, this approximation is effective only for lognormal processes. The valuation results are broadly confirmed by the prices of swing/recall options in the OTC markets. Usually the early exercise premium is close to zero.

In the case of power, the valuation can be significantly simplified, even for more complex processes. As we discussed in Chapter 4, power prices often exhibit regime-switching behavior. The prices can either remain in the normal $30 range or the abnormal, and infrequent, spike range (say, $300). In those situations, the optimal boundary will be very easy to determine. Whenever the price exceeds some threshold sufficiently far away from $30 (say, $100) we should exercise the swing.

Under those circumstances, valuation of the swing comes down to correctly determining the distribution of the number of spikes and their amplitude; that usually gives us 99% of the value of the option.

Swing Options versus Index/Daily Options

The value of a swing option comes from two sources:

- **End-of-period premium:** The ability to exercise the option at the end of the contract period: this is important especially in markets with significant contango (forward price increasing with the term). The contango suggests that the expected price at the end of the contractual period is higher than the average price for the period. This can be captured by looking at the forward price for the contractual month and the following month (in other words calculating the convenience yield: see equation 8.4). Also the contribution from volatility is the highest at the end of the term.
- **Early exercise premium:** (Discussed in the previous section)

If we look at the market quotes of daily options and swing options the overall difference is significant. It can be easily as high as 50%. Table 8.1 shows an example of actual quotes for a contract with five swing rights for a couple of natural gas liquid points.

TABLE 8.1   Quotes for Natural Gas Liquid Points

	Index Option (premium per exercise right)	Swing Option (premium per exercise right)	End-of-Period Option (premium per exercise right)
Henry Hub, July 2002	$0.16	$0.25	$0.23
NGPL, Dec 2002	$0.29	$0.45	$0.41
NGPL, Dec 2001	$0.29	$0.44	$0.40
Chicago City Gate, Dec 2001	$0.36	$0.92	$0.90

The end-of-the-period premium is calculated by using GBM assumptions and cash volatility implied from the index options. If, for example, the true underlying process is mean-reverting, and the effect is strong enough on the time-scale of the tenor, for example, of the contract (one month), then the volatility will not grow with time as rapidly, effectively making the end-of-the-period option less valuable and by implication making the early exercise premium higher.

Swing Options in Practice: Hedging

There are two liquid instruments with which we can hedge swing options. BOM (or possibly prompt forward contracts), forward options and index/daily options. We can always super-replicate the payoff of swings by selling/buying a strip of index/daily options for the full volume of the swing option. The fewer swing rights we have, the more expensive this solution appears. In certain power markets in the summer months, however, a recall with only a couple of swing rights is roughly equivalent to a strip of daily options, since almost all the value of the strip of dailies will come from the possibility of spikes.

If we decompose the value of the swing option into end-of-period and early exercise premium, we can use prompt month forward options to hedge the end-of-period part of the value and BOM and index options to hedge the early exercise premium. The first part of the overall hedging strategy will usually work much better than the second part.

Multiperiod Swing Options

Our discussion of swing options has not been explicit about the length of the optimization horizon. Although we formulated the problem in abstract terms, the analysis implicitly assumed that we considered one-period swings. The term "period" refers to the resolution of forward markets, for options or price contracts. In the United States forward markets trade at a minimum resolution of one month; in Nord Pool, the minimum resolution is one week.

TABLE 8.2   Values of the Swing Options

	Swing Premium	Daily Option Premium
September	$0.69	$0.67
October	$0.72	$0.70
Multiperiod	$0.75	

The resolution of the forward market is immaterial if we build a valuation model based on spot price. We just need to make sure it is consistent with the available forward curves, and we can apply the tree or Monte Carlo methodology.

However, in a multiperiod setting we do not need to resort to dynamic programming techniques at all. Furthermore, we can limit the degree to which we have to worry about spot price behavior. If we have forward contracts for the different subperiods of the optimization, we can usually split the optimization into forward optimization and inside-the-period optimization.

We do not go into a formal proof of the fact (see Wolyniec, 2001). An example of how to implement the procedure in practice is given in the section on storage later in the chapter, as well as in Chapter 9 when we discuss the long-term constraints on power plants.

EXAMPLE 8.3   *Multiperiod swing premium*

Consider a two-month fixed strike-price swing option with one swing right. We evaluate the option at the beginning of the year. The swing option covers September and October. The current forward prices are in both months equal to $3.70/MMBtu. The daily volatility for both months is 57%. The fixed strike price is equal to $3.70/MMBtu. The values of the swing options will be given in Table 8.2.

Related Swing Structures: Take-or-Pay Provisions

The swing structure described in the previous section appears in many forms. Take-or-Pay provisions include restrictions on the minimum and maximum amount taken over the life of the contract and penalty provisions for violating those restrictions. The presence of the cumulative constraints introduces an additional decision variable: the exercised volume. We can handle this with the tree methodology by adding the exercised volume as another dimension to the tree. We can discretize the possible volume choices at exercise. We can now formulate the critical boundary as a function of time, number of remaining swing rights and the exercised volume. (For implementation issues along with the inclusion of the penalty see Jaillet, Ronn, and Tompaidis, 2001 or Clewlow and Strickland, 2000.)

Nominations

Nomination options are quite similar to swing options in that they offer the holder the right to change the volume received K ($< N$) times during the contract period. The difference is that the level of the volume is adjusted upwards (or downwards) for the remainder of the contract until the next nomination right is exercised.

For example, the original nomination specified 10,000 MMBtu of natural gas every day. If the holder of the option exercises another nomination right and doubles the volume to 20,000 MMBtu, he will receive 20,000 MMBtu a day for the rest of the tenor of the contract, unless the holder has another nomination right and changes the volume again.

Unlike swing options, nomination options typically allow a very limited number of nomination rights. Often, the timing of the exercise is actually prespecified. For example, a contract may give the option holder the right to nominate the volume at the beginning of every month, up to the option expiration month. Also, there might be no limitations on the minimum or maximum size of the "swing" but only the cumulative constraint on the minimum and maximum volume taken over the life of the contract, typically a calendar year.

Recalls

Recalls are essentially swing options. The different terminology comes from the different usage of those rights. As was described, recalls are used to interrupt delivery under stressful circumstances, while swings are used for managing demand. In practice, the most frequent version of the swing option is the one with the number of swing rights K equal to the number of exercise periods N. Recalls, on the other hand, typically have the number of "swing" rights substantially smaller than N.

Economic and Uneconomic Exercise

As we discussed, swing options are at times not exercised optimally. This may be due to several reasons. It may be physically impossible to vary required volume with the prices. If the contract specifies delivery at a specific city gate, which itself is not a liquid point, it might be impossible to turn around and sell the unneeded volume to gain the exercise premium. In principle, the received gas can be transported to a liquid hub and sold there. However, some pipeline systems might not physically allow that. Even if the operation is feasible our valuation must account for the cost of the transportation capacity required. We do not elaborate on this point here because pricing derivative products at illiquid locations introduces a number of complexities (due to dependencies among structures), which are beyond the scope of the present discussion. In the extreme case, when the customer exercises no control over the swing exercise (i.e., whenever the exercise is driven solely by the commodity demand the customer faces) the nature of the structure changes radically. We are not dealing with an option anymore but with a load management contract, which we discuss in detail in a later section.

In practice, many counterparties will follow mixed policies: sometimes optimizing the exercise to the spot price, and responding to the demand changes at other times. Those behavioral characteristics make valuation and hedging dependent on the specifics of the counterparty.

ASIAN OPTIONS

The Asian option structures come in two flavors: average price and average strike. The payoff functions for the Asian calls are given by the following expressions:

$$V_{AP} = \max(A_T^\tau - K, 0)$$

$$V_{AS} = \max(S_T - A_T^\tau, 0)$$

$$A_T^\tau = \frac{\sum_{i=\tau}^{T} S_i}{T - \tau} \tag{8.6}$$

The averaging period can start at the inception of the contract or at some later date. The forward start Asian options are the rule rather than the exception in energy markets. Often the contracts do not have a fixed strike price but are struck at the first-of-the-month index price (see Chapter 1). A forward-start Asian option with floating strike can be seen as a forward start call on a swap, with the strike price set to the value of the swap price just before the start of the averaging period.

EXAMPLE 8.4 *Asian options as a price protection mechanism*

A local delivery company (LDC) is charged with supplying residential customers. The company is concerned with the cost of supplying gas during the month of January, its highest demand period. There are several alternatives the company can choose from to protect itself from high prices. For example, it can enter today into a forward contract to fix the price of its future base-load needs. However, the utility believes that there is a good chance that, if there are no major disruptions in the pipeline system, the spot prices will be much lower than currently suggested by the forward market. The company wants to benefit from lower prices, but at the same time it wants a measure of protection in case there is a disruption. The natural solution is to buy a call option on the average spot (daily index) price in January, struck at the current forward price. In this way, when prices fall as expected, the LDC will enjoy the benefit of cheap delivery. On the other hand, if prices increase, the utility will have to buy in the expensive spot market, but its higher cost will be offset by the payoff from the option it bought for protection.

Related Asian Structures

In the energy world, Asian options appear under many guises and in combinations with other structures. The frequent extensions are volume-weighted Asian options (e.g., in Canadian AECO location) and multi-asset Asian options.

The floating strike options described in the previous section can physically deliver at another location, and the floating strike price will be defined as a spread to the first-of-the-month index at a nearby liquid location. Then we will be dealing with a multi-asset forward-start Asian option with floating strike:

$$V_{AS} = \max(A_T^\tau - I^2 - d, 0)$$

$$A_T^\tau = \frac{\sum_{i=\tau}^{T} S_i^1}{T - \tau} \tag{8.7}$$

Superscripts 1 and 2 refer to the different assets (locational indices).

Often, the arrangement is such that the commodity is delivered physically to a location that does not have a liquid spot market. In that case, the formula (8.7) is not directly applicable, since we do not know what S^1 is. The way to get around this problem is to construct a proxy for S^1 by considering the nearest liquid location and the cost of transport to the point of interest.

We consider two modifications of the standard Asian payoffs: volume weighted and multi-asset. The payoff functions are given by:

$$C_{VW} = \max(B_T - K, 0)$$

$$C_{MA} = \max(S_T^2 - A_T^1, 0)$$

$$B_T = \frac{\sum_{i=t}^{T} V_i S_i}{\sum_{i=t}^{T} V_i}$$

$$A_T = \frac{\sum_{i=t}^{T} S_i^1}{T - t} \tag{8.8}$$

Here V_i is the trading volume on i-th day of the averaging period. Superscripts 1 and 2 refer to the prices of two different assets. In natural gas markets, the different indices refer to the different index prices (locational prices).

Asian Options: Valuation and Hedging

We begin this section by reviewing the main techniques of valuation for the standard Asian structures given in (8.6).

Assume that the spot price follows the standard geometric process:

$$\frac{dS}{S} = \mu dt + \sigma dW \tag{8.9}$$

This warrants some justification. As we saw in Chapter 3, energy prices do not follow a GBM (or even mean-reverting GBM). However, we will develop pricing formulas under this unrealistic assumption in order to find a first approximation. This approach allows us to use the substantial body of literature on Asian options available in the financial markets. Later we will analyze the impact of non-lognormal behavior on the Asian option prices.

The value of the average price Asian option is given by the following general formula:

$$V_{AP} = E_t^*[e^{-r(T-t)}\max(A_t^\tau - K, 0)] \tag{8.10}$$

where the expectation is given under the appropriate risk-neutral measure.

An aside here: the choice of the risk premium depends on whether the market for the underlying commodity is complete or not. In other words, the question centers on the issue of having enough other products with which to hedge out the risks associated with the Asian option. The forward contract itself is not sufficient since it settles at the beginning of the month, instead at the end of the month, when the average price is determined. The time basis (the differential between the forward contract and the average) can be very substantial; in power markets it can be as high as 400% (see Chapter 3). In some markets, however, there is a liquid balance-of-the-month (BOM) market. The liquidity of the BOM market in PJM, for example, is better than that of the forward contracts there. The presence of BOM contracts can help enormously with effective dynamic hedging of various structures and especially of Asian options. In many markets, however, the liquidity in the BOM contracts is quite limited (e.g., NEPOOL, several gas locations).

Under these circumstances, and if there are liquid forwards available, we must price in the time basis risk. Additionally, there can be more than one source of risk. Beyond the level risk that we can handle with forwards and/or BOM contracts, we might be exposed to implied volatility smiles and skews, which, as we saw in Chapter 3, are present in all energy markets. The liquidity of the volatility smile markets (options) can be substantial, but those options are often written on the forward at expiration. Consequently, hedging volatility exposure suffers from the same time-basis problem that affects hedging with forwards. Using daily (power) or index (natural gas) options can partially alleviate this problem, but those options suffer from lower liquidity and do not usually offer quotes except for ATM options. Additionally, using the cash month options for hedging generally requires a dynamic strategy—and this, in turn, is largely impossible due to the low liquidity.

Despite those drawbacks, a strategy combining forward, BOM, and index option hedging, with the forward positions dynamically adjusted and the option position held statically, will perform quite well.

After this lengthy introduction we are ready to price the forward-start Asian option. The distribution of individual prices of the average is lognormal. A known closed-form formula for the distribution of lognormal variates does not exist. Consequently, it will not be surprising that no closed-form solutions exist for the value of the arithmetic Asian options (the only ones trading). Therefore, we must content ourselves with approximations and numerical procedures.

The simplest approach is a Monte Carlo simulation, but given its relative slowness, this solution should be used as a last resort. It can be somewhat improved by using variance reduction techniques. For Asian options, an obvious choice for a control variate is the value of the geometrically averaged option; it has a closed-form solution.

An alternative is to use analytical approximations. We consider two of them: one from Vorst (1990) and the other from Curran (1992). The advantage of the former is its simplicity, and the latter, its superior performance.

Vorst Method

The Vorst approach approximates the value of the arithmetic average Asian option with a geometric average option. Geometric average is given by the following:

$$G = \sqrt[n]{\prod_{i=1}^{n} S_i} \tag{8.11}$$

The product of n lognormal variables is itself lognormal; consequently G will be lognormally distributed with the following parameters:

$$\mu_G = \ln S_0 + (r - q - \tfrac{1}{2}\sigma^2)\frac{T + \Delta t}{2}$$

$$\sigma_G^2 = \sigma^2\left(\Delta t + (T - \Delta t)\frac{(2n - 1)}{6n}\right) \tag{8.12}$$

where $\mu = r - q$ is the drift (see (8.9)), q is the convenience yield, T is the time of expiration and Δt is the length of the time interval between the price fixings (prices used to compute the average value). With these coefficients we can easily use the Black-Scholes formula to price a call on the geometric average:

$$C_G = e^{-rt}[e^{\mu_G + \frac{1}{2}\sigma_G^2}N(d_1) - e^{-rt}KN(d_1 - \sigma_G)]$$

$$d_1 = \frac{\mu_G - \ln K + \frac{1}{2}\sigma_G^2}{\sigma_G} \tag{8.13}$$

Here, t is the start of the averaging period. We can now bound the arithmetic average, using the geometric option price.

It is well-known that the geometric average G is always less than the arithmetic average A. Consequently, the call on geometric average C_G must always be worth less than the call on the arithmetic average C_A. On the other hand, we can easily show that given

$$\max(A - K, 0) \le \max(G - K, 0) + A - G$$

we have

$$C_G \le C_A \le C_G + e^{-rt}\left(E[A] - E[G]\right) \tag{8.14}$$

We have thus established bounds on the arithmetic average option with the geometric average option. The averages are given by the following formulas:

$$E[G] = e^{\mu_G + \frac{1}{2}\sigma_G^2}$$

$$E[A] = e^{(r-q)\Delta t}\frac{(1 - e^{(r-q)n\Delta t})S_0}{(1 - e^{(r-q)\Delta t})n} \tag{8.15}$$

Given the above definitions, the Vorst approximation is given by the following:

$$\hat{C}_A = e^{-rt}[e^{\mu_G + \frac{1}{2}\sigma_G^2}N(d_1^*) - e^{-rt}K^*N(d_1^* - \sigma_G)]$$

$$d_1^* = \frac{\mu_G - \ln K^* + \frac{1}{2}\sigma_G^2}{\sigma_G} \tag{8.16}$$

$$K^* = K - (E[A] - E[G])$$

Hence, the approximation of an arithmetic Asian option consists of evaluating a geometric Asian option, and correcting for bias by adjusting the strike price of the option. The adjustment effectively increases the mean of the geometric average to match that of the arithmetic average. Given the bounds mentioned before, the error of the approximation is given by

$$|\hat{C}_A - C_A| \le e^{-rt}(E[A] - E[G]) \tag{8.17}$$

This error is not small, however, and it increases with the cumulative volatility. In practice, the Vorst method does not perform very well. It is described here as a "quickie" tool, and as a useful introduction to a superior method proposed by Curran that also uses the concept of geometric average.

Curran Method

The Vorst approach uses information about the differences between the means of arithmetic averages and geometric averages to arrive at an approximation. However, with more information about the relationships between the two distributions we might be able to develop a better approximation.

We have shown that the logarithm of the geometric average $\ln G$ is normally distributed with the mean and variance given by (8.12). Similarly, we know that for every fixing period the logarithm of the underlying price $\ln S_i$ is also normally distributed. We can also show that the two variables, $\ln G$, $\ln S_i$, for every i will be jointly normally distributed. Using the standard properties of the joint normal distribution we can show that $\ln S_i$ conditional on $\ln G = x$ will be also normally distributed:

$$(\ln S_i | \ln G = x) \sim N\left(\ln S_0 + (r - q - -\tfrac{1}{2}\sigma^2)t_i + (x - \mu_G)\rho_i \frac{\sigma_i}{\sigma_G}, (1 - \rho_i^2)\sigma_i^2\right)$$

$$\sigma_i^2 = \sigma^2 t_i \tag{8.18}$$

$$\rho_i = \frac{\sigma^2 \Delta t((2n + 1)i - i^2)}{2n\sigma_i\sigma_G}$$

It follows, then, that S_i conditioned on the $\ln G = x$ is lognormally distributed with the parameters given above.

We can now write the arithmetic option price as a conditional expectation on the geometric average G:

$$C_A = e^{-rt}E[\max(A - K,0)] = e^{-rt}E\{E[\max(A - K,0)|G]\}$$

$$= e^{-rt}\left\{\int_0^K E[\max(A - K,0)|G = x]f(x)dx + \int_K^\infty E[\max(A - K,0)|G = x]f(x)dx\right\}$$

$$\tag{8.19}$$

Since $A > G$ we can see that the second term in the last equality is

$$C_2 = \int_K^\infty E[\max(A - K,0)|G = x]f(x)dx = \int_K^\infty E[A - K|G = x]f(x)dx$$

$$\tag{8.20}$$

$$= \frac{1}{n}\sum_{i=1}^n \int_K^\infty E[S_i|G = x]f(x)dx - K\int_K^\infty f(x)dx$$

The second term in this expression is simply the strike price times the lognormal probability of $\ln G > K$, and the first term is just a sum of exponential terms integrated with respect to the lognormal distribution. We can easily obtain a closed-form solution for both terms.

The first term in the last equality in (8.19) does not have an analytical expression, so we resort to an approximation:

$$C_1 = \int_0^K E[\max(A - K,0)|G = x]f(x)dx \geq \int_0^K \max[E(A - K|G = x),0]f(x)dx$$

$$= \int_{LB}^K E(A - K|G = x)f(x)dx = \widehat{C}_1$$

$$LB = \arg\min[x|E(A|G = x) = K]$$

$$E[A|G = x] = \frac{1}{n}\sum_{i=1}^{n}\exp\left[\ln S_0 + (r - q - \tfrac{1}{2}\sigma^2)t_i + (\ln x - \mu_G)\rho_i\frac{\sigma_i}{\sigma_G} + \tfrac{1}{2}(1 - \rho_i^2)\sigma_i^2\right]$$

$$(8.21)$$

To find an appropriate LB we must equate the conditional expectation above to K, and find x that meets the condition. To achieve that, we need a numerical procedure. The solution is usually easy to obtain with simple linear searches (e.g., bisection, see Bazzara and Shetty, 1979).

Putting our results together, we get the following expression for the Curran approximation:

$$\widehat{C}_A = e^{-rt}(\widehat{C}_1 + C_2)$$

$$= e^{-rt}\left[\frac{1}{n}\sum_{i=1}^{n}\exp(\ln S_0 + (r - q - \tfrac{1}{2}\sigma^2)t_i + \tfrac{1}{2}\sigma_i^2)\Phi\left(\frac{\mu_G - \ln LB + \rho_i\sigma_i\sigma_G}{\sigma_G}\right)\right.$$

$$\left. - K\Phi\left(\frac{\mu_G - \ln LB}{\sigma_G}\right)\right]$$

$$(8.22)$$

This is highly accurate for a wide range of input parameters. We recommend it as the best, given the trade-off between accuracy and speed.

Other Asian Structures

The Curran approximation was developed for the average price Asian options. We can use the results to price average strike Asian options outside the averaging period. For GBM (Geometric Brownian Motion) the following symmetry result applies (see Henderson and Wojakowski, 2001).

$$V_{AS}^{Call}(S_0,\lambda,r,d,0,T) = V_{AP}^{Put}(\lambda S_0,S_0,d,r,0,T)$$

$$V_{AP}^{Call}(K,S_0,r,d,0,T) = V_{AS}^{Put}\left(S_0,\frac{K}{S_0},d,r,0,T\right)$$

$$(8.23)$$

where

$$V_{AS}^{Call}(S_0,\lambda,r,d,0,T) = e^{-rT}E[\max(\lambda S_T - A_T,0)]$$

$$V_{AP}^{Call}(K,S_0,r,d,0,T) = e^{-rT}E[\max(A_T - K,0)]$$

and d is the dividend rate. (We refer the reader to Lipton [1999], Hoogland and Neumann [2000] for a detailed description of the use of symmetries for pricing Asian and other exotic options).

Multivariate and volume-weighted Asian options generally require numerical methods such as Monte Carlo. However, the methods for the standard Asians work quite well as first approximations.

Other Methods

Recently a number of powerful methods based on inverse Laplace and other transforms have been developed for pricing Asian and other exotic options (e.g., see Geman and Yor, 1993; Geman and Eydeland, 1995; Linetsky, 2001; Lipton, 2001; Lipton, 2002). The principal advantages of these methods are due to the fact that they can be applied to a wide range of underlying processes, including jump-diffusion processes, and that they produce the closed-form pricing formulas for Asian options, albeit in the integral form. The pricing algorithms based on these formulas are efficient and accurate, but their implementation requires a certain degree of sophistication.

It is worth mentioning that in the case of GBM, we still recommend to use Curran's algorithm if the implementation speed is the objective, since in practice it approximates the true value very well (see Nielsen, 2001).

Nonlognormalities in Asian Option Valuation

Now that we have examined the valuation of Asian options under the assumptions of GBM, we can extend the Curran approximation to the mean-reverting case. This is because for the mean-reverting GBM process, individual prices S_i are still lognormal, and consequently, $S_i|G$ is also lognormally distributed. We can recover the Curran approximation by adjusting volatilities and correlations in (8.22).

In principle, for more complex processes, we must resort to simulations or the transform-based techniques mentioned in the previous paragraph to properly value Asian options. In practice, however, the use of a lognormal approximation with the appropriately chosen implied volatility performs quite well.

For example, monthly options in natural gas and power markets are essentially average price Asian options. The underlying is the price of the contract that settles against the average spot price inside the contract month. The only problem is the time basis we mentioned before; this can be managed by trading BOM contracts inside the month. Consequently, we can approximate the value of Asian options with monthly averaging periods by using the appropriate implied volatilities along with one of the lognormal approximations such as Curran.

Forward Volatility Skew versus Daily/Index Volatility Skew

In Chapters 2, 3, and 4 we discussed the option markets in energy products. We noted that the liquidity of those markets, especially for OTM options, is quite limited. However, we often observe a significant difference in liquidity, depending on the type of option involved. In natural gas markets, forward volatility skew is extensively traded, at least at Henry Hub. On the other hand, the corresponding daily/index options show significant liquidity only for ATM options. The question we pose in this section is whether we can use the information in the forward volatility smile to recover the daily volatility smile. The issue is of interest in pricing and especially in hedging structured gas products.

We noted before that the forward contract is effectively settled against the average spot price inside the contract period—most often a month. This obviously suggests that an option on the forward price can be treated as a forward-start Asian option with the averaging period corresponding to the forward contract period (a month). Given this, we can attempt to recover the implied volatility of the underlying spot process from forward option prices by treating them as Asian options. We will calculate the *implied Asian volatility skew* by finding spot volatility that, when put into an Asian pricing formula, recovers the currently quoted forward option prices. We can use the Curran approximation (8.22).

$$C_{Market}(K) = \widehat{C}_A(\sigma_{IAV}^K) \qquad (8.24)$$

We will call the implied volatility curve, defined by this equation as a function of strike price K, implied Asian volatility skew.

We want to use the implied Asian volatility skew as a proxy for the unavailable implied daily volatility skew, but there are two limitations to the procedure. First, the forward options settle before the averaging period, and hedging inside the period is more complex. Hence a risk premium may be due to the unhedgeable time basis. Second, Asian option prices are affected not only by the local volatility of the process, but also by the effective correlation structure between the prices on individual days. (Note that under GBM, returns are not correlated, but prices are.) Consequently, there is not necessarily a one-to-one relationship between Asian implied volatility and local volatility. As a minimum consistency check, we should always investigate whether ATM implied Asian volatility agrees with the quoted ATM daily volatility. Table 8.3 shows the ATM implied Asian volatility versus the quoted daily implied volatility for natural gas contracts (Henry Hub).

As we can see the agreement is basically flawless. Also, the volatilities agree very well no matter when we choose to observe them. For power prices, the implied Asian volatilities and daily implied volatilities are far apart. Fortunately, we are interested in drawing conclusions about daily skew from monthly skew only in natural gas markets. In power markets, the

TABLE 8.3 ATM Implied Asian Volatility versus Quoted Daily Implied Volatility for Natural Gas Contracts (Henry Hub)

	Daily Volatility	Asian Implied Volatility
Feb–2001	79%	77%
Jul–2001	47%	48%
Oct–2001	53%	53%
Jan–2002	66%	65%

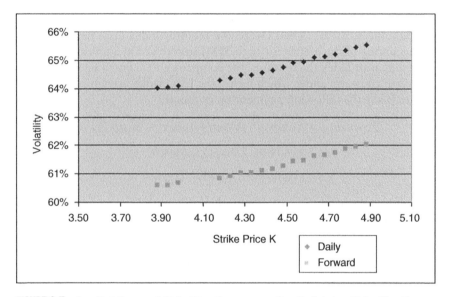

FIGURE 8.5 Implied Forward Volatility Skew versus Implied Asian Volatility Skew

volatility skew does not usually trade very liquidly, and if it does (e.g., in the Cinergy market) it is primarily daily skew that is quoted.

Figure 8.5 compares the implied forward volatility skew with the implied Asian volatility skew for natural gas contracts (Henry Hub).

SWAPS, SWAPTIONS, AND EXTENDIBLES

In this section we consider a variety of swap structures that appear in energy markets. We discussed the forms of widely traded swaps in Chapter 2; here we analyze the extensions of the standard product often encountered in the OTC markets.

Plain Swap (Contract-for-Differences)

The standard fixed-for-float swap involves an exchange of cash flows or commodities. One party pays a fixed, predetermined price for a set of payments or deliveries at a sequence of dates in the future.

EXAMPLE 8.5 *Financial swaps as price protection*

A local delivery company (LDC) requires a stable supply of natural gas for the next winter season (November through March) at predictable prices. The volume the company expects to serve is 10,000 MMBtu per day throughout the season. The LDC pays a monthly index price determined at the beginning of the month for each MMBtu received in a given month. To protect against index fluctuations, the company enters into a financially settled swap contract, under which terms, the LDC will receive from the swap counterparty the following payment every month:

$$Payments_i = Volume_i {}^* (MonthlyIndex_i - Swap\ Price)$$

$$i = Nov., Dec., \ldots, March$$

$$Volume_i = 10,000 {}^* Days_i$$

where $Days_i$ is the number of days in the i-th month.

The LDC clearly benefits from the arrangement when the index prices exceed the swap price, by recovering what it paid for gas above the swap price. Conversely, the company must pay extra whenever index prices are below the swap price. This structure gives the LDC precisely the benefit it seeks. When prices are high, it receives additional cash flow to help offset the higher costs of natural gas. The cost of this protection is an inability to take advantage of any low prices that might appear.

We discussed pricing basic swaps in Chapter 2.

EXAMPLE 8.6 *Physical swaps*

A power marketer is asked to make market in winter swaps in natural gas markets at an illiquid location. The swaps will be settled against the winter index, the arithmetic average of monthly indices. There is no forward basis traded for the location, and the spot market itself is quite spotty. The natural solution for pricing (and hedging) is to consider a nearby liquid point that has a liquid forward basis traded. To construct the proper product we must also secure the transportation capacity from the liquid point to the contract location. Given the cost of the capacity and the forward basis market for the liquid location, we can price the swap as the sum of the NYMEX Henry Hub contract plus the forward basis and the per unit cost of transportation capacity. Clearly, given the physical dimension of the problem, the swap price will depend on the physical assets available to the power marketer (we develop this point more fully in Chapter 10).

Differential Swap

A differential swap can be seen as a plain-vanilla fixed-for-float swap, in which the floating leg is the difference between the prices of two assets. Pricing differential swap does not differ much from pricing standard swaps. Instead of using one forward curve, we use the difference between two forward curves.

EXAMPLE 8.7 *Differential swaps as margin protection*

A power generator in PJM owns several gas-fired units with a heat rate of 7,000 (see Chapter 2). The generator expects a hot summer and predicts that his unit will be running at peak capacity throughout the on-peak hours of every summer month (May through September). Despite these attractive prospects, the generator is concerned about the impact of the fuel cost volatility on his margin. To remove this risk, the generator enters into a (spark spread) differential swap, whereby he will pay the fixed leg and receive the floating leg. The floating leg will be settled against the difference between the forward price at PJM West at expiration and the product of the heat rate and FOM index at Transco Zone 6 (Non-New York). The swap price is thus given by:

$$Swap\ Price = \frac{\sum_{i=May}^{September} df_i \cdot Volume_i \cdot (F_i^{PJM} - HR \cdot F_i^{Transco})}{\sum_{i=May}^{September} df_i \cdot Volume_i} \qquad (8.25)$$

We can see from our example that differential swaps can be used to fix production margins in power generation, oil refining (crack spread swaps), and so on. Additionally, we can use differential swaps to fix basis differentials between locations, called *basis swaps*.

Participation Swap

A standard swap gives the fixed-side party full protection against adverse price moves. The cost of this protection is the loss of the opportunity to benefit from advantageous price moves. This problem can be alleviated by a *participation swap* allowing the fixed leg holder to participate in the advantageous price movements. This is a standard swap with the additional provision that a certain percentage of upside price move will be retained by the fixed-leg holder. The payoff function of the swap is given by:

$$ParticipationSwap_i = \begin{cases} Volume_i(F_i - ReferencePrice_i) & \text{if } F_i \geq ReferencePrice_i \\ (1 - P)Volume_i(F_i - ReferencePrice_i) & \text{if } F_i \leq ReferencePrice_i \end{cases}$$

$$ParticipationSwap = \sum_i ParticipationSwap_i \qquad (8.26)$$

P is the participation percentage. We can see that the participation provision is equivalent to the reduction of the payments the fixed-leg holder will have to make. The pricing of a participation swap proceeds from the fact that it is essentially a combination of a standard swap and a strip of put options. For a given set of reference prices the value of a swap can be written as follows:

$$Value = \sum_i df_i \cdot Volume_i(F_i - ReferencePrice_i) + \sum_i df_i \cdot Volume_i E^*[\max(ReferencePrice_i - F_i, 0)]$$

$$(8.27)$$

This expectation is written with respect to the risk-neutral expectation (hedgeable value).

To determine the fair reference prices of the structure, we choose them so as to make the above value equal to zero. In the simplest case we can designate all the reference prices as equal, and call this price again the swap price. To find the price, we must use some simple numerical optimization routine, since there is no closed-form solution for the swap price. The task of finding the swap price can be achieved easily by varying the swap price manually. Given the monotonicity of the value function, the solution can be readily found.

EXAMPLE 8.8   *Participation swap as cheap price protection*

An LDC enters into a participation swap for the delivery of natural gas in winter (November through March). The company expects the volumes to be flat throughout winter at 10,000 MMBtu per day. The contract will be settled against the FOM indices, and the participation percentage is 50%.

TABLE 8.4 Inputs for Valuation

	Forward Prices	Forward Volatilities
November	$3.10	50%
December	$3.20	55%
January	$3.30	60%
February	$3.20	50%
March	$3.10	50%
Plain Swap Price	$3.18	
Participating Swap Price	$3.60	

Table 8.4 summarizes the inputs for valuation and compares the swap prices for the participating and plain-vanilla swap. The swap price for the participating swap is higher. This reflects the cost of the upside of the fixed-leg holder receives.

Multi-assets and Other Complex Swaps

A great variety of swap products are available in OTC energy markets, and we cannot do justice to the complexity and richness of the market in a couple of short pages. For a flavor of the types of products, consider the example of a Btu swap. In this fixed-for-float swap, the receiving party pays a fixed amount and receives the value of a set amount of energy (measured in Btu, hence the name). The source of the energy can be any number of fuels (e.g., natural gas and heating oil). The supplier will obviously deliver the cheapest form of energy. In the financially settled contract, the payoff to the receiving party is given by:

$$BtuSwap_i = Volume_i[\min(HC_G F_i^G, HC_O F_i) - SwapPrice)]$$

$$BtuSwap = \sum_i BtuSwap_i \qquad (8.28)$$

where HC_G and HC_O are the heat contents of natural gas and heating oil, respectively.

We can decompose the Btu swap into a natural gas swap and strip of spread options:

$$BtuSwap_i = Volume_i[(HC_G F_i^G - SwapPrice) - \max(HC_G F_i^G - HC_O F_i^O, 0)] \quad (8.29)$$

We now see that the fixed-leg holder receives the natural gas swap, and at the same time sells a strip of options on the spread between natural gas and heating oil. The benefit is that the swap price is lower than for the pure natural gas swap. The swap price is given by:

$$SwapPrice = \frac{\sum_i df_i Volume_i \cdot (HC_G F_i^G) - \sum_i df_i Volume_i E^*[\max(HC_G F_i^G - HC_O F_i^O, 0)]}{\sum_i df_i Volume_i}$$

(8.30)

The expectation is taken with respect to the risk-neutral (hedgeable) distribution. We will investigate the proper way to value spread options in a later section.

This structure can also be physically settled, a product appealing to dual-fuel generating plant owners who can take delivery of either fuel, depending on market conditions.

Swaptions

Swaptions are options (calls or puts) on swaps. For single-period swaps, swaptions reduce to the standard calls/puts (plain-vanilla swaptions), standard spread options (differential swaptions), or compound options (participating swaption).

In this section we will analyze multiperiod plain-vanilla swaptions, whose payoff function is given by the following:

$$Swaption = \max\left(\frac{\sum_i df_i Volume_i F_i}{\sum_i df_i Volume_i} - K, 0\right)$$

(8.31)

This appears structurally similar to the payoff function of the arithmetically averaged Asian option in equation (8.6). The difference is that the terms in the summation in (8.31) correspond to separate assets, while (8.6) shows prices of the same underlying assets at different point in time. This difference, although important from the hedging standpoint, might not be so crucial in the valuation process. Moreover, for some Asian options there is no difference: For example, in Asian options on spot power, the individual terms in the average do not correspond to any one underlying asset. Due to the nonstorability of power, electricity at two different points in time is two different assets.

In practice we often encounter embedded swaption contracts of a more complex nature than the plain-vanilla swaptions described above—for example, swaptions built into extendible swaps (see next section). Other examples include swaptions on differential swaps or swaptions on participating swaps. The former is essentially an option on a sequence of spreads; the latter is an option on a plain-vanilla swap and a portfolio of options. This makes the swaption a complex compound option (see upcoming section "Compound Options") whose valuation is not easy and often requires numerical techniques. The most popular one in this context is Monte Carlo simulation; its popularity is due to its ability to handle virtually any payoff function, no matter how complex. The disadvantage is its very slow convergence, induced by the complexity and instability of hedge coefficients. These problems can be partially alleviated by a judicious choice of control variates, but that is no panacea.

The alternatives are tree-based methodologies or, more generally, numerical approximations to the appropriate partial differential equations (e.g., see Wilmott, Howison, and Dewynne, 1995). Their advantage is the ability to handle the early exercise provisions swaptions often carry. Their disadvantage is the significant computational cost and complexity of the approximation for complex payoff function, especially in the context of multifactor models.

Extendible Options and Extendible Swaps

Extendible swaps are contracts in which one party has the option to extend the term of the swap on the same or modified terms. Related products include callable swaps, in which either the receiver (the fixed leg) has the right to shorten the term of the swap, and puttable swaps, in which the floating leg has that right. Oftentimes, the exercise of this right requires payment of a termination fee.

In this section we concentrate on analysis of the extendible swap because of its popularity in the energy markets. An analysis of callable and puttable swaps is essentially identical. We can treat them as extendibles with the initial term appropriately shortened.

EXAMPLE 8.9   *Extendibles as cheap alternatives to standard swaps*

An LDC, concerned about gas volatility, plans to fix its fuel cost by taking on the fixed-leg side of a plain-vanilla swap. The term will cover the whole calendar year and will be settled against the respective monthly (first-of-the-month) indices. A gas marketer quotes a price that the LDC finds too high. The marketer then proposes to lower the swap price if the LDC grants it the right to extend the contract term for an additional year. Moreover, the marketer even offers to lower a swap price for the extension year. Expecting a long-term decline in gas prices, the LDC decides that the potential gain is worth the risk and enters the deal.

The ability to lower the price comes from the fact that the LDC in Example 8.9 receives a swap for the first year and sells a swaption for the second year. The marketer is able to lower the swap price and hence decrease the value of the first-year swap, because in exchange it receives the swaption, whose value will offset that decrease. The value of the extendible swap for a given set of fixed swap prices will be:

$$ExtendibleValue =$$

$$\sum_{i=Jan/Year1}^{Dec/Year1} df_i \cdot Volume_i \cdot (F_i - Swap\ Price_1) - E^* \left\{ \max \left[\sum_{j=Jan/Year2}^{Dec/Year2} df_j \cdot Volume_j \cdot (F_j - SwapPrice_2), 0 \right] \right\}$$

$$(8.32)$$

The choice of swap prices 1 and 2 is made in such a way that the initial value of the contract is zero, providing us the fair value of the extendible. This problem is analogous to the one we solved for participating swaps in an earlier section, with the complication that we must perform it with two variables. In practice, the way to approach this is to fix the second swap price at some attractive level (e.g., the level corresponding to the other party's expectation of the price level in the second year.) Then the swap price is given by:

$$Swap\ Price_1 = \frac{\displaystyle\sum_{i=Jan1}^{Dec1} df_i Volume_i F_i - df_i E^* \left[\max \left(\sum_{j=Jan2}^{Dec2} Volume_j^* (F_j - SwapPrice_2), 0 \right) \right]}{\displaystyle\sum_{i=Jan1}^{Dec1} df_i Volume_i}$$

$$(8.33)$$

The swap price in the first period is lowered by the value of the swaption. The valuation of extendibles comes down to the valuation of standard swaps and swaptions, which have been addressed in previous sections.

This is considered the simplest extendible option on a plain-vanilla swap, but extension provisions are also often found in more complex swap contracts—extendible differential swaps, participating swaps, and a variety of others. In all these, the basic analysis is the same. The complex extendible decomposes into a complex swap and a complex swaption. (See the previous sections for more information.)

COMPOUND OPTIONS

Swaptions, or options on swaps, are just one example of a class of derivative products called *compound options*. By definition, a compound option is any option whose underlying is another derivative. Most typically, a compound option is a call or a put on a certain, often complex, derivative structure. In the case of a call, at the exercise date an option holder has the right (but not the obligation) to buy the underlying derivative structure for a specified payment (strike price). Similarly, a put allows the holder to sell the underlying derivative for a specified strike price.

Compound options frequently encountered in the financial markets are captions and floortions. A *caption* is a call on a cap. (A cap is a derivative structure that can be represented as a series of calls with different exercise dates and strikes.) Thus, at the exercise date the caption holder should decide if the value of a cap is higher than the strike price. A *floortion* is a call on a floor, that is, a series of puts.

To understand the mechanics of compound options, consider a simple example, a call on a call. It is a call option whose underlying is another call option. More formally, a holder of this compound option has the right (but not the obligation) at time T_0 to pay the strike price K for a call with exercise date T_1 and strike X. Denoting the value of this call at a given time t by $C(t, S_t; T_1, X)$, where S_t is the price at t of the asset underlying the call, we can express the payoff of the compound option at the exercise time T_0 as

$$\Pi_{compound} = \max\left[C(T_0, S_{T_0}; T_1, X) - K, 0\right]$$

It means that at time T_0 the compound option will be exercised if the value of the underlying call at that time exceeds the strike K of the compound option. Once the payoff is known, the value of the compound options is obtained by computing the risk-neutral expectation of this payoff with respect to S_{T_0}.

Under certain conditions this expectation can be computed explicitly leading to Black-Scholes-type closed-form expressions for compound option values. For example, the Geske (1979) formulas for calls or puts on plain-vanilla calls or puts were developed under the assumption that the evolution of the underlying assets (stocks) is governed by GBM. In this case the European call-on-call value at time t is given by the expression

$$C_{call\text{-}on\text{-}call} = S_t N\left(h_1 + \sigma\sqrt{T_0 - t}, h_2 + \sigma\sqrt{T_1 - t}; \sqrt{(T_0 - t)/(T_1 - t)}\right)$$

$$- Xe^{-r(T_1 - t)}N\left(h_1, h_2; \sqrt{(T_0 - t)/(T_1 - t)}\right) - e^{-r(T_0 - t)}KN(h_1)$$

where

$$h_1 = \frac{\ln(S_t/S^*) + (r - \sigma^2/2)(T_0 - t)}{\sigma\sqrt{T_0 - t}}$$

$$h_2 = \frac{\ln(S_t/X) + (r - \sigma^2/2)(T_1 - t)}{\sigma\sqrt{T_1 - t}}$$

where $N(x,y;\rho)$ is the standardized bivariate cumulative normal distribution, and the value S^* is the solution of the equation $C(T_0,S^*;T_1, X) = K$. The values of a European call-on-put, put-on-call and put-on-put are given by similar expressions. (See details and generalizations in Geske, 1979; Rubinstein, 1991; and Nelken, 1996.)

It is interesting to note that although the call $C(t, S_t; T_1,X)$ is the underlying of the compound option, we did not use the distribution of its values to compute the value of the compound option. Instead, we used the distribution of the "underlying of underlying," S_{T_0}. This choice can be explained by a practical consideration that the asset used in valuation will be also used in hedging. Therefore, given a choice, we should prefer to use a more liquid instrument in valuation formulas.

Compound Options in Energy Markets

Many compound options developed in financial markets found their way into energy markets as well. However, the most frequently used ones are unmistakably energy-specific. They are options on spread options or on more complicated spread-dependent structures, such as energy assets. Thus, instead of call-on-call used in financial markets, we are more likely to encounter *call-on-toll*.

Call-on-toll.   This common compound option allows its holder to enter, if he or she so chooses, into a tolling agreement at some future date T_0 in exchange for a specified payment K. Tolling contracts were described in Chapter 2. Fundamentally, a tolling contract can be viewed as a financial replication of a long-term lease or ownership of a physical asset, such as a power plant. Therefore, a call option on a toll is a relatively inexpensive way to have an access to a power plant in the future. This opportunity may be quite useful, especially if one believes in the cyclicality of commodity prices. Using call-on-toll option at the bottom of a price cycle is a natural and not capital-intensive strategy to bet on the improvement of the price environment in the future.

Tolling contracts can be represented as a series of options on spreads between power and fuel prices with the variable being the strike. In the next section we will give a detailed description of the issues related to valuation of spread options. Here, suffice to say that the value of the tolling deal at time t is determined by the forward and volatility curves for power and fuel:

$$V_{toll} = S\left(t, F_1^{power}, \ldots, F_n^{power}, F_1^{fuel}, \ldots, F_n^{fuel}, \sigma_1^{power}, \ldots, \sigma_n^{power}, \sigma_1^{fuel}, \ldots, \sigma_n^{fuel}, VOM\right)$$

In this equation S is a spread option evaluator, forward contracts cover the duration of the tolling deal and volatility parameters denote both monthly and cash volatilities. With this definition the payoff of the call-on-toll option at the exercise date T_0 is given by the expression

$$\Pi_{call-on-toll} = \max\left[S\left(T_0, F^{power}_{T_0,1}, \ldots, F^{power}_{T_0,n}, F^{fuel}_{T_0,1}, \ldots, F^{fuel}_{T_0,n}, \sigma^{power}_{T_0,1}, \ldots, \sigma^{power}_{T_0,n}, \sigma^{fuel}_{T_0,1}, \ldots, \sigma^{fuel}_{T_0,n}, VOM\right) - K, 0^{TM}\right]$$

This expression means that the payoff of the call-on-toll option is determined by the forward price and volatility data observed at the future time T_0. Assuming that the volatility is not stochastic, the price of this option is obtained by computing a risk-neutral expectation over all possible realizations of power and fuel forward curves at T_0. If the duration of the tolling contract is large, it means computing high-dimensional integrals in the space of forward prices. Two methods can be suggested to achieve this goal.

1. Monte Carlo simulations. This is a standard approach to computing high-dimensional integrals. It consists of generating a number of samples of vectors of forward power and fuel prices, computing the corresponding payoffs and taking their average. The forward price samples are generated under specified assumptions on their expectation and covariance structure.

2. Dimension reduction. The Monte Carlo method, while simple and robust, has one drawback—it is usually a challenge to use it for American-style options, that is, for options that allow early exercise (before T_0). Although progress to adapt Monte Carlo for this purpose has been made in recent years, backward induction (implemented commonly on a binomial or trinomial tree) is still the most popular technique for pricing American- or Bermudan-style options. If the early exercise feature is present in the compound option and we want to use backward induction, there is no choice but to reduce the dimension of the problem. This can be done by imposing a certain low-dimensional structure on movements of the power and fuel forward curves from today to T_0. For example, we may use HJM-type techniques described in Chapter 5, provided that we can demonstrate that movements of the forward curves are fairly well approximated by a combination of a small number of basis functions (i.e., principal components). In this case the backward induction technique can be implemented since it can be reduced to low-dimensional integration. See Eydeland (1996), Jamshidian and Zhu (1997) for more details on this approach.

Call-on-toll is one example of a fundamentally energy compound option. More complex examples include options on forward acquisitions of assets, such as turbines, plants, storage, or options allowing one to make a decision in the future whether to start a new construction of a power plant.

SPREAD OPTIONS

In this section we analyze methodologies developed for pricing and hedging basic spread options. Our focus on these options is motivated by the fact that in energy markets, unlike in financial markets, spread options and other correlation products are critically important. For example, the majority of generation assets can be seen as complex versions of spread options. For this reason, and also because the literature on financial derivatives generally does not adequately cover them, we present a detailed analysis of these options.

First we look at spread options in the Black-Scholes world.

Spread Options in the Black-Scholes World

It might seem strange that, after arguing extensively about severe limitations of the Black-Scholes analysis as applied to energy and (especially) electricity markets, we find a new devotion to this simple model when it comes to pricing spread options. The reason is mainly pedagogical; valuable intuition can be gained about the unique behavior of spread options even within a simple framework. In fact, the qualitative behavior of spread options and their risk measures are quite robust with respect to the selection of the price distribution.

The payoff of a spread option is given by the following equality:

$$SpreadOption = \max(F_1 - F_2 - K, 0) \tag{8.34}$$

For the simplest case of the European spread option on forward contracts with no strike price (i.e., exchange option: $K = 0$), the value is described by the following formula from Margrabe (1978):

$$C_S = e^{-rt}(F_1 N(d_1) - F_2 N(d_2))$$

where

$$d_1 = \frac{\ln(\frac{F_1}{F_2}) + \frac{\sigma^2 t}{2}}{\sigma\sqrt{t}}$$

$$d_2 = d_1 - \sigma\sqrt{t} \tag{8.35}$$

This formula is almost identical to the Black formula for the value of a call on a futures contract, with the price of the second contract put in the place of the strike price. The only substantial difference is that the volatility used in the formula is given by:

$$\sigma = \sqrt{\sigma_1^2 + \sigma_2^2 - 2\rho\sigma_1\sigma_2} \tag{8.36}$$

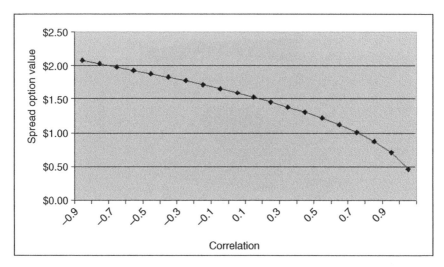

FIGURE 8.6 Spread Option Value As a Function of Correlation

Figures 8.6 and 8.7 illustrate the behavior of spread option values as a function of its parameters.

Figure 8.6 shows that the spread option price decreases with correlation. This behavior is universal and does not depend on the values of volatilities, prices, and so on. The highest sensitivity to correlation comes at high correlation levels and when the component volatilities are close in magnitude. We can define a new sensitivity coefficient:

$$\pi = \frac{\partial C_S}{\partial \rho} = -v \frac{\sigma_1 \sigma_2}{\sigma} \tag{8.37}$$

v is the vega of the standard Black formula. That is, it is the derivative of formula (8.35) with respect to σ defined in (8.36). Since correlation effectively changes the "volatility" of the spread, it is not surprising that sensitivity to correlation is at its highest for out-of-the-money options. Figure 8.7 shows the dependence of π to volatility levels. For ATM options, π is at its highest for the set of volatilities and correlation described by the following equation:

$$\sigma_1^2 + \sigma_2^2 - 2\rho\sigma_1\sigma_2 = \frac{\sqrt[3]{16}}{T} \tag{8.38}$$

In the case of standard options (calls and puts), the option value is always an increasing function of the volatility of the underlying process. This is often expressed by saying that its vega—sensitivity with respect to volatility—

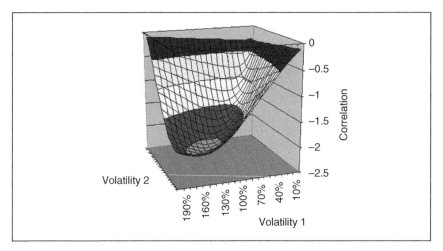

FIGURE 8.7   Correlation Sensitivity π As a Function of Volatilities

is positive. However, this property does not hold for spread options, as we can see directly by calculating the two respective vegas:

$$v_1 = \frac{\partial C_S}{\partial \sigma_1} = \frac{\partial C_S}{\partial \sigma}\frac{\partial \sigma}{\partial \sigma_1} = v\frac{\partial \sigma}{\partial \sigma_1} = v\frac{(\sigma_1 - \sigma_2\rho)}{\sqrt{\sigma_1^2 + \sigma_2^2 - 2\rho\sigma_1\sigma_2}}$$

$$v_2 = \frac{\partial C_S}{\partial \sigma_2} = \frac{\partial C_S}{\partial \sigma}\frac{\partial \sigma}{\partial \sigma_2} = v\frac{\partial \sigma}{\partial \sigma_2} = v\frac{(\sigma_2 - \sigma_1\rho)}{\sqrt{\sigma_1^2 + \sigma_2^2 - 2\rho\sigma_1\sigma_2}} \quad (8.39)$$

where v stands for the vega of the standard call. The vega of the first asset will become negative if the following holds:

$$\sigma_1 \leq \sigma_2\,\rho \quad (8.40)$$

A similar condition will hold for the vega of the second asset. Figure 8.8 presents this regularity in graphical form. We can see that if volatility 1 is small while volatility 2 is high, the vega 1 will be substantially negative. Hedging coefficients can also exhibit counter-intuitive behavior in response to changing volatility, as Figure 8.9 shows.

The absolute value of the individual deltas tends to be similar at moderate levels of volatility. If the volatility levels become substantially different, the absolute value of the long-leg delta becomes significantly higher than the short-leg deltas. The higher the volatility, the stronger the effect.

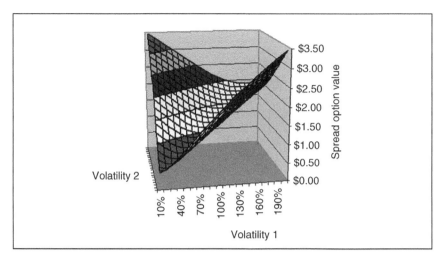

FIGURE 8.8 Dependence of the Spread Option Value on the Volatilities of Both Assets

In practice these issues are encountered when hedging peaking plants in the summer. Those plants can be described as spread options between on-peak (possibly hourly) power prices and natural gas prices (the primary fuel). Even if a plant is substantially in-the-money, we often find that with the very high (hourly) power volatility and relatively low gas volatility, our power positions will be substantial, while the corresponding gas positions will decrease. This situation can seem a little counter-intuitive, especially for operators accustomed to hedging the physical needs of plants. With a plant substantially in-the-money, it would seem only natural to buy the required gas supplies on a forward basis to assure smooth operation and lock in the spread. This solution is erroneous, however, because it ignores that fact that what is or is not deep in the money is not a question of absolute price differences, but rather of volatility and the correlation between the different assets. (Distance in prices should be measured in units of volatility.)

Nonzero Strike Prices in Black-Scholes World

At present there is no closed-form formula for pricing spread options with nonzero strike price, but several approaches can address this valuation problem. The simplest involves an approximation using the Margrabe formula with an adjusted volatility, and an adjustment as a function of the strike price.

$$C_K = e^{-rt} \left(F_1 N(d_1) - (F_2 + K) N(d_2) \right)$$

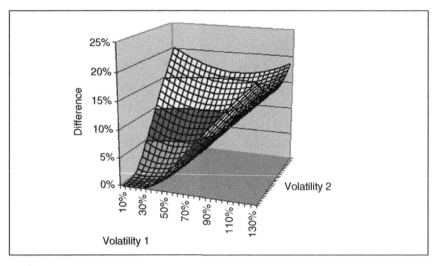

FIGURE 8.9 The Difference between the Absolute Values of the Long-leg and Short-leg Deltas As a Function of Volatilities

where

$$d_1 = \frac{\ln\left(\dfrac{F_1}{F_2 + K}\right) + \dfrac{\sigma^2 t}{2}}{\sigma\sqrt{t}}$$

$$d_2 = d_1 - \sigma\sqrt{t} \qquad (8.41)$$

$$\sigma = \sqrt{\sigma_1^2 + \left(\sigma_2 \frac{F_1}{F_2 + K}\right)^2 - 2\rho\sigma_1\sigma_2 \frac{F_1}{F_2 + K}}$$

The adjustment consists in replacing the forward price F_2 with $F_2 + K$ and multiplying volatility σ_2 by the factor $F_1/(F_2 + K)$.

This approximation performs quite well in comparison to other numerical techniques. The values and the hedges it generates come very close to their true values. Also, the qualitative behavior of the values and hedges does not change much in comparison with the case of zero strike price.

Another alternative is to use semi-analytical techniques (see Pearson, 1995) based on transforming the two-dimensional problem into one-dimensional integration by conditioning in the following way:

$$C_K = e^{-r(T-t)}E_t^*[\max(F_1 - F_2 - K, 0)]$$

$$= e^{-r(T-t)}\int\int[\max(F_1 - F_2 - K, 0)]f(F_1, F_2)dF_1dF_2 \qquad (8.42)$$

$$= e^{-r(T-t)}\int\int[\max(F_1 - F_2 - K, 0)f(F_1|F_2)dF_1]f(F_2)dF_2$$

$$= \int C_{BS}(F_2)f(F_2)dF_2$$

$BS(F_2)$ is the properly adjusted Black-Scholes formula. The (8.42) equalities exploit the fact that the conditional distribution of F_1 conditioned on F_2 is lognormal as long as the joint distribution is lognormal; we used this fact in Asian options. The numerical savings of the reduction can be substantial. The method performs very well for valuation and hedging and is generally superior to the adjusted Margrabe presented above. However, its improved performance may not justify its higher computational expense.

The most powerful method is obviously Monte Carlo, but its slow convergence often disqualifies it as a feasible alternative in daily operations—real-time marking of a trading book and the like. Tree-based methodologies, on the other hand, although marginally faster, can have significant problems in dealing with high-correlation cases. These can become especially severe in convergence of the hedge coefficients, but this can be avoided by using more sophisticated lattice/grid methods (see Eydeland and Mahoney, 2002). The advantage of tree/lattice methods is the ability to value American spread options.

Spread Options in the Non–Black-Scholes World

As we argued in previous chapters, the behavior of energy prices seldom follows the joint lognormality assumption of the previous section. We concentrated a good deal of effort on understanding the behavior of spread options in the chapter on correlation. Here we present a quick overview of relevant pricing techniques.

Modeling the Spread Directly

One of the early methods is based on the assumption that the spread itself is lognormally distributed (Wilcox, 1990). This assumption has the downside of excluding the possibility of negative spreads; its primary motivation is the computational efficiency, because it lets us use all the standard Black-Scholes formulas.

Making the lognormality assumption is not very realistic, but the idea of modeling the spread directly is tempting in itself. It lets us avoid the thorny problem of explicitly understanding the dependence structure (correlation).

In assuming that the spread follows a given process, while the component prices follow another, one concern might be the potential for inherent inconsistency. For example, when individual prices follow geometric Brownian motions, it is impossible for the spread to follow a geometric Brownian motion. On the other hand, if we assume that the individual prices followed arithmetic Brownian motion, there is no inconsistency in assuming arithmetic Brownian motion for the spread. Furthermore, in general, even if there is some inconsistency in the assumptions about the underlying process, we are usually able to choose the parameters of the spread process that ensure an approximate matching of the distribution.

However, even if we succeed in choosing a process for the spread (whether one factor or multifactor), using it for pricing and hedging the spread option is not usually feasible. The fundamental problem is that the hedging instruments are the individual underlying components. As we have seen in the previous section, correlation and leg volatilities can have dramatic impact on hedges. In Figure 6.3 we showed that the difference between the component deltas can widen and narrow significantly with changes in volatility or correlation. The alternative delta hedge, with a constant ratio between the individual underlying contracts generated by the method that models spreads directly, will usually result in significant losses in hedging efficiency.

The above consideration is obviously not an absolute one. The statistical properties of the spread might be more stable than those of the individual underliers (see the discussion of cointegration in Chapter 6). In such a situation, the estimation of the model can be much easier, and the hedging issues of lesser importance. Additionally, in some cases it is the spread itself that trades (e.g., basic swaps). In those situations using spread models can be a superior solution.

Multifactor Spread Models

In Chapter 6 we discussed the concept of implied correlation to illustrate the deviations of the actual pricing of a spread option from its joint-lognormal benchmark. Here we review a couple of models that explicitly account for the deviations.

In principle we can make any distributional assumptions and integrate the resulting expression by using Monte Carlo techniques. For multifactor models, this is often the only feasible solution. Computational cost can be very high, however, limiting our ability to mark and hedge the books in real time. With some distributional assumptions we may be able to reduce the computational effort significantly.

We can try to apply expansion methods, such as Edgeworth expansion or Hermite polynomials, which are a natural basis for expansions around normal variables (see Jackwerth, 1999, and also Abken, Madan, and Ramamurtie, 1996). This procedure involves computing correction terms to the standard Margrabe formula. The general problem is that the adjustments can result in negative probability densities. The issue is especially acute in energy markets, where deviations from normality can be substantial. For example, in Edgeworth expansions the correction terms are proportional to the higher cumulants of the distributions. However, highly leptokurtotic distributions with high kurtosis (as high as 40 for power) and skewness (used in energy markets) imply large correction terms, which often result in negative probability densities. This is obviously unacceptable, so we find those methods of limited use.

For the class of affine jump-diffusion processes (see Chapter 6), we can develop relatively fast numerical techniques that rely on the closed-form characteristic function of the joint process. The idea is analogous to the pricing result for the Heston model, which we presented in Chapter 4 (see Dempster and Hong, 2000).

DIGITAL OPTIONS

In this section we give a quick overview of digital options. Digital options come in two main flavors (calls):

- **Cash-or-nothing:** If the underlying exceeds the strike price at exercise, the holder of the option will receive a fixed amount of money:

$$Payoff = X \cdot I_{\{S>K\}}$$

- **Asset-or-nothing:** If the underlying exceeds the strike price at exercise, the holder of the option will receive the underlying asset:

$$Payoff = S \cdot I_{\{S>K\}}$$

In financial markets digital options are used as protection against discrete events along with their cousins: barrier options (see Taleb, 1997 for an extensive analysis). In energy markets, digital options do not trade as such. They are, however, implicit in the payoff functions of some physical assets as we will see in Chapter 9. Instead of standard digital options, we encounter spread digital options (calls):

- **Spread cash-or-nothing:** If the spread exceeds the strike price at exercise, the holder of the option will receive a fixed amount of money:

$$Payoff = X \cdot I_{\{S-G>K\}}$$

- **Spread asset-or-nothing:** If the spread exceeds the strike price at exercise, the holder of the option will receive either the underlying spread or one of the assets:

$$Payoff = (S - G) \cdot I_{\{S-G>0\}}$$
$$Payoff = S \cdot I_{\{S-G>0\}}$$

Similar definitions apply to put options.

Valuation

In the Black-Scholes world, the valuation of standard digital options can be done by using the Black-Scholes formula for standard calls. For cash-or-nothing calls, we need to only find the (risk-neutral) probability of ending in the money. This is given by the second term of the Black-Scholes formula: $N(d_2)$. Consequently, the value of the calls will be given by the following:

$$C_{Cash\text{-}or\text{-}nothing} = df \cdot X \cdot N(d_2)$$

$$d_2 = \frac{\ln(F/K) - \sigma^2(T - t)/2}{\sigma\sqrt{T - t}}$$

where F is the forward price.

Similarly we can find the expression for the value of the standard asset-or-nothing calls:

$$C_{Asset\text{-}or\text{-}nothing} = df \cdot F \cdot N(d_1)$$

$$d_1 = \frac{\ln(F/K) + \sigma^2(T - t)/2}{\sigma\sqrt{T - t}}$$

Finally, the expressions for the spread digital calls will be given by the appropriate adjustment in the Margrabe formula:

$$C_{Cash\text{-}or\text{-}nothing}^{Spread} = df \cdot X \cdot N(d_2)$$

$$d_2 = \frac{\ln(F_S/F_G) - \sigma^2(T - t)/2}{\sigma\sqrt{T - t}}$$

$$\sigma^2 = \sigma_S^2 + \sigma_G^2 - 2\rho\sigma_S\sigma_G$$

Hedging

In general digital options exhibit striking behavior in their hedging parameters. The vega of the option is almost always negative unless the option is deeply out-of-the-money. However, the biggest problems with digital options appear when we attempt to hedge the structure with the underlying close to expiration (low volatility).

For at-the-money digital options, the delta can become very high. Unlike standard calls, there is no limit to how high the delta can become. Additionally, under those circumstances, the gamma of the option can also become extremely high and abruptly switch signs. This makes it difficult to effectively manage the risks associated with digital structures. We will discuss examples of the problem in Chapter 9.

GAS/OIL STORAGE

Storage is probably one of the most complicated option structures in the energy markets. Its complexities exceed even those of power generation. Not surprisingly, then, hedging and valuation of storage facilities is a challenging undertaking. We start by describing typical storage facilities and contractual arrangements.

Storage facilities are time machines that let us move the production capacity from one point in time to a later one. This mechanism enables smoothing of the supply response to demand fluctuations.

For example, natural gas markets tend to have high prices in the winter and low prices in the summer—a reflection of relatively higher use of natural gas in the winter and lower in the summer. Note, however, that winter prices are usually only 25% to 30% higher than in the summer. This is very different from electricity prices, which can be many times higher during the summer peak-use period than during the winter.

The difference between the two markets is the availability of relatively cheap storage for gas, which allows shifting the cheap but idle summer production capacity into winter at a relatively low cost. This points out the first major function of storage in fuels markets: *seasonal cycling*.

Demand for gas during winter can be highly volatile. All the fuel that we have brought from the summer will be of little value if we cannot respond quickly to changing conditions and control the peaking demand. This results in another storage activity: *peaking service/peaking deliverability*. Again, the advantage of a fast-turning storage facility is that it obviates the need for fast production facilities that may be very expensive.

The need for quick deliverability can also be driven by disruptions in the pipeline system that create a need for *balancing service*.

These three main uses are the major economic drivers behind the development of storage facilities. All the services and contractual arrangements ultimately can be traced to these considerations.

It is obvious that, given the role it plays in managing relationship between supply and demand, storage has a major impact on price formation in the fuel markets, especially for natural gas. However, all our subsequent analysis of pricing and hedging will be carried out under the assumption that the impact of our decisions on price is negligible. In other words, we assume that the unit of storage we price and hedge is marginal, otherwise the pricing problems become much more complex. We discuss the general problem in more detail in a later chapter, but here we simply mention that, due to the geographical fragmentation of the natural gas markets at certain less liquid locations, this assumption can be easily violated.

The modeling issue is seriously affected by these considerations, especially in the development of new facilities. In network industries, changes of supply-demand balance in one location can propagate widely throughout the system, leading to significant changes in the price formation process. In extreme cases, they can render all historical data useless, greatly complicating estimation of valuation models. In those circumstances, standard analysis requires an explicit accounting for the supply-demand characteristics of the system and its topology. We must augment standard derivative analysis with some measurement of the impact of the new development on the nontradable and tradable value factors. This is normally achieved through some sort of scenario analysis, where the scenarios are generated by a fundamental model of the pipeline system (see our discussion of fundamental models in Chapter 7).

Storage Characteristics

Three main operational characteristics describe a storage facility:

- **Capacity:** in natural gas markets it is measured in Bcf (1 Bcf = 1,000,000 MMBtu)
- **Withdrawal rate (Withdrawal Daily Quantity, WDQ):** often expressed in MMBtu per day, or percentage of total capacity per month
- **Injection rate (Injection Daily Quantity, IDQ):** often expressed in MMBtu per day, or percentage of total capacity per month

These quantities, to a large degree, determine the operational flexibility of a storage facility. As such, they have a major impact on the optionality, and consequently the value, of a unit.

Additional characteristics are:

- Unit injection and withdrawal cost (pumping and transportation)
- Fuel injection and withdrawal losses

TABLE 8.5 Categories of Physical Gas Storage

Facility	Description	Injection	Withdrawal	Operating Costs	Major Use
Aquifers	Low deliverability, low cycling, high capacity,	120–200 days	60–120 days	High, some fuel losses	Seasonal cycling
Depleted fields	Low deliverability, low cycling, high capacity	120–200 days	60–120 days	High, some fuel losses	Seasonal cycling
Salt domes (caverns)	High deliverability, high cycling (up to 12 inventory turns per year), low capacity	20 days	5–20 days	Low, minimum fuel losses	Balancing and peaking service
Pipelines	wide variety of operational characteristics				Balancing and peaking service

- Ratchets, WDQ and IDQ are usually not constant, but depend on the inventory level.

These performance characteristics fully define a storage facility, or at least its financial dimension, and although driven by physical limitations, they can be determined through contractual arrangements. An owner of a storage facility can lease part of it and assign a certain part of deliverability (WDQ and IDQ), not necessarily in proportion to the capacity leased.

Physical storage facilities usually fall into the categories shown in Table 8.5.

Storage Contracts

Contractual arrangements often involve either leasing empty storage facilities for a prespecified term, or leasing storage facilities with a number of restrictions on operation or services required. We present several examples:

- **Peaking services**
- **Summer fill:** the lessee receives an empty facility and returns it full at the end of the term (i.e., summer, which is the end of October)

- **Seasonal cycling:** the lessee receives an empty facility and returns it empty
- **Storage carry:** the lessee receives the storage facility full at the beginning of the term and returns it full at the end of the term.

EXAMPLE 8.10   *Storage contract*

An LDC owns a storage facility with the total capacity of 5 Bcf. It's currently March, the end of the peak season, and the facility is half full. To avoid the high costs of carrying the gas until the next peaking season, the company decides to lease the facility to a marketer for the next year. To make sure it has access to a sufficient amount of gas during the next peaking season, the LDC stipulates that the lessee is required to have the facility 75% full at the end of summer (i.e., end of October). The extra gas will be paid for at the summer index price, minus a discount. The discount will represent the savings generated by giving up the control of the facility. Additionally, the LDC requires that during the peaking season the minimum inventory level cannot fall below 30%. The LDC retains the right to withdraw any amount of gas, up to 75% of the total capacity, at its discretion during the peaking season. When the LDC does not use the facility, the marketer has full control of its deliverability and capacity.

The arrangement in Example 8.10 represents a combination of peaking services, summer fill with some additional features. The valuation and hedging issues of structured contracts of this type are discussed in the section on asset management deals. Here we point out just a couple of issues.

If the withdrawals (peaking services) are driven by the demand faced by the LDC and not by price considerations, the valuation of the contract should be split into valuation of the load contract (see a later section), and the valuation of the storage facility with restrictions. This conclusion applies as long as the cash market is liquid and does not exhibit a significant bid-ask spread (see asset management deals section).

Storage valuation involves initial inventory and a series of minimum inventory restrictions: 75% minimum inventory at the end of October and a series of daily minimum inventory limits during winter. This is just a sample of possible contractual complexities in storage contracts. In the following section we start by analyzing the valuation and hedging of empty storage facilities. In later sections we consider extensions.

Valuation Approaches

There are four main approaches:

- Forward optimization
- Forward dynamic optimization: (spread) option portfolio (linear and nonlinear optimization)
- Stochastic dynamic programming: (backward induction on trees, Lagrangian relaxation, and so on)
- Combinations

Forward Optimization

In this approach, we optimize injection and withdrawal schedules given the current forward prices and the storage constraints. Example 8.11 will illustrate the approach.

EXAMPLE 8.11 *Forward valuation of storage*

A marketer leases a storage facility with the following operational characteristics:

Total capacity: 1 Bcf
WDQ: 20,000 MMBtu/day
IDQ: 10,000 MMBtu/day

The above rates mean that it takes around 3 months to fill the facility and it takes around 1.5 months to empty it.

The term of the contract is from April of current year through end of March of the following year. For the time being we will ignore ratchets and round-trip costs. The forward curve is given by Table 8.6. The July and August are the optimal injection months, while January and February the optimal withdrawal points. The cost of injection is given by the arithmetic average of the three injection points on the curve, since it will be spread over the three months equally:

$$\text{Injection Cost} = (\$2.27 + \$2.31 + \$2.25)*\text{Total Capacity}/3$$
$$= 2.28\$/\text{MMBtu}*1,000,000 \text{ MMBtu} = \$2,280,000$$

The withdrawal revenue is a weighted average of the two withdrawal points. Given that it takes 1.5 months to withdraw the inventory, we will try to withdraw as much as possible in January (and the rest in February). We have then:

$$\text{Withdrawal revenue} = (\$2.92 *2/3 + \$2.81/3)*\text{Total Capacity}$$
$$= 2.89\$/\text{MMBtu}*1,000,000 \text{ MMBtu} = \$2,890,000$$

TABLE 8.6   Forward Curve

	Forward Curve ($/MMBtu)	Discounted Curve
April	$2.40	$2.39
May	$2.30	$2.27
June	$2.35	$2.31
July	$2.40	$2.34
August	$2.32	$2.25
September	$2.50	$2.41
October	$2.50	$2.40
November	$2.80	$2.67
December	$2.95	$2.80
January	$3.10	$2.92
February	$3.00	$2.81
March	$2.85	$2.66

The total value of the facility over the term is given by:

Storage Value = Withdrawal revenue − Injection cost = (2.89 − 2.28)

$/MMBtu · 1,000,000MMBtu = .61$/MMBtu · 1,000,000 MMBtu = $610,000

The optimal strategy in this example was to turn the inventory only once. Depending on the shape of the forward curve it might be optimal to turn the facility more than once as shown in Table 8.7. Light shading represents injection and dark shading, withdrawal. In this case it is optimal to turn the facility 4/3 times. The total value increases from $610,000 to $690,000. The above strategy relies only on the monthly relationships on the forward curve. It presupposes that we are operating on monthly strategies, and we will not exploit any strategies available in the cash markets.

The value of the forward optimization strategy can be described formally in the following way:

$$ForwardValue(\overline{F}_t;TC,IDQ,WDQ,t) =$$

$$= \max_{\overline{V}} \left\{ -<\overline{F}_t,\overline{V}> = -\sum_i F_t^i V_i; \underset{i \geq 0}{\forall} \ - WDQ \cdot n_i \leq V_i \leq IDQ \cdot n_i, \underset{j \geq 1}{\forall} \sum_{i=0}^{j} V_i \leq TC \right\}$$

(8.43)

where

F_t is the vector of the forward prices at time t

n_i is the number of days in month I

TABLE 8.7 Forward Curve Optimization

	Forward Curve ($/MMBtu)	Discounted Curve
April	$2.40	$2.39
May	$2.30	$2.27
June	$2.35	$2.31
July	$2.45	$2.39
August	$2.45	$2.38
September	$2.30	$2.22
October	$2.30	$2.21
November	$2.80	$2.67
December	$2.95	$2.80
January	$3.10	$2.92
February	$3.00	$2.81
March	$2.85	$2.66

V_i is the volume of gas moved; positive value indicates injection while negative value indicates withdrawal

TC is the total storage capacity

These two conditions correspond to the three types of operational restrictions imposed on the storage facility: maximum injections, maximum withdrawals, and total capacity. We can easily show that the value is a convex function of the forward prices.

For the simplest case, the resulting optimization is a straightforward linear program. We can easily incorporate additional constraints as required: minimum inventory, initial and final inventory conditions, negative inventory options, and scores of others result only in additional linear constraints. They obviously have an impact on the value, but the principle of the optimization problem is not changed. Certain other constraints might introduce nonlinearities and require more sophisticated treatment—ratchets, for example. In practice, however the nonlinearities can be approximated by perturbations of the linear problem (Lagrangian relaxation).

We can reformulate the above optimization problem in a way that will prove useful later. Instead of formulating it in terms of the net volumes for a given month (V_i), we can use as decision variables net volumes for a given spread. Table 8.8 presents an example of the results of optimization on the curve from the second part of the preceding example.

We zeroed out the negative spreads because they can never enter the optimal solution; the shadings indicate the optimal spreads. Note that the solution for the spreads is not unique. Had we swapped the May to July and June to January spreads with May to January and June to July, we

TABLE 8.8 Monthly Discounted Spreads

		April	May	June	July	Aug	Sept	Oct	Nov	Dec	Jan	Feb	March
		$2.39	$2.27	$2.31	$2.39	$2.38	$2.22	$2.21	$2.67	$2.80	$2.92	$2.81	$2.66
April	$2.39	$ —	$ —	$ —	$0.01	$ —	$ —	$ —	$0.29	$0.41	$0.54	$0.43	$0.27
May	$2.27		$ —	$0.04	$0.12	$0.11	$ —	$ —	$0.40	$0.53	$0.65	$0.54	$0.38
June	$2.31			$ —	$0.08	$0.07	$ —	$ —	$0.36	$0.49	$0.62	$0.50	$0.35
July	$2.39				$ —	$ —	$ —	$ —	$0.28	$0.41	$0.53	$0.42	$0.26
August	$2.38					$ —	$ —	$ —	$0.29	$0.42	$0.54	$0.43	$0.28
Sept	$2.22						$ —	$ —	$0.45	$0.58	$0.70	$0.59	$0.44
Oct	$2.21							$ —	$0.46	$0.59	$0.72	$0.61	$0.45
Nov	$2.67									$0.13	$0.25	$0.14	$ —
Dec	$2.80										$0.13	$0.01	$ —
January	$2.92											$ —	$ —
February	$2.81												$ —
March	$2.66												

would have obtained the same value. Given the nonuniqueness of this solution, performing the optimization directly is usually more efficient. We explain the motivation for introducing this technique in the section on storage optionality.

Formally we can write the value of the forward optimization in terms of the optimal spread choices in the following way:

$$
\begin{aligned}
&ForwardValue(\overline{F}_i;TC,IDQ,WDQ,t) \\
&= \sum_{j>i} \Delta F_t^{i,j} V_{i,j}^*(\overline{F}_i;TC,IDQ,WDQ,t)
\end{aligned}
\tag{8.44}
$$

where $V_{i,j}^*$ are the optimal spread volumes.

This valuation procedure immediately suggests a hedging strategy. We enter into long positions in the summer contracts and short positions in the winter contracts, allowing us to completely hedge the price exposure associated with the changing forward markets. The resulting hedging positions will be static—we will set up the hedge strategy, and revise it only to account for discounting effects. Once we enter the hedge positions, our cash flow is locked in and will not change, no matter what happens to the forward prices afterwards.

Note, however, that the actual physical decision depends not on our hedging portfolio, but only on the prices of forward contracts at injection. If the spread is negative at that time, we won't ever inject gas into storage, no matter what hedging strategy we have in place. This is a manifestation of a larger principle, which we discuss at length at the end of the chapter: *a hedging strategy almost never affects operational decisions—hedges almost never affect the exercise decision.* The qualifier "almost" in this statement refers to situations of limited liquidity, significant bid-ask spreads, or both.

Forward Dynamic Optimization: (Spread) Option Optimization

We have considered two examples of forward optimization for two different forward curves. We saw that the value of the facility increased by $80,000 when the forward curve shifted a certain way. This suggests another strategy to increase the value of the storage facility:

1. We enter into the forward positions suggested by the optimal injection/withdrawal schedule for this forward curve.
2. If the forward changes favorably, we readjust our positions to capture the positive difference. If the curve moves in an unfavorable way, we do nothing.

We continue this strategy throughout the term of the contract; note that it always has a positive value because we change our positions only when the spread between the new and old schedule is positive. As such, the strategy is an option position.

The value of this complicated option depends on the variability of the forward curve. This, in turn, is determined by the volatility of the individual contracts and the correlation structure between them. Intuitively, the higher the volatility of individual forward contracts and the lower the correlation, the higher the value of our option.

Exercise of the optionality is a relatively easy undertaking. The challenge is to properly value it up front, and properly hedge the additional option value (the extrinsic or time value of the option). Formally we can describe the value of the option in the following way:

$$OptionValue = ForwardValue(\overline{F_{t_0}};TC,IDQ,WDQ,t_0)$$

$$+E_{t_0}^*\left\{\sum_{i=t_0+1}^{T}\max[ForwardValue(\overline{F_i};i) - ForwardValue(\overline{F_{i-1}};i-1),0]\right\}$$

$$(8.45)$$

where $ForwardValue(F_i;t)$ is defined by equation (8.43).

This formulation brings out the fact that the value of storage options is essentially a portfolio of complex spread options. The expectation used in valuation is risk-neutral. The value of the spread option is a function of the values of the forward contracts and as such it should be fully hedgeable, as long as volatilities and correlations are hedgeable, or at least constant.

The direct way of evaluating this expectation is through a Monte Carlo simulation: We simulate several thousand paths of the forward curve evolution, and evaluate the optimization on every path and at every time step. Next we collect the payoffs on every path and calculate appropriate averages. Since we are dealing with the evolution of the forward curve, we can apply the models of forward curves discussed in Chapter 5.

This brute force approach can be computationally expensive, mainly because of the numerous reoptimizations we must perform. Below we present an approximate methodology that can substantially reduce the computational cost, but at the price of underestimating the true value.

In addition, we must account for the high cost of calculating hedges with respect to all forward contracts, and possibly volatilities if tradable. This last problem can be partially avoided by using a forward model with fewer factors than the full number of forward contracts. In this way we can reduce the dimensionality of the problem and calculate the hedges with respect to fewer factors. This solution, although attractive, may not always be feasible, since the values of some facilities can be very sensitive to the correlation between specific contracts, as a result of specific operational constraints.

Let's rewrite the value of the reoptimization option (8.45) using the spread optimization formulation (8.44):

$$OptionValue = ForwardValue(\overline{F_{t_0}};TC,IDQ,WDQ,t_0)$$

$$+E_{t_0}^*\left\{\sum_{i=t_0+1}^T \max[ForwardValue(\overline{F_i};i) - ForwardValue(\overline{F_{i-1}};i-1),0]\right\} =$$

$$= ForwardValue(\overline{F_{t_0}};TC,IDQ,WDQ,t_0)$$

$$+E_{t_0}^*\left\{\sum_{i=t_0+1}^T \max\left[\sum_{k>l}\Delta F_i^{k,l}V_{k,l}^*(\overline{F_i};TC,IDQ,WDQ,i)\right.\right.$$

$$\left.\left. - \sum_{k>l}\Delta F_{i-1}^{k,l}V_{k,l}^*(\overline{F_{i-1}};TC,IDQ,WDQ,i-1),0]\right\}\right. \tag{8.46}$$

We can rewrite the (8.46) optimization problem in the following format:

$$Option\ Value = E_{t_0}^*\left[\sup_\tau\left\{\max_V\left(\sum_{k>l}\max(\Delta F_\tau^{k,l},0)V_{k,l}\right)\right\}\right]$$

$$= E_{t_0}^*\left[\sum_{k>l}\max(\Delta F_{\tau^*}^{k,l},0)V_{k,l}^*\right] \tag{8.47}$$

τ^* represents the optimal exercise time of the storage optimization problem, while V^* are the optimal gas volumes. It would seem that the expression is very different from (8.46), however, one can show that the two formulations are identical (see Wolyniec, 2002).

Notice one important difference from the formulation (8.46). Instead of using spreads themselves, we optimize with respect to the positive spreads only. As we mentioned, negative spreads will never enter the optimal solution, hence we are justified in dropping them altogether.

Since the optimal value of a linear program is convex in the prices (here, positive spreads), we have by Jensen's inequality:

$$E_{t_0}^*\left[\sup_\tau\left\{\max_V\left(\sum_{k>l}\max(\Delta F_\tau^{k,l},0)V_{k,l}\right)\right\}\right] \geq \max_V\left(\sum_{k>l}E_{t_0}^*[\sup_\tau\max(\Delta F_\tau^{k,l},0)]V_{k,l}\right)$$

Notice that:

$$E_{t_0}^*[\sup_\tau\max(\Delta F_\tau^{k,l},0)]$$

is the value of an American spread option. In other words we show that the optimal value of the storage facility will be higher than the value of the statically optimized portfolio of American spread options.

If we can assume that injection/withdrawal costs are zero then we can show that the approximation with spread options is exact (see Wolyniec, 2002). This flows from the fact that the value of a storage facility is linear with respect to the spreads under those circumstances. This result may be a little bit surprising, since, in general, for any linear optimization problem the optimal value is convex in the prices. However, the storage optimization problem has a unique structure: namely that the value of a spread over three time periods is always smaller than the sum of the spreads for the component spreads:

$$\max(F_3 - F_2, 0) + \max(F_2 - F_1, 0) \geq \max(F_3 - F_1, 0)$$

Notice that the condition holds only if there are no injection/withdrawal costs. Consequently, the equivalence fails in the presence of those costs.

It turns out that the portfolio of spread options can generate a sufficiently tight lower bound for non-zero costs. The advantage of this is that evaluation of the optimization of the portfolio of spread options is hundreds or thousands of times faster than full-blown simulation.

The approximation works in the following way: Instead of optimizing the value given the current spreads, we optimize the value given the prices of spread options with the strike prices adjusted for injection/withdrawal costs. The optionality flows from the fact that we have the right but not an obligation to inject gas for later withdrawal. This creates the additional time value of the option.

Compare Table 8.9 to Table 8.8.

Table 8.9 shows the option values for the same forward curve as shown in Table 8.7. These are calculated assuming 50% volatility for all the contracts, and .98 correlation among all the contracts. The dark fields mark the old optimal positions, which themselves increased in value. The light fields show the extra value from the additional positions we can now take. Previously, these had no value because their corresponding spreads were negative. However, out-of-the-money options always have positive value, which we can exploit by putting on the additional positions.

The total extra value accruing from the optionality is $40,000. For this specific case, the value is around 6% of the intrinsic value. The time value of the option can range from one or two percent to multiples of the intrinsic value.

The main drivers of the additional value are:

- **Shape of the curve:** the flatter it is, the higher the relative increase in value
- **Volatility and correlation levels:** the higher the volatilities and the lower the correlation, the higher the relative increase in value
- **Operational flexibility:** the more flexible the unit (i.e., the higher IDQ and WDQ), the higher the relative increase in value—although the intrinsic value is also higher

TABLE 8.9 Spread Option Values

	April	May	June	July	Aug	Sept	Oct	Nov	Dec	Jan	Feb	March
	$2.39	$2.27	$2.31	$2.39	$2.38	$2.22	$2.21	$2.67	$2.80	$2.92	$2.81	$2.66
April $2.39	$ —	$0.02	$0.03	$0.06	$0.05	$0.01	$0.01	$0.29	$0.41	$0.54	$0.43	$0.27
May $2.27			$0.07	$0.14	$0.12	$0.03	$0.03	$0.40	$0.53	$0.65	$0.54	$0.38
June $2.31				$0.11	$0.10	$0.02	$0.02	$0.36	$0.49	$0.62	$0.50	$0.35
July $2.39					$0.05	$0.01	$0.01	$0.28	$0.41	$0.53	$0.42	$0.27
August $2.38						$0.01	$0.01	$0.29	$0.42	$0.54	$0.43	$0.28
Sept $2.22							$0.05	$0.45	$0.58	$0.70	$0.59	$0.44
Oct $2.21								$0.46	$0.59	$0.72	$0.61	$0.45
Nov $2.67									$0.15	$0.26	$0.16	$0.06
Dec $2.80										$0.15	$0.07	$0.02
January $2.92											$0.03	$0.00
February $2.81												$0.01
March $2.66												

The great advantage of the spread option approximation lies in our ability to use all the well-known valuation and hedging techniques for spread options:

- It gives us an easy static hedging strategy if we can sell spread options directly.
- It allows us to easily calculate all the dynamic hedge coefficients very efficiently.
- It allows us to incorporate the impact of volatility smiles and correlation skews on the value and hedges directly.
- It allows the trader to easily understand storage facility in terms of spread options.

This last point should not be underestimated. The reduction to simpler contracts, even if only approximate, has value independent from computational considerations. As we mentioned in the introduction to Chapter 4, we should always strive to find the best static hedges we can, and only then worry about the residual. For example, if we wanted to directly investigate the impact of the volatility smile on the value of storage, we would have to develop a reduced-form model of the evolution of the forward curve that would either directly incorporate the underlying stochastic volatility/jump effects, or impose parametric restrictions on the process to match the volatility surface—a nontrivial and demanding undertaking. In general, reducing a structure to simpler constituents lessens the burden of modeling. In Chapter 4 we showed an example of how using forward contracts allowed us to avoid direct modeling of mean reversion. Similar issues apply here.

Obviously, the crucial question at this stage is: How good is the approximation? This depends on the same factors that determine the contribution of the time value of the spread option, the shape of the curve, volatilities, correlation, and degree of flexibility. However the crucial factors are the operational costs (injection/withdrawal and fuel costs, bid-ask spreads, and so on). Under certain circumstances, however, high operational costs can lead to a substantial error when using the spread option approximation.

We can improve the approximation by extending its dimensionality, that is, by including additional optionality on top of the direct spread options considered above. We won't elaborate on this point further, but will note that we can develop better and better approximations by extending the size of the optimization. We face a tradeoff between the size of the optimization and the size of the simulation, and it might be more efficient, at some stage, to perform the direct simulation, rather than continue developing higher dimensional approximations (see Wolyniec, 2002).

Cash Market Strategies

These modeling approaches concentrate on the value available from trading with monthly strategies (forward curve–based strategies), but they can be extended to handle intramonth value contributions, especially in the markets that trade liquid BOM or balance-of-the-week contracts.

These strategies have significant contributions for facilities with high flexibility (i.e., high deliverability). Salt domes, with their one-month turnaround capability, can have a high intramonth value. The incorporation of liquid BOM markets in the above modeling methodology is straightforward, equivalent to adding an additional month to the analysis with a variable number of days. To account for the spot market optionality, we can consider strategies that exploit spreads between the spot price, the BOM price, and the forward value of existing inventory as determined by the models from the previous section.

For example, consider cash-BOM spreads: Whenever the current spot price is sufficiently higher than the BOM price—to cover the operational costs of injections and withdrawal—the strategy is to sell gas from the current inventory and inject it later at the lower price. If the opposite holds, we buy gas now and sell it on the BOM market for delivery during the rest of the month.

A similar spread strategy can be pursued between the spot market and the forward value of the current inventory. In both cases, the value of the strategy is given by a spread option. In the first case, it's simple: it involves the prices, volatilities, and correlations of spot and BOM markets. In the latter case, it's more complicated.

With no BOM markets, we can value intramonth flexibility as a swing option with minimum and maximum volume restrictions. For details, refer to the section on swing options.

Stochastic Dynamic Programming Approaches

An alternative to the forward-based valuation approach is the stochastic dynamic approach that relies on direct modeling of the spot process, possibly calibrated to the forward prices, along with the development of the optimal exercise rule for storage flows given the dynamics.

This approach is equivalent to valuing a multiperiod swing option. The swing option in question can, obviously, have fairly complex constraints. We will briefly review the methodologies used to solve the resulting SDP, and then discuss its applicability and relationship to the forward-based approaches discussed in the previous section. The discussion of solution techniques will be limited, since we address the general issues involved in other parts of the book (see Appendix B).

SDP Formulation

The optimal value is given by the solution of the following Bellman equation:

$$V(t, I) = \arg \max \{CF_t(f;g_t) + e^{-rdt} E_t[V(t + 1, I_{t+1})]\}$$

such that

$$(1) -WDQ \leq f \leq IDQ$$
$$(2) I_t + f = I_{t+1}$$
$$(3) 0 \leq I_t \leq TC$$
$$(4) I_T = 0$$
$$(5) CF_t(f;g_t) = g_t f$$
$$(6) dg_t = \mu (g_t,t)dt + \sigma (g_t,t)dW \qquad\qquad (8.48)$$

where

I_t is the inventory level at time t

f is the amount of flow in any given period (day)

g_t is the fuel price at time t

The first constraint guarantees that the flow does not exceed the maximum injection or withdrawal rate. The second constraint gives the evolution rule of the stored inventory: it simply says that the inventory in the future is the sum o of (the current inventory) and the current flow f. The third constraint assures that the total inventory is never greater than the capacity of the facility (and never less than zero). Constraint 4 makes sure we do not leave any inventory at the end of the term. Constraint 5 gives us the cashflow function and 6 shows the evolution equation for the gas price.

We can impose additional restrictions as needed, of course. Note that the terminal condition $I_T = 0$ is not needed, since it is never optimal to leave any fuel in storage at the end of the term.

Solution Approaches

The most direct and straightforward way to solve equation (8.48) is by backward induction. The easiest implementation is through the binomial (or trinomial) forest approach described in our discussion of swing options. The difference in the decisions variable lies in the inventory level, and not in the exercise rights.

The method is feasible only if the underlying process for fuel evolution does not have too many dimensions, in which case incorporating stochastic volatility or jumps might prove to be very cumbersome.

Even in the simplest case, the efficiency of the solution is not high. Its advantage is its simplicity, but it is usually advisable to use more sophisticated methods. We review a number of methodologies used for solving stochastic dynamic programming in Appendix B, where we discuss the valuation of power plants. The optimization problem we face here can be considered a simplified version of the general problem we analyze there.

Performance and Relationship to Forward-based Valuation

As long as the forward markets for price and volatility are relatively efficient, multiperiod swing valuation techniques cannot result in valuations that are substantially different (risk-adjusted) from forward-based techniques augmented with one-period (intramonth) swing valuation (see Wolyniec, 2002).

The downside of this method is its lack of direct conditioning on forward market information, resulting in problematic calibration for the spot process (see Chapter 4 for details) as well as in problems calculating and executing hedging strategies. The optimal decision surfaces generated by the solution to the SDP problem (8.48) can be very sensitive to changing forward market conditions, which often results in unstable hedge parameters—something to avoid, if only it were possible.

Again, direct modeling of spot prices is challenging. It often leads to unstable parameterization of the process (even if implied from the forward market). Note also at this point that, either directly or indirectly, we must incorporate the forward price evolution into the evolution of spot prices—technically to derive the risk-neutral evolution of spot prices—as long as we plan on using forward contracts for hedging the storage value. Failure to do so results in inconsistent pricing: It's akin to using the actual return of the stock in valuation of an option, and then arguing that we can also hedge the exposure associated with the price variability. The presence of the hedge usually changes the expected return, which, in complete market, is equal to the risk-free rate. Consequently, one cannot separate valuation from the hedging decisions.

Stochastic dynamic approaches can suffer from this oversight. Great care must be taken when specifying and calibrating spot processes for the use in optimization, so that they are consistent with the hedging strategy to be pursued. Additionally, even for a given set of forward information, the critical surface may exhibit unstable behavior that renders it of limited use as a hedging tool.

TRANSPORTATION AND TRANSMISSION

In Chapter 2 we described the common terms associated with transportation deals in natural gas and power markets. Here we concentrate on the firm capacity transactions. These transactions involve the release of *firm transportation capacity*, that is, the receiver gains the control over the flow of the fuel through the pipe.

This is in contrast to an *interruptible capacity* transaction, in which the seller has the discretion to flow the gas through the pipe on a best-effort basis. Valuation of those contracts is much more complex, because it requires a thorough understanding of the behavior of the specific counterparty. Valuation can be seen as the valuation of firm capacity with a certain set of recall provisions. The trouble is that the number of recall rights is unknown. We can obviously try and approximate the likely number of exercise rights and use the standard valuation tools for recalls. The limitation is that the number of recall rights is likely to be correlated with the size of the price spread between locations.

Firm capacity transaction involves effectively granting the buyer the right, but not the obligation, to flow gas between two points in the system. If the two points are liquid, then it comes down to that of a daily strip of spread options, for one-directional deals, or a strip of spread chooser options. Spread chooser option payoffs are given by the following formulas:

$$SpreadChooser = \max\left[\max(G_2 - G_1 - K,0), \max(G_1 - G_2 - K,0)\right]$$

$$= \max(G_2 - G_1 - K,0) + \max(G_1 - G_2 - K,0) \quad (8.49)$$

In the chooser option, two spread options correspond to the right to flow fuel in each direction. Since the two options are mutually exclusive, the valuation can be split into two separate valuations, one for each direction. For clarity of exposition, we will analyze only one-directional flows, since an extension to two directions is trivial.

The typical transportation deal will have the following characteristics.

EXAMPLE 8.12   *Gas transportation contract*

A power generator owns a plant located in Virginia.

Receipt point: El Paso Permian

Delivery point: Malin (California)

Maximum daily quantity (MDQ): 20,000 MMBtu

Commodity charge (CC): .03 $/MMBtu

Fuel losses (FL): 2%

Term: July of the current year

The above terms should be self-explanatory: Receipt point refers to the source of the commodity, while the delivery point is the location where the fuel will be received.

Two points to note here:

- The commodity charge is levied on the actual commodity flown and not on the capacity held (MDQ).
- The fuel losses refer to the difference between the amount of the fuel at the delivery point and the receipt point.

The value of the contract is then given by the following expression:

$$V_t = MDQ \sum_{i=1}^{3l} e^{-r(T-t)} E_t^* [\max((1 - FL)S_{Delivery}^i - S_{Receipt}^i - CC),0)] \quad (8.50)$$

It is essentially a strip of spread options, whose valuation we discussed in a previous section. The only nonstandard feature is the presence of the multiplicative factor $(1\text{-}FL)$. As long as the process for the evolution of the $S_{Delivery}$ is multiplicative. in the mean (or current forward price), this feature is easy to handle.

The practical problems in valuing transportation are the choices of correlation and volatility parameters. Estimation on historical data can be quite challenging, especially for illiquid points in the pipeline system. We've discussed those topics at length in previous chapters; here we simply point out that the behavior of the spread can be affected by the topology of the pipeline network. The crude assumptions of joint lognormality can be fully inapplicable. The spreads are not likely to widen without limit, since there are other routes through which the commodity can be sent, so natural boundaries for the joint price behavior are likely. On the other hand, at locations where no alternative transportation routes exist, the spreads can reach very high values, as was the case in California in the winter of 2000 to 2001.

The above considerations suggest the need to augment the standard reduced-form approaches with the fundamental considerations along the lines of the hybrid models we developed in Chapter 7 for power prices. We do not engage in such an undertaking in this book, due to limited space, noting only that such an approach would be quite challenging.

Electrical Transmission

Transmission contracts in power markets (FTR, TCC; see Chapter 2) can also be analyzed in terms of spread options. The only difference between them is that in wheeling power from one location to another, we cannot be assured about the exact route the power travels to reach its destination. There are always differences between scheduled flow and actual physical flow because the optimal path is driven by system-wide conditions. To manage this uncertainty, transmission contracts often specify a path, which is used for financial reconciliation of all transmission charges incurred along the way. The effect of this difference is that the strike price of the spread option does not have a straightforward structure.

LOAD- AND DEMAND-SERVING CONTRACTS

In this section we analyze valuation and hedging of load-serving contract in natural gas and power markets. The working assumption of our analysis is that the demand centers are located at liquid price points where the bid-ask spread on the underlying commodity is sufficiently small. As we explain in the section on asset management deals, this assumption is sufficient to analyze the pricing and hedging of load/demand contracts independent of the presence of generation, transportation and other assets in the portfolio. In later sections we consider the more complex case.

Load-serving Contracts

There are many kinds of load-serving contracts in both natural gas and power markets. In its basic form, the structures involve serving a load at a given location. A crucial assumption is that the supplier controls the physical dispatch rights of the load, ensuring that the amount of load to serve is not directly determined by the exercise policy of the demand "owner." In other words, we must make sure that we are serving the actual physical load and not the net load after the load "owner" has exhausted cheaper sources of delivery. The motivation for this framework is our attempt to separate embedded option structures from the physical load one serves. Since the pricing techniques are quite different, the approach provides clarity. More importantly, under our working assumption of a liquid pool market, we can separate valuation and hedging of the load-serving part of the contract from that of the embedded options. Consider the following example.

EXAMPLE 8.13 *Price options versus load-serving*

A local utility in NEPOOL enters into a load-serving agreement in which a power marketer is obligated to deliver an amount of power specified by the utility at the beginning of every hour during the life of the contract. If the contract specifies a fixed price for every megawatt/hour delivered, the above contract will be equivalent from the point of view of the utility to buying a very expensive strip of hourly power options. Note that, depending on the characteristic of the true load itself, the cost of serving the load directly (i.e., of simply buying the power in the spot market) might be much lower than the cost of the option. The difference arises from the utility's right to call on the delivery of power when true demand is low and the price is very high.

In this situation, the analysis of load-serving contracts must account for the implicit or explicit optionality embedded into it, but in this section we assume that no additional optionality is present. If the load is located at a liquid point, the additional features can be analyzed separately.

Load-serving Contracts in Power Markets

There are several types of load-serving contracts in power markets.

Full-requirement Deals

In full-requirement deals the delivering party takes on all obligations associated with serving the load. Beyond the energy requirements, these might include paying for or supplying installed capacity (NEPOOL, PJM, see Chapter 1), ancillary services and the like.

The variable energy portion of the requirement is served in its entirety throughout the term of the contract, including off-peak, peak and super-peak hours (see Chapter 1). The cost of serving the energy requirement is given by the following:

$$\text{Cost-To-Serve} = \sum_{i=StartMonth}^{EndMonth} \sum_{j=StartDay(i)}^{EndDay(i)} \left(\sum_{k=StartOffPeakHour(j)}^{EndOffPeakHour(j)} P_k L_k + \sum_{n=StartOnPeakHour(j)}^{EndOnPeakHour(j)} P_n L_n \right)$$

$$(8.51)$$

As we can see, the cost-to-serve is simply the sum of products of (uncertain) prices and loads. To understand the cost to serve on the forward basis we must understand its distribution. That's an imprecise statement in many respects. We must first ask what distribution we have in mind. The actual "empirical" distribution might not be relevant if we intend to hedge our exposure.

If we choose to value the contract (say, a fixed-price contract) in a mean-variance framework—given the linearity of the contract, this can be made consistent with the pricing of other power derivatives—we first have to determine the mean and the variance of the cash flow CF:

$$E_t[CF] = E_t\left[\left(\sum_i \sum_j \left\{ \sum_k [(P_k - P_{Contract}^{OnPeak})L_k + (F_T^{OnPeak} - P_k)\Delta_T^{OnPeak}] + \sum_n (P_n - P_{Contract}^{Offpeak})L_n \right\} \right) \right]$$

$$(8.52)$$

where

$P_{Contract}$ is the contractual price

Δ_T is the forward hedge position at the expiration of the forward contract

We assume that we take a static delta position into the month. In principle, we can adjust the hedge with BOM contracts if they are sufficiently liquid. We can see we have terms corresponding to the expected prices and loads and the cross term that we can rewrite for individual terms in the following way:

$$E_t[P_k L_k] = E_t[P_k]E_t[L_k] + \mathrm{cov}(P_k, L_k) \qquad (8.53)$$

We analyzed the estimation of forward covariance for problems of this type in Chapter 6.

The optimization required to find the optimal hedge position is quite straightforward. In a dynamic framework we can split the overall optimal hedge problem into two steps:

1. Optimize the cash flow in (8.52) statically with respect to the choice of the optimal hedging block at the expiration of the forward contract
2. We treat the resulting cash flow as a function of the optimal hedge block, forward prices, volatilities and correlations. It can then be hedged dynamically before the expiration of the forward contract (and possibly options) by calculating the appropriate deltas (for proof of this see Gao and Wolyniec, 2002).

The resulting cash flow can be sensitive to the forward/daily volatility and, obviously, to prices. As we saw in Chapter 6 forward covariance can depend on forward prices and volatilities. This can lead to nonzero gammas and vegas of the hedging portfolios.

Interruptible Contracts

Interruptible contracts are variable energy contracts that contain provisions for the interruption of service, for a given amount of load a set number of times during the life of the contract. As such, they can be decomposed into the standard load-serving contracts analyzed in the previous section, and the standard swing/recall contracts addressed in the section on swing options.

It is worth repeating here that valuation of recall options in power markets tends to be simpler than in other markets, while hedging is quite challenging. The major challenge in valuation of swing options, with relatively few swing rights, is determining the optimal exercise boundary. But, in spiky power markets, the rule is almost trivial: Exercise whenever a spike occurs. Any gain in value that results from trying to optimize exercise under nonspiky conditions is usually negligible. Consequently, the valuation of interruptibles comes down to determining the conditional distribution of the

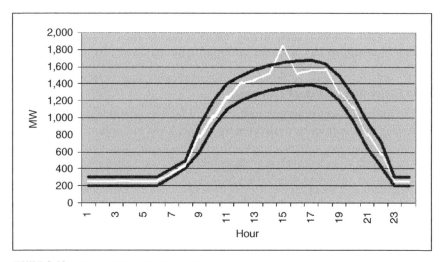

FIGURE 8.10   Banded Hourly Shaped Energy

amplitude and frequency of spikes—a challenging task, but not specific to the valuation of interruptibles.

Banded Hourly Shaped Energy

This contract specifies an hourly load range, within which the energy delivered will be sold at a set price, possibly indexed to the forward curve at expiration. Outside this range, the differential is priced at the current spot price (see Figure 8.10).

The dark, heavy lines in Figure 8.10 indicate contractual bands, and the white line shows one realization of load. At 4 PM the load moves outside the band: the actual load is 1,826 MW, as against the contractual max of 1,670 MW for that hour. The load up to the maximum will be settled according to the contractual pricing formula (e.g., a set on-peak or RTC price). The balance of 156 MW will be settled at the prevailing cash price.

Block Power

A block power contract involves a transaction of a set amount of power throughout the tenor of the agreement. Examples include standard on-peak forward contracts, as well as their variations: round-the-clock (RTC), off-peak, peak, super-peak, and the like.

Fixed Shape

The fixed shape product differs from the block product in that the everyday shape within the contractual period (e.g., on-peak) can vary. It's also similar to the banded hourly shaped energy product, except that the delivered amount is known with certainty at the inception of the contract. It's essentially a banded product with the minimum and maximum bands equal.

Load Factor with Look-back Provisions

In unbanded variable energy products, load factor is defined as the average load over the contract term divided by the peak (or maximum) load.

$$\Lambda = \frac{AverageLoad}{PeakLoad}$$

For banded variable energy products, the definition of load factor is given as the ratio of the averaged load and the maximum contractual load.

Many variable-load contracts contain look-back provisions on realized load factors, which adjust pricing terms depending on the actual load factor.

This mechanism assures that pricing is relative to the realized load level. To see why pricing (or replication cost) changes with changing load factor, consider an example of a variable load contract with a maximum load level.

The cost-to-serve for such a contract will be given by:

$$Cost\text{-}To\text{-}Serve = \sum_n P_n \max(L_n, L_{max}) = \sum_n P_n \max(\Lambda s_n, L_{max})$$

$$= \Lambda \sum_n P_n \max\left(s_n, \frac{L_{max}}{\Lambda}\right) \tag{8.54}$$

where Λ is the load factor and $S_n = L_n/\Lambda$.

We can start the analysis of the pricing by noting that, since the price charged depends on the specific realized load factor, the relevant quantity in the valuation, at least at first approximation, is the expectation conditioned on the load factor:

$$E[Cost\text{-}To\text{-}Serve|\Lambda = \lambda] = E\left[\Lambda \sum_n P_n \max\left(s_n, \frac{L_{max}}{\Lambda}\right)\Big|\Lambda = \lambda\right]$$

$$= \{if\ \lambda \approx 100\%\} = L_{max}E\left[\sum_n P_n\right] \to \lambda \tag{8.55}$$

$$= \{if\ \lambda \ll 100\%\} = E\left[\sum_n P_n \Lambda s_n\right]$$

We consider two limiting cases in (8.55):

- Load factor close to 100%. Obviously that means that the contractual load is just a flat block of power.
- "Low" load factor; a low factor sufficiently low that given the conditional volatility of hourly loads, the probability of touching the band is very low. Pricing under those circumstances is equivalent to pricing an hourly shaped energy product.

This suggests that, as long as the covariance structure of load and price is independent of the load level, the valuation for different load factor levels can be calculated independently, since the conditional means (and conditional distributions) are independent of the load factor distribution.

Unfortunately, matters are not that simple, even if all these assumptions hold. The problem is that, as our cardinal rule says, we cannot separate pricing from hedging. We must form the hedge portfolio before the load factor is known, using contracts that are not sensitive to the load factor; this induces dependency of the pricing on the load factor distribution. We can see that easily by noting that if the load-factor is high, the optimal (or nearly optimal) hedging position in the available forward markets is to enter into a long position of the forward contract with volume of L_{max}. For low load factors, we might want to use fixed-shape products properly adjusted for the covariance structure (see the section on variable load). Knowing the optimal "conditional" hedges and the distribution of the load factor, we can find the optimal hedge and conditional price.

If we use the variance minimization of cash flow as the criterion for the choice of an optimal strategy (although this is not usually consistent, see Chapter 10), this analysis can be formally performed as follows:

Using the unconditional variance decomposition in Chapter 4:

$$Var(CF) = E_\Lambda[Var(CF|\Lambda)] + Var_\Lambda(E[CF|\Lambda]) \qquad (8.56)$$

where the cash flow function is given by the following:

$$CF = \sum_n [(P_C(\Lambda) - P_n)\max(\Lambda s_n, L_{\max}) + VF] \qquad (8.57)$$

V is the volume of the forward position and $P_c(\lambda)$ is the pricing schedule.

The next step in the valuation is to find the optimal pricing schedule and optimal hedging volume. The hedging position is generally dynamic. Consequently, optimization should be performed in a dynamic framework, where possible approaches include solving a corresponding dynamic program to find the optimal hedging strategy and (static) pricing schedule. This optimization can be greatly simplified if we make strong assumptions about the relationship between forward prices and cash variance (see Chapter 4 for details), that is, if we assume independence between forward and "cash" variance (not prices). It can be performed in two steps:

1. Static optimization of the "cash" variance of the cash flow (i.e., the choice of the forward position at expiration of the forward contract)
2. Minimization of the forward variance of the cash flow (i.e., the choice of a dynamic hedging strategy in the forward contract, between the inception of the contract and the expiration of the forward contract).

The formal derivation of this result can be found in Gao and Wolyniec (2001).

Pricing Load Contracts in Practice

Previous sections presented the theoretical approach to pricing load deals. The crucial part of effectively optimizing a portfolio is knowledge of the underlying (joint) distributions. Optimal hedges and pricing schemes often depend very sensitively on the specific parameters of the distribution. For example, in the preceding section the optimal hedge was sensitive to assumptions about the variability of the load factor (or more specifically the variability of the average monthly load).

Considering this sensitivity, we must have an efficient and stable estimate of the parameters of the underlying distribution. We met this problem in discussing power price products, but the problem is even more severe in dealing with load products. Currently, data for specific loads span at most two years, and often only the load shape—the average expected load shape is available. This obviously provides no information about the variability of the load itself.

Even with two years worth of data, estimation of parameters contain significant standard errors, especially since the load behavior often exhibits substantial seasonal variation.

EXAMPLE 8.14   *Load contracts and parameter estimation*

A power marketer enters into a load-serving contract with maximum power provisions and load-factor look-back. The optimal hedge, and consequently the optimal pricing structure, depend on the distribution of the load factor, but that is difficult to reliably extract from the available data: Two years of data gives only 24 observations of the load factor. If we try to estimate the distribution on the sample, the standard errors can be significant.

The solutions to the estimation problems can be categorized into four types:

1. Hiding or ignoring the problem
2. Expanding the data set by aggregation
3. Expanding the data set by relating one variable to another
4. Changing the criteria of performance

The first solution comes in many guises. One entails choosing parameters somehow, by guessing, estimating, "modeling," and optimizing—guaranteeing precisely the wrong result Another approach involves ignoring all the optimization niceties and making an educated guess. For it to be truly educated, it is still worthwhile to go through the modeling exercise (as in the previous section) to understand the structure of the problem and the associated sensitivities. This is a superior way of handling things, since, at the very least, it is computationally efficient (i.e., it takes no time at all, or maybe years of experience), while the results are identical. The solution can be justified by portfolio effects for a shop with a large volume of short and long power positions where those effects can assert themselves. But this only works if all the other participants are equally unsophisticated about risk. If other shops bidding in the marketplace have superior ability to manage risks, less sophisticated players will fall victim to the winner's curse: they will pick up undesirable business. Their returns are likely to be substandard. It would be advisable for such players to start thinking about the wisdom of participating in risk-management business, which involves separation of risks and their efficient management.

The second solution involves including more data for estimation. For example, we can perform time aggregation of the sample. We have already seen examples of the procedure in Example 8.15. We formed a sample of 24 observations of load factor (average load). This, obviously, presupposes that the distributions of load factor are identical in different years and in different months. Even if the previous assumption is known not to be true, there are ways to pre-process the data to eliminate estimation biases. If, for example, the load is known to have a strong year-on-year growth rate, we can detrend the data and form one sample. Also, depending on the parameter of the distribution we are after, the nonstationarity of the data might not induce any biases of import.

We can also perform other types of data aggregation. If we have data for "similar" loads in the region, after proper rescaling, we can aggregate them and perform estimation. The crucial question is the meaning of the term "similar"; the proper definition again depends on the parameters we are trying to estimate. We can, for example, aggregate loads of the same customer type (e.g., residential, commercial, or industrial) from the region, and we can form proper subcategories depending on the availability of data. As always, we must trade off the efficiency of our estimates against our use of conditional information.

The third solution involves using the available sample to produce a statistical relationship to a variable for which we have much more data and for which we can perform the requisite estimation efficiently. For example, we can estimate the correlation structure between the contractual load and the system load. If the correlation is very high (or at least the dependence is), we can treat the contractual load as (possibly nonlinear) transformation of the system load. Usually, the system load shows several years of data. We can use this data to estimate the parameters of the (joint) distribution: If the two loads are jointly normal and the correlation between the loads is close to 1, then we have:

$$L_{Contract} \approx \frac{st.dev.(L_{Contract})}{st.dev.(L_{System})} L_{System} \qquad (8.58)$$

If this is the case, to find the distribution of the cost to serve, we only need to find the distribution of the system-cost-to-serve:

$$\sum P_n L_{System}^n \qquad (8.59)$$

The crucial part of the methodology is the availability of a variable that is very highly correlated with the variable we are trying to estimate. It does not even have to be the load itself. We might attempt to relate, for example, the cost-to-serve and the system-cost-to-serve directly.

The final solution to the problem consists in changing the goal of the whole undertaking Note that if you don't know the optimal minimal variance hedge, you might avoid the problem entirely by forming a hedge to protect against large risks. In the case of Example 8.14, we would enter into a forward contract with the volume equal to the load cap. A hedge like that guarantees that we will never suffer catastrophic losses due to spiking power prices.

Since the effective management of the risks involved requires optimization of strategies and values, a natural question emerges about the quality of data needed for the description.

Hedging Load Contracts

We continue Example 8.14, looking more closely at hedging issues again.

As we saw in the previous section, the choice of the correct hedging strategy depends on the distribution of the load factor. If the load factor tends to be high with little variability, the optimal hedge will be to enter into a long forward position equal to the load cap. On the other hand, even if expected load factor is close to 100% but its variability is high, the optimal hedge factor is substantially lower. Note that this hedge effectively trades off the risk of having too much power and having to sell it at a low price, against the risk of having too little power and having to buy at a high price. Consequently, the optimal hedge can be quite different depending on the criterion for the optimization. If, for example, instead of optimizing the variance of our cash flow, we optimize skewness and kurtosis of the distribution, the hedge tends to be close to the load cap, whatever the distribution of the load factor is. If our main concern is the possibility of suffering a rare but very significant loss, then the optimal hedge is the load cap. This is essentially an insurance approach to pricing and risk-management. Obviously, if this is our primary concern, there might be better ways of managing this risk. Buying far out-of-the-money calls on power will supply the requisite protection. Which solution is preferable depends on specific market conditions—prices and profiles of available contracts.

In previous sections we performed the analysis of load contracts under the assumption of mean-variance optimization. As the basic instrument we chose the forward contract. The choice is motivated by the high liquidity of the contract and low transaction costs that make dynamic hedging possible. We can supplement the trading strategy by including daily power options, fuel contracts (see Chapters 7 and 9), and other structures. We can also use combinations of load contracts to manage other load contracts. For example, we can use fixed-shaped energy contracts instead or in conjunction with the forward contract to hedge variable hourly shaped energy contracts. We do not analyze in detail the specific combination. The analysis should follow similar structure of the examples we have seen in previous sections.

Hedging Load with Weather Derivatives

Finally, we comment briefly on the use of weather contracts in hedging load contracts. These seem to offer significant potential for hedging load exposures. As we have shown in previous chapters, power load is driven largely by weather factors, especially temperature. Consequently, it seems only natural that weather contracts can be an important risk management tool. However, this optimism is usually not justified. Once we hedge out the price risk using the available price products (e.g., forwards, options, and so on), the residual weather risk may not be significant. If the correlation (or more accurately the dependence) between load and price is high, the optimal price hedges will also hedge out most of the volumetric risk.

As we know from Chapter 7, the relationship between load and price tends to be strong for low and intermediate prices, but it usually breaks down for high prices. Consequently, we might be led to believe that when prices are high, for example in the summer months, weather hedges offer a sizable contribution. However, with the deterioration of the load-price relationship comes another effect: The volatility of power prices increases significantly and

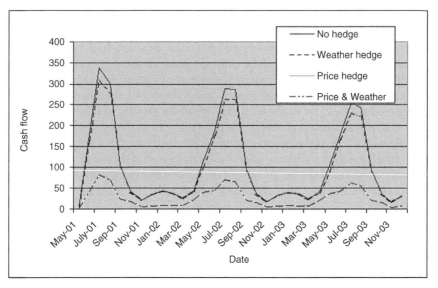

FIGURE 8.11   Weather and Price Hedging Performance

drives most cash-flow variability, and its associated risks. Once we hedge out the price risks, the residual volume risk is relatively small, though not small in absolute terms. However, to remove the residual volumetric risk, we must understand in great detail how the residual responds to weather. This can be difficult to achieve, since small errors in the optimal price hedge, given its relatively large size, can completely change the nature of the exposure: A one or two percent increase in the size of the price hedge can turn a short weather position into a long one. There is usually no reliable way of deciding what the weather hedge should be, making weather hedging largely infeasible.

EXAMPLE 8.15   *Performance of weather hedges*

In this example we look at the absolute and residual cash-flow variances of an actual load in one of the NERC regions (see Figure 8.11).

If we used weather hedges instead of price hedges, we could achieve some reduction in risk. However, given the greater liquidity of the price products, and their structure's greater amenability to effective hedging, it is almost always more efficient to use price hedges.

This logic does not apply to hedging natural gas demand. Gas load can be also highly correlated with weather, while locational spot prices do not have a strong dependence on weather. With its relatively lower price volatility, using both price and volumetric hedges might be worthwhile. (It might be puzzling why, despite the strong dependence of demand on weather, the price-weather relationship is not very strong. The fact is driven by the complexity of the topology of the pipeline network.)

ASSET MANAGEMENT DEALS

In this section we analyze pricing and hedging of structured deals, often built around physical assets. We give two examples: one from the natural gas market and the other from the power world.

We will lay out the main principles governing the analysis of derivative product portfolios. We must define the terms clearly: By liquid markets, we mean markets in which prices are not affected by volumes transacted, and where the bid-ask spread is negligible.

And now for our principle: *In liquid markets, values and hedges are additive.*

The main consequence of this principle is that valuation (and hedging) of a complex deal or structure can be done by splitting them into smaller and simpler parts, finding their values (and hedges) separately and ultimately aggregating these values (and hedges). The advantage is that the values and hedges of simpler components usually can be computed more efficiently.

More fundamentally, in liquid markets, as long as there are no operational dependencies among various assets, there will be no cash flow, hedging, or even more general risk dependencies. Consequently, all the component assets can be analyzed and managed separately.

EXAMPLE 8.16   *Interaction of power generation and fuel storage*

A power merchant owns a gas-fired generation unit in PJM. The unit has a gas storage facility, which is located at a liquid point. Let's assume that the gas price on any given day is G_t. The price is two-way for purchases and sales, that is, there is no bid-ask spread.

When valuing (and hedging) the two facilities, we have two alternative ways:

- We can assume that we source all the needs of the generation unit from the storage facility, and we optimize the storage facility so as to meet the demand of the generation unit and trade the surplus (or shortfall) in the spot market.
- Alternatively, we can assume that we always source the fuel for the generation unit from the spot market, and manage the storage facility independently.

Although, the second method may seem a bit artificial, we can easily show that the cash flows (and consequently hedges) for the two cases will be identical. To see this, note that on any given day, if the unit is generating and requires one unit of natural gas, the cash flow will be:

$$CashFlow = P_t - G_t$$

If we source from the spot market it is obvious that the cash flow will be given by the preceding equation. However, even if we source from the storage facility, the cash flow is also given by this equation. Since, the opportunity cost of using the gas from the storage facility is the price for which we could sell the gas in the spot market, the cost is given by G_t. Consequently, the two methods of valuing the two facilities are equivalent, since all the cash flows are identical.

Note that the Example 8.16 result relies on the assumption that we can buy and sell at the same price. If the assumption fails, the equivalence no longer applies. On the other hand, we can measure the possible gains from joint optimization of assets by looking at the size of the bid-ask spread (induced by transportation costs to and from the liquid point). The tighter the spread, the smaller the gain from joint optimization.

The principle applies as readily to financial assets as to physical ones. More specifically we can show that under the liquid markets assumption, operational decisions are not affected by hedges we hold.

EXAMPLE 8.17   *Interaction of hedges and operational decisions*

A gas marketer enters into a delivery contract at a liquid location for a tenor of one month. The volume is variable and nominated every day by the counterparty. The price is fixed at P_c. To manage its risk the marketer buys a forward position (at F) for the contractual month with the fixed volume of 1 MMBtu. On a certain day t, the counterparty nominates the volume of 1 MMBtu. The marketer has two possible strategies:

- Take the delivery from the forward contract and pass on the natural gas: the cash flow is then: $P_c - F$.
- Buy the gas in the spot market, and deliver it to the customer. Sell the gas received from the forward contract delivery to the spot market. The resulting cash flow will be: $(P_c - G_t) + (G_t - F) = P_c - F$

We can see that as long as the bid-ask spread is negligible, the two strategies result in the same cash flow. The upshot is that we can treat the delivery part of the contract and the hedge independently, that is, we can operate as if the hedge contract was not in place and our operations will not be changed. What does change is the cash flow.

The two preceding examples lead to the following conclusions:

1. In liquid markets, the physical asset operations are not affected by hedging strategies, but the cash flows are.
2. In liquid markets, portfolio of physical and financial assets can be analyzed separately.
3. In illiquid markets, the values and hedges of individual structures are dependent on the entire portfolio.
4. In illiquid markets, the physical asset operations are affected by hedging strategies and should be jointly optimized. (The gains from the joint optimization are bounded by the size of the bid-ask spread.)

CHAPTER 9

Power Plants and Other Cross-commodity Derivatives

In this chapter we present a number of cross-commodity derivatives along with a host of issues related to their hedging and valuation.

POWER PRICE AS A CROSS-COMMODITY DERIVATIVE

In our extensive analysis of hybrid models of power prices, these models gave us a representation of the joint distribution of cash power prices (and the relevant fuels) in terms of several dynamic factors and related liquid tradables. We can formally represent the behavior of power prices and major fuels such as oil and natural gas by the following expression as well as other factors:

$$p_t = s(D_t, g_t, l_t, \overrightarrow{\Omega_t}, \overrightarrow{E}^t, \overrightarrow{\Im_t}, \overrightarrow{OPC_2^t}) + \varepsilon_t \qquad (9.1)$$

where

ε_t is the stochastic error term.

OPC_t is the vector of operational characteristics of the stack at time t that parameterizes the stack transformation.

s is the deterministic stack transformation.

The upshot of this analysis is that power price itself can be treated as a fuel derivative. What this means in practice is that even pure power contracts have fuel sensitivities. We can easily see that a large oil-fired power plant, under certain circumstances, can have significant natural gas exposure. As higher natural gas prices in many situations imply higher power price volatility (see Chapter 7), the plant can be long natural gas.

This conclusion might be puzzling, because, if we are already using power price contracts to hedge our exposure, it seems natural that the power price hedge would eliminate direct exposure to the underlying fuels. But this is true only if we have enough power price tradables to eliminate all the risk. Fuel prices have an impact on the volatility, as well as the volatility skew, of power prices. Since the skew is not traded, we can try to substitute fuel contracts to increase the effectiveness of our hedging strategy.

GENERATION ASSETS: THERMAL

A number of technologies are used in generating electricity. The technology involved usually is not of much interest to us here. The main technical characteristics that impact valuation and hedging, such as start-up costs, ramp rates, heat curves, fuels used, and emission rates will be sufficient to characterize the financial impact. Using those categories we can distinguish three main families of thermal generating units:

1. Baseload
2. Cycling
3. Peaking

Table 9.1 illustrates the bundles of operating characteristics that define the categories listed above.

The technology used in different classes of generation units can be based on a variety of principles. In Chapter 1 we reviewed the types of fuels used for generation. We must mention that some power plants have multi-fuel capabilities, that is, the ability to switch between different fuels, depending on operational or cost considerations. In some cases, the switch can be made without delay and at a low cost, but in others it might involve a shutdown and all the consequent costs.

The following list recaps the main performance characteristics of generation units and analyzes them in detail in the context of the merit characterization in Table 9.1.

TABLE 9.1 Bundles of Operating Characteristics

	Baseload	Cycling	Peaking
Start-up costs	High	Moderate	Moderate
Fuels	Gas, coal, oil, nuclear	Oil, gas	Oil, gas
Ramp rates	Low	Low to moderate	High
Heat rates at maximum capacity	Low	Moderate	High

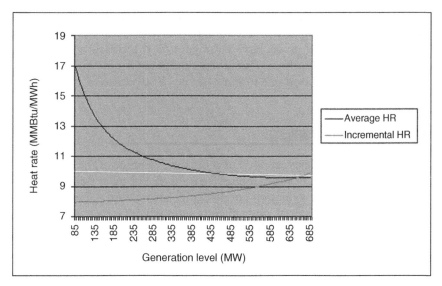

FIGURE 9.1   Baseload Heat Curve

Capacity. Maximum power output of the unit expressed in MW (megawatts). The number can change with seasons and/or ambient temperature. Typical ranges for different technologies are as follows:

Nuclear: Over 1,000 MW

Coal: Over 500 MW

Gas/oil baseload: 200 MW–800 MW

Gas/oil peakers: 50 MW–200 MW

Heat Rate. A measure of efficiency of the unit; its ability to convert fuel energy content, expressed in British thermal units (Btu), into electrical energy, expressed in kWh (see also Chapter 2). Hence heat rate is expressed as Btu/kWh. A unit's heat rate is dependent on its generation level. The curve describing this relationship is called, not surprisingly, the heat curve. The typical values of the heat rate (at maximum generation) are shown by the following examples:

Baseload coal—9,500 Btu/kWh

Combined cycle—7,000 Btu/kWh

Combustion turbine—12,000 Btu/kWh

Examples of average heat curves (as opposed to incremental heat curves) are given by Figures 9.1 and 9.2.

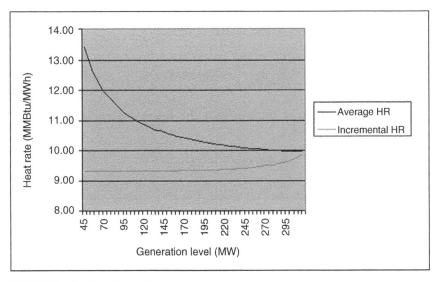

FIGURE 9.2 Peaking Heat Curve

Average Heat Rate at Generation Level q ($AHR(q)$). The average amount of fuel (expressed in MMBtu) needed to produce 1 kWh of electrical energy for all the levels of generation between min generation level C_{min} and the generation level q. The average heat rate multiplied by the generation level gives us the total amount of fuel needed to generate q kWh over the period of one hour.

Incremental Heat Rate at Generation Level q ($IHR(q)$). The incremental amount of fuel (expressed in MMBtu) needed to produce an additional 1 kWh of electrical energy at the generation level q.

We have that the total fuel generation cost is given by:

$$Fuel\ Cost = q \cdot AHR(q) \cdot Fuel\ Price$$

Incremental heat rate is related to the average heat rate by the following relationship:

$$ImpHR(q) = \frac{\partial[q \cdot AHR(q)]}{\partial q} = AHR(q) + q \cdot AHR'(q)$$

We can see that the incremental heat rate is equal to the average heat rate plus a term, which is equal to the product of the generation level q and the slope of the average heat curve. Note that given the fact that incremental heat rate times the fuel price is the slope of the cost curve, the optimal generation point q^* will be given by the first order condition:

$$\frac{Power\ Price}{Fuel\ Price} = ImpHR(q^*)$$

The above applies if q^* is within the feasible generation interval $[C_{min}, C_{max}]$. If we have

$$ImpHR(q^*) \le AHR(q^*)$$

then, it is optimal to shut the unit down. The above condition is always met as long as the slope of the average heat curve is negative.

Variable O&M Costs. Variable operational and maintenance costs, per unit of generation.

Min/Max Generation Level. Maximum generation level is the unit's capacity. Minimum generation level is the technically feasible minimum level. For steam units, the min levels are around 30% to 50% of total capacity; for some combustion turbines they can be as high as 80%. This characteristic has a major impact on a plant's flexibility, and consequently its optionality.

Availability (Forced and Planned Outages). These fall into two categories:

- **Scheduled outages.** Planned downtime for maintenance. Units typically require 2 to 4 weeks of downtime annually.
- **Forced outages.** Unplanned downtime caused by a technical failure of the unit. Expressed as equivalent forced outage rate (EFOR), which is defined as the number of outage hours in a measurement period divided by the number of available hours in that period (see details in Chapter 3). Outage rates depend on the unit's technology, its age, and its operating conditions. The outage rate can run from 3% to more than 20% for some units. In general, the timing of individual outage events can be influenced to some degree by operating decisions, and individual outages can be delayed by certain actions. However, this can entail substantial cost down the road or a higher outage rate later. Outage rates have an impact on the value of the plant, because they limit the total amount of energy available from a unit. More importantly, outage rates can have a substantial impact on the risk profile of a unit's cash flow. Given an extreme "spikiness" of power prices, one ill-timed event, coupled with outstanding short positions (obligations to serve or deliver), can result in catastrophic losses.

Ramp Rate. The rate at which the generation level can be changed, expressed in MW per minute. Fast-ramping units have rates of around 5 MW/min. This characteristic has a major impact on the flexibility of a plant, and consequently on its ability to capture hourly and other short-term optionality.

Start-up/Shutdown Costs. The costs of starting up or shutting down a unit can be of three types:

- Fixed dollar cost per event
- Fuel consumed in a start-up
- Electricity consumed in a start-up

For large baseload units, fixed start-up costs can run into tens of thousands of dollars, and we must differentiate between various start-ups. Depending on the state of the unit, a start-up can be cold, warm, or hot. This classification refers to the state of the boiler in steam-powered units: The colder the boiler is, the more expensive it is to heat it up again. The cost of start-up increases accordingly.

The size of these costs has a substantial impact on the value of flexibility associated with the unit. It tends to have a disproportionately high impact on the risk profile of the unit cash flow, and it can also tend to induce significant hedging costs. In trader's jargon, high start-up costs tend to induce significant gamma.

Min/Max Runtime, Min/Max Offline Time. For technical reasons, various restrictions on the length of runtime and/or offline time can be present. Those restrictions can significantly affect a unit's flexibility and thus its ability to exploit optionality.

Operational costs of units are affected by the following items:

- Fuel costs
- Variable O&M
- Emissions costs and emission restrictions (they can have cumulative instead of marginal character)
- Transmission costs (depending on the market design)

Economic Dispatch and Bidding of Generation Units

Depending on the structure of the market, the dispatch of a generation unit can be significantly different.

In pool markets, where we have one market clearing price (at least for energy), the optimization of dispatch is greatly simplified. As our examples in Chapter 8 showed, in systems with one price (pools), the optimization of generation assets is independent of any load obligation, storage facilities, and any financial (or even physical) contractual arrangements. It follows that the operation of a unit is by and large not affected by any hedges the generator might hold. As will be seen in the next section, the above is strictly true only for risk-neutral operators. For certain market designs, hedging strategies can influence operational decisions through the impact of risk-reduction on the optimal dispatch decisions. For example, if an operator enters into contracts that guarantee that at least the start-up and no-load (minimum generation level) costs will be recovered—something it cannot be otherwise sure of—the operator will be willing to start up the unit more frequently.

This consideration, however, depends on the specifics of the pool design. In some pools (NYPOOL), the market structure offers the option of a three-dimensional bid: energy, start-up, and no-load. This mechanism supplies an insurance scheme to the generator, ensuring that it will be made whole on its commitment decision no matter where energy prices end up. This setup effectively displaces any need for start-up cost hedging strategies.

In bilateral markets, dispatch involves optimizing generation, given contractual load constraints and fuel prices. It can also involve selling excess power or buying needed resources in the cash market. The problem in purely bilateral markets is that the price discovery process can be quite inefficient. We might not be able to consistently contract for a specific service. Also, depending on the side of the market we are on, we might face different prices. In other words, we will see an effective bid-ask spread.

In the rest of this chapter we concentrate on valuation and hedging in pool markets. This choice is motivated by the growing popularity of the solution. Additionally, analysis in pool markets has the virtue of simplicity compared with the full-blown bilateral market case. We will point out major differences and considerations along the way.

In pool markets there are four types of bidding decisions to consider:

Structure of the Bid.   Some markets offer a choice between market-based schemes and cost-based schemes. Another example is the choices required in the multidimensional bid markets—for example, energy, no-load, start-up.

Timing of the Bid.   In multisettlement pools (e.g., PJM, NYPOOL, and so on), one deals with day-ahead markets and day-of or real-time markets. Although the former can be considered as financial (one-day) forward markets (since they are usually settled financially), their role in the efficient operation of the pool market is different from that of the real-time market. The day-ahead market serves the purpose of securing slow-starting units (e.g., steam, and so on) for service the following day (i.e., unit commitment), while the day-of market is used mainly for rebalancing, with upward revisions in demand often requiring the start-up of inefficient quick-start units. Market participants can elect to self-schedule and receive a real-time price. However, early commitment gives the ISO an advantage in planning reserve resources (i.e., ancillary services) as well as controlling start-up risks—a consideration of significant import to generators. The economic drivers lead to differential behaviors by the prices. Consequently, their relationship cannot be understood simply in terms of the risk-adjusted expectation of the other. In this sense the day-ahead price should not be seen as the forward price of the real-time price. The arbitrage between the two cannot be carried out by, for example, slow-starting steam units. Additionally, the market set-up offers implicit options to generators who commit in the early market: Whenever the real-time price drops below the generation costs, the generators have the option of ramping down their units and delivering from the spot market (actually in some markets this option is automatically exercised by an ISO on behalf of the generators).

Choice of the Market. Beyond energy markets, a supplier has also the choice of selling its capacity into the ancillary markets (see Chapter 1). On the load side, load-serving entities (LSEs) must also bid for capacity resources apart from the energy requirements.

Time Structure of the Bid. In many pool markets the day-ahead auction involves bidding for all the hours of the day. In this sense, a market participant deals not with one energy market but with twenty-four separate ones. Although the auction may be conducted independently for each hour, the generation costs across the day are not independent: The presence of start-up costs and finite ramp rates produces interdependencies in the marginal generation costs across the different hours.

We cannot offer clear-cut rules about the proper bidding choices; the topic is vastly complex. To find an optimal bidding strategy we must consider all the structural issues we just listed, as well as the characteristics of the price distributions of all the elements. The problem is quite challenging in its general mathematical formulation; however, the mathematical problem is not the most important one. The biggest challenge lies in achieving a robust understanding of the underlying distributions and risks, as we have seen in the previous chapters, the challenge remains a formidable one.

Economic Dispatch, Uncertainty, and Valuation: An Introduction

In other chapters of this book we analyzed contractual arrangements and physical assets in terms of their financial structure. We treated the problems of valuation and hedging of energy assets no differently from equity or FX markets.

Let us examine now a general approach to valuing financial derivatives. The first step usually involves describing the payoff function of a structure at hand and calculating its intrinsic value. The next step entails finding the proper distribution with which to evaluate the necessary expectation and thereby find the unambiguous value. In previous chapters we have seen that finding the proper distribution for energy assets can be a lot of hard work. Now, however, we face another problem: *What is the intrinsic value of a generation unit? Or, what is the payoff function?*

An example will clarify the issues. Consider a gas-fired generation unit with a specified constant heat rate. The operator of the unit must determine the optimal operation of the unit for the next day, as well as its level of generation. Since the unit requires a costly start-up, and a time lag until it comes online, the operator must make these decisions today in order for the unit to be ready to generate power tomorrow. After he has made the commitment decision, he will have to make the operating decision. How does the operator make his decision?

Assume that tomorrow's prices are known with certainty; then the generator will start up the unit as long as the following holds:

$$C(\hat{P} - HR \cdot \hat{G}) \geq SC \tag{9.2}$$

where

C is the unit capacity

HR is the unit heat rate (assumed to be constant)

SC is the start-up cost

$\hat{P}$ and $\hat{G}$ are tomorrow's power and gas prices

We can rewrite the above to yield the payoff function of the generation unit

$$Payoff = C \max\left(\hat{P} - HR \cdot \hat{G} - \frac{SC}{C}, 0\right) \tag{9.3}$$

We can see that the payoff is identical to the spread option payoff (see Chapter 8) with strike price given by SC/C (or start-up cost per unit of capacity). The crucial difference between spread options and generation, however, is that under uncertainty the nature of the exercise decision will change. This is due to the interaction of the commitment, risk aversion, and operating level decisions.

Let's assume now that tomorrow's prices are uncertain, and that the expectations of the prices are as follows:

$$E[P] = \hat{P}$$

$$E[G] = \hat{G}$$

In other words, the expectations are equal to the certain prices we used before. Now, is it optimal to use the rule given in equation (9.2) to start up the unit? We can see now that we might find ourselves in a situation where we will suffer losses, if the actual spread (as opposed to the expected one) is not sufficient to compensate us for the costs. However, if we optimize the expected value of the spread, the optimal decision still falls under the rule above as long as we have no operational flexibility. The conclusion will change if the operator is risk-averse and requires compensation for risk taken. Under those circumstances, the optimal decision will be given by the following rule:

$$(\hat{P} - HR \cdot \hat{G}) - \frac{SC}{C} \geq RP \geq 0 \qquad (9.4)$$

where RP is some positive risk premium.

On the other hand, even if the operator is risk-neutral, the optimal decision rule can change due to the presence of operational flexibility. If the operator can shut down the unit to avoid the negative cash flows resulting from negative spreads, the optimal decision rule will be given by the following:

$$(\hat{P} - HR \cdot \hat{G}) - \frac{SC}{C} \geq k$$

$$k \leq 0 \qquad (9.5)$$

where

$$k = -E[\max(HR \cdot G - P, 0)] \qquad (9.6)$$

We can rewrite the expected payoff function in the uncertain case in the following way:

$$Payoff = C\left(\hat{P} - HR \cdot \hat{G} - \frac{SC}{C}\right)I_{[\hat{P} - HR \cdot \hat{G} - \chi > 0]} = C\max(\hat{P} - HR \cdot \hat{G} - \chi, 0) - (SC - C\chi)I_{[\hat{P} - HR \cdot \hat{G} - \chi > 0]}$$

$$\chi = \chi(\hat{P}, \hat{G}, \sigma_P, \sigma_G, \rho; \overrightarrow{OPC}, RP) = RP + \frac{SC}{C} - E[\max(HR \cdot G - P, 0)] \qquad (9.7)$$

where

$I_{\{ \}}$ is an indicator function

function χ is the start-up shadow price

Conceptually, this quantity is analogous to the critical price (or boundary) in the valuation of American options. As we can see, the shadow price depends on the distributions of the prices, operational characteristics of the unit, and the risk premia the generator requires. The value of the shadow price can be negative or positive; the higher the risk premium, the bigger (more positive) the shadow price will be. Also, we can see that the start-up cost is essentially a premium we must pay to be able to exercise operational flexibility. We decomposed the expected value of the generation unit into a spread option struck at the shadow price and an additional term, which can be interpreted as a short position in a digital spread option with unit payoff equal to the difference between the start-up cost and the product of the shadow price and capacity.

Given the payoff function, we can now find the value of the generation facility by calculating the appropriate risk-neutral expectation of the payoff function. We start by noting that our expected prices are one-period conditional expectations of the cash prices:

$$E_T[P_{T+1}] = \hat{P}$$

$$E_T[G_{T+1}] = \hat{G}$$

Consequently, the value of the generation asset at time t_0 will be given by the following:

$$\text{Value} = E_{t_0}(\textit{Payoff}_T) = CE_{t_0}\{\max[E_T(P_{T+1}) - HR \cdot E_T(G_{T+1}) - \chi, 0]\} - E_{t_0}[(SC - C\chi)I_{\{\hat{P} - HR \cdot \hat{G} - \chi > 0\}}]$$

$$= CE_{t_0}\{\max[E_T(P_{T+1}) - HR \cdot E_T(G_{T+1}) - \chi, 0]\} - SC \cdot E_{t_0}[I_{\{\hat{P} - HR \cdot \hat{G} - \chi > 0\}}] + C \cdot E_{t_0}[\chi I_{\{\hat{P} - HR \cdot \hat{G} - \chi > 0\}}] \quad (9.8)$$

Note that we express the payoff function in terms of conditional expectations and not in terms of realized prices, as we usually do with standard structures, because the exercise of the option is performed in terms of conditional expectations and not solely in terms of realized prices.

The above example considers a simple one-period valuation with a very simplified set of operational characteristics. The general problem is much more complex, involving a number of constraints we analyze in subsequent sections. On the other hand, the overall structure of the valuation problem remains unchanged. In many cases we can formulate the problem in terms of shadow prices, and valuation and hedging can be analyzed as an extension of spread option analysis.

Valuation

The optimization of economic dispatch is a challenging undertaking. The presence of complex physical constraints induces dependencies across price paths seen by the unit. Below we consider the general problem of economic dispatch, and investigate the impact of various constraints on valuation and hedging in significant detail.

The crucial feature of the electricity market is that the cash markets into which the generation units sell power are not directly traded on a forward basis. This fact has serious consequences for valuing, hedging, and risk-managing generation assets. Unlike with the usual derivative contracts in financial markets, the dispatch of a unit often happens before all the relevant quantities are known. In other words, one exercises a generation option before the prices are known.

Consequently, the realized cash flow from a dispatch decision can be negative—a situation that never occurs with financial options. Therefore, depending on the amount of uncertainty left, and the trading (or dispatching) view and risk preferences of the dispatcher, the plant can be dispatched quite differently.

Below we show that in some situations the presence of different operational constraints induce significant deviations from the simple spark-spread–based models. Those differences are visible in valuation, but they are especially severe in hedging parameters.

For example, gas units with sizable start-up costs can exhibit negative sensitivity to volatility even when standard spark-spread option analysis suggests otherwise. Furthermore, for certain popular choices of dispatch heuristics, delta positions can become very high and very sensitive to small price changes. In trading language, the plant will exhibit negative vega, deltas exceeding 100%, and extremely high (and possibly negative) gammas.

This underscores the challenge of energy markets we mentioned earlier; the choice of the exercise policy itself is not a trivial issue. The high gamma and delta are a function of the selected dispatch heuristic; for other dispatch strategies, the gamma and deltas might become much more manageable. However, this increased tractability exacts a price: Falling gamma will, in this case, entail falling hedgeable value. On the other hand, as is well known, trying to chase high gamma in markets with limited liquidity can be quite dangerous, exposing the trader to greater risk and higher costs. In these situations we see three possible solutions:

- **The heroic one:** try to maximize the value by the choice of a dispatch policy, and aggressively hedge the exposure.
- **The stoic one:** try to maximize the value by the choice of a dispatch policy, and statically hedge the exposure—ignoring the gamma and letting chips fall where they may.
- **The safe one:** choose an easily hedgeable heuristic and let the value be what it is.

Our personal preference would be the middle-of-the-road choice of the stoic position, but we are not traders and we may be more willing to accept the wildly fluctuating mark-to-market value of our asset portfolio. We are not sure every trader would share our equanimity.

The dilemma of choosing between value and risk is obviously well known in financial markets. The trading rules of thumb for the early exercise of American options parallel the problem we face here (see Taleb, 1996). In energy markets, problems of this type are much more pervasive and relatively more severe.

Stochastic Dynamic Programming and Spark-spread Options

In this section we begin an analysis of the general problem of valuing and hedging power generation units. As we set up the problem, we must remember that any valuation of interest has to provide us some way of monetizing (hedging) the value associated with the optimization technique. Without this, the proposed value is just an opinion, greatly dependent upon specific assumptions about power price behavior.

Complex models are not always very useful as production tools, because of the significant data and computational resources they require for robust valuation and risk management. However, they can be helpful as a technique for developing insight into the structure of the problem. In other words, they can tell us what approximations are likely to work under what circumstances.

We systematically review the detailed mathematical issues involved in valuation of generation in Appendix B. Here, we first analyze the basic spark-spread option–based valuation and then move on to extensions based upon approximations to the general stochastic dynamic program.

Simple Spark-spread Option Valuation

If we can assume that start-up costs, minimum/maximum runtimes and downtimes have no significant impact, and that the heat curve is flat, the analysis of generation plants can be reduced to that of a strip of daily (or block) spread options. This setup corresponds to the assumption that the optimal shadow prices are equal to zero.

Given the above, the value of a power plant is given by the following formula:

$$V_0 = \sum_{n=1}^{N} \sum_{m=t_n}^{M} e^{-r(m-t_0)} E_{t_0}^* \left[\max\{M_m C_{max}(P_m - HR_{max} G_m - VOM), 0\} \right] =$$

$$\sum_{n=1}^{N} \sum_{m=t_n}^{M} e^{-r(m-t_0)} E_{t_0}^* \left[M_m C_{max} \max(P_m - HR_{max} G_m - VOM, 0) \right] \quad (9.9)$$

The *n* summation covers months, while the *m* summation covers periods within the month (on-peak, off-peak blocks or possibly all hours). M_m stands for the magnitude of a forced outage derate of available capacity.

If forced outages are independent of prices—an assumption that can only be safely made in months when the system is not unduly constrained (e.g., winter months in the United States, summer months in Scandinavia)—we can rewrite equation 9.9 in the following way:

$$V_0 = \sum_{n=1}^{N} \sum_{m=t_n}^{M} e^{-r(m-t_0)} E_{t_0}^*[M_m] C_{max} E_{t_0}^*[\max(P_m - HR_{max}G_m - VOM, 0)]$$

$$= \sum_{n=1}^{N} \sum_{m=t_n}^{M} e^{-r(m-t_0)} C_{max}^{eff} E_{t_0}^*[\max(P_m - HR_{max}G_m - VOM, 0)] \qquad (9.10)$$

where

$E_{t_0}^*[M_m]$ is a risk-adjusted expectation of outage (expected derate)

C_{max}^{eff} is the effective (outage-adjusted) capacity of the unit

We can see that under this assumption, the impact of forced outages is reflected through changes to the effective capacity of the unit. Given that outage rates overall exhibit at most seasonal structure, the effective capacity changes from season to season.

With those assumptions in place, the analysis of valuation and hedging of generation plants boils down to an analysis of spread options. We reviewed extensively the issues involved in valuation and hedging spread options in Chapters 6 and 8. We address the practical issues involved in hedging power plants in a later section of this chapter.

Here we present an extensive example of valuing power plants with spark-spread options using the results from Chapters 4, 5, 6, and 8.

EXAMPLE 9.1 *Spark spread option valuation of a generation plant*

A company AYC owns a cycling gas-fired generation unit with a max Heat Rate (HR) = 10,000 and max capacity C_{max} = 300MW. The variable O&M is zero. The company intends to hedge the value of the asset for the next calendar year. Table 9.2 gives the current forward curves.

The implied heat rate is simply the power forward price divided by the primary fuel price, indicating the heat rate of the marginal unit (the one setting the price). The moneyness is the ratio of the implied heat rate and the unit heat rate (max capacity). It indicates where our unit is in relation to the

TABLE 9.2   Forward Curves for Example 9.1

	Power On-peak	Power Off-peak	Gas	On-peak Implied HR	Off-peak Implied HR	Unit On-peak Moneyness	Unit Off-peak Moneyness
Jan	$34.00	$18.00	$3.90	8.7	4.6	87%	46%
Feb	$32.00	$17.00	$3.75	8.5	4.5	85%	45%
Mar	$28.00	$22.00	$3.40	8.2	6.5	82%	65%
Apr	$34.00	$24.00	$3.10	11.0	7.7	110%	77%
May	$42.00	$26.00	$3.25	12.9	8.0	129%	80%
Jun	$58.00	$26.00	$3.20	18.1	8.1	181%	81%
Jul	$89.00	$28.00	$3.35	26.6	8.4	266%	84%
Aug	$92.00	$28.00	$3.48	26.4	8.0	264%	80%
Sep	$49.00	$27.00	$3.50	14.0	7.7	140%	77%
Oct	$30.00	$22.00	$3.49	8.6	6.3	86%	63%
Nov	$28.00	$18.00	$3.68	7.6	4.9	76%	49%
Dec	$33.00	$19.00	$3.80	8.7	5.0	87%	50%

marginal unit. Moneyness over 100% indicates that our unit is in-the-money as its heat rate is lower than the marginal heat rate. In other words, we can now sell forward the generation from our plant and earn a (unit) margin equal to the difference between the market implied heat rate (ImpHR)and the plant heat rate multiplied by the fuel (forward price):

$$\text{Forward Plant Margin} = F_P - HR_{Plant} \cdot F_G = F_G \cdot (ImpHR - HR_{Plant})$$

$$ImpHR = \frac{F_P}{F_G} \tag{9.11}$$

If the moneyness is less than 100%, then the forward margin is negative and the spark spread option is out-of-the-money. To value the unit properly the company needs to evaluate its monthly values. Those in turn are given by the summation of the values of daily spark-spread options.

For any given month we must evaluate a collection of standard on-peak and off-peak spark-spread options. We account here only for the block optionality. This is to say we treat the plant as if it was dispatched to the average on-peak and off-peak prices ignoring the contribution of hourly optionality. This simplification is not as unreasonable as it looks. We rarely deal with plants that can exploit the full measure of hourly optionality. Additionally, in practice, the impact of hourly volatility is significant only for peaking units with high heat rates.

Returning to the main line of analysis, the monthly option value is composed from two types of terms, off-peak and on-peak:

$$V_n = V_n^{OffPeak} + V_n^{OnPeak}$$

$$V_n^{OnPeak} = \sum_{s=t_n}^{S} e^{-r(s-t_n)} C_{max}^{eff} E_{t_0}^* [\max(P_s - HR_{max} G_s, 0)] \qquad (9.12)$$

$$V_n^{OffPeak} = \sum_{m=t_n}^{M} e^{-r(m-t_n)} C_{max}^{eff} E_{t_0}^* [\max(P_m - HR_{max} G_m, 0)]$$

The individual expectations in the sum are the values of spark-spread options. We can express the values of the options in the following way:

$$V_n^{OnPeak} = \sum_{s=t_n}^{S} SS(F_P^{OnPeak}, F_G^{OnPeak}, \overrightarrow{\sigma}_P^{Daily}, \overrightarrow{\sigma}_G^{Daily}, \overrightarrow{\theta}, \tau = s - t_0; HR_{max}) \quad (9.13)$$

$\overrightarrow{\sigma}_P^{Daily}$ —implied volatility smile for power

$\overrightarrow{\sigma}_G^{Daily}$ —implied volatility smile for fuel (gas)

$\overrightarrow{\theta}$ —model parameters (e.g., correlations, etc.)

We can hide all the complexity associated with non-lognormal models by using the Margrabe formula for spark-spread options with appropriately modified parameters (see Chapters 6 and 8):

$$SS(F_P^{OnPeak}, F_G^{OnPeak}, \overrightarrow{\sigma}_P^{Daily}, \overrightarrow{\sigma}_G^{Daily}, \overrightarrow{\theta}, \tau = s - t_0; HR_{max}) =$$

$$SS_M\left(F_P^{OnPeak}, F_G^{OnPeak}, \sigma_P^{Daily}\left(\frac{ImpHR}{HR_{max}}\right), \sigma_G^{Daily}\left(\frac{ImpHR}{HR_{max}}\right), \rho_I^{Daily}\left(\frac{ImpHR}{HR_{max}}\right), \tau = s - t_0; HR_{max}\right)$$

$$(9.14)$$

We rewrote the general spark spread formula in terms of implied volatilities and correlation corresponding to the moneyness of the option.

Lognormal case. Now we start with the assumption that all the prices are jointly lognormally distributed. In this case, the volatilities and correlation do not depend on moneyness. The volatilities are constant and equal to the

TABLE 9.3   Daily Volatilities and Correlations

	Power On-peak Daily ATM Volatility	Power Off-peak Daily ATM Volatility	Natural Gas Daily ATM Volatility	Natural Gas - On-peak Daily ATM Correlation	Natural Gas - Off-peak Daily ATM Correlation
Jan	75%	30%	70%	90%	50%
Feb	70%	25%	65%	90%	50%
Mar	65%	25%	40%	90%	50%
Apr	60%	25%	45%	90%	50%
May	70%	25%	45%	90%	50%
Jun	140%	30%	45%	50%	50%
Jul	140%	30%	45%	50%	50%
Aug	80%	30%	45%	50%	50%
Sep	60%	30%	45%	50%	50%
Oct	60%	30%	55%	90%	50%
Nov	60%	30%	60%	90%	50%
Dec	60%	30%	60%	90%	50%

ATM implied volatilities (they can change from month-to-month). Correlation is also constant and should be estimated as in Chapter 6.

We need to use daily volatilities (see Chapters 2 and 4) for our estimation. In power markets daily volatilities are often quoted with the liquidity as good as or better than the monthly volatility. We can then use the direct quotes.

With daily volatilities calculated from the market data, and correlation estimated from historical data (remember to use sample of a minimum of a hundred observations when estimating correlation, see Chapter 6), we can now plug them into the Margrabe formula to obtain the option values. Table 9.3 shows the ATM daily volatilities and correlations used for all the months.

Using the Margrabe formula (see Chapter 8), we can now calculate the value of the daily spark-spread options for the year. We assume that the evaluation takes place on October 1 of the previous year. For simplicity we assume that the discount rate is equal to zero. The value of the generation facility will be then given by Table 9.4.

Table 9.4 compares the intrinsic value of the spark spread with its option value. We can see that the difference, which comes from the ability to shut down the unit when the spark spread is negative in the future, is significant. The value increases by 20%. The increase in value in the top of the summer (July, August) is modest at most 10%, as the options are deep ITM. Some shoulder months see an increase from 20% to 50%. Obviously, the contribution of optionality depends on the correlation and volatilities cho-

TABLE 9.4 Spark Spread Valuation for the Lognormal Case

	On-peak Spark Spread (Intrinsic)	Off-peak Spark Spread (Intrinsic)	On-peak Daily Spark Spread Option	Off-peak Daily Spark Spread Option	Total Value
Jan	$ (5.00)	$(21.00)	$ 0.68	$0.01	$ 73,158
Feb	$ (5.50)	$(20.50)	$ 0.62	$0.02	$ 68,306
Mar	$ (6.00)	$(12.00)	$ 0.68	$0.06	$ 78,843
Apr	$ 3.00	$ (7.00)	$ 4.30	$0.71	$ 533,305
May	$ 9.50	$ (6.50)	$10.41	$1.13	$1,223,663
Jun	$26.00	$ (6.00)	$32.99	$1.46	$3,644,637
Jul	$55.50	$ (5.50)	$60.75	$1.99	$6,635,603
Aug	$57.20	$ (6.80)	$58.14	$1.89	$6,348,003
Sep	$14.00	$ (8.00)	$17.28	$1.70	$2,012,309
Oct	$ (4.90)	$(12.90)	$ 1.47	$1.15	$ 282,594
Nov	$ (8.80)	$(18.80)	$ 0.77	$0.59	$ 147,043
Dec	$ (5.00)	$(19.00)	$ 2.06	$0.77	$ 302,407

sen for our example. In many markets, correlations are lower, implying a proportionally higher contribution of optionality.

Non-lognormality and Power Plants

The formulation in terms of spread options has the advantage of giving us clearer insight into the impact of non-lognormality on valuation and hedging. We devoted Chapter 6 to an analysis of correlation and the consequences of non-lognormality. Here we review the consequences of those considerations for hedging and valuation of power plants.

One of the primary (or popular) considerations in valuing spread options is the presence of power price spikes (or excess kurtosis). We reviewed a number of models in previous chapters that can generate price spikes in a more or less robust way. We have not investigated the impact of the choice of different models on the valuation of power plants, but it is easy to see that depending on the choice of the model and the calibration of its parameters, we can generate wildly varying valuations (e.g., see Clewlow, Strickland, and Kaminski, 2001). The big question is then what model to use. The answer is as simple as it is useless: the right one. But there is another answer: none.

The ability to properly model price spikes and the like might seem all-important. However, this issue is fundamental only for modeling and hedging power options (monthly or especially daily). Spread options do not necessarily require any specific modeling of spikes or kurtosis. If we have access to liquid power option markets, the difficult job of accounting for spikes and the like has been performed for us by the market maker. If we can actively hedge with power option contracts, our exposure to model assumptions is significantly diminished. This is a welcome development, since it can help us steer clear of sterile discussions about what the true mean-reversion or spike probabilities are.

The procedure, in valuation stages, consists in using the appropriate implied volatilities, choosing the correct (implied) correlation and inserting it into the standard spread option formula (e.g., Margrabe formula, see Chapter 8). How does this procedure hold up when we attempt to hedge our exposures with the model of this type? The answer is that if we consistently use the implied quantities (volatilities), and frequently recalibrate the model to the new volatilities, the hedging program is likely to perform well. As we argued in Chapter 4, in practice, a frequently recalibrated Black-Scholes model performs quite well as a hedging strategy (for the theoretical justification, see Berkowitz, 2001).

There is only one fly in the ointment: correlation. Implied correlation is not traded, so we cannot know what to use. This consideration helps explain the obsessive attention we give to correlation in this book. As we saw in Chapter 6, we cannot escape the behavior of the marginal distributions when we attempt to find implied correlation. Implied correlation depends on the whole volatility surfaces of the underliers. By themselves, however, those are not enough to determine what the implied correlation should be—the shape of implied volatility surface creates only broad restrictions on the implied correlation curve. For this we need an explicit model of the behavior of the whole joint distribution (including marginals). However, due to the frequent absence of reliable models of the underlying prices, we may resort to approximate rules of thumb.

In our experience, implied correlation curves tend to be relatively stable over time (if changes in the volatility are accounted for), but they can be sensitive to the structure of the market (see implied correlation curves in Chapter 7). Consequently, they can differ among the NERC regions. In Chapter 6 we presented a procedure that can help us find an appropriate implied correlation, so long as certain assumptions about the structure of the price processes are satisfied. We also identified broad conditions under which it is not possible to adjust the available simple tools, and we must use explicit models or risk serious errors in valuation, and potentially very ineffective hedges.

A further warning is in order. Even though the frequent recalibration technique can work for simple structures, it does not follow that it also works for more complex ones. This theoretical consideration is amply confirmed in practice. For example, Asian options are not correctly priced by using implied volatility smiles extracted from standard calls. The implication is that, when we deal with generation plants that cannot be easily reduced to a collection of spark-spread options, the recalibration technique is not likely to work. A simple example would be a slow-ramping generation plant, unable to capture the full measure of sudden, quickly reverting price spikes. This suggests that using implied volatility from hourly, or even daily, options can be misleading.

There is another consideration in attempting to form an option-based hedge. We know from our basic analysis of spread options for the Black-Scholes case, that sensitivities to volatility (vegas) can switch signs depending on the individual leg volatility and correlation levels. As we know from Chapter 8, this effect is most likely to appear if the correlation is high and the two volatilities are of similar magnitudes. In the U.S. markets, there are several regions in which one fuel (natural gas) is almost always the marginal one (e.g., California, ERCOT). If the loads remain on the flat part of the stack (see Chapter 7), the correlation is high, and volatilities are roughly similar. Those conditions tend to occur in winter and shoulder months. Consequently, it might be a serious problem to set up an effective volatility (vega) hedge during those months, because of limited liquidity in forward and especially daily ATM power options. Flips in vegas, in principle, require switching between long and short option positions, and vice-versa. This can be quite expensive, since we are forced to cross the substantial option market bid-ask spread, and it often leads to reluctance on the part of asset traders to use volatility hedging strategies.

Obviously, this issue is driven by the limited liquidity in the volatility market, which also points to a larger theme that the recalibration strategy relies on liquid volatility markets in the first place. In many power markets, liquidity in volatility products is limited and we must resort to explicit modeling (see Chapter 7), with all its attendant risks.

We now continue the analysis of Example 9.1 by including non-lognormal behavior into our analysis. We follow the approach described in Chapter 6.

EXAMPLE 9.2 *Power plant valuation in the presence of non-lognormalities*

We now return to the representation of the value of spread option given in equation (9.14). Formally, the only difference in our analysis is the introduction of implied volatilities and correlation that depend on the moneyness of the asset. We analyzed the issues in Chapter 4 (volatilities) and 6 (correlations). Here, we quickly review the conclusions. The goal of using the implied correlation and volatility representation is to separate the structure of the cash flow/payoff function of the structure at hand (power plant in our case) from the distributional assumptions. Also, using the approach allows us to clearly see the deviations from the standard lognormal assumptions and measure them not in terms of generalized statistical concepts (e.g., standard

TABLE 9.5   Spread Options in the Nonlognormal Case

	Correlation (lognormal)	Correlation (non-lognormal)	On-peak Spread Option	On-peak Spread Option (non-lognormal)	Difference
Jan	90%	78%	$ 0.68	$ 1.57	$0.89
Feb	90%	78%	$ 0.62	$ 1.50	$0.88
Mar	90%	78%	$ 0.68	$ 1.15	$0.47
Apr	90%	71%	$ 4.30	$ 5.54	$1.24
May	90%	62%	$10.41	$12.03	$1.62
Jun	50%	17%	$32.99	$34.63	$1.64
Jul	50%	15%	$60.75	$62.60	$1.85
Aug	50%	15%	$58.14	$59.36	$1.22
Sep	50%	27%	$17.28	$18.61	$1.33
Oct	90%	74%	$ 1.47	$ 3.26	$1.78
Nov	90%	73%	$ 0.77	$ 2.47	$1.70
Dec	90%	74%	$ 2.06	$ 4.35	$2.29

error, and so on) but in terms of the relevant metrics: cash flows and hedges. The use of the implied formulation allows us also to use the information available in the market directly and consistently with the available hedging strategies (volatility smiles).

Below, we use (daily) volatility and correlation smiles for gas and power. The daily gas volatility smile is generated from the actual forward one using the technique described in Chapter 8. The power volatility smile is generated from a version of the hybrid model we described in Chapter 7. It does not represent quoted contracts. The model correctly prices all the available liquid contracts (forwards, ATM options and OTM options where available). The correlation smile is derived through a stochastic volatility jump-diffusion model that matches the above volatility smiles.

After adjusting for correlation skew (and term structure) we obtain the values of the spread options in the non-lognormal case as shown in Table 9.5.

The overall increase in value over the lognormal case is around 10%. This is not necessarily representative of the usual contribution of nonlognormality. The additional value can easily increase (or decrease) by 30% to 40% for some units in certain markets. The above serves only as a generic example of the analysis involved.

Operational Constraints and Stochastic Dynamic Programming

The spark-spread approximation only works under the assumption that a host of operational constraints can be assumed away. The standard way to handle this problem consistently is to use a stochastic dynamic programming

(SDP) representation of the problem. We present all the details of valuation and solution techniques in Appendix B; here we briefly discuss the structure of the problem.

The expected value of a generation unit in this framework can be expressed by the value function: $V(U^{on}, P, G, M, T; t)$. This expresses the value of the facility at time t, conditioned on the current operational state of the unit, current prices, and other state variables. Since we are dealing with conditional expectations about the future condition of the state variables, we can use other price- and nonprice-conditional information. For example, we could include current BOM prices, current forward/futures prices, option prices, and the like. In practice, the horizon of the optimization rarely extends beyond one month (with important exceptions, explained shortly). Consequently, we rarely need to condition on more than BOM and prompt forward prices. Note that we use the additional information, even if we do not explicitly plan to commit our generation resources in the BOM market—we use it only to obtain better information about the spot price behavior. Quite apart from the optimization issue, the fact that we can use BOM information to perform better dispatch also implies that we can use those contracts as an inside-the-period hedge.

The solution to the problem of finding the optimal value function (and an associated operational strategy) is given by the first order optimality condition, which results in the following recursive equation (Bellman equation) for the value function:

$$V[P_{(t,i)}, G_{(t,i)}, M_{(t,i)}, \Im_{(t,i)}; U^{on}_{(t,i)}, d^{shutDown}_{(t,i)}, d^{startUp}_{(t,i)}; (t,i)] =$$

$$\max_{q_{(t,i)}, u_{(t,i)}} \{q_{(t,i)}[P_{(t,i)} - AHR(q_{(t,i)}, \Im_{(t,i)})G_{(t,i)} - VOM]\}$$

$$-u^{on}_{(t,i)}(SC(d^{shutDown}_{(t,i)}) + FSC(d^{shutDown}_{(t,i)}) \cdot G_t + PSC(d^{shutDown}_{(t,i)}) \cdot P_{(t,i)})$$

$$+ e^{-r\Delta t}E^*_{(t,i)}\{V[P_{(t,i)+1}, G_{(t,i)+1}, M_{(t,i)+1}, \Im_{(t,i)+1}; U^{on}_{(t,i)+1}, d^{shutDown}_{(t,i)+1}, d^{startUp}_{(t,i)+1}; (t,i) + 1]\} \quad (9.15)$$

(See list of constraints in Appendix B.) The above formulation is shown here mainly for its scary looks. Detailed explanation can be found in Appendix B.

Stochastic Dynamic Program as an Approximation to the "True" Problem

As we analyze approximations to the solutions of the optimization problem formulated in equation (9.15), we must be aware that we might not be able to formulate the problem robustly in many situations. Our knowledge of the distribution of all the information sources we use in dispatch (that is, BOM prices, temperature, market rumors, and so on) is usually quite limited. For certain units, the optimal dispatch policy can be sensitive to the choice of parameters of the distributions. To cope with the problem, traders use simple heuristics for dispatch; more sophisticated analysis rarely achieves significant improvement. If we decide to use the simple solution, we must also use it consistently in the forward evaluation of the plant. A more sophisticated approach in forward valuation will result in misvalued assets and, more ominously, very misleading hedges.

Spark-spread Options versus Stochastic Dynamic Programming

Historically, spark-spread option valuation techniques came to the energy industry with a wave of Wall Street talent. For Wall Street analysts, the natural way to understand risk management of power plants was in terms of the spread option, a structure that can be relatively easily analyzed and hedged.

The downside of this technique is that it misrepresents the operational characteristics of power plants, potentially leading to valuation errors *and* poor hedging performance. Stochastic dynamic programming techniques have been applied to the problem to handle the limitation. With this added sophistication, however, comes added complexity. Understanding the behavior of values and hedges becomes much more challenging. Additionally, using SDP models for hedging can actually lead to dangerous results if followed too closely. This is due to the instability of hedge parameters.

On the other hand, spark-spread formulation allows us to arrive at the optimal hedging strategies in a much more efficient manner than if we do it directly by perturbing SDP solutions. This is not a trivial consideration.

In the rest of this chapter, we approach the problem of power plant valuation from both angles. Reducing generation plant analysis to spread options and its derivatives can help us understand the impact of price behavior on values and hedges. Solving a full-blown SDP problem and its approximations is helpful in identifying the interaction of operational constraints.

Examples of Valuation and Hedging Analysis with Extended Spark-spread Model

Armed with an understanding of the optimization problem we are trying to solve, we return to Example 9.1 and analyze the issues of valuation, and especially hedging, in terms of the extended spark-spread model. This approach does not obviate the need to solve or approximate the stochastic dynamic program in equation (9.15), but it affords us a better view of the structure of the problem, and it brings to bear the option pricing methods we analyzed in previous chapters.

We analyze a simplified problem with three operating constraints that cause it to deviate markedly from the basic spark-spread valuation.

We consider a unit with the following characteristics:

- Fixed start-up costs: FSC
- High ramp rates
- Minimum capacity: C_{min}
- Minimum runtime: $D_{min} = 8$ hours

- Start-up/shutdown time: $D_{start-up} = D_{shutDown} = 8$ hours
- Heat curve: two optimal levels of generation with the corresponding heat rates given by:

$$HR_{min} > HR_{max}$$

We can choose to model the facility with a time resolution equal to the smallest decision unit allowable by the above constraints (i.e., $\Delta t = 8$ hours). This corresponds to using 8-hour averages as a proxy for the price in the decision blocks. This formulation undervalues the unit, since it recognizes only the block optionality and does not account for hourly optionality. Hourly optionality, however, does not have a significant impact on the value of most types of units; exceptions might be very high heat-rate ($> 17,000$) peaking plants in summer months. Additionally, we can easily account for hourly optionality by replacing the expectation of the average options with the sum of the expectations of the hourly options.

We also split the optimization into monthly sub-problems corresponding to liquid hedging instruments at our disposal. This is an approximation that works reasonably well as long as we have no long-term cumulative constraints (e.g., emission caps), and the minimum runtime, downtime, and average length of a forced outage are not longer than a couple of days.

Given the above characteristics we can describe the value of the plant in the following way:

$$\text{Value}_{t_0} = E_{t_0}^* \left[\sum_{n=1}^{N} \hat{V}_n(F_n^{OnPeak}, F_n^{OffPeak}, F_n^G, \overrightarrow{\sigma_n^{P;Monthly}}, \overrightarrow{\sigma_n^{P;Daily}}, \overrightarrow{\sigma_n^{G;Monthly}}, \overrightarrow{\sigma_n^{G;Index}}; t_n) \right] \quad (9.16)$$

where

$$\hat{V}_n = V_n[P_{t_n}(F_n^{OnPeak}, F_n^{OffPeak}, \overrightarrow{\sigma_n^{P;Monthly}}, \overrightarrow{\sigma_n^{P;Daily}}), G_{t_n}(F_n^G, \overrightarrow{\sigma_n^{G;Monthly}}, \overrightarrow{\sigma_n^{G;Index}}); t_n] \quad (9.17)$$

The vector notation for volatilities refers to volatility smiles for power and gas prices (see Chapter 4). The monthly value functions V_n are given by the following:

$$V_n = \sum_{m=t_n}^{M} e^{-r(m-t_n)} \{ \max[M_m C_{max}(P_m - HR_{max}G_m - VOM),$$

$$C_{min}(P_m - HR_{min}G_m - VOM)]U_m - FCS \cdot \max[(U_{m+1} - U_m),0] \} \quad (9.18)$$

where

$$U_m = I_{(M_m C_{max} > C_{min})}[I_{(P_{m-1} - HR_{max}G_{m-1} - VOM - \frac{x_{m-1}}{C_{max}} > 0)} \cdot (1 - U_{m-1}) +$$

$$U_{m-1} \cdot (1 - I_{(P_{m-1} - HR_{max}G_{m-1} - VOM + \frac{\phi_{m-1}}{C_{max}} > 0)})] \quad (9.19)$$

U_m is the indicator function that is equal to 1 if the unit is on and 0 otherwise

χ_{m-1} is a start-up shadow price

ϕ_{m-1} is a shutdown shadow price

In equation (9.18) we have two terms. The maximization term represents the value of the operational choices: running at maximum or minimum capacity. The second term represents the cost of starting up a unit. A start-up is represented by the transition from the offline state $U_{m-1} = 0$ to the online state $U_m = 1$.

The transition equation for U_m is derived as follows: if there is a full outage, the unit is turned off and $U_m = 0$. This is the meaning of the first multiplicative term.

In the braces we have two terms. The first corresponds to the start-up decision: If the unit is off, $U_{m-1} = 0$, and the current relevant spark spread exceeds the shadow price χ_{m-1}, we start up and $U_m = 1$. The second term corresponds to a shutdown decision: If the unit is on, $U_{m-1} = 1$, and the current relevant spark spread is smaller than the shadow price ϕ_{m-1}, we shut down the unit and $U_m = 0$.

Shadow prices are, in general, functions of current prices (time $m-1$), or possibly even prices before $(m-2)$ and all the other available information: BOM prices, volatilities, correlations, and so on. Note that unlike Example 9.2, the start-up shadow price can be negative. This is due to the fact that we have a delay in the start-up decision. It might therefore be optimal to start up the unit even though the current spark spread is negative. On the other hand, the shutdown shadow price must always be positive, since it is never optimal to shut down the unit if we have a positive spark spread.

Considering that the time steps cover three distinct periods—off-peak, peak and super-peak—the start-up decision often depends more on the previous peak and super-peak spark spreads than on the off-peak one. We have seen in previous chapters that prices during off-peak and on-peak hours can behave quite differently, with little correlation between the two. Consequently, the decision to start up will be based mainly on the spark spread during the last on-peak period. Furthermore, if the price process exhibits very weak autocorrelation (e.g., a very fast mean reversion from the "spiky" state) during the month, then the decision to start up will be based only on the parameters of the process (e.g., forwards at expiration, volatility smile at expiration, and so on).

Shutdown decisions will be based on the trade-off between losses in the upcoming off-peak period and savings on start-up costs, if it turns out to be optimal to have the unit on in the following on-peak period. Consequently, the shutdown shadow price will depend both on current off-peak prices (i.e., we assume we can shut down the unit at the same time we observe off-peak prices) and on previous on-peak prices (i.e., as a proxy for the future on-peak prices).

After all this rigorous hand waving we are left with two extreme cases:

1. Constant start-up decision
2. Constant shadow prices (at most dependent on the forward prices and volatilities at expiration)

The first solution can become optimal only under very unrealistic assumptions about price behavior. The second approximation performs quite satisfactorily in many contexts and for many types of units, and in the section that follows we concentrate on it.

Extensions of Spark-spread Option Formulation to More Complex Cases

We now investigate the behavior of generation plant values in the presence of physical constraints. In this section, we use an approximate formulation of the valuation using constant shadow prices. As we know from previous analysis, this approximation works only under certain circumstances. We use it for even more complex cases to gain at least an approximate understanding of the behavior of hedges and values in response to changing market conditions.

We formulated the approximation in (9.18). By rearranging terms, and assuming away outages, we can express the formula in the following way:

$$V_0^n = \sum_{m=t_n}^{M} e^{-r(m-t_n)} E_{t_0}^* (\{\Delta C \max [P_m - \Delta HR \cdot G_m - VOM, 0) +$$

$$C_{min}(P_m - HR_{min} G_m - VOM)]\} U_m - FCS \cdot \max [(U_{m+1} - U_m), 0]) \quad (9.20)$$

where

$$\Delta C = C_{max} - C_{min}$$

$$\Delta HR = \frac{C_{max} HR_{max} - C_{min} HR_{min}}{\Delta C}$$

U_m is given by (9.19)

So far we have rearranged the value of the power plant into a combination of a spark spread on the incremental capacity (between min and max level), the incremental capacity-weighted heat rate, the forward spark spread at minimum heat rate, and the fixed start-up cost. All are obviously conditioned on the state of the facility U_m.

Using the law of iterated expectations and the properties of conditional expectations, we can exploit the fact the U_m depends only upon information at time $m-1$ (absent outages):

$$V_0^n = \sum_{m=t_n}^{M} e^{-r(m-t_0)} E_{t_0}^*(\{\Delta CE_{m-1}^*[\max(P_m - \Delta HR \cdot G_m - VOM, 0)] +$$

$$C_{min}[E_{m-1}^*(P_m) - HR_{min} E_{m-1}^*(G_m) - VOM]\} U_m - FCS \cdot \max[(U_{m+1} - U_m), 0]\})$$

$$(9.21)$$

If we make the unrealistic assumption that we always shut down the unit at the end of the on-peak period and restart it during off-peak if the previous on-peak spark spread exceeded the shadow price (and we aggregate super-peak and peak hours into on-peak), we get:

$$V_0^n = \sum_{m'=t_n}^{M'} e^{-r(m'-t_0)} E_{t_0}^*(\{\Delta CE_{m-1}^*[\max(P_{m'}^{OnPeak} - \Delta HR \cdot G_{m'}^{OnPeak} -$$

$$VOM, 0)] + C_{min} E_{m'-1}^*(P_{m'}^{OnPeak}) - HR_{min} E_{m'-1}^*(G_{m'}^{OnPeak}) - FSC\} \cdot U_{m'})$$

$$(9.22)$$

where the summation m' now covers only on-peak periods (off-peak contributes only start-up cost so we roll them into the on-peak period). Given this assumption, $U_{m'}$ is given by

$$U_{m'} = I_{\{E_{m-1}^*[P_{m'}] - \Delta HR \cdot E_{m'-1}^*[G_{m'}] - VOM \geq \chi'\}}$$

$$(9.23)$$

Here we express the dispatch rule in terms of conditional expectations instead of previous term prices. This formulation is actually more general; we can formulate the optimal start-up rule in many ways. The particular description we use is motivated by ease of analysis. Assuming that χ is positive, we can rewrite equation (9.22) as:

$$V_0^n = \sum_{m'=t_n}^{M'} e^{-r(m'-t_0)} E_{t_0}^*(\{\Delta CE_{m-1}^*[\max(P_{m'}^{OnPeak} - \Delta HR \cdot G_{m'}^{OnPeak} - VOM, 0)] +$$

$$C_{min} E_{m'-1}^*(P_{m'}^{OnPeak}) - HR_{min} E - FSC\} \cdot I_{[E_{m'-1}^*(P_{m'}) - \Delta HR \cdot E_{m'-1}^*(G_{m'}) - VOM \geq \chi']}) =$$

$$\sum_{m'=t_n}^{M'} e^{-r(m'-t_0)} E_{t_0}^*[\{\Delta CE_{m-1}^*[\max(P_{m'}^{OnPeak} - \Delta HR \cdot G_{m'}^{OnPeak} - VOM, 0)$$

$$I_{[E_{m-1}^*[P_{m'}] - \Delta HR \cdot E_{m-1}^*[G_{m'}] - VOM \geq \chi']} + C_{min}[E_{m'-1}^*(P_{m'}^{OnPeak}) - HR_{min} E_{m'-1}^*(G_{m'}^{OnPeak}) - VOM]$$

$$I_{[E_{m'-1}^*(P_{m'}) - \Delta HR \cdot E_{m'-1}^*(G_{m'}) - VOM \geq \chi']} + FSC \cdot I_{\{E_{m'-1}^*(P_{m'}) - \Delta HR \cdot E_{m'-1}^*(G_{m'}) - VOM \geq \chi'\}}] \quad (9.24)$$

If we ignore the differences in optimal exercise regions, we can approximate the first term of the above sum by the following:

$$V_{0;m'}^n \approx C_{max} \cdot \left[SS_{t_0}^{m'}(\Delta HR, VOM + \chi') - \left(\frac{FSC}{C_{max}} - \chi' \right) DSS_{t_0}^{m'}(\Delta HR, VOM + \chi') \right] +$$

$$e^{-r(m'-t_0)} E_{t_0}^* \left[(\Delta HR \cdot E_{m'-1}(G_{m'}^{onpeak}) - HR_{min}) I_{[E_{m'-1}^*(P_{m'}) - \Delta HR \cdot E_{m'-1}^*(G_{m'}) - VOM \geq \chi']} \right]$$

$$(9.25)$$

where
SS is a standard spark-spread option with ΔHR heat rate and the strike price shifted by the shadow price. DSS is a digital spark spread with identical parameters.

The monthly value of the facility is then given by the following:

$$V_0^n = \sum_{m'=t_n}^{M'} V_{0;m'}^n \qquad (9.26)$$

We managed to decompose the value of the unit into a strip of digital and standard spark spread options. As long as our risk aversion is not significant, the shadow price will be positive and smaller than fixed start-up costs per unit of capacity. This obviously shows that our exposure is composed of one strip of long spark-spread positions, and another strip of short digital spark-spread option positions.

The above formulation is written in terms of daily time intervals, but we can extend to weekly or monthly start-up decisions. This actually reflects the decision cycle of many utilities that usually make weekly start-up and shutdown decisions only at the end of the week, or if prices during the week decrease considerably.

We can easily extend the above analysis by introducing four weekly start-up decisions. This would result in individual (weekly) terms having the following form:

$$V_{0;m}^n \approx \sum_{k=t_m}^{K} \left\{ C_{max} \cdot \left[SS_{t_0}^k(\Delta HR, VOM + \chi') - \left(\frac{FSC}{KC_{max}} - \chi' \right) DSS_{t_0}^k(\Delta HR, VOM + \chi') \right] \right.$$

$$\left. + e^{-r(m'-t_0)} E_{t_0}^* \left[(\Delta HR \cdot E_{m'-1}(G_{m'}^{onpeak}) - HR_{min}) I_{[E_{m'-1}^*(P_{m'}) - \Delta HR \cdot E_{m'-1}^*(G_{m'}) - VOM \geq \chi']} \right] \right\} \quad (9.27)$$

The above sum covers all the subperiods within the week (off-peak and on-peak). The expression is in principle a random sum (*K* is a random variable) since, by assumption, we can shut down the unit during the week if spreads (or their expectations) fall too low. This consideration can significantly complicate the analysis, because *K* is correlated with the payoffs of the component spread options. We do not elaborate further on this point, since that would take us far afield.

As long as the likelihood of a shutdown is not high, the approximation should work well (K = maximum number of periods). This clearly is driven by the structure of price distribution: if current (forward) spreads are positive and volatilities are not too high, the approximation can work well. Even if volatility is high, but option prices exhibit significant skew for OTM options (e.g., spikes), the approximation is still applicable.

In the previous chapter we examined the behavior of digital options, and noted their very unstable behavior close to expiration and around at-the-money. Consequently, if we hedge a unit close to expiration—a month or two away—with the heat rate close to the implied heat rate of the market, we should expect a very significant gamma. This implies that small changes in the spark spread lead to large changes in deltas, but this does not exhaust the list of challenges: the gamma of digital options is not only high, but it can also potentially switch signs. A similar situation applies to vegas: they can switch their signs as well. For ATM digital options the gamma and vega are negative. Since we implicitly own a short digital option position, the gamma and vegas are positive. When the options move into the money our gamma position becomes negative while the vega position stays positive. This implies that if we implement ATM daily option positions to hedge out the gamma and vega risks, as the option moves ITM the vega hedge still works but the gamma hedge deteriorates. This problem can be nontrivial, because the only effective hedging instruments are ATM daily gas and power options. Their liquidity is limited, though, so trading in and out is not cost-effective. One possibility is to take a quasi-static position and readjust it infrequently. For more details about hedging digital options see Taleb (1996).

We will see in later sections that the behavior of hedging parameters, even in the more general case, qualitatively resembles the behavior of a short digital option position. Equation 9.27 helps us understand the drivers of this behavior in simple terms, while allowing a reduction of even the most complex constraints.

Operational Characteristics and Their Interaction with Price Behavior

Under what circumstances, and for what types of units, must one worry about the limitations imposed by various operational characteristics of the units? We cannot give an answer to this question; the possible combinations are endless. Our goal here is to illustrate the issues by using the methodologies developed in previous sections and in Appendix B.

The theme of the analysis is that the operational constraints on a unit ultimately represent limitations on its available optionality. Consequently, in situations where the time value of an option is a large part of the overall value of a unit, we can expect the relative impact of any of the constraints to be high. It is always worthwhile to start any analysis of a unit by looking

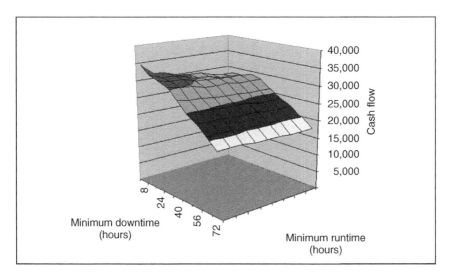

FIGURE 9.3 Peaking Unit Cash Flow As a Function of Minimum Runtime and Downtime

at the simplified spark-spread analysis (see previous sections). If the time value of the option is a large percentage of its value, we should model all the relevant constraints fully and accurately.

This suggests a complementary look at the issue: We must investigate the distributional properties of prices as well as the operational constraints. To put the issue in a very simplistic way: High volatility is likely to interact closely with physical constraints.

We present the analysis by showing the response of monthly cash flows to perturbations in physical constraints, using representative summer and winter months. We examine three types of units: a gas baseload unit with a heat rate of 7,000, a gas peaking unit with a heat rate of 11,000, and a gas cycling unit with a heat rate of 9,000. The unit characteristics are shown in Table 9.6.

Given our earlier argument, we should expect the peaking and cycling units to exhibit high sensitivities.

Figure 9.3 shows the impact of changes in minimum runtimes and minimum downtimes for the peaking unit.

The impact of increasing minimum downtime is significantly higher than that of minimum runtime. This reflects the fact that even if we cannot shut down the unit, we can still make operational decisions to minimize losses by ramping it down. There is no comparable flexibility when the unit is down. Since the unit is close to the money, this ability to exploit the operational flexibility is a large part of the value of the plant. This makes minimum downtime restrictions very expensive. As we can see, increasing minimum downtime from eight hours to three days (though arguably an unlikely case) halves the value of the plant. Similar behavior applies for the cycling unit.

TABLE 9.6 Unit Characteristics

	Capacity (MW)	Minimum Run Capacity (MW)	Ramp Rate (MW/min)	Forced Outage Rate (%)	Heat Rate at Maximum (Btu/kWh)	Heat Rate at Minimum (Btu/kWh)	Variable O&M $/MWh	Start-up Cost (fixed) ($/start-up)	Minimum Downtime (hours)	Minimum Runtime (hours)
Baseload	500	100	12	4.50%	7,000	7,000	0.5	10,000	8	8
Peaking	100	50	12	4.50%	11,000	11,000	0.5	2,000	8	8
Cycling	500	100	12	4.50%	9,000	15,000	0.5	10,000	10	10

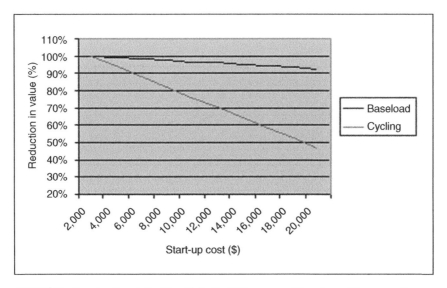

FIGURE 9.4 Baseload and Cycling Unit Cash Flow As a Function of Start-up Costs

For the baseload plant, the impact of the constraints will be relatively small, at most 10%, because the unit is deeper in the money and the constraints do not impose significant costs by restricting its available flexibility.

Figure 9.4 shows relative cash flow changes as a function of increasing start-up costs for cycling and baseload units (peaking is quite similar to cycling).

As before, the value of the operational options is relatively higher for cycling or peaking units. Consequently, start-up costs, which can be seen as the price of exercising this flexibility (the option premium), have a relatively larger impact on the value of this type of unit. Finally, Figure 9.5 shows the impact of minimum generation levels on the cash flow of a cycling unit.

The response of the cycling unit is quite significant, reflecting that the volume of the available optionality drops with increasing minimum capacity. This makes the remaining volume relatively more expensive, while the start-up cost (the premium) stays the same.

This also suggests an interaction with minimum downtime and start-up costs: As those two items increase, the sensitivity of cash flow to minimum dispatch level increases. This is obviously driven by the fact that as the cost of making operational options available increases, we are less likely to reacquire them (start the unit up) and more likely to cycle the unit down to avoid shutting it down altogether.

The baseload unit is significantly in-the-money; consequently the ability to lower the dispatch level contributes little to its value.

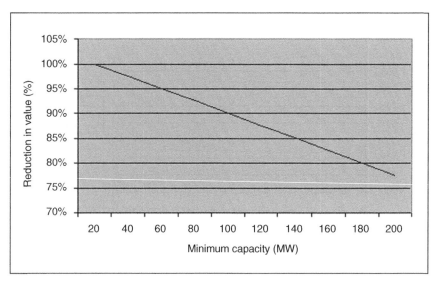

FIGURE 9.5   Cycling Unit Cash Flow As a Function of Minimum Generation Level

The peaking unit, on the other hand, is significantly out-of-the-money. It generates power only if the (spot) spark spread increases significantly. Sufficiently high spark spreads are likely to occur only during on-peak hours. During off-peak hours the peaking unit incurs significant losses even if it runs at a minimum dispatch. Therefore, it is optimal to shut down the unit during off-peak—and also during on-peak if the cash spark spread becomes negative for any number of hours. The ability to cycle down is not worth much in this context. If we increased the cost of start-up significantly, the sensitivity would increase as well. Again, this is because start-up costs can be seen as the premium we pay for gaining access to the spark-spread options. If the premium is very high we are willing to incur the off-peak losses, in order to retain the option without paying the premium over and over again.

These considerations bring out another dimension of generation plant valuation: compound option structure. Start-up costs can be seen as the strike price of the overlying call on a strip of spark-spread calls. In this light, shutting a unit down can be seen as selling a strip of spark-spread options as well as avoiding a negative cash flow from the spark spread at the minimum capacity.

Hedging Power Plants

In this section we review a number of useful hedging coefficients, which should not be confused with model sensitivities. The goal of looking at hedging parameters is to understand the formation and evolution of a hedging portfolio. Naturally, the model choice and hedging are related. Hedging achieves two things, however: it removes risk and limits exposure to model assumptions. The more products we use for hedging, the less we must worry about model assumptions. Hedging is a buy-one-get-one-free policy in reverse: sell risk and sell assumptions about risk.

For example, correlation is not a quantity that trades, and consequently we are not interested in a correlation hedge coefficient. On the other hand, by convention, implied volatilities do trade, so it is useful to look at the corresponding hedges (vegas).

As we saw in equations (9.25) and (9.26), the value of a power plant can be represented as a strip of daily (and hourly) digital and standard spark-spread calls (and potentially compound options). The liquid tools usually available for hedging are BOM contracts inside of the month, forward contracts, and monthly and daily options outside the month.

From Chapter 2 we know that the highest liquidity can be found in on-peak forward and BOM contracts. On-peak monthly and daily options rank second in liquidity, while off-peak forwards and BOM contracts trade only sporadically. Off-peak options basically do not trade at all.

Deltas

On-peak deltas are the deltas of the cash flow with respect to forward contracts (or BOM contracts). Using the formulations in problems (9.25) and (9.26), we can calculate the deltas by differentiating the monthly cash-flow function with respect to the underlying on-peak and off-peak forward contracts:

$$\Delta_n^{OnPeak} = \frac{\partial V_0^n}{\partial F_n^{OnPeak}}$$

$$\Delta_n^{OffPeak} = \frac{\partial V_0^n}{\partial F_n^{OffPeak}} \tag{9.28}$$

$$\Delta_n^{Fuel} = \frac{\partial V_0^n}{\partial F_n^{Fuel}}$$

Figure 9.6 shows a series of on-peak deltas for peaking, cycling, and baseload units as a function of the price level.

The forward gas price used for the above calculations is such that the baseload unit is ATM at $30, the cycling unit is ATM at $37, while the peaking unit is ATM at $45. The cycling and baseload units both have similar ATM deltas, but the peaking unit's ATM delta is significantly lower.

In our experience, forward hedges alone can remove around 30% to 40% of cash flow volatility; when combined with forward volatility hedges,

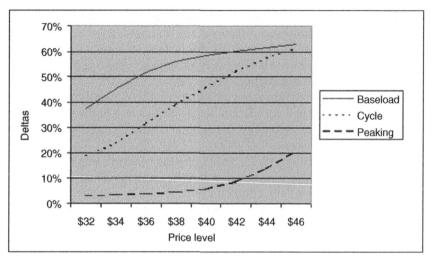

FIGURE 9.6   Generation Unit Deltas

the percentage can grow to 50% to 60%. One of the challenges of forward delta hedging is the substantial basis between forward prices and average intramonth spot prices (see Chapter 3). Spot prices can average $40/MW in the spot market, while the forward expires at $140/MW and, vice versa, with significant impact on the performance of forward hedges. The solution is to use BOM contracts for hedging inside the month. Although the correlation of BOM and spot prices is not that high, the performance of the combined hedging strategy (usually augmented by trading daily/index options and possibly some structured products) can be quite good. Again, in our experience (which is by no means applicable in every circumstance), the combined strategy can remove upwards of 80% of cash flow variance.

An aside here: The fact that the BOM hedge is so effective, despite at times weak correlation with spot prices, may be a little puzzling. The reason is that the volatility of BOM contracts is quite high in some markets (at times as high as 70% of spot on-peak volatility). We can treat BOM hedges as effective forward sales in the BOM market. Since the volatility is not much smaller, the option value of generation in the BOM market is correspondingly high. Additionally, we always have the ability to exploit the optionality between the BOM and spot markets from which we can collect additional revenue.

Finally, we must be careful about the use of heuristics and approximations in dispatch when considering hedging parameters. Hedges, unlike values, are very sensitive to the choice of approximation, a result of their high sensitivity to operational characteristics.

Consider the following example. If a unit has a constant marginal heat curve, then the optimal operation levels—assuming infinite ramp rates—are maximum or minimum capacity. If the heat curve exhibits even the slightest nonconstancy (say, a very small linear term), there are intermediate optimal operational levels. Assume that the optimal levels are C_{min}, C_{max}, and $(C_{max} + C_{min})/2$. If the market implied heat rate (power price divided by fuel price) is close to the unit (average) heat rate, the resulting delta position will differ markedly depending on the approximation chosen for the heat curve. If the unit is in-the-money, the delta will be close to the maximum capacity for the constant heat curve; on the other hand, using linear approximation, the delta is much closer to mid-point capacity. For a large unit, the difference might be as high as several hundred megawatts. The difference in the value induced by the heat curve differences is not significant (at most 10%), while the hedges can be increased or lowered by 50%.

Ultimately, the problem underscores the need to align hedging strategies closely with operational ones. The impact of the misalignment need not be significant though. In the above example, we are exposed to the risk of ending up with a (physical) short position equal to the capacity of the unit, while the optimal operational level finds the unit generating, for example, only half of that. Obviously, if the approximation with a flat marginal heat curve is very close, the gain from operating at the lower level is small. That in turn implies that the loss from a mismatch between hedges and generation is small as well, and that it exactly offsets the operational gain.

The ultimate impact of the mismatch is then the financial unwinding of the operational strategy. The financial effect is such that the cash flow from our portfolio (plant plus hedges) is equal to the cash flow of a plant operating at maximum capacity. We succeeded in turning a plant with a linear heat curve into one with a flat heat curve, and lost money in the process. Yes, financial technology can change the world. However, our success is only a financial one: In pool markets, there is only the financial effect, and the operational strategy is unchanged. The missing megawatts are supplied from the market, and since there is only one market clearing price, the financial effect is identical to that of our increasing generation to meet the short position. In bilateral markets, where we are faced with an effective bid-ask spread, we are better off increasing generation from our unit to supply the short position. This strategy lets us avoid paying the (cash) bid-ask spread. All of this reflects a larger principle: In pool markets, hedges have no impact on operations; in bilateral markets, the impact is driven by the cash bid-ask spread.

As we can see, if the extra value from optimal operations is significant, we must pay close attention to calculating hedges accurately. This lets us recover additional value, but there are limits to our ability to do that. Nonlinear effects in operational constraints tend to induce significant gammas. Large gammas imply significant trading costs induced by the need to adjust our deltas as forward prices move. The effect is strong close to expiration for assets with heat rates close to the market implied heat rate (ATM spark-spread options). Consequently, we are going pay the forward bid-ask spread to avoid the cash one. The trade-off between effective hedging of the additional value (monetizing the value) and the costs involved is driven by the relative sizes of the two bid-ask spreads, as well as by the volatilities of the prices and moneyness of the unit in question.

The upshot of this argument is that under certain circumstances it literally pays to ignore the operational complexities.

Gammas

Monthly gammas of the generation plant are given by a familiar expression:

$$\Gamma_n^{OnPeak} = \frac{\partial^2 V_0^n}{(\partial F_n^{OnPeak})^2}$$

$$\Gamma_n^{OffPeak} = \frac{\partial^2 V_0^n}{(\partial F_n^{OffPeak})^2} \tag{9.29}$$

$$\Gamma_n^{Fuel} = \frac{\partial^2 V_0^n}{(\partial F_n^{Fuel})^2}$$

In Figure 9.6 we showed the evolution of deltas over time to expiry. As we can see the peaking unit exhibits significant changes in deltas close to expiration. This obviously is expected, since the short digital option position, due to start-up costs, induces high gamma close to expiration. For baseload units the gamma is much more manageable, since the option is substantially in-the-money.

The high gamma close to expiration is a significant challenge in effective hedging. The implication is that we must frequently trade in and out of our positions. This carries two costs: the bid-ask spread and slippage. We are forced to travel through the bid-ask spread frequently, and the market can have limited depth, with which comes the problem of prices moving against a trader in a transaction of significant volume (slippage). Some forward markets have little ability to handle more than a couple hundred megawatts before the price is significantly affected.

Off-peak–On-peak Cross Delta

The cash flow representation in equation (9.26) contains both on-peak and off-peak terms. We can rewrite the individual terms of the sum in terms of on-peak and off-peak contributions:

$$V_0^n = V_0^{n;OnPeak} + V_0^{n;OffPeak} \tag{9.30}$$

This separation can be useful in achieving a better understanding of risks and sources of value. When we make such a separation, however, we must account for cross delta effects, that is, for the impact of forward off-peak prices on on-peak cash flows, and of on-peak prices on off-peak values. A useful measure is the cross delta(s):

$$
\Delta_n^{OnPeak;OffPeak} = \frac{\partial V_0^{n;OnPeak}}{\partial F_n^{OffPeak}}
$$

$$
\Delta_n^{OffPeak;OnPeak} = \frac{\partial V_0^{n;OffPeak}}{\partial F_n^{OnPeak}}
$$

(9.31)

The cross effects are induced by the dependencies among cash-flow components, which in turn are induced by start-up and runtime constraints. For example, cycling units are quite unlikely to run during off-peak hours if off-peak prices are low. An increase in off-peak prices may make it optimal to run the unit during those hours and to run it longer. This higher utilization level gives us an opportunity to exploit high prices during on-peak hours more frequently. It is easy to see that higher off-peak prices mean higher on-peak cash flow. We find then that the on-peak–off-peak delta is positive.

Again, conceptually, off-peak hours are the premium we pay for helping ourselves to on-peak optionality (i.e., the margin is negative). If the premium is lower we are more likely to buy the option (i.e., run the unit) and consequently, to make more money overall.

Month-to-Month Cross Delta

The representation in (9.26) is an approximation of (9.15). The difference lies in the impact of decisions in one month on another. As we mentioned before, this effect is relatively small as long as there are no cumulative constraints and runtime constraints are limited. Another way of expressing the same fact is by saying that the monthly cross delta (and possibly cross vega) is small:

$$
\Delta_{n;k}^{OnPeak} = \frac{\partial V_0^n}{\partial F_k^{OnPeak}} \approx 0
$$

(9.32)

There is one important issue associated with cross-delta, and with month-to-month dependence: Intertemporal correlations between forward contracts have no impact on valuation or hedging power plants if equation (9.32) is true. This is a simple consequence of the fact that the month-to-month operations of power plants are not dependent on each other—with little operational dependence, there is little cash flow dependence. From this it follows that the overall cash flow and hedges are not dependent on intertemporal correlations. Since we are not able to hedge out all the risks associated with power plants, the overall variance of cash flow may still be affected by the correlations. This is the case, however, only if the portfolio

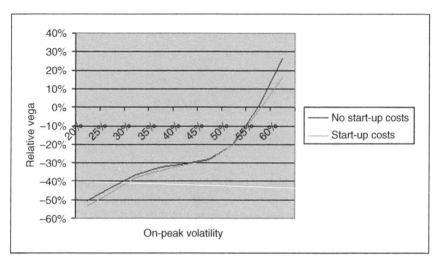

FIGURE 9.7 Baseload Unit ATM Implied Vega

cash flows (i.e., generation unit plus all the hedges) are correlated across various months. If correlations or spikes across various months were correlated, for example, then we would expect the variability of the overall portfolio cash flow to be affected by the intertemporal correlations.

On-peak Monthly (Power) Vegas

Monthly vegas are cash-flow sensitivities with respect to implied monthly volatility:

$$v_n^{Monthly} = \frac{\partial V_0^n}{\partial \sigma_n^{Monthly}} \qquad (9.33)$$

The above measure should not be confused with sensitivities to the parameter of the model called volatility. The relationship between implied volatilities and parametric volatilities may not be simple (see Chapter 4 for details). We are interested here in hedging coefficients, and not in sensitivities to model parameters. The two are potentially very different things. Vegas with respect to implied volatilities give us the appropriate option ATM hedging positions scaled for forward prices. Figures 9.7 and 9.8 show the response of baseload and peaking units to changes in monthly volatilities.

We express the vegas as a percentage of the unit value. We can easily see that the relative impact of changes in volatility is much higher for the peaking unit as one would expect for an out-of-the-money option.

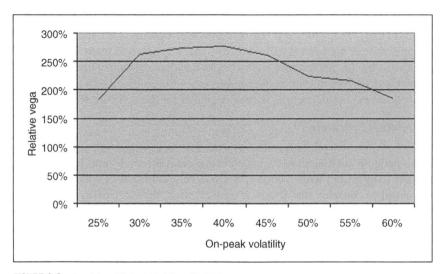

FIGURE 9.8   Peaking Unit ATM Implied Vega

The peaking unit is long volatility, while the baseload unit is actually short volatility. This surprising effect comes from the fact that the vega of a spread option can depend on its moneyness. Since we are looking at the sensitivity of the spread option value with respect to the ATM implied volatility, the standard rules for the sign of spread option vegas (see Chapter 8), must be modified by the sensitivity of OTM and ITM "implied" volatilities to changes in ATM implied volatility. If this sensitivity is negative, the sign will change.

For our example we chose a market (NYPOOL) in which sensitivities are negative for ITM options and positive for OTM options. Consequently, baseload units are likely to have negative vegas (short ATM volatility), while peaking units tend to have positive vega (long ATM volatility). There is also an impact on implied correlation to consider, but if the change in implied volatility is not too dramatic, in our experience, this consideration is rather small.

Again, we underscore that quantities such as implied OTM volatility are not necessarily traded contracts. We develop a model for the evolution of prices, and from the resulting distributions we construct volatility and correlation surfaces. In other words, the terminology of implied volatilities and correlations is just a language with which we describe our model. The choice of language is not accidental, however: it helps us naturally express the behavior of assets and financial contracts in terms of tradables.

As we saw in previous sections, generation units can be represented approximately as a sum of a long spark-spread call position and a short digital spark-spread call. The digital almost always has a vega opposite in sign to the standard call, except for deep out-of-the-money options (see Chapter 8). This suggests that in the presence of start-up costs, a generation plant should have a higher vega (in magnitude) than should an identical unit without start-up costs. Figure 9.7 shows the graph of vega when the baseload unit has no start-up costs. As expected, the vega is always smaller for the unit with start-up costs.

Correlation Sensitivity?

A discussion of correlation sensitivity is a bit unconventional, since we analyze a hedging coefficient here, which is usually quite irrelevant. In the Black-Scholes (Margrabe) world, correlation has an unambiguous meaning, but in the world of complex distributions we deal with, there are many correlation coefficients among factors (see Chapter 6 for details). Analyzing all their sensitivities, although instructive, may not be fruitful. We can analyze the sensitivity of cash flow with respect to implied correlation instead. The problem with this suggestion is that implied correlation is a function of not only the dependence structure but also of the marginal distributions. It follows then that changes in implied volatilities imply changes in implied correlations.

To be able to separate the "pure" correlations effects and volatility effects ordinarily requires a model. We can see the vicious circle closing in on us. However, the procedure that we employed in Chapter 6 for adjusting historical estimates of correlations (and covariances) can be employed to adjust the implied correlations in response to changes in implied volatilities. This method demands fewer assumptions about the behavior of prices than constructing explicit models.

Overall, the sensitivity of implied correlation to small changes in implied volatilities tends to be quite small.

Plant Operation: Risk and Hedging in Practice

The overriding consideration in the practical applications of the techniques described above is the stability of the resulting values, dispatch policies, and hedges.

Our knowledge of the underlying distributions and processes is quite limited. In situations where the details of our operating strategy depend heavily on the specifics of the distribution, exact optimization might not be called for.

This is further complicated by the problem's large dimension. As described in Chapter 1, the power market often consists of many separate (although related) cash markets. Apart from the standard energy product, an operator can be faced with as many as seven ancillary services markets (e.g., NEPOOL).

Furthermore, the cash markets often operate in multisettlement arrangements (see Chapter 1) where the decision of when to commit the resource in question can be a nontrivial one.

Also in several markets the very structure of the commitment decision can be subject to an operator's decision. In NYPOOL, for example, the structure of the bid can be three-dimensional: the generator can bid separately the energy, no-load, and start-up components. In PJM, a generator has a choice of bidding in the so-called "market" or "cost" schemes. Depending on its choice, the payments received and the risks taken on can vary dramatically.

Additionally, the highly skewed (spiky) nature of power prices makes optimization in expectation a potentially hazardous undertaking. When committing a unit in early settlement stages, we often take the outage risk upon ourselves. If the cash prices explode to very high levels in real-time and at the same time the merchant unit in question undergoes a forced outage—however unlikely the joint occurrence—the generator can suffer catastrophic losses. This exposure arises from the generator's commitment to supplying certain amount of power. If it's not available from its own physical unit, the merchant is forced to deliver by buying the needed power in the cash market.

No matter how attractive the early commitment might look in expectation, rare extreme events can significantly impact even the viability of an operator.

If anyone thinks that this is just a fancy theoretical possibility, they should consider the fate of a number of power marketers caught short one bad afternoon in the summer of 1998 in ECAR.

The extreme left skewness of cash-flow distribution can have significant impact on the optimal strategies pursued by a merchant. The dispatch decision is affected, and the effect can induce dependencies in the dispatch strategies of a portfolio of units. The generator will likely hold part of his portfolio for later dispatch as a physical hedge against an extreme event.

Consequently, we will be faced with a joint portfolio dispatch problem, with the objective function having terms corresponding to the relevant risks (e.g., kurtosis of the cash flow). The multidimensional nature of the problem, coupled with its nonlinear structure, will greatly complicate the optimization problem.

Finally, the information traders rely on to dispatch the units is not limited only to the price information (which is scarce as it is). As we discussed in previous chapters, there is usually a great wealth of other information such as short-term weather forecasts, rumors about pending or occurring outages, and short squeezes. These can all have impact on the optimal strategies.

In principle, the only thing that matters for dispatch is the future price distribution. Ultimately, nonprice information is used to form conditional forecasts of the price distribution. Consequently, if we could only calibrate a sufficiently rich conditional price process, we could plug it into our stochastic optimization and optimize away.

Hopefully, after reading Chapters 3 and 4, the reader will understand how challenging this task is likely to be.

This overwhelming complexity leads to simplified approaches, in which one uses heuristics to help manage the complexity and to dispatch plants reasonably well. In point of fact, the simplistic assumption of constant shadow prices, which we used in a previous section as an illustration of the concept, is actually more realistic than the full-blown stochastic optimization problems.

This is not to imply that more sophisticated approaches cannot be used. Far from it: In certain markets, where the structure of the cash markets is simpler, they can be very robust. Also, in some cases we might be able to reduce the complexity of the problem by first considering the simplified problem, and then adjusting (fudging) the results to reflect the additional considerations—performing a poor man's (or woman's) Lagrange relaxation, as it were.

Long-term Cumulative Constraints

The analysis in the preceding sections relied on the assumption that decisions made in one month do not have much impact in subsequent months. This enables us to separate valuation and hedging into smaller subperiods.

The approximation fails when we consider cumulative operational constraints. The simplest example is an annual emission cap. In certain markets emissions are not managed through a pricing mechanism (see Chapter 1), but through plant- or subsystem-specific restrictions on total volume of emissions. Emission credits are essentially a market-wide opportunity cost of emissions. In the explicit scheme, individual operators have to explicitly optimize the operation given this constraint.

We can always reformulate our stochastic program and include additional constraints. The price implied by the extension, however, can be very steep in computational performance. Effectively, every generation decision made by the operator must be weighed against its long-range impact. We can again employ some shadow price heuristics to include the opportunity cost, but it is not easy to find an approximation that performs well under many circumstances.

Fortunately, there is a direct way of resolving the problem. Unlike with the dispatch decision in the short term, we usually have forward-looking information on future prices and volatilities in tradable form. Instead of performing a stochastic optimization (or its approximation), we can perform a static one on the trade-off between operations today and the value of future operations, as estimated from the current values of forward prices and volatilities. The following example will make those issues clearer.

EXAMPLE 9.3 *Multi-period constraint valuation*

Consider a three-month valuation problem, for a simple generation unit with no operational constraints. The current operational value is given by the current (spot) spark-spread option. The emission cap is such that it allows us to run our unit two out of the three available months. The value of the plant in the individual months is given by the following:

$$V^1 = \max(P_1 - HR \cdot G_1, 0)$$
$$V^2 = \max(P_2 - HR \cdot G_2, 0)$$
$$V^3 = \max(P_3 - HR \cdot G_3, 0)$$

In principle we must now perform a stochastic dynamic optimization (as described in Appendix B). However, due to the presence of forward markets, we can turn the dynamic optimization into a static one, by optimizing concurrently with respect to the current spot price and current forward prices and volatilities.

The optimization proceeds as follows: When we arrive at time 1 we evaluate the following three quantities:

$$V^1 = \max(P_1 - HR \cdot G_1, 0)$$
$$V_1^{2;F} = E_1[\max(F_2^P - HR \cdot F_2^G, 0)]$$
$$V_1^{3;F} = E_1[\max(F_3^P - HR \cdot F_3^G, 0)]$$

The F stands for forward prices. Note that the expectations in the above are with respect to forward prices (the hedgeable value) and not spot prices. Since the forward prices and volatilities for future periods 2 and 3 are known, we can evaluate the expectations at time 1. Now we perform the optimization by sorting the values from highest to the lowest and choosing the two highest. If the V^1 is among the two chosen, it is optimal to consume one unit of emission allotment at time 1. We continue forward to time 2. If at time 2 the following holds:

$$V^2 \geq V_2^{3;F}$$
$$V^2 = \max(P_2 - HR \cdot G_2, 0)$$
$$V_2^{3;F} = E_2[\max(F_3^P - HR \cdot F_3^G, 0)]$$

we use up the second part of the allotment at time 2. Otherwise, we wait until time 3 to generate. As long as the forward markets are reasonably efficient, the resulting value will be equivalent to the one derived through a dynamic program (and backward induction) on a risk-adjusted basis. For detailed exposition of the topic, see Wolyniec (2002).

The presence of forward markets allows us to turn a backward induction problem into a forward induction one. The big advantage of the latter is its reduction of the dynamic optimization problem into a static one.

Forward induction is much easier to implement efficiently, and an ideal tool for this purpose is a Monte Carlo simulation. The price we pay for the reduction is an increase in the size of the static problem, and increase in the dimensionality of the price process. Instead of dealing with one spot process we must introduce the joint evolution of spot prices and the forward curve(s).

The approach discussed in Example 9.3 is essentially equivalent to the valuation problem of a multi-period swing (recall) option and storage facilities we considered in Chapter 8.

The hedging implications of the long-term constraint are the increase in month-to-month cross deltas and cross vegas.

Portfolio Valuation

As we argued repeatedly in previous sections, in pool markets individual units can be analyzed in isolation from other units or physical assets (e.g., fuel storage, load contracts, and so on.)

The conclusion does not follow under the following circumstances:

- Common operational constraints
- Nonzero effective bid-ask spread in (cash) fuel and power markets (bilateral markets)
- Finite price elasticity in response to our operational decisions

System-wide (marginal) restriction on emissions, or generation levels directly, can induce operational dependencies. For example, if we have two units fired by two different fuels (e.g., oil and gas) with system-wide marginal emission caps, a decision about which unit to run depends not only on the relevant spark spreads (power-to-oil and power-to-natural gas), but also on the emission efficiency of the units. If their emission rates are constant, and the cap is such that we can run only one unit at full capacity while the other is limited to only half capacity, a decision on which unit runs depends on both the relevant spark spreads and the oil–natural gas spread.

Nonzero cash bid-ask spreads lead to joint optimization of resources. For example, if we have a storage facility located at an illiquid location close to our generation plant, we might be able to extract additional value by using fuel from the storage facility instead of sourcing in the spot market. The value contribution is only as large as the effective bid-ask spread (possibly induced by transportation costs to and from a liquid point). Consequently, the usual way of accounting for those effects is to value the portfolio separately at bid-and-ask prices. The difference is the maximum gain (never attainable) we can extract from joint optimization of resources.

The final consideration is the impact of our dispatch and other operational decisions on prices. If we are perfect price takers, there is no issue. If, however, prices react to our dispatch decisions—adversely, as they usually do—we must take it into account, as long as it is legal to do so.

Up to now we have been concentrating on the value (cash flow) portfolio effects. We might want to consider the impact of the structure of the portfolio and operational decisions on risk. However, we must be careful how we do this. As long as there is no cash flow impact, there is no impact on hedge coefficients. It follows then that if we can hedge out all the risk, there is no portfolio effect whatsoever. The reason is that, with perfect hedging, the values of the subcomponents of the portfolio become certain. If there is no risk, there is no portfolio effect. This suggests that portfolio effects exist whenever there is correlation between *residual* risks. In other words, if the (uncertain) residuals of the values of the different subcomponents of the portfolio are correlated, we will see portfolio effects on the risk side.

HYDRO UNITS, REFINERIES, AND OTHER PHYSICAL ASSETS

The methodology of real options, which we applied to thermal generation in the previous section, can be readily extended to other physical assets. We review quickly a couple of simple examples.

Refineries

Refineries process (crack) crude oil into several oil products. Among them we find gasoline, heating oil, fuel oil, residual oil, and so on. Although forward markets in the crude oil are well developed, not all products in the forward market actively trade. This makes effective risk management a challenge. The usual operational flexibilities associated with refineries, which in turn lead to financial optionality tend to have slightly different character from that of power generation. There is the standard crack-spread optionality, fully analogous to the spark spread optionality. Usually, however, the ability of a refinery to vary production levels is quite limited. Minimum production levels are 80% to 90%. The more significant part of optionality comes from the ability to mix the fuel input, that is, different grades of crude, which then can lead to different output mix. Additionally, refineries often have the optionality to further process lower-value product in a higher value one. We do not develop the analysis any further, leaving it as an application of the techniques discussed in the rest of the chapter.

Hydro Units

Hydro generation is especially important in the American Pacific Northwest and in Scandinavia. Only units with reservoirs that can store the water runoff can be fruitfully analyzed with the techniques of the book. For hydro units for which the major portion of energy is generated from the so-called run-of-river, the valuation comes down to understanding the flows of the relevant river. No operational decisions affect generation. Units with reservoirs can be analyzed as storage facilities (see Chapter 8) for which the injection part is uncertain and driven by the river flow. The operational decisions come to timing the withdrawal (the flow) of water from storage to produce electricity. The timing optionality can be analyzed on the seasonal time resolution or even time block one (off-peak–on-peak). We do not offer detailed analysis, referring the reader to Chapter 8 for the details of modeling storage facilities.

WEATHER-CONTINGENT PRODUCTS

Weather Derivatives

In the developing market for weather derivatives, temperature derivatives are the primary types of products trading. However, the basic trading underlying is not the temperature itself but heating-degree days (HDDs) and cooling-degree days (CDDs). The definitions are as follows:

$$HDD_t^T = \sum_{i=t}^{T} \max(65°F - \Im_i, 0)$$

$$CDD_t^T = \sum_{i=t}^{T} \max(\Im_i - 65°F, 0)$$

(9.34)

The OTC markets trade various forward (swap) and option contracts on HDDs and CDDs for a variety of locations and tenors. The most liquid instruments are summer and winter forward contracts, which, in contrast to other energy markets, usually have capped payouts.

EXAMPLE 9.4 *Weather derivatives as a risk management tool*

An LDC decides to control its risk associated with variable gas demand in its service area during the winter. Since the gas demand increases as the number of HDDs is increasing, the company sells a winter (November–March) HDD swap. If, in the coming winter, the number of HDDs is lower than the 10-year average, the company will pay the counterparty $5,000 per one degree of deviation. If the actual number of HDDs exceeds the 10-year average, the company will receive $5,000 per one degree of the difference. The maximum payout is capped at $5,000,000.

The valuation of the basic weather instruments is performed using two main approaches:

Burn Analysis (Historical Simulation). We choose a suitable collection of historical data, calculate the suitable payoffs (averages for swaps) for every year in our sample and then average the results. In the example above, the swap is implicitly priced at the 10-year average. It is in fact a common market practice to quote the prices of swaps as an offset to 10-year averages. Of course, the procedure can become more complicated for options and is probably more suitable for simple linear products. For contingent products, especially OTM options, we must be careful to use sufficiently large samples. Notice, however, that HDD/CDD swaps are usually not linear products (independent of volatility) because of the cap provisions.

Monte Carlo Simulation. This procedure first involves a selection of a suitable process for the evolution of temperature (often estimated on historical data). Then the process is simulated and the average payoffs of the structure in question are calculated to give us the estimate of its fair value.

(Semi) Analytical Approaches. Instead of using simulation we can use some of the analytical methods we analyzed in Chapter 4. We noted there that some GARCH model extensions offer a surprisingly robust fit to temperature data. For example, we can use Fourier-based inversion techniques to value weather structures quickly and efficiently (see Chapter 4).

Once we have derived the fair value of the structure under consideration we need to risk-adjust the resulting value. Both procedures are two different approaches to historical estimation. In general we can attempt to include forward-looking information into pricing. One way is to do it by using forecasts. Usually, the flow information about future weather conditions starts only relatively close to the beginning of the term of the structure. Before then (usually three months), the most sophisticated forecasts are not that much better than long-term historical averages. Incidentally, this suggests that the standard delta-hedging techniques used in derivative markets (both financial and energy) are not likely to work well.

The above analysis concentrates on absolute pricing, more suitable for the insurance world. Relative pricing (the realm of derivative pricing) is complicated by the fact that the weather itself is not a tradable commodity. Consequently, CDD and HDD swaps are not derivative securities in the strict sense. We can attempt to price options in relation to the swaps. The approach is complicated by the fact that the market is fairly fragmented and there are no benchmark liquid products one can use at least for proxy hedging (attempts to establish transparent exchange-based markets in the swaps fizzled). This implies that replication arguments used in pricing options in financial and even energy markets (delta hedging) will largely fail. Also, note that because of the cap provisions on the swaps, even if we had a liquid swap market, the delta-hedging of option contracts would be quite different from the standard procedures.

We can still use the swaps to statistically hedge options. Obviously, the efficiency and details of implementation are dependent on the specifics of the available swap contracts. (Readers interested in learning more about weather derivatives should refer to Geman, 1999 and Banks, 2002.)

Weather Cross-commodity Derivatives

Other weather-related products gaining in importance are cross-commodity products. The attraction of this market is the better fit of those products to the correlated exposures faced by end users. As we argued in Chapter 8 when we discussed load hedging, pure weather contracts are not necessarily useful for hedging volumetric exposure either because of their relative unimportance or the inability to separate price and volumetric risk. This consideration can seriously impede the adoption of the weather products. However, the solution to the second problem are weather cross-commodity products that enable the end user to lay off the price and weather risk at the same time, without worrying about the separation of the component risks. This last task is left to the market makers (energy marketers).

The selection of available products is quite substantial and we cannot cover all the permutations. The most popular are either standard or digital weather contingent options on power or natural gas. The payoffs of those structures are given by the following:

$$C_{\Im,G} = \max([G_T - K_G],0)\max[(\Im_T - K_\Im),0]$$

$$C_{\Im,G}^{Digital} = \max([G_T - K_G],0) \cdot I_{[\Im_\tau - K_\Im > 0]}$$

$$C_{HDD,G} = \max[(HDD_t^T - K_{HDD}),0]\max\left[\left(\sum_{i=t}^{T}\frac{G_t}{T-t} - FOM\right),0\right]$$

$$(9.35)$$

We now consider an example of an actual structure.

EXAMPLE 9.5   *Synthetic peaker*

XTC is a load serving entity in Rhode Island. The utility is concerned about high power prices during periods of high demand in both the summer and winter. They have arranged for a baseload power contract of 400 MW. XTC would like to remove the risk associated with the temperature/load relationship. To achieve this purpose the company enters into the following contract.

Deal specifications

- Price location: NEPOOL
- Price strike: $75
- Temp strike: 83°F
- Deal cap: $5,000,000
- Volume: 200
- Terms: May–September and November–March
- Settlement: Financially settled on an hourly basis during on-peak hours

Deal Structure

$$Payoff = Volume \cdot \max(\Im_t - 83°, 0) \cdot \max\left(P_t - 75\frac{\$}{MW}, 0\right)$$

Valuation of the structures can be always performed with Monte Carlo simulation or burn analysis. The challenge is the integration of the forward looking market information. The correlation issues we discussed in Chapter 6 apply to the weather cross-commodity as well. The natural computational technique for those structures is the one developed by Dempster and Hong (2000) for spread options. In fact, their approach applies more naturally to the above structures than to spread options proper.

CHAPTER 10

Risk Management

RISK ADJUSTMENT

As we amply documented in the previous chapters, the scale of risks facing energy market participants is unprecedented. In this light, the importance of proper managing, or at minimum proper understanding, of the risks is critical for one's ability to make proper investment, operational, and contractual decisions.

In standard corporate finance practice, the adjustment for risk involved discounting the cash flows under consideration with an appropriate risk-adjusted discount rate. The standard approach is only consistent for symmetric cash flows, that is, for cash flows for which the probability of loss is equal to the probability of gain. The fact suggests that for nonlinear derivative products the procedure will not be appropriate. This is, indeed, the case. For nonlinear derivative products, there is no one consistent rate that we can use to discount risky cash flows (see Dixit and Pindyck, 1994). More specifically, if we have two different options (say ATM and OTM) on the same underlying, there is no way of finding one rate to properly discount the two options. There is, however, a consistent way to adjust for risk that we illustrate in the following example. Take two options with two different strike prices K_1 and K_2. The expected cash flows from the two options are given by the following expressions:

$$
\begin{aligned}
V_1 &= E_P[\max(S - K_1, 0)] \\
V_2 &= E_P[\max(S - K_2, 0)]
\end{aligned}
\qquad (10.1)
$$

A proposed risk adjustment involves changing the distribution of the underlying price S (that is, risk neutralizing the distribution; see Duffie (1992), or Hull (1999). Assume that the price S follows the GBM process:

$$
\frac{dS}{S} = \mu dt + \sigma dW
\qquad (10.2)
$$

where

μ is the drift

Then the values of the two options follow this process:

$$\frac{dV_1}{V_1} = \mu_1 dt + \sigma_1 dW$$

$$\frac{dV_2}{V_2} = \mu_2 dt + \sigma_2 dW \tag{10.3}$$

We can easily show (see Hull, 1999) that the following has to hold:

$$\frac{\mu_1 - r}{\sigma_1} = \frac{\mu_2 - r}{\sigma_2} = \lambda \tag{10.4}$$

These ratios are not dependent on the nature of the derivative. For both options the value of the ratio is the same. We denote it by λ and call it *price of risk*. The value depends only on the underlying asset S and not on the specifics of the derivative structure. As such it can be called the price of S risk λ_S. The price of risk is the excess return per unit of volatility. This quantity can be used for consistent adjustment for risk for derivative products on a specific underlying.

If we require a specific excess return over the risk-free rate (per unit of volatility) for S risk, then we should value all derivative products with underlying S by using the risk-adjusted process:

$$\frac{dS^*}{S^*} = (\mu - \lambda_S \sigma)dt + \sigma dW \tag{10.5}$$

Here, λ_S is independently given constant. We use it to adjust for the S risk present in any derivative product. By (10.4), we know that the risk-adjustment will be consistent across all the derivatives that depend on S. Consequently, for (risk-adjusted) pricing of S-derivative products we should consistently use process (10.5), instead of (10.2).

If S is a tradable asset, the value of any derivative is fully hedgeable and then the following has to hold:

$$\lambda_S = \frac{\mu + y - r}{\sigma} \tag{10.6}$$

where y is the net convenience yield (including storage costs). If the S-risk is not fully hedgeable the choice of λ_S depends on the circumstances.

The preceding analysis concentrated on the risk adjustment for standard geometric Brownian motion. For other processes we considered in Chapter 4, the adjustments will have the following structure: In jump-diffusion processes, we need to adjust the jump rate λ

$$\lambda \to \lambda^*$$

to account for the jump-timing risk. We also need to adjust the mean of the jump-size distribution

$$k \to k^*$$

to account for the jump-size risk. As we saw in Chapter 4, we use the compensated jump-diffusion process, and the net drift rate is affected by the product of λ and k. In complete markets (i.e., where all the risks are hedgeable), the relationship between the risk-neutralized parameters of the jump process and the observed actual (empirical) drift μ of the process will be given by the following:

$$\mu - \lambda^* \cdot k^* = r - y$$

If the jump risks are not hedgeable, those parameters are chosen as the free parameters of the process (corporate risk adjustment).

For stochastic volatility processes, we need to adjust the mean-reversion rate of volatility κ:

$$\kappa \to \kappa^*$$

In the fully hedgeable case, we can extract this value from option prices (for example ATM options). If we cannot hedge, the mean-reversion rate becomes a free parameter.

The next two sections examine the issues involved in choosing the appropriate price of risk. In general the risk-adjustment procedure involves the shifting of the drift of the underlying process by the price of risk.

Market Price of Risk

We can recover the so-called market price of risk λ_M from prices of liquidly trading derivatives on the S underlying by using (10.4). The market price of risk corresponds to the aggregate risk preferences of market participants. The issue of recovering of the market price of risk from tradables is given a lot of attention in academic literature (e.g., see Duffie, Pan, and Singleton,

1999). The motivation for this vast effort is the fact that if we can identify all the underlying factors (e.g., price, stochastic volatility, jumps, and so on) and their corresponding market prices of risk (e.g., market price risk for prices, volatility market price of risk, jump market price of risk, and so on), by the results of the previous section, we will be able to price any derivative product consistently with market preferences. In practice, the estimation of market price of risk is a very challenging undertaking. The choice of the factors can have a significant impact on the estimates of the various market prices of risk.

If we have sufficient number of tradables to hedge out all the risks, the search for market price of risk becomes moot. The market price of risk is then implicit in the tradables, but we do not have to know it to be able to price (and hedge) any new products. The new products can be reduced to (possibly dynamic) combinations of the tradables (see Baxter, 1996).

If the number of tradables is insufficient to remove all the risk, then we have to determine the market price of risk to find out what the price of any new product would be if it traded liquidly.

Another use of the concept is in comparing historical (objective) distributions with market-implied ones. The connecting link is exactly the market price of risk. At times we may be interested in knowing the quantity to be able to reconcile the two distributions (see Chapter 4 for examples).

Corporate Price of Risk

The commercial goal of pricing is not to find out what the market would trade at, if it actually traded, but to see whether a given product is a good deal. For that, we only require the knowledge of the available hedging instruments, the residual risk and our personal (corporate) appetite for a specific risk. With these in hand we can easily set our bids and offers without any reference to the esoteric quantities such as market price of risk. Ultimately, we are interested in the commercial viability of our deal-making (and risk management) and not in divining pricing mechanisms of nonexistent markets. Consider Example 10.1.

EXAMPLE 10.1 *Risk adjustment in market-making*

A power marketer is approached by a utility that is interested in buying a power forward contract for ten years in the future. The market-based approach involves finding the price by developing the distribution for the spot price 10 years in the future and then adjusting the resulting expectation by the market price of risk. We usually attempt to extract the market price of risk from the visible part of the forward curve, and then project it 10 years forward. However, this effort may be unnecessary, if the goal is to find out what price the marketer should offer to the utility. Instead of finding market price of risk we can adjust our expected spot projections by the corporate risk premium. The risk premium (corporate price of risk) depends on the organization's risk preferences (as measured by RAROC, and so on). As such it is a reflection of the company's policies. Consequently, it does not require any analysis nor modeling.

Risk Premia, Market Inefficiencies, and Risk Management Process

If we believe that the underlying plain-vanilla products are mispriced, and mispriced in such a way that it is profitable (on the risk-adjusted basis) for the organization to pursue the opportunity, then the hedging strategy for the structured products will be affected. Take the example of the barrier option in Chapter 4: We argued that the value of the barrier down-and-in call was given by the value of the OTM put struck at the barrier. Assume that we sell the structure. Let's also assume that we have a (good) reason to believe that the puts are "expensive," meaning that we believe that the future realized volatility will be substantially lower than the implied volatility the quote suggests. Then, it's obvious that we will never buy the static hedge, that is, we will never buy the put to hedge our barrier option. Instead we will pursue the delta-hedging strategy.

This simple insight, even though not often acknowledged, is widely pursued in the investment world. The organizational setup of many trading entities directly implements this trading/hedging structure. The split of the trading operations into structured desks and price (vanilla) desks is a direct reflection of the principle. The structured desk forms the best hedges it can, given the available basic tradables/underlyings. However, the price desk makes the internal market in the underlyings. Then, effectively, the organization's net hedge is a sum of the flat hedged position of the structured desk and the view on the market expressed by the price desk.

To follow our example again, even though the structured desk is going to be flat in the underlyings in the internal market, the risk of actually hedging will be sold off to the price desk. The price desk, in turn, will not be buying the puts if they believe the puts are too "expensive." In this way, the organization will not be buying the "expensive" puts as a hedge, exactly following the reasoning we went through in the previous two paragraphs. On the other hand, the value of the structure will be marked-to-market and any gains (or losses) from actually not pursuing the static hedge will accrue to the price desk.

Until now we have been mainly focusing our attention on how to account for risk when we value a particular derivative structure. Equally, if not more important, is the question of assessing the risk of a portfolio of such structures, that is, the question of devising a consistent measure of the aggregate portfolio risk. There are a number of approaches to measuring portfolio risks, among which VaR methodology is presently the most popular.

VALUE-AT-RISK AND OTHER RISK MEASURES

The use of value-at-risk (VaR) by financial institutions as a risk measure of their portfolios can be traced back to the 1980s. The popularity of VaR grew dramatically after J. P. Morgan introduced the RiskMetrics system in 1994 in an attempt to standardize risk measurement methodology. By 1995, 60% of pension funds surveyed by the New York University Stern School of Business reported the use of VaR (Linsmeier and Pearson, 1996). Another push toward the recognition of value-at-risk was given by regulators when in 1995 the Basle Committee on Banking Supervision released a proposal that under certain conditions banks may use their VaR models to determine the capital requirements. It was followed by similar proposals issued by the U.S. Federal Reserve, the U.S. Securities and Exchange Commission, and the European Union regulators.

VaR

A typical procedure for computing VaR of a portfolio P consists of four steps:

1. Identify risk factors

$$f_1, f_2, ..., f_m$$

and specify a procedure for computing a portfolio value as a function of these factors,

$$P = P(f_1, f_2, ..., f_m) \tag{10.7}$$

This procedure can be an analytical formula or a complex Monte Carlo simulation.
2. Given the current state of the random factors, determine their joint distribution over a certain predetermined holding period, that is, determine the joint distribution of the factors at the end of the period conditional on their values at the beginning of the period. (The holding period can be a day, a week, a month, or even longer depending on the liquidity of the market). Again, the distribution can be computed analytically or through simulations.

3. Using the distribution of the random factors over the holding period and expression find the distribution of ΔP, where ΔP denotes the change in the portfolio value over the holding period.
4. Once the distribution of ΔP is found, compute VaR at a given confidence level α using this definition

$$\Pr\{\Delta P \le -VaR\} = -\alpha \qquad (10.8)$$

Implementation of the VaR Methodology in the Energy Markets

Due to the importance of the subject, the VaR methodology has been extensively covered in the financial literature, especially in recent years. (For example, see RiskMetrics™, 1995, Duffie and Pan, 1997; Shimko, 1997) The use of VaR in the energy markets has been described in Pilipovic, 1997 and Clewlow and Strickland, 2000. It would not be an exaggeration to say that by now the methodology, its benefits and shortcomings, as well as various implementation issues are well understood. Therefore, we are not going to give a detailed examination of the VaR methodology, instead referring the reader to the previously-mentioned publications. We will simply present an outline of key concepts linked to each step of the VaR methodology and briefly comment on specific issues arising when this methodology is used in energy applications.

Choice of Risk Factors

There is no universal set of risk factors and their choice usually depends on a portfolio composition, on the markets and on particular risk attitudes. Frequently an expert opinion is sought to determine the most effective and appropriate selection. Naturally the risk factors should be in agreement with the formulas and algorithms used to value a given portfolio, since ultimately what is required is the representation (10.7) connecting the portfolio value with the risk factors. For example, if only price and volatility data is used to value portfolio, temperature cannot be selected as a risk factor.

At this stage the greatest implementation challenge is posed by the exceptionally high amount of factors that determine the value of a real-life portfolio. Consider, for instance, a portfolio of an energy trading company. If it trades in gas and power, potentially it may mean having position at no less than 50 liquid locations. Each liquid location is characterized by its own forward curve (or even several forward curves as is the case of on-peak and off-peak power prices), and each curve is defined by, say, 20 to 30 points. Thus, in prices only we may be looking at a thousand or more portfolio value drivers. Adding volatility curves at each location, and then, on top of that, oil, coal, and emission price and volatility curves, we may be facing close to two thousand factors.

Finally, if we need to consider temperature or load, that may mean an addition of another couple of thousand drivers. Indeed, there are more than a thousand weather stations in the United States of which more than a hundred are located close to main population centers and hence are expected to be included in the list of portfolio value drivers. Each location has its own temperature curve, which means, even with coarse monthly resolution, 12 factors. Furthermore, we must add to this number a similar amount of volatility factors.

All in all we have several thousand possible variables, which is a substantial number even for the most powerful computers especially if time-consuming Monte Carlo simulations are used to compute the joint distribution of these variables.

Two methodologies are usually considered for dealing with the challenge of high dimensionality.

Mapping on the Reduced Set of Principal Risk Factors. This mapping involves aggregation of factors into "buckets," both locational and temporal. For example, we may choose not to differentiate the monthly prices within the second quarter of the next year, thus creating a quarterly bucket. The quarterly price will then be a risk factor. If we need to map the changes in the quarterly price to the changes in the monthly prices, this can be achieved, for example, by assuming perfect correlation between quarterly and monthly price movements.

Principal Components Method. This technique of complexity reduction is conceptually similar to the methods described in Chapter 5. Instead of separate points along the forward curve, now the risk factors are the magnitudes of perturbation of the whole curve. If we can identify principal movements of the forward curve, this approach can result in a dramatic reduction in the number of risk factors. (See Jamshidian and Zhu, 1997 for an example of successful application of this methodology. For some complications, see Chapter 5.)

Representation of the Joint Distributions of Risk Factors

At the second stage we need to compute the joint distribution of the risk factors over the holding period conditional on their current state. Three methodologies commonly used to determine this distribution are historical, analytical, and Monte Carlo.

Historical Simulation

In this method the changes in the factor values over the holding period are sampled from the past history and applied to their current state to compute joint distribution samples. For example, assume that the holding period is one day. Then the samples of the joint distribution of the risk factors are computed according to this procedure.

1. Consider the history of the risk factors spanning the period of L days. For each day in the history compute the daily changes in the risk factors

$$\Delta f^\ell_1, \Delta f^\ell_2,..., \Delta f^\ell_m, \qquad \ell = 1,2,..., L$$

2. Given today's risk factors, $f^0_1, f^0_2,..., f^0_m$ compute L samples of the next day risk factors.

$$(f^\ell_1, f^\ell_2,..., f^\ell_m) = (f^0_1 + \Delta f^\ell_1, f^0_2 + \Delta f^\ell_2,..., f^0_m + \Delta f^\ell_m), \ell = 1,2,..., L \quad (10.9)$$

The corresponding sample distribution is a representation of the next day joint distribution.

Needless to say, this approach is based on the assumption that historical data is rich enough to contain a reasonable representation of possible changes in factor values. This, plus a certain stationarity of factor evolution, provides justification for the historical simulation method.

Pros.   Provided that the conditions necessary for the method applicability hold, the benefits of the historical simulations are easy to identify. First, it is the simplicity of implementation. Indeed, unlike the Monte Carlo method (see Appendix A), the historical simulations do not require complex matrix operations. To be precise, computationally there is no difference between two methods at the portfolio evaluation stage. It is at the joint distribution simulation stage that historical method is more efficient numerically. Second, the historical simulations do not require identifying and modeling a risk factor correlation structure, which is a very valuable feature, especially if the joint distribution of the factors is far from a standard normal-like distribution.

Cons.   The main drawback of the method of historical simulations is that the conditions for its applicability, namely, wealth of data and stationarity, are difficult to satisfy in most markets. And in energy markets, as we know, the situation is practically hopeless. Another general weakness of the historical simulations stems from the fact that historical data is always conditional on the contemporary state of the world. In financial markets these conditions may be of political or macroeconomic or similar nature. In power markets we are particularly concerned about the structure and specification of the existing generation supply stack. If the current state of the world is significantly different from the past one (e.g., due to a substantial build-up in a new efficient generation capacity), the use of historical data may be inappropriate and misleading.

Analytical Method

In this method the joint distribution of risk factor deviations, Δf_i, over the holding period is chosen from a certain parametric family of distributions. Naturally, the most common choice is a multi-dimensional normal distribution. However, even in this case we face a formidable task of determining distribution parameters, namely, a covariance matrix. Chapter 4 and, particularly, Chapter 6 contained enough evidence of how difficult this task can be in the energy markets and how complex the covariance structure may be. Complexities aside, however, in practical implementation of VaR methodology the most frequently used algorithms for forecasting covariance structure are quite straightforward. They are the method of exponentially weighted moving averages (EWMA) and the generalized autoregressive conditional heteroskedasticity method (GARCH).

- **EWMA.** An N-period EWMA method gives the estimate of the covariance matrix at time t by the formula:

$$\hat{\Sigma}_t = \frac{\Sigma_t + \lambda \Sigma_{t-1} + \lambda^2 \Sigma_{t-2} + K + \lambda^N \Sigma_{t-N}}{1 + \lambda + \lambda^2 + K + \lambda^N}$$

where

$$\Sigma_{ij,t} = E[(\Delta f_{i,t} - \mu_i)(\Delta f_{j,t} - \mu_j)]$$

$\lambda = 1$ corresponds to equally weighted average and $\lambda = 0.94$ is the value used in RiskMetrics™.

- **GARCH.** In its general form GARCH(p,q) model was introduced by Bollerslev (1986). In practice, a simple GARCH(1,1) seems to be adequate for applications and is used frequently. The GARCH(1,1) model is given by this recursive formula:

$$\hat{\Sigma}_t = \omega + \alpha \Sigma_t + \beta \hat{\Sigma}_{t-1}$$

Which approach is better? As was mentioned in Chapter 6, when answering this question one should pay attention to the use of forecasted quantities. The longer-term valuation tasks require different correlation estimates than shorter-term VaR calculations. In Chapter 6 we concluded that the use of historical estimates of the EWMA or GARCH type for the purpose of computing VaR is reasonable provided that the size N of historical data used in estimation is sufficiently large. Alexander and Leigh (1997) compared these methods on a wide range of test data and concluded that, with some exceptions, GARCH and equally weighted moving average models are superior to exponentially weighted moving averages.

Pros.   The analytical method is efficient and easy to implement. Of particular importance is its ability to handle a very large number of risk factors.

Cons.   The principal drawback of the method is that it imposes a joint distribution structure which most likely does not correspond to reality, especially in the energy markets.

Monte Carlo Simulations

Similar to the Analytical Method the method of Monte Carlo simulations requires the knowledge of joint distribution. Once it is given, the L samples of changes in the values of the risk factors over the holding period

$$\Delta f_1^\ell, \Delta f_2^\ell, ..., \Delta f_m^\ell, \ell = 1,2,...,L$$

are computed using an appropriate simulation technique (for example, see Appendix A). After that the samples of new risk factors are computed using equation (10.9).

Unlike historical simulations, Monte Carlo simulations are not limited by the number of entries in the historical time series and can generate an arbitrarily large set of risk factors. This feature of the method is useful from the accuracy point of view.

Computing the Change in Portfolio Value

We now are at Step 3 of the VaR methodology—computation of the change in the portfolio value in response to the change in the risk factors.

$$\Delta P^\ell = P(f_1^\ell, f_2^\ell, ..., f_m^\ell) - P(f_1^0, f_2^0, ..., f_m^0) \qquad (10.10)$$

Again we separate the simulation methods from the analytical method.

Historical and Monte Carlo Simulations

In both historical as well as Monte Carlo simulations the portfolio value change is computed for each simulated set of risk factors by substituting it into the portfolio pricing formulas and algorithms. The fact that the value change is computed exactly constitutes a significant advantage of the simulation methods, especially when portfolio value is strongly nonlinear in the risk factors. In the case of nonlinearity, approximations and shortcuts may fail dramatically, hence a method that values the portfolio exactly will be quite advantageous. On the other hand, this is also the main weakness of the simulation methods, since exact portfolio valuation may be a time-consuming proposition, especially when one needs to run Monte Carlo simulations for this.

For example, consider a portfolio of power deals and assume that the hybrid model of Chapter 7 is used for its valuation. Suppose we need to know the effect of changing fuel prices on the power portfolio value. To achieve that we first have to generate samples of new risk factors, and then for each sample we have to run Monte Carlo simulations required by the hybrid model to obtain a new power price and with it a new portfolio value. It is clear how such methodology can become prohibitively expensive, particularly for a large number of risk factors.

Analytical Method

In a frequently used implementation of the variance-covariance method the change in portfolio value is approximated using first terms of Taylor expansion:

$$\Delta P \approx \sum_{i=1}^{m} \delta_i \Delta f_i \qquad (10.11)$$

where δ is the vector of first derivatives (deltas) of the portfolio value with respect to the risk factors,

$$\delta_i = \frac{\partial P}{\partial f_i}(f_1^0, f_2^0, ..., f_m^0)$$

Because of the use of deltas in the approximation (10.11) this method is frequently called the *delta-VaR* method.

The advantages of the delta-VaR method are in its simplicity and ease of implementation, as well as the ability to handle large size portfolios and a large number of risk factors. On the negative side, since (10.11) is a linear approximation, the method works well only if a given portfolio is linear or close to linear. The term "linear portfolio" means that it consists of products that depend linearly on the risk factor changes. For example, a portfolio consisting of futures, forwards, and swaps is a linear portfolio. On the other hand, if there are many options in the portfolio it may be far from being linear. From the discussion in the previous chapters it is clear that, in fact, an energy portfolio is expected to be very nonlinear, especially if there are many asset-type deals (e.g., storage, generation, load service, and so on). In this case, linear approximation (10.11) may be missing big changes in the portfolio values due to nonlinearity.

A frequently used methodology designed for a better representation of changes in the values of a nonlinear portfolio uses second order Taylor approximation:

$$\Delta P \approx \sum_{i=1}^{m} \delta_i \Delta f_i + \tfrac{1}{2} \sum_{i,j=1}^{m} \Gamma_{ij} \Delta f_i \Delta f_j$$

where

$$\Gamma_{ij} = \frac{\partial^2 P}{\partial f_i \partial f_j}(f^0_1, f^0_2, \ldots, f^0_m)$$

This "delta-gamma-VaR" method can be reduced to a regular delta-VaR method if the usual deltas are replaced with certain modified deltas (see Rouvinez, 1997, for a detailed description of this method).

Computing VaR

This is the most straightforward step of the VaR procedure. If simulations, either historical or Monte Carlo, are used to generate samples of changes in the portfolio value, then the sample distribution should be used in equation (10.8) to determine VaR. If an analytical method, for example, delta-VaR model, is used, then assuming that changes in risk factors are normally distributed, we obtain that ΔP is normally distributed as well. Therefore, for a given level α

$$VaR = c_\alpha \sqrt{\Delta f' \; \hat{\Sigma} \; \Delta f}$$

where c_α is a constant. For example, $c_\alpha = 2.32$ for $\alpha = 99\%$.

Summary

In the case of energy applications we see only Monte Carlo simulations and analytical (variance-covariance) models as competitors in the implementation of the VaR methodology. The use of historical simulations is not recommended due to the issues discussed previously.

The advantages of Monte Carlo simulations include the ability to model any evolution of risk factors over the holding period. Particularly, all the processes of Chapters 4, 5, and 7 can be modeled using the Monte Carlo simulations. Furthermore, there is no need to approximate portfolio values in this method—they are computed exactly. Hence, the method can be used for estimating VaR in the most nonlinear portfolio, which is a valuable characteristic for energy portfolios with assets.

On the negative side, the curse of the dimension, that is, a large number of risk factors even in a medium size energy portfolio, can make Monte Carlo simulations very expensive computationally. Various aggregation techniques can help, from the numerical efficiency point of view, although they result in the reduction of accuracy of the method.

It is a fact that Monte Carlo simulations are gaining popularity as a methodology for risk measurement largely because of their ability to capture portfolio value better than alternative methods. However, we have to caution the reader that the benefits of more precise portfolio valuation can be completely negated by the imprecision in defining underlying stochastic processes or their parameters. For example, VaR calculations require the use of a physical world drift (and not the one in the risk-neutral world—a frequent error, unfortunately). Estimating this drift parameter is a challenge. Similarly, obtaining estimates of correlation parameters can be very difficult (see Chapter 6). Clearly, without good parameter estimates, precise portfolio valuation may be of no use, thus, making Monte Carlo methodology less appealing.

The benefits of analytical methods stem from their ability to deal with a very large set of risk factors. They are efficient and easy to implement. The methods such as delta-gamma-VaR model can capture nonlinearity of mildly nonlinear portfolios reasonably well.

The shortcomings of analytical methods are due to their approximate nature and the need to make simplifying assumptions along the way to achieve computational efficiency. For example, the use of covariance matrix implies a particular normal-type behavior of the joint distribution of risk factors, which normally is a very crude approximation in the energy applications. Moreover, even the second order approximations (delta-gamma-VaR) may be insufficient for a reasonable approximation of portfolio values due to severe nonlinearity of energy assets and extreme movements of certain risk factors, such as power prices.

Finally, VaR itself as a measure of risk may be insufficient in the case when the distribution of portfolio changes has fat tails, which is precisely what we expect from energy portfolios. The problem is that value-at-risk only tells us that potential portfolio losses over the holding period will not exceed a certain threshold with probability 1-α. However, it does not tell us what to expect if the losses fall below the threshold, which is very important to know in the case of fat-tailed distributions. Indeed, a common interpretation of 95% VaR is that it is violated twenty days a year. Then it is only natural to ask what happens when it is violated, and how severe is the magnitude of the losses? VaR, by definition, cannot answer this question.

Another, more subtle problem with VaR is that it has some objectionable properties, such as lack of sub-additivity, that is, VaR of a two-asset portfolio can be greater than the sum of individual VaRs of these assets (see Artzner et al., 1999). It means that as a risk measure VaR may not agree with the principle of diversification, since diversification may result in the increase in the portfolio risk as measured by VaR.

These are the reasons why a modification of VaR has been introduced—a risk measure called conditional value-at-risk (CVaR).

CVaR

In general terms, CVaR is a weighted average of VaR and the conditional expectations of losses strictly exceeding VaR. We refer the reader to Rockafellar and Uryasev (2000) and Bogentoft, Romejin, and Uryasev (2001) for precise definitions and properties of CVaR. The following properties separate CVaR from VaR.

- CVaR provides a measure of losses beyond VaR
- CVaR is subadditive, that is, diversification of the portfolio decreases the risk as measured by CVaR
- CVaR is a convex measure allowing one to develop efficient portfolio optimization procedures (see Uryasev, 2000).

Despite their differences, conceptually VaR and CVaR are quite close. There are, however, alternative risk measures that are substantially different. One such measure is cash flow at risk (see Linsmeier and Pearson, 1996).

Cash Flow at Risk

This risk measure has been gaining popularity, particularly among nonfinancial corporations for whom the VaR approach to risk assessment may be too limited. The main difference of the cash flow at-risk methodology is that it considers the impact of risk factors on the cash flows (i.e., quarterly, annual, and so on) and their distributions and not on the mark-to-market portfolio value. Therefore, the period over which the impact is considered is significantly longer than the holding period of VaR calculations. Furthermore, the set of factors used in this methodology is much broader than the one used to compute VaR. It may potentially include all the drivers that affect the operating cash flow and not just market factors used in VaR methodology. For example, in the case of a power plant they may include, in addition to price and volatility factors, the factors corresponding to generation growth, changes in demand, technology, demographics, macroeconomic conditions, and so on.

The main drawback of this method is that it relies too heavily on expert guidance. The choice of the driving factors, their impact on operating cash flow, and the cash flow model itself—all this is based on the developer's judgment and knowledge. Moreover, there should be consistency between operating and market factors used for modeling cash flow distribution. For example, factors representing the addition of new capacity should be in agreement with the volatility factors. Despite the drawbacks, the cash flow at risk methodology can supply useful insights into the long-term risks of a corporation.

Credit VaR

Credit risk in energy markets, that is, the risk that a transaction counterparty will be unable to meet its contractual obligations, has drawn a lot of attention recently, particularly after the demise of Enron. In financial markets the importance of assessing this risk has been appreciated for some time and a number of credit risk measures, such as Credit VaR of J. P. Morgan's CreditMetrics™, have been developed. Clewlow and Strickland (2000) give a comprehensive introduction to various credit risk measurement techniques in energy markets. The basic concepts of Credit VaR are similar to the ones used in VaR methodology. The only difference is that now when constructing the distribution of changes in the portfolio value we must also take into consideration the probability of arrival of credit events. These events include default and change of credit quality (i.e., credit rating). Probabilities of credit events are typically provided by the credit rating agencies. As a rule, Credit VaR is computed using the Monte Carlo technique when the distribution of market risk factors is simulated together with the arrival of the credit events. After considering these general risk adjustment and measurement strategies we now concentrate on the application of the tools to physical assets.

PHYSICAL ASSETS AND LONG-TERM FORWARD CURVES

Future Spot Prices and Forward Curves: Modeling Long-term Forward Curves

For any given period in the future for which we have a quoted forward/futures price, the difference between the forward price and expected spot price is due to risk aversion (at least in reasonably efficient markets) of market participants that require compensation for taking one or the other side of the transaction. The difference in the prices is called the risk premium. The size and sign of the premium is determined by the relative risk aversion (i.e., risk tolerance) of the various market participants.

In Chapter 5 we analyzed the models of the evolution of the quoted forward curve. In Chapter 4 we also showed that under certain assumptions about the relationship between the spot price and the corresponding forward price we can express the value of the forward contract in terms of the spot process. We suggested that this theoretical possibility is of little practical value since usually we have a better grasp of the behavior of the forward price than that of the spot price itself. Crucially, the use of the spot price concept is limited in the risk-management practice, since forming hedge position with the spot product is quite complex. Therefore, we used forward prices as given and only modeled their evolution over time. The natural question is then what to do if we do not have (liquidly) traded forward contracts. This issue is quite important in energy markets because we often deal with long-lived physical assets, while the liquid forward contracts presently do not extend beyond five years.

Before we answer this question, we need to understand how to use a forward curve. The forward is the price of a contract for future delivery of an asset transacted today. The contract enables us to lay off the risks associated with holding long (or short) future positions. We can see that the value of forward contract rests on its availability today. The forward price may not be a good forecast of the future spot prices (see Chapter 3 for more details) but this is not necessarily a problem. The contract enables us to monetize the future cash flow today (this is reflected in the concept of mark-to-market accounting). Given that forward contracts enable us to shift future cash flows to today (or at least lock them in), it is unclear what the point of a procedure of projecting forward price for the nontraded part of the curve might be. We can obviously produce a number through a host of techniques. However, this number has a very different meaning from the quoted price. We can try to use the projected forward prices as predictions of the future spot prices. In general, however, the forward prices might be biased forecasts of future spot prices. Forward prices contain (market) risk premia. Those, as we argue elsewhere, are not of much interest.

Therefore the preferred procedure is to develop a model of future spot price behavior, add the corporate risk premium and use the resulting values as the projection for all pricing. We will call this price the projected spot price. Again, it has to be clear that the resulting number has to be treated differently than actual forward quotes. For example, risk exposure (as measured by VaR) for positions covered by the projected spot analysis is much higher than for those covered by the actual forward quotes. In the latter case we can substantially remove the exposure within days or weeks by transacting in forward markets. In the former case no strategy of this kind is available until we come sufficiently close to the period of interest, and liquid forward markets open up. This implies that we carry months or even years worth of exposure. One-day or ten-day holding horizons often used in VAR analysis are wholly inapplicable to positions of this kind. The risks associated with such positions will be magnitudes higher than those associated with positions covered by liquid forward curves.

Physical Assets as Derivative Products: Market Perspective

In Chapters 8 and 9 we toiled heavily trying to show how various physical assets (e.g., generation, storage, transportation) can be analyzed in terms of certain more or less exotic financial structures. We found that those assets can be understood as bundles of various forwards, options, spread options, and digital option positions.

There are often heated discussions about what the proper market line is for acquisition of new assets. Should one use expected spot prices or forward prices in initial valuations? This argument flows from the recognition of the fact that the forward prices and expected spot prices might not be equal for a variety of reasons. Oftentimes great effort is invested in trying to investigate which way the difference goes. However, as we will see shortly, this effort is misdirected in the case of new asset acquisition. As we will see, no matter what drives the difference, as long as the forward markets are reasonably liquid, the proper value benchmark is given by the forward curve. Before we go to the heart of the argument, let us look a little more closely at the difference between forward and expected spot: $D = E[S] - F$. The difference can be due to two factors:

- Inefficiency in the forward market
- Risk premium in the forward market

In the first case we think that the forward market does not properly account for the presence of some information. In the second case, the presence of required risk premia leads to the difference. Obviously, both factors can play a role in any given situation. In the first situation, as long as our risk aversion is not higher than the market one, we have a clear incentive to exploit the mismatch by acquiring a suitable position in forward contracts or by acquiring a physical asset (with identical resulting exposure). In the second case the difference will be an attractive opportunity as long as, again, our risk aversion is lower that the one exhibited by the market. And again as before we could exploit it by acquiring a suitable position in the forward markets or by acquiring an equivalent physical position.

What unites these two strategies (physical and financial) is the ability to extract the perceived value by transacting in the forward markets. This fact is crucial for our analysis. The physical alternative suggested in the above description, however, is not symmetric. The forward (financial) strategy is virtually cost-less to execute, while the physical strategy requires significant outlays. The consequence, then, is obvious: the cheaper alternative is always the preferred one. Now, the question we might want to ask is: How does this fact relate to asset valuation and acquisition?

The answer is: If we can exploit the difference between forward and spot for free, the value accruing from the difference cannot be a part of the value of the assets to be acquired (as long as we have to pay something for the asset). In other words, we should not be willing to invest capital into something we can get for free (or at least relatively cheaply) anyway. Consequently, in valuing assets for acquisition we should not be including the extra value. It means that only the forward curve should be used for valuation of assets (for acquisition). Obviously, once the asset is acquired we should recognize the additional value by marking (projecting) it appropriately for risk-management purposes. Notice, however, that if we intend to sell the asset, our reservation price is again given by its forward value and the expected spot is irrelevant.

Physical Assets as Liquidity Plays: Market Making

All the previous analysis assumes liquid forward markets. If some of the markets do not trade the only way to acquire the exposure is to own the asset. Under such circumstances, the valuation of the asset is not related to the nonexistent forward markets.

We mentioned in Chapter 2 that some of the power option markets are not very liquidly traded because of extreme volatility and the lack of tradable underlying, which would enable selling of covered calls. One solution to the problem is to acquire a source of the underlying such as generation assets to be able to make markets in volatility. We can then think of assets as completing the market and offering the ability to make markets in products not otherwise liquidly traded.

Therefore, we can see assets as a strategy for acquiring exposure to illiquid markets while laying off exposure to liquid ones. For example, if we are interested in making markets in OTM volatility, we acquire the physical asset (say a peaking plant) and hedge out the level (forward price) exposure while retaining the volatility exposure.

Physical Assets As Long-term Investments: Valuation, Investment, and Modeling

We can also see physical assets as bets on the future prices that are not traded at all. This is a related rationale to the one elucidated above; however, the thrust of the investment strategy is not related to market making or risk-management but to taking long-term directional positions with all the attendant risks.

Valuation of long-term bets of this nature is a very challenging problem. As we argued previously, forward curves are not available and modeled forward curves are not of much use.

The situation is even more complicated for long-term asset modeling. There are no primitive tradables to use for relative valuation. The various forward curves are presumably long gone by the time our problem begins. And, as we run out of the forward curves, the advantages of risk-neutrality are gone too and we are on our own.

Consider the valuation of a generation unit over the next ten years. We know that the value of the plant ultimately comes down to market heat rate and the market reserve margin in ten years. This, in turn, is driven by load-growth and stack additions. Projecting those quantities is not easy. We can build sophisticated models of market price formation trying to account for the dynamics of stack additions and load growth. However, no matter how sophisticated the models are, they will not be able to overcome the need for robust determination of inputs. The practice is that models of this kind are extremely sensitive to the slight changes in assumptions about investment behavior of market participants. A 5% change in the investment rule will cumulate over the years to yield prices and volatilities differing by orders of magnitude. Obviously, we can argue that those models give us an approximate estimate of the future expected spot prices. However, it is not clear how much effort we should put into deriving forecasts with 500% standard errors.

These concerns may be partially alleviated by the fact that we are not just interested in valuation for one individual year. Over several years, broad equilibrium conditions should assert themselves, giving us more faith in our estimates. Obviously, our knowledge of equilibrium conditions may not be much better. To top it off, for an investing organization, it is critically important which route to equilibrium is taken. There is a possibility that an initial period of very low prices may result in an undue strain on the financing capabilities of the organization. The organization may not be around to enjoy the following period of high prices. It is of little comfort to know that the average market participant earns its cost of capital while one watches from the sidelines. Ultimately, this should not be construed to mean that long-term investment is not advisable. Quite the contrary, there is a need for enterprising organizations to take on the enormous risks. However, simple models of supply and demand are usually all that is required. Incremental value from sophisticated modeling is not high. What is needed is a significant capital base capable of withstanding the overwhelming risks of long-term investing.

Physical Assets As Long-term Investments: Risk

The previous section introduced a number of techniques for estimating VaR (and its derivatives). However, to use the tool effectively one has to understand the applicability of the concept itself. This issue is especially pressing when we are dealing with illiquid markets. It is crucial to understand that VaR is a reasonable measure of risk only in liquid markets. If we don't have tradable forward curves in relation to which we can evaluate VaR, the concept has little meaning.

VaR assumes using the holding period concept to analyze the market price risk over a period of time in which we should be able to unwind a losing trade. If there is no ability to unwind the trade (like in long-dated energy contracts), VaR is a meaningless measure of risk.

This concern can be handled by properly extending the holding period. However, this is often not feasible nor even desirable. Consider the case of a merchant power producer that owns a generation unit. What are the risks associated with holding the asset?

The economic life of the asset extends beyond the liquid part of the power curve (presently five years at the most). The risks associated with the liquid part of the curve can be understood in terms of VaR and some reasonable holding periods. Obviously, in this context unwinding a trade does not involve the physical sale of the unit, but changes in the portfolio composition to remove the risks. For example, we might own an asset and a portfolio of static forward positions as a rough hedge. We will ordinarily bear a substantial amount of volatility risk. We can calculate the associated VaR on the principle that in case the forward volatility declines we can stop our losses by selling/buying a suitable portfolio of options. If the volatility market is reasonably liquid, this should be achievable within days or weeks. At worst we can always try and enter into a short-term tolling agreement to remove our risks.

The situation is dramatically different for the part of the value of the plant beyond the first five years. We have at least two difficulties:

First: we do not have any products to remove the risk from our portfolio. We can obviously try to sell the plant; however, it's unclear how long this would take; more importantly though, we do not know at what value we might be forced to sell the plant.

Second: no tradable conditional information. Unlike the case of the liquid part of the curve, now the changes in the value of the unit do not come about because of changes in the tradable underliers. The changes occur due to the arrival of some information (e.g., regulatory changes, changes in stack projections, and so on). In other words, the changes are due to changes in modeling assumptions.

In principle, for a product that does not have any underliers and that will be carried to maturity, the measure is not the conditional distribution of the value (as in VaR) but the terminal distribution of value. VaR gives us the risk associated with the changes in the conditional distribution, while the unhedgeable risk should be measured with the unconditional distribution of value.

Inasmuch as the forward markets are efficient, the VaR measures for the furthest visible point on the forward curve should give us the lower bound for the illiquid risk. However, this is only true for storable commodities; it will not apply to power commodities.

HEDGING

Throughout this book we have encountered situations where we could not hedge out all the risks associated with a position (whether physical or financial). Assume we are interested in hedging a European natural gas option that expires at a future time T. The payoff of the option at expiration is given by the expression:

$$Payoff = \max(g_T - K, 0) \tag{10.12}$$

where g_T is the spot price at T.

If the gas exposure is fully hedgeable, we can write the value of the option in this way:

$$Value_t^T (F_{t,T}^g) = df_t^T \, E_t^*[Payoff] = df_t^T \, E_t^*[\max(g_T - K, 0)]$$

$$F_{t,T}^g \text{—natural gas forward price}$$

$$df_t^T \text{—discount factor} \tag{10.13}$$

$$E_t^* \text{—risk-neutral expectation}$$

As long as the forward price process and the payoff function are relatively well behaved (see Duffie, 1992), the optimal (delta) hedge position will be given by:

$$\Delta_t = \frac{\partial V(F_{t,T}^g)}{\partial F_{t,T}^g} \tag{10.14}$$

If we follow a dynamic hedging strategy suggested by (10.14), we will remove all the risk and lock in the value (at least approximately).

In general, the value of this option is not fully hedgeable. We can use a variety of instruments to try and control the exposure. What is the optimal hedging strategy? The topic is vast and we expand on the general issues in the following subsection, here we just concentrate on the extensions to the hedging strategy just mentioned.

Assume now that spot gas price can be decomposed into the hedgeable part and the unhedgeable basis that is uncorrelated with the hedgeable part:

$$g_T = g\,(F_{t,T}^g; T) + \varepsilon_T^g$$

$$\text{cov}(g(F_{t,T}^g; T), \varepsilon_T^g) = 0 \tag{10.15}$$

The value of the structure will now be given by the following expression:

$$\widetilde{V}(F_{t,T}^g) = \widetilde{Value}_t^T (F_{t,T}^g) = df_t^T \, E_t^*[E_{\varepsilon_T^g}^{RA}[Payoff]] \tag{10.16}$$

The first (risk-neutral) expectation in this equation is identical to the one in (10.13). The second expectation is the risk-adjusted expectation of the unhedgeable basis. Technically, it is also a risk-neutral expectation, but we call it risk-adjusted instead to make clear that it requires explicit input of our (corporate) risk preferences.

Since we are assuming that the basis is independent of forward prices, the local variance minimizing hedge will now be given by this formula:

$$\widetilde{\Delta}_t = \frac{\partial \widetilde{V}(F_{t,T}^g)}{\partial F_{t,T}^g} \tag{10.17}$$

In general we have:

$$\tilde{\Delta}_t \neq \Delta_t \tag{10.18}$$

Formally, the two expressions are identical. However, because the values (10.13) and (10.16) are in general different, the hedge coefficients will have different values. The difference comes about because of the presence of the variability (and possibly nonzero mean) of the basis. In practice, we need to adjust the volatility of the underlying to account for those effects. This also suggests that no adjustment will be required for linear products, such as swaps, since they are not affected by volatility directly. There can be an indirect effect through the risk-adjustment mechanism. This points out the larger issue. The particular choice of risk adjustment for the unhedgeable part of the exposure will affect the hedge coefficients.

The formal result (10.17) is not dependent on the particular representation (10.15). If, instead of price, we decomposed the return into hedgeable and unhedgeable parts:

$$\ln g_T = \ln g(F_{t,T}^g; T) + \zeta_T^g \tag{10.19}$$

the result would be no different.

The assumption of lack of correlation between the hedgeable and unhedgeable part is not as limiting as it seems. Assume that the true decomposition of the gas price is:

$$g_T = F_{t,T}^g + \xi_T^g$$
$$\text{cov}(F_{t,T}^g, \xi_T^g) \neq 0 \tag{10.20}$$

We can almost always find such a transformation g that equation (10.15) holds. Then all the hedging results apply.

The bigger challenge is the issue of independence of the different factors (hedgeable and unhedgeable ones). For jointly normal variables, zero correlation (or covariance) implies independence. For other distributions this result does not hold. If the two factors are dependent, yet correlation is zero, the above procedure may not be directly applicable. Strictly speaking, if correlation is always zero, the local variance minimizing hedge will always be given by equation (10.17). However, for nonnormal distribution, factor dependence will make correlation a stochastic process (or at least, deterministic function of the marginals; see Chapter 6). Thus, even if correlation is zero on average, the optimal local variance minimizing hedge will depend on the distribution of correlation. For more on this topic see Wolyniec (2002).

EXAMPLE 10.2 *Variance minimizing hedges for linear products*

To understand why the issues just discussed are important, consider the standard way of hedging linear products. Consider a forward contract F_P, which we intend to hedge with another forward contract F_G. Assume that the prices are jointly arithmetic Brownian motion with correlation ρ:

$$dF_P = \sigma_P dW_P$$

$$dF_G = \sigma_G dW_G \qquad (10.21)$$

$$dW_P dW_G = \rho dt$$

The optimal (local-variance) hedge is then given by the following (e.g., see Hull, 1999):

$$\rho \frac{\sigma_{F_P}}{\sigma_{F_G}} \qquad (10.22)$$

Note that as long as the correlation and volatilities are constant, the optimal hedge is constant. This is due to the linearity of the structure. We can recover this result by following the procedure we described in equation (10.17). First let us decompose F_P into the hedgeable and uncorrelated unhedgeable part:

$$dF_P = \sigma_P dW_P = \sigma_P(\rho dW_G + \sqrt{1 - \rho^2}d\widetilde{W}) = \rho\frac{\sigma_P}{\sigma_G}dF_G + \sigma_P\sqrt{1 - \rho^2}d\widetilde{W}$$

$$dF_G = \sigma_G dW_G \qquad (10.23)$$

Integrating this equation and taking the expectation as in equation (10.16) we get (we assume no discounting for ease of exposition):

$$V_t^{F_P}(F_G^t) = E_{F_G}^*[E_{\widetilde{W}}^{RA}[F_P^T]] = \rho\frac{\sigma_P}{\sigma_G}E_{F_G}^*[F_G^T] + \sigma_P\sqrt{1 - \rho^2}E_{\widetilde{W}}^{RA}[\widetilde{W}^T]$$

$$= \rho\frac{\sigma_P}{\sigma_G}F_G^t + \sigma_P\sqrt{1 - \rho^2}E_{\widetilde{W}}^{RA}[\widetilde{W}^T] \qquad (10.24)$$

where
F^t and F^T are forward prices observed at times t and T respectively

Now, using (10.17), the hedge coefficient will be given by:

$$\Delta_t = \frac{\partial V_t^{F_P}(F_G^t)}{\partial F_G^t} = \frac{\partial\left\{\rho\frac{\sigma_P}{\sigma_G}F_G^t + \sigma_P\sqrt{1 - \rho^2}\,E_{\widetilde{W}}^{RA}[\widetilde{W}^T]\right\}}{\partial F_G^t} = \rho\frac{\sigma_P}{\sigma_G} \qquad (10.25)$$

which is identical to equation (10.22). The approach described here may seem a little roundabout way of deriving the result. However, the simple expression in (10.22) applies only to linear products. For options, the correct procedure requires going through all the intermediate steps. For more extensive exposition see Wolyniec (2002).

Hedging in Incomplete Markets

In many chapters of this book we have encountered situations where we could not hedge out all the risks associated with a position (whether physical or financial). When calculating hedges we followed the standard procedures used for complete markets (hedgeable assets). In the complete market case there is only one correct way to hedge an exposure (even though it may be hard to find it). In the incomplete case the correct hedging strategy depends on the risk appetites of the hedging entity. The risk appetites themselves need a clearer definition. The standard finance framework (CAPM) concentrates on minimizing systematic variance (covariance with the appropriate risk proxy, e.g., stock market returns) while retaining the highest possible return (mean-variance optimization). This may not be always applicable: in many situations we may be interested in managing the catastrophic risk of power spikes (minimization of kurtosis). Still, using mean-variance optimization can be a proxy for other types of risk minimization and has the advantage of having a highly developed analytical framework.

In the rest of this section (in fact in almost all the book) we pursue an approach concentrating on mean-variance optimization.

Mean-Variance Optimization

There are two general concepts of mean-variance optimization in a dynamic framework:

- **Local optimization:** we minimize one-step variance between rebalancing of the hedge portfolio
- **Global optimization:** we minimize the total variance.

Ultimately, the second concept is more natural as we usually are interested in reducing our overall exposure. The problem with the concept is that finding the optimal hedging strategy is often quite a challenging problem and requires significant computational resources. Additionally, in some situations an optimal hedging portfolio does not exist. On the other hand, in many situations, local and global optimization are equivalent. Also, the local optimization procedure is guaranteed to exist and is much more tractable (see Föllmer and Sondermann, 1986). In the rest of the book we use almost exclusively the local version of the problem.

Hedging with Hybrid Models

The approach to hedging in incomplete markets, which we discussed in previous sections can be extended to hybrid models that we analyzed in Chapter 7.

We can formally represent the behavior of power prices and major fuels (for example, oil and natural gas) by the following expression:

$$p_t = s^{bid}(D_t, g_t, l_t, \overrightarrow{\Omega_t}, \overrightarrow{E_t}, \overrightarrow{\Im_t}, \overrightarrow{OPC_t}) + \varepsilon_t \qquad (10.26)$$

where the following are dynamic variables (random variables):

D_t is the system demand at time t

g_t is the natural gas price at time t

l_t is the oil price at time t

Ω_t is the vector of outages at time t

E_t is the vector of emission prices at time t

$\Im_t$ is the vector of weather at time t

ε_t is the stochastic error term.

While the following are the deterministic parameters:

OPC_t is the vector of operational characteristics of the stack at time t that parameterizes the stack transformation

s^{bid} is the deterministic stack transformation

We can express the values of dynamic variables in terms of more fundamental variables, which in turn can be expressed in terms of their tradables:

$$D_t = d(\Im;t) + \varepsilon_t^D$$

$$g_t = g(BOM_{exp}^{gas}, \overrightarrow{C_{exp}^{GasMonthly}}, \overrightarrow{C_{exp}^{GasDaily}};t) + \varepsilon_t^g$$

$$l_t = g(F_{exp}^{oil}, \overrightarrow{C_{exp}^{OilMonthly}};t) + \varepsilon_t^l \qquad (10.27)$$

$$E_t = E(F_{exp}^{Emissions};t) + \varepsilon_t^E$$

$$\Im_t = \Im(Swap_{exp}^{HDD}, Swap_{exp}^{CDD};t) + \varepsilon_t^\Im$$

The preceding equations are analogous to equation (10.15). The difference is that we may use more than one tradable. For example, for gas prices we have:

$$g_t = g(BOM_{\exp}^{gas}, \overrightarrow{C_{exp}^{GasMonthly}}, \overrightarrow{C_{exp}^{GasDaily}}; t) + \varepsilon_t^g \qquad (10.28)$$

We express the values of the underlyings (e.g., gas spot price) in terms of tradable contracts at expiration. The approach attempts to reduce the value of underlying prices to the payoff functions of liquidly tradable contracts.

We have expressed natural gas price at time as a deterministic function of liquidly-traded natural gas contracts at expiration and a stochastic error term: $BOM_{\exp}^{gas}$ stands for the price of the balance-of-the-month contract price at expiration (alternatively, we can use the corresponding forward price, if BOM is not available or not very liquid). The vector $C_{exp}^{GasMonthly}$ represents a vector of monthly option prices on natural gas at expiration for different strike prices. Similarly, $C_{exp}^{GasDaily}$ represents a vector of daily option prices on natural gas at expiration. We can obviously use index options, if they are more liquid or offer better hedging performance. The choice of tradables is driven by two considerations: liquidity and hedging performance. The latter is measured in turn by the "size" of the stochastic error term ε_t^g: the smaller its variance, the better.

The specific functional representation we chose in equations (10.27) and (10.28) might not be a natural one. We can rescale option prices, for example, and instead of using forward and option prices, we can use forward prices and implied volatilities (volatility smiles). The particular choice of representation will depend on ease of implementation.

If all the residuals have zero variance, any derivative written on the power price can then be priced as an expectation with respect to the risk-neutral distributions of the tradables. The value will be fully hedgeable with the underlying tradables, and the hedging strategy can be derived by using Ito's lemma and finding appropriate "deltas."

If the variances are not zero, and as long as all residuals are *independent of the values of tradables at expiration*—lack of correlation is not enough—the value of any derivative written on power price will be given as an expectation with respect to the risk-neutral distributions of the tradables, and the risk-adjusted distribution for the unhedgeable risks (e.g., forced outage, residua). The optimal dynamic hedging strategy (in terms of mean-variance optimization) will be given by Ito's lemma applied to the expectation above.

The calculations of hedges in both cases are identical, although the interpretation of the results is a bit different. In the first case we have a riskless value and hedging strategy; in the second, the value itself is risky (random), and the hedging strategy gives only an optimal (local variance minimizing) dynamic statistical hedging strategy.

Multidimensional Monte Carlo Simulation with a Given Volatility and Correlation Structure: The Case of GBM

Given N commodities. The forward curve for the i-th commodity at a time t is denoted by F^i_{t,T_k} where T_k, k = 1,2,. . .,K, is a discrete set of settlement dates of the forward contracts constituting the forward curve. If $Z^i_{t,k} = \log F^i_{t,T_k}$ then by the assumption that the evolution of F^i_{t,T_k} is governed by GBM, the variables

$$\Delta Z^i_{t,k} = Z^i_{t+\Delta t,k} - Z^i_{t,k}$$

are normally distributed with the expectations $\mu^i_{t,k}$ and covariance matrix C_t,

$$\mu^i_{t,k} = (E\Delta Z^i_{t,k})$$

$$C^{i,j}_{t,k,l} \equiv E(\Delta Z^i_{t,k}, \Delta Z^j_{t,l}) = \rho^{i,j}(t,T_k,T_l)\sigma^i_{t,k}\sigma^j_{t,l}\Delta t$$

$$i,j = 1, \dots, N, \quad k,l = 1, \dots, K, \quad 0 \le t \le T_k \le T_l$$

where $\sigma^i_{t,k}$ is the instantaneous volatility of $Z^i_{t,k}$ at time t, and $\rho^{i,j}(t, T_k,T_l)$ is the matrix of correlation coefficients across all commodities and all forward contracts. Since the values of $Z^i_{0,k}$ are known from the initial forward curves, the Monte Carlo simulation of the evolution of the variables $Z^i_{t,k}$ is performed by generating the random increments $\Delta Z^i_{t,k}$ with the given expectations and the covariance matrix.

We will describe now a step of this procedure at a given time t. Assuming that at the time t we know $Z^i_{t,k}$, we will show how to simulate $Z^i_{t+\Delta t,k}$

numerically. Let k_t be the index of the first forward contract expiring after t, that is,

$$T_k > t \text{ for } k \geq k_t$$

Introducing the discrete volatility and correlation matrices

$$\sigma_t^i = \begin{bmatrix} \sigma_{t,k_t}^i & 0 & \cdots & 0 \\ 0 & \sigma_{t,k_t+1}^i & \cdots & 0 \\ \vdots & \vdots & \ddots & \vdots \\ 0 & 0 & \cdots & \sigma_{t,K}^i \end{bmatrix}$$

$$R_t^{ij} = \begin{bmatrix} \rho^{ij}(t,T_{k_t},T_{k_t}) & \rho^{ij}(t,T_{k_t},T_{k_t+1}) & \cdots & \rho^{ij}(t,T_{k_t},T_K) \\ \rho^{ij}(t,T_{k_t+1},T_{k_t}) & \rho^{ij}(t,T_{k_t+1},T_{k_t+1}) & \cdots & \rho^{ij}(t,T_{k_t+1},T_K) \\ \vdots & \vdots & \ddots & \vdots \\ \rho^{ij}(t,T_K,T_{k_t}) & \rho^{ij}(t,T_K,T_{k_t+1}) & \cdots & \rho^{ij}(t,T_K,T_K) \end{bmatrix}$$

we can now construct the covariance matrix

$$C_t = \begin{bmatrix} \sigma_t^1 & 0 & \cdots & 0 \\ 0 & \sigma_t^2 & \cdots & 0 \\ \vdots & \vdots & \ddots & \vdots \\ 0 & 0 & \cdots & \sigma_t^N \end{bmatrix} \begin{bmatrix} R_t^{1,1} & R_t^{1,2} & \cdots & R_t^{1,N} \\ R_t^{1,2} & R_t^{2,2} & \cdots & R_t^{2,N} \\ \vdots & \vdots & \ddots & \vdots \\ R_t^{1,N} & R_t^{2,N} & \cdots & R_t^{N,N} \end{bmatrix} \begin{bmatrix} \sigma_t^1 & 0 & \cdots & 0 \\ 0 & \sigma_t^2 & \cdots & 0 \\ \vdots & \vdots & \ddots & \cdots \\ 0 & 0 & \cdots & \sigma_t^N \end{bmatrix} \Delta t$$

and perform its Cholesky decomposition

$$C_t = L_t L_t'$$

where L_t is a lower triangular matrix, and L_t' is its transpose. The Monte Carlo simulation step consists of first generating a random vector ε, normally distributed with mean zero and standard deviation one,

$$\varepsilon = (\varepsilon_1, \ldots, \varepsilon_{(K-k_t+1)N})'$$

where $\varepsilon_i \sim N(0,1)$, and then computing the increment vector

$$\Delta Z_t = \mu_t + L_t \varepsilon, \quad \Delta Z_t = \{\Delta Z_{t,k}^i\}, \quad \mu_t = \{\mu_{t,k}^i\}$$

It is a simple exercise to show that this vector has all the necessary statistical properties. Finally,

$$Z_{t+\Delta t,k}^i = Z_{t,k}^i + \Delta Z_{t,k}^i$$

Optimization of Operations of Physical Assets

In this section we describe the general mathematical problem of optimizing power generation. This general technique can be used in valuation of storage and other energy assets. As we go through the exercise of setting up the problem, we must remember that any valuation of interest has to give us some way of monetizing (hedging) the value associated with the optimization technique.

We will use the following notation:

$HR = HR(q, \Im)$—marginal heat rate as a function of the generation level q and ambient temperature $\Im$

C_{min}—minimum generation level; so-called no-load generation level.

$C_{max} = C_{max}(\Im)$—maximum generation level as a function of ambient temperature. The max capacity can also vary as a function of the dispatch process. The Automated Generation Control max capacity is usually lower than the manually dispatchable one.

SC—fixed start-up cost: a function of the time from the latest shutdown

FSC—fuel start-up cost: the amount of fuel required for a start-up. A function of the time from the latest shutdown

PSC—power start-up cost: power consumption at start-up (from the grid). A function of the time from the latest shutdown

VOM—variable O&M expenses; expressed in terms of $/MWh

RR—ramp rate expressed in MW/hr

D_{min}—minimum runtime

$D_{start-up}$—start-up duration; the time from the decision to start-up to unit availability.

$D_{shutdown}$—minimum time after a shutdown at which one can attempt a start-up again.

λ—the forced outage frequency rate. The rate can be influenced by operating decisions at significant cost down the road. Consequently, the rate is only approximately constant. Additional characteristics of outage distribution are duration and the size of the operational derate.

The decision variables will be given by the following:

q—generation level
u^{on}—start-up decision
1—start-up
0—no start-up
u^{off}—shutdown decision
1—shutdown
0—no shutdown

The state variables are given by the following:

P_{ti}—power price on day t at hour i.

G_t—natural gas fuel price on day t.

L_t—oil fuel price on day t.

$\Im_{ti}$—temperature on day t at hour i

M_{ti}—derate multiplier due to forced outage; with the range of 0%...100%

U_{ti}^{on}—operational status online or offline

U_{ti}^{off}—operational offline status: cold, warm, hot

$d^{start-up}$—time from the latest start-up

$d^{shutdown}$—time from the latest shutdown

Before we formulate the problem, we must clearly understand the dispatch and commitment process in pool markets. For a multisettlement system, the bulk of unit commitment decisions are performed in the day-ahead market (see Chapter 1). Consequently, an operator can structure a bid so that he is assured of nonnegative payoff; he either gets a positive payoff, if he is dispatched, or gets zero if his bid is out-of-merit and the unit will not be committed.

This bidding structure retains operational flexibility but removes the risk of negative cash flows (or rather makes future prices operationally perfectly foreseeable). Obviously, this consideration matters only for day-ahead decisions. Start-up decisions, however, usually have consequences beyond a one-day horizon. Therefore, the issue of the interconnection between operational flexibility and risk we illustrated in Chapter 9 comes into play.

In the deterministic case, if we know all the prices, outages, and so on, the optimization problem can be formulated as the following mathematical program (everywhere $(t,i)-1$ means the previous decision period):

$$OF = \max_{q,u} \sum_{(t,i)=StartDay}^{EndDay} [q_{(t,i)}(P_{(t,i)} - HR(q_{(t,i)}, \Im_{(t,i)})G_t - VOM)$$

$$-u_{(t,i)}^{on}(SC(d_{t,i}^{shutDown}) + FSC(d_{t,i}^{shutDown})^*G_t + PSC(d_{(t,i)}^{shutDown})^*P_{(t,i)})]$$

such that

Operational Constraints

1. $U_{(t,i)}^{on}C_{min} \leq q_{(t,i)} \leq M_{ti}U_{(t,i)}^{on}C_{max}$

2. $q_{(t,i)-1} - RR \leq q_{(t,i)} \leq q_{(t,i)}-1 + RR$

State Transition Constraints

3. $U_{(t,i)}^{on} \leq U_{(t,i)-1}^{on}$ if $d_{(t,i)}^{shutDown} < D_{shutDown}$

4. $U_{(t,i)}^{on} \geq U_{(t,i)-1}^{on}$ if $d_{(t,i)}^{start-up} < D_{min} + D_{start-up}$

5. $U_{(t,i)}^{on} = \begin{cases} 0 & \text{if } M_{(t,i)}C_{max} \leq C_{min} \text{ or } u_{(t,i)}^{off} = 1 \\ 1 & \text{otherwise and if } d_{(t,i)}^{start-up} = D_{start-up} \\ 0 & \text{if } d_{(t,i)}^{start-up} < D_{start-up} \end{cases}$

6. $d_{(t,i)}^{shutDown} = \begin{cases} 0 & \text{if } U_{(t,i)}^{on} - U_{(t,i)-1}^{on} = -1 \\ d_{(t,i)-1}^{shutDown} + 1 & \text{otherwise} \end{cases}$

7. $d_{(t,i)}^{start-up} = \begin{cases} 0 & \text{if } u_{(t,i)}^{on} - U_{(t,i)-1}^{on} = 1 \\ d_{(t,i)-1}^{start-up} + 1 & \text{otherwise} \end{cases}$ (B.1)

The objective function contains two terms: one for the operational cash flow and the other for start-up costs.

We review the meaning of the various constraints:

1. The generation level is within feasible boundaries.
2. The changes in the generation level are only those allowed by the ramp rates.
3. The unit remains off if not enough time has elapsed since the most recent shutdown.
4. The unit stays on if the minimum run time has not yet elapsed.

5. Defines under what conditions the unit must be (or cannot be) online: It cannot be on if there was a sufficient outage to shut down the unit, if not enough time has elapsed since start-up for the unit to come online, or if the unit was shut down. It must be on if the time since start-up is exactly equal to the required time.

6. Defines the evolution of the variable measuring time since last shutdown: it is zero only if the unit has gone offline, but otherwise the time is the previous time plus one.

7. Defines the evolution of the variable measuring time since last start-up: If the unit was off and it has come online, the variable is zeroed out; otherwise it is incremented by one period.

We do not include equations for the evolution of the exogenous state variables, that is, prices and forced outage events.

The problem (B.1) accounts for a number of typical operational constraints. The list is by no means exhaustive. This structure also excludes a number of operational flexibilities we find in many markets and operating units: multi-fuel capability, optimization across power markets (energy, ancillary services) as well as optimization across settlements (day-ahead versus day-of) and so on (see Chapter 9). The incorporation of those considerations in the framework would be fairly straightforward.

The above program is a feasible description of the operational problem only if we have perfect foresight of all the future prices and outage events. But in making the operational decisions we must account for uncertainty. We can reformulate the problem in terms of a stochastic dynamic program (with recourse). In this framework, we reflect the impact of uncertainty on our decisions by optimizing our choices with respect to the (conditional) expectations of the impact of our decisions on the future cash flows.

The expected value of a generation unit in this framework can be expressed by the value function: $V(U^{on}, P, G, M, \Im; t)$. This expresses the value of the facility at time t conditioned on the current operational state of the unit and current prices and other state variables. As we are dealing with conditional expectations about the future condition of the state variables we can use other price and nonprice conditional information. For example, we could include current BOM prices, current forward/futures prices, option prices, and the like. In practice, the horizon of the optimization rarely extends beyond one month (see important exceptions later). Consequently, we rarely have a need to condition on more than BOM and prompt forward prices. Notice, that we use the additional information, even if we do not explicitly plan to commit our generation resources in the BOM market. We use it only to give us better information about the spot price behavior. Quite apart from the optimization issue, the fact that we can use BOM information to perform better dispatch also implies that we can use those contracts as an inside-the-period hedge. We will examine the issues later in this appendix.

The solution to the problem of finding the optimal value function (and associated operational strategy) is given by the first order optimality condition, which results in the following recursive equation (Bellman equation) for the value function:

$$V[P_{(t,i)}, G_{(t,i)}, M_{t,i}, \Im_{(t,i)}; U_{(t,i)}^{on}, d_{(t,i)}^{shutDown}, d_{(t,i)}^{start\text{-}up}; (t,i)] =$$

$$\max_{q_{(t,i)}, \mu_{(t,i)}} [\{q_{(t,i)}(P_{(t,i)} - HR(q_{(t,i)}, \Im_{(t,i)})G_{(t,i)} - VOM)$$

$$-u_{(t,i)}^{on}(SC(d_{(t,i)}^{shutDown}) + FSC(d_{(t,i)}^{shutDown})^{*}G_{t} + PSC(d_{(t,i)}^{shutDown})^{*}P_{(t,i)}) +$$

$$e^{-r\Delta t}E_{(t,i)}^{*}\{[V[P_{(t,i)+1}, G_{(t,i)+1}, M_{(t,i)+1}, \Im_{(t,i)+1}; U_{(t,i)+1}^{on}, d_{(t,i)+1}^{shutDown}, d_{(t,i)+1}^{start\text{-}up}; (t,i) + 1]]\}$$

Operational Constraints

$$U_{(t,i)+1}^{on}C_{min} \leq q_{(t,i)+1} \leq M_{(t,i)+1}U_{(t,i)+1}^{on}C_{max}$$

$$q_{(t,i)} - RR \leq q_{(t,i)+1} \leq q_{(t,i)} + RR$$

State Transition Constraints

$$U_{(t,i)+1}^{on} \leq U_{(t,i)}^{on} \text{ if } d_{(t,i)+1}^{shutDown} < D_{shutDown}$$

$$U_{(t,i)+1}^{on} \geq U_{(t,i)}^{on} \text{ if } d_{(t,i)+1}^{start\text{-}up} < D_{min} + D_{start\text{-}up}$$

$$U_{(t,i)+1}^{on} = \begin{cases} 0 & \text{if } M_{(t,i)+1}C_{max} \leq C_{min} \text{ or } u_{(t,i)}^{off} = 1 \\ 1 & \text{otherwise and if } d_{(t,i)+1}^{start\text{-}up} = D_{start\text{-}up} \\ 0 & \text{if } d_{(t,i)+1}^{start\text{-}up} < D_{start\text{-}up} \end{cases}$$

$$d_{(t,i)+1}^{shutDown} = \begin{cases} 0 & \text{if } U_{(t,i)+1}^{on} - U_{(t,i)}^{on} = -1 \\ d_{(t,i)}^{shutDown} + 1 & \text{otherwise} \end{cases}$$

$$d_{(t,i)+1}^{start\text{-}up} = \begin{cases} 0 & \text{if } u_{(t,i)}^{on} - U_{(t,i)}^{on} = 1 \\ d_{(t,i)+1}^{start\text{-}up} + 1 & \text{otherwise} \end{cases} \tag{B.2}$$

In the above, we optimize with respect to properly risk-adjusted expectation. Given the solution to the problem, this is to say the value function at the beginning of the operation period t_{start}, we can now find the value of the facility today (at time t_0) by calculating the following expectation:

$$\text{Value} = E_{t_0}^*[e^{-r(t_{start} - t_0)} V(P_{t_{start}}, G_{t_{start}}, M_{t_{start}}, \Im_{t_{start}}; U_{t_{start}}^{on}, d_{t_{start}}^{shutDown}, d_{t_{start}}^{start-up}; t_{start})]$$

$$= E_{t_0}^*[e^{-r(t_{start} - t_0)} V(P_{t_{start}}, G_{t_{start}}, M_{t_{start}}, \Im_{t_{start}}; 0, 0, 0; t_{start})] \qquad (B.3)$$

As before, we calculate the value with respect to the (conditional) risk-neutral expectation of all the underlying stochastic factors (prices, outages, temperature, and so on).

Even though it is not explicit in the formulation of the optimization problem, the solution of the equation (if it exists) is optimal only if the price processes are Markovian (e.g., see Stokey, Lucas, and Prescott, 1989). The Markov property of a process is defined by the following relationship:

$$E[x_t | x_{t-1}, x_{t-2}, \dots] = E[x_t | x_{t-1}]$$

The Markov property states roughly that in forecasting future values of a process, the only information we need is the current state of the process and not its past values.

However, if we define the power price process as a sequence of hourly prices throughout the day, the resulting process will not be Markovian. To show this, we note simply that future on-peak prices can be closely correlated with past on-peak prices, but only weakly correlated with current off-peak prices. Consequently, if one tries to forecast the on-peak prices of the coming day, the current off-peak prices will be insufficient. One must make use of the past data on recent on-peak prices.

This problem points to the challenge of using spot price processes for modeling power prices. It can be overcome by redefining the state space and price processes. If we define two spot processes—one off-peak and one on-peak—we can turn the optimization problem into a Markovian one. There is a vast amount of literature dealing with optimization and Markov processes (For references see Stokey, Lucas, and Prescott, 1989; we refer the reader to the sources for further details.)

This discussion may seem to be a theoretical nicety, but the proper formulation and representation of the problem have a significant impact on the efficiency of the numerical solutions we discuss in the next section. Those issues should not be underestimated. Proper formulation of the problem can result in a much more efficient solution. Additionally, proper formulation in terms of tradables can significantly aid the process of finding the optimal hedge portfolio and measuring its performance.

In general, we can avoid the problem entirely by conditioning on something other than current prices. BOM on-peak prices are often the best source of information, especially if they are augmented with temperature and system outage information. These processes have approximately Markovian structure. The problem with using this formulation is that we must have a robust model of the joint distribution of the conditional information (BOM, and so on) and "spot" power prices. The hybrid processes discussed in Chapter 7 are ideally suited for this task. Let us also note that this formulation has advantages beyond computational issues. Since the formulation in terms of BOM, temperatures, and so on uses a richer set of information, it can help us find better values than the direct method would. However, this is not the main consideration in introducing the method; the improvements in values are usually small, the bigger advantage lies in our ability to find better hedges and evaluate their performance.

SOLUTION METHODS

In this section we consider generic solution strategies. Then we will deal with the practicalities of obtaining the solution.

Backward Induction in Binomial/Trinomial Forests

The most direct and simplest way of finding the solution is to use the binomial/multinomial forest representation of the problem and solve through backward induction. The procedure is identical to the one applied to swing options in previous chapters. For application of this methodology to power generation see Gardner, Zhuang (2000). We represent the evolution of the underlying prices as a trinomial tree, at minimum two dimensional, or a multinomial grid (see for example Eydeland, Mahoney, 2002). We also introduce additional dimensions for the decision variables of the optimization problem—generation level q and start-up/shutdown decision u—and for nonprice state variables (e.g., time since last start-up, and so on).

To implement the forest efficiently we must discretize our decision variables, which is quite natural. For example, we can divide the generation level into units measured by maximum possible adjustment within one time unit allowed by the unit ramp rate (e.g., one hour). The other system variables are discrete variables in any case.

The valuation/optimization proceeds as follows:

1. We start at the terminal set of nodes at time T. In every trinomial tree, corresponding to a different combination of the state variables, we calculate operational cash flow.
2. We step back one time period to $T-1$ in all the trees. We calculate the discounted (conditional) expectation of cash flow at time T in every individual tree. This corresponds to an assumption that all the state variables remain essentially unchanged.

3. Next, we calculate the conditional expectations between feasible trees. That is we calculate collections of conditional expectations for feasible pairs of current (time T–1) and future (time T) states. For example, if we are in state $U_{T-1}^{on} = 1$, $d_{T-1}^{min} > D_{min} + D_{start-up}$, $q_{T-1} = C_{max} - 2RR$. Then we will have to calculate three different expectations for the following future conditions:
   a. $U_T^{on} = 1$, $d_T^{min} > D_{min} + D_{start-up}$, $q_T = C_{max} - RR$
   b. $U_T^{on} = 1$, $d_T^{min} > D_{min} + D_{start-up}$, $q_T = C_{max} - 3\,RR$
   c. $U_T^{on} = 0$, $d_T^{min} > D_{min} + D_{start-up}$, $q_T = 0$
4. Given the three expectations above in step 3 and the discounted conditional expectation in step 2, we will choose an operational decision with the highest one, considering the impact of the decision on the current (T−1) cash flow.
5. We calculate the total cash flow (current operational cash flow plus the optimal expectation) for every combination of (feasible) operational states.
6. We continue the same procedure with the next step back, and we roll back through the price tree until we arrive at the valuation time. The initial value (time t_0) will give us the optimized value of the generation plant.

The above prescription generates the optimal value. We can also output the critical exercise surfaces: $K_i(P,G,M,\Im;U,d,q;t)$ for various decisions (i.e., start-up, shutdown, ramp-up, ramp-down). The surfaces indicate the optimal decision, given the state variables. This quantity is directly analogous to the critical exercise price in an American option, as well as to the shadow price χ we analyzed in Chapter 9.

The above method is relatively simple and can be easily implemented in a spreadsheet. A significant challenge is the computational performance of the method. Given the many constraints, we might be able to significantly improve the basic algorithm by using an efficient representation of the problem.

We will have a potentially large number of trees in the forest. We can eliminate a certain number of unfeasible combinations right away: for example, if the unit is off the generation level must be equal to zero.

As it is true with trees in general, the computational performance of the method deteriorates as the number of exogenous uncertain factors increases. In our simple formulation, we dealt with power and gas prices, temperatures, and forced outages. Considering that price processes themselves can have complex multifactor structure (i.e., stochastic volatility, jumps, and so on), the dimensionality of the problem can be high. The computational burden of the tree method increases exponentially with the number of factors, as we must keep adding dimensions to our simple trees. We can easily find ourselves with ten factors to represent. At those dimensions, tree-based approaches become extremely costly.

Monte Carlo Simulation for Bermudan Options: Backward Induction

An alternative method of implementing the backward induction is through Monte Carlo simulation. The algorithm works as follows:

1. We start at the terminal set of nodes at time $T-1$. We simulate the conditional distribution of all the uncertainties at time T conditional on the information (price and otherwise) available at time $T-1$.
2. To evaluate the optimal conditional expectations, we can follow the binomial tree prescription and evaluate the various expectations for all the feasible pairs of states at time T and time $T-1$, and then find the maximum over the possible decisions. This would obviously be very expensive computationally, since we would have to do so for every set of information at time $T-1$. An alternative is to try to evaluate the critical exercise surfaces directly. One way is to find such a set of current $(T-1)$ price and nonprice information about which we are indifferent as to taking one decision or doing nothing:

   - $E_{T-1}[V(U_T = 1)|P_{T-1}, G_{T-1}, M_{T-1}, \Im_{T-1}] = E_{T-1}[V(U_T = 0)|P_{T-1}, G_{T-1}, M_{T-1}, \Im_{T-1}]$
   - In cases when we have only two prices, the critical surface can be approximated with simple methods. In more general cases, we can use for example the approach proposed by Schwartz and Litzenberger (1999). In their approach, one approximates the critical boundary at every step by running a regression on a number of variables. The variables chosen are functions of conditional information: power and gas prices, temperatures, and the like.

3. Having determined the critical boundary at time $T-1$ we perform an identical procedure at time $T-2$.
4. We roll back through the tree until time t_0.
5. With the critical surface(s) in place, we can now roll forward to evaluate the optimal cash flow.

The previous method, developed for American options, has been applied to valuation of swing options by Ghuieva, Lehoczky, and Seppi (2001) with encouraging results (for stability tests see Moreno and Navas, 2001). Applications to power generation can be found in Tseng and Barz (1999).

The substantial advantage of the Monte Carlo–based backward induction is its ability to easily incorporate multidimensional price processes—something that is very hard to accomplish efficiently on trees.

Lagrange Relaxation

Solving the general stochastic dynamic programming (SDP) problem does not have to involve backward induction. One powerful method that has found wide applicability in optimization is Lagrange relaxation. The method consists in simplifying the problem by removing complicated constraints and solving a simpler problem, with the objective function adjusted by the values of the deviation from the feasible solution of the relaxed (removed) constraints. The literature on the topic is vast. There are also a number of papers examining the application of various methods to power plant operation (e.g., see Takriti, Supatgiat, and Wu, 2001 and Takriti, Birge, and Long, 2000).

Iterative Solutions

We can also attempt the solution by finding the critical surfaces by an iterative procedure. We start with a reasonable guess for the critical surfaces, which we put it into our simulation (or tree) and find the corresponding value. Next, we perturb the surfaces in such a way that the resulting value is higher than the starting one. We continue until we cannot find an improving perturbation. The idea is simple; however, efficient implementation of the method is nontrivial because we must ensure that our final solution is feasible, and that the search in the space of the feasible surfaces is done efficiently. Given the high dimensionality of the surface, efficient procedures are not easy to come by. If the payoff structure and the constraints are linear, we can reformulate the problem as a sequence of linear programs. However, dispatch problems have at best mixed linear-integer structure. This requires the application of integer programming methods (Branch and Bound, Bender decomposition. See Nemhauser and Wolsey 1999.) that are usually quite complex computationally.

Heuristics and Approximations

Solving the optimization problem exactly may prove very expensive, and in many situations, solving it exactly is not necessary or even useful. Here, we concentrate on the approximation of the problem itself, as well as heuristic methods for solving the problem.

Time Aggregation

In many cases, the true problem has hourly resolution (or even 15-minute, in European markets). We can approximate the true solution by aggregating the time dimension into 4-, 8- or even 16-hour blocks. The performance of the approximation will depend on the physical constraints and the distribution of prices.

Horizon Division

Valuation of generating plants often involves a horizon of several months or even years, making the optimization problem very large in size. One way of coping with the computational complexity is to subdivide the tenor of valuation into smaller subperiods and optimize them separately; natural choices are weekly or monthly horizons. The weekly choice is motivated by the standard operating procedures of plant dispatch, in which the dispatch decision is usually made on Monday and the unit is usually shut down by the end of the week when prices tend to fall. Obviously, this procedure can be sensible only for some units and only for certain sets of expected prices and volatilities.

Another choice is to use a monthly resolution. This is frequently a natural solution, since it directly corresponds to the resolution of forwards and options contracts (at least in U.S. markets; the situation is different in Scandinavian markets that use weekly resolution). Unless there are significant cumulative constraints present (e.g., annual emission caps), or the minimum runtimes and start-up costs are very high, this approximation works very well in terms of both values and most crucially hedges (small cross gamma).

State Aggregation

Depending on the operational characteristics of a unit, we may be able to reduce the dimension of the state space by aggregating several states into larger units. For example, if the heat curve of a unit is sufficiently steep, we can show that it is always optimal to run either at minimum or maximum capacity (bang-bang solution). If the ramp rate of the unit is sufficiently high, we can then reduce the state space to only two levels of feasible generation levels (we also must add a penalty term due to finite ramp rates). The approximation can also work well in estimating the value of a plant even if the optimality of the bang-bang solution is only approximately true. However, one has to be very careful when calculating hedges for the approximate case. Hedges can be extremely sensitive to true heat-curve behavior so that even seemingly innocuous approximations can lead to incorrect hedges.

Direct Approximations of the Critical Surfaces

This fancy name refers to using simple rules for operational decisions. For example, we might use a rule that as long as the BOM price for power is sufficiently higher than the BOM price for fuel:

$$BOM_t^P - BOM_t^G \geq \chi$$

where χ is the shadow price. In general, it can be a function of volatilities and other characteristics of the (joint) price distribution. We can improve this initial guess by performing a couple of iterations (this is obviously an approximate iterative solution).

bibliography

Abken, Peter A., Dilip B. Madan, and Sailesh Ramamurtie. "Estimation of Statistical and Risk-Neutral Densities by Hermite Polynomial Approximation." Federal Reserve Bank of Atlanta, Working Paper Series, 1996.

Abramovitz, Milton, and Irene S. Stegun. *Handbook of Mathematical Functions.* Dover, 1965.

Alexander, Carol. *Market Models: A Guide to Financial Data Analysis.* John Wiley & Sons, 2001.

Alexander, Carol, and C. T. Leigh. "On the Covariance Matrices Used in Value at Risk Models." *The Journal of Derivatives* 4 (1997): 50–62.

Arranz, Miriam A., Álvaro Escribano, and Francesc Marmol. "Effects of Applying Linear and Nonlinear Filters on Tests for Unit Roots with Additive Outliers." Working Paper 00-86, Statistics and Econometrics Series, Universidad Carlos III de Madrid, 2000.

Artzner, Phillippe, Freddy Delbaen, Jean-Marc Eber, and David Heath, "Coherent Measures of Risk." *Mathematical Finance* 9 (1999): 203–228.

Banks, Eric, ed. *Weather Risk Management: Markets, Products and Applications.* Element Re Capital Products, Inc., 2002.

Bates, David S. "Pricing Options Under Jump-Diffusion Processes." The Wharton School, 1988.

———. "Testing Option Pricing Models." in *Handbook of Statistics.* G. S. Madala and C. R. Rao (editors) Vol. 14, Elsevier Science (British Version) 1996.

Baxter, Rennie. *Financial Calculus.* Cambridge University Press, 1996.

Bazzara, Mokhtar S., and C. M. Shetty. *Nonlinear Programming: Theory and Algorithms.* John Wiley & Sons, 1979.

Beidleman, Carl R. *Interest Rate Swaps.* McGraw-Hill, 1990.

Berkowitz, Jeremy. "Frequent Recalibration of Option Pricing Models." University of California, Irvine Working Paper, 2001.

Bessembinder, Hendrik, and Mike Lemmon. "Equilibrium Pricing and Optimal Hedging in Electricity Forward Markets." *Journal of Finance,* 2001.

Black, Fischer. "The Pricing of Commodity Contracts." *Journal of Financial Economics* 3 (1976): 167–179.

Bogentoft, Erik, Edwin Romejin, and Stanislav Uryasev. "Asset-Liability Management for Pension Funds Using CVaR Constraints." Research Report 2001-10, Risk Management and Financial Engineering Lab Center for Applied Optimization, Department of Industrial and Systems Engineering, University of Florida, Gainesville, 2001.

Bollerslev, T. "Generalized Autoregressive Conditional Heteroscedasticity." *Journal of Econometrics* 31 (1986): 307–327.

475

Borenstein, Severin, James Bushnell, and Steven Stoft. "The Competitive Effects of Transmission Capacity in a Deregulated Electricity Industry." *Rand Journal of Economics,* 31, no. 2 (2000): 294–325.

Boswijk, P. H., "Testing for a Unit Root with Near-Integrated Volatility." Working Paper, Department of Quantitative Economics, Universiteit van Amsterdam, 2000.

Box, G. E. P., and D. R. Cox. "An Analysis of Transformations" (with discussion), *Journal of the Royal Statistical Society,* Series B 26 (1964): 211–252.

Brace, Alan, Dariusz Gatarek, and Marek Musiela. "The Market Model of Interest Rate Dynamics." *Mathematical Finance* 7, no. 2 (1997): 127–155.

Briys, Eric, Mondher Bellalah, Huu Minh Mai, and François de Varenne. *Options, Futures and Exotic Derivatives.* John Wiley & Sons, Inc., 1998.

Broadie, Mark, and Paul Glasserman. "Pricing American-Style Securities Using Simulation." *Journal of Economic Dynamics and Control* 21 (1997): 1323–1352.

Buraschi, Andrea, and Jens Jackwerth. "The Price of a Smile: Hedging and Spanning in Option Markets." *The Review of Financial Studies* 14, no. 2 (1998): 495–527. This paper was circulated earlier under the titles "Explaining Option Prices: Deterministic vs. Stochastic Models" and "Is Volatility Risk Priced in the Option Market? Empirical Evidence and Implications for Deterministic and Stochastic Option Pricing Models."

Chernov, Mikhail, and Eric Ghysels. "Estimation of Stochastic Volatility Models for the Purpose of Option Pricing" in Y. S. Abu-Mostafa, B. LeBaron, A. W. Lo, and A. S. Weigend (editors), *Computational Finance – Proceedings of the Sixth International Conference, Leonard N. Stern School of Business,* MIT Press, (2000): 567–582.

____. "A Study Towards a Unified Approach to the Joint Estimation of Objective and Risk Neutral Measures for the Purpose of Options Valuation." *Journal of Financial Economics* 56 (2000): 407–458.

Chibisov, Boris, Uriel Scott, Tsvetan Stoyanov, and Krzysztof Wolyniec, Mirant Research Notes (2001). The paper is available on www.commodityrisk.com.

Clewlow, Les, and Chris Strickland. *Energy Derivatives: Pricing and Risk Management.* Lacima Publications, 2000.

____. "A Multi-Factor Model for Energy Derivatives." *QFRG Research Paper Series* 28 University of Technology, Sydney, 1999.

Clewlow, Les, Chris Strickland, and Vincent Kaminski. "Sparking Confidence." *Energy and Power Risk Management,* October 2001.

Cox, John, and Mark Rubinstein. *Option Markets.* Prentice Hall, 1985.

Culp, Christopher, and Merton Miller, editors. *Corporate Hedging in Theory and Practice, Lessons from Metallgesellschaft.* Risk Books, 1999.

Curran, Michael. "Beyond Average Intelligence." *Risk* 5, no.10 (1992): 60–63.

Das, Sanjiv R,. and Rangarajan K. Sundaram. "Of Smiles and Smirks: A Term-Structure Perspective." *Journal of Financial and Quantitative Analysis* 34, no. 2 (1999): 211–239.

Davidson, Russell, and James G. MacKinnon. *Estimation and Inference in Econometrics.* Oxford University Press, 1993.

Davis, Mark. "Pricing Weather Derivatives by Marginal Value." *Quantitative Finance,* 1 (2001): 1–4.

Davison, Matt, C. Lindsay Anderson, Ben Marcus, and Karen Anderson, "Development of a Hybrid Model for Electrical Power Spot Prices." PE-332PRS (12-2001), IEEE, 2001.

Dempster, Michael A. H., and Hong, S. S. G. "Spread Option Valuation and the Fast Fourier Transform." Judge Institute of Management Working Paper 26, *Proceedings of the First World Congress of the Bachelier Finance Society*, Paris (2000).

Deng, Shijie. "Stochastic Models of Energy Commodity Prices: Mean-Reversion with Jumps and Spikes." 1998.

Derman, Emanuel. "Regimes of Volatility." *Risk* 4, no. 4 (1999): 55–59.

Derman, Emanuel, and Iraj Kani. "Riding on a Smile." *Risk* 7, no. 2 (1994): 32–39.

Dixit, Avinash, and Robert Pindyck. *Investment Under Uncertainty*. Princeton University Press, 1994.

Duan, Jin-Chuan. "The GARCH Option Pricing Model." *Mathematical Finance* 5, (1995): 13–32.

Duan, Jin-Chuan, and Stanley Pliska. "Option Valuation with Co-Integrated Asset Prices." University of Toronto, Working Paper, 2001.

Duffie, Darrell. *Dynamic Asset Pricing Theory*. Princeton University Press, 1992.

Duffie, Darrell, and Jun Pan. "An Overview of Value-at-Risk." *The Journal of Derivatives* 4 (1997): 7–49.

Duffie, Darrell, and Philip Protter. "From Discrete to Continuous Time Finance: Weak Convergence of the Financial Gain Process." *Mathematical Finance* 2, no. 1 (1992): 1–15.

Duffie, Darrell, Jun Pan, and Kenneth Singleton. "Transform Analysis and Asset Pricing for Affine Jump-Diffusions." *Econometrica* 68 (2000): 1343–1376.

Duffie, Darrell, Stephen Gray, and Philip Hoang. "Volatility in Energy Prices." *Managing Energy Price Risk*, 2nd ed. Risk Publications, 1999.

Dumas, Bernard, Jeff Fleming, and Robert E. Whaley. "Implied Volatility Functions: Empirical tests." *Journal of Finance* 53, no. 6 (1998): 2059–2106.

Embrechts, Paul, Alexander McNeil, and Daniel Straumann. "Correlation and Dependence in Risk Management: Properties and Pitfalls." in *Risk Management: Value at Risk and Beyond*, Michael A. H. Dempster (ed.) Cambridge University Press (2002): 176–223.

Escribano, Álvaro, Peña, J. Ignacio, and Villaplana, Pablo. "Modelling Electricity Prices: International Evidence." Working Paper, Universidad Carlos III de Madrid, (2001).

Eydeland, Alexander. "A Spectral Algorithm for Pricing Interest Rate Options." *Computational Economics* 9 (1996): 19–36.

Eydeland, Alexander and Hélyette Geman. "Fundamentals of Electricity Derivatives." *Energy Modelling and the Management of Uncertainty*. Risk Books, 1999.

Eydeland, Alexander, and Dan Mahoney, "Fast Convolution Method for Pricing Derivatives." Mirant Research Notes (2002). The paper is available on www.commodityrisk.com.

Föllmer, Hans and Dieter Sondermann. "Hedging of Non-redundant Contingent Claims." in *Contributions to Mathematical Economics*, Werner Hildebrand, Andreu Mas-Colell (eds.), 205–223. North Holland, 1986.

Frey, Rüdiger. "Derivative Asset Analysis in Models with Level Dependent and Stochastic Volatility." *CWI Quarterly*, 10, no. 1 (1996): 1–34.

Gao, Yan, and Wolyniec, Krzysztof. "Pricing and Hedging Load Contracts." Mirant Research Notes, 2002. The paper is available on www.commodityrisk.com.

Gardner, Doug, and Yiping Zhuang. "Valuation of Power Generation Assets: A Real Options Approach." *ALGO Research Quarterly* 3, no. 3 (2000): 9–20.

Gatheral, Jim. "Stochastic Volatility and Local Volatility." Case Studies in Financial Modelling Course Notes, Courant Institute of Mathematical Sciences, Course Notes, available on the Courant Institute server 2001.

Geman, Hélyette, ed. *Insurance and Weather Derivatives: From Exotic Options to Exotic Underlyings*. Risk Books, 1999.

Geman, Hélyette, and Alexander Eydeland. "Domino Effect." *Risk* 8, 1995.

Geman, Hélyette, and Andrea Roncoroni. "A Class of Marked Point Processes for Modelling Electricity Prices." Working Paper. ESSEC, 2002.

Geske, Robert. "The Valuation of Compound Options." *Journal of Financial Economics* 7 (1979): 63–81.

Ghuieva, Cristian, John Lehoczky, and Duane Seppi. "Using Least Squares Monte Carlo to Value Swing Options." Presentation at 5th annual EPRM Congress, 2001.

Ghysels, Eric, Andrew Harvey, and Eric Renault. "Stochastic Volatility." *Handbook of Statistics* 14, Statistical Methods in Finance, 1997.

Gourieroux, Christian, and Joann Jasiak. *Financial Econometrics: Problems, Models, and Methods*. Princeton University Press, 2001.

Greene, William H. *Econometric Analysis*. 4th ed. Prentice Hall, 2000.

Hahn, Gerald J., and William O. Meeker. *Statistical Interval*. John Wiley & Sons, Inc., 1991.

Hamilton, James D. *Time Series Analysis*. Princeton University Press, 1994.

Harvey, Scott M., and William M. Hogan. "On the Exercise of Market Power Through Strategic Withholding in California." LEGG, LLC, May 2001.

Heath, David, Robert Jarrow, and Andrew Morton. "Bond Pricing and the Term Structure of Interest Rates: A New Methodology for Contingent Claim Valuation." *Econometrica* 60 (1992): 77–105.

Henderson, Vicky, and Rafal Wojakowski. "On the Equivalence of Floating and Fixed-Strike Asian Options." *Applied Probability Trust*, 2001.

Heston, Steven L. "A Closed-Form Solution for Options with Stochastic Volatility with Application to Bond and Currency Options." *Review of Financial Studies* 6 (1993): 327–343.

Heston, Steven L., and S. Nandi. "A Closed-Form GARCH Option Pricing Model." Working Paper 97-9, Federal Reserve Bank of Atlanta, 1997.

Hobson, David. "Stochastic Volatility." Working Paper, University of Bath, 1996.

Hoogland, Jiri, and Dimitri Neumann. "Asians and Cash Dividends: Exploiting Symmetry in Pricing Theory." Report Number: mas-r0019, CWI (National Research Institute for Mathematics and Computer Science in the Netherlands), 2001.

Huisman, Ronald, and Ronald Mahieu. "Regime Jumps in Electricity Prices." *ERIM Report Series: Research in Management* ERS-2001-48-F&A, 2001.

Hull, John. *Options, Futures and Other Derivatives*. 4th ed. Prentice Hall, 1999.

Hull, John, and Alan White. "The Pricing of Options on Assets with Stochastic Volatilities." *Journal of Finance* 42, (1987): 281–300.

Jackwerth, Jens. "Option Implied Risk-Neutral Distributions and Implied Binomial Trees: A Literature Review." *Journal of Derivatives* 7, no. 2 (1999): 66–82.

Jaillet, Patrick, Ehud Ronn, and Stathis Tompaidis. "Valuation of Commodity-Based Swing Options." *Preprint available on the Internet* at *http://uts.cc.utexas.edu/~jaillet/research/swing.pdf*.

Jamshidian, Farshid, and Yu Zhu. "Scenario Simulation: Theory and Methodology." *Finance and Stochastics* 1 (1997): 43–67.

Jarrow, Robert. *Modelling Fixed Income Securities and Interest Rate Options*. Kamakura Corporation, 1995.

Jarrow, Robert, ed. *Over the Rainbow: Development in Exotic Options and Complex Swaps*. Risk Publications, 1996.

Johnson, Blake, and Graydon Barz. "Selecting Stochastic Processes for Modelling Electricity Prices" in *Energy Modelling and the Management of Uncertainty*. Risk Books, 1999.

Jones, Phillip E. "Option Arbitrage and Strategy with Large Price Changes." *Journal of Financial Economics* 13, no. 1 (1984): 91–113.

Kaminski, Vincent, and Stinson Gibner. "Exotic Options." *Managing Energy Price Risk*. Risk Publications, 1997.

Kennedy, Douglas P. "The Term Structure of Interest Rates as a Gaussian Random Field." *Mathematical Finance*, 4 (1997): 107–118.

Knittel, Christoper R., and Michael Roberts. "An Empirical Examination of Deregulated Electricity Prices." mimeo, Boston University. *POWER Working Paper PWP-087*. UCEI, University of California, Berkeley, 2001.

Koekkebaker, Steen, and Fridthjof Ollmar. "Forward Curve Dynamics in the Nordic Electricity Market." Working paper, Norwegian School of Economics and Business Administration, 2001.

Kolb, Robert. *Options, Futures and Swaps*. 3rd ed. Blackwell Publishers, 1999.

Kolb, Robert. *Understanding Futures Markets*. 5th ed. Blackwell Publishers, 1997.

Kosecki, Roman. "Fuel Based Power Price Modelling." *Energy Modelling and the Management of Uncertainty*. Risk Books, 1999.

Kou, Steven G., and Wang, Hui. "Option Pricing Under a Double Exponential Jump-Diffusion Model." Presentation at conference, Institute for Operations Research and Management Sciences, 2001.

Krapels, Edward N. *Electricity Trading and Hedging*. Energy Security Analysis, Inc. Risk Books, 2000.

Lari-Lavassani, Ali, Mohammadreza Simchi, and Anthony Ware. "A Discrete Valuation of Swing Options." *Canadian Applied Mathematics Quarterly* forthcoming (2001).

Lindgren, Bernard W. *Statistical Theory*. 2nd ed. The Macmillan Company, 1968.

Linetsky, Vadim. "Closed-Form Pricing of Asian Options." Preprint. Department of Industrial Engineering and Management Sciences, McCormick School of Engineering and Applied Sciences, Northwestern University, 2001.

Linsmeier, Thomas J., and Neil D. Pearson. *Risk Measurement: An Introduction to Value at Risk*. University of Illinois, 1996.

Lipton, Alexander. "Self-Similarities and Similarities of Path-Dependent Options," *Risk* 12, no. 9 (1999): 101–105.

____. *Mathematical Methods for Foreign Exchange.* World Scientific, 2001.

Longstaff, Francis A., and Eduardo S. Schwartz. "Valuing American Options by Simulation: A Simple Least-Squares Approach." *Review of Financial Studies* 14, no. 1 (2001): 113–147.

Managing Energy Price Risk. 2nd edition. Risk Books, 2000.

Mansur, Erin. "Pricing Behavior in the Initial Summer of the Restructured PJM Wholesale Electricity Market." *POWER Working Paper-083* http://www.ucei. berkeley.edu/ucei/PDF/pwp083.pdf, 2001.

Margrabe, William. "The Value of an Option to Exchange One Asset for Another." *Journal of Finance* 33, no. 1 (1978): 177–186.

McMillan, Lawrence G. *Options as Strategic Investment.* 3rd ed. Prentice Hall, 1992.

Merton, Robert C. "Option Pricing When Underlying Stock Returns Are Discontinuous." *Journal of Financial Economics* 3 (1976): 125–144.

Moreno, Manuel, and Javier F. Navas. "On the Robustness of Least-Squares Monte Carlo (LSM) for Pricing American Derivatives." Working Paper, Universitat Pompeu Fabra and Instituto de Empresa, 2001.

Nelken, Israel. *Pricing, Hedging, and Trading Exotic Options: Understanding the Intricacies of Exotic Options and How to Use Them to Maximum Advantage.* McGraw-Hill, 1999.

____. "Square Deals." In *Over the Rainbow,* Robert Jarrow, ed. Risk Books, 1996.

Nelsen, Roger B. *An Introduction to Copulas.* Lecture Notes in Statistics139, Springer-Verlag, 1999.

Nelson, Daniel B. "ARCH Models as Diffusion Approximations." *Journal of Econometrics* 45, (1990): 7–38.

Nemhauser, George L., and Laurence Wolsey. *Integer and Combinatorial Optimization.* Wiley-Interscience, 1999.

Nielsen, Lars B., "Pricing Asian Options." Masters Thesis, AArhus University (Denmark), 2001.

Oksendal, Bernt. *Stochastic Differential Equations.* Springer Verlag, 1998.

Pan, Jun. "The Jump-Risk Premia Implicit in Options: Evidence from an Integrated Time-Series Study." *Journal of Financial Economics* 63 (2002): 3–50.

Pearson, Neil D. "An Efficient Approach for Pricing Spread Options." *Journal of Derivatives* 3, (1995): 76–91.

Pilipovic, Dragana. *Energy Risk: Valuing and Managing Energy Derivatives.* McGraw-Hill, 1997.

Pindyck, Robert S. "The Long-Run Evolution of Energy Prices" *The Energy Journal* 20, no. 2 (1999).

Pirrong, Craig, and Martin Jermakyan. "Valuing Power and Weather Derivatives on a Mesh Using Finite Difference Methods." *Energy Modelling and the Management of Uncertainty,* Risk Books, 1999.

Press, William H., ed., et al. *Numerical Recipes in C++: The Art of Scientific Computing.* Cambridge University Press, 2002.

Rebonato, Riccardo. *Interest-Rate Option Models: Understanding, Analyzing and Using Models for Exotic Interest-Rate Options.* 2nd ed. John Wiley & Sons Ltd., 1998.

____. *Volatility and Correlation.* John Wiley & Sons, Inc., 1999.

Reiner, Eric. "Volatility Rules and Implied Processes." Presentation at Risk Conference, 1998.

Renault, Eric, and Nizar Touzi. "Option Hedging and Implied Volatilities in a Stochastic Volatility Model." *Mathematical Finance* 6, no. 3 (1996): 279–302.

RiskMetrics™. 3rd ed., J. P. Morgan, 1995.

Rockafellar, R. Tyrrell, and Stanislav Uryasev. "Optimization of Conditional Value at Risk." *The Journal of Risk* 2, no. 3 (2000).

Ross, Stephen A. "Hedging Long-Term Exposures with Multiple Short-Term Futures Contracts." in *Corporate Hedging in Theory and Practice*. Risk Books, 1999.

Rouvinez, Christophe. "Going Greek with VaR." *Risk* 10, no. 2 (1997).

Rubinstein, Mark. "Double Trouble." *Risk* 4 (1991): 53–56.

_____. "Implied Binomial Trees." *Journal of Finance* 49, no. 3, (1994): 771–818.

Samuelson, P. A. "Proof that Properly Anticipated Prices Fluctuate Randomly." *Industrial Management Review* 6 (1965): 41–49.

Sapatgiat, Chonawee, Rachel Q. Zhang, and John R. Birge. "Equilibrium Values in a Competitive Power Exchange Market." *Computational Economics* 17 (2001): 93–121.

Schroder, Mark. "Computing the Constant Elasticity of Variance Option Pricing Formula." *Journal of Finance* 44 (1989): 211–219.

Schwartz, Eduardo S. "The Stochastic Behavior of Commodity Prices: Implications for Valuation and Hedging." *Journal of Finance* 52, no. 3 (1997): 923–73.

Schwartz, Eduardo S., and James E. Smith. "Short-Term Variations and Long-Term Dynamics in Commodity Prices." *Management Science* 46, no. 7 (2000): 893–911.

Scott, Uriel, and Krzysztof Wolyniec. "Conditional Correlation Structure in Energy Markets." Mirant Research Reports (confidential and proprietary) 2002. The paper is available on www.commodityrisk.com.

Seppi, Duane J. "A Survey of Stochastic Methods for Energy and Commodity-Linked Contingent Claim Valuation." Working Paper, Carnegie Mellon University, 1999.

Shimko, David. "What is VaR?" in *VaR: Understanding and Applying Value-at-Risk*, Risk Books, (1997): 331–332.

Skantze, Peter L., and Marija D. Ilic. *Valuation, Hedging and Speculation in Competitive Electricity Markets: A Fundamental Approach*. Kluwer Academic Publishers Group, 2001.

Stokey, Nancy L., Robert E. Lucas Jr., and Edward C. Prescott. *Recursive Methods in Economic Dynamics*. Harvard University Press, 1989.

Stoll, Harry G. *Least-Cost Electric Utility Planning*. John Wiley & Sons, 1989.

Sturm, Fletcher J. *Trading Natural Gas*. Pennwell Publishing, 1997.

Taleb, Nassim. *Dynamic Hedging*. John Wiley & Sons, 1996.

Takriti, Samer, Chonawee Supatgiat, and Lilian S. Wu. "Coordinating Fuel Inventory and Electric-Power Generation Under Uncertainty." *IEEE Transaction on Power Systems* 16, no. 4 (2001): 603–608.

Takriti, Samer, John R. Birge, and E. Long. "A Lagrangian Relaxation Approach Coupled with Heuristic Techniques for Solving the Unit Commitment Problem." To appear in *IEEE Transactions on Power Systems*.

Toft, Xuan. "How Well Can Barrier Options Be Hedged by a Static Portfolio of Standard Options?" *Journal of Financial Engineering* 7, no. 2 (1998).

Tseng, Chung-Li, and Graydon Barz. "Short-Term Generation Asset Valuation."
Proceedings of the 32nd Hawaii International Conference on System Sciences,
1999.
Uryasev, S. "Conditional Value-at-Risk: Optimization Algorithms and
Applications." *Financial Engineering News* 14 (2000):1–5.
Vorst, Tom. "Prices and Hedge Ratios of Average Exchange Rate Options."
International Review of Financial Analysis 1, no. 3 (1992): 179–94.
Wilcox, D. "Energy Futures and Options: Spread Options in the Energy Markets."
Goldman Sachs, 1990.
Wilmott, Paul. *Paul Wilmott on Quantitative Finance.* John Wiley & Sons, Inc.,
2000.
Wilmott, Paul, Sam Howison, and Jeff Dewynne. *The Mathematics of Financial
Derivatives.* Cambridge University Press, 1995.
Wolyniec, Krzysztof. "Storage Valuation: Spread Options and Alternative
Approaches." Mirant Research Notes, 2002. The paper is available on
www.commodityrisk.com.
_____. "Forward Markets, Spread Options and Intertemporal Optimization." Mirant
Research Notes, 2002. The paper is available on www.commodityrisk.com.
_____. "Correlation, Volatility and Joint Distributions." Mirant Research Report,
2001. The paper is available on www.commodityrisk.com.
Wood, Allen J., and Bruce F. Wollenberg. *Power Generation, Operation and
Control.* John Wiley & Sons, 1984.
Zhu, Jinxiang, Gary Jordan, and Satoru Ihara. "The Market for Spinning Reserve
and Its Impact in Energy Prices." GE Energy Services Reports, 2000.

index

Printed and bound by CPI Group (UK) Ltd, Croydon, CR0 4YY

23/04/2025

14660925-0004